Children's Language and Learning

Second Edition

Judith Wells Lindfors

University of Texas, Austin

Prentice-Hall, Inc., Englewood Cliffs, New Jersey 07632

Library of Congress Cataloging-in-Publication Data

LINDFORS, JUDITH WELLS.
Children's language and learning

    Bibliography: p. 475
    Includes index.
    1. Language and languages. 2. Language acquisition.
3. Learning, Psychology of. 4. Communicative competence. 5. Language and languages—Variation. I. Title.
P106.L534 1987   401'.9   86-22624
ISBN 0-13-131962-0

Editorial/production supervision and
   interior design: Marianne Peters
Cover design: Wanda Lubelska Design
Manufacturing buyer: John B. Hall

Printed in the United States of America

10 9 8 7 6 5 4 3 2 1

ISBN 0-13-131962-0   01

Prentice-Hall International (UK) Limited, *London*
Prentice-Hall of Australia Pty. Limited, *Sydney*
Prentice-Hall Canada Inc., *Toronto*
Prentice-Hall Hispanoamericana, S.A., *Mexico*
Prentice-Hall of India Private Limited, *New Delhi*
Prentice-Hall of Japan, Inc., *Tokyo*
Prentice-Hall of Southeast Asia Pte. Ltd., *Singapore*
Editora Prentice-Hall do Brasil, Ltda., *Rio de Janeiro*

To Dad
who shared language and learning
with the child I was

In Memoriam

Contents

12   Communicative Competence:
Teachers and Children   355

section five   language variation

13   Dialect Variation   394

14   Dialect Variation: Teachers and Children   414

15   Different Languages: Teachers and Children   435

References   475

Index   487

Preface

Not long ago I got a phone call from a local kindergarten teacher who was most eager for me to come and visit the four kindergarten classrooms in her school. She wanted me to see their new language program, a program of which they were very proud. The four kindergarten teachers were pilot testing some sort of new language kit. As she explained, "Every day each child does four boxes."

"Oh," I said. "And do the children ever get to choose their activities?"

"Oh yes," came the enthusiastic reply. "If a child gets a box wrong, he then does three remedial activities, and he gets to do them in whatever order he wants to."

This wasn't what I meant by "choice," but I refrained from saying so, mainly because she went right on.

"I've been teaching kindergarten for eleven years and this is the best year I've ever had; I can *see* the children learning." And then came these terrifying words: "This program assures that there will be no gaps in the children's learning."

Well, I never went to see the kindergarten language program, so I never found out what was in the daily four boxes. I know it wasn't language. Language never has lived in boxes and it never will. But mostly I didn't go because that teacher and I have nothing to say to each other. I'm sure we would both say we're interested in children, in language development, in learning, in teaching. But she was not talking about children, about language, about learning, about teaching as I know these.

I picture you browsing in a bookstore. I assume you've picked this book up and started glancing through it because you assume from the title that it's a book about children, their language, and their learning. And you're right, of course. But it's about what *I* mean by these. The kindergarten teacher with the boxes would write a very different book, though she might give it the same title. So before you plunk a goodly sum down on the counter and purchase this book, I'd better tell you what I mean by these, for it may be that I have nothing to say to you, just as I have nothing to say to the kindergarten teacher.

A reviewer of the first edition of this book criticized it for being "biased." I would prefer to use some other term—to call it a book with an "orientation," perhaps, or maybe a "philosophy" or a particular "set of basic assumptions." But whatever the term chosen, the reviewer was right: the first edition was most definitely *that* sort of book. When I wrote the first edition I had every intention of suggesting that all ways of viewing children and language and learning are not equal: some are "more equal than others." The reviewer's remarks alerted me to the fact that, in this second edition, I must make my "bias" explicit.

> I see children as shapers of their own knowing, their own languaging.
> I see children's development of language as a creative construction process they carry out in their constant and continuing experience in a social world.
> I see children's learning in *all* areas as an active sense-making process— necessary and inevitable and individual.

Which brings us to teaching, for I see teaching as our sensitive and supportive response to the powerful learning processes of children. I have called the kindergarten woman with the boxes a "teacher." She isn't. Not in my view, anyway. She's a technician. It's technicians, not teachers, who order boxes, store them, dispense them, move children through them on schedule. And only a technician could see this box business as "assuring that there will be no gaps in the children's learning." For the technician, it doesn't matter who the particular child is or how she is going about the business of making sense of the world. In a way, there is no individual child or individual sense-making process: one box fits all.

A teacher is different from a technician. I guess I'd have to call the difference "sensitivity." "Sensitivity" is a tricky word. We tend to think of sensitivity as something that just sort of showers down from the sky and if we happen to be standing in the right place we get a lot of it, and if we're standing in the wrong place, we don't. But I don't think it's like this. To some considerable extent, sensitivity involves knowledge, awareness, understanding—all of which we build on the base of our own *beliefs*, of course. We can increase our awareness and understanding. We see children's behaviors in certain ways because we have developed certain notions about the kinds of thinking, feeling, and interacting people that children are and the kinds of processes that learning and languaging involve. To increase our understanding is to change our ways of viewing children— which behaviors we notice, how we interpret those behaviors, how legitimate we feel those behaviors to be, how we value those behaviors. To increase our understanding of children's ways of learning and languaging is, perhaps, to increase our ability to see the child's behavior from his or her point of view—as making sense on its own terms and not simply in terms of its fit with our adult ways. I think we can get better at seeing the child's language and learning from the child's point of view. That's sensitivity. I think that's what this book is about. The reviewer who found the first edition biased would probably disagree. The box woman would *certainly* disagree. And you? I wonder what you'll think if you decide to go with me through to the end of this book.

Those of you who are familiar with the first edition will find substantial changes here, especially in three areas: this edition deals more with literacy development, has more substantial classroom implications chapters, and includes some information from important recent sociolinguistic research. Your voices have haunted me as I've worked on this second edition: You've groaned, complained, wailed, and railed at me, but rarely if ever have you lauded a change. I'm sorry if your favorite explanation or example is gone and if the parts you found most boring or unclear are still here. The orientation itself, however, will be the one you knew in the first edition.

Glenda Bissex helps me sum up that orientation. She has written a book called *GNYS AT WRK.* The book is a description of her son Paul's writing development from age five to age eleven. The book's title comes from one of Paul's early written messages, a sign on his workbench: DO NAT DSTRB. GNYS AT WRK.

I believe that the child developing language—the child *inventing* language—IS a genius. And she is a genius AT WORK. It is for us, her teachers, to understand the nature of that genius and of that work, and— understanding it—to recognize it, believe in it, appreciate it, encourage it, support it, extend it. It is the work of creatively constructing language in a social world.

This is the bias—or orientation—of this book.

Judith Wells Lindfors
University of Texas, Austin

Acknowledgments

"You're working on a second edition? Hey, easy," joked one colleague. "Just put on a new cover and sprinkle in a few recent studies."

I'd like to begin by acknowledging those who made it impossible to do this. They're the people whose recent work has had profound implications for us in education and made it impossible for me to work within the existing framework of the first edition. They have made my job of writing this second edition far more difficult than I ever anticipated, for their work has necessitated massive amounts of new writing. It's their work that I can "blame" for this manuscript getting to the publisher fully a year and a half later than I expected. Though a number of people are in this category and will find themselves in subsequent pages, I would especially thank Shirley Brice Heath, Donald Graves, Vivian Paley, and for making my work on this edition so very difficult.

Encouragement in this project has come from many sources. I am grateful to the Modern Language Association for awarding the first edition the Mina Shaughnessy Medal, and to D. F. Shaughnessy who personally encouraged me to undertake a second edition. Many colleagues and friends have helped in different ways, some of which they may be unaware of. I thank:

Courtney Cazden for her early positive response to the first edition and her upbeat interest in the progress of the second edition;

Carole Edelsky for being—*always*—my most helpful critic/supporter/responder;

Lily Fillmore for giving me the opportunity to get to know her three-year language project from the "inside";

Barbara Flores for her readiness—no, eagerness—to share recent work;

Jerry Harste (and Jean Ann Clyde) for extensive comments on the first edition and suggestions for the second;

Cyndy and Sarah Hoffman for letting me "listen in," and thus better understand language acquisition at work;

Sarah Hudelson for being such a helpful reader and support team when I needed it;

Mary Lou Serafine for always being ready to listen and respond to my ideas, groans, enthusiasms.

I also thank those on whom I rely for the tedious business of making a readable manuscript out of messy drafts: Bette Hinol and Susan Milburn. That they should have done this with good humor is more than I deserved.

My debt to my students is enormous and is present on every page of this book. They have been unfailingly generous in letting me include examples from their work, and in interacting with me in open, honest, and challenging ways. My students are ever an important and constant source of my own growth. They keep me in touch with my audience, for they ARE my audience (conversational partners?). They keep me in touch with what it's all about. More importantly perhaps, with why.

I must ever be thankful to my own children, Brenda, Susan, and Erik (now young adults) who more than anyone else, must be responsible for having shaped my notions of children, their language, their learning.

And there's Ben; there's always Ben. He believed this project was worth pursuing, though neither of us realized how major the commitment was to be. I acknowledge him. When the struggle of the work is farther behind me, I may even thank him.

An Overview of Five Dimensions of Language

INTRODUCTION

Language is always everywhere with us. It pervades every area of our waking lives—our family relationships, our friendships, our working relationships, and even our aloneness. And those of us who carry on lively conversations or write great poetry in our dreams would argue that language pervades our hours of sleep as well as our hours of waking.

The more that researchers study child language acquisition, the more they become aware of the amazing language abilities children have by the time they come to elementary school. These abilities are what this book is about. At the very least, the five-year-old

> has a well-developed system for relating meaning and expression in language (Section One);
>
> has acquired this system of language structure by using powerful processes of creative construction (Section Two);
>
> uses this system of language structure for cognitive purposes (Section Three);
>
> uses this system of language structure for social purposes (Section Four);
>
> and may control more than one dialect or language system (Section Five).

LANGUAGE STRUCTURE

Many language scholars have tried to understand and describe the structure of language, that "system by which sounds [expression] and meanings are related" (Fromkin and Rodman 1974, p. 2). What are the parts of language? How do they interrelate to form that integrated system which every language user knows and draws on in his oral and written interactions with others? Clearly, there must be some set of organizational principles for every language, which enables its speakers both to produce meaningful expression and to grasp the intended meanings in the expression of others.

Language has various types of units. Every language has its own set of possible sounds, sound combinations, words, and word combinations; not all selections and combinations of them convey meanings. If you doubt this, write down a straightforward sentence abut ten words long. Now read the words in some other order, for example, in reverse. It is clear that there is no randomness in what constitutes the significant parts of any language and the possibilities for their combination. There is structure; some basic set of organizing principles is involved. Without an orderly, nonrandom system of organizational structure, we would not have language, but only a conglomeration of verbal noises or written symbols. Every language has a structure that serves, in highly complex and abstract ways, to relate expression and meaning.[1] One way to characterize the language dimension being focused on here (and treated at length in Section One) is with the questions "What is the structure of language?" and "What are the parts of language and how are they organized and related?"

It is important for us, as teachers, to understand language structure. Children's control of the structure of their language, largely mastered by the time they come to kindergarten, is basic to all their learning. Their understanding of what they hear and what they read, and their ability to express what they know in speech and in writing, depend in no small part on their knowledge of the relationships between expression and meaning in their language. Much of what we do as teachers involves expansion and further development of cognitive, attitudinal, and social meanings. For example, "pounds" and "ounces," "liberty and justice for all," "less," "sinister," and "multiply" may be new meanings for a child, but once he[2] grasps these meanings and their labels, they find a ready home in his total language system. We take it for granted that children will tell us "I multiplied them" but not "I sinistered them." They may talk of "ten pounds" or "six ounces," but not "ten justices" or "six sinisters." The child knows, without our telling him, the kind of language unit the new concept/term is, and he readily incorporates it into his well-developed existing linguistic framework.

Children demonstrate their knowledge of language structure in many ways, but we see their behavior as evidence of this knowledge only if we know to look at their behavior in this way. For example, children often quite naturally play with elements of language structure—with sounds, with words, with combinations of words.

Four-year-old Emily is eating lunch while her mother is nearby making soup.

C: Get the old sugee bowl, the old sugee bowl.
M: Get the old what?

---

[1]In the case of some handicapped people, other means than verbal expression are employed, for example, sign language for the deaf and mute. However, the basic principle is the same— our overt expression system relates to our intended meanings in systematic ways.

[2]Throughout this book, generic he and generic she alternate by chapter.

C: The old sugee. That's sugar. (laughs) I said it funny. (sing-songy voice, to herself) Get the sugar buger muger. Sugar, bigger pigger.[3]

Two four-year-old boys are painting at an easel in their nursery school classroom.

C-1: What are you painting?
C-2: Inside of a body. Inside of a potty.
C-1: Quit teasing, you boo-boo.
C-2: I'm not a boo-boo, you silly.
C-1: Ah-choo, a-a-ah-choo a boo boo boo. (Both laugh and start chanting.)
C-1/C-2: I'm making a body, I'm making a potty.[4]

These examples could easily be dismissed as idle babblings of children who are "just acting silly." If we attend closely, however, we can see that these children in their play reveal a great deal of knowledge about the meanings and expression possibilities of their language.

Children also demonstrate their knowledge of language structure when they use developmental forms, that is, forms which are different from those the adult uses but which reflect the child's knowledge of how his language works. Consider the following excerpt from a story that one five-year-old told his mother as they looked at Mercer Mayer's wordless storybook *Hiccup*.

> The drink accidently got on her, and she was mad at him. But she forgived him . . . . And they hollered at each other and they keeped on hiccuping . . . And she kicked him into the water. And she was alaughin' at him, and sticked her tongue out at him.[5]

If we did not know better, we could easily dismiss this child's "forgived," "keeped," and "sticked" as mistakes, and fail to recognize these forms as evidence that the child has discerned some important regularities in the ways that past tense is expressed in his language. Worse yet, we might see this as the "perfect opportunity" to "teach past tense," and proceed to correct the child's unconventional forms and put him through repeat-after-me drills—all of which would do nothing to hasten the child's use of adult irregular verb forms and would do much to dampen his enthusiasm for creating stories—at least when we were around.

The child's language play and use of developmental forms are only two of many typical demonstrations of the child's well-developed language structure. We'll consider these and other types of evidence in Section One. However, perhaps the very best evidence of the child's knowledge of language structure is the one we most often overlook: The child expresses his meanings in predictable ways that have much in common with adult expression. He also understands what we say to him, for the most part. This means that his language structure system is much like ours. His

[3]I am indebted to Julie Niehaus for this example.
[4]I am indebted to Sally Scott for this example.
[5]I am indebted to Judy Muery for this example.

expression is predictable in the sense that it usually conforms to our expectations of how utterances are structured—what elements are included and how they are arranged. Notice what the five-year-old above did not not say in his story.

> Her him on drink at accidently made the got and was she. Forgived but she him . . .

We take it for granted that our children don't talk to us this way. But perhaps it is not to be taken for granted. If the child did not have an organizational system, then any order of these words would be equally likely. Clearly, this child, like most five-year-olds, shares with us a basic organizational system for relating meaning and expression. If we are, as we so often say, intent on knowing "where the child is," then we must recognize the evidence in the child's daily language behavior that indicates "where he is" in language, the system he will use more than any other in his learning.

It is also important for us to understand language structure so that we can differentiate between the child's *knowledge* of language structure, on the one hand, and his ability to *talk about* that knowledge, on the other. The child's knowledge of language structure lives at an unconscious level, an intuitive level. The young child *does* language; he does not talk about language or reflect upon it in a conscious way. (Notice that this is to some extent the case with many adults as well. You may find it challenging in chaps. 2 and 3 to focus in a conscious, analytical way on that very structure of language which you know so intuitively.) Some examples might help to clarify this distinction between intuitive and conscious knowledge of language structure.

A second-grade teacher I know wanted her children to ask questions, so she tried to engage them in a game: "I'll tell you an answer, and you tell what the question is that my statement is an answer to." She was dismayed to find that the children could not do this, even though, as she told me, "I know they ask questions all the time. I hear them do it." And she is right, of course. They do ask questions, and those questions are formed in ways that demonstrate organizational principles at work that are much like the adults', for example, a question word at the beginning (what, where, who, how, when), and a reversal of subject and first element of the verb phrase (Where *are you* going? not, Where *you are* going?). But their knowledge of the selection and ordering of elements so as to ask a question is at an intuitive level. They cannot dredge it up in response to terms like "question," "statement," "answer." In her direction, the teacher in essence said, "Identify a particular type of language form (question) that my particular form (statement) is a particular kind of response (answer) to." This is to require children to reflect on language forms consciously, rather than to use those forms spontaneously to express meaning. Our children aren't much into this reflection. Rather, they ask questions—real ones—to get answers. Here are a few of the questions a kindergarten group asked their teacher as she read them *The New True Book of Reptiles*:

Is that a turtle there?

What is that one? (referring to a picture)

What's that one right there?

If you was a turtle and you called a loggerhead, what you do?

Is he dead?

Is that a boa constrictor?

Is he scaring another snake away?

This snake won't hurt you? (checking to confirm something that was said)

Which one is the harmless snake?[6]

Similarly, they are into using words, not talking about them. Words, of course, include consonant and vowel sounds, are composed of syllables, express particular meanings, and so on. Our children's talk about dinosaurs, space, hospitals, computers, baby sisters, and pet fish is clear evidence of their knowledge of the sounds of language, of particular words expressing particular meanings. But using words to tell people things is very different from finding CVVC(consonant-vowel-vowel-consonant)-pattern words in print or identifying long and short vowel sounds or two-syllable words or diagraphs.

The goal in Section One is to increase our own conscious awareness of language structure in all its fascinating complexity so that we can recognize its presence in the children we teach. My hope is that

we will become more aware of, and more appreciative of, the complexity of language structure knowledge the young child has;

we will see evidence of the existence of this complex knowledge in the child's diverse language behaviors in interactions through talk and writing;

we will recognize when we are engaging that knowledge in a *doing* way—the way that is most natural for the child—and when we are asking him instead to reflect consciously upon that knowledge and to focus on language form as *form*, standing apart from the purposeful expression of meaning.

LANGUAGE ACQUISITION

The mental abilities of a little child seem to be rather limited in many ways, yet he masters the exceedingly complex structure of his native language in the course of a short three or four years. (Slobin 1979, p. 74)

We know that young children are not formally instructed in the abstract complexities of language structure, complexities which trained linguists understand only imperfectly and most parents of young children understand far less. Yet without such instruction, virtually all children master the structure of at least one language system, and they do so in a remarkably short time and across a wide range of diverse environments. Whether more or less fortunate intellectually, economically, socially, or

[6]I am indebted to Linda Owen for these examples from her data.

physically, children learn the language of their community and do so at a time when their overall cognitive functioning appears far less complex than language learning seems to require. How does this happen?

Again, we look at the child's use of developmental forms. We have already seen that these forms give evidence of the content of the child's knowledge—*what* the child knows (for example, the child who says "sticked" and "forgived" knows that past tense is generally expressed as the suffix "ed" added to the base form of the verb). Developmental forms also tell us much about *how* the child develops spoken and written language—the process itself. The term "creative construction" is one that will become very familiar to you as you read this book. It is the term that I feel most aptly characterizes the active process in which the child engages in figuring out how language works, how meanings and expression relate. Both words, "creative" and "construction," are important. "Construction" suggests that the child actively builds a language system. One of the most striking characteristics of children's learning of language is that it is learning without "teaching" in the usual sense. Adults do not give children explicit instruction in language, nor do they plan a sequenced curriculum for the language-learning child. Rather, they interact with the child in many different contexts and they use language with others in the child's presence. Out of this diverse experience of language in use, the child constructs a complex system relating the expression he hears with the meanings he understands.

We sometimes hear children imitate language forms they hear. Yet the child's construction of his language system is more "creative" than it is imitative. The child uses forms that are not—that *cannot* be—the result of imitation, for they are forms adults in the child's environment do not use. Here are some examples from the talk of children of different ages as they tell stories for wordless storybooks.[7]

A four-year-old and his mother (who is blind):

C: An' an' the dog came, looked madly at the turtle.
M: Does he look mad at the turtle?
C: Yeah.

A five-year-old:

C: But when he was in here he was afraid, but then he lost his fraidness . . .

A second grader:

C: He was flying over the south-west-east thing. (weather vane)

---

[7] I am indebted to Debra Baker, Chris Grannan, Alicia Koury, and Sandra Longoria for these examples.

A fourth grader:

C: And then they got off-board. (The characters pictured are stepping out of a rowboat.)

These examples and the earlier "forgived," "keeped," and sticked" examples suggest a very cognitively active and innovative learner and learning process. Clearly, the children in these examples have discerned patterns, that is, regularities, in the language in use around them, and they are using these patterns to guide their creation of specific forms they have never heard and thus could not possibly be imitating. And they do this without explicit instruction, without drills, without a sequenced curriculum, without periodic tests. This characterization of the language learner as actively and creatively constructing a language system for himself is terribly important for us as teachers to understand, for it stands in striking contrast to our traditional notions of how children learn. We have traditionally maintained that a child will learn more effectively if we (1) structure the content to be learned so that it moves in a sequence from more simple to more complex items; (2) "reward" correct responses, thus strengthening them, and "punish" incorrect responses (for example, correct them), thus making them less likely to recur; (3) maximize the likelihood of successful responding, so that errors will not occur and be imprinted in the child's responding patterns; and (4) provide ample opportunity for the practice of correct behaviors so that they will be strengthened. But careful study of children acquiring language has made us reconsider the significance of these principles for language learning.

(1) Observing the language that surrounds children and is used with them, we see that, although many adults do simplify their speech to children in somewhat predictable ways, there exists nothing like the carefully structured simple-to-complex sequence that is used in school to teach subjects like math. And yet without this careful sequencing, far more children are successful in learning to speak a language than are successful in learning to multiply.

(2) Substantial research on children learning language in natural situations indicates that adults do not give or withhold reinforcement on the basis of the formal correctness of what children say, but rather on the basis of the truth of the message. Yet without the provision of reinforcement contingent on the correct use of language structure, all children, except those who are severely handicapped, develop, over time, the ability to create and use sentences which the adult would call grammatically well formed.

(3) As children learn language, they say many sentences that are different from adults' forms. Earlier structures like "all gone sticky" and "Where he is going?"; earlier pronunciations like "cwackers" and "twuck"; earlier word forms like "comed" and "goed," "mans" and "sheeps"; and earlier overgeneralized references like "doggie" used to refer to cats, dogs,

sheep, and cows alike—these are all in time replaced by adult forms. These developmental forms are not imprinted in the child's response patterns; but, without any drilling or special direct instruction designed to eradicate them, they drop out as the child matures, and are eventually replaced by adult forms.

(4) Language acquisition research demonstrates that children early use adult irregular forms like "went," "came," and "children." However, despite their practice of these adult forms, children later replace them with the forms "goed," "comed," and "childs" when they become aware of regular patterns for expressing past tense and plural in English (Ervin 1964). The early practice of the adult forms in these (and other similar) instances does *not* strengthen them. Thus sequenced content, reinforcement contingent on correctness of form, error-free responding, and practice of correct forms—whatever their relevance may be for other areas of learning (and some question their importance in any areas of learning)—clearly do not contribute significantly to the child's learning of language in any simple, obvious way.

Humans are apparently endowed with innate propensities for processing the language expression they encounter in meaningful contexts so as to construct for themselves the complex underlying system by which people in their linguistic community relate that expression to meaning. The young child actively uses his special language-learning abilities to discern regularities in the language he encounters, to construct working hypotheses based on them, and to continually revise his earlier hypotheses in the light of conflicts revealed through further interaction with others. Thus, his system over time is continuously revised and refined until it ultimately matches the adult system. It is crucial that we understand the nature of language acquisition in the child—both the developmental sequence involved and the processes that the child employs—in order that we move with this very strong current rather than interfere with it.

The goal of Secton Two is for us to understand better the sequence and, especially, the processes and situations of language development in children, and to consider possible classroom implications of this increased understanding. The assumption in Section Two is that the most effective situations for language development in school, as at home, are those that continue to engage the child fully in meaningful oral and written interactions that support the child's creative construction in talk and print and that treat the the child as a real conversationalist, reader, and writer.

LANGUAGE AND LEARNING

Language is inextricably entwined with our mental life—our perceiving, our remembering, our attending, our comprehending, our thinking—in short, all of our attempts to make sense of our experience in the world. In Section Three we'll consider how language can support children's ongoing learning. Three kinds of support have particular importance for teachers.

First, it is through language that our school children encounter a wider world of ideas than they have known at home. Through talk and print, they interact with others in new worlds of thought, knowledge, and feeling. In school these encounters with new ideas often fall into categories we designate as "literature" or "science" or "social studies"; but just as often they do not. There's the intriguing idea raised by the child's friend at lunch or on the playground, or the chance encounter the child has with a particular book while browsing "aimlessly" in the school library, or the interesting imagining the child reads in a story written by an unknown child in another class. In all these instances, language makes possible the child's encounter with the new idea.

Second, it is through the child's own talk and writing that he often "encounters" and shapes his own ideas. Language enables the child to make his idea into a *thing*, an object, an entity that he can refine, consider, shape, and act on, much as he might act on clay. As with clay, the child can shape and *re*shape—can play with possibilities, can explore alternatives, can create new worlds of his own mind.

And third, the child's expression of his thought is our most important means of knowing what kind of sense the child is making of his experience. It is in children's use of exploratory language—the language of their wondering, their inquiring, their conjecturing, their considering, their imagining—that we are occasionally able to glimpse through windows into our children's thought.

In the following conversation, a class of kindergarten children (with their teacher) discuss this question: "If you were in charge of the world, would you make only one language or many languages the way it is now?" (Warren is from a Chinese background, and Akemi is Japanese.)

TANYA: One language. Oh Yes! Then I could understand everyone in the whole world.
EDDIE: No, let it stay this way so different countries keeps on being not the same. Then you take trips to see what those countries are like and how they talk.
ELLEN: I like the world the way it is but I don't like fighting.
TEACHER: Is that because they have different languages?
ELLEN: Well, if they can't understand each other they might think good words sound like bad words.
WALLY: She means like if someone says, "Let's play," in French, then in Chinese they might think he said, "Let's fight."
WARREN: Keep it this way because if you're Chinese you would have to learn English.
TEACHER: Would English have to be the language everyone learns?
WARREN: I don't know what God likes to talk. Wait, I changed my mind. Let everyone say the same language. Then when my mommy and daddy speak quietly I could understand them.
TANYA: I changed my mind too. Better not have the same language. Here's why: whenever this whole world had the same language everyone would say they want their language to be the one everyone has to have. Then everyone would blame someone else for giving them the wrong language.

AKEMI: If everyone speak Japan, everyone have to live there. My country too small for the big America.

WARREN: Everyone can come to China. It's much bigger. Let Chinese be the language. No, I changed my mind. Let my mommy and daddy talk English all the time. (Paley 1981, pp. 119-20)

It is through language that these children pool their ideas, thus making a wider range of ideas available to all the children; it is through language that they respond to one another's ideas—put their own ideas up against another's ("No, let it stay this way," "She means . . .," "Everyone can come to China"); it is through language that they shape and *re*shape their ideas ("Wait, I changed my mind," "I changed my mind too"); and it is through the children's language that the teacher is able to glimpse the thinking behind the talk.

The basic notion of Section Three is that the child is constantly engaged in actively trying to make sense out of experience. As teachers, we stand in a particularly good place to support the child's sense-making efforts: by assuring the child's talk and print interaction with a wide world of ideas, by sustaining and extending the child's use of language to shape his own developing ideas, and by observing, interpreting, and responding to the child's ideas as they are reflected in his talk and writing.

LANGUAGE USE IN SOCIAL CONTEXTS

Section Four focuses on social aspects of language, that is, language in communication as children interact with others, through talk and print, for a range of different purposes and in a range of different situations.

From the child's very beginnings, he is typically involved in interaction with others. Adults who engage the infant in conversation express many communication purposes; for example, they use language to soothe or comfort the child, to comment on ongoing events, to restrain the child, to encourage him, to entertain him, and so on. But many adults not only express their communication purposes but also often respond to the child's behaviors (gestures, facial expressions, babbles) as conveying communication intentions, for example, as the child requesting something or expressing impatience. Many children are treated from the beginning as full conversational partners making purposeful contributions to the conversation and, over time, become competent, communicatively purposeful partners.[8] In short, the child learns early on that "language is put to a multiplicity of purposes" (Hymes 1972, p. xxii), just what many of those purposes are, and how one expresses them. The toddler uses language to request, to inquire, to initiate contact, and so on.

---

[8]Ways of interacting with infants and young children show considerable variation from culture to culture. See Heath (1983), Ward (1971), and Philips (1983) for examples of adult-child interaction patterns that are different from the Anglo middle-class pattern described here.

Within the child's ongoing interactional experience, in addition to learning how to express different purposes in communication, the child also develops a range of communication styles, that is, different ways of expressing himself in different situations.

Children learn, somehow, to take into account a host of social factors in each communication situation, and to use the appropriate expressive style for that occasion. For example, the age, status, and relationship of the person with whom a child is speaking, and the context in which the communication is taking place, will significantly influence what the child says (or does not say) and how he says it.

How can we explain that young children acquire, without special tutoring, not only the structure of language but the subtle variations in the social use of language as well? For example, how do they come to know that "Shut up, stupid" is an OK communication to a younger sibling, but not to a visiting grandparent? How does the child come to know that his mother's gentle "Bobby, are you almost ready for bed?" is not simply a question calling for a yes or no answer, but that it also conveys her desire that he move more efficiently toward that goal? In short, what is the meaning provided by the social context of the message, and how does a child learn to recognize it and adapt his language appropriately?

The child entering elementary school demonstrates his considerable knowledge of speaking styles. He modifies his way of speaking, for example, when he talks to a younger child or to an outside visitor to the classroom or to a close friend on the playground. He readily slips in and out of different roles in dramatic play—now a baby, now Batman, now parent, now teacher—and his talk is appropriate to each role. And think of the literature we read to children, literature involving a range of speaking styles—different characters in different situations and relationships, expressing different moods.

Section Four focuses on the child's development of communication abilities, that is, the development of his ability to express a range of communication purposes in ways that are appropriate to different social contexts. We'll consider the support the classroom offers for the child's social language development as the child adds new purposes and styles to his range, including purposes best served by written expression with its own stylistic range.

LANGUAGE VARIATION

All natural human languages are similar in important ways. For example, they all involve the association of verbalized sounds with conceptualized meanings; they all provide for making statements, questions, requests, equational propositions; they all include both vowel and consonant sounds. And yet, within the bounds of what constitutes human language, there is a range of diversity which has been a source of fascination for many scholars. We know that an Englishman does not talk like an Iranian; we say they speak different languages. But we know, too, that English people do not talk like Americans, though most would agree that they do speak the same language. And what of the differences among English, a single language, as spoken in Australia, Ireland, and Canada? We do not even need to go that far. What about the English spoken by a Bostonian, a Texan, a Brooklyner, an Alabaman, a Los Angelean? These dialect differences are geographically based. There are also dialect differences relating to ethnic and social groups—what of the dialects of English spoken by Navajo children in Albuquerque, by Mexican-American children in San Antonio, by black children in Harlem, by Puerto Rican children in Miami?

As our classrooms increasingly include children from diverse social backgrounds learning together, we hear more of these language variations in our children's talk. Here are some kindergarten children in a dramatic-play area.

Here they are playing with dolls:

C-1:   My baby, she cryin'.
C-2:   I'm goin' gi' huh some foo (food).
C-3:   (talking to a doll) Lil' boy you better shut yo mouf an' git up dere and eat, boy fo' you git hit on da head.
C-1:   Dat's V———'s baby.

Now they are playing with toy cars.

C-1:   Tol'ya dat's woner bug, he rollin' by hisself, ain't he? Woner bug, he a bad lil' ol cah. He be catchin' all up wit you. Cause I . . .
C-2:   Bettah watch out, boy!
C-1:   Woner bug, he'll 'tack dat cah, righ'?
C-3:   Um-uh. Woner bug is *mean!*
C-1:   He'll be mean ta . . .
C-2:   A-o-o-o-o he fixin' to dribe (drive) hisself. Rum-m-m-m.
C-3:   Git 'way from baby wit dat cah, gir'. My baby, she, she want dat cah.

C-1:   Dat's my baby's bottle. I put some milk in here fo' mah baby.
C-2:   Here dat kine (kind). You bettah hush you mout.
C-1:   Leabe her 'lone. She sleepin'.[9]

And here are some other kindergarten children enacting with puppets a story that had been read to them.

C-1:   "¿Cómo estaba la escuela? ("How was school?")
C-2:   No, dijo la mamá, "¿Cómo te ha ido en escuela?" Dijo, "Maaa, todos los niñós se burlaron de mí. Porque dijo . . . me dijeron que . . . que . . ." (No, the mother said, "How did things go at school?" He said, "Maaaa, all the children made fun of me. Because he told me . . . they told me that . . . that . . .")

[9]I am indebted to Brenda Cone for these excerpts from her data.

C-1: "No me debo de poner este ropa en . . . para ir a la escuela." ("I shouldn't wear these clothes in . . . to go to school.")

C-2: "No te preocu . . ." ("Don't you worr . . .")

C-1: "No te pacupes. Te hago algo. Te hago una chaqueta." ("Don't you worry. I'll make you something. I'll make you a jacket.")[10]

Though we may hear differences in the children's talk, we may be unaware of the subtle but pervasive influence that children's varying language and behavior styles has on our attitudes toward them and on our expectations regarding their intellectual and social potential. Whether we like it or not, different language styles foster different attitudes toward people who use them. Some language styles (dialects, languages, or whatever) convey "nice, but not too bright"; others convey "intelligent, but cold"; others "quick, but stuck up or hostile"; others "slow, but it's not *his* fault (poor thing)," depending on who we are, what our language and lifestyle happen to be, and what sort of familiarity we have with members of various social and linguistic groups.

We may also be unaware of deeper-level differences than the talk itself, the various pronunciations, particular word forms, and sentence structures our children use. Research is accumulating that indicates that children from different social backgrounds interpret quite differently many of the interaction events that are so typical in classroom instruction, for example, whole-group instruction or one-to-one interaction with the teacher. What constitutes appropriate ways of interacting with others differs among social groups. Some of these differences have special importance in school. We can assume that children differ in their notions of when to speak and when to be silent, of how to interpret teachers' questions (Is the teacher seeking information she doesn't have, is she testing to see if you know something, or is she criticizing your behavior, for example, "Are you talking again?"). When our notions of appropriate classroom interaction differ from the child's, we run the risk of misinterpreting the child's behavior, thus, for example, interpreting the child's respectful silence as evidence of the child's being uncooperative or ignorant.

Many classrooms provide opportunities for children to extend their language range to include more than one language. In Section Five we'll consider the nature of the task of second-language learning and how we might best support the children's learning.

Whatever problems we still have in learning to understand, accept, and effectively teach *all* the children in our increasingly diverse classrooms, there are encouraging signs that we are coming to realize that this diversity does not confuse children or contaminate their language, cognitive, and social growth; rather, it contributes positively to the rich environment we know is most conducive to that continuing growth. How effectively we capitalize on that richness for children's learning will depend in no small part on how well we understand it.

[10]I am indebted to Pat Seawell for this example from her data.

FINALLY

The goals of this book are two: (1) to better understand language and how children acquire and use it and (2) to better relate that understanding to the classroom.

To better understand

the complexity of the child's knowledge of language structure, knowledge that enables him to express meanings and to grasp the meanings expressed by others (Section One);

the processes by which the child's remarkable knowledge of language structure has been, and continues to be, accomplished, processes by which the child creatively constructs language through interaction with others (Section Two);

the uses the child makes of language in his learning about the world— his use of language to shape his own ideas and to encounter new ideas from others (Section Three);

the many communication purposes for which the child uses language and the many ways he shapes his language to be appropriate in various social contexts (Section Four);

the diverse social backgrounds our children bring to school—the various ways in which they understand and participate in interaction (Section Five).

To better relate our understanding to the classroom in order to actively

build on the child's language knowledge in helping him move on, building new understandings and ways of expressing them in talk and print (Section One);

support the child's processes of creative construction as he extends his language expression further into oral and written channels (Section Two);

invite the child's use of language for learning—to inquire, to conjecture, to wonder, to imagine (Section Three);

engage the child in purposeful and diverse interactions with others in talk and print (Section Four);

engage the child in interacting meaningfully with others from a wide range of language and social backgrounds (Section Five).

We owe all our children no less than this.

2

Native Speaker
Abilities

INTRODUCTION

This is a book about children's language—what it is like, how children develop it, how they use it. Yet we begin by exploring our own knowledge of language. As adults, we represent a sort of end point.[1] We all "know" at least one language. Virtually every child, like ourselves, comes to know at least one language. What is that knowledge that we have as adults and that the children we teach are in the process of developing?

To know a language is to know many things, some of which will be considered in subsequent sections. The aspect of language knowledge that we are concerned with in the present section is our knowledge of language structure. Buildings have structure. So do bicycles, political organizations, and philosphical theories. This is to say that they all have identifiable components, or parts, that relate to each other in systematic ways. You know what the parts of bicycles are—seat, handle bars, brakes, pedals, and so forth. You also recognize that the total set of parts alone does not comprise a bicycle, but only a heap of parts. It is only when the parts are arranged, related, organized in certain expected ways that they become an instance of the structure we call a bicycle.

So, too, in language. The structure of language is far more complex and abstract than the structure of bicycles, but it too involves parts and relationships among them. You already know what some of the parts are—words, sounds, meanings that we express. You also are aware that the parts don't go together in just any old way. Language isn't a heap of parts. Rather, it involves ways of organizing the parts, ways of putting them together, ways of relating them.

None of us can remember developing the amazingly complex knowledge we have of language elements and the possibilities for their organiza-

---

[1]"End point" is, of course, a relative term. We never reach an end point in our development of language. We continue throughout our adult lives to encounter unfamiliar words and new communication situations that place new demands on our use of language.

tion. Certainly no one ever taught us this. Yet, just as certainly, we learned it. And so it is with every child we teach.

We begin, then, by considering the complex knowledge of language structure that virtually every human child develops for at least one language. We look first at ourselves and our own complex knowledge. That is where it is most real for all of us. The amazing thing is, your knowledge of language structure is far more vast and intricate than you ever dreamed. You know, unconsciously, intuitively, far more than you ever suspected. Basic to this section is the premise that your knowing involves two levels: the level of meaning and the level of expression. That is, you know many meanings—for example, categories, ideas, entities, attributes, and relationships—that are expressed in your language; you also know how those meanings connect with expression possibilities—specific sounds, words, and word combinations. To have knowledge only of meanings but to be unable to relate these meanings to expression of them is not to have a language. You may have had the experience of wanting to ask a speaker of another language some question or to make some comment to her, but though you had a clear and simple meaning to convey and knew that that meaning was easily graspable by her, you lacked the knowledge of the expression associated with that meaning in that person's language—that is, you did not know her language.

Yet to be aware only of expression possibilities is not to have a language either. When you listen to someone speak a language you do not know, you hear verbal sounds. To you it sounds like noises, like babbling. With practice, you might become able to mimic those sound strings, much as parrots or parakeets mimic. This would not make you a "knower of the language," however. Expression alone is not sufficient. What exists for the speaker of the language you don't know, and exists for you in *your* language, is knowledge of the relation of that expression (those sequences of sounds) to meanings.

Knowledge of meaning, expression, and the relations between them—all this is, necessarily, present in your mind for the language(s) you know. It is this knowledge that we begin to explore in this chapter. This is to begin our story of language development at the end, with the adult, with *you*. To understand the richness and complexity of this aspect of language is (1) to recognize it in its developing form in the children we teach; (2) to appreciate the incredible accomplishment of every child in developing the structure of language; and, above all, (3) to become aware of ways to build on our children's knowledge of language structure in their classroom experience.

RECOGNIZING GRAMMATICAL AND UNGRAMMATICAL SENTENCES

As a speaker of English, you have the ability to judge which strings of words are acceptable arrangements of appropriate parts and which strings are not. The kind of "acceptability" we are concerned with here does not have to do with use of polite words rather than rude ones, but rather with the organization of language parts to convey intended meanings. Speakers of any language will judge some strings to be OK organizations of parts and others not to be. Further, these judgments will, in the vast majority of cases, be the same for all speakers of that language. Here are some examples for you to judge. Put a check mark beside those sentences in the group that follows that you feel are unacceptable English sentences.

1. Mary married a drunken sailor.
2. It was a drunken sailor that Mary married.
3. It was Mary that married a drunken sailor.
4. That was it Mary married a drunken sailor.
5. It was drunken that Mary married a sailor.
6. It was nice that Mary married a sailor.
7. It was sailor that Mary married a drunk.
8. It was strange that Mary married a drunk.
9. It was a drunk that Mary married strange.
10. It was drunk that Mary married a strange.
11. It was a drunk that strange Mary married.
12. That Mary married a drunken sailor was strange.
13. That Mary married a strange sailor was drunk.
14. That Mary married a drunk was sailor.
15. That Mary married a drunk was inevitable.
16. Mary's marrying a drunken sailor came as a surprise to us.
17. Mary's drunken sailor came to surprise us.
18. Sailor Mary's drunken to surprise us came.
19. What shall Mary do with a drunken sailor?
20. What with a drunken sailor Mary shall do?
21. Shall Mary do drunk with what a sailor?
22. Shall Mary have fun with such a sailor?
23. With what a sailor shall Mary do drunk?

I checked 4, 5, 7, 9, 10, 13, 14, 18, 20, 21, and 23, and my guess is that you did too. It would be interesting to take this set of sentences (or better yet, some set of sentences that you make up) and try them out on other speakers of English to see whether their judgments are the same as yours. Chances are they will be similar, if not identical, to your own.

What I am calling your ability to judge the acceptability of sentence strings, many linguists call the ability to judge the grammaticalness of sentences. But we need to be careful of the term "grammatical" here because for many of us this word conveys a notion of "correctness" that contemporary linguists do not intend. Probably most of us had at least one English teacher, usually somewhere between fifth grade and ninth grade, who tried to give us "good grammar" with the same kind of determination and noble intentions with which our parents had earlier tried to give us castor oil or vitamin pills. We labeled words as verbs, adjectives, nouns, interjections; we avoided ending sentences with prepositions (at least during English class);

we diagrammed sentences; and we spouted definitions abut "name of a person, place, or thing" on demand. Some of our teachers seemed to feel that these activities would make us "educated" and well-rounded as adults; others seemed to feel that such activities would lead us to increased social status and better paying jobs; and still others seemed convinced that these activities would build character, as the endurance of hardship is felt, by some, to do.

But if we are going to use the term "grammar," we need to rid ourselves of our traditional notions—our seventh-grade labels, definitions, shoulds and shouldn'ts of speaking, and our memories of classroom tedium and drudgery. We use "grammar" here as a neutral term, referring simply to what you know intuitively about the basic meaning and expression units of your language and the possibilities for their combination—the structure of your language. To say, then, that you recognize some sentences of your language to be "grammatical" and others to be "ungrammatical" is only to say that you will judge some to be sequences of language elements which are in accordance with your intuitive knowledge of the organizational possibilities of English units, and others not. In the present case, some of these sentences are in accordance with your notions of meaning-expression relations, and some violate your notions. For some of these sentences you cannot relate any meaning to the expression; for others, though you understand the meaning, its expression is organized in a jarring, unexpected way. Both cases are "ungrammatical" for you. They do not fit your expectations.

Notice that your judgment of the grammaticality of a sentence does not depend on whether or not you have ever actually encountered that particular sentence before, but rather on whether you feel that such a sentence is an acceptable possibility for your language. Notice, too, that your grammaticality judgments do not depend on your ability to talk about why or how you made them, nor on your ability to label sentence parts.

How do we account for the overwhelming (though not total) agreement among the speakers of a language as to which sentences are and are not grammatically possible in that language? When you know a language, you intuitively know a set of structural possibilities for sentences (possibilities for selection and organization of parts and expression of them), and you recognize particular sentences as being consistent or inconsistent with that set, even though you are probably not able to actually describe the set of principles against which you are "checking" each sentence. Whatever this set of principles is, it is clearly one you share with other speakers of your language, for they, for the most part, make grammaticality judgments similar to yours, though they—like you— cannot describe the set of organizational principles against which they judge the grammaticality of each sentence.

RECOGNIZING MORE AND LESS GRAMMATICAL SENTENCES

We have considered two extremes: grammatical and ungrammatical. Actually, the situation is more complex and far more interesting than this. Some of the sentences we encounter are difficult to categorize simply as grammatical or ungrammatical; we might want to put them in a "well . . . sort of OK" area. Much of poetry and humor lives in this middle region where sentences are often structured somewhat deviantly in order to create special effects and convey special meanings. As speakers of English (or any language, of course) there would be considerable agreement among us as to which of several sentences is "more grammatical" and which is less so — that is, which sentences conform more nearly to our notions of what constitutes acceptable arrangements of parts in the expression of meanings in our language. A well-known trio follows, and most speakers of English would rank the three sentences from most to least grammatical as they are ordered here:

> John plays golf.
> Golf plays John.
> John plays symmetrical.

One university student, obviously more concerned about math than about golf, offered this trio as a substitute:

> I'm taking math.
> Math's taking me.
> I'm taking symmetrical.

Whichever set you prefer, you will probably find the first sentence of each straightforward enough, that is, clearly in accordance with the set of principles you have regarding meaning-expression relations. For the third sentence in each set, you probably feel a need to change it in some way to make it a message-carrying structure. For example, you might want to change it to "John plays symmetrica*lly*" (we might picture John lining up a course for himself in which both sides were identical, and he played item 1 on one side and then item 1 on the other, and so on) or to "John plays *Symmetrical*" in which "Symmetrical" is the name of a new game that has just come on the market. But the sentence as it stands is simply puzzling. There are a number of things one can "play"—golf, second fiddle, the piano, tricks, Parcheesi, sick, host, Hamlet, hop scotch—but one cannot play "symmetrical." One can take math, a coffee break, a joke, her book, tennis lessons, an aspirin, but one cannot take "symmetrical." We may want to ask, "You're taking symmetrical *what?*" We look for a something to be played or taken, and "symmetrical" alone just will not do.

But what about the middle sentence of each set? Here is where the fun is. We expect some*one* to be playing/taking some*thing*, but we find the reverse—the some*thing* is somehow controlling (playing/taking) the some*one*. It is as if we have attributed human characteristics to golf or math. We might hear John's wife, who knows her husband is not a promising golfer, say, "Golf plays John." We might hear a frustrated university student sigh, "Math's taking me." But notice that the something/someone switch in the second sentence of each set—a switch from one kind of noun to another— is much less drastic than the switch in the third sentence of each set, from a "something" (played or taken) to a descriptor word—from a noun to an adjective.

Some linguists refer to this ability of native speakers as the recognition of "levels of grammaticality." But whatever you choose to call it, the fact is that we realize when sentences violate our structural expectations in interesting ways that still convey meanings (and often add special ones), and when they violate our expectations so drastically that they cease to convey meanings at all. Poets and humorists often express themselves in deliberately deviant ways in order to achieve special effects. From A.A. Milne's *Winnie-the-Pooh* comes this:

> "And how are you?" said Winnie-the-Pooh.
> Eyore shook his head from side to side.
> "Not very how," he said. "I don't seem to have felt at all how for a long
time."(Milne 1956, p. 43)

And from James Thurber's *The 13 Clocks*, this:

> The Duke is lamer than I am old, and I am shorter than he is cold, but it
> comes to you with some surprise that I am wiser than he is wise. (Thurber
> 1950, p. 63)

And Dylan Thomas's *Fern Hill:*

> Now as I was young and easy under the apple boughs
> About the lilting house and happy as the grass was green,
>   The night above the dingle starry,
>   Time let me hail and climb
>   Golden in the heydays of his eyes, . . . (Thomas 1953, p. 178)

Notice again that your ability to rank sentences for grammaticality levels, like your ability to judge clear cases as simply grammatical or ungrammatical, is attributable to your knowledge of meaning possibilities, expression possibilities, and the relations between them.

RECOGNIZING RELATIONS WITHIN SENTENCES

A key concept in language, as in any structured system, is that of relatedness—relationships among the parts. For now, we can think of the words of our language as being its major parts (though we will want to modify this later). We know that sentences in our language are not randomly ordered strings of words. If they were, then different arrangements of the same set of words would mean the same thing and there would be no difference in meaning between, for example, "The squirrel was looking for a nut" and "The nut was looking for a squirrel." But in English, as in many languages, the order of words does make a difference in expressing meaning. It is largely in the ordering of the parts in sentences that relationships among the meaning parts are expressed. The following sentences all contain the same set of words, but the differences in the order of words correspond to differences in relational meanings (and in fact, some orders convey very little if any meaning at all).

> The teacher spanked the rude girl.
> The girl spanked the rude teacher.
> The rude teacher spanked the girl.
> The rude girl spanked the teacher.
> Rude the the spanked teacher girl.
> Spanked the girl the teacher rude.

George Miller has said, "The meaning of an utterance is not a linear sum of the meanings of the words that comprise it" (Miller 1965, p. 18). Much of the meaning of the sentence is relational, and clearly the order of the parts in the expression helps to convey those relational meanings. We would all pretty much agree as to what is meant by "girl," "rude," "teacher," "spanked," and "the," but the arrangements of these meaning parts convey, in addition, another essential kind of meaning—who is doing the spanking, who is getting the spanking, who is rude. The arrangement of the elements in the expression provides the answers: "rude girl" attributes the characteristic of rudeness to the girl; "rude teacher" attributes it to the teacher. The ordering ". . . teacher spanked . . ." makes the teacher the spanker, relating these parts as agent and action, while the order ". . . spanked . . . girl" makes the girl the spankee, relating these parts as action and recipient. Reversal of "teacher" and "girl" in the sentences changes the relationships so that the girl becomes the agent of the spanking and the teacher the receiver. Who is doing what to whom is largely expressed by the ordering of those parts (words) which name the doer, what is done, and to whom.[2] Miller, attempting to demonstrate that the ordering of words in sequence gives clues to their relationships, once used this example: "A Venetian blind is not the same as a blind Venetian" (Miller 1965, p. 16).

Another way to approach this important point about sentence meaning relating to the arrangement of the individual words in expression as well as to their individual meanings, is to take the individual word meanings out of a "sentence" and see what kind of meaning, if any, is left. Here is a sentence that contains little in the way of word meanings but much in the way of relational meaning.

> The blugy chinzels slottled prasily on the flubbish wub. (Campbell and Lindfors 1969, p. 106)

---

[2]Notice that the same ordering of the three important words "teacher . . . spanked . . . girl" indicates different relationships—the who is doing what to whom—if we make some additional changes in the sentence, for example, "The *teacher* was *spanked* by the *girl*." Clearly, word order is not the only expressive means by which we convey relationships of sentence parts, but it is a major way.

You can ask and answer a number of appropriate questions relating to this expression without having any meanings at all for the basic "words": "blugy," "chinzels," "slottled," "prasily," "flubbish," and "wub". (Try to make up your own questions and answer them before looking at the questions that follow.)

1. What did the blugy chinzels do?
2. How did they slottle?
3. Where did they slottle?
4. What kind of chinzels were they?
5. What slottled?
6. What kind of wub did the chinzels slottle on?

What does your ability to ask and answer these questions tell you about your knowledge of the relationships in the sentence? That you can ask and answer questions 1 and 5 indicates that you understand "the blugy chinzels" to be the doers of the action of "slottling." Being able to ask and answer question 2 shows that you recognize "prasily" as indicating the way in which the action was carried out. If you can ask and answer question 3, you clearly understand that the phrase "on the flubbish wub" tells where the action occurred. And your ability to ask and answer questions 4 and 6 indicates that you recognize "blugy" to be an attribute of the "chinzels" and "flubbish" to be an attribute of a particular "wub." The relationships of agent-action, action-manner, action-location, and attribute-object are indentifiable even in the absence of familiar word meanings. Notice that there are other questions you would *not* have asked about the original sentence; for example: "How did the flubbish blugy?" "Where did the prasily chinzels?" "Where did the slottled wub?" Why not?

The order of the "words" in our nonsense sentence gave you important clues to the relational meanings in the sentence. But you are no doubt aware that it was not *only* the word order that provided clues. Suffixes on some of the words helped you a lot. Can you find all five suffixes that gave you clues to the function various (non)words were serving in the sentence? Two very important ones are the "s" of "chinzels" and the "ed" of "slottled." Many English words which are not plural nouns are written with a final "s" (pronounced like a /z/[3] in "Chinzel*s*") as in goe*s*, i*s*, Marie'*s*. However, the final letter "s" (with different pronunciations as in buss*es* /əz/, truck*s* /s/, and train*s* /z/) often does indicate a plural noun, and in this case you interpreted the "s" in this way. And though there are many English words which we write with "ed" as the last two letters and which are not past tense verbs (r*ed*, se*ed*, Fr*ed*), many English words that end this way in writing *are* past tense verb forms (with the "ed" variously pronounced as /t/ in hopp*ed*, /d/ in tri*ed*, and /əd/ in want*ed*), and you interpreted "slottled" as

---

[3]We will use the symbol / / to indicate that we are talking about sounds in words rather than about spellings. The symbol /ə/ represents the "uh" sound that we often insert as a hesitation in conversation, or the unstressed word "a" in, for example, "They bought *a* new house."

a past tense verb form. The "y" of "blugy" and the "ish" of "flubbish" follow adjective suffix patterns familiar to you, and the "ly" of "prasily" doubtless reminded you of this familiar pattern found in a host of manner adverbs you know—briskly, sluggishly, laughingly, aggressively. So, though you had never before encountered the major content words of this sentence and thus had no experiential meanings for them, you were able to glean considerable information from the arrangements of the parts in the expression (the sentence itself) and from the suffixes of some of the words. The word order and suffixes suggested a familiar organizational framework of sentence relationships to you.

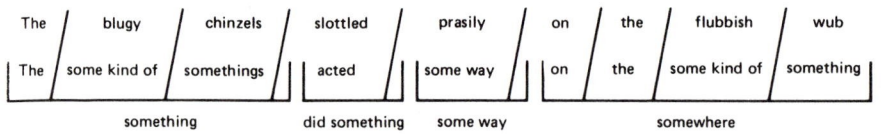

Clearly, then, there is far more to your understanding of the possible sentences of your language than the meanings of the individual words that comprise them. In a sentence like "The teacher spanked the rude girl," it is surely important to know what a teacher is; but it is just as important and necessary to know how "teacher" functions in relation to the other sentence elements.

If you were given a straightforward, routine sort of English sentence and asked to divide it into its major parts, there would be considerable agreement among you and your fellow English speakers as to where the major breaks would occur. And there would be virtually total agreement as to where major breaks could not occur. Try these English examples:

1. The little boy was bouncing a red ball.
2. Put your coat in the closet.
3. Joan fled when she saw her mother coming around the corner carrying a heavy sack of groceries.

Most speakers of English would probably see the major divisions of the first sentence as "the little boy" and "was bouncing a red ball" and would probably put a secondary break between "was bouncing" and "a red ball." Asked to describe your reason for dividing the sentence as you did, you would probably say something like "Well, 'the little boy' tells who was doing something, and 'was bouncing the red ball' tells what he was doing, and within that, 'the red ball' tells what it was that he was bouncing." Probably no native English speaker would divide that sentence exactly in the middle, with four words on each side of the break: "The little boy was" and "bouncing a red ball." In explaining this you would say perhaps that "the little boy was" is an incomplete part and does not seem to function as any kind of sensible unit. Probably no English speaker would have regarded "a little" or "a red" or "bouncing a red" or "boy was bouncing a" as major cohesive sentence parts either.

Of sentence 2 you would perhaps say something like "'Put' tells you what to do, and 'your coat' tells you what you're going to 'put,' and 'in the closet' tells where you're going to put it." But probably no English speaker would divide the sentence as "Put your" + "coat in" + "the closet."

How about the third sentence, now, a considerably longer one? Most English speakers will see this sentence as a combination of parts, each of which is like a sentence itself and thereby potentially divisible into the same kinds of parts that we could identify in our first two sentences—doers, things done, locations of things done, things that get done to (recipients of action). Most would agree that one major part of this longer sentence has to do with Joan's fleeing, another with her seeing her mother, another with her mother coming around the corner, and another with her mother carrying a sack of groceries. Thus, we get something like

> Joan fled
> when she saw her mother
> (her mother was) coming around the corner
> (her mother was) carrying a heavy sack of groceries.

We need not worry at this point about the repeated "her mother was," which I have put in parentheses. These repeated portions are present in the meaning of each major sentence part. However, English, like most languages, deletes repeated expression of the same meaning elements when shorter sentences are combined into longer ones.

You might well ask, "Yes, but don't we all tend to divide the sentences in similar ways because of those teachers we had who drilled us so hard on all that business about subjects and predicates, direct objects and adverb phrases, and because of all those exercises where we had to 'Draw one line under the subject and two lines under the predicate' for endless lists of sentences?" It is a good question, but the answer is "Probably not." Probably you divide the sentences into major parts as you do in spite of, rather than because of, your seventh-grade English teacher's efforts. Your divisions, and your *non*divisions, reflect your grasp of the important functional units of sentences. You know that certain words cluster and work as a kind of unit in the sentence, and that those units can often be further subdivided into finer relationships among their parts.

It is interesting to note in passing that many early utterances of young children, whatever the language they are acquiring, express the basic relationships that your sentence divisions reflect. (This will be discussed more fully in Section Two.) Somewhere around two years of age, children go through a period in which many of their sentences are two-word constructions. Here are a few examples of types of early two-word utterances of children, which demonstrate some important basic relationships present in their earliest combinings.

> Throw ball (Meaning "Throw me the ball." Action-object relation)
> Doggie chair (Meaning "My toy dog is on the chair." Object-location relation)
> Daddy go (Meaning "Daddy is going." Agent-action relation)
> Go bye-bye (Meaning "I want to go outside." Action-location relation)
> Baby little (Meaning "The baby is little." Object-attribute relation)
> Mommy juice (Meaning "It's Mommy's juice." Possessor-object relation)

Notice what the child's two-word utterances do *not* include: me the, doggie is, on the, to go. It appears that relations of major sentence parts play a crucial role for the child as she attempts to construct the set of organizational principles of the language of her community, those principles that somehow hold together and account for the diversity of the specific sentences she hears. No seventh-grade English teacher has as yet gotten hold of the two-year-old child and put her through her subject-predicate paces. Our sensitivity to the relationships in the sentences of human language runs much deeper than anything any teacher ever "gave" us. It is more likely that it was our sensitivity to sentence relationships that enabled us to identify "subjects" and "predicates," rather than that our "being taught to" identify subjects and predicates enabled us to grasp relationships within sentences. Our teachers may have given us some labels and they may have brought to a conscious level the relational meanings and their expression in our language—meanings and expression that we had already grasped intuitively, but they did not put these relational understandings in our heads in the first place. We built those understandings for ourselves as we interacted with others as children and in those interactions figured out how language works.

Summing up, we find that we recognize basic parts of sentences and how they are related. We recognize some subparts of sentences as forming clusters, as belonging together as single units that serve some special relational function in the sentence. We get clues to the relationships within sentences from the order or arrangement of the words in sequence, as well as from the particular forms of some of the words. We know that both the meanings of particular words (which we know) *and* the meanings conveyed by their forms and their arrangements in strings are crucial to the total "meaning" of a sentence. That is quite a bit of knowing! And that knowing accounts for our ability to divide sentences of our language into major parts and subparts. But as considerable as that knowledge is, it represents only a small fraction of what we know and what all children learn as native speakers of a language.

RECOGNIZING RELATIONS AMONG SENTENCES

Your knowledge of relationships in language extends beyond your recognition of the interaction of the parts of individual, single sentences. You also recognize some sentences as being what Fromkin and Rodman call "stylistic variants" of other sentences (Fromkin and Rodman 1974). That is, you recognize some sets of sentences as being related in that they represent various ways of expressing the same general meaning.

1. John's little sister kicked him in the shins.
2. John's younger female sibling kicked him in the shins.
3. It was John's little sister who kicked him in the shins.
4. What John's little sister did was kick him in the shins.
5. John was kicked in the shins by his little sister.
6. The one who kicked John in the shins was his little sister.

If you examine these sentences, you will see that each one contains the same set of propositions (meanings), namely that (1) John has a sister, (2) she is younger than John, (3) she kicked him in the shins, and (4) it happened at some time in the past. Each sentence in the set, each "stylistic variant," (particular expression) may focus our attention more on one aspect of the message than on another, but they all contain the same basic set of meaning elements and meaning relationships.

What kinds of differences are there among the sentences of the preceding set? You will see that some sentences include additional words not present in the first sentence, which is the simplest, most direct, and unelaborated version of the message; for example, "It was . . . that," "What . . . did was . . . ," ". . . was . . . by," "The one who . . . was. . . ." You will also notice that in some of the sentences the parts are ordered differently—in sentences 5 and 6 the one kicked (John) is mentioned before the kicker (his little sister). Sentence 2 refers to John's little sister as his "younger female sibling," a phrase which, although slightly different in tone, identifies the same person. But they are all different expressions of the same basic meaning.

Now here is another set of sentences for you to contrast with the preceding set. You will see that these are *not* related structurally, as was the case with the first set; they are not different expressions of the same meaning.

1. John's little sister kicked him in the shins.
2. John's little sister kicks hard.
3. John dislikes his little sister.
4. John's leg is in a cast.
5. John kicked her back.
6. Little sisters can be dangerous.

Each sentence of the set relates to the original in some important way, but not (as with the earlier set) as a stylistic variant of it. You might want to see if you can characterize in your own words how each of sentences 2 through 6 relates to sentence 1. You will see that each is conveying a new message rather than expressing the original message in a different way.

RECOGNIZING AMBIGUITIES

Knowing that we can express the same message in different ways is an important part of our knowledge as native speakers of a language. Equally important, perhaps, is our knowledge of the reverse—a single sentence structure can express more than one meaning. It will not be difficult for you to find several meanings for each of the following sentences.

1. The bill was large.
2. I walked beside the bank.

3. That's really cool.
4. That movie was far out.

5. They are eating apples.
6. Did you ever see a horse fly?
7. That's a beautiful woman's handbag.
8. Orkin—world's largest pest control company.
9. The astronauts are taking underwear and spices to season their food.

10. His cooking upsets me.
11. Visiting relatives can be a nuisance.
12. Dress optional.

The sentences have been grouped into three sets because though they all are single sentences that can be interpreted in different ways, the variability of possible interpretation depends on different characteristics for each set. You can see that, in the first set, the sentences are ambiguous (have more than one possible interpretation) because of the various possible meanings of a particular word. What was it that was large? The amount you had to pay for a purchase or service? The denomination of the paper currency you had? The actual size of the paper currency in question? The mouth part of a duck? Or even, in some areas of the country, the front flap of a cap. And did you walk beside a river bank or beside the bank where your money is kept? Does the coolness of the object in sentence 3 refer to its temperature or to how much the speaker admires it? And what about the movie—is it some distance from town, or is it very contemporary and appealing to teenagers? In these examples, the multiple meanings of the particular words "bill," "bank," "cool," and "far out" account for the ambiguity.

Try this one. What is the crucial word on which the ambiguity hinges in this children's joke from Bennett Cerf 's *Book of Laughs*?

> Another day Marvin ran into his house. He let a fly come in.
> Then Marvin ran out of the house.
> He let in another fly.
> Marvin ran into the house again.
> Another fly came in.
> At last his mother said, "Marvin, I wish you would not run in and out of the house. I do not like all of these flies in here."
> Marvin said, "All right, Mother, show me which flies you do not like, and I will make them go out." (Cerf 1959, pp. 6-7)

What is Marvin's meaning of the word "all"? What is his mother's meaning for this same word?

For the sentences of the second group (5 to 9), it is not the meanings of the individual words that make the sentences ambiguous. The crucial question about each of these sentences is, How do the words cluster into phrases and how do the parts relate to each other? Notice that in sentences

5 and 6 you actually say the sentence differently for each of the two possible meanings. Your voice reflects the phrases and relations in the stress and rhythm you use when you say each one. (If you doubt this, try saying each of these two sentences with one of its possible meanings to a friend to see if you can communicate the meaning you intend just by the way you say it.)

| They | are eating | *apples.* |
| They | are | *eating* apples. |

The first of this pair could be an appropriate answer to the question, "What are they eating?" The second could be an appropriate answer to the question, "What kind of apples are they?" Now can you describe the differences in the way you say the horse fly sentence, depending on whether you are asking about an insect or whether you are asking about a horse that flies?

Sentence 7 make us want to ask, "What is it that is beautiful, the handbag or the woman?" That is, what does "beautiful" cluster with or belong with? Is it a beautiful handbag belonging to a woman? Or a handbag belonging to a beautiful woman? There is a relation of attribution here, and the question is, is "beautiful" to be attributed to the woman or to the handbag? The situation is similar in the Orkin sentence: What is it that is the "largest"? What does "largest" cluster with, or what is "largest" an attribute of? Is Orkin the control company for the "world's largest pests"? Or is it the "world's largest company" for controlling any pests, regardless of their size?

In sentence 9 (actually spoken by a newscaster), two organizations or groupings of the words are possible:

The astronauts are taking underwear   and spices to season their food.
The astronauts are taking   underwear and spices   to season their food.

For each of the sentences of the second group, then, two different organizations in the groupings and relations of the sentence parts are possible, and each carries a different meaning.

The special shared characteristic of the sentences of the third group (10, 11, and 12), which makes them all ambiguous may be harder to detect than that of the first two groups. It helps us understand their special character, I think, if we rephrase these sentences a bit, beginning each one with "something":

10. Something upsets me.
11. Something can be a nuisance.
12. Something is optional.

Now we can ask what the something is in each case. Is it *that* he cooks or *how* he cooks that upsets me (notice that in the one case my upset is psychological and in the other case probably physical)? Is it relatives *coming* to visit me, or me *going* to visit relatives that can be a nuisance? Is it *how* to dress or *whether* to dress that is optional? In each case we seem to have a reduced version (his cooking, visiting relatives, dress), and we cannot tell what it is a reduced version of; the reduction could have had two possible original sources.

In summary, then, an item might be ambiguous because (1) one word or phrase in the expression can have several different meanings, (2) the sentence can reflect several different relations of the parts, or (3) there are two different possible original meaning sources for part of the sentence, and it is not clear which one the sentence part is a reduced version of. Can you find and describe the ambiguities in the following headline and cartoons?

Disappearance Of Man in Lake Called Strange

© 1975 Newspaper Enterprise Association, Inc.

© 1974 United Features Syndicate, Inc.

© King Features Syndicate, Inc. 1974

© 1975 Newspaper Enterprise Association, Inc.

© King Features Syndicate, Inc. 1975

"Why did Mr. Allen say the scenery's nice? I don't see
any scenery."

"The Family Circus" by Bil Keane, reprinted courtesy The
Register and Tribune Syndicate, Inc.

© 1975 Newspaper Enterprise Association, Inc.

© 1974 Newspaper Enterprise Association, Inc.

© 1975 Newspaper Enterprise Association, Inc.

© Field Enterprises, Inc., 1975

© 1974 United Features Syndicate, Inc.

© Field Enterprises, Inc., 1975

Usually when we meet ambiguous sentences in our everyday lives, their meaning is clear from the situation in which we encounter them. (I say "usually," remembering the student who told me he vividly recalls as a child begging his mother not to buy "toilet water" from a cosmetics saleswoman who came to the door.) The point that is important for us here is the insight that our understanding of ambiguity can give us into what we know about the structure of our language. We know that certain words in our language express different meanings, and we pretty much agree on what those words and meanings are (though, of course, no one knows all the words of a language, let alone all the meanings of all the words). But we are also aware of various possible relations of meanings which underlie the actual strings of words we say or hear (expression). We know, for example, what kind of food apples are and we know that eating involves intake of food; but we also know that the relational meaning of "eating apples" in "They are eating apples" can be either the action of eating plus what is being eaten, or apples that are of a kind that are good for eating. These are relational meanings. The structure of our language clearly is not simply words in a string. We know, we have access to, and we use some set of principles for relating parts of sentences, and these relationships are not always immediately obvious from the expression itself. And finally, our recognition of some ambiguous sentences shows us that we know that certain phrases or parts within sentences could possibly be expressions of several more fully specified meanings—that they are, in a sense, traceable to more than one original relational meaning source. Our understanding of ambiguity is one reflection of our very complex intuitive understanding of the structure—the parts and putting-togethers— of our language.

CREATING NOVEL SENTENCES

The abilities discussed so far are quite remarkable, but they are not nearly as remarkable as another ability you have which lies right at the heart of human language. You have and use the ability to endlessly create and understand sentences which you have never encountered before. Except for a small set of ritualized kinds of exchanges—such as greetings ("Hi" or "How are ya' "), conversation openers ("Know what?"), leave-takings ("See ya' later," "Take care," or "Say 'hi' to your family for me")—you communicate with specific sentences which are entirely novel in your experience and which are the result of your own creation. Search your memory for five sentences you have said so far today that are repeats of sentences you have heard, spoken, read, or written before. Now search for five sentences that people have said to you so far today that you have encountered previously. Chances are that except for the kinds of ritualized exchanges cited above, you will not be able to think of a single sentence you have spoken or heard today that was not novel to you.

If you find it difficult to scan today's communication events so far, just listen to a conversation. To what extent are the participants using sentences they, or you, have encountered before? Yet they understand each other and you understand them, though the sentences of the exchange are completely novel to your experience and theirs. Or list five sentences from this book or from today's newspaper (not including ads) that you have never encountered before in speech or writing. Easy enough. But now list five that you *have* heard, read, written, or spoken before. Impossible.

How does it happen that I can say sentences to you that are new to both of us, and yet you will immediately comprehend my intended meaning and reply with another sentence that is also new to both of us yet is a sentence I immediately comprehend? Whatever language *is*, one thing it surely *is not:* It is not some supply or storehouse of specific sentences ready to be pulled out and used on appropriate occasions. The human mind could neither learn nor store such a set. We communicate by creating new sentences, not by pulling old ones out of mothballs.

CONCLUSION

All the language abilities you've explored in this chapter point to the existence of a deep, abstract, and complex system you have for relating meaning and expression in your language.

> To designate some expressions of meaning as "grammatical" is to recognize that they conform to your system; conversely, to designate other expressions as "ungrammatical" is to recognize that they conflict with your system in some way, that they violate your expectations; to designate one expression as

"more" or "less" grammatical than another is to recognize degrees of conformity to your system for relating meanings and expression of them.

Your recognition of relations of parts within sentences indicates that your knowledge includes not only specific elements of meaning and expression of those specific elements (as words) but that it also includes relational meaning and its expression (for example, as word endings or as particular orders and arrangements).

Your recognition of various sentences expressing the same meaning (stylistic variation), and of single sentences expressing various meanings (ambiguity) are two sides of the same coin. Both attest to your language knowledge involving meaning, expression, and principles for relating them.

As intriguing as these abilities are as demonstrations of our knowledge of a meaning-expression system, even more awesome is our constant creativity in language. How often do we hear people say, "Oh, I never was very creative." Not so in language! There, our knowledge of a limited set of principles for relating meaning and expression enables us to produce and understand an endless set of sentences, spoken and written, that are novel in our experience. It is primarily through novel sentences that we communicate with others. Communication is a highly creative endeavor.

We move now to consider in more detail in Chapter 3 the components of the knowledge system we all developed as children, the knowledge that accounts for our creative capacity in language. Every child we teach, whether sixth grader or kindergartner, has already made impressive progress in developing just such a meaning-expression system.

3

Components
of Language
Structure

INTRODUCTION

One major goal of linguistics has been to describe the knowledge speakers have of the structure of their language. You can see that this would be an extremely difficult task for several reasons. First of all, the system is a complex one. However, we know that many complex systems have been described—the system of U.S. federal, state, and local government, computer systems, ecological systems. What makes description of language structure more difficult than these is that it is highly abstract as well as complex. It is a system of knowledge that individuals have. We can directly observe individuals' behavior, but we can't directly observe individuals' knowledge. The enormous task facing linguists has been to consider peoples' language behaviors and then answer the question , What would someone have to know in order to behave in these ways? Some of the relevant behaviors are those that occur quite naturally, people communicating with each other in speech and in writing, for example. It becomes immediately apparent that they don't talk or write in random, jumbled ways. Their production and comprehension in language are orderly, organized, predictable. What is the knowledge that serves as the basis for this organization?

Linguists also consider less natural and more contrived behaviors of native speakers, such as those we considered in Chapter 2: speakers' reflections on language, for example, their judgments of the grammaticalness of sentences, and their recognition of ambiguity and of relations within and among sentences.

Not surprisingly, different linguists have described this complex and abstract system of knowledge in different ways. Some descriptions have focused more on expressive elements and sequences (words and word parts), others more on meaning elements (the notions that get expressed in language), others more on various kinds of relationships among elements, and so on. Our concern here is not to learn about the specifics of these various descriptions, nor is it to commit to one description as being "the one" that best characterizes language knowledge.[1] Rather, our purpose is to consider some components of language knowledge that most linguists would agree are important. These include (1) the semantic component, which involves the speaker's knowledge of meaning elements; (2) the syntactic component, which involves the speaker's knowledge of relational meaning; and (3) the phonological component, which involves the speaker's knowledge of expression possibilities for conveying meaning in his language.

SEMANTIC COMPONENT

Semantic Categories and Labels

A British woman teaching English composition to a class of secondary school Kenya students once asked her class to write a composition about the English language—a "What English Means to Me" composition. The opening sentence of one student's composition was "English is a language which is full of words." And so it is! One of the three major components of native speakers' knowledge of the structure of their language relates to the meaning parts of their language and the words that represent these meaning parts or concepts—their "mental dictionary." The speakers of any language know the way the people of their community view the world, the way they divide reality into significant categories and label them in their language.

No two language-culture communities view reality the same way, and each community's language reflects its world view, what it regards as the significant categories and relations of experience.[2] Though all humans are endowed with the same types of perceptual and cognitive mechanisms, each group represents reality differently, assigning to its experience of the world different significance, groupings and relationships. Examples are legion of different groups dividing and labeling reality differently. The color continuum that English divides into the six categories labeled purple, blue, green, yellow, orange, red, some American Indian languages divide into four labeled categories and others into only two categories. English speakers regard "snow" as a single category, but Eskimos have many categories for "snow," depending on the kind of snow it is. English speakers see one (singular) and more than one (plural) as significant categories. But many languages differentiate between one (singular), two (dual), and more than two (plural). In English, "this" and "that" indicate near and not near spatial divisions. But some languages label spatial areas much more specifically with categories, for example, for "near me but not near you," or "far

---

[1]If you are interested in learning more about some linguistic descriptions, you might want to see Slobin 1979, Chapter 1, or Fromkin and Rodman 1978.

[2]This is, admittedly, an oversimplified discussion and does not deal with the problem of defining "community." I am simplifying the social aspect here to enable you to focus in greater depth on the linguistic one.

away from both of us," or "out of sight of both of us," or "near both/all of us." Much of what English categorizes as a "that" (inanimate), some languages categorize as a "who" (animate).

Every human being is born into a community that views reality its own way and whose language reflects that world view. As a member of that community, the human learns that particular world view as he learns the language which expresses the groupings and relations it labels. Because we live with the categories our language uses, we tend to feel that these categories and labels are somehow God-given or inherently logical in the objects and experiences themselves. But this is clearly not so, for if our categories and labels were inherently logical, then all languages would encode the same categories. As we have seen, they do not. Each culture simply groups diverse objects, experiences, and events so that its members, in a sense, agree to regard as the "same" or equivalent some sets of unidentical things that share certain features and to regard as "different" other events, experiences, and objects not possessing certain crucial features, that is, to regard them as belonging to different classes or categories. The words of our language convey our categories.

Every language represents reality differently; you know the way your language does it. It is intriguing that our bases for grouping objects into categories are so variable. Those "crucial features" on which we base our particular categorizations are hardly predictable. We categorize now according to one dominant feature, now according to another. All objects that we identify as "round" share a perceptible attribute, a readily recognizable shape. But notice that similarity of appearance is not the dominant feature in categorizing which animals are and are not "dogs." If appearance were crucial to "dogness," how could German shepherds and chihuahuas end up in the same general category "dog," but German shepherds and wolves end up in different categories? We place A, $\mathcal{A}$, a and a , in the same category: They are all "a's" (Or are they all "A's"? " $\mathcal{A}$'s"? or " a's"?), but we insist that " a " and "o" and "c" belong in different categories, as do "b" and "d," though "B," " $\mathcal{B}$," "b," and " b " belong in the same category, and "D," " $\mathcal{D}$," "d," and " d " do also. And of course there is always "G," " $\mathcal{G}$," "g," and " g ." Appearance, though an important basis for some categories, is less important for others. A feature of tameness (the result of historical development) is crucial to the dog-wolf distinction, and functional considerations are crucial in the alphabet letter examples. And so, as we categorize, we seem to be focusing now on one important dimension and now on another, sometimes on a perceptible characteristic (shape, size, contour, texture, weight, hue, sound), sometimes on function, sometimes on structural similarity, and so on.

Let's summarize for a minute. The speakers of a particular language view reality in similar ways, in terms of categories and the relationships among them. The words of their language reflect their categories (dog, wolf, loud) and relations (bigger, less, because). The speakers of English basically agree on what actions constitute the categories "jumping," "eating," "sleeping." That is, the domain of experience labeled by these words is similar (though not identical) for most speakers of English. English speakers would agree on what it means to "own" something, to "think" something, to "throw" something. They would also basically agree on which items in the world are or are not "lizards," "daughters," "benches," "preferences." They share common meaning associations for "happy," "pretty," "energetic," "sluggish," "slovenly" (though they might disagree as to which particular people should be described as possesssing these characteristics). The semantic knowledge of a speaker of a language includes knowledge of how the world of his community is categorized and labeled. These labels constitute his lexicon or mental dictionary. He shares with other speakers the words—lexicon—that express specific, basically agreed upon meanings or domains of experience. A language is indeed "full of words" and full of the meanings that those words express.

That we have dictionaries at the ready and consult them frequently is sufficient evidence that we never learn all the words and all the meanings of all the words in our language. We frequently have the experience of interacting with people who speak the same language we do but whose domains of daily activity are different from ours, and thus their semantic knowledge—the meanings and the words that express them—are different too. I am reminded of these differences whenever my doctor tells me "what ails me" or my auto mechanic tells me what ails my car, when the plumber or electrician tells me what my house problems are, or when the TV sportscaster tells me about the day's sporting events—talk of "bogies" and "eagles" and "hat tricks," all words that express very little meaning for me. And I wonder, "Do we really speak the same language?" Of course, any of these folks might be prompted to wonder the same thing if I started talking to them about their "semantic component of linguistic knowledge." But we do speak the same language, the auto mechanic, doctor, plumber, electrician, sportscaster, and I; our somewhat different semantic systems reflect the different experiences on which our semantic knowledge is based. No individual can have all possible experiences within a community, so of course no individual can have all possible meanings and words to express those experiences.

There are other reasons, also, why we will never know all the words and meanings in our language. New words enter the language to express new meanings—the results of new explorations, discoveries, inventions, concerns, and interests. "Byte" and "rom," "bulimia" and "anorexic," "space capsule" and "lift off" have entered the language during our lifetimes. New words also enter the language as borrowings from other languages whose speakers we are in contact with. Food terms come to mind immediately. What English speaker's lexicon does not include "chop suey," "pizza," and "enchilada"? You can see that our semantic development never ends. Nevertheless, the mental dictionaries of adult speakers of any language are significantly similar.

Inflectional Morphemes

Notice that in the semantic component, it is not only total words that express meaning. Words can also contain smaller elements of meaning of various kinds, and this is part of our semantic knowledge also. The words in each of the columns in the accompanying table, although distinctly different in the total meaning they express, share a common element of meaning. Can you identify it?[3]

1	2	3	4	5	6
cupcakes	came	feels	its	bigger	jumping
women	walked	has	Susan's	better	crying
provisions	ran	is	their	prettier	studying
children	went	hopes	person's	friendlier	chewing
jealousies	schemed	says	people's	worse	waving
people	strutted	supposes	Jack's		wondering
glasses	thought	does	the Jones's		
			mine		

It is helpful to think of these words as exemplifying changes from some basic, unmarked word form. Then we can ask, "What is the meaning change or meaning addition expressed in each set?" In the first set, the meaning element "plural" or "more than one" is expressed in each word. If we think of the singular form as being the basic unmarked form, then we can say that the meaning of plural has been added and expressed in each.

It's important to distinguish between the meaning and its expression (a word or part of a word). The meaning of plural is common to each item in the first group, but notice how variously that meaning can be expressed: as /s/ in cupcakes, as /z/ in jealousies and provisions, as /əz/ in glasses, as /rən/ and a vowel change in children, as two vowel changes in women, and as a totally new sound string in people. And do you ever count sheep to help you fall asleep? The meaning of plural is in sheep, but this meaning does not change the basic word form in any way. You could say that it is silent. Of course, the idea is not new to you that in language a meaning can be present without having a specific pronounceable item to express it.

Is it any wonder that we hear children say "mans" and "sheeps" where we would say men and sheep? Of course not. They recognize that English differentiates between one of something and more than one of it, and that the meaning of more than one is generally expressed by adding /s/ ("cupcakes"), /z/ ("jealousies"), or /əz/ ("glasses") to the basic form. What they have not yet learned, but will in time, is (1) that there are specific cases where the meaning of plural is expressed in some other way, (2) just what those other ways of expressing plural are, and (3) just which words they apply to. All of this is part of the adult English speaker's knowledge of his language, and over time it becomes part of the child's knowledge as well. Rather than being struck by children's failure to express irregular plural forms appropriately, we should be impressed that at a tender age they (1) grasp the notion of plural and differentiate between one and more than one, (2) know (unconsciously) that the notion of plural is usually expressed as an addition of /s/, /z/, or /əz/ to the base form, and (3) usually select appropriately between the three typical expressions of plural, adding the appropriate ending to a word whose plural form they have not heard before.

[3]Remember that the expression discussed in these paragraphs is oral expression, not written expression.

The common meaning element expressed in various ways in the words of the second set is the meaning "past." In walked, schemed, and strutted, past is expressed according to the regular pattern of adding /t/ (walked), /d/ (schemed), or /əd/ (strutted) to the unmarked form of the verb. But the meaning "past" is expressed by a vowel change in ran and came, and by a totally different form in went and thought. As with the meaning element plural, the meaning element past can be "expressed silently" as in "She put her books in her desk." In view of the variety of expression possibilities for past, it is rather remarkable that young children, without special tutoring, conceptualize a present-past distinction, express that distinction in their speech, discern that the usual way of expressing past is through the addition of /t/, /d/, /əd/ to a base form (as children's "putted," "comed," "goed," "thinked" clearly indicate), and that in time, through continued verbal interaction with others, they come to recognize which verbs are the exceptional cases that do not follow the general pattern for expressing the notion past and to understand how those idiosyncratic cases work.

The common meaning conveyed in the third group is simply that the subject of each verb is a third person singular (he, she, it, John, or Mary, but not we, they, or you) and that the verb is in the present tense. One cannot help wondering, if "run" is a perfectly OK form to go with "I, you, we, they, John, and Mary," why it is not a perfectly OK form to go with "he, she," and other third person singular subjects. But this is idle wondering. The fact is that historically, English has developed in such a way that the information "third person singular subject" is expressed by a special verb form (as well as by the subject itself). Notice that the usual expression is the addition of /s/ (hopes), /z/ (feels), or /əz/ (supposes) to the base form, the same sounds we generally add to nouns to express the meaning element plural. Note again, though, that the one meaing—third person singular—is expressed in various ways besides the regular set (vowel changes in says and does, substitution of /z/ for /v/ in has, and a special form in is). How surprised would you be to hear a four-year-old say, "He haves a lot of them"? Why?

The familiar /s/, /z/, /əz/ pattern occurs in group 4, this time as the usual expression for the meaning "possession." (Note the /z/ of Susan's, people's, and person's; the /əz/ of the Joneses' and the /s/ of its and Jack's.) Note again that the common meaning element, possession, can be expressed in other ways as well—mine and their suggesting just two of the possibilities.[4]

The common meaning element expressed in the words of group 5 is sometimes called the "comparative." Again, though that notion is most often expressed by a certain change of a base form (adding "er" to the

---

[4]Given the /z/ regularity of "They're yours/his/hers/ours/theirs," is it any wonder we sometimes hear young children say, "They're mines"? This is not a sign of lack of intelligence. Quite the reverse. It is further evidence of children's remarkable ability to discern and utilize regularities in language.

adjective or preceding it with "more"), irregularities occur, as in better or worse. (Have you ever heard children say "gooder" or "badder"?)

The words in group 6 are striking for their lack of irregularity in expression. The common meaning element contained in all of them you doubtless recognize as what is sometimes called "progressive" or "continuous"—action actually in progress. That meaning is always expressed in English through the addition of /iŋ/ (usually spelled "ing") to the basic verb form. Notice that these forms also require that a form of "be" precede the verb. Not surprisingly, expressions like "I jumping" and "Daddy coming," in which the "be" preceding the verb is missing, are typical at an early stage of language acquisition in children.

Clearly, your mental dictionary or lexicon includes meanings like plural, past, possessive, comparative, third person singular, and continuous, as well as meanings like "goat" and "scratch." The term "morpheme" is helpful here.

A morpheme is the smallest meaning unit in language. Basic meanings like goat and scratch (which are expressed as words) are morphemes; meanings like plural and past (which typically are expressed as parts of words) are morphemes also. You understand the words women, ran, supposes, bigger, Bob's, (be) wondering each to be a complex morpheme containing two morphemes or meaning units: woman + plural, run + past, suppose + third person singular subject, big + comparative, Bob + possessive, wonder + continuous.

The six morphemes we considered in the preceding groups (plural, past, third person singular, possessive, comparative, and continuous) combine with other morphemes. They all belong to a class of morphemes called *inflectional* morphemes.[5] We inflected the verb "run" for past when we changed it to "ran," that is, when we added the information *past*. "People" includes the inflectional morpheme *plural*. With inflected forms, an original morpheme has been further refined through the addition of some meaning like possessive, comparative, plural.[6]

Derivational Morphemes

Now let's look at another type of morpheme. The words in the accompanying table express complex morphemes (morpheme combinations). The words in each group include a common meaning element. Can you find and characterize it?

[5]Throughout this discussion, the term "inflection" refers to the adding of meanings to basic morphemes. Some people also use "inflection" to mean the rise and fall of the voice in speaking. To avoid confusion, I use the term "intonation" for this meaning (rise and fall of the voice) and reserve "inflection" for "additional meanings."

[6]Remember that there is a distinction between the meaning unit itself (a morpheme) and its expression. Thus, past is a morpheme, and /əd/ is one possible expression of it; "cat" is a morpheme, and /kæt/ is the expression of it; "cats" is a complex morpheme composed of two simple morphemes, the first expressed as /kæt/ and the second expressed as /s/, and the new complex morpheme expressed as /kæts/. However, in other works, you may encounter the term morpheme used to refer to the meaning *and* its expression or to the expression itself.

1	2	3	4	5
teacher	flexible	generosity	waspish	foxy
baker	adaptable	sincerity	impish	wily
singer	replaceable	blindness	foolish	crafty
player	responsible	scarcity	clannish	sneaky
preacher	expendable	messiness		sloppy
	audible	purposefulness		hasty
		foolishness		
		irregularity		
		stupidity		
		kindness		

These complex morphemes include only a few examples of the many simple morphemes called *derivational* (in contrast to the inflectional ones we considered earlier). These derivational morphemes, which are usually expressed as suffixes added to a base form, most often change the class to which the word belongs. "Teach" is a verb, but adding the "er," to convey the meaning "one who does it," changes the original verb form to a noun (teacher) comprised of two morphemes. The addition of "er" *derives* a noun form from what was originally, in its basic unmarked form, a verb. The addition of the derivational suffix "ible/able" changes a verb base form to an adjective; the addition of "ity" or "ness" generally changes an adjective form to a noun, whereas the addition of "ish" does the reverse, generally changing a noun (wasp, fool, imp, clan) to an adjective. The addition of "y" generally changes the original noun to an adjective.

You can see that both derivational and inflectional morphemes are similar in that they combine with basic morphemes (they do not occur alone) and in that they modify the original meaning. However, they differ in the ways they modify that original meaning: Inflectional morphemes add meaning to the original meaning (for example, the meaning of past or plural or continuousness of action), whereas derivational morphemes change the word class of the original (for example, from verb to noun or from noun to adjective).

It would be lovely if the distinction between inflectional (adds meaning) and derivational (changes word class) were perfect and always held true. But it is not that neat. There is an intriguing set of items generally called derivational morphemes and expressed as prefixes (coming before, rather than after, the base form), which do not change the word class of a base morpheme. These morphemes largely have to do with meanings of recurrence and negation: *re*group, *re*convene, *re*assert; *in*compatible, *in*escapable, *un*important, *in*edible, *in*comprehensible, *im*possible, *in*complete, *ir*replaceable, *un*scientific; *anti*social, *anti*climactic, *anti*septic, *anti*histamine; *mis*understand, *mis*trust; *dis*trust, *dis*appear.

If inflectional morphemes pose "problems"[7] in the variation of their

---

[7] I put "problems" in quotes here because, in fact, our learning of this part of our language does not seem to be problematic. We learn it, as we do the rest of our language, with no apparent difficulty or even conscious awareness. It only looks "problematic" when we stand back, as we are now doing (and as children do not do), and see how complex a system we have actually mastered.

possible irregular expressions, just think of all the possible expression "problems" derivational morphemes raise, as they are considerably less patterned and predictable than inflectional morphemes. If someone is lovely, it is her loveliness, not her loveliosity or lovelicity that impresses us. But if she is sincere, it is her sincerity, not her sincereness, that impresses us. I can be hasty or unhasty, but can I be slow or unslow? I can be mindful or unmindful, but can I be wonderful or unwonderful? I can be clear or unclear, but can I be understood or ununderstood (which is different, of course, from being misunderstood). If I am ambitious, I have ambition, not ambitiousness or ambitiosity. If I am generous, I have generosity, but if I am a genius I do not have geniosity.[8] And if someone can be uncouth or incorrigible or unwitting, why can he not also be couth or corrigible or witting? If I can redo or regain things, why can I not relose or refix things? I can like, dislike, or hate someone, but I cannot dishate him. I can unwind or rewind things, but I cannot unfind or refind things. Given this extreme variability in the expression of derivational morphemes, would you expect children to master inflectional or derivational morphemes earlier?

You know what kinds of morphemes—meanings—can combine to form more complex morphemes; you know what forms of expression they will take in combination; and you also know how they will be ordered: irregular-ity, not ity-regular-ir. You use your knowledge of possibilities of morpheme combinations to create and understand new forms. I have heard students describe acquaintances as being "sort of cute-ish" or as having "no couth" or a lot of "stick-to-it-ive-ness."

Cartoonists often capitalize on our knowledge of inflectional and derivational morphemes, and their possible expression, for humorous purposes. Consider the accompanying cartoon.

© 1974 United Features Syndicate, Inc.

It is worth noting that particular pronounceable items like /z/, /s/, /t/, "er," and "un"[9] do not always express inflectional or derivational meanings. The /z/ in bug*s* expresses plural, but the /z/ in buz*z* or i*s* has no special significance; it is merely part of the pronunciation of a simple morpheme. The /s/ in hat*s* expresses a morpheme, but the /s/ in bu*s* does not. The "er" in preach*er* and the "un" in *un*doing express morphemes, but the "er" in h*er* and the "un" in s*un* do not. There is no simple, one-to-one, always-and-only correspondence between morphemes and their expression, even as there is no such simple correspondence between sentence meaning and expression, as we saw in earlier examples of ambiguous sentences (in which

[8]I am indebted to Mildred Miran for this example from a university student learning English as his fourth language.

[9]I am representing these in their spelled form so as to avoid using unfamiliar phonetic symbols for vowel sounds that you will readily recognize from their spellings. But remember that we are still concerned with *sound*s, not with written forms.

one expression had several meanings associated with it), and sets of related sentences (in which various expression possibilities could relate to one meaning structure).

Compounds and Idioms

Besides including base morphemes and their expression like "tree" and "stand," inflectional morphemes like past and plural, and derivational morphemes changing an item from one word class to another, your semantic knowledge includes compounds and idioms and ways to express them. These are lexical items clearly composed of subparts, each with its own meaning in isolation but which, when the subparts are combined, often convey new and special meanings. Football is more than the meaning of "foot" plus the meaning of "ball." It identifies a type of object and a type of game. A restroom is not simply the meaning of "rest" plus the meaning of "room." The combination names a type of room which is probably not primarily a room for resting at all.

The relatedness of the morphemes expressed in compounds is generally obvious to us though it can be quite varied. Note these examples from Fromkin and Rodman:

> . . . a *bedchamber* is a room where there is a bed, *bedclothes* are linens and blankets for a bed, *bedside* does not refer to the physical side of a bed but the place next to it, and *bedtime* is the time one goes to bed. . . . A *houseboat* is a boat which is a house, but a *housecat* is not a cat which is a house. A *boathouse* is a house for boats, but a *cathouse* is not a house for cats, though by coincidence some cats live in cathouses. A *jumping* bean is a bean that jumps, a *falling star* is a "star" that falls, and a *magnifying glass* is a glass that magnifies. But a *looking glass* isn't a glass that looks, nor is an *eating apple* an apple that eats, nor does *laughing gas* laugh. (Fromkin and Rodman 1974, p. 120)[10]

But notice that, with some compounds, the combination expresses a new and unpredictable meaning whole. Again some examples from Fromkin and Rodman:

> A *jack-in-a-box* is a tropical tree, and a *turncoat* is a traitor. A *highbrow* doesn't necessarily have a high brow, nor does a *bigwig* have a big wig, nor does an *egghead* have an egg-shaped head. . . . if one had never heard the word *hunchback*, it might be possible to infer the meaning. But if you had never heard the word *flatfoot* it is doubtful you would know it was a word meaning "detective" or "policeman." (Fromkin and Rodman 1974, pp. 120-21)

With idioms, the relationship between the individual morphemes and the new total combination meaning is even less obvious—sometimes nonexistent. Even though you are not an acrobat or an infant, you can "put your foot in your mouth." If someone "has two left feet," we do not order special

---

[10]Do not be troubled because some compounds are written with a space between the two parts (laughing gas) and some are not (houseboat). We are concerned here, not with the written symbolization for our language, but with the oral expression of morpheme combinations.

shoes. When someone "kicks the bucket" we are more likely to head for the funeral home than for the mop closet.

My favorite example comes from a Tanzanian student of mine who relates an incident he remembers from a dinner party he attended as a secondary school student. One of his teachers, a British woman, had invited a select group of students to her home for dinner. When she encouraged one of the guests to have seconds, he refused in a way that he thought was very polite. He said, "Oh no, Madam. I'm *fed up*." Quite unknowingly, he had stumbled on an idiom that, despite his perfectly reasonable expectation that it conveyed his meaning of being fully satisfied, conveyed instead the meaning that he was disgusted. You can see why it is challenging for an adult acquiring a second or foreign language to learn to express himself "idiomatically" in that language. Idioms are apparently entered in the native speaker's mental lexicon as wholes, not as the meaning of each part plus the usual relations among the parts.

Semantic Features

When we think of simple morphemes like "lamp" or "break" or "itch," we may feel as if the meaning of each is a kind of indissoluble whole. But in fact, it may be more accurate to think of these morphemes as clusters of meaning features or aspects of meaning that some linguists have called *semantic features*. If I asked you to tell me what "break" means, you would probably say something like, "It means to come apart or to become damaged." Fine. We say of many things that come apart or become dysfunctional, that they broke.

The lawn mower broke.
The plate broke.

But there are many other things in our world that come apart, but we do not say of them that they broke.

The paper broke.
Her dress broke.

Textural properties of the object involved seem to be important to the meaning of break. Only some objects are breakable. Perhaps our notion of break includes a semantic feature of brittleness of texture (though notice that thread, which is not brittle, also breaks).

Break also seems to entail a certain specificity and completeness. A complex mechanism or organism (a car or a person, say) can go from a state of being fully functional to being damaged, but we do not generally say, "The car broke" or "Mary broke." We either use break and specify the particular part that is no longer functional ("The fan belt broke" or "Mary's arm broke") or else we indicate a more general kind of breakage with an expression like "break down": "The car broke down" or "Mary broke down." When we do use break with a complex organism, as in "Mary broke under pressure," it has the force of suggesting a completeness in the breakage.

It is interesting to consider the many kinds of breaking (destructing?) we identify in English. Though all are similar in including the notion of coming apart, each includes some specific meaning feature(s) which differentiates it from the others. Consider these few:

> If an item breaks by changing from a solid to a liquid through the action of heat, it "melts" (butter, ice cream, jello).
>
> If an item breaks suddenly, through ignition from within itself, it "explodes" (bomb, firecracker).
>
> If an item breaks in such a way that it blends with the surrounding liquid medium, it "dissolves" (sugar in coffee).
>
> If an item breaks as the result of a ripping motion, often leaving a jagged edge, it "tears" (cloth, paper).

Notice how the features of the literal interpretation are present when we use the breakage terms metaphorically:

> I melt every time he looks at me.
>
> She exploded when she heard what he had done.
>
> He dissolved into tears.
>
> Janet tore their argument to shreds.

Some features or aspects of meaning that differentiate among morphemes are fairly obvious. The feature of being animate or inanimate differentiates the meaning bundles we represent as "hippo," "ape," "spider," "Brenda," "mailman," "old maid," and "chairperson" from other meaning clusters (morphemes) we express as "refrigerator," "rock," "pencil," and "mud." The feature of being human or nonhuman differentiates "hippo," "spider," and "ape" from "Brenda," "mailman," "old maid," and "chairperson." The feature of being male or female separates "Brenda" and "old maid" from "mailman" and also separates "rooster" from "hen" and "billy goat" from "nanny goat." The feature of being concrete or abstract differentiates "Brenda," "rooster," and "rock" from "idea," "freedom," and "love."

But other features that differentiate meanings are more subtle. Study this set of words listed in *The New Roget's Thesaurus* (1964, p. 533) under "Verbs. walk."

amble	stroll	parade	hobble	trudge
canter	stride	prance	shuffle	wade
pitter-patter	strut	stalk	stagger	tiptoe
saunter	swagger	limp	reel	

All these words include the same basic set of semantic features that defines the general term "walk." Stated informally, these would include at least the following set: action, locomotor movement, animate (that is, action of an animate being), alternating feet continuously. But the word "walk" is more general in meaning than the words in the above set. Each of the more specific walk words above contributes some additional semantic feature to "walk." "Stagger" adds unsteadiness, "stroll" adds slowness and leisureliness, "wade" adds through water, "prance" adds high stepping, and "tiptoe" adds on toes with heels not touching the ground. Can you describe the specialness of each specific walk word, the semantic feature(s) it includes that sets it apart from the more general "walk"? You can see that the more specific a morpheme is the greater the number of semantic features that characterize it and set it apart from other morphemes in the language.

Here's another example. It comes from my blender. How would you differentiate among the following words that the blender manufacturer has printed under the row of buttons: stir, beat, puree, cream, chop, whip, crumb, mix, mince, grate, crush, blend, shred, grind, frappe, liquefy? (Everyone should have such a blender!)

The point is that your semantic knowledge is wonderfully complex, more complex than you probably suspected. Your knowledge of subtle meaning features—"shades of meaning," as one student called them—is part of that complexity. Put informally, the entries in your mental dictionary seem to be "defined" as composites of meaning features or elements. These elements contribute to your awareness of which morpheme combinations are and are not possible. We generally take it for granted that butter melts, bombs explode, sugar dissolves, and paper tears. But when we encounter unusual morpheme combinations, we are jarred into an awareness of the magnitude of our semantic knowledge and of what some of the semantic features we are using might be. My favorite nonnative example comes from a Kenya secondary school student. He was complaining in a written composition about his class leaders' unfortunate habit of making announcements, during meals, about the dirty condition of the school latrines. He argued, very persuasively, that mealtimes were not the proper times for such announcements, which "lessened one's taste for eating considerably." He painted a dire picture of students in great numbers falling ill from lack of food if such announcements continued to be made at mealtimes. He concluded his argument with this statement: "And so, if this continues to happen, many people's normality will be impeded, owing to underfeeding." We recognize this instantly as a sentence that a native speaker of English could hardly have come up with, mainly because of the co-occurrence of "normality" and "impeded." Part of the meaning that normality has for us is that it is a state or condition someone or something is in, and part of the meaning that impeded has for us is interference with active movement toward some goal. A state of being is not something which moves toward a goal; therefore it is not something which can be impeded. We understand the student's meaning because we share with him some of the meaning aspects (semantic features) of normality and impeded (the notion of interference in impeded and the notion of a healthy or right kind of condition in normality). But the knowledge we have of subtle features of meaning constrains combination possibilities, and thus, for us, normality cannot be impeded.

Conclusion

We have barely begun to explore your semantic knowledge, but we know that it includes a knowledge of (1) how your community of language speakers views reality—categorizes it, relates the categories, and labels those categories and relationships; (2) the various kinds of meanings your language encodes, some heavy in referential content (like "cat," "see," "ugly"), others adding further refinement to basic meanings (inflectional morphemes like "plural" or "past"), others changing the word class of a morpheme so that it can relate differently to other morphemes (derivational morphemes), and others combining morphemes which, taken together, provide new meanings (such as compounds and idioms); (3) the possibilities for morpheme combinations, both within complex morphemes (which simple morphemes can combine to form complex ones and what the ordering principles are for these combinations), and also as co-occurrence possibilities within sentences; and (4) aspects of meaning which combine in morphemes (though this is often quite unavailable to consciousness). And this is only the barest beginning.

The growth and development of our semantic knowledge never ends. As our experience continues, our meanings increase. New experiences bring new meanings and expand and refine old ones. As teachers interacting with children in new and stimulating experiences, we are doing more about children's semantic growth than about their growth in the other two linguistic structure components (syntax, phonology). Interestingly, the prevailing view among many teachers is that their greatest contribution to children's language development in elementary school is in syntax (giving children grammar exercises designed either to teach them to identify parts of speech or to provide them with more adultlike sentence structures) *or* in phonology (giving children a knowledge of the sounds of their language through phonetic approaches to the teaching of reading, or trying to substitute more mature for less mature pronunciations). But nothing could be further from the truth. It is in the semantic domain that children's growth is most vigorous during the elementary school years. It is in new and rich shared experiences, which are part of the child's school life, that new meanings are born and expressed and familiar ones live and grow. This is the base of the child's continuing semantic growth. And because the semantic domain, so embedded in continuing experience, is an area where we too are learners, it is here that we may be doing our most important "teaching," for it is here that we, as real *learners* ourselves, demonstrate what continuing learning is.

SYNTACTIC COMPONENT

In the semantic component, the key notion is the morpheme, the basic meaning unit. In the syntactic component, the key notion is the sentence, the basic organizational unit. The term "sentence" is a bit tricky in that it means different things in different contexts. We are perhaps most familiar with school contexts in which children are told that a sentence is "a group of words expressing a complete thought" (a definition which would be helpful only to a child who already knew what "a complete thought" was) or that it is a sequence of written words "beginning with a capital letter and ending with a period." Both of these are definitions of *expressed* sentences, that is, sequences of spoken or written words. But the notion of sentence which is crucial for us is that which underlies expression. We can call this the *underlying* sentence. It is a mental construct, our sense of a string of morphemes comprising a proposition. It is our intuitive sense of "a complete thought"—our basis for deciding where to put capital letters and periods. It involves relational meanings, the relations that hold among the morphemes in combination. We have a sense of verb morphemes being the core of each proposition or underlying sentence. In fact, though linguists' descriptions differ in many ways, many try to capture this sense that speakers have that a verb element is the nucleus of the underlying sentence. Other major sentence elements can be characterized in terms of their relation to the verb element. Consider the expressed sentence that follows:

> The little girl powerfully kicked the soccer ball into the street with her left foot.

If asked to describe the relations among the parts you might say something like this: "Well, 'the little girl' tells who did something, and 'kicked' tells what she did, and 'the ball' tells what got kicked, and 'powerfully' tells how the little girl kicked the ball. 'Into the street' tells where she kicked it and 'with her left foot' tells what she used to kick it with. And 'little' describes the girl and 'soccer' tells what kind of ball it was and 'left' tells which foot the girl used." Your ability to describe the expressed sentence in this way resides in your sense of the underlying sentence as a composite of related parts, your sense of a someone who acted on something someplace in some way and so on. This ability also demonstrates your knowledge of meaning-expression connections, that is, your awareness of how the underlying sentence and the expressed sentence match.

Notice that we can take any expressed sentence, however complex, and sense the underlying sentences or propositions that comprise it. We can decompose it mentally.

> Coming around the corner, I saw the little girl who lives across the street and comes over for dinner every Friday, kick the soccer ball her father gave her into the street to show that she was angry.

Identifying the underlying sentences that comprise this expressed sentence, we get something like this set.[11]

> I came around the corner.
> I saw the girl.
> The girl was little.

[11] The set of specific underlying sentences will differ slightly from one linguistic description to another.

The girl lives across the street.
The girl comes over every Friday night.
The girl comes for dinner. (reason)
The girl kicked the ball into the street.
The ball was a soccer ball.
Her father gave her the ball.
The girl showed something.
The girl was angry.

Notice that some of the elements in this underlying set get deleted in the expressed sentence; for example, "the girl" and "I" and "be" are expressed only once. Also, some elements in the expressed sentence substitute for elements in the underlying sentence; for example, "who" substitutes for "the girl" in the expressed sentence. "That" gets included in the expressed sentence, though it does not occur as a morpheme in the underlying sentences. Further, the overall arrangement is different in the expressed sentence and the underlying set of sentences. Do you perhaps begin to get a sense of how complex your knowledge is of the underlying sentence structures of your language and their expression singly and in combination? This is syntax.

It helps to grasp the difference between semantic and syntactic knowledge if you consider examples like the following:

I meant what I said
And I said what I meant . . . .
An elephant's faithful
One hundred per cent! (Seuss 1968, unpaged)

"You should say what you mean," the March Hare went on.
"I do," Alice hastily replied; "at least—at least I mean what I say—that's the same thing, you know."
"Not the same thing a bit!" said the Hatter. "Why, you might just as well say that 'I see what I eat' is the same as 'I eat what I see'!"
"You might just as well say," added the March Hare, "that 'I like what I get' is the same thing as 'I get what I like'!"
"You might just as well say," added the Dormouse, which seemed to be talking in his sleep, "that 'I breathe when I sleep' is the same thing as 'I sleep when I breathe'!" (Carroll n.d., pp. 75–76)

"Now let me see," the Golux said. "If you can touch the clocks and never start them, then you can start the clocks and never touch them. That's logic, as I know and use it." (Thurber 1950, p. 106)

Horton, the elephant speaker in the first example, is not saying the same thing twice in the first two lines even though the individual words—the expressed morphemes themselves—are the same. "Meaning what you say" *is* different from "saying what you mean"; but they're different, not because of the individual words they include, but because of the relations among them. The Mad Hatter and the March Hare draw on their awareness of the difference between semantic (morphemic/elemental) and syntactic (relational/combinational) meaning in the second example. And it is precisely because the Golux (in the third example) recognizes the difference between touching clocks without starting them and starting clocks without touching them, that he saves the day and the Prince and Princess live happily ever after!

Now see what you can do with this more mundane example:

She fed her dog biscuits.

Already you can see it is ambiguous: It could be an answer to the question "What did she feed her?" (answer: dog biscuits) or to the question "What did she feed her dog?" (answer: biscuits). And if we thought of "biscuits" as the name of her dog ("Biscuits"), we would have yet another meaning. But now take the word "only" and insert it at different points.

Only she fed her dog biscuits.
She only fed her dog biscuits.
She fed only her dog biscuits.
She fed her only dog biscuits.
She fed her dog only biscuits.
She fed her dog biscuits only.

What's happening here? The meaning that "only" expresses by itself (its morphemic meaning) does not change, nor does the meaning expressed by the other single words. What changes are the groupings or clusterings of the words within the sentence, that is, how the elements go together. This is relational meaning and its expression.

Notice how often we consider contrived and specialized examples in an attempt to become more consciously aware of our sense of syntax. In our typical daily conversations, we don't generally talk like Horton, Mad Hatters, March Hares, or Goluxes. Nor do we converse in sentences such as the many examples we used in Chapter 2: sets of grammatical and ungrammatical sentences, cartoons, nonsense sentences, deliberately deviant sentences, and cleverly ambiguous sentences. We use such examples because the language knowledge we are exploring, especially our knowledge of syntax (relations among morphemes in combination) is so much a part of us and resides at such a deep intuitive level that we have difficulty recognizing its presence in our usual talk. This knowledge is something we take for granted, rather like we take our left little finger for granted until we sprain it. Not until it is in an unusual state do we notice it. So it is with this part of ourselves, our knowledge of language structure: We need special devices and contrived examples to bring it to conscious awareness as an object of our reflection.

And we go about our daily activities, chattering away with friends, reading newspapers, jotting notes to ourselves and others, rarely if ever reflecting on the deep and complex knowledge system we have for relating meaning and its expression—the very system that plays such an important part in making our communication experiences possible.

PHONOLOGICAL COMPONENT

The human being is capable of making a wide range of sounds with his vocal apparatus. He can cough, whistle, sing , sneeze, and wheeze. He can also talk. Considering the diverse set of sounds all human beings can make so easily by means of an air stream passing up through the vocal tract and out through the mouth and/or nose, it is interesting that only a subset are the sounds of talk in any language. If we listen to a person speaking a language with which we are totally unfamiliar, a language for which we have no expression-meaning correspondences at all, we are still likely to recognize which of the sounds he produces are language sounds and which are not.

All the sounds used in human languages, however diverse they may appear, can be described in terms of a limited set of sound features relating to, for example, whether or not the vocal cords vibrate; whether the air stream passes through the mouth, or nose, or both; the position of the tongue in the mouth; the shape of the mouth; the position of the lips; whether the air stream passes through the mouth continuously (as in /s/) or whether its passage is stopped (as in /b/). We can indentify a set of signifi- cant sound features that all languages draw on. Clustering these features into various bundles, each language emerges with an inventory of basic consonant and vowel sounds (called phonemes) that the native speakers recognize as being significant in conveying meanings in their language. What is paricularly interesting, however, is that these basic sounds (signifi- cant sound feature bundles) are not clearly demarked in the actual stream of speech. The sounds in "She fell into the river but he grabbed her ankle and pulled her out just in time" form a continuous stream when spoken in natural conversation. But however continuous this sound stream is in time, the English speaker can break it into a set of significant sound units. You would say that the first word, "she," is a combination of a consonant sound /š/ and a vowel (V), the next word is the sound /f/ plus a V plus /l/, "into" is a V + /n/ + /t/ + V, "the" is the sound /ð/ + V, "grabbed" is a /g/ + /r/ + V + /b/ + /d/, "ankle" is a V + /ŋ/ + /k/ + V + /l/, and so on.

The intention here is not to present a special set of written symbols for representing the basic sounds of English that the native speaker knows. For our purposes, V is a stand-in for a variety of specific vowel sounds. But it is important to emphasize that our concern here is with language *sounds*, not with the written symbols our alphabet uses (not always consistently) to represent them. Many languages have no written system of expression at all; they are no less languages for that. English does have a written system of expression and anyone who has ever been concerned with teaching a child to read it is aware that the written symbolization does not represent the sound system of our language through any simple set of one-to-one, sound-symbol correspondences. A given sound may be represented by different written symbols (the vowel sound of ra*i*n, re*i*gn, c*a*me or the /š/ sound of *s*ugar, *Ch*icago, sta*ti*on, *sh*ape). The reverse is also true; a single written symbol may represent various pronunciations (the different vowel sounds in f*i*n and f*i*ne and the "th" in *Th*omas, *th*igh, and *th*y). What the speaker recognizes as a single basic sound may be represented by a combination of written symbols, as in the *Th*omas, *th*igh, and *th*y cases, in the /f/ written as "gh" in enou*gh* and as "ph" in ele*ph*ant, or in the /ŋ/ written as "ng" in ki*ng*.

The important point here is that the sound system and written system are two different expressive systems, each with its own structure and conventions and uses. We often hear people unintentionally confuse the two systems. When I ask my students how we typically express plural when we speak (phonological system), they often answer with information about the written system: "We add 's' or 'es' to the noun." My students, influenced by their knowledge of the written system of English, tend to hear "king" as having four sounds, the last two being /n/ and /g/, rather than as having three: /kVŋ/. (Contrasting Ki*m*, ki*n*, and ki*ng* helps to make the singleness of the /ŋ/ evident.) We hear people explain the casual pronunciations of "walking" and "having" as "dropping the g," and in fact we often see these pronunciations represented in literature as "walkin'" and "havin'." Was there ever a /g/ in these words? What we mean is that in casual speech we often substitute final /n/ for /ŋ/. Sometimes people pronounce the past tense of "walk" without verbally expressing the addition of the past tense morpheme (/t/). We hear it said that they "dropped the ed." But of course, this is a description of the written form, not of the pronunciation. People speak of "the *t* sound" in the middle of the word "little." In fact, there is rarely a /t/ in the middle of "little." (Notice that "middle" and "little" rhyme.) These are all examples of individuals confusing the expressive system of speech and the expressive system of print.

It is the sound system of your language, then, not the written system, that you recognize as being comprised of an inventory of significant or basic sounds—the sound bundles you pay attention to to differentiate meaning. For example, /bæt/, /pæt/, and /mæt/ are all pronunciations of English morphemes. The initial sound of each differentiates it from the other two. Notice that the initial sounds share some features but are different in others; /b/, /p/, and /m/ are all made with the lips closed. But /m/ is nasal (made with air passing through the nose) while /p/ and /b/ are oral sounds (made with air passing through the mouth); /p/ is voiceless, while /m/ and /b/ are voiced (vocal cords vibrate during their production); /bæt/, /bæd/, and /bæn/ are all pronunciations of English morphemes also. The final sounds /t/, /d/, and /n/ differentiate them and in fact form an analogous set to the /p/, /b/, /m/ trio. Can you describe the features of similarity and difference in the set /t/, /d/, and /n/ in terms of tongue position, nasality, and voicing?

The final sounds that differentiate "but," "bus," and "buzz" (/bət/, /bəs/, /bəz/) demonstrate another sound feature that is significant in characterizing basic sounds of any language. The tip of your tongue is in a similar position for all three of the final sounds. The voicing of /z/ sets it apart from the voiceless /t/ and /s/, but notice that the /s/ and /z/ are very different from /t/ in the way the air stream passes through the mouth. The air stream is completely blocked in the production of /t/ (thus /t/, like /b/, /p/, /d/, /k/, and /g/, is sometimes called a *stop* consonant), while for /s/ and /z/ the air stream passes continuously through the mouth (and not surprisingly, these sounds are sometimes called *continuants*). We can account for all the basic significant sounds in your sound inventory as clusters of a limited set of sound features, no two basic sounds (sound feature clusters) being identical in their total sets of features but each one sharing some sound features with other basic sounds. We have considered only a few consonant sounds here; vowel sounds as well share some features (such as voicing and continuousness) and differ in others (such as shape of the mouth, position of the lips, and position of parts of the tongue).

It is easy to see that you know the basic significant consonant and vowel sounds of your lanuage. It is less easy to see that you have knowledge (though possibly not at a conscious level) of specific sound features. The fact is, however, that for some purposes you treat various basic sounds in similar ways because of some shared sound feature. You pluralize chur*ch* (/č/), jud*ge* (/ǰ/), bu*s* (/s/), gara*ge* (/ž/), a*sh* (/š/), phra*se* (/z/) in the same way— by adding the syllable /əz/—because of a sound feature shared by all, and only by the set /s/, /z/, /š/, /ž/, /č/, /ǰ/. These are the "hissing" or "shushing" sounds of English, the class of sounds called *sibilants*. You may not have thought about this sound feature before, but given a nonsense word ending in any one of these six basic sounds (and only these six), you would have provided a plural form by adding /əz/; that is, you are treating diverse basic sounds in the same way—classifying them—on the basis of a shared specific sound feature. In pluralizing nouns ending with nonsibilant sounds, you classify them for the property of voicing, selecting voiceless /s/ for those ending with voiceless sounds (ha*t* + /s/, mo*p* + /s/), and selecting voiced /z/ for those ending with voiced sounds (bo*y* + /z/, gir*l* + /z/).[12] Likewise, you regularly add the /əd/ past tense only to verbs ending in /t/ (strut) and /d/ (fade)—the two English sounds which are nonnasal and stops and made with the tongue at the gum ridge. For other verbs, you select voiced /d/ for those ending in voiced sounds (tr*y* + /d/, hu*m* + /d/), and voiceless /t/ for those ending in voiceless sounds (ho*p* + /t/, dan*ce* + /t/). Again, you are responding to particular sound features which you are not consciously aware of but which you intuitively know.

You also know which combinations of basic sounds are possible— which combinations the sound system of your language "allows." Asked to select an English name for a newly discovered object, from this possible set of names:

slenk   blenk   tlenk   glenk

there is one which you certainly would not choose. Which one is it? You would probably say that "tlenk" is impossible because of the combination "tl." You are right. You may say that the combination "tl" is too difficult to pronounce. Clearly, this is not the case, as the sound combination /tl/ occurs in other languages than English. English combines /l/ with other stop con-

---

[12]I am including here only regular forms and excluding irregular plurals such as "children," "sheep," and "data."

sonants; notice the /bl/ of black, the /pl/ of plaque, the /gl/ of glass, and the /kl/ of class. But /tl/ and /dl/ do not cluster in English syllables. This is not a constraint imposed by human possibilities of pronunciation; it is simply a constraint from within a particular language. It is a simple fact of the language, and it is a fact that you know, although, as with so much of your language knowledge, you may be unaware that you know it.

If you try to pronounce the Swahili word for drum, *ngoma* (/ŋVmV/), you may become aware of another important aspect of your phonological knowledge. In English, the sound /ŋ/, as in ri*ng* or thi*ng*k, can occur at the end or in the middle of words but not at the beginning. Though all sounds in *ngoma* also occur in English, you would know immediately that this could not be an English word. What is important here is, not that you would know that it is not, in fact, an English word (after all, there are lots of English words you do not know), but rather that you would know that it *could not be* an English word. You know the constraints on the positions in which basic sounds can occur, and one of these is that in English the sound /ŋ/ does not occur at the beginning of words.

Another fascinating aspect of your phonological knowledge is how the pronunciation of certain sounds changes, depending on what sound(s) precede or follow them. If you pronounce the following three pairs

*p*ill	*sp*ill
*t*ill	*st*ill
*k*ill	*sk*ill

you may be aware of a difference in your pronunciation of /p/, /t/, and /k/ when these sounds occur initially and when they are preceded by /s/. If you do not notice a difference, hold your hand in front of your mouth as you say each pair. You will probably be aware that the /p/, /t/, and /k/ in the first column are accompanied by a puff of air (aspiration) when you say them, while in the pronunciation of these "same" sounds preceded by /s/, the puff of air is absent. Here is a harder pair:

"cat"/kæt/   "cad"/kæd/

Can you hear any difference in the vowel sound as you pronounce the two words? The vowel sound of "cad" is longer in duration than the vowel sound of "cat." Notice that when we say a vowel sound is "long," we are not using this term as the reading teacher does to mean an alphabet symbol that "says its own name" or that Webster writes with a "-" above it. We are talking about the duration of the sound in time.

So far we have talked about only a small part of your knowledge of particular sounds and how they combine. You also know much about the "tune" of the sentences of your language, the ups and downs, the stresses, the pauses, and the various meanings conveyed by these sentence features. One way to attune your ears to the intonation possibilities (ups and downs of the voice) of your language is to consider the simple one-word sentences "Oh" and "No." Various intonation patterns differentiate between the "oh" of uncertainty (. . . well . . . I don't know really), the "oh" that means "How beautiful!" the "oh" of understanding (. . . so *that's* what it means), the "oh" of disappointment, and the "oh" of knowing a sly secret. The situation is similar with "no": Different intonation patterns convey different meanings including at least the "no" of shock (You didn't!), of warning (mother to young child who is moving slowly, deliberately toward the forbidden object), of hesitation and uncertainty (. . . but . . .), of finality, and the straightforward negative reply to a question. You might want to try some of these "ohs" and "nos" out on friends or fellow students to see whether they can tell the meaning that your intonation conveys. But be warned! This can become very frustrating when you discover that these various meanings that you convey so easily and naturally in everyday conversation are more difficult to convey out of context when you concentrate on them so consciously. You will probably also be surprised to see how much you use nonverbal clues (facial expressions or the shrug of your shoulders) in addition to intonation patterns to convey your meanings.

Read these words aloud:

saw
who
yesterday
know
do
I
you

Now read this arrangement of the same words aloud:

Do you know who I saw yesterday?

The list and the question probably sounded very different. Perhaps you read the list with a rising intonation on each word, followed by a pause, and then a falling intonation on the last word (rise-pause, rise-pause, . . . fall). But when you read the sentence, you probably lost the pauses that were part of your list reading and gave the sentence an overall rise, indicating that you were asking a certain type of question. The rhythm and intonation of the question were different from the rhythm and intonation of the list. Can you describe the rhythmic and intonational differences in the two possible readings of the ambiguous sentence

Did you ever see a horse fly?

(Sometimes it helps to substitute "la la la" for the words.)

You know which intonation patterns and rhythms are appropriate in conveying meanings in your language. You also know how to use and understand the feature of stress (emphasis). If you intended a neutral, strictly informational meaning, you would probably stress the words "told" and "tomorrow" slightly in the sentence

He told me they'd be arriving tomorrow.

But if you wanted to convey a special meaning, you would apply extra stress on various words, depending on your meaning:

He told me they'd be arriving tomorrow (Not *she* or you, but *he*)

He *told* me they'd be arriving tomorrow (He didn't *ask* me, he *told* me, or despite the fact that it didn't happen, he *told* me it would)

He told *me* they'd be arriving tomorrow (*Me*, instead of you or someone else)

He told me *they'd* be arriving tomorrow (Not *he* or *she*— one, but *they*—a group)

He told me they'd be *arriving* tomorrow (Not leaving, but *arriving*)

He told me they'd be arriving *tomorrow* (Not next week, but *tomorrow*)

This extra stress, which adds a special meaning to the neutral informational message, is called *contrastive* stress, for it focuses on one element as it contrasts with some expected meaning. As a speaker of English, you use and respond to this phonological feature of English with facility. Knowledge of stress, intonation, and rhythm are all important aspects of your phonological knowledge, every bit as important as your knowledge of the particular sounds of your language and the possibilities for their combination and pronunciation.

You know a lot about what matters in the phonological subsystem of your language—which particular sounds, out of all the possible sounds a human can make, are significant; what arrangements of sounds are possible; how sounds alter in combination; what stress, intonation, and rhythm patterns are appropriate. You also know what aspects of verbal sounds do not matter in the business of conveying meanings. The speed with which we say something, for example, does not alter the basic content of our message, nor does the pitch, quality, volume, or breathiness of our voice. It surely is the case that these voice features are sometimes associated with emotional or social meanings. We may, for example, speak more rapidly when excited, with higher pitch when upset, or more quietly when telling a friend a secret. These are important meanings: I'm excited; I'm upset; I don't want to be heard. But we need to look beyond the rules of language structure to account for them. Voice quality, speed, volume, and pitch do not alter the meanings of the propositions you make, the commands you give, or the questions you ask.[13]

It seems strange that the very stream of speech sounds that is so full of meaning for the speaker of a given language, is just so much noise to the outsider. "Sounds are given meaning by the language in which they occur"

---

[13]You will recognize the difficulty here in limiting ourselves to "language structure." This is an important difficulty, as it underscores the fact that language is for communication; language structure does not actually exist in a pure form—in some sort of vacuum, apart from its use by real people in real situations to talk to each other about real experiences—to be sarcastic, to parody, to persuade, to show respect. But language structure is an important part of the whole, and by understanding this aspect more fully, we may ultimately come to better understand the whole, even though it is admittedly artificial, to some extent, to try to examine it out of the context of real communication.

(Fromkin and Rodman 1974, p. 3). I process the sound stream of Chinese, Yoruba, or Amharic as noise, while the speaker of Chinese, Yoruba, or Amharic processes the same sound stream as meaning conveying—in fact, is probably unaware of the *sound* at all, so closely related is that sound to meaning and so completely is his attention focused on that meaning.

The linguist's choice of the phrase "sound stream" is apt, for the sounds of spoken language do indeed flow continuously. Speakers sometimes pause for breath or for emphasis or to get their thoughts in order, but overall there is a continuous flow of sounds in speech. It is easier to hear this continuousness of the speech stream if you listen to people speaking a language you do not know than if you listen to people speaking your own language. When you listen to your own language, the meaning "gets in the way." You tend to feel "breaks" in the speech stream that are not present in the sound signal itself but are very much present in your mental organization of the sound signal you hear. To know a language is to know how the (physically) unbroken speech stream is (mentally) broken—the organizational structure of sounds, meanings, and relations that the language system imposes. It is precisely because the sounds and meanings of your language are so inextricably entwined for you that it is difficult to focus simply on the sound stream; for you it is not only a sound stream but a meaning stream as well.

Do you begin to wonder how it is possible that an infant, exposed to the continuousness of the sounds of language, ever manages to figure out the organization of that stream and its relation to meanings? Yet over time, virtually *every* child does build a mental organization for the language that matches that of the adult in the language community. From an initial exposure to what, for the infant, must be noise, to the development of a full-fledged, highly complex, abstract language system matching the adult's seems an incredible journey, but it is one that every child makes for at least one language. This must surely stand as one of the greatest accomplishments of every human life.

THE WHOLE

We have focused on the knowledge speakers have of three components of language structure: semantic (knowledge of morphemic meaning), syntactic (knowledge of relational meaning), and phonological (knowledge of the sound system). Now we need to consider some important characteristics of the whole—all three components intergrated into a total meaning-expression system. What kind of a system is this, considered in its entirety?

First, it is a *two-level* system, one level involving meaning (often called deep structure) and the other involving expression (often called surface structure). To know a language is necessarily to know both the meanings in that language (morphemic and relational) and expression possibilities for those meanings within that language. It's fairly easy to demonstrate that there are these two levels in language structure. We all encounter expression in various forms each day—spoken or written or signed (as in deaf sign) sentences—and we instantly relate these to meanings. We also express meanings each day through these same expressive channels. Clearly, we could neither comprehend nor produce messages if we did not have a knowledge system of both meanings and expression possibilities, as well as of the relations between them.

But there is further evidence for this two-level system. There is no simple one-to-one correspondence between deep and surface structure. A single surface structure often relates to more than one deep structure. Consider these examples:

> /z/ expresses plural in "cookie*s*," possessive in "John'*s*," and third person singular in "run*s*."
>
> /Vr/ expresses "the one who does it" in "teach*er*" but expresses comparative in "bigg*er*."
>
> The word "runs" expresses different meanings in "He batted in three *runs*," "She has *runs* in her hose," and "Every morning Willard *runs* to catch the bus."
>
> And the expressed sentence, "She fed her dog biscuits," conveys several different meanings, as discussed earlier.

The opposite is also true: A single deep structure often relates to more than one surface structure.

> The meaning "more than one" (plural) is expressed as /z/ in "cookies," as /s/ in "hats," as /əz/ in "glasses," as no change in "sheep," and in a Variety of irregular ways in "mice," "data," and "leaves."
>
> The meaning of comparative is expressed as /Vr/ in "bigger" but as "more" in "more beautiful."
>
> A single meaning is expressed as both "small" and "little."
>
> A single meaning is expressed as "died," "passed away," and "kicked the bucket."

And any underlying sentence can relate to a variety of expressed sentences ("John's little sister kicked him in the shins" was our earlier example).

We also find instances in which an element of meaning or expession is present at one level and absent from the other. Commands offer the clearest examples here. If I say to you, "Put your shoes on" or "Take the trash out," there is no doubt about who is to perform the action, even though I have not named a doer in the string of sounds I have uttered. The fact that you respond to these commands—that you put your shoes on or that you angrily shout, "Take it out yourself"—indicates that it is clear to you that you are the doer in that sentence. My eighth-grade English teacher used to call this "*you* understood." Not a bad description, perhaps. Where is that "you"? Clearly not in the expressed sentence (surface structure), but just as surely present in the underlying sentence (deep structure). It is "understood" to be there. We know it is "there" in the deep level of structure.

We also find cases where elements in the surface structure are difficult to relate to specific meanings. If someone said to you, "It's mine," it would make perfectly good sense to ask, "What's yours?" But if someone said to you, "It's raining," it would make no sense at all for you to ask, "What's raining?" "It" just has to be there in the surface structure for the expressed sentence to be an OK (grammatical) sentence of English, but it does not correspond to any specific meaning element. And what about "to" in "I asked him to come"? We would not think of leaving it out, any more than we would think of including it in "I saw him (to) come." It does not really *mean*, it just *is* because the sentence *is* an OK English sentence with it, and it is not an OK English sentence without it.

Finally, we can think of sentences that are very similar (though not identical) at the surface level (expressed sentences) but distinctly different in the relations of the underlying sentence.

John is	easy eager	to please. (N. Chomsky 1964, p. 66)
Mary's sisters	begged asked persuaded told promised	her to clean the room.
She	asked told	him what to paint. (Based on C. Chomsky 1969, p. 100)

One word substitution in the expressed sentence—substituting one adjective or verb for another—conveys a radically different relational meaning, a markedly different organization of the entire sentence. Can you describe the differences in relations expressed in the sentences of each group from the preceding examples? For the first, the crucial question is, Who is doing the pleasing and who is being pleased? Is John pleasing someone else, or is someone else pleasing John? The second involves the question of who it is who is going to clean the room in the "promise" case, as opposed to the other cases: Is it Mary or her sisters who will do the cleaning? And the crucial queston for the last sentence pair is, Who is doing the painting?

Notice here that the changes do involve the substitution of one meaning part for another; for example, "easy" and "eager" are different meanings as are "begged" and "promised." However, the rest of the sentence in each case remains unchanged in form. Yet the relational meaning of the parts changes drastically for the entire sentence, not just for the meaning of the particular substituted word. By making one seemingly small change, substituting one member of a word class for another member of the same class, we totally change the organizational relations for the entire sentence. Though remarkably similar at the surface level, the sentences in question are vastly different at their deeper level of organization, a further argument for the existence of two levels of language structure. Clearly, then, our language system does not involve only one level of structure. Horton, the elephant, and the rest of us, can both *mean* and *say*.

Second, the system is *arbitrary* in that the particular expression symbols we relate to particular meanings are in no way "given" in the meanings themselves. There is nothing about the object we sit on in the park that would require our calling it a "bench" rather than calling it by some other name. A "rose by any other name would smell as sweet," and a bench by any other name would still be for sitting on in the park. In fact, in other languages it is called by some other name. Nor is there any logical reason to call human locomotor movement on one foot "hopping." People who speak other languages sometimes move about in this way, but they do not call this action "hopping." And so it is with all the words we use; they are arbitrary expresssive symbols—historical accidents, if you will—in no way dictated by the entities, actions, or characteristics they represent. The situation is similar with relational meaning. There is no inherent logic in expressing an attribute relationship by placing an adjective before the noun it modifies ("a red apple," "a little girl"). In fact, many languages express this relationship by placing the adjective after the noun;[14] still others use particular affixes rather than order.

Our expression is arbitrary, but—just as important—it is also, third, *conventional*. It is as if all speakers of a particular language have "agreed" to relate meaning and expression in the same ways. To be a member of a language group is to mean and express in the same way that others in the group do. Without this shared system, communication would be impossible.

I am particularly struck by the arbitrary and conventional nature of language each time I hear young children create some version of a game in which they deliberately change labels for familiar meanings. "Hey, I know. Let's do it this way. When we say 'yes' that means 'no,' and 'no' means 'yes.' " And they proceed to play this out with great giggling. But notice the importance of convention here. The game works only if all partners agree to use the same labels in the same way. In fact, it is this convention that places some individuals within the group and makes others outsiders. And so with "real" language: We are *in* the language group whose conventions we share.

Finally, language is a system that is at once *finite* and *infinite*, finite in that it includes a limited set of principles for relating meaning and expression, yet infinite in that that finite set of principles accounts for a literally infinite set of particular possible sentences. We have a mental scheme for the possible designs that expressed sentences may take, yet within these designs, innumerable specific expressed sentences can occur. Thus, every expressed sentence we encounter or produce is both new and not new—new in its specifics, but familiar in its design.

We are familiar with systems in other areas of our lives, in which a finite set of principles accounts for an infinite set of specific instances. We all know a multiplication system, a set of relationships among elements. It is a finite system, yet it enables us to deal with a literally infinite set of pairs of specific numbers. We are able to comprehend and produce specific cases

---

[14]Notice that English also uses the order noun followed by adjective in constructions like "The girl is little."

that we have never encountered before. They are familiar in that they conform to our mental scheme, yet they are new in their specifics.

One of the important principles of language structure that accounts for this infinite aspect is that any possible sentence can easily be made into another and longer sentence. If "That man is old" is a possible sentence of English, then so is "That man is very old" and so is "That man is very, very, very old." (I shall never forget my high school drama coach who, when distressed with some aspiring actor's poor performance at a rehearsal, would say, "That performance was absolutely the most wishy-washy, willy-nily, shilly-shally, run-of-the-mill, bottom-of-the-barrel . . . etc. . . . performance that I have ever seen.") If "That man is his father" is a possible sentence of English, then so is "I know that that man is his father" and so is "You know that I know that that man is his father."(How many times have you heard children engage in this "I know that you know that I know . . ." game? Does that tell you anything about their language knowledge?) If "That boy is his son" is a sentence, then so is "That boy, who is a very good friend of mine, is his son" and so is "That boy is the son of the man I like very much but wish would stop smoking those foul-smelling cigars." The examples here are trivial, but the point is not. It is always possible to include a sentence within a sentence, and thus language must be, by definition, infinite.

Including a sentence within a sentence is called *recursion*; and, of course, all languages have this recursive property. However, we do not generally communicate using sentences that are very recursive—sentence within sentence within sentence (although we do play games with such sentences as in "This is the house that Jack built"). Communication requires that out of the structurally possible set of sentences, we use those which will be processed readily in actual life situations. But it is important to understand, as a basic fact about language, that there is no limit to the set of sentences accounted for by a finite set of structural principles, even though many of the theoretically possible sentences are ones we would be unlikely to use in conversation.

It is, finally, this largely unconscious, two-level, arbitrary and conventional finite-and-infinite system that enables us (and the children we teach) to mean and to say, and to do so in novel ways.

WRITTEN LANGUAGE

The title here announces an important fact: Writing *is* language. So far we have mainly considered the verbal expression system, with the barest mention of the written system. There are two reasons for this. First, children's literacy development is a major concern of elementary teachers— especially in the early grades—and even of parents and others in the larger society. It is easy for us to become so preoccupied with children's reading and writing that we focus on this almost to the exclusion of a concern for oral language development. (Notice the cover of this book. The designer represents the "language" of the title as alphabet letters, that is, written symbols.) A righting of the balance between written and verbal expression seems to be in order. Second, linguists have been particularly interested in describing characteristics that all (or at least, most) languages share, "linguistic universals" as they are called. All human languages have verbal systems of expression,[15] but only some have written systems of expression as well. Thus, linguists have described verbal expression systems more fully than written ones.

However, in literate societies such as ours, we use the expressive system of writing to convey meanings in many different situations. We have two major systems of expression, talk and print, and they do different kinds of intellectual and social work for us.

We have described the structure of language as two-level, including both a meaning level and an expression level. You can readily see that this description accounts as well for writing as it does for speech. The written system of English happens to be alphabetic; that is, the expression symbols (letters) relate to phonemes of the language, rather than to syllable units (as in the syllabic systems of some languages) or to morphemes as in some ideographic systems.[16] Because the English system uses an alphabetic principle, it is often seen as somehow parasitic on the sound system of English. That is, many people (teachers among them) feel that it is necessary to "go through" the verbal system to process the symbols of the written system. But surely accomplished readers and writers relate symbols of print directly to the meanings those symbols express; theirs is not a two-step process of relating symbols to sounds and then relating sounds to meanings. All written systems, whether alphabetic, syllabic, or ideographic, are language in that they are part of a two-level system of relating meaning and expression.

Further, written language is language in that it is an arbitrary and conventional system of expression. There is no logical "reason" that "c" and "q" and "x" and "u" should have become expressive symbols in English rather than ͮ‿   ᘓ ⅄ . Nor is there any particular logic in the relationship between the selected symbols and the elements they represent. The written system is, like its parallel verbal system, arbitrary in the symbols and their use. And, like the expressive system of speech, it is conventional: In order to communicate shared meanings in written form, we all "agree" to represent those meanings in similar ways in writing. If I want my conversational partner to know I am talking about my furry four-legged pet that laps up milk, climbs uninvited into my lap and purrs, and catches unwary mice, I'll express it orally as /kæt/. If I want the friend to whom I'm writing a letter to know I'm referring to the same object, I'll

---

[15]I am excluding specialized systems such as deaf sign, secret coding systems, drumming languages, and so on.

[16]It is important not to oversimplify here. Many people, quite mistakenly, believe ideographic writing, as in Chinese, to be sequences of little simplified pictures, and they believe alphabetic writing, as in English, to be sequences of symbols directly representing language sounds. In fact, neither of these beliefs is true.

express it as "cat."[17] My conversational partner and my long-distance friend and I all share a system of conventions for relating oral expression symbols to meaning, and also a system of conventions for relating written expression symbols to meanings.

Finally, the written system is language in that it involves a finite system of principles that generates a literally infinite set of meaning-expression possibilities. The astonishing creativity of language once again! We daily encounter particular written forms (items we read, items we write) that we have never encountered before. Yet because they conform to a finite set of principles we know for relating meaning and written expression, we readily understand and are understood. However mundane our behavior may be in other areas of our lives, in our language— oral and written—we are endlessly creative after all.

---

[17]Unless, of course, I am a child, in which case I may for some period of time refer to this animal in some other way(s) in talk and writing. More of this in Section Two.

4

Language Structure: Teachers and Children

INTRODUCTION

"What one sees depends on how one looks" (Cazden in press). There are different ways of looking at, and seeing, the children we teach. One prevalent way is to see school children as bundles of deficiencies, lacks, and problems. We are typically advised to begin each new school year by diagnosing problems in our students and then providing experiences designed to eradicate those problems—diagnose, prescribe, and treat. This approach is often called "meeting the needs of the individual child," a seemingly innocuous expression, but one which frequently masks a view of children as deficient beings. "Diagnose," "prescribe," and "treat" are medical terms and suggest that we view the child as an unhealthy, poorly functioning organism. After all, we seek our doctors' diagnoses, prescriptions, and treatments when we are ill, not when we are in good health. If unhealthy is what we look for in children, then unhealthy is what we see.

But in the area of language, the child is an extraordinarily healthy organism who will continue to flourish in the rich environment we can provide. We are not trying to rid the child of language "problems," but rather to enhance her remarkable continuing language development. Typically the child's language is alive and well, at whatever developmental stage we first encounter her—preschool, primary, or intermediate level—and our job is to provide an environment in which it will thrive.

The preschooler, given the opportunity and the desire, tells us about objects and events, asks a variety of questions, and requests or demands what she wants. It takes a well-developed linguistic system (as well as a sophisticated knowledge of how to use it appropriately in various situations) to do this, and a well-developed linguistic system is exactly what preschoolers have. This is not to say that four-year-olds always formulate their sentences as adults do. Clearly, they do not. Their language includes pronunciations, word combinations, and vocabulary items which are different from the adult's, as will become more apparent to you when you read Section Two. But these are more accurately seen as the healthy and necessary developmental differences of language growth in progress than as a set of "problems." Adults get around by walking, and eight-month-old babies get around by crawling. But notice that we do not view the eight-month-old's crawling as a "walking problem"; rather, we delight in the substantial accomplishment of mastering crawling, though we realize that the child will not crawl forever. Why, then, do we view the young child's far more impressive language accomplishment as being full of "problems" simply because it does not yet match our own? This is a faulty way of looking and results in our forming inaccurate notions of children developing and using their language. But not only are the resulting notions inaccurate; they are also unhelpful for the teacher. Presumably the teacher's goal is to help the child extend her abilities as a language user. To do this, the teacher can only use what the child has, for it is what the child *has*, not what she lacks, that enables the child to go beyond.

We often hear that a teacher should "Start where the child is." I find it interesting, and discouraging, that this advice is often interpreted as "Find out what's wrong with the child, so we'll know what to 'work on.' " We would do better to interpret this advice as "Find out what the child has so we can use it to support her going beyond."

Our way of looking (and seeing) is informed by our knowledge of what language is and how children use it. Only when we are guided by this knowledge can we see children's language behaviors as evidence of what children *know*, *have*, and *do* as language users. To paraphrase our opening statement: What one sees depends on how one looks, which depends on what one knows. And so we move now to look at school children's language behaviors on the basis of our knowing, our understanding of language structure. Looking in this way we will see healthy, able children.

ORAL LANGUAGE EXAMPLES

We cannot begin to consider here all types of oral evidence of children's language knowledge, but three important kinds of evidence are (1) children's self-corrections when talking, (2) children's play with elements of language, and (3) children's enjoyment of language play in the literature we read to them.

Children's Self-Corrections

As adults, we frequently correct ourselves when we speak. We may, for example, modify our pronunciation of a word or alter our syntax or select a different word. Whatever the change, it is the result of our sensing a mismatch between what we actually said and our notion of what we "should have said." That is, the change attests to the presence of an ideal system in our minds against which we match our speaking performance.

And so it is with children. The young child's organizational system for language may not exactly match the adult's; nevertheless, the child has a system, a set of expectations for the selection and arrangement of language elements to express meanings. Sometimes the child corrects her talk in light of that system, which, of course, shows that she *has* such a system. Consider these examples of self-corrections by five- and six-year-old children in conversation with an adult.

ORIGINAL UTTERANCE	CORRECTED FORM
a. We can't go no more	We can't go anymore
b. They was going	They were going
c. I know what them are	I know what they are
d. I pulled off his hat off	I pulled his hat off
e. You put down it	You put it down
f. What you're doing?	What are you doing?
g. He didn't wash hisself	He didn't wash himself
h. He growed bigger	He grew bigger
(Rogers 1983, p. 78)	

What I find particularly impressive here is that all of the original utterances are entirely comprehensible to a speaker of English. All convey the child's intended meanings quite adequately. In every case the child's correction involves a rather sophisticated minor refinement of form, a sort of "nicety," that makes the utterance more conventional by adult standards. (The one exception here is h.) Examples a, b, and c are especially striking "nicety" examples. Notice that "any" (in a) in English is a special negative form. Many of us had well-intentioned teachers who told us that in standard English negative is expressed only once per sentence. Clearly, this is not the case: Contrast "I want *some*" and "I *don't* want *any*"; "We're going to do that some more" and "We're *not* going to do that *any*more." The children in examples b and c also correct by selecting particular forms that "go together" with other words in the sentence in certain conventional ways, in the adult system. In all three examples (1) the original utterance expresses the child's meaning in a clear and unambiguous way, showing that the child's basic meaning-expression system is quite intact and much like ours; (2) the correction goes quite beyond the basic system to a minor form change in the direction of adult standard English convention; and (3) the correction involves the child's taking into account a larger domain than just the particular word, for in each case the child's correction involves combinations ("any" goes with "n't," "were" goes with "they," and "they" goes with "are").

Examples d and e involve combinations also. The children in d and e obviously know quite a bit about ordering nouns and pronouns with two-word verbs ("put down" and "pull off"). Notice that in adult standard English we order two-word verbs and nouns in either of two ways:

I called John up last night.
I called up John last night.

but only one way with pronouns

> I called him up last night.
> I called up him last night.

Child d's original utterance, "He pulled off his hat off," reflects both noun orders used by adult standard English speakers. She adjusts her utterance by selecting one of them. In e, the child self-corrects by splitting up the two-word verb ("put down") and inserting the pronoun, resulting in a form that more nearly matches the adult's convention. As in cases a through c, the original sentences d and e show a well-developed meaning-expression system at work, and the changes are minor modifications of form that involve combinations of words within the expressed sentence.

The original sentence f is a developmental form that we encounter frequently with young children. (You will become more familiar with questions of this form in Section Two.) Notice that the original utterance demonstrates at least the following adult-type knowledge: "What" plus "do" queries the action phrase, "what" goes at the beginning of the expressed sentence, "you" refers to the person being spoken to, "be" before the verb (expressed as "are" with "you") plus "-ing" after the verb expresses action in progress, "do" is the all-purpose verb for action, and "you're" is an optional variant of "you are." That's quite a bit of knowing! But in her correction the child goes beyond this to rearrange elements in the more usual adult order. "What you're doing" apparently does not match her sense of order as well as "What are you doing?"

The last two original utterances, g and h, show overgeneralizations on the child's part. That is, they show that the child has discerned a regular pattern in the language and is applying that pattern, or rule, to specific cases that are exceptions in the adult language. Notice the possessive form of the pronoun in the following:

I washed *my* -self	We washed *our* -selves
You washed *your* -self	You washed *your* -selves

The child's "hisself" attests to the child's recognition of that underlying regularity in English. The minor correction the child makes suggests that her knowledge system includes a particular exception to the general rule.

Example h is my favorite. The child's correction attests to her knowledge of the regular way of expressing past tense in English. This child senses the original "grew" as mismatching how it "should be." In this instance, the child's change is in a nonadult direction; but this change, just as fully as the others, shows that the child has a complex and orderly system for relating meaning and expression in language, and that that system guides her speech.

I well remember a breakfast conversation some years ago when my son was nine years old. He said that he had "aten" something, and immediately his eleven-year-old sister pounced on him: "*Aten*?! *Aten*?! You don't say 'aten,' Erik. You say 'eaten.'" He gazed out the window, shaking his head, and said to himself in a most puzzled way, " 'Eaten.' 'Eaten.' That sounds weird." Notice his appeal to his sense of sound. He had a language system no less than his sister. They were simply different systems. "Eaten" belonged in one system and was "weird" in the other, but the belonging and the weirdness both were attributable to the (different) set of expectations each child had for meaning-expression relations.

Some people seem to think that adults have a language system but children don't and that is why children's talk is "chaotic" and "full of mistakes." It should be clear to you by now that this is inaccurate. The child's language system may be different from the adult's system in some identifiable ways, but it *is* a system nonetheless. Children, like adults, correct themselves precisely because they sense a mismatch between their utterance and their system. Children's self-corrections tell us that they have a system of language structure, and a very complex system at that, and also give us clues as to what that system is like. But we see (hear?) children's self-corrections as evidence of this language system at work only if we know to look—and listen—for it.

Children's Language Play

Adults play—using cards, using tennis racquets, using sailboats, using language. From our corny puns to our sophisticated witticisms, we use "language as a toy" (Garvey 1977). Children do too, and their language play, like our own, reveals substantial knowledge of language elements and relationships. To use language in a deviant way deliberately, as we do in language play, is to give evidence of our awareness of "the usual." Obviously, we cannot deliberately deviate from a norm unless we have a norm.

Consider these examples of language play by four-year-olds in a nursery school class. For each example, try to identify what knowledge the child has about language structure that enables him or her to play in this way.[1]

a. *C-1:* You're a boo!
    C-2: You're a shoe!
    C-3: You're a boo, too!

b. *C-1:* You're a crazy nut head.
    C-2: You're a coo-coo brat head.
    C-1: Well, you're really a boo-boo bat bed.
    C-2: You're a foo-foo fat head.

c. *C-1:* (hopping along in a squatting position) Guess what kind of animal I am. Rib-bit, rib-bit, rib-bit.
    C-2: A frog.
    C-1: No. Rib-bit, rib-bit, rib-bit.

[1] I am indebted to Judith Blalock, Cynthia Postel, and Ellis Scaff for these examples.

C-2:   A toad.

C-1:   No. Rib-bit, rib-bit.

C-2:   I don't know, then.

C-1:   A rabbit.

C-2:   Uh-uh (meaning *no*).

C-1:   Uh-huh (meaning *yes*). This rabbit says rib-bit. (laughs)

d.   C-1:   My babies are over here. My babies are over here! I have to get them.

C-2:   (with feather duster) I'm a duster lady.

C-3:   (grabs a duster, giggles and starts a chant) Mamadee-humadee, mumadee-humadee, mumadee-humadee, mumadee-humadee. (giggles)

C-1:   (loudly) *I have to go to a party!*

C-2:   We'll have to share these *bee*bies. (giggles)

C-1:   We are going to the *potty* and then . . . to the *party*. (giggles)

e.   C-1:   (a boy, pointing to other boys) You're a girl; you're a girl; you're a girl. (Pointing to C-2, who is a girl) You're a boy. (laughs)

C-2:   If I'm a boy, you're a girl!

C-1:   Oh no! We mixed it all up! I'm a girl! (speaks in a high voice) I'm a girl! I'm a girl!

f.   C-1:   What's this baby's name?

C-2:   na-ma.

C-1:   What's this one's name?

C-2:   Naked Baby. (laughs)

C-1:   What's this blanket's name?

C-2:   Uhhhhhhh, Bla-bla.

C-1:   Bla-bla? Bla-bla? (laughs)

g.   C-1:   Do you love hot dogs?

C-2:   Uh-huh. (meaning *yes*)

C-1:   Then why don't you marry it? (laughs)

h.   C-1:   I eat milk.

C-2:   I drink chicken. (both laugh)

The children in a and b are clearly playing with the sounds of language. The children in a insert rhyming words into a single frame ("You're a *(rhyme)*"). The children in b use a more complex frame that involves rhyming sets of words ("coo-coo brat head," "boo boo bat bed," and "foo-foo fat head"). In their final two rhyme sets, they are playing with alliteration as well as rhyme, in C-1's use of initial /b/s and C-2's use of initial /f/s. The knowledge these children have of the sound system of their language is considerable, as demonstrated in their sound play. They know basic sounds of their language, and these are what they substitute as they move from rhyme to rhyme. And when they create new words, they create within the English possibilities for sound combinations. "Foo-foo" is not an English word, but it *could* be in the sense that that consonant-vowel combination can occur within the English sound system.

The children in c and d are also playing with elements of the sound system. The children in c play within a frame; however, it is not a line frame, repeated in each turn, but a conversational frame. Call it "the guessing game frame." The sound play turns on the similarity of sounds in the two "real" words "rabbit" and "ribbit." The children in d make a joke of the similar sounding "potty" and "party" and also deliberately distort "babies" to "beebies." Notice that the children's laughter in c and d occurs after each of these points of sound play.[2]

Play with language meanings is particularly evident in examples e–h. The children in e are playing with meaning-label pairings by deliberately switching them, christening boys "girls" and girls "boys." This play suggests some sense the children have of the arbitrariness of labels. This same sense of the arbitrariness of labels is evident in f as the children assign verbal labels to their dolls and whether "real words" or nonsense syllables (which syllables, of course, conform to possible sound combinations of English). The children in e and f are drawing on their awareness of language as conventional in that they seem to be agreeing to accept certain labels for certain entities.

In g, C-1 is obviously playing with two meanings of "love": food preference and person preference. And what about the children in h? They are playing with a feature of meaning that differentiates "eat" and "drink." Both "eat" and "drink" involve taking food into the body for nourishment, but in one case the food is solid, and in the other case it is liquid. So, it is funny to "eat milk" and "drink chicken." Incredible! And all of these children have been alive for less than five years.

Notice that in all these examples, the play partners clearly share a similar language system. Each of these episodes is jointly constructed. No parallel play here; rather, what we see are sequences of conversational turns each of which picks up on and extends the play focus of the partners. To be able to play the same language game successfully, the children must be using similar language rules, that is, they must be drawing on a similar base of meanings and expressions and relations among them.

This sharing of a language structure system and using it to construct jointly a language play episode is evident in the next example also, in which two five-year-olds are playing with objects *and* with the derivational suffix "y."

C-1: (inspects stuffed animals) Teddy bear's mine.

C-2: (busy with suitcase) The fishy fishy is mine.

C-1: No, the snakey snakey is yours. (wandering) 'Cause it's fishy too. 'Cause it has fishes.

C-2: And it's snakey too 'cause it has snakes and it's beary too because it has bears.

C-1: And it's . . . and it's hatty 'cause it has hats. (Adapted from Garvey 1977, pp. 70–71)

---

[2]Children's laughter can be most informative. My advice: Always take children's laughter seriously, as it tells us so much about the child's sense of ongoing events.

It would be easy to dismiss children's language play as "nonsense," but if we look and listen, we are awed by the enormous amount of *sense* in this kind of "non"-sense—children's sense of sounds, rhythms, words, arrangements, and meanings. It is this *sense* of language that provides the elements, the toys, of the children's language play. Without this rich *sense* of language children could not create *non*sense.

Children's Enjoyment of Language Play in Children's Literature

Many children's authors have capitalized on children's delight in language play by providing a rich literature of rhymes and riddles and language surprises of all sorts. We read this literature aloud to young children and they hear[3] playful novel words and names:

> We find out how many, we learn the amount
> By an Audio-Telly-o-Tally-o Count.

> Do you know who's asleep
> Out in Foona-Lagoona . . . ?
> Two very nice
> Foona-Lagoona Baboona.

playful sound sequences:

> Up at Herk-Heimer Falls, where the great river rushes
> And crashes down crags and in great gargling gushes,

> Our chap counts these balls as they plup in a cup.

> Moose juice, not goose juice, is juice for a moose
> And goose juice, not moose juice, is juice for a goose.
> So, when goose gets a mouthful of juices of moose's
> And moose gets a mouthful of juices of goose's,
> They always fall out of their beds screaming screams.

novel word combinations and forms and arrangements:

> And the old drawbridge draw-er just said with a yawn,

> All this long, happy day, they've been honking about
> And the Hinkle-Horn Honkers have honked themselves out.
> But they'll wake up quite fresh in the morning. And then . . .
> They'll start right in Hinkle-Horn honking again.

> So, every so often, one puts down his hoop,
> Stops hooping and does some quick snooping for soup.
> That's why they are known as the Hoop-Soup-Snoop Group.

---

[3]The first three sets of examples all come from a single treasure-chest of a book, *Dr. Seuss's Sleep Book* (Seuss 1962).

play with ambiguities involving particular words:

> In her employer's absence, Amelia Bedelia, a housemaid, is instructed to "Draw the drapes when the sun comes in": and she dutifully takes pencil and paper and draws a picture of the drapes. (Parish 1963)
> She is instructed to "dress the chicken" and indeed she does—with clothing. (Parish 1963)
> She is told to "pare the vegetables" and she arranges them two-by-two. (Parish 1964)

play with syntactic ambiguities (in which the double meanings depend on relations among the words):

> One day Marvin went to a farm. "Would you like to take this hen home to eat?" the farmer asked Marvin.
> "Oh, I would, I would!" said Marvin. "But tell me—what does it eat?" (Cerf 1959, p. 3)

> Sammy told Marvin, "One time my father shot an elephant in his pajamas."
> Marvin asked, "How did the elephant ever get into your father's pajamas?" (Cerf 1959, p. 54)

We read this playful literature to children, and we readily see that they enjoy it. It is tempting to conclude that the child's appreciation of the combination "old drawbridge draw-er" rests on her sense of "-er" indicating the doer of the action; or that her appreciation of the combination "Hinkle-Horn Honkers" rests on her recognition that these are individuals who honk horns of the Hinkle type, and so on. But we can't attribute such specific knowledge to the child in these instances on the basis of the child's general overall expressed delight. Specific knowledge that the child draws on is more apparent when the child produces the language play than when she responds appreciatively to language play created by others. But the fact of the child's obvious delight and attentiveness to the language play in children's literature is evidence enough for me that the child's sense of language is importantly involved. I believe that it is the unexpected in the language of these books that is most engaging to the child. To call the sound sequences and word combinations of this literature "unexpected" is, of course, to say that the child has expectations. Those expectations are the child's developing knowledge of language structure.

With an ever-increasing concern in our society for basics, accountability, student achievement measured by test scores, and teachers' merit pay based on that student achievement, there is real danger that we will be under pressure to rid our classrooms of such "nonsense." But it is an intriguing and persuasive idea that language play, as created by both children and authors, focuses on those very language elements that the young school child will later be encouraged to consider in a more conscious, analytic way when she learns *about* language. This play may be an important precursor to the child's subsequent, more conscious understanding of language structure. We see a pattern in other areas of children's learning whereby their physically acting upon entities precedes and enhances a later, more abstract understanding. Science offers a good example. Some leaders in science education advocate that teachers make specific provision for an initial "messing about phase" when children encounter an unfamiliar phenomenon (the pendulum, for example) in order to "build an apperceptive background, against which a more analytical sort of knowledge can take form and make sense" (Hawkins 1965, p. 6). It may be that in their language play, children are building a similar apperceptive background that supports their moving from a more intuitive toward a more conscious sense of language structure. It may be that play with language elements strengthens the base on which the child will build her more reflective consideration of language later on.

WRITTEN LANGUAGE EXAMPLES

1. Take a piece of paper and cover up the indented passage that follows.
2. Now slide the paper slowly down the page, uncovering the passage line by line as you read it aloud one line at a time.

> The boys' arrows were nearly gone so they sat down on the
> grass and stopped hunting. Over at the side of the wood they saw
> Henry making a bow to a small girl who was coming down the road.
> She had tears in her dress and tears in her eyes. She gave Henry
> a note which he brought over to the group of young hunters. Read
> to the boys, it caused great excitement. After a minute, but rapid
> examination of their weapons they ran down to the valley. Does
> were standing at the edge of the lake, making an excellent target.[4]

Can you see how you are using your knowledge of meaning-expression relations as you read? There is good, and increasing, evidence that children draw heavily on their knowledge of language structure when they read also.[5] In one well-known reading study of one hundred first-, second-, and third-grade children, the researcher first determined each child's reading level and then gave each child words to read orally at that level (K. Goodman 1967). The words for each child came from a story at his or her grade level, but from a story in a basal series that the child was not using in the classroom so that the story would be new to the child. Each child read the words in two conditions: First the child read the words in a list (with no comment or correction by the researcher), and then the child read the story including those same words. In the second condition (reading the story), on the average, the first graders read correctly approximately two-thirds of the words they had missed when they read the list; the second graders read correctly approximately three-fourths of the words they had missed in the list reading; and the third graders read correctly

---

[4]Guy T. Buswell, *An Experimental Study of the Eye-Voice Span in Reading,* Supplementary Educational Monographs, No. 17 (Chicago: The University of Chicago Press, 1920), p. 87.
I am grateful to Kathleen Copeland for calling this passage to my attention.

[5]It is important here to differentiate between "reading"—the construction of language meanings in relation to printed symbols—and "word calling"—the pronouncing of words in left-to-right sequences on the page.

approximately four-fifths of the words they had read incorrectly in the list-reading task. Why? How are we to explain the fact that a child correctly reads in context the very same words that she reads incorrectly on a list? One important factor is that the full context of the story allows the child to use her knowledge of language structure, especially her semantic and syntactic knowledge. To say that the child *uses* this knowledge is, of course, to say that she *has* it. (Does this research finding make you wonder about the advisability of the teaching practice we see so often, in which the teacher introduces the new words in a basal story by presenting those words on flash cards or in a list before the children read the story?)

The example here of children's language structure system at work as they read comes from a research study. However, further evidence of children using their language knowledge in reading is directly available to teachers day after day as they listen to children read aloud. Children make changes in the text. These differences between the text and the child's oral reading of it are called "miscues." They can be most informative—*if* we know to observe in these changes the child's language knowledge at work. Consider the following miscue examples and try to identify the knowledge that the child demonstrates in her alteration of the original text. (The child's reading appears in italics above the printed text.)

      Look at the little red toy.
a.   Look at the little red train.

      In the morning, she went to school.
b.   In the morning, she walked to school.

      Give it to Mommy.
c.   Give it to Mother.

      He was standing next to the fence.
d.   He was standing beside the fence.

      Bring me the big one.
e.   Bring me the little one.

      They crept into the circus.
f.   They crept into the circus tent.

      "Well, I'll try," said John.
g.   "Well, I'll try," John said.

      It was raining so she took her umbrella.
h.   It was raining. She took her umbrella.

      Yes, I can't d . . . I can do it.
i.   Yes, I can do it.

      I think the will . . . they wi . . . I think she will come.
j.   I think she will come.

In a–e, the child substitutes for the original another word from the same word class, a noun for a noun, a verb for a verb, a preposition for a preposition, or an adjective for an adjective. In a and b, the miscue begins with the same letter as the original word, but obviously that is not the only cue the child is using, since there are many other words the child does not choose that also begin with the same letter and/or are more similar in appearance to the original (for example, "try" or "rain" for "train" or "wanted" for "walked"). Clearly, the child's language knowledge is at work here: Some words contribute to sensible meaning while others do not. In c the child's miscue suggests that the meaning-expression relation she is using is a very personal one, thus "Mommy" for "mother." In d and e the substituted words are graphically very different from the originals, suggesting that in these cases the child's reliance on semantic and syntactic information is greater than her reliance on graphic information. In d the child gives a synonym for the original while in e she gives an antonym. Nonetheless, both readings are meaningful, provide substitutions in the same word class, and suggest that syntactic phrases (prepositional phrases and adjective phrases) cohere for the child.

In f (an ommission) and g (a rearrangement) the child's miscues are alternative expressions that preserve the meaning of the original. But in h the child actually improves on the text, preserving the meaning but expressing it in a more flowing and natural way than does the original text. And in i and j the child corrects her own reading when that reading, her expression, does not relate to meaning in a way that makes sense within her language system.[6]

"Written language *is* language." You have read this before. This means, among other things, that written language, like spoken language, relates expression and meaning.[7] These children's miscues demonstrate that they know written language to be language in this sense. Their miscues demonstrate that they are processing print in terms of well-developed expectations (rules) for these relations.

Children's writing, like their reading, gives abundant evidence that they are bringing their knowledge of language structure to bear on their writing activity. Five-year-old Brian demonstrates his awareness that writing expresses meaning graphically as he explains the following two figures to his teacher:

That's Jim. And that's Jim too. (Dyson 1983, p. 889)

[6]Not all reading miscues are semantically or syntactically based, as in these examples. Children use other types of knowledge as they read also (for example, how a printed word looks— "went"/"want"— or what letters a word has—"was"/"saw").

[7]Like all language, written language involves other aspects as well such as, for example, social context, diverse communication purposes, and specific expressive symbols.

The following written messages both show considerable specific knowledge of the conventions of written language. Obviously, these children belong to the same writing community that we do and they are participating (expressing) as members of that community. That's why we can read what they write.

A mother tells her four-year-old son that if he wants to go out before she wakes up in the morning, he must leave her a note telling her where he is. So he does.

I MGOEGTAB
AWTSID

(Y. Goodman 1982, p. 435)

A Spanish-dominant child, in second grade, starts her five-page story this way.[8]

wuants ap an a taim ther
wuas a dragan Thet livd
en a maunten he wuaz
May Frend he wazente
min he wuaz nais I f yust
to gevem ascrm The
pipl was Min to hem

These children understand that writing is language: Like speech, writing expresses their messages. These children are using a finite set of principles, *their* principles, to create—that is, to express *novel* messages that they have

[8]I am grateful to Sarah Hudelson for this example.

not encountered before in this specific form. This is to grasp the most basic fact of all about language: that it is a system of endless creative potential.

CHILDREN'S QUESTIONS ABOUT TALK AND PRINT

I am repeatedly struck by the considerable knowledge that children's questions reflect. Those questions tell us more about children's knowledge than about their lack of it. This is as true of the child's questions about the physical and social world as it is true of the child's questions about language, of course. But the examples that follow all deal with aspects of language structure knowledge.

Four-year-old Jill asks many questions as her mother reads *Curious George Goes to the Hospital*; many are questions about language, including these:[9]

M: (reading) "What could be in it? George could not resist."
J: What does resist mean?

  (The picture in the book shows children in hospital beds. Each bed has a name card with the child's name facing the child. Some cards are pictured on the name side, and some are pictured from the back side. Jill's question refers to the pictured children whose cards are pictured from the back side.)

J: Why they don't got their names?
M: Well, their names are on those cards but they're going that way. It's on the other side and we can't see in the book.

M: (reading) "By the time the attendant came with the stretcher—"
J: What is it? Why do you call it a stretcher?

M: (reading) " 'We'll let him sleep,' said Nurse Carol. 'The more he sleeps, the better.' "
J: What does 'the better' mean? The better he gets, I don't know—the better he gets—the better what?

Four-year-old Sarah asks many questions as her mother reads *Sarah's Unicorn*. Some of her questions focus on print and speech as two expression systems for meaning:

M: (reading) "He will take her on his back, and they will ride to dawn, dancing on the moon beams. Unicorns can do that you know."
S: Is that the word or are you saying it?
M: What, honey? Unicorns can do that? It's the words in the book.
S: How come?
M: Well, that's what the author wanted to write. "Unicorns can do that you know."
S: Unicorns can do that you know.
M: Uh-huh.

[9]I am indebted to Carol Peterson for these examples.

S: That word?
M: This is the word "unicorn."[10]

Children demonstrate a great deal about their knowledge of language structure. We find evidence of that knowledge in their talk and in their response to talk (in their self-corrections, in their language play, in their response to playful literature), in their oral reading, in their writing, and in their questions about oral and written language. But they show and tell us of their knowledge only if we know to look and listen, believing that it is there.

TEACHERS AND (NON) LANGUAGE

Children know very well that oral and written language express meaning. Outside of the classroom, teachers know this too. Inside the classroom, we sometimes forget. Compare the two whole-class discussions that follow, the first from a third grade, and the second from a kindergarten.

T: Who remembers what we call these things that hang down from the ceiling? Do you remember . . . (pause) . . . what we just saw . . . on the slides? . . . (pause) . . . Okay, I'm going to say it, and say it after me. Stalactites. They have to hang on tight. Stalactites. Everybody.
CHILDREN: Stalactites.
T: Okay, now we can see something else in this picture. It starts in the bottom. Who remembers the name for these? They go up from the floor . . .
CS: Stalagmites.
T: Good. Stalagmites. Let's all say it.
CS: Stalagmites.
T: Then, we see something that goes from the bottom of the cave all the way to the top, or from the top all the way to the bottom. Who remembers the name for this?
C: I know. I know.
T: What is it:
C: Stalagmites.
T: Well, a stalagmite starts at the bottom . . . what could be coming off the bottom?
C: Stalagmites.
T: Stalagmites. And what could be coming down from the top?
CS: Stalactites.
T: Good, stalactites. And what could be maybe starting at the bottom and going up to the top and starting at the top and going all the way to the bottom? What could be called that? . . . (pause) . . . do you remember? Columns. Let's say that.
CS: Columns.
T: Columns.[11]

[10]I am indebted to Miriam Martinez for this example from her dissertation data.
[11]I am indebted to Mimi Miran for this interaction.

TEACHER: How do you know if somebody likes you?

TANYA: When you think there's someone that doesn't like you . . . well, you don't have to worry about that so much. You could have some other friends.

KIM: Maybe they might not like you but later they will.

FRED: When they grow up they could be friends.

ELLEN: If someone says to you, "I don't like you," and then you say, "I don't care," and then you know they don't like you.

LISA: When people think that no one's being nice to anybody you should just ignore them.

TEACHER: It sounds as if it's easier to talk about people who don't like you. But how can you tell if someone *does* like you?

WALLY: Watch a person and see if they stay and play.

JILL: And lots of people get in fights and they act like they're not being nice but the next day they want to be friends again.

EDDIE: If he talks to you a lot he likes you.

DEANA: I can tell if someone doesn't like me. I like someone who doesn't like me. I chase him and he doesn't run after me. He tries to hit me and I duck.

EDDIE: I know the boy next door is my enemy because we know we're enemies.

ELLEN: They say bad words to you if someone doesn't like you. (Paley 1981, pp. 150-51)

These two class discussions differ in many ways, but one important difference might be called the "parrot-people distinction." We can train parrots to speak particular fixed words or phrases on cue. The children in the first discussion seem to have been so trained. Three times in this short episode the teacher tells the children to repeat a word after her, apparently assuming that if the children can verbalize a particular label, then they have the underlying meaning that the teacher associates with that label. But this is not to be assumed. Children can, like parrots, make the appropriate noises with little or no concept relating to those noises. (I am reminded of a whole-group lesson in which a student teacher worked very hard to teach her Texas first graders about reptiles. She did this basically by lecturing to the children, trying to place reptiles within the animal kingdom. She talked of vertebrates and invertebrates, cold-and warm-blooded thises and thats, on and on, but all in a vacuum, totally removed from the children's experiences of snakes and such—and Texas children know snakes, if anybody does! At the end of the lesson, intending a kind of grand climax, she said to the children, "And so, today we've learned all about re— (hopeful pause), about re—" And in loud chorus, the children shouted, "*rec-tangles!*"—something they had "learned about" in a similar setting a few days before. (The student teacher learned a painful, but important, lesson that day.)

The emptiness in the first "discussion" above is evident: There is empty space where *meaning* should be. The children repeat words as the teacher directs, and they also play a sort of guessing game: "Guess what word the teacher wants and say it. If she doesn't like one, try its opposite." There are verbal noises and they occur in the proper slots, but I get no sense of these verbal noises expressing children's meanings, anymore than I do when the parrot at the zoo says, "Polly want a cracker."

In sharp contrast to the first "discussion," which is meaning-empty, the second discussion is meaning-full. There is no question here but that the teacher and children are engaged in purposeful language—meaning and expression both. This is people talk, not parrot talk. It is important for us to be able to hear the difference, for to engage children in mere verbalization is not to engage them in language. Language, unlike parrot talk, necessarily involves meaning.

LEARNING ABOUT LANGUAGE

The children in both discussions above *have* well-developed systems of language structure. The children in the second discussion are using that system (and much more) to the full. This is language structure in use, and it is very different from learning *about* language structure. All too typically, school children's classroom experience, especially in curriculum areas designated "language arts" and "reading," involves *reflection on* language, rather than *use of* language to achieve effective communication. Workbook and worksheet exercises offer examples like these:

> Draw one line under the subject and two lines under the predicate in the sentences below.
>
> In each row, circle the words that have a long vowel sound.
>
> Beside each word in the list, write the number of syllables it has.
>
> In the blank in each sentence below, write one of the adjectives given in the box.

Teachers' talk offers examples like these:

> And what is that sound? Is it long or short a?
>
> Can you find a CVC (consonant-vowel-consonant) word in that sentence?
>
> I need a definition for "organized." Who can tell us what "organized" means?

There are more effective and less effective ways to help children build their conscious awareness of language structure, and these will be discussed in subsequent sections. The essential point here is to differentiate between the child's having (and using) a system of language structure, on the one hand, and the child's being able to *talk about* that system of meaning and expression, on the other hand.

Following are some statements that teachers have made to me that express their bafflement over their children's language behavior. In each case the teacher mentions children being able to use language in some way but being unable to talk about (or respond to another's talk about) language. In each case the bafflement is caused by the teacher's failure to realize that knowing language and knowing about language are different. Can you identify the knowing language–knowing about language confusion in each example?

"My second graders can't ask questions. I told them to 'Ask me a question' and they couldn't do it."

"My sixth graders just can't write complex sentences because they don't know parts of speech."

"Vicky just doesn't have any vocabulary. Whenever I ask her, 'What does that word mean?' she can't tell me."

"Sammy's having reading problems. He can read the stories in the basal—he's on grade level—but he doesn't know vowel sounds. He calls long vowels 'short' and short vowels 'long.'"

"My students this year are going to learn to write! We're going to do *grammar*!"

Questioning and producing questions in response to the term "question" are different; writing and identifying parts of speech are different; using words and defining them are different; reading words that, necessarily, have vowels in them and identifying vowel sounds as "long" and "short" are different; writing and "doing grammar" are different. In each case the teacher first mentions a behavior that engages the child's *knowing* language structure and then mentions a behavior that involves the child's *knowing about* language structure.

I include one final example to demonstrate the difference between unconscious and conscious knowledge of language, the difference between knowing language and knowing about language. It is a personal example, a memory that is painful still. I was in third grade and my teacher, Mrs. McKenzie, daily had us read the basal story and then write answers to questions "in complete sentences with a capital letter at the beginning and a period at the end." (Sound familiar?) I became aware that if I wrote something very long as an answer, it was "a sentence," but if I wrote something very short, it wasn't, though it seemed to me to answer the question perfectly well. Suppose the question was "Did Tom and Janet like the new puppy their father brought them?" If I wrote, "Tom and Janet liked the new puppy their father brought them," I was sure to be right; but if I wrote, "Yes" (with a capital Y and a period at the end), I was sure to be wrong because though in my view this answered the question completely, it wasn't, in Mrs. McKenzie's view, "a complete sentence." But I was puzzled most about the middle-length responses. What about these?

Yes, they did.
Yes, they liked it.
They liked the new puppy.
Tom and Janet liked it.
They liked the puppy he brought them.
Tom and Janet liked their new puppy.

If I chose a middle-length response, I was taking my chances. Sometimes it was marked right and sometimes wrong, but I saw no pattern to it. So middle-length was a route to take only if I was in a hurry.

Puzzling over this one day, I figured I must have missed something crucial, the key to the mystery, that Mrs. McKenzie had given in my ill-timed absence. So I decided to solve the mystery for myself once and for all. I'd ask Mrs. McKenzie about it. This turned out to be a fatal mistake.

ME: Mrs. McKenzie, I think I was absent the day you told us what a sentence is. Could you please tell me what a sentence is?

Her response came in an angry, piercing shout—at least in my eight-year-old-in-front-of-my-friends perception:

MRS. MCKENZIE: What do you mean "What is a sentence?" We've been working on sentences ever since the first day of school . . .

On and on it went, loud and long.

What I understand now that I didn't understand then is that I *did* most deeply know what a "sentence" was. It was precisely this deep intuitive knowledge of that basic propositional unit composed of a sequence of morphemes—my sense of sentence—that enabled me to recognize a large set of longer and shorter expression possibilities as stylistic variants. But Mrs. McKenzie was working on something quite different. She was focusing on a very conscious kind of knowledge, specifically, knowledge of a particular subset of types of expressed sentences which she felt to be appropriate for a particular type of writing task. Her goal was that I and my classmates should consciously produce a particular type of language structure in response to her direction, "Write the answers *in complete sentences.*"

I wish that Mrs. McKenzie and I had both understood the nature of the task we were engaged in; I wish that we had recognized what I did know and what I needed to learn. Her response to my question did not clarify the "sentence" situation for me. It did, however, convince me that I should play it safe and stick with long written sentences. It also convinced me that I shouldn't ask questions when I was confused.

Another important consideration here is Mrs. McKenzie's missed opportunity. If I was puzzled about this written task, she might have wondered whether other students were also puzzled. I have no doubt that she would have discovered that I had company in my confusion. (As an adult, I have observed many third graders experience this same confusion.) Had she recognized what kind of knowledge I and my classmates *had* of "sentence," and also what kind of knowledge we did not have, she might have used this in interesting ways. The real issue here is larger than Mrs. McKenzie realized: It is the matter of different types of expressed sentences being appropriate in different contexts. What is an appropriate "sentence" in one context may not be in another. Yet typically, when teachers "teach sentences" to their third-grade reading groups, they, like Mrs. McKenzie, ignore the crucial matter of context. They teach "sentence" in a vacuum, quite removed from language as the child knows it. I observe discussions like the following in one classroom after another.

TEACHER: I have some cards here, and I'll read what's on each card. You tell me if you think it's a sentence or not. If it is, we'll need to put a capital letter at the beginning and a period (or question mark or exclamation point) at the end. "The boy got up." Do you think that one is a sentence?

C-1:   Yes, because it's a complete thought. You know, like "the boy" tells you who did something and "got up" tells you what he did.

TEACHER: Does everybody agree?

C-2:   No, 'cause it doesn't tell when he got up. It should be "The boy got up in the morning."

TEACHER: OK. Well, that one is a bit tricky. Let's come back to that one after we've done a few more. How 'bout this one? "They were playing in the street"? Sound OK? Is it a sentence?

C-3:   Well, it doesn't say who was playing and it doesn't tell what they were playing. I don't think that one is.

C-4:   Yeah, but it can still be a sentence. A sentence doesn't have to tell you *everything*.

TEACHER: What do you think, Jeremy? We haven't heard from you yet.

JEREMY: Well, I think it all depends. Like, like, well, it *could* be a sentence, but, well, it just all depends. I can't explain it.

Jeremy is exactly right, of course: It all depends. What Jeremy is grappling to explain is that it all depends on context. Expressed sentences (which is what the teacher is trying to teach here) do not occur on 3 x 5 cards. They occur in conversations, stories, ads, TV news broadcasts, songs, sermons, plays, arguments, riddles, jumprope rhymes, and scoldings. To ask children to deal with "sentences" in a vacuum is to ask them to deal with nonlanguage. What the teacher has on her 3 x 5 cards is not language at all, but only, on each card, a "figment of [her] curriculum" (Edelsky and Smith, 1984). "Teaching" episodes like the preceding one must surely leave children more puzzled than they were before the session began.

Children's comments in "sentence" discussions invariably indicate, as in the previous example, that the children have a very well-developed sense of sentence—*felt* sentence—that is, their intuitive notion of the underlying whole that is expressed variously in different contexts. But often teachers fail to recognize this underlying knowledge which the children's comments reflect. So, instead of building on this deep sense of sentence to extend the children's knowledge into a conscious domain of the different styles, sounds, and forms of expression sentences take in different contexts, the teacher stays with the safety of her nonsentences (nonsense?) on 3 x 5 cards while the children struggle to tell her the basic truth which she has apparently forgotten: It all depends. Meanwhile, the children watch the teacher's face closely for indications of whether the correct response to her card is "Yes, it is" or "No, it isn't."

The matter of "felt sentence" (deep structure) and spoken sentence and written sentence (surface structure) is fascinating and lends itself to rich explorations of how sentence meanings are expressed in different situations and for different purposes. So back to Mrs. McKenzie and her missed opportunity. She was concerned with written sentences, especially those appropriate to a particular type of written task.[12] But the real and fascinating question (though I think Mrs. McKenzie was not aware of this) was the much larger one of context: What kinds of sentences are appropriate to different communication contexts? So what might Mrs. McKenzie have done?

I can imagine her sending us out as sentence explorers: "You already know that people write sentences with a capital letter at the beginning and a period (or question mark or exclamation point) at the end. But there are just all different kinds of sentences. Do you think "yes" could ever be a sentence? Or "OK"? Or "because"? What about this: "This is the cat that caught the rat that ate the malt that lay in the house that Jack built"? Is that written down somewhere with a capital at the beginning and a period at the end? If so, somebody thinks it's a sentence. I want you to go exploring and find as many different kinds of written sentences as you can, whatever ones are interesting to you. Maybe some long ones, or short ones, funny ones, mysterious ones, ones that give information you think is interesting. Maybe some you don't like—some that are boring or silly or mean or not true. I'm giving you each a big grocery sack 'cause you'll have to bring the written material back so we can see your selected sentences right in their own places. You'll want to look in books—all different kinds of books—but remember that there are lots of written sentences that are in places other than books." I can imagine us exploring the school (individually? with a friend or two?), accumulating our favorites and lugging our sacks back to the pooling area (a carpeted area of the room perhaps, designated as the expedition center?) and then going off again. The materials in the expedition center would soon include all sorts of books—joke books, poetry collections, dictionaries, phone directories, biographies, mysteries, science fiction, textbooks, songbooks, workbooks, plays—but also pamphlets, notices, newspaper articles, record jackets, ads, written interviews, public announcements, and appliance manuals. (If I had been Mrs. McKenzie, I would have been sure to slip e. e. cummings's "hist whist" onto the stack, just to add to the fun.) I can see us sharing the selected sentences from these various sources. But in the hunting and gathering and sharing, we would have been actively engaged with many specific, authentic examples of written sentences. Our intuitive knowledge of stylistic variation would have been validated: There *are* many ways of expressing things in writing as in speech, as we well knew. From our active engagement and our innundation with so many examples of so many types of expression, we would have been building on our intuitive, unconscious knowledge, extending that knowledge into the area of conscious awareness of particular styles being appropriate to particular contexts or types or purposes or writing. I can see games developing. "I'll find a sentence in one of these sources, and

---

[12]It is important to say here that I am not advocating this task of having children read basal stories and write out answers to comprehension questions. In fact, I can think of few more effective ways of "making children hate reading," as John Holt puts it (Holt 1969).

I'll read it out loud, and you tell me whether you think it comes from this dictionary, this songbook, or this play." The focus here is sentence-in-a-context. Or, "I'll read a sentence and you tell me which of these items that we've gathered you think it *sounds* like it could come from." The purpose here is to identify, not which source it *does* come from but which source it *could* come from. This would have been to appeal to our *sense* of language. I wonder if some of us would have wanted to interview people—parents, other children, school personnel—to gather definitions of "sentence" and then to see how well the various definitions applied to the actual written sentences we had gathered. Might some of us have gotten interested in gathering spoken sentences in various situations? This would have involved our attending closely to suprasegmentals (for example, pauses and intonation contours) just as professional language researchers do. What differences might we have discovered between sentences of talk and sentences of print?

The specifics of these imaginings are unimportant. You can readily supply your own what-could-have-happened ending to the Mrs. McKenzie story. But the point is that activities such as these would have built on the deep understanding my friends and I had of underlying sentence and stylistic variation while extending that knowledge to a conscious level in a particular domain. Also, these activities would have engaged us in real language, not in the phony "language" of teachers' 3 x 5 cards.

Well, none of this happened. What did happen was that I was confused, I asked a question, I was scolded, and I withdrew. And, of course, I did somehow come to know which types of sentences to write for Mrs. McKenzie and which types to avoid, but I did this without Mrs. McKenzie's help.

Mrs. McKenzie missed a rich opportunity. She missed it for a number of reasons but one important one was her failure to recognize the intuitive knowledge I and my classmates had, on the one hand, and on the other, the conscious knowledge of written conventions that she was trying to help us gain. Being unaware of this, she was unable to use the intuitive knowledge we did have to help us build the conscious awareness we did not have.

FINALLY

Children's language knowledge is everywhere evident in classrooms. As teachers, we can become more language sensitive in our interactions with children:

> We can learn to recognize evidence of children's language knowledge—its presence and influence in all our children's encounters in talk and print.
>
> We can learn to recognize when we are engaging our children in meaningful language, and when we are engaging them only in empty verbalizations.

We can learn to recognize when the tasks we engage children in require them to *know* language, and when those tasks require them to *know about* language.

SUGGESTED EXERCISES AND PROJECTS

1. *Recognizing the conscious awareness of language required by school "language" materials.*

Select a reading or language arts workbook for children in second or third grade. Examine the written instructions closely and then select and list at least twenty-five words that require conscious awareness of language on the child's part in order for the child to complete the workbook exercises. (For example, "word," "vowel," "syllable," and "letter" would all be good candidates for your list.)

2. *Recognizing demonstrations of language knowledge in children's talk.*

Equipped with a hefty pack of 3 x 5 cards, go to a place where you can hear children talking freely, with no adult present (for example, free play on the school playground). (Obviously, you would need to secure permission.) Write down at least twenty-five child utterances you hear that demonstrate some aspect of the child's language knowledge that is of interest to you. Write each utterance on a separate card. (You will want to add notes about the conversational context also, in order to recall the situation later.) As soon as possible, get together with a fellow student or two to consider the aspect of language knowledge demonstrated in each child utterance you have collected. This will work particularly well if your fellow student(s) have also gathered children's utterances, and you can all contribute and compare examples. You might all want to collect examples in different situations or from children of different ages. Modify the activity in any way you and your fellow student(s) choose in order to make it maximally interesting to you.

3. *Playing with playful literature.*

Select a children's book (several, perhaps) that is rollicking-frolicking full of language play—nonsense, puns, jokes, riddles—whatever is fun for you. (I find children's librarians in public libraries to be very helpful in getting me to a variety of playful books that children enjoy.) Next, select some children you like to be with. Read your selected book(s) to your selected children (individually or in small groups) and . . . well . . . just see what happens and enjoy it. (You might also want to read one or two of these books to an adult whom you think would appreciate this literature and/or to an adult you think would not.)

4. *Creation of novel sentences.*

We have said that creativity is basic to language; communication proceeds mainly through the creation and use of specific sentences which are novel to both the speaker and the hearer. We recognize that creativity is basic to adult communication. But is it also basic to communication among children? Do they, too, interact mainly through the creation and use of novel sentences? To explore this question, tape record about thirty minutes' worth of children's interaction in as natural a situation as possible, *with no adult* in the immediate environment. (Needless to say, this will be most interesting if you study the children you actually teach.) You may have to tape the children several times to get them accustomed to the tape recorder, and also to get a total thirty minutes' worth of audible conversation. (It does not all have to come from a single taping session.)[13]

As you will discover, taping is not easy. Two important things to remember are (1) to tape a situation or activity that children do in a localized area, so that your microphone will pick up most of their conversation (for example, housekeeping corner or table where three or four children usually sit to work; avoid the playground) and (2) to keep your taping equipment as unobtrusive as possible.

When you have thirty minutes' worth of audible taped interaction, transcribe it as exactly as you can, with all the "uhs," all the giggles, all the pauses, and all the inevitable inaudible spots where you simply indicate that you cannot hear what was said. Then study your transcript, trying in your written paper to answer questions like the following: Do children communicate mainly through the use of novel sentences or through memorized ready-made ones? What are some examples of each type from your data? What proportion of the children's utterances is novel sentences? What proportion is memorized imitations? In what sense are the "novel" sentences new creations; that is, do the children create new vocabulary or new syntactic structures? What kinds? Or do they create within a predictable set of already established syntactic and semantic principles? What is the evidence here? For what purposes do the children use nonnovel (ready-made) language?

An interesting extension of this study is to compare the language creativity of your children's interaction with that of an adult interaction (taped and transcribed the same way that you did your children's conversation).

5. *An exercise in differentiating meanings.*

Pick a synonym cluster from Roget's *Thesaurus* and try to differentiate the meanings of the particular words within your selected cluster. Can you identify the semantic feature or features which distinguish each entry from the others? What semantic features do all the words in their synonym cluster share (what makes them synonyms)? (This works particularly well as a small-group discussion exercise.)

One interesting variation on this exercise is to try it with your intermediate-level students. Can they tell the "special meaning" of each item?

A second variation to use with children is to ask your primary or intermediate-level children to act out selected items from a synonym cluster, for example, various "walk" words.

If you and several of your fellow students or colleagues try one of these variations with children, you may want to get together afterwards to compare notes on your experience. What kind of linguistic knowledge did the children's behavior imply?

6. *A discussion exercise on interestingly, intentionally deviant language.*

Each member of a group (about five or so) brings several favorite examples of language used in interestingly not-quite-grammatical ways. Good places to look for such items include advertising, adult or children's literature, adult or children's

---

[13]One university student had considerable success with this project by suspending the tape recorder microphone from a light fixture above the center of a small play-dough activity table in the nursery school where she was working. Because the children were localized in the small area around this table, the microphone picked up most of their conversation. Also, the situation proved to be a very natural one, as the children became quite involved in working with play dough, conversing informally as they worked. The student wisely set up this taping arrangement and left it there for several weeks—sometimes with the tape recorder on, sometimes with it off—before she started taping the conversations she was going to study. By that time, the suspended microphone had become just another piece of classroom furniture to the children, and they were quite unaware of it.

conversation, and adult or children's writing. Together consider what the creator of that language item has done that makes it interesting in a special and unexpected way. What language rule(s) has he or she broken or bent? Why?

It is particularly interesting here to use children's favorite items from children's literature (what understanding must they have of language structure if they appreciate the author's deliberately deviant use of language?) or from their own oral or written language. However, note that the exercise deals with the intentional use of deviant language to provide special effects. Do not include items spoken by young children, which are simply the result of an early stage of language acquisition—deviant utterances which are not deliberately so.

7. "Your own thing."

Design your own learning experience relating to the ideas in this section, discuss it with your instructor or an acquaintance knowledgeable in this area, and execute it.

SUGGESTED FURTHER READING

A source dealing with the structure of language, which is solid in its content, readable in its presentation, and appropriate for readers who are not professional linguists, is

FROMKIN, V., AND R. RODMAN, *An Introduction to Language.* (2nd ed.). New York: Holt, Rinehart and Winston, Inc., 1978.

5

Perspectives on Language Acquisition

INTRODUCTION

For centuries parents, scholars, and teachers have been fascinated and amazed by the phenomenon of language acquisition in children. How are we to account for the fact that *virtually every child, without special training, exposed to surface structures of language in many interaction contexts, builds for himself—in a short period of time and at an early stage in his cognitive development—a deep-level, abstract, and highly complex system of linguistic structure and use.* And that is only the beginning. In addition to acquiring the structure of the language of his community, the child acquires the complex underlying rule system governing its use: how and when to say what to whom. Let's think a minute about our italicized sentence above.

Virtually every child . . .

Except for those physical and cognitive skills which are clearly biological in their base, it is very difficult to think of abilities that all humans develop. It is "given" in our biological inheritance as members of the species "human" that (almost) all of us eventually develop the ability to walk on two legs, to grasp objects with thumb and fingers juxtaposed, to make associations between events. But only some of us will learn to play an instrument, to multiply, to turn cartwheels, to whistle, to sail. You probably know some young people or adults who cannot drive, swim, or play chess, but how many do you know who cannot understand and use language? Even when we look at the disabled members of the population (those with intellectual, physical, or emotional handicaps), we still find that most of them understand and use some form of language for communication. It appears that acquiring a language is a basic part of our human-ness: More and less intelligent children acquire language, more and less economically fortunate children acquire language, more and less physically able children acquire language, more and less emotionally healthy children acquire language. Whether a child grows up in a "traditional" society or in a "technological" one; whether in a large extended family or in a small nuclear one; whether on a Pacific island, in an urban ghetto, or in a tribal farm compound; whether in a villa, a straw hut, an apartment, or a tent; whether with or without formal schooling; whether in a wet, dry, hot, or cold climate—the child will acquire the language of his community. Humans vary in which languages and dialects they acquire, in how rapidly they acquire them, in how many languages and dialects they acquire, in how talkative they are, in what they use language for, and in how effectively they express themselves in speech and/or writing. But virtually all of them acquire at least one linguistic system for relating meanings and overt expressive symbols (usually verbal sounds).

Further, there is striking similarity in how all learn children learn their language. Naturally the specifics of the learning differ depending on characteristics of the language being learned, as well as on some other environmental factors. But it is possible to sketch a predictable general sequence of stages that children follow in acquiring language, as well as to describe certain cognitive processes that children seem to use as they figure out how the verbal sounds they hear relate to the meanings they understand. Researchers speak with greater confidence about the "how" of sequence than about the "how" of process in language acquisition, and it is easy enough to see why. Describing a developmental sequence involves observing children's language behaviors and making generalizations about those observed behaviors. But positing mental processes the child is using involves inferring from the observed behavior, that is, conjecturing about what might be going on in the child's thinking that would account for the observed behavior. This is necessarily a more tenative endeavor. But even though our statements about process are very cautious and couched in phrases like "the child *appears* to be operating according to a principle like X" or "the child behaves *as if* he is using a rule such as A," still the similarities across children are impressive.

The idea of being able to sketch a general developmental sequence of stages for some area of children's growth is probably not new to you. Piaget has been a leader in suggesting a sequence of stages children move through in their cognitive growth. We are all aware of a sequence of stages in children's physical development as well—we recognize that children hold their heads up before they sit up unaided, and that they stand alone before they walk alone. The suggested physical and cognitive development sequences are the result of careful observations of many children in a variety of both structured and naturalistic settings. And so it is in language acquisition. Though formal study of children's language as a separate discipline is more recent than formal study of children's physical and cognitive development, still the basis of the suggested developmental sequence is the same: It is a set of generalizations based on observations of what many children of various ages and backgrounds *do* and *say* as they learn language.

On reflection, the possibility of sketching a general sequence of stages of language acquisition for "all" children should be no more surprising than the possibility of sketching general developmental sequences for physical or cognitive growth for "all" children. Language acquisition involves a language and a learner. Human languages, however diverse they are in their surface details, are all remarkably similar in their basic elements and organizational schemes. For example, similar syntactic devices (affixes, word order) signal relationships in many languages; the same sentence types—statements, questions, negatives, commands—occur in many languages; similar sound features and combinations occur in the verbal expression systems of many languages, and so on.

As there are deep-level similarities across diverse human languages, so there are deep-level similarities across the diverse humans who acquire them. Similar physical and cognitive structures are part of the makeup of all of us, whatever kind of environment we happen to be born into and raised in. Clearly, language acquisition is deeply rooted in the physical and cognitive structures and possibilities all humans share. Thus it should not be too surprising that we note a similar general developmental sequence and similar general learning processes at work across virtually all children acquiring language.

. . . without special training . . .

In many areas of children's learning, a goal is set and activities are provided to assure its attainment. We typically (1) divide the learning into "chunks" (such as subskills and basic concepts); (2) sequence the subskills or concepts in a simple-to-complex set of steps; (3) present them to the children and provide practice activities so that they will attain mastery of the concepts, skills, or processes; (4) test periodically to check for mastery and to guide subsequent learning activity. If we wanted a child to be able to add and subtract numbers up to six and to understand addition and subtraction as inverse processes, some of the sublearnings included might be the notion of each number up to six, the notion of set, the notion of set combination, the notion of subsets. We would sequence the sublearnings in some reasonable order and would give the child many opportunities to work with objects in different amounts and to combine, uncombine, and recombine them. We would give him tasks to perform that would inform us of his progress toward mastery of the learnings, and we would use this feedback to guide our subsequent instruction.[1]

It is possible, though strange, to conceive of ways we could provide this kind of direct instruction for young children learning language. It would be possible to divide the language to be learned into basic parts—"parts of speech," types of sentences, types of sounds, labels from categories of things in the child's environment. We could sequence these in some logical simple-to-complex series and provide opportunites for the children to practice each. We could periodically test for mastery as we went along. It would be posssible in theory (but probably not in practice) to do this. But we *do not* do this, and it would probably be disastrous if we did! John Holt

---

[1]This is not to deny, of course, that much of the learning that occurs in our culture and in other cultures does not follow this pattern. People often learn by observation, modeling, trial and error, and so on.

speculates about the absurdity and the disastrous outcome of such a procedure.

> Bill Hull once said to me, "If we taught children to speak, they'd never learn." I thought at first he was joking. By now I realize that it was a very important truth. Suppose we decided that we had to "teach" children to speak. How would we go about it? First, some committee of experts would analyze speech and break it down into a number of separate "speech skills." We would probably say that, since speech is made up of sounds, a child must be taught to make all the sounds of his language before he can be taught to speak the language itself. Doubtless we would list these sounds, easiest and commonest ones first, harder and rarer ones next. Then we would begin to teach infants these sounds, working our way down the list. Perhaps, in order not to "confuse" the child . . . we would not let the child hear much ordinary speech, but would only expose him to the sounds we were trying to teach.
>
> Along with our sound list, we would have a syllable list and a word list.
>
> When the child had learned to make all the sounds on the sound list, we would begin to teach him to combine the sounds into syllables. When he could say all the syllables on the syllable list, we would begin to teach him the words on our word list. At the same time, we would teach him the rules of grammar, by means of which he could combine these newly-learned words into sentences. Everything would be planned with nothing left to chance; there would be plenty of drill, review, and tests, to make sure that he had not forgotten anything.
>
> Suppose we tried to do this; what would happen? What would happen, quite simply, is that most children, before they got very far, would become baffled, discouraged, humiliated, and fearful, and would quit trying to do what we asked them. (Holt 1967, p. 56)

We know that the most important people in the young child's language environment, his family members and caregivers, do not provide him with a rigorous language-learning "curriculum." Rather, they engage with him and with each other (in his presence) in real communication in a wide range of contexts and situations. These interactions typically involve linguistic structure far more complex than the child controls. Much of the language of his environment is not directed to him. But for many children, much of it is—people explain to him, scold him, describe things to him, tell him anecdotes, wonder and speculate aloud with and for him, play with him, warn him, coax him, threaten him, answer him. Always there is language, verbal (or written) expression living in contexts which provide clues to the cognitive and social meanings the expression conveys.

> *. . . exposed to surface structures of language in many interaction contexts, builds a deep-level system of linguistic structure and use.*

An infant is exposed to a wide range of sounds—birds singing, objects falling, airplanes roaring, water running, people sneezing, people whistling, people talking. One wonders how the infant sorts out the sounds that convey language meanings from the sounds that do not. But consider the diversity within just the verbal strings. The child is exposed to a language "sample" including language addressed to him and language addressed to others, sentences which constitute well-formed (grammatical) strings and sentences which do not, sentences which involve linguistic structure he has mastered and sentences which are beyond his developing system, and strings spoken by a wide range of individuals in a wide range of contexts. But one thing is common to them all: Each verbal string is an expression of some meaning. How does the child, *every child*, sort out which strings are well formed (grammatical) and which are not? How does he figure out how the noise strings are broken into meaning hunks? How does he figure out the principles according to which the strings of elements are organized? Above all, how does he figure out how those verbal strings relate to particular meanings?

The child's language environment includes a set of specific sentences, but it is not this set of specific sentences that he acquires. Rather, he deduces from these particular sentences as an underlying set of organizational principles and sound-meaning relationships. He seems to understand that specific sentences are particular examples of basic principles, and it is those principles he works on. Children, even as young as two, do not talk to us by simply using the specific sentences that they have heard, but rather by constructing sentences according to their own early version of organizational principles *underlying* the specific sentences they have heard. The child's early linguistic system is different from the adult's and thus results in sentences like Why you play with that? I not like it, and He gave it to me.

The child will continue to revise his system as he interacts with other language users in many different social situations. Over time his sentences will become more adultlike. But what is noteworthy about these early sentences is that they are not simple repetitions of the specific sentences he has heard, but are rule-governed constructions of his own created according to the underlying principles he has deduced. Every child is exposed to surface structures in interaction—particular expression sequences used in particular communication events. From this experience, he builds a system relating that expression to meaning, though he is never directly exposed to that abstract system of expression-meaning relations. This deep and abstract system is one which he . . .

builds for himself . . .

Many adults believe that children learn language because adults teach it to them. I vividly recall an informal conversatoin I had several years ago with an acquaintance who is a sociology professor and the father of three children. It went something like this:

ME: It's interesting, isn't it, that we don't really "teach" a child his language. He learns it for himself.

DR. X: (annoyed) What do you mean he learns it for himself? I *taught* my children their language, and that's how they learned it.

ME: Oh? And how did you do that?

DR. X: What do you mean "how did I do it?" I pointed to a book and said, "Book. Book. Book. Say it. Book." And the child said it. Then I pointed to a table and said, "Table. Say it. Table. Table." And he said it. That's how my kids learned English.

ME: Oh.

This parent far underestimates the complex system that a language is. Like many adults, he is mistaking a limited set of verbal labels for *language*, the endless creation of sentences according to a finite set of structural principles. He also far underestimates his children's abilities for language learning. But though there is a sense in which he overestimates his contribution to his children's language acquisition, there is also an important sense in which he *under*estimates his contribution. He has doubtless been far more important to his children's learning of language than he has ever dreamed, though not at all in the way that he supposes. He has been an important source of rich and varied language examples for his children; he has interacted with them verbally and nonverbally in various contexts and situations; he has provided opportunities for them to explore and "mess about" with their world and thus build the meanings basic to language; he has responded to and encouraged their communicative attempts. He may, as he claims, have taught his children some labels. Most parents do. But how minor that contribution is in comparison to his role as a rich language provider and interactant in communication with his children.

The young child learning language is sometimes called "a little linguist." This metaphor is helpful because it focuses on the child as the active party in learning a language. The young child is seen as a field linguist trying to figure out a language which is new to him. He hears unfamiliar verbal strings in particular contexts. The child, like the linguist, attends to the unfamiliar verbal expressions and the contexts in which they occur, and builds "hypotheses" (hunches?) about the sound-meaning relationships present. He "tests" his hypotheses, or hunches, by further observation, or by producing new sentences, trying them out, and seeing "how they fly." He is constantly getting feedback relating to his hypotheses, and also further exposure and interaction, both of which lead him to revise his hypotheses. This "little linguist" analogy does not mean that the child is aware of what he is doing (as the linguist is); rather, it offers an interactive model of the child and his environment which eventually results in the development of a complex abstract system of linguistic structure which moves steadily toward a closer match with the adult's. It is the child himself who processes the sounds of speech in his community so as to derive underlying structure. We expose the child to language and interact with him through language, but he acquires linguistic structure through his own cognitive and social activity.

. . . in a short period of time . . .

We are not surprised to find that entering kindergarteners are able to ask a variety of questions, to tell about things they've done and seen and things they like and don't like, to request things they want, and to direct others to do things. In short, though there is a range in rates of development across children and a range in styles and purposes for which they have used language in the preschool years, five-year-olds typically can use complex and varied language structures to serve a variety of purposes in their lives. Their language growth is still in process, but they generally have substantial control of language structure and use. Attaining this high level of control in such a short time is remarkable, given the complex system that a language is, and the fact that the child begins life as an infant immersed in a sea of undifferentiated sensations. Is there any other area of our lives where we accomplish something so complex so quickly? The kindergartener's language abilities don't surprise us; maybe they should.

. . . at an early stage in his cognitive development . . .

A great deal of a child's acquisition of linguistic structure occurs during the first five years of life. This is the period when he is most active in discerning a set of underlying organizational principles of language from the expression that surrounds him. It is puzzling that one so young is able to engage successfully in activity that seems to demand so much abstracting from direct experience. All instances of language that the child encounters are contextualized; that is, they are particular spoken or written words in particular sequences and used for particular purposes in particular settings. The child must somehow extract from this wide array of particular examples the underlying principles—the unifying design—that accounts for all the instances. The principles are, of course, not directly observable; only the specific instances of language in use are observable. Thus the child must derive the unobservable from the observable. This is not to suggest that the child does this in any conscious, reflective way. However, it is to suggest that this seems a Herculean task for one so young, and a task that is cognitively complex, involving abstracting, relating, synthesizing, and integrating at an impressive cognitive level. This is a type of mental activity that children are not often given credit for in psychologists' descriptions of young children's thinking.

Let's end this introduction where we began it—with our initial italicized sentence. That sentence probably seemed innocuous enough at first, but you may now be aware that it raises fascinating and powerful questions about the incredible phenomenon of language acquisition:

> *Virtually every child, without special training, exposed to surface structures of language in many interaction contexts, builds for himself—in a short period of time and at an early stage in his cognitive development—a deep-level, abstract, and highly complex system of linguistic structure.*

PERSPECTIVES ON LANGUAGE ACQUISITION

The Behaviorist View

Through the first half of this century, there was a prevalent view that language learning, like other kinds of learning, occurs as the result of the environment shaping an individual born with a given IQ (an innate general learning potential). This "behaviorist" position held that an individual is reinforced (positively or negatively) for responses to various stimuli. By administering positive reinforcement (praising, smiling) when a desired behavior occurs and administering negative reinforcement (scolding, correcting) when an undesired behavior occurs, one presumably strengthens the desired behavior and makes it more likely that that behavior will recur. Let's take a classic hypothetical example involving infants and language. Suppose a baby is lying on his back, happily babbling in his crib. Mother appears and begins to play with him. In the course of his babblings, the baby hits on the syllables "ma-ma" (an occurrence which, given the fairly predictable sequence of phonological development in infants, is quite likely). He gets a very positive response from his mother, as any mother knows only too well. He is hugged, cuddled, and nuzzled, perhaps, all to the accompaniment of the mother's delighted squeals and chatterings. Surely any baby worth his salt will in time come to produce the sounds ma-ma in the presence of his mother and cause a repeat of the pleasurable "aftermath." This view of language learning maintains that as a child grows older, reinforcement becomes progressively more contingent on how nearly the child's language matches the adult's. That is, whereas ma-ma is positively reinforced as an appropriate response in an infant, it is likely that a mother will positively reinforce only utterances that are considerably more complex and adultlike when the child is three or four. Thus, as positive reinforcement is employed only for progressively more adultlike utterances, the child moves steadily toward a more complex adult language system.

This description of the behaviorist view of language acquisition is somewhat simplistic and general. It does not do justice to the range of specific positions held within this school. Some behaviorists emphasize one aspect, some another, and certainly they elaborate the details of this general position differently, one from another. However, there is an area of common ground that justifies our speaking, at a general level, of "the behaviorist position." This common ground includes the belief that (1) children are born with a general learning potential which is part of their genetic inheritance (but without any specific learning abilities, such as a special innate capacity for acquiring language); (2) learning (including the learning of language) occurs entirely through the action of the environment shaping the individual's behavior; (3) behavior (including language) is shaped through the reinforcement of particular responses emitted in the presence of particular stimuli; (4) in the shaping of very complex behavior such as language, there is a progressive selection or narrowing of responses which are positively reinforced; although more simple and general responses receive positive reinforcement initially, such reinforcement is later given for responses which are more complex and which more nearly match the ultimate behavioral goal.[2]

At first glance this view is very persuasive. It squares with some of our own informal observations and intuitions about what children are and how

[2]For additional reading relating to this view see Skinner 1957, N. Chomsky 1959, and Staats 1971.

they grow. Those of us who work with children doubltess feel that children do differ in their general learning abilities; that regardless of their environments, some are simply born with greater learning potential than others. Further, this view tells us that the environment plays a crucial part in one's learning, and that, too, is something we all feel is true. And no one would deny that important people in the child's world—parents, teachers, friends—do positively reinforce some behaviors (with smiles, hugs, praise, increased allowance, special privileges) and negatively reinforce other behaviors, and that they reward and punish different behaviors in seven-year-olds and in two-year-olds. And finally, children do learn language, and this view tells us that they will.

Is the Behaviorist View Adequate?

Over the past several decades, scholars have gained richer insights into the complexity and creativity of human language, the language acquirer, and the processes of language acquistion. These insights have raised crucial questions that the behaviorist view has difficulty answering.

First, it is difficult for the behaviorist view to account for the uniformity of language acquisition throughout the human species—virtually all children acquire a language, and they do so in some strikingly similar ways. (This is what people mean when they say that language acquisition is "species uniform.") If language acquisition were simply the result of an innate general learning capacity plus a shaping environment, we would expect differences in language acquisition to reflect the wide range of IQ differences and environmental differences of young children. In fact, we would expect some children not to acquire language at all. Yet we see that even many mentally retarded children acquire language, though they do not learn some other things. And though there are many specific differences from child to child in the learning of language, those differences are not nearly so vast as a behaviorist theory would predict. If language acquisition were simply a matter of environment shaping the child's language, the resulting shapes and sequence and processes leading to those resulting shapes would be far more diverse than they in fact are.

Second, there is the other side of this "species uniform" coin, the "species specific" argument. The behaviorist position would predict that intelligent beings other than humans could acquire language too. If language acquisition is a function of innate IQ plus environmental shaping, we should be able to take intelligent chimps, put them in a language shaping environment, and end up with chimps that communicate through humanlike languages.

A number of researchers tried to do just this. The question was not, "Do chimps have a system of communication they use for conveying messages to one another?" It was well known that members of other species *do* communicate among themselves. The crucial question concerned the *type* of communication involved. The accepted view was that the communication systems of other species involved a limited set of messages, each of which was signaled always and only in the same way. This system would, of course, be quite different from the human system with its unlimited set of messages, each of which can be expressed in many ways. This is the difference between a closed expression system and an infinite expression system. It had been asserted that an infinitely generative type of language system was the distinct province of humans. But if chimps could be taught a human type language, then it would seem that human language was not species specific and behaviorist notions of general-IQ-plus-shaping-environment could perhaps account for language acquisition after all.

Notice that the question was not, "Can chimps learn to talk?" It was recognized that the vocal apparatus of chimps is different from that of humans and is not adapted to produce the sounds of human speech. But many humans do not speak either, yet they develop a human language. Many individuals who are deaf and/or mute communicate by means of hand signs. So, why not try to teach chimps the sign language of the deaf as the expressive means? And this is what some researchers did. Others taught chimps to arrange small objects on a magnetic board, and still others taught chimps to type geometric designs. Whatever the expressive means, however, the question was the same: Can other species learn a language system in which the user creates (produces and understands) novel messages governed by a finite system of rules; *or* are other species limited to a specific set of messages, each one expressed by a particular signal?

At first the efforts with chimps seemed very promising. It was reported that some chimps responded appropriately to complex commands such as "Sarah" (chimp's name) "insert apricot red dish, grape (and) banana green dish" (Fleming 1974, p. 35) and that they responded differently to "Roger tickle Lucy" (chimp's name) and "Lucy tickle Roger" (p. 46), demonstrating a grasp of underlying organizational relations. Some chimps were reported to invent "words." One, seeing a duck for the first time, signed "water bird" (p. 38); another, who had used the sign "food" for radish, finally tasted a radish and thereafter signed it either "cry hurt food" or "hurt food" or "cry food" (pp. 44, 46). Researchers reported that their chimps generalized labels learned in particular contexts to new contexts. For example, after learning "more" in the context of tickling, one chimp started using the "more" sign when she wanted more of a variety of actions and objects (p. 32). Some chimps were reported to string "words" (signs or manipulable tokens) together into combinations they had not been taught so as to express new meanings.

But serious objections began to be raised about this line of research, perhaps the most persuasive objections coming from a researcher who had himself engaged in this kind of work for five years (Terrace 1979). He had started working with his chimp (Nim Chimpsky), confident that chimps could be taught a human type language. He had "hoped to demonstrate that apes can, indeed, form sentences . . . and show that grammatical rules are needed to describe many of an ape's utterances" (p. 65). In short, he was a believer. However, "after analyzing videotapes of Nim's 'conversations' with his teachers, I discovered that the sequences were subtle imitations of the teacher's sequences. I could find no evidence confirming an ape's grammatical competence, either in my own data or those of others, that could not be explained by simpler processes" (p. 67).

Close examination of photos and videotapes of various apes with their trainers revealed that the trainers, quite inadvertantly, were giving subtle, nonverbal cues to the chimps that influenced the animals' performance. This is the well-known "Clever Hans phenomenon," so named after a horse that supposedly could count to high numbers by tapping his foot but, in fact, was found to be cueing on signs from the trainer, for example, the tension in the trainer's body until Hans reached the correct number and then the trainer's visible relaxing, at which point Hans would stop his tapping. It was the trainer, not Hans, that was counting. This subtle cueing was discovered to explain Hans's "counting" only after a careful study which began when it was found that Hans "counted" correctly only when his trainer was visible. Examination of the ape photos and videotapes revealed many nonverbal cues (including specific gestures, small versions of the desired signs, body postures, and facial expressions). Also, the chimps have been found to perform differently with different trainers, and significantly worse with outsiders, further suggesting that the chimps' performance depends on signals from the trainer.

The trainers cue in another way, also, one which is built into the procedure itself. The trainer typically prompts the chimp to give a response and in the prompt uses both the required signs and the required sequence. Thus, the chimp can often respond correctly by imitating the trainer's prompt. It seems more reasonable to explain the chimp's correct responses in terms of imitation than in terms of an understanding of syntax. In Nim's case, 20,000 sign combinatons that were not imitations were examined. Every one of them either made no sense or else could be "adequately explained by simpler, nonlinguistic processes. . . ." (Sebeok and Umiker-Sebeok 1980, p. 21).

Critics of the chimp research have pointed out that much of the chimp behavior goes unreported. The research reports often describe selected anecdotes (typically from only "prize pupils"), rather than accounting for all the relevant behaviors of all the ape subjects. Critics assert that the choice anecdotes offer good examples of overinterpretation by the researchers, a problem critics feel is pervasive in this work. Take the "water bird" example. The trainer signs the question, "What's that?" in the direction of water with a duck swimming in it. The chimps signs "water" and then signs "bird." Terrace argues that there is no external evidence that the chimp was expressing an adjective-noun relationship ("water bird") rather than two unrelated signs: "Water." "Bird." Without some independent evidence—at least some pervasive pattern of such expressions in the entire body of data—it is not justifiable to make such an interpretation. It is the researcher who is making a syntactic relation here, not the chimp.

There is overinterpretation of another kind as well. Researchers/ trainers tend to assume that the chimps' spontaneous signs (that is, signs not in response to the trainers' prompts) are intentional rather than random, and then they go on to provide (create?) meanings for the possibly random signs. But this might be more a test of the trainers' ingenuity than of the chimps' meaningful expression. What is the basis for the original assumption that the chimp intends to convey some specific meaning?

In some of the ape research the researchers have interpreted the ape's unexpected responses as "jokes" or "lies" or "insults" or "teases" or "metaphors."[3] You can see the problem here: If every accurate response is considered correct and every inaccurate response is also considered correct (being explained as "lying" or "joking" or "teasing"), then the researcher has set up a situation in which there is no possibility of the ape being incorrect. This is hardly an objective scientific procedure.

Terrace points out some further striking differences in the process of language development in chimps and in children over time. Both chimp and child increase their vocabularies, but only the young child moves steadily from producing shorter sentences to producing longer ones that are elaborations of the earlier versions (for example, going from sentences like "Dat dolly" to sentences like "That's my dolly."). Over time the chimps accumulate labels to use to get rewards, but they do not seem to develop syntax. Also, whereas for a child the proportion of creative utterances increases and the proportion of imitated utterances decreases over time, for Nim the reverse was true: The proportion of imitated sentences increased while the proportion of nonimitated sentences decreased.[4]

The debate is not over. But the species-specific argument holds strong. Human language does appear to be special (specific) to our species, especially in the domain of syntax. This means that IQ, some overall general intelligence potential, plus a shaping environment cannot adequately account for language acquisition as behaviorists would claim. There must be something more or other than this. If it were not so, chimps would be able to learn a human type language, and thus far it has not been demonstrated that they can.

Third, the behaviorists' heavy reliance on stimulus-response-reinforcement learning poses serious problems. Children eventually come to use full adult forms of language, forms produced in accordance with an underlying system of structural principles like the system of the adult. Yet in the natural communicative interaction that forms the basis for the child's language learning, very rarely is he verbally reinforced positively or negatively for the forms he uses. The early work of Brown and his colleagues demonstrates that parents verbally reinforce their children according to the truth value of what they say, rather than for the forms they use. One study took language samples of three children who were observed extensively in their homes, and

> contrast(ed) the syntactic correctness of the population of utterances followed by a sign of approval—*That's right, Very good,* or just *Yes*—with the population

[3]See, especially, the work of Francine Patterson. One readable description of this work is F. G. Patterson, "Conversations with a Gorilla," *National Geographic*, 154, no.4 (1978), 438–65.

[4]I am focusing here only on the linguistic differences between Nim's language and the child's. However, Terrace identifies some additional conversational differences, for example, the fact that Nim failed to follow turn-taking patterns in conversation and the fact that Nim (and other chimps) use "language" for only one purpose: to get specific rewards. The young child, in striking contrast, early (even prelinguistically) develops a turn-taking pattern in interactions with others and even in a one-word stage uses language for a variety of purposes.

of utterances followed by a sign of disapproval—*That's wrong* or *No*. The results are simply stated: there is not a shred of evidence that approval and disapproval are contingent on syntactic correctness. (Brown, Cazden, and Bellugi-Klima 1971, p. 409)

The parents of the three children did give verbal signs of approval and disapproval for what the children said, but the approval and disapproval were contingent on the truth value of the child's utterance, not on the form. Two examples of utterances given verbal approval by the mother are "He a girl" (spoken in reference to the mother) and "Her curl my hair" (spoken while the mother was curling the child's hair). Two examples of utterances given verbal disapproval are "There's the animal farmhouse" (spoken of a lighthouse) and "Walt Disney comes on, on Tuesday" (the program came on on a different day). Brown, Cazden, and Bellugi-Klima conclude:

> It seems, then, to be truth value rather than syntactic well-formedness that chiefly governs explicit verbal reinforcement by parents—which renders mildly paradoxical the fact that the usual product of such a training schedule is an adult whose speech is highly grammatical but not notably truthful. (1971, p. 410)

The behaviorist position claims that correct (adultlike) structures come to prevail as immature forms drop out due to the reinforcement they receive. But this claim does not square with systematic observations of parents actually reinforcing their children's utterances. Children's language forms become steadily more adultlike, despite the fact that children are not specifically reinforced for form.

Occasionally a child is corrected for using a form, however. The following two well-known examples demonstrate the difficulty a child has recognizing what, specifically, he is being corrected *for*.

CHILD: Nobody don't like me.
MOTHER: No, say "nobody like**s** me."

CHILD: Nobody don't like me.
   (eight repetitions of this dialogue)
MOTHER: No, now listen carefully, say *"nobody likes me"*.
CHILD: Oh! Nobody don't like**s** me. (McNeill 1966, p. 69)

> "Want other one spoon, Daddy"—"You mean, you want THE OTHER SPOON."—"Yes, I want other one spoon, please, Daddy."—"Can you say 'the other spoon?'"—"Other . . . one . . . spoon."—"Say . . . 'other.'"—"Other."—"Spoon."—"Spoon."—"Other . . . spoon."—"Other . . . spoon. Now give me other one spoon?" (Braine 1971, pp. 160-61)

According to the behaviorist view, reinforcement is contingent on specific behavior. It is difficult to see how negative reinforcement could be playing an important role in the child's learning of form, for when it is given (and remember, it very rarely is), it is very general; it is given in response to a form that has many elements, any one or several of which could be wrong. How could the child make use of this global negative reinforcement to increase the likelihood of his using more mature forms? This kind of reinforcement lacks the specificity that most behaviorists would claim is important.

Also, as a child learns a language, we see many earlier adult forms drop out, only to be replaced by less adult forms, which are in turn eventually replaced by the original adult forms. For example, early in his development a child uses adult irregular verb and noun forms (came, went, ran, men, feet) but then replaces them with overregularizations (comed, goed, runed, mans, foots) and eventually goes back to the appropriate irregular forms (Ervin 1964). Surely the child was not negatively reinforced for his earlier adultlike irregular forms and positively reinforced for the nonadult regular forms. Yet his earlier adult forms are replaced by nonadult ones. A view of language learning that sees developmental changes in form as the result of reinforcement is hard put to explain this very predictable sequence in children learning English.

Fourth, as mentioned previously, the child is exposed to many particular sentences, yet what he learns is not those specific sentences, but the organizational principles underlying them. What young children say is in the main not sentences that are repetitions of those they have heard, but rather sentences they have created according to their own rule system. It is difficult to see in what sense the young child is being— or *could* be—reinforced here. He utters specific sentences that he has created. If positively reinforced, how could he know that that reinforcement is contingent, not upon the specific sentences themselves, but on the principles underlying them? If the child is unable, when corrected, to recognize what in his sentence the correction applies to, how can we expect him to take the enormous abstract leap of linking reinforcement to his building of a deep-level system of linguistic structure?

Fifth, how could the child learn a system so complex in such a relatively short period of time if he begins at level zero, with nothing given but a general learning capacity? There are other, far less complex learnings that he masters less well despite rigorous stimulus-response-reinforcement training schedules. It seems incredible that given only general intelligence as a starting point, language acquisition could occur in such a short time.

The final problem also concerns the behaviorist notion of general intelligence capacity as the only mental ability present at birth: It is the young age at which children engage in language acquisition. It seems quite remarkable that virtually all children, whatever the language they are learning and whatever the environment in which they are learning it, are so universally successful in deriving the unobservable from the observable, but this is what happens: Out of their direct experience of language in use, they figure out the underlying structure of the system itself. Many young children falter on figuring out far less complex and abstract matters than language, yet they are invariably successful in this complex business during the very years when they are cognitively the least mature. How can general intelligence and a shaping environment alone account for this?

In summary, many child language scholars have found the behaviorist account of language acquisition untenable, as it is unable to account for (1) the species uniformity of language acquisition, (2) the species specificity of language acquisition, (3) the independence of language development from reinforcement for form, (4) children's inferring of deep-level structure from an exposure to surface structure, (5) the relatively short period of time, and (6) the early stage in children's lives, during which they acquire so much of a complex linguistic system.

The Innatist View

Partly in response to these apparent inadequacies in the behaviorist view, another view of language acquisition gained ground, called the "innatist" position because it gives increased importance to innate factors in language acquisition.

Pendulums swing in the field of language acquisition no less than in other disciplines. Thus, the earliest shapers of and spokesmen for the innatist view (particularly Noam Chomsky) articulated a strong version of this position, perhaps partly as a reaction to the strongly prevalent behaviorist view of the time. Chomsky maintained that every child is born with universals of linguistic structure "wired in." That is, the child does not have to learn those features common to the structure of all human languages, for he is born with the skeletal framework of linguistic structure innately specified; the semantic, syntactic, and phonological possibilities of human language are already present. According to this view, the child presumably does not have to learn, for example, that the verbal strings he hears relate to meanings; that those strings affirm, negate, question, command; and what the basic syntactic elements of language are. These features are common to all languages and thus relate in some way to shared physical and mental characteristics of all humans. Being a human, the child already has a start on "knowing" what kind of system a language is in its basic design. He has a start on cracking the particular linguistic code of his speech community because he already "knows" what kind of system that code must be. His job, then, is to figure out how the particular language system of his community actualizes linguistic universals. He does not have to learn *that* one can ask information questions in his language, but rather *how* one asks information questions in his language: Does one use question words? What are they? Does one rearrange sentence elements? How? He does not have to learn that one expresses meanings through verbal expression, but rather what the particular set of distinctive sounds are (out of all the possible ones) that his linguistic community uses. Which basic sounds are used? How do they combine? How do they modify each other in combination? In short, he knows what kind of system human language can be, and his job is to discover which particular subset of the semantic, syntactic, and phonological possibilities his language community happens to use.

This strong version of the innatist position received support from biologically based research relating to language development. Lenneberg (1964) drew attention to some important ways in which language acquisition is more akin to genetically determined skills (such as walking on two legs) than to culturally transmitted ones which are the result of training. Using language, like walking on two legs, is a behavior which shows (1) limited variation within the species (wide individual variation in the specifics of its execution but striking similarity in its basic design throughout the species); (2) no beginning point for the behavior within the evolutionary history of the species (we cannot find a point in the history of our species when humans began to walk on two legs or began to use language as we know it); (3) "evidence for inherited predisposition" (Lenneberg 1964, p. 584)—humans are "biologically constituted" for a certain type of locomotion and for symbolic communication through language; (4) apparent existence of organic correlates (language acquisition, like walking, follows a predictable course of maturational development, more than a course predicted primarily by type or amount of training).

Lenneberg pointed out some correlations between stages in language development and stages in physical maturation (for example, motor coordination, structural and biochemical changes in the brain). In studying language recovery in adults and children who had incurred brain injury, Lenneberg found the prognosis to be "directly related to the age at which insult to the brain is incurred" (Lenneberg 1967, p. 142). If the injury to the language area of the brain occurs in the early years, the brain is still "plastic" enough that another area can take over the function of language acquisition. However, this does not seem to be the case after puberty, the time of life at which the brain has stabilized. Lenneberg posited a "critical period" for language acquisition, ending at puberty, by which time the brain has matured (structurally, biochemically, neurophysiologically), and after which time "automatic acquisition from mere exposure to a given language seems to disappear . . . and foreign languages have to be taught and learned through a conscious and labored effort" (Lenneberg 1967, p. 176).[5]

Thus, Lenneberg's work linking language acquisition to biological maturation supported the innatist claim that genetic inheritance for mental abilities was not simply a general ability to learn but, rather, that it included a specific predisposition for language acquisition.

Notice, however, that Lenneberg at no time claimed that language acquisition was an entirely inherited phenomenon.

> The appearance of language may be thought to be due to an innately mapped-in *program* for behavior, the exact realization of the program being dependent upon the peculiarities of the (speech) environment. As long as the child is surrounded at all by a speaking environment, speech will develop in an automatic way, with a rigid developmental history, a highly specific mode for generalization behavior, and a relative dependence upon the maturational history of the child. (Lenneberg 1964, p. 600)

According to Lenneberg, exposure to language in the environment is a necessary and sufficient condition for language acquisition in children. But

---

[5]For more recent research relating to Lenneberg's ideas, see Krashen 1973, whose study suggests that brain lateralization occurs much earlier than Lenneberg proposed, possibly by around age five.

in drawing attention to the characteristics of language acquisition that are biologically based, rooted in our species membership, Lenneberg's work supported the view that children are born with an innate predisposition for language acquisition, a special capacity apart from general IQ.

Obviously, human language crucially involves the brain and the speech organs. Both of these show special evolutionary adaptations particularly well suited to human language, adaptations that do set us apart from other primates. When we speak, we use mouth, tongue, lips, breath passing from the diaphragm, and so on. Other animals have these same body parts, but they are not "designed" to produce the sounds of speech as ours are.

> In the case of Homo sapiens, it can be shown that our oral and respiratory systems did not just evolve to serve functions of eating and noisemaking, but to serve the particular functions of producing articulate speech. Chimpanzees . . . cannot learn to speak because they are not built to do so. This suggests that, a very long time ago, there were selection pressures for hominids who could voluntarily produce strings of distinctly different sounds in rapid sequence.[6] (Slobin 1979, pp. 114-15)

Not only have we as a species evolved physical structures adapted for producing this type of speech, we have also evolved brains that can process such speech and also can regulate the production of such speech. In humans, large areas of the brain are involved in controlling the speech organs, whereas in monkeys, larger areas of the brain are involved in controlling hands and feet (and tail) and relatively less brain area is devoted to control of the mouth. Further, the human brain, unlike the brains of other species, is asymmetrical. This asymmetry appears to be directly related to language. Though both hemispheres are concerned with language functions, they control different aspects of language, with the larger left hemisphere being more crucially involved, especially in analyzing and interpreting sequences of information units. Thus, our brains have larger areas devoted to language and more specialization within these areas than is the case with other species. Both anatomically and neurologically, then, our species is specifically adapted to produce and process temporal sequences of distinct speech sounds. Biological evidence strongly supports the notion of an innate capacity specifically for language in human beings. Slobin summarizes it this way:

> Special features of our brain and our articulatory apparatus make it clear that the language capacity has a distinct biological foundation in our species. Species-specific behavior, accompanied by distinct neural and anatomical structures, is good evidence for the special evolution of those capacities, preserved in the genetic code which makes us mature into speaking creatures. The uniquely human biological foundations of language thus support the

---

[6]For discussion of specific anatomical differences between humans and other primates, see Slobin 1979, Chapter 5.

theoretical and empirical arguments for inborn language capacities in human beings. . . .[7] (Slobin 1979, p. 114)

Clearly, biological evidence attests to the presence of a special innate capacity for language in humans. However, it does not suggest what the specific nature of such a capacity might be. Chomsky, speaking from within a purely theoretical framework, argued that that special innate capacity was content, that is, a body of unconscious knowledge of language universals already "wired in." When a child was exposed to the language of his community, his "language acquisition device" would be "triggered" and would proceed along a largely predetermined course resulting in the child's becoming a speaker of the particular language of his community.

But the accumulating data from direct and intensive observations of children learning language over time in natural settings suggests an active, figuring-out child more than a triggered "language acquisition device." The special capacity of children for acquiring language may be special processing abilities for figuring out how language works. Slobin contrasted this "process approach" with the Chomskyean "content approach."

> It seems to me that the child is born not with a set of linguistic categories but with some sort of process mechanism—a set of procedures and inference rules, if you will—that he uses to process linguistic data. These mechanisms are such that, applying them to the input data, the child ends up with something which is a member of the class of human languages. The linguistic universals, then, are the *result* of an innate cognitive competence rather than the content of such a competence. The universals may thus be a derivative consequence of, say, the application of certain inference rules rather than constitute the actual initial information in terms of which the child processes linguistic input. (Slobin 1966, pp. 87–88)

Some developmental psychologists, considering children's language development from the larger perspective of overall cognitive development, have contributed a somewhat different idea about children's language learning. They located children's ability to figure out language within a larger, more general ability to " 'make sense' of things, and above all make sense of what people do, which of course includes what people say" (Donaldson 1978, p. 33). These psychologists suggest that children have a general capacity for inference. This is the crucial capacity, rather than a specific capacity for language per se. ". . . the child's ability to interpret situations . . . makes it possible for him, through active processes of

---

[7]Further interesting research support for a strong innate base for language acquisition comes from the study of language development and, especially, language invention, by deaf children. Young deaf children have been observed to use novel signs for new toys and other objects, and also to use specific multisign phrases before their mothers used these sign combinations in communicating with the children. It seems that handicapped humans invent human language naturally, while specially trained chimps do not. For a readable introduction to this work on deaf children, see S. Goldin-Meadow and H. Feldman, "The Development of Language-Like Communication without a Language Model," *Science, 197* (1977), 401—3.

hypothesis-testing and inference, to arrive at a knowledge of language" (Donaldson 1978, p. 33).

And so the debate goes on. Notice, though, that the debate does not center on whether or not there is an innate capacity in humans that enables almost all members of the species to be successful in this incredible feat of learning a language. Rather, the discussion centers on the nature of this innate ability. Is it some sort of advance knowledge that is activated by language exposure? Is it processing abilities? If it is processing ability rather than content, is it an ability specific to language or is it a more general sense-making ability? Or are both a more general *and* a more specific ability involved in language learning?

> Does the child have strategies which were specifically evolved for the task of language acquisition, or can one account for this process on the basis of more general human cognitive capacities (which also have their own innate bases)? . . . I suspect that both general cognitive principles and principles specific to language are at play in the child's construction of his native language. (Slobin 1979, p. 100)

We can only speculate about how human language originated, but surely human language was the creation of human intelligence. The only kind of language system that humans could create is one that human intelligence can process and learn. In an important sense, human language is created anew by every human child. As members of the human species, we clearly have an "in."

The Interactionist View

Behaviorist and innatist views of language acquisition focus on cognitive aspects of the learner and his language-learning activity. The role of environment is variously seen as shaping language learning through the reinforcement of selected responses, as "triggering" the child's language acquisition device, or as providing "data" from which the child can discern underlying rules. But ongoing systematic observations of children learning language in natural settings, have forced us to locate language acquisition more squarely within a social framework. The child is indeed a cognitive being, making sense out of his world, including the world of language. But the child is just as deeply a social being, and his learning of language both reflects and uses his social self. The innatist view, especially in its process version, sees the language-learning child as a cognitive activist; but we have come to see the language-learning child increasingly as a social activist as well.

This perspective on language acquisition that brings social aspects of the learning into prominence is called by some the "interactionist" view (Genishi and Dyson 1984). It is a helpful term. Think about it: *action* which is *inter*, that is, an active child well endowed for learning language, in active engagement with his physical and social world. Every instance of language that the young child encounters is contextualized. That is, it occurs in some real situation for some real communication purpose. It is an example of how particular meaning is expressed, but clearly the meaning is *social* as well as propositional. Thus, every instance of language provides an example of how language is used to express certain propositions in particular social settings and for particular communication purposes— of persuading someone, perhaps, or of entertaining with language or of sympathizing or complaining or complimenting or arguing or challenging or daring or greeting or . . . you can think of many more. The interactionist view brings into sharper focus the social nature of the learning of language. In fact, the suggestion is gaining ground that the child's sense of people's social intentions—his own and other's—enables him to work out the propositional meanings that are expressed. For example, his understanding that a particular situation is one in which someone is trying to get another person to do something enables him to attend to how a request is expressed; his understanding that a particular situation is one in which someone is trying to get information from another person enables him to attend to how an inquiry is expressed; and so on. The child learning language is actively engaged in a social world of language in use.

IN CONCLUSION

In the 1960s, Chomsky denounced the behaviorist characterization of language and how it is learned by children. Chomsky's assertion was that humans have a special innate capacity for human language. From the sixties on, child-language researchers have systematically observed children learning language in natural settings in order to gain a clearer picture of just what kind of process language acquisition is. This fact of ongoing systematic observations of children is important. The innatist view (stressing the importance of an innate capacity for human language) and the interactionist view (characterizing the child's language learning as an ongoing interaction between the innately endowed child and his social world) were not dreamt up out of the blue to thwart behaviorists. They grew out of insightful observations of many real children in diverse settings learning and using language. It is not simply convenient to say that language acquisition is species uniform and species specific; rather, it has been noted by many observers of children that they all learn language and do so in a variety of natural settings by following an impressively similar general course, and that members of other species do not naturally acquire a communication system that allows for endless creativity within a finite set of organizational principles. It is not simply convenient to say that reinforcement for form is not crucial to acquiring a complex linguistic system. Rather, extensive research has provided ample evidence that children are not typically reinforced for form, and that on those rare occasions when they are, they are unable to make use of the reinforcement. It is not simply convenient to say that children devise a deep-level system for relating expression to propositional and social meanings on the basis of the contextualized language samples that people around them use. Rather, researchers say this based on their observations of children across a wide

range of diverse settings, learning and using language. Further, it is sometimes claimed that while the behaviorists rely on empirical evidence, basing
their conclusions entirely on actually observed behavior, the innatists and
interactionists are "mentalistic," relying heavily on unfounded conjectures
about what is going on in children's minds. But in fact all three views of
language acquisition are rooted in actually observed behavior. The difference among them is a difference in how to interpret the behavior that is
observed. Is this observed behavior the result of innate general IQ plus
reinforcement for responses to stimuli, or is it the result of special innate
processing abilities plus constant interaction with the environment?

Continuing study of children learning language in different contexts
and settings will further our understanding, of course. For now, however,
we are left with some inescapable assumptions about language acquisition,
and these will provide the framework in the next two chapters for our
study of the sequence and processes of language acquisition:

> The child is the active party in the learning process.
>
> The child, as a member of the human species, is well endowed for learning
> human language.
>
> The child is a cognitive being and his language learning involves active sense
> making, that is, the building of a deep-level system relating expression and
> propositional meaning.
>
> The child is a social being and his language learning involves his active obser-
> vation of and participation in interaction with others, from which experience
> he constructs a system relating expression and social meaning.
>
> The environment in which language is learned is purposeful (purpose-full);
> the child encounters language in use for various purposes and in various
> specific contexts.

Chapters 6 and 7 focus on the sequence and processes of language
acquisition, and Chapter 8 focuses on classroom implications that this
knowledge of language acquisition has for us. As you study the sequence
and processes of language learning in children (chaps. 6 and 7) you might
want to keep in mind the key question of Chapter 8: How can our knowledge of children's language acquisition help us as teachers to contribute to
this healthy, active, powerful development in children?

6

Language Acquisition: Developmental Sequence

INTRODUCTION

In language development, as in some other important areas of children's development (physical and cognitive, for example), it is possible to describe a predictable general course that virtually all children follow, though at varying rates. In this chapter we'll consider first an overall sketch of the sequence of preschool language development, then a more detailed discussion of that early developmental sequence, and finally some aspects of language development during the school years.

Sequential development considered simply as a list of accomplishments over time can be rather boring in the way that any list is boring, but a study of developmental sequence becomes quite interesting and engaging if you keep the question *why* uppermost in mind: "*Why* do certain developments precede others?" Does the sequence make sense somehow; would I have expected this sequence? How do earlier developments relate to later ones? Are earlier developments "easier" and later ones more "difficult"? How? It is reasonable to expect developmental sequences to demonstrate continuity over time. Look for continuities as you consider the developmental sequence presented in this chapter.

PRESCHOOL DEVELOPMENT: A SKETCH

Over time, the language forms that children use become more like those used by the adults in the community. Following are seven excerpts from mother-child interactions selected to demonstrate a typical progression in language acquisition. These short episodes involve different child-mother pairs. However, all include children from similar background (middle-class Anglo), and all episodes were gathered in as natural a setting as possible (in the home, with mother and child engaging in an activity that was typical of their daily interactions). Study the seven episodes to see what differences you notice from one to the next. What changes do you see as the child progresses? Jot down your observations of each episode, if you choose, before going on to read the discussion. (Episodes 4 and 5 should be considered together, as they represent the same stage of development but demonstrate different language features of that stage.)

As you study the episodes, try to keep two things in mind. First, what is being demonstrated is a general developmental sequence characteristic of early language growth in children. Though the general course of development is similar across children, the specifics of that development and also the rate at which children develop are highly variable.[1] I have not included the ages of children in the episodes, so that you will not be tempted to make age-related statements about "the language of three-year-olds" or "the four-year-old stage," but rather will be able to focus on a developmental progression which children go through at different rates, though in the same basic sequence.

Second, remember that we are attempting to describe the child's developing linguistic structure, and this means describing something which she has, not something which she lacks. It is tempting to look at an episode involving a child's early language and say, "She doesn't have articles" or "He makes mistakes in verb tenses" or "She has trouble with plurals." To say this would be to say that the young child's language system is different from the adult's, and we knew that already. When we finish listing features of adult language that the child "does not have" or "has trouble with" (that is, uses differently than we do), we have said nothing about what the child *does* have, what she does do, what her language system *is* —the very thing we are supposedly attempting to describe. We know that the child's early language is a system of some sort. Her early sentences are designed, non-random, patterned; they are constructed in accordance with the child's rule system. Our question is, What is the nature of that system? What is language from the child's point of view? How does it change over time?

As you study these episodes, try to avoid describing the children's language as a set of deficiencies ("The child lacks . . .," "He makes mistakes with . . .," "She has trouble/difficulty with . . ."). Here are some sentence frameworks that might help you focus your expression and your thinking on the nature of the language system the child does have:

> This child expresses _____ (possession, plural, information questions) through the pattern _____.

> This child combines units of type _____ with units of type _____ in the order _____.

> In this episode the child is using elements like _____, _____, and _____ that were not present in earlier episodes.

---

[1]Even in a single child, one can observe what appear to be faster and slower periods of development, though the "spurt" or "slack" is doubtless more apparent than real, for the internal development that we cannot observe may be proceeding very steadily and what we call "spurt" or "slack" may simply be the appearance of the overt behavior reflecting that steady development.

EPISODE 1[2]

C: Nununuhnuh
M: You wanta get down? Huh?
C: Dahdah mummun nunah nahnahmah
M: Where you goin'? Where you goin'? Where you goin'? No, no, no, no.
C: Mamama
M: Come here.
C: Dahdah
M: Daddy's lunch. Daddy's lunch. Daddy's lunch.
C: Nanana dedah dede
M: Get back.
C: Nuhna nahnuhnuh
M: No. (Child is fooling with tape recorder.) Huh? Where you goin', huh? Where you goin', huh? Where you goin', huh? Where you goin', huh? See this baby? See this baby?
C: Dede
M: You're gonna fall off. No, see the baby? Here, H——, H——, H—— (child's name). Here, let me have that. Let me have it.
C: (Fusses.)
M: Did you get all that out? You can't have that, darlin'.
C: (Fusses.)
M: No, come on. Find something else to play with. Come on. Here. Here you go.

EPISODE 2[3]

M and C are playing in yard in child's sandbox.

M: Do you want to swim in your swimming pool today? Do you want to get in the pool? Or not? (pause) Do you know where your teaspoon is? The big one.
C: (Looks around but does not try to find spoon.)
M: Here it is. Whee. (Dumps some sand out.)
C: (inaudible)
M: Want to use this? Can you fill up the spoon first?
C: (Fills a container, patting it with a shovel.)
M: Are you ready to turn it over? Want to turn it over?
C: (Starts turning it over during M's questions.) Yeah.
M: OK, pat it some more.
C: (Pats some more.) Me.
M: OK. Turn it over. Oh. Quick. Quick. Turn it over quicker or it's all going to fall out.
C: (Turns it over quickly.)
M: That's a girl. Oh, it all came apart. Oh, too bad. Too bad. Let's do this one. (Picks up another container.) Here you want to help fill that up?
C: (inaudible)
M: You want to use that one?
C: (Looks at tape recorder.) Carole.

[2]I am indebted to Chris Leach for this episode.
[3]I am indebted to Carole Urzúa for episodes 2, 3, and 5.

M: Carole's. That's not a radio.
C: (Returns to filling container.)
M: Shall we turn it? (pause) Do you want to turn it now?
C: Here.
M: Right over here? Poop.
C: Pow.
M: Are you going to go bang and pow mine down? Oh, don't do that. Don't do that!
C: (Steps on the sand castles.) Off. Off. Off.

EPISODE 3

M and C are playing with toys in C's room.

M: I'm going to build a tower. (Begins building with blocks.)
C: (Pushes tower over.)
M: What did you just do?
C: Me . . . tower fall down.
M: Tower fell down. Yeah. Will you build a tower?
C: (inaudible)
M: You build one.
C: (Builds tower.) One tower.
M: One tower. You want to build two towers?
C: (Gets up to look into cylinder that contained blocks and is now empty.) Allgone.
M: All gone? There's plenty around here, I think. Enough for you to do something else.
C: (Puts cylinder over her own head.) Allgone.
M: Where's D———? (Picks up cylinder from front of C's head.) There she is!!
C: (Puts cylinder back on her head again.)
M: Where's D———? Oh. She disappeared for good. (Lifts cylinder.) Oh, there she is!
C: (Indicates her toy doll named Judy.) Judy.
M: Judy? You want to play it with Judy?
C: Hat on. (Puts cylinder on doll.)
M: Hat's on. Judy's hat's on.
C: Horsie do it.
M: Horsie do it? OK. You go over there and see if you can do it with the horsie.
C: (Puts cylinder over top of big horse on springs.) Hi. Hi, horsie. (Looks back at M and smiles.)
M: Did you get the horsie?
C: (Sees duck.) Duck?
M: Kiss the duck. (Extends duck to C.)
C: (Comes over and hugs M.)
M: You know what I see over there? I see your big bus is over there and it's turned over. Do you know that?
C: Mommy. (Puts cylinder over M's head.)
M: Mommy? OK.
C: Where Mommy?

M: Where's Mommy? (Lifts cylinder.) Boo.
C: (Squeals delightedly.) Wear hat.
M: Wear a hat? Are you going to wear a hat? That hat's too big for you to wear.
C: (Puts cylinder on top of her own head. Squeals.)
M: You squealer.

C: Sit down.
M: Sit down?
C: (Puts cylinder over her own head.) Where? Where?
M: Where's D——? She's gone. She's all gone.
C: Allgone Mommy. (Takes off cylinder.)
M: Mommy all gone. Hey, where's the cow? (M puts cow under the cylinder.)
C: See cow.
M: The cow's all gone.
C: Cow allgone. (Looks around.)
M: Where is it? Where is the cow? Do you know where the cow is? (Lifts cylinder.) Huh. D——, look at this.
C: See cow. (Laughs.)

EPISODE 4[4]

M and C are playing in C's room. C has stuffed rabbit.

M: Is this yours?
C: Mommy gave me that.
M: Does it have a name?
C: Uh uh.
M: What color is he?
C: It's a bunny.
M: Are you going to undress your black baby? What does she have on?
C: Some pants.

C: (at scribble book) I draw the puppy.
M: What, L——?
C: I draw the puppy's nose.

M: Oh, you know what?
C: You know what? I can draw two puppies.
M: OK. You do that for me. Is that one puppy right there?
C: Uh uh.

M: Tell me something about the goblins.
C: Goblins scare me.
M: When did the goblins come and scare you?
C: Goblins scare me.
M: What do they look like?
C: (no response)

[4]I am indebted to Suzy Heitzeberg for this episode. (Consider episodes 4 and 5 together.)

M: What does Santa Claus look like?
C: Um, my mouth.
M: What does he have that's real big and white?
C: A chin.

EPISODE 5

C: Mommy, can I have a Butter Crunch? (from an ad)
M: No, honey.
C: Can I have a Hershey bar?
M: No, honey.
C: What I can have?
M: How 'bout some raisins?
C: OK.

C: I say no.
M: No what?
C: Not like.
M: You don't like cabbage?
C: No.
M: Well, just leave it there, OK? Just leave it there.
C: Eat the fish.
M: You can eat some fish.
C: Put the cabbage here.
M: (Puts cabbage where child indicated.) Yeah, let's put the cabbage . . . let's put the cabbage like you do when you don't care for something. You just sorta leave it there. You taste it and you be polite and you taste it and then you just put it there and then you just eat everything else. Would you like some more fish?
C: I like more fish.
M: All right. Child, you're gonna have table manners yet!

EPISODE 6[5]

Heidi and her mother are watching some small pill bugs crawling around on a table. The nearby tape recorder gets Heidi's attention first.

C: What is it?
M: That's the tape, going around and round.
C: Well, I want you put this on.
M: Well, it is on right now. We'll listen to it in a minute to see how we sound.
C: Ah, Heidi don't wants to.
M: You don't want to listen to it?
C: No.
M: OK. Well, you don't have to listen to it, but don't pull on it, OK? OK.

Now Heidi turns her attention to the pill bugs.

---

[5]I am indebted to Paula Brock for this episode.

M: Now be careful.

C: Why we gotta be careful for?

M: 'Cause I don't want the bugs to get down on the floor in the carpet.

C: Why they can't for?

M: 'Cause then we'd lose them and couldn't find them. What are the bugs doing?

C: They playing. They doing a sommersault.

M: They're doing a sommersault? Do you like to play with bugs?

C: Wet's put 'em back in the pan 'cause we tired.

M: 'Cause we're tired. Does Tammy play with bugs?[6]

C: Nooooooo.

M: Who plays with bugs?

C: Heidi dos and Tammy dos. ("Dos" pronounced to rhyme with "shoes.")

M: Heidi does and Tammy does?

C: Yes.

C: Now I want to put the bugs back in there.

M: OK. Does Tammy have any bugs like that at her house?

C: Uh-uh, her don'ts.

M: She doesn't?

C: No.

EPISODE 7

M: What did you do at school today?

C: Working—just was working. Teacher has a magnet game. Some things are magnet and some things are not. The ones that are sticky stick and the ones that are not sticky don't stick.

M: Did you play on the jungle gym today?

C: No, I'm a watcher.

M: What's a watcher?

C: I watch everybody fall off and if they do, I go and get the teacher.

M: Did you have a nice ride on the school bus?

C: Yes. Do you know what Mr. B———(the bus driver) says?

M: No, what?

C: "Shut up, R——— " (child's name) and he turns the radio up real loud.

M: What do you want to be when you grow up?

C: I am a fireman!

M: What do firemen do?

C: They put out fires, rescue people if they fall from a real tall building and go in spook houses and if someone is missed, like a fireman, the ambulance and the rescue people, they find him.

M: What's your favorite kind of sandwich?

C: A mustard sandwich. Take some bread and fold it up and put some mustard in the middle of it. Don't you know?!?

[6]Tammy is Heidi's friend.

M: What do you want for breakfast tomorrow?
C: After this night?
M: Yes.
C: Cheerios in a bowl with milk on top.

M: It's time to go to bed, R———.
C: If you say, "It's time to go to bed, R——— " one more time, you are going to
    upset me.
M: I'm sorry, but it is time.
C: You're upsetting me!

    You might question whether C-1's language is language at all (throughout this discussion I will refer to the child in each episode with C- and the number of the episode). Isn't this just a baby making noise? No, it is something more than random noise making. The baby repeats a limited set of syllables in this sample, most of them consonant + vowel combinations. This repetition shows some articulatory control that was not present earlier for this child. Earlier verbal noise making is more diverse and does not show the patterning evident here, either in consonant + vowel syllable structure or in deliberate syllable repetition. C-1's language demonstrates some nonrandomness, which is a characteristic of language.
    In this first episode one wonders whether C-1's "Mamama" and "Dahdah" are words. How can we tell when "Dahdah" is a repetition of two syllables and when it is a word, a deliberate sound string intended to convey a particular meaning? The mother in this episode responds to "Dahdah" as a meaningful utterance, since the child speaks it in the presence of the father's lunch and, the mother assumes, with some reference to that. Generally when we begin to observe the child uttering particular sound sequences in particular situations, we assume that the child has established some sound-meaning connection. It is this assumed connection that distinguishes words from verbal noises. The crucial question is, "Is there a particular sound-meaning connection for this child?" We would have to observe the child's use of these sound strings in diverse contexts to be sure. However, it would seem, even from this very limited episode, that the child is at least at the brink of "wordness."
    Often a sound-meaning connection is different for the child than for the adult. It is not unusual to hear a mother say of her child, "———is the word she uses for———." Here the sound sequence may be quite unlike that which the adult would use to express that meaning. On the other hand, a child's early word may sound very much like an adult's yet denote a different area of meaning, as is the case, for example, with the child who calls all animals "doggie."
    Notice the turn taking in this first conversation. We often take it for granted that two participants in a conversation take turns when they interact. If for some reason both speak at the same time, they tend to apologize and one gives the floor to the other ("Sorry. Go ahead"), thus acknowledging that both know that the appropriate way to dialogue is to take turns speaking. But turn taking in an interaction is behavior which develops over

time. The baby's earliest cooing and gurgling often overlap with the mother's verbalizations. In episode 1 there is some evidence of verbal turn taking.

In episode 2 there is no question as to whether or not the child is communicating with words, that is, deliberate sound sequences which *mean*. The child's "me" following her mother's "OK, pat it some more" might mean "Me—I'm the one who's patting it." Her "Carole" as she looks at the tape recorder possibly means "That's Carole's," and her "here" possibly is said to indicate "I want to turn it over right here." This child is getting considerable mileage out of a few one-word utterances. Notice the absence of sound-making "fillers" (though if we looked at a larger segment of this child's language in a wide range of situations, we might find some "playing with sounds"). We also see in this episode a rooting of the child's language in her action, a characteristic typical of early language. It helps us to understand what the child is saying if we can also see what she is doing—"pow" as she moves to pow the sandcastles, "off, off, off" as she step, step, steps on them.

We know that a child's language growth doesn't have to do only with what she says, but at least as importantly it has to do with what she comprehends in the speech of others. But the question, What language does the child comprehend? is the most difficult of all, and the earlier the stage of language development, the harder it is to answer. C-2 does not overtly respond to the mother's opening series of questions, though it would seem the mother is using these forms precisely to get some sort of verbal or nonverbal (action) response from her child. After her mother asks, "You want to use that one?" (referring to a container), C-2 looks at the experimenter's tape recorder and says, "Carole." Does C-2 behave in this way because she did not understand what her mother was saying or because she did not understand a crucial *part* of what her mother was saying or because she was not even listening or because she preferred to do something else? There is usually no way to tell for certain.

On the other hand, Mother says, "Turn it over. Oh. Quick. Quick" and C-2 does turn it over quickly. Mother says, "OK, pat it some more" and C-2 does. Is this because she understands her mother's verbal suggestions or simply because it is in the nature of the game itself to pat the sand and turn it over quickly? Or did she understand some nonverbal signal, a gesture or facial expression, and not comprehend or perhaps not even attend to the verbal signal itself? To attempt an answer, one must observe a child extensively to note overall patterns in the child's verbal and nonverbal behavior in different situations. Even then the question of comprehension remains tantalizing. Our overriding tendency is to assume that the child's responses, being similar to those *we* would make in that situation, indicate that she understands what *we* would understand in that particular situation. Maybe . . . but then again, maybe not.

Overall, movement from episode 1 to episode 2 involves movement toward "wordness." In episode 1, repeated sound sequences and tentative hints of words play an important part in the interaction. In episode 2, words—items we can identify with confidence as sound-meaning relations—have emerged to play an important part in interaction.

Particularly noteworthy in episode 3 is the child's word combining. Some researchers consider this early combining the beginning of syntax for the child. And what powerful use C-3 makes of this expressive device. In a total of twelve word combinations for the child in this short episode, we find her using language for different purposes. She reports and comments on her actions: "tower fall down" (presumably meaning something like "I made the tower fall down"), "one tower" ("I'm building one tower"), "sit down" ("I'm going to sit down"), "see cow" (spoken both when she does see the cow, suggesting a meaning like "I see the cow," and when she doesn't see it, suggesting a meaning like "I want to see the cow"). She initiates and maintains games: "hat on," "horsie do it," "where Mommy," "allgone Mommy," "wear hat." She greets: "hi, horsie." Structurally we find constructions involving verbs expressing actions, nouns as agents (doers) of actions and also as objects, and locational expressions ("on," "where," "down"). This child seems to use to the full whatever expressive devices she has, in this case two or three words in combination. The young child wrings tremendous expressive potential out of simple two-word combinations, expressing through them a variety of meanings and relationships.

In episode 3, as in episode 2, the child's saying and doing are of a piece; her words live in her physical actions. It is through her saying and doing together (and with the willing participation of a very sensitive, cooperative mother!) that C-3 initiates and controls throughout this episode.

You'll notice that "allgone" is written as one word for the child but as two ("all gone") for the mother. This is not a misprint, but an attempt to convey how the item functions differently for the child and for the adult. The mother's lexicon includes two separate items, "all" and "gone," each of which enters into various combinations with other words. But study of the large body of language data collected on this particular child reveals that "allgone" works for her at this stage as a single, inseparable unit denoting absence. Remember, our question is, "What is the child's language system?" and in the system of this child at the time of this episode, "allgone" functions as the expression of a single morpheme.

Episodes 4 and 5 demonstrate what Roger Brown has called "an intricate sort of ivy" that begins "to grow up between and upon the major construction blocks, the nouns and verbs" that are the predominant elements in early speech (Brown 1973, p. 249). You can notice an increased length in the utterances of C-4 and C-5 over those of C-3. It is partly this "ivy" that accounts for the increase in length. C-4 and C-5 include in their utterances a variety of grammatical morphemes, those bits and pieces that are not heavy carriers of semantic content but which refine meanings and contribute to smoothness and fluency. Now there are articles ("a," "the," "some"), "be" forms ("It's a bunny"), plural morphemes ("mittens," "bears"), possessive morphemes ("puppy's"), prepositions ("on," "with," "through"), and auxiliaries like "can."

C-4 and C-5 are using a variety of sentence types—affirmatives, negatives, interrogatives, imperatives. Notice the variety in negatives: "Uh uh," "I can't," "I didn't," "No," "Not like." The interrogatives occur in the fixed routine sequence in episode 5. Notice that C-5 says the two yes/no questions as they occur in the ad: *"Can I have X?"* But when she asks the information question, "What *I can* have?" she doesn't invert the subject-verb order as it occurs in the ad. Clearly, she is not simply imitating the ad but, in this instance, is structuring the expression according to her own developing system of rules. This unreversed subject-verb order in information questions is a familiar phenomenon in children's development of interrogative forms.

Notice C-4's responses to the adult's questions. She responds to the yes/no questions ("Is this yours?" "Does it have a name?" "Is that one puppy right there?") by supplying an affirmative or negative reply, which is what the adult would also do. She also gives adultlike responses to the repetition question ("What,——?") and to the two questions that ask about an object ("What does she have on?" and "What does he have that's real big and white?"). Notice, though, that, when asked, *"What color is he?"* she treats it as if it were another direct object question, answering by naming the object ("It's a bunny") rather than by giving a color (a particular attribute of the object). Labeling an object in response to a question is apparently an earlier development for this child than specifying a particular characteristic of an object in response to a question. Notice, too, C-4's responses to the adult's "What do they look like?" and "What does Santa Claus look like?"—syntactically rather complex questions that attempt to elicit characteristics of objects. And what about the adult's "when" question: "When did the goblins come and scare you?" Can you see that this question is complex in two ways: Besides being a two-clause question (involving "coming" and "scaring"), it focuses on that very abstract notion time. Cognitively, "when" is more complex than "what." Notice, finally, C-4's response to the adult's social question, "You know what?" a question that generally serves to get the next conversational turn for the speaker. Instead of replying, "What?" and thus giving the conversational turn back to the original speaker, C-4 repeats the question, thus getting the speaking turn for herself. I wonder whether her response indicates that this social convention question has not yet become part of her repertoire, or whether C-4 chooses to take over this question form and use it to her purpose of getting the turn so she can tell the adult something instead of listening to what the adult has to say.

A major new question is evident in C-6's conversation with her mother, the "why" question (expressed as "Why . . . for" by this child). This question was noticeably absent in the earlier conversations. The younger children's questions were yes/no types and questions seeking identification or locations of actions or objects—all very concrete kinds of information. But clearly C-6 is interested in reasons that lie behind the concrete, the reasons behind requested actions and behaviors. C-6 uses both inverted and noninverted question forms: inverted in "What *is it*?" and uninverted in her questions "Why *we gotta be* . . .?" and "Why *they can't* . . .?" Later in this section you'll find that "why" questions are more complex than the earlier questions in several ways, but already you can see that the kind of information they seek is more cognitively demanding than that required by "what" and "where" questions.

The presence of alternative forms coexisting as choices for the child is an interesting phenomenon. C-6's grammatical system includes both inverted and non-inverted forms of questions.[7] Adults also have alternative forms in their grammars; for example, both "I called up John" and "I called John up" are possibilities. You can see that the particular set of alternatives that C-6 has as part of her grammatical system (for example, "Why can't I" and "Why I can't") is different from the adult's set; nonetheless, having alternative expressive forms within one's grammar exists for both child and adult.

C-6 expresses third person singular in a consistent way. She clearly distinguishes between first person and third person verb forms: "I want" but "Heidi/Tammy dos" (rhymes with "shoes" and follows the pattern I do/you do/he or she dos) and even "Heidi don't wants" and "Her don'ts."

A dramatic new development in C-6's conversation is her combining of several propositions in a single expressed sentence: for example, "Heidi dos and Tammy dos" and "Wet's put 'em back in the pan 'cause we tired," "I want you put this on," and "Now I want to put the bugs back in there."

Complex combining of several propositions in a single sentence is a striking feature of C-7's talk. Surely the most structurally complex utterance in this episode is C-7's reply to his mother's question "What do firemen do?": "They put out fires, rescue people if they fall from a real tall building and go in spook houses and if someone is missed, like a fireman, the ambulance and the rescue people, they find him." This reply includes at least the following underlying propositions. (Analyses here will differ slightly, depending on how some adjectives and adverbs are treated.)

Firemen put out fires.
Firemen rescue people.
People fall from a building.
The building is (real) tall.
Firemen go in houses.
The houses are spooky (type).
Someone misses someone.
Someone misses a fireman.
The ambulance finds the fireman.
The people find the fireman.
They are rescuers (type).

Also notice that whereas the earlier conversations focused mainly on the here-and-now, this conversation is less dependent on the immediate situation. In this informal, before-bed conversation, C-7 and his mother talk about the child's actions earlier in the day, about the child's immediate

[7]In the larger body of data, C-6 uses both inverted and uninverted forms of "why" questions. Thus, it is not a case of her consistently inverting in one type of question ("What is it" questions) and not inverting in another type of question ("Why . . ."). She varies within a single question type.

future (tomorrow's breakfast) and his distant future (becoming a fireman), and about things that are not right there (Cheerios, mustard sandwich).[8]

The seven episodes included here span a four-year age range: C-1 is under one year, and C-7 is under five. Already, from just this preliminary sketch of a language-development sequence in the early years, you can recognize some basic dimensions of change over time. Length is perhaps the most obvious. You can see that the children's utterances lengthen over time from single-word utterances to short combinations to longer sequences of words in the later episodes. You may also have noticed changes in the kinds of units that the child's utterances include. In the earlier episodes, the children use mainly nouns and verbs, which are major language building blocks and heavy carriers of meaning. The later episodes include further refinements: articles, prepositions, and grammatical morphemes (for example, past tense, plural, the -ing of action in progress). Thus, the utterances in the later episodes sound smoother and more complete to the adult's ear. Perhaps you can also see that the later episodes show an increase in the types of sentences the child expresses syntactically. Children's one-word sentences may function as commands or as questions or as statements, but these meanings are conveyed by the situation itself and the child's intonation. In later episodes, however, the child uses specific linguistic devices to express these various sentence types (for example, question words like "what" or "why," negative elements like "not" or "can't," and word order) so that the sentence type is clear from the spoken words.

Sentence combining is another dimension of change evident in these episodes. Did you notice that in the earlier episodes each child utterance expresses a single proposition, a unit that could be considered an early version of a simple sentence, whereas the child utterances in episodes 6 and 7 combine several propositions into complex sentences? And finally, you may have noticed that the talk in the earlier episodes is entirely limited to the situation of the moment, to the objects and the actions actually present. But C-4 moves beyond the present situation in talking about goblins and Santa Claus, C-6 talks about an absent person (Tammy), and C-7 talks entirely about past and future events. Over time, children's language becomes less dependent on the immediate situation and can stand more on its own.

Obviously, more mature speakers of a language do not use only long utterances or only complex sentences or only talk focusing outside of the present situation. Even as adults we often use one-word sentences about the here-and-now. Conversational sequences like "Coming?" "Yup," "OK" are not uncommon. Language development is not so much a matter of trading in some linguistic devices for others, but a matter of extending one's repertoire of expressive possibilities. The child's development is a gradual, continuous—at times even imperceptible—move, more like the

---

[8]For further discussion of the young child's move away from dependence on the immediate context, see Sachs 1977.

continuous swelling movement of an incoming tide than like the separate hops one makes through a set of clearly demarked boxes in a hopscotch game.

PRESCHOOL DEVELOPMENT: A CLOSER LOOK

Prelinguistic Development

There is a tendency to think that a child's language development begins when she says her first word, which word mother dutifully records in the child's baby book. But infant research compels us to reject this notion and to recognize evidence of communication development from birth.

Infancy research suggests a strong innate base for language. Two types of evidence researchers cite in support of their innateness claims are: (1) the presence at birth of structures which are well adapted for language (though initially not used for language) and (2) the presence of general social behaviors and also language-specific abilities in the first few months of life.

With regard to the first type of evidence, the presence of adapted structures at birth, Trevarthen (1977) cites the newborn's "organs [being] in a strange anticipatory state of adaptation, with intrinsic organization in excess of essential function at that time" (p. 229). This statement takes some thinking about at first, but let's consider two examples, smiling and hand movements, that will help to clarify Trevarthen's statement. Initially a smile expression just happens; the infant at first does not smile intentionally in order to signal some state. Yet the smile, present from birth, is an expression "uniquely adapted to affect other persons" (p. 233). During the second month of life, the smile becomes functional; that is, it becomes a communicative signal. Thus, the smile is a "structure" that is *there*—in place and ready to become functional in communication—before the child actually uses it in this way. The newborn's hand movements include waving and finger pointing. It is simply a given that human hands move in these ways, but these movements, over several months, become intentional signaling gestures, and by about eight months the child reaches toward an object to signal that it is of interest. Before long the reaching gesture becomes a specific finger pointing (Bruner, Roy, and Ratner 1982). Remember that the movements are *there* at birth, available for the child to use later as signals in communication with another. Smiles and hand movements are thus two structures that are "in an anticipatory state of adaptation," structures that have within them the potential for being used as specific communication expressions for the child.

Some behaviors of infants in the first few months suggest that the human child is innately "primed" for social interaction in general and for language in particular. It is well documented that the infant prefers the real human face, or a representation of it, to a real or represented object. By two months the child responds quite differently to persons and objects (Trevarthen 1977). This early person-object distinction and preference for humans bespeaks a social orientation in the newborn. Clearly, such an orientation is the basis for communication development. But in addition to this general social tendency, the infant demonstrates abilities quite specific to language. For example, the one-month-old is able to make subtle distinctions between very similar sounds (/ba/and /pa/) which are used to differentiate meanings in talk (Eimas et al. 1971).

From the beginning, many behaviors of mother and child exhibit a pattern of alternation, a kind of synchrony involving both partners. This alternating, or turn-taking, pattern is evident in physical movement of mother and child, a pattern of one moving and then being more still while the partner's movement increases. Vocalizations of mother and infant show this complementary pattern to some degree also.[9] The mother-child pairs studied tend to take turns in vocalizing: When mother is more quiet, the infant vocalizes more, and mother tends to speak more in the pauses between the infant's vocalizations. Some overlaps occur, with mother and child vocalizing at the same time, but these overlaps are likely to occur in particular situations, as, for example, when both partners laugh or when mother suddenly warns the child while the child is vocalizing or when the child is distressed and mother's soothing talk overlaps the child's fussing (Schaffer, Collis, and Parsons 1977). By the end of the child's first year, these turn-taking patterns have become elaborated into extended game sequences or routines, for example, peek-a-boo or give-and-take games. However, whether in nonverbal or verbal interaction, and whether in less or more elaborated sequences, mother and infant seem to be coordinating their moves in interaction with one another.

During the first year the child develops many concepts and abilities that are important prerequisites to linguistic expression. The child develops an understanding of self and other as distinct entities, an understanding one would have to have if "self" is going to communicate with "other." As mentioned already, the child early differentiates between persons and objects, but beyond this, the child builds concepts of agents (people causing things to happen) and of objects people do things to or with, and of the actions people engage in as distinct from the people and objects themeselves. Obviously, these basic relationships (agent, action, and object) are encoded in language. The young child builds a notion of separate entities in physical space, a necessary prerequisite for reference. Toward the end of the first year the child comes to grasp means-end relationships, a notion that is an important foundation for the child's early use of language to request, that is, to get someone (the means) to do something (the end) for the child. Earlier in the first year, the child is able to orient to one entity at a time, for example, either to caregiver or to an object. But by the end of the first year the child can relate to caregiver and object; thus, the child can focus *with* another person *on* some object—a preliminary sort of "conversation" with a "topic" of joint focus.

---

[9]One caution is necessary here. The subjects in this mother-infant research have been mainly Anglo and middle class. Some recent language research on early caregiver-child interaction reveals that there is considerable variation from one culture to another in the ways that mothers and children interact, and in the extent to which they interact verbally. See, for example, Heath 1983 and Ochs 1983. The mainstream patterns described here are well documented, but it is not yet clear in what ways and to what extent they may be limited to specific cultural groups.

There is more, much more, in the first year, but the examples here should be sufficient to demonstrate that the child's early development is crucial to subsequent linguistic development. This is not to say that the "reason" (in the universal order of things) for these developments is so that the child will subsequently develop a full linguistic system, but it is to say that there are many developments in the first year that contribute to the child's ongoing development of language. By the end of the first year, typically, the child has developed a rich base of cognitive understandings: concepts of self and other, of persons and things, of means and ends. Also, the child has built a rich base of social and interactional understandings: of initiating and responding, of attending, of signaling, of turn-taking. Both the cognitive and the social aspects are important bases for further language development.

One-Word Stage

1. Write ten words that you think are likely to be in a child's vocabulary in the one-word stage (that is, when a child's verbal expression is limited to single words rather than word combinations).

2. Now think of a situation in which your hypothetical child might say each word on your list, and write an adult type sentence that would express the child's meaning in that situation. For example, you might have included "dog" on your list. A situation in which that word might occur is one in which mother and child are looking at a picture book and the child points to a picture of a dog and says "dog," a meaning the adult might express as "That's a dog." Another situation might be the child gesturing toward her toy dog and saying to her mother "dog," a meaning the adult might express as "I want the dog" or "Get the dog for me"—that is, some sort of request for that object. The point is that it is necessary to think of a particular situation because the child's single word might express different meanings, depending on the situation.

3. Now go on reading, but keep your list nearby.

It is a common notion that the child in a one-word stage goes along accumulating names for things and people in her world. This is true as far as it goes; most children's early vocabularies do include a substantial proportion of nouns. But typically the child's early vocabulary includes other types of words also. It is usual to find action words (for example, "go," "fall," and "eat"), social expressions (like "hi" or "bye-bye"), locational words (like "here," "there," "up," and "down"), and describing words (such as "hot" or "big").[10] "No" is often an early word and may be used to reject (meaning something like "I don't want that" or "Stop doing that to me") or to signal absence of something expected or to deny something (for example, as a response to a question such as "Did you do that?"). Many children

---

[10]You might want to see Katherine Nelson's study (1973) in which she characterizes some children as "referential" in their early vocabularies and other children as "expressive." Also see Nelson 1981 for a discussion of individual differences identified in the early vocabularies of children by various researchers.

have an early word to request a repeat of something they like ("more" or "again") and many have a word for signaling absence of something (for example, "allgone," which functions as a single word for the child). Your list of ten words probably includes some, but not all, of these types of words. (Which ones do you have?) You can see that the child does much more than simply accumulate object labels. Though the child's early words are of different types, they have one feature in common: They do important communiation work for the child. It is easy to see that many words would not carry such significant social or propositional meaning for the child. Articles ("the" and "a") or auxiliary elements (the "may" of "He *may* come" or the "has" of "She *has* gone") would not convey as much meaning as "hi" and "doggie," "fall" and "no," or "down" and "allgone." It is likely that you did not include on your list either articles or auxiliaries, words that add minor refinements to basic meanings.

In addition to the diversity in the kinds of words children use in the one-word stage is the diversity in the ways they use them. With a relatively limited set of words, a child can express a variety of meanings and relations in different contexts. By the end of the one-word stage, the child may use nouns to identify objects (for example, in a picture book "naming game" with an adult), to draw someone's attention to something, or to indicate something that she wants. Sometimes she uses the noun to identify the one who is doing something (agent), sometimes to identify the object of an action, and sometimes to identify the receiver (for example, someone she is giving something to). The child may use a noun to indicate a location (for example, "table" or "shelf" as the place where some object is to be put) or to indicate a person associated with a present object (for example, "Daddy" spoken with reference to an object belonging to or used by him). "Up" or "down" can be used to name an occurring action (spoken as the child is being lifted up or down) or to request that action, or to name a location in answer to a question (for example, "Where did it go?"). "No," as mentioned, can signal rejection, absence, or denial, three quite distinct uses. (Which of these uses do you find on your own list?) You can see that the situation in which the single word is spoken is crucial to adults as they try to interpret the child's meaning. The situation is, of course, also necessary to the child as she expresses meaning: It is in her word-and-situation taken together that she is able to convey her meaning.

The child takes the situation into account in another way, also, during this period. Some research has suggested that when the child has developed a variety of words and ways to use them to express different meanings, she tends to select, in a given situation, the word that is most informative (Greenfield 1978). For example, if the object being used in a game is obvious to the child (for example, it is in her hand) but the action—what is to be done with the object—is in question, then the child's one word will name the action, the uncertain element in the situation. But if the action is obvious—the known or "given" element in the situation—but the object to be used is in doubt, then the child will name the object. This assumes, of course, that the child has a word for the action and also for the object and "selects" one. The suggestion is that though the child in this stage is limited in her expression to single-word utterances, she understands a larger set of relationships (for example, agent-action-object) in the situation and expresses the most informative part of the whole.

It is somewhat problematic to know just how much and what kind of knowledge to attribute to the young child on the basis of her observed single words and actions in particular situations.[11] When the child says "Mommy" in a given situation, for example, does the child simply have a label or does she have a sense of Mommy as an agent, that is, the performer of an action? Cases like this are matters of debate. Does one favor a "rich interpretation," crediting the child with more knowledge, or a "lean interpretation," crediting the child with less knowledge? Though some specifics are uncertain, however, it is clear that the one-word stage is not a simple monolithic period, but a time of interesting and important development from the beginning of the period to the end. The child does not, at the beginning of this stage, use single words to express the whole range of meanings described here. Rather, throughout this period she increases her range of uses for her single words. Further, certain uses seem to precede others in a somewhat predictable order. Earlier in this stage the child's action and object words relate to her own actions and the object involved, and only later does she use these same words in relation to the actions of others (decentration). Many words occur first as accompaniments to actions which the child is engaged in at the moment (for example, saying "down" as she is being lifted down) and only later are they used apart from the action (for example, saying "down" as a request to be lifted down). Earlier in the stage the child uses words in isolation and later as answers to the partner's questions, thus connecting (relating) her single-word utterance to another's previous utterance. (You might want to look at your own list again and decide which of the words and situations you listed would occur earlier and which ones later in the one-word stage.) It is not so important to remember the specific developmental details of this period as it is to understand that this stage, like all stages, is developmental rather than static.

I find it most impressive that the child in a one-word stage is able to express so much with so little. Only single words in specific situations, yet what a lot of communication mileage the child gets from these limited means. The kinds of words the child uses—such heavy carriers of content—plus the diverse uses she makes of them in different situations, plus the selection she makes for maximum informativeness—all suggest the human's thrust toward making and expressing meaning in a social world.

Early Combinatory Speech

Mean Length of Utterance (MLU).   Brown and his colleagues closely observed the early language development of three children over a period of several years (Brown et al. 1973). It became apparent to them that the length of a young child's utterances was a better indicator of language

---

[11]See C. Howe's review of Greenfield and Smith 1976 in the *Journal of Child Language*, 4, no. 3 (1977), 479–83.

development than was chronological age. If we describe the language system of several children of the same age, we find marked differences. But if we describe the language system of several children whose utterances (spoken sentences) average the same length, we find impressive similarities. Brown and his colleagues used the child's average number of morphemes per utterance as their length measure (mean length of utterance or MLU). They posited five stages in early language acquisition, each stage defined by MLU. For each stage they also suggested an upper bound (UB), that is, what would typically constitute the longest utterance (in morphemes) in the child's sample. One can view Brown's stages as MLU spans as well as central MLU points.

STAGE	MLU (POINT)	MLU (SPAN)	UB
1	1.75	1.5—2.0	5
2	2.25	2.0—2.5	7
3	2.75	2.5—3.0	9
4	3.50	3.0—3.5	11
5	4.00	3.5—4.0	13

Based on Brown 1973, p. 56.

Up to Stage 5, an MLU of 4.0, increasing length reflects increasing complexity. Typically, a young child might say, "Daddy go" and later "Daddy going" and still later "Daddy is going." As the child's combinatory speech develops, it moves from a system which at most combines two or three uninflected, heavy content items (especially nouns and verbs) to a system that incorporates expression of inflections like past tense and plural, grammatical morphemes like articles and prepositions, and embedded and conjoined constructions, all of which contribute to both length and complexity of expression. Because of this length-complexity relationship, MLU is a good indicator of early language growth and many child-language researchers have used Brown's stages.

After an MLU of 4.0, however, utterance length is no longer a very helpful measure of language growth. You can probably already guess why. Just think of all the shortened forms we regularly use in conversation. If someone asks you, "Are you going to be able to make it to the party by 8:00?" you may simply answer, "Yup." But that one "yup" that you actually speak relates to a much more complex underlying structure that you have access to and are drawing on—something like "I am going to be able to make it to the party by 8:00." And so it is with children. After an MLU of 4.0, the length measure does not reflect the complexity of what children know, the system that enables them to produce deleted forms.

Stage 1. This period marks the child's move from one-word speech into combinatory speech (MLU 1.5–2.0). We have already seen that the child's one-word speech expresses a variety of meanings. Those meanings are present in Stage 1 as well, but gradually the constraint of being able to express only one element verbally seems to lift and the child increasingly verbalizes more than one element. Thus, the continuity in children's meanings from one-word speech into combinatory speech is as noteworthy as the change in how children express their meanings.[12]

Some researchers have dubbed the language of this period "telegraphic," as the morphemes the child expresses tend to be heavy carriers of content—nouns, verbs, some adjectives and adverbs—just as would be the case in a telegram where we pay by the word and thus select the heaviest content carriers we can find. There is a noticeable absence of grammatical morphemes like articles (a, the, some), auxiliaries (can, will), "be" forms as main verbs (It *is* red), and "be" forms which precede verbs in adult constructions (*is* going). C-3, for example, expresses the meaning "The cow is all gone" by saying, "Cow allgone." She conveys her meaning very satisfactorily, as she would not have done had her two uttered morphemes been "the is." Though every child's language development is unique in its details, the general similarity across children at this stage, expressing their meanings through heavy content items in short combinations, is striking.

Equally striking is the general similarity in *what* it is that Stage 1 children express. Again, the specifics differ from child to child, and there is an increase in propositional complexity during the stage. However, it is possible to identify a limited set of major meanings and relations that account for a high proportion of the utterances of most Stage 1 children.[13] This may not surprise us if we assume that early cognitive development is similar across children and that "children learn language as a means of representing or coding information that they have already acquired about objects, events, and relations in the world" (Bloom, Lightbown, and Hood 1974, p. 3). If children's early understanding of the world is similar, then the content of their early talk will be similar, for their talk expresses this common understanding.

And what are these "major meanings and relations" expressed in early combinations? Independent research studies show considerable agreement that they include existence, nonexistence, and recurrence. Here are some examples.

Existence (also called nomination or labeling):

a. Adult says, "What's this?" Child answers, "*This doll.*"
b. Adult and child are looking at a picture book. Child points to a picture of a house and says to adult, "*See house.*"

---

[12]C-3 is an example of a child in Stage 1. Of course, a far more substantial sample of the child's language than is present in episode 3 is necessary to establish a child's MLU. This episode has been extracted from a large body of data for C-3, and her MLU for that larger body of data places her in Stage 1.

[13]Key studies here include Brown 1973; Bloom, Lightbown, and Hood 1975; and Miller 1982. See Slobin 1979 (pp.85–90) for a discussion of increasing propositional complexity during Stage 1.

    c. Adult asks child, "Where's the baby?" Child touches doll nearby and answers, *"Here baby."*

Nonexistence:

    a. Child stops turning a toy wheel that had been making noise when he turned it, and says, *"No more noise."*

    b. Child looks at empty breakfast plate and says, *"Allgone egg."*

    c. Mother and child are inside with the front door open. Mother closes the door and child says, *"Allgone outside."*

Recurrence:

    a. Child begins turning a toy wheel in order to make noise, and says, *"More noise."*

    b. Mother has some raisins. Child extends open hand toward mother and says, *"'Nother raisin."*

    c. Child and mother have been walking outside. Mother starts toward the house. Child pulls on mother's hand so she'll keep walking and not go inside. Child says, *"More bye-bye."*

Existence involves the child identifying things in her world by labeling them. She may be simply naming an object, or she may be providing a label in answer to a question, or by way of calling another's attention to the object or person in order to introduce a "topic" of "conversation." In nonexistence the child expresses her awareness of the absence of something; while in recurrence, requesting more of a pleasurable experience, the child expresses an awareness that entities and events can exist again, can be repeated.

    These meanings have to do with being: things being (existence), not being (nonexistence), or being again (recurrence). But children's early combinations also express attributes of objects and association of objects with people, for example.

Attribute:

    a. Child reaches for a microphone, draws back suddenly, and says, *"Microphone hot."*

    b. Adult says to child, "Bring me a book to read to you." Child brings a book about animals and says, *"Animal book."*

    c. Child and mother are looking at a picture of Cinderella's stepmother. Child says, *"Her mean."* (Miller 1982, p.179)

Association:

    a. Child and her mother are eating lunch. Child reaches for a piece of cheese on her high chair tray and says, *"My cheese."*

    b. Child points to her father's place at the table and says, *"Daddy chair."*

    c. Child touches her mother's nose and says, *"Mommy nose."*

In attribute expressions the child conveys at least a beginning awareness that particular people and objects have certain characteristics. Some researchers would call the preceding association examples "possession" rather than "association," and you can see why: From the adult's perspective they can be interpreted as "X belonging to Y." If the adult said these things, possession is what the adult would mean. But from the child's perspective—the perspective we are most interested in—association may more accurately characterize what the child means, as it may be too much to credit the child with the abstract notion of ownership that possession assumes. Whether the child actually has the notion of ownership here or whether simply of association, it is certain that in these expressions the child is connecting (relating) two entities as belonging together in some way.

Many of the child's combinations during this period express two elements of a basic agent (doer) + action + object string. Interestingly, all two-element combinations occur, and they occur in the order the adult would expect. Here are some examples:

Agent + action:

a. Mother is writing a letter. She asks child, "What's Mommy doing?" Child answers, "*Mommy write.*"
b. Mother is dressing child (Kathryn) and encouraging her to stand up so mother can pull her overalls on. Child says, "*Kathryn stand up.*"
c. Child is trying, unsuccessfully, to open a box. She extends the box toward her mother and says, "*Mommy open.*"

Action + object:

a. Child is preparing to throw a ball. Child says, "*Throw ball.*"
b. Child is "feeding" a toy cat a raisin and says, "*Eat raisin.*"
c. Child is preparing to pull a Teddy bear in a toy wagon. Child says, "*Pull Teddy.*"

Agent + object:

a. Mother is busy making bread. Child looks at her and says, "*Mommy bread.*"
b. Adult says to a child (Kathryn), "Throw me the ball." Child answers, as she prepares to throw the ball, "*Kathryn ball.*"
c. Mother is putting child's book away on the shelf. Child says, "*Mommy book.*"

Notice how important the context is in interpreting the child's meaning in the agent + object examples. Without taking the situation into account, one could easily misinterpret these as association (or possession) expressions.

Locational expressions play an important role in the child's Stage 1 utterances and they are closely related to action. The child expresses locations of actions, objects, and agents, in situations where change of movement is involved and also in situations where location is static, for example,

a. Child is carrying her doll to the doll bed. Child says, *"Doll bed."*
b. Child's doll is in the doll bed. Mother asks, "Where's your doll?" Child answers, *"Doll bed."*
c. Child is putting different-shaped blocks in corresponding holes in a toy mailbox. Child says, *"Put box"* (meaning "I'm putting this in the box").

Later in Stage 1 the child uses nouns in some new relationships as well, for example, to name the one who receives something ("Ball Mommy", meaning "I'm giving the ball to Mommy") or to name the object used as an instrument ("Hit hammer," meaning "I'm hitting this with the hammer"). Many children in this stage begin to ask labeling and location questions, for example, "What dat?" and "Where X?"—which certainly makes sense, given the child's focus on existence and location expression in this period.

Remember that the speech of the child in the one-word stage names people and objects and actions and places and characteristics within various situations. The fact that the child during that period tends to verbalize the one word that is most informative in the situation suggests that she has a preliminary grasp of underlying sentence relations (such as agent-action-object). With the advent, and increase, of combinatory speech in Stage 1, we can be more confident in attributing to the child a grasp of these syntactic relations. In the one-word stage the child may say the single word "Mommy" in different situations, but in Stage 1 the child may say

Mommy throw ("Mommy throws the ball.")
Hit Mommy ("I hit Mommy.")
Mommy dress ("That's Mommy's dress.")
Mommy. (In answer to the question, "Who's that?")
Mommy kitchen. ("Mommy's in the kitchen.")
Book Mommy ("I give the book to Mommy.")

Not only is this verbal behavior more elaborated and more explicit than one-word speech; it also demonstrates regular order in the elements the child verbalizes. It is patterned and nonrandom. Such verbal behavior clearly demonstrates developing syntax in the child. Indeed, researchers call Stage 1 speech "the beginning of syntax." But as with so many aspects of the continuous development of language, how can you tell when syntax "begins"? I wonder.

In Chapter 7 we'll focus on the cognitive base of the child's early combinatory speech, but think about it for a minute. The Stage 1 child has been described as one who talks of objects and people, of their existence, nonexistence, and recurrence; she talks of properties of objects and she associates particular objects with particular individuals; she talks of actions, of the people who perform them, and of the objects they act upon; and she talks of locations—of people, of things, of actions. Is this the talk you would expect of this young child? Does this talk express the kind of understanding of the world that you would expect the young child to have built out of her experience? Why (not)? Notice what is absent from the child's expression: We have not found expression of time relations ("then," "before," "since," "after," "while") or of cause ("why," "so," "if," "because") or of amount ("lots," "few," "three"). Does this surprise you? Why (not)?

One cannot help but be impressed by the evidence of pattern in this early period in the child's language development. The child's language is clearly rule governed and creative. The child seems to be, not imitating others' comments, but expressing her own meanings creatively, within the set of structural possibilities her system allows. That is exactly what we do as adults, of course, only we create within a different system of structural possibilities for relating sounds and meanings.

Stage 2.   Brown defines Stage 2 as centering on an MLU of 2.25 and including the span of 2.0 to 2.5. What accounts for the increase in the MLU? What expressive devices are children now using that make their sentences longer? We can identify three that are important here: (1) the emergence of grammatical morphemes included in the child's speech, (2) the stringing together of two-term relations, and (3) the expansion of a term in a relation.

I mentioned in the brief discussion of episodes 4 and 5 the grammatical morphemes that begin to be in evidence as the child's MLU exceeds 2.0—Brown's "ivy" that creeps in and around the heavy content items that are the building materials of Stage 1 speech. Brown and his colleagues have studied the emergence and development of fourteen grammatical morphemes, including present progressive ("-ing"), the prepositions "in" and "on," plural, regular and irregular past tense, regular and irregular third person singular forms (he or she goes, skips, rises, says, does), possessives, articles, auxiliary *be* (*is* going), and *be* as a main verb (Brown 1973).

It is important to recognize that though many of these grammatical morphemes first appear in Stage 2, they do not suddenly occur in all contexts where the adult would use them. It may be many months between the child's first use of the preposition "in" to express containment ("put in," "in box") and use of this preposition for all containment situations where the adult grammar would require "in." Sometimes it is as if a rule which is obligatory for the adult is optional for the child. The "as if" here is a deliberate hedge in that we cannot know just what rules the child operates with. We do know, however, that alternative forms (constructions expressing containment with and without the use of "in") do occur and seem to live quite happily side by side in children's language for a period of time (the period of time differing from morpheme to morpheme and from child to child). More or less gradually the child's use of the particular grammatical morpheme comes to resemble the adult's use, reflecting a progressive modification of the child's underlying rule system toward that of the adult.

A second factor accounting for increased length of the utterances in Stage 2 is the stringing together ("concatenation") of constructions which would earlier have stood as complete utterances for the child. Taking an example from our earlier episodes, we find in episode 5 "Put the cabbage here," an action + object + location construction. At an earlier point, two terms of this construction would have been typical: action + object (put cabbage), entity + location (cabbage here), or action + location (put here). Here is another example from episode 4: "I draw the puppy," a three-term construction (agent + action + object) composed of two-term relations familiar from Stage 1: "I draw" (agent + action), "draw puppy" (action + object), or even "I puppy" (agent + object).

It is hard not to ask *why*. If the child can express a set of two-term relations at a given point in her development, why can't she express those very same relations in a string? Why only one by one? Is this the result of some sort of memory constraint or of some processing limitation? Again, we don't know for sure. However, the movement toward increased combinatory capacity is a developmental phenomenon that occurs quite predictably in children's acquisition of language.

The following two examples from episodes 4 and 5 demonstrate a third major factor accounting for the increase in MLU in Stage 2.

I draw the puppy's nose.
I like more fish.

Here we again have concatenation in that the child has strung together

agent	+	*action*	+	*object*
I		draw		the puppy's nose
		like		more fish

But in addition to concatenation, we find that within one term of this relationship, the object, the child has produced an expanded construction. Note that the expansions clearly grow from Stage 1; the expressions "more fish" and "puppy nose" would be no surprise in Stage 1. What is new is their incorporation within a major term. A hierarchical structure is evident here in that a major component (the object) has subcomponents.

The continuity of the child's growth through Stage 1 and into Stage 2 is impressive. We see clearly in the speech of the Stage 2 child that she has incorporated, refined, elaborated, and expanded the meanings and expressive devices available to her in Stage 1. The child does not leap from one stage to the next; rather, she grows steadily in language, at every point building on what has preceded. Thus, familiar meanings find more explicit expression (possessive inflection, use of "a," "the"), new expressions suggest that earlier meanings have become more refined (verb + -ing), earlier structures are combined (agent + action + object) and elaborated (object that is a phrase), but the seed from which these developments have grown is clear.

LATER COMBINATORY SPEECH

Major Developments

Already at Stage 2, it begins to be difficult to stay with a stage-by-stage description of the child's developing language. We have said that grammatical morphemes begin to appear in Stage 2. However, the child's adultlike mastery of them typically develops steadily over several years after their first appearance. When we move beyond Stage 2, this continuousness in the development of complex aspects of language is even more striking, especially in three areas: the development of negatives, interrogatives (questions), and sentence combining.

Development of Negatives

What do we mean when we use negatives, when we say no? Clearly, we mean different things:

Yes, we have no bananas.
No, I don't want that.
That is not true.

At the very least, our meanings for negatives include nonexistence, rejection, and denial, as in the preceding sentences. The semantics of negation include these meanings for at least some children in the one-word stage, that stage the following examples come from. (Remember that the one-word stage includes some multiword utterances, but the child's MLU is less than 1.5.)

NONEXISTENCE

No more cleaner (said when the cleaner was gone).
No more juice (said when the juice was gone).
No pocket (said on finding her mother's skirt lacked a pocket).

REJECTION

No (said while pushing object away).
No dirty soap (said while pushing worn sliver of soap away in bathtub). (Bloom 1970, pp. 172-73)

DENIAL

No dirty (said with reference to a clean sock the mother had just said was dirty). (Bloom 1970, p. 149)

What about the syntactic devices that develop to express the child's meanings of no? Klima and Bellugi-Klima (1971) have sketched a developmental sequence for negation. They identify a first period during which the main device for expressing negation is to affix a "no" to the beginning of a sentence as in

No money.   No singing song.
No sit there.   No play that.

This device is used for various meanings of "no," as in the following examples of rejection and denial:

ADULT: Get in your high chair with your bib, and I'll give you your cheese.
CHILD: No bibby.
ADULT: Oh, you don't want your bibby?

ADULT: Well, is the sun shining?
CHILD: No the sun shining.
ADULT: Oh, the sun's not shining? (Klima and Bellugi-Klima 1971, p. 418)

Later the child begins to insert the negative element within the sentence, and the set of negative words expands to include "don't" and "can't" as single, inseparable units in addition to the earlier "no" and "not."

That no fish school.   I can't see you.
There no squirrels.   You can't dance.
He no bite you.   I don't want it.
I no want envelope.   I don't know his name.
That not 'O,' that blue.   (Klima and Bellugi-Klima 1971, p. 418)

Still later, elements like "can't" and "don't" separate for the child; that is, she uses "do" and "can" alone in interrogative structures, and therefore we assume that she has now analyzed "can't" and "don't" as the morpheme and combinations "can" + "not", "do" + "not."

Later still, we observe "negation spread," as in these examples from a child with an MLU of 4.7:

I'm not scared of nothing.
Little puppies can't bite no one, right?
Don't never leave your chair.
He can't have nothing.
I never have none. (Bellugi 1971, p. 105)

And, finally, the special set of indeterminates that adults use in negative sentences ("anything," "anyone," "any") find their way into the child's system.

This syntactic development occurs over a period of several years and, as you might expect, the changes are gradual. In time, certain forms come to prevail over others, but various negative forms will exist side by side in the child's emerging system at any particular time.

Development of Interrogatives

Questions are generally requests for information.[14] There are three main interrogative structure types in English for asking questions. Here are a few examples of each type:

YES/NO

Have you seen him recently?
Can you come tomorrow?
Are you coming down with the flu?
Did you get your A in statistics?

INFORMATION

What are you taking?
What are you doing?
When are you going?
Why are you going?
Where are you going?
How are you getting there?
Whose is it?
Who won?
What fell?

POLAR

Did you talk to Mark or Jim?
Did Mary or Jim answer?
Did you talk to Mary yesterday or the day before?
Did you talk to Mark about that, or did you decide to just skip it?

As the name implies, yes/no questions are used by adults to elicit from the listener either agreement or disagreement with the proposition in the question. Such questions generally involve a reversal of the subject and the first part of the verbal element from standard sentence word order. This reversal is sometimes called the "flip-flop transformation." *"You have* seen him recently" becomes *"Have you* seen him recently?" *"You can* come . . ."* becomes *"Can you* come . . . ."* Questions including some form of "do" can be described in reversal terms, also, even though the related simple

---

[14]We frequently use interrogative structures for purposes other than to gain information. For example, "Can you reach my pencil?" or "Could you hand me that?" are not requests for information; yes or no would be inappropriate responses. They are requests for action. When teachers ask questions like "What is the capital of Montana?" they are not seeking the information the question implies, but ascertaining whether the student knows what the capital of Montana is. "Tag questions" like "It's hot, isn't it?" or "You like that, don't you?" do not really seek information but mainly serve to engage one in conversation. (The form/function distinction will be elaborated in Section Four.)

declarative sentence "You got your A in statistics" does not include the "do" element in its surface structure. It is as if the "do" element is inserted and then reversed (*"You did* get your A . . . ." *"Did you* get your A . . .?"). Sometimes we ask yes/no questions without this syntactic reversal, conveying by intonation alone that we have asked a yes/no question: "You've seen him recently?" "You can come tomorrow?"

Information questions generally seek fill-in-the-blank information:

You are taking (*something*).
You are doing (*something*).
You are going (*some time*).
You are going (*for some reason*).
You are going (*some place*).
You are getting there (*some way*).
It is (*someone's*).
(*Someone*) won.
(*Something*) fell.

The first seven sentences in the preceding list can be viewed as undergoing three changes to become the related information questions: (1) The appropriate question word is selected to fill in the blank (what, where, whose); (2) that word is moved to the beginning of the sentence; and (3) the subject and first verbal element are reversed, just as they were for yes/no questions, resulting in sentences like "What *are you* doing?" (rather than "What you are doing?"). There are, of course, many more kinds of information questions than are given in the set of examples (how much or how many, what kind, how big, which, which one), but the structural principles for them are all similar. A few questions, like the last two in the list, require only the substitution of the appropriate question word for the blank:

(Someone) won.	Who won?
(Something) fell.	What fell?

Polar questions are choice questions. The speaker provides several choices and assumes the listener will select the accurate one. We use polar questions when we think the answer is one of several possibilities, and we're just not certain which one. Notice that the choice, _____ or _____, can involve any basic portion of the sentence—subject, verb, object, location, time, or entire clause.

Children must learn which utterances are questions, what questions mean, and how to express them. And, as with negation, their development of interrogatives changes over a period of several years.

Young children seem to be in a good environment for learning about questions, since a high proportion of the speech of many mothers to their young children is in the form of questions. In fact, it is not surprising to find in the literature reports of observations of mother-child pairs in which 50 percent of the mother's utterances to her child are questions (Savić 1975).

Ervin-Tripp has suggested that children recognize questions early and respond to them differently than to other sentence types: "The age for studying the initial discrimination of questions must be from the very onset of speech, at least well before 1:9, when we find such discrimination already well established in our youngest subject" (Ervin-Tripp 1970, p. 81). Indeed, by 1:9, children typically ask a variety of questions themselves. It is interesting that young children will respond to a question by providing information—that is, they will respond to a question as if it *is* a question, even though they will sometimes provide the wrong type of information, the kind of information required by a different question type. The child in the following example seems to be answering the adult's attribute questions ("What color," "What kind") as if they are identification questions ("What is X?").

M: What color is he? (referring to child's stuffed rabbit)
C: It's a bunny.

M: What kind of house did the little pig build?
C: A house.

And these next two examples come from Ervin-Tripp (1970).

ADULT: Who's watching Daddy?
CHILD: Shaving.

ADULT: Who's eating?
CHILD: Meat.

Here the child apparently interprets the first question as a question about the father's action and the second as a question about what is being eaten. Clearly, children comprehend certain types of questions earlier than others. Though they may know that an utterance is a question and seeks information, they may not recognize what kind of information the particular question seeks. Then they may respond by giving information that would be required by a type of question already in their repertoire.

Not surprisingly, the child generally comprehends a given question type before she produces it. However, comprehension and production sequences seem to be similar; those questions understood earlier are those produced earlier, and those understood later are produced later, with the production lagging some months behind the comprehension.

The work of different researchers who have studied children's acquisition of the semantics of questioning is not exactly comparable, as different researchers have studied slightly different sets of questions and they have studied them in somewhat different ways (Brown 1968; Ingram 1970; Ervin-Tripp 1970; Savić 1975; Tyack and Ingram 1977; Cairns and Hsu 1978). However, there is general agreement about some important question types. "What" (direct object), "where," and "yes/no" questions are among the earliest comprehended and produced, with "why," "how," and especially "when" questions coming much later, and "who," "whose," and "what-do" questions generally falling somewhere in between.[15]

When you think back to the child's Stage 1 meanings and relations, this general acquisition sequence for the semantics of questions is not surprising. "What" and "where" questions focus on naming and on location. Remember that naming objects and expressing location of actions and entities are an important part of Stage 1 language. The intermediate questions, "who," "whose," and "what-do," relate to the child's early meanings also. "Who" asks about agents (or objects), "whose" about possession, and "what-do" about action. These meanings, too, are basic to the child's early expression. But the meanings required by "why" (causal relations), "how" (means or instrumentation of action), and "when" (time concepts) occur later in children's understanding and in their verbal expression.

Klima and Bellugi-Klima (1971) have studied children's acquisition of the syntactic structures of questioning. They find children to go through a predictable sequence that spans several years. They have examined the syntax of questioning in children at three periods, roughly corresponding to Brown's Stages 1, 3, and 5. Here are some examples of yes/no and information questions of children in the three periods they studied (Klima and Bellugi-Klima 1971, pp. 421-23).

	YES/NO QUESTIONS	INFORMATION QUESTIONS
Period 1 (around Stage 1)	Mommy eggnog?	What(s) that?
	I ride train?	What cowboy doing?
	Sit chair?	Where kitty?
	Ball go?	Where horse go?

In this period the child expresses yes/no questions by speaking a sentence with rising intonation. Without that intonation contour, each of the preceding examples would be a simple statement for the child. (Note the familiar Stage 1 meanings and relations in these questions.) Information questions at this point include only "what" and "where" types and are of the form "what X," "what X doing," "where X," and "where X go."

	YES/NO QUESTIONS	INFORMATION QUESTIONS
Period 2 (around Stage 3)	See my doggie?	Where baby Sarah rattle?
	Mom pinch finger?	What me think?
	You can't fix it?	What the dollie have?

---

[15]"What" direct object questions are questions about the direct object portion of the sentence. "What did he eat?" Answer: "A steak." Not all questions with "what" ask about the direct object (*"What* broke?" or *"What* kind of ice cream do you want?" or *"What* one do you like best?"). "What-do" questions ask about the entire verb phase (predicate) of a sentence, as in "What did he do?" Answer: "Ate a steak."

	YES/NO QUESTIONS	INFORMATION QUESTIONS
	This can't write a flower?	Why you waking me up? Why not . . . me can't dance?

In Period 2, though the sentence + rising intonation is still the main device for asking yes/no questions, modals like "can't" and "don't" are in evidence along with the heavy content words. Information questions have expanded to include additional types ("why," "why not"), and the question word often precedes a full-blown sentence (for example, "Why" + "You waking me up").

	YES/NO QUESTIONS	INFORMATION QUESTIONS
Period 3 (around Stage 5)	Does the kitty stand up? Is Mommy talking to Robin's grandmother? Did I saw that in my book? Oh, did I caught it? Will you help me? Can't it be a bigger truck?	Where I should put it when I make it up? What I did yesterday? What he can ride in? Why kitty can't stand up? Which way they should go? How he can be a doctor?

Period 3 is particularly interesting. In yes/no questions the child's use of auxiliary elements has expanded considerably (note "does," "did," and "will" in the examples). Especially noteworthy is the child's reversal of subject and first verbal element—the "flip-flop"—in yes/no questions. But notice that this reversal is not present in the child's information questions. (C-5 is a good example of a child in Period 3.) This is puzzling. Why would this flip-flop occur regularly in the one question type (yes/no), and just as regularly not occur in the other (information)? Obviously, the information questions are more difficult in that they require (for adults) other adjustments in addition to the reversal. They also require the selection of an interrogative word and its placement at the beginning of the sentence. But if the different situation for the two question types were merely a matter of how many adjustments must be made, then we would expect that, with information questions, sometimes the child would make one adjustment, and sometimes another; sometimes she would say, "What you are doing?" (placement of question word at beginning, but no reversal), and other times, "Are you doing what?" (reversal, but no placement of question word at the beginning). But this is not what happens. Children have not been observed to use questions of the latter type ("Are you doing what?"), but quite predictably ask questions of the former type ("What you are doing?"). We don't know *why* it happens this way; we know only *that* it happens this way, the question word apparently being more salient to the child than the reversal is.

Development of Sentence Combining

Another important aspect of children's language development that spans a period of several years is the combining of several propositions into a single sentence.[16] As adults we accomplish this combining in a variety of ways. Consider a few ways we can combine propositions:[17]

a. This is the house and Jack built it. (Two clauses or propositions of equal status are combined.)

b. This is the house that Jack built.
    This (thing) that Jack built is the house. (One proposition is given prominence and the other elaborates a noun in that proposition.)

c. When Jack built the house, rats were all about.
    Rats were all about when Jack built the house.

    Before Jack built the house, he was troubled by rats.
    Jack was troubled by rats before he built the house.

    After Jack built the house, the rats ate the malt.
    The rats ate the malt after Jack built the house.

    (Two propositions of unequal status are combined in a time relationship.)

d. Jack killed the rats because they ate the malt.
    Because the rats ate the malt, Jack killed them.

    If the rats get in the house, they will eat the malt.
    The rats will eat the malt if they get in the house.

    (Two propositions of unequal status are combined in a cause-result relationship.)

e. Jack's building the house surprised me. (From "*Something* surprised me.")
    Jack likes to build houses. (From "Jack likes *something*.")
    You know that Jack built the house. (From "You know *something*.")
    (One proposition "fills in the blank" in another.)

Acquiring the capacity to combine propositions in these various ways would seem to be a very complicated business, but the first few conversational turns of C-7, in our earlier example, show that this four-year-old is using many of these proposition-combining devices, often in combination with each other.

M: What did you do at school today?
C: 1. Working—just was working. 2. Teacher has a magnet game. 3. Some things are magnet and some things are not. 4. The ones that are sticky stick and the ones that are not sticky don't stick.
M: Did you play on the jungle gym today?

[16] I have relied heavily in this section on Clark and Clark's (1977) very clear and informative discussion of work in this area. You may want to read their discussion after you have read Chapter 7 of this text.

[17] Remember, a good way to find the propositions within a sentence is to find the verbs. Each one will generally be the nucleus of a proposition.

C: 5. No. I'm a watcher.
M: What's a watcher?
C: 6. I watch everybody fall off and if they do, I go and get the teacher.
M: Did you have a nice ride on the school bus?
C: 7. Yes. 8. Do you know what Mr. B——(the bus driver) says?
M: No, what?
C: 9. "Shut up, R——," and he turns the radio up real loud.

In sentences 3, 4, 6 (twice), and 9, the child combines propositions with "and," giving them equal status (as in example a from the preceding list). In sentence 4, one proposition elaborates a noun in the other (as in examples b): "ones that are sticky," "ones that are not sticky." In sentence 6, he combines propositions in a cause-result relation (as in examples d): "if they do, I go." And in sentences 6 and 8, he combines propositions by making one "fill in the blank" in the other (as in examples e): "I watch *something*→ I watch *everybody fall off*"; "You know *something*→ You know *what Mr. B—— says*."

 Some research suggests an earlier preference for combining propositions in an equal way (as in example a), rather than in ways that give one prominence over the other. Slobin and Welsh (1973) gave a two-year-old called Echo sentences to repeat after a model. Some of them included unequal clauses. "Repeating" these after the model, Echo restructured them either by repeating only the main clause, as in

MODEL: Mozart (name of child's bear) who cried came to my party.
REPETITION: Mozart came to my party. (p. 487)

or else by joining them as two equal clauses:

MODEL: Mozart who cried came to my party.
REPETITION: Mozart cried and he came to my party. (p. 493)

MODEL: The owl who eats candy runs fast.
REPETITION: Owl eat a candy and he run fast. (p. 494)

MODEL: The man who I saw yesterday got wet.
REPETITION: I saw the man and he got wet. (p. 494)

In their spontaneous, nonelicited speech, young children first combine propositions as equal clauses, typically using "and" or "and then." Later they begin to combine propositions of unequal status, using adverbials like "before," "after," and "because."

 In addition, children's acquisition of complex structures shows an earlier preference for keeping clauses intact and not interrupting them by inserting other clauses. Sentences of the type

 This is the house *that Jack built.* (uninterrupted main clause)

would typically precede sentences of the type

This (thing) *that Jack built* is the house. (interrupted main clause)

We would assume that C-7 was using structures like

I have the ones *that are sticky*. (uninterrupted main clause)

before structures like

The ones *that are sticky* stick. (interrupted main clause)

C-7's "I watch everybody fall off" and "Do you know what Mr. B———says?" are further examples of uninterrupted clauses in combination.

Eve Clark has noted another developmental trend in the acquisition of sentence combining. When two events are mentioned in a sentence, young children assume that the one mentioned first occurred earlier in time than the event mentioned second. Given sentences to act out with toy objects, for example,

> The boy patted the dog before he kicked the rock.
> After the boy patted the dog, he kicked the rock.
>
> Before the boy kicked the rock, he patted the dog.
> The boy kicked the rock after he patted the dog. (Clark and Clark 1977, p. 359)

younger children will make the boy pat the dog and then kick the rock for the first pair but will make the boy kick the rock and then pat the dog for the second pair. A reasonable assumption is that children's earlier productions of complex sentences relating events in time will reflect this comprehension pattern, that is, that their earlier sentences with time adverbials will mention events in the order of their occurrence. The comprehension-precedes-production assumption is not foolproof by any means, but it usually works.[18] Clark and Clark (1977) found the children's earliest adverbials to be "when," "if," and " 'cos" (because), and later to include "before," "till" (until), and "after" (p. 358).

Limber has studied the development of combining devices like those in examples e earlier (called complements) in which a clause fills the "something" blank. Studying children from two to three years of age, he identified an early set of verbs children were using, including a "want" group ("want," "need," "like") and a "watch" group ("watch," "lookit," "see"), as in

> I don't want you read this book. (I don't want *something*.)
> Watch me draw circles. (Watch *something*.)
> I see you sit down. (I see *something*.)
> Lookit a boy play ball. (Lookit *something*.) (Limber 1973, p. 177)

[18]For an interesting discussion of production preceding comprehension see Berko Gleason and Weintraub's (1976) paper on the "trick or treat" routine.

At an earlier stage these verbs typically occur in the child's speech followed by simple nouns—"want that," "see Mommy." Limber suggests that the step from verb + noun ("want + juice" or "watch + me") to verb + clause ("want + you fix it" or "watch + me do it") is a small one, often occurring within a month after the child's first use of the particular verb in any construction (p. 175). (Recall C-6's "I want you put this on.") As Limber's subjects approached three, their repertoire of verbs taking complements ("something" -blank fillers) expanded to include a variety, for example, "think," "said," "remember," "wonder," "wish," and "pretend" (p. 176).

In summary, a child's development of sentence-combining devices shows movement along several dimensions: (1) from a stringing together of equal clauses toward a joining of clauses of unequal status, (2) from uninterrupted main clauses toward use of interrupted ones (insertion of subordinate clauses within main clauses), (3) from order of mention coinciding with order of occurrence toward variable order of clauses, and (4) from use of small semantic-syntactic sets (of adverbials, of complement verbs) toward more expanded sets.

But now let's get back to real children and their talk. The following is a "simple" conversation between two four-year-olds as they are playing. They use a variety of negatives, interrogatives, and combined sentences. See which ones you can identify and describe. (C-1 and C-2 here are not the children of episodes 1 and 2.)

C-1:   What's that gonna be?
C-2:   That's the thing that keeps the door closed.
C-1:   And what this gun' be?
C-2:   That's the (inaudible).
C-1:   (They begin to play house.) Now, Mommy! I don't want to.
C-2:   Well, you have to.
C-1:   I don't want to go to sleep. OK?
C-2:   You have to.
C-1:   What?
C-2:   You have to.
C-1:   Well, I'm gonna play this game all night.
C-2:   You better not 'cuz I'll spank you.
C-2:   (Sneezes.)
C-1:   Bless you, Mommy! (Both laugh.)
C-1:   Now, Mommy.
C-2:   What?
C-1:   I'm doing all this all night, so spank me.
C-2:   (Spanks her.)
C-1:   What you going to do now?
C-2:   Put you to sleep. Now, go to bed.
C-1:   (Makes loud noise.) Mommy?
C-2:   What?
C-1:   I'm not going to . . . go to sleep. I'm going to pop you in the tummy.
C-2:   I'll *punch* you in the tummy. (Both laugh.)

C-1: Now, I'm not going to put my pants on under my 'jamas, OK? Mommy. (calling) It's morning time. I didn't go to sleep. What's gonna happen now?
C-2: You're gonna have to go to sleep.
C-1: In the daytime?
C-2: Yeah. Take a nap.
C-1: I'm not going to.

C-1: Look out the window. Oh! Hey Mommy! A ghost outside! OK, Mommy? OK, Mommy? (Meaning, "Do you agree to pretend there's a ghost outside?")
C-2: OK.
C-1: There's a ghost outside. Look out the winda. See a ghost?
C-2: Yes.
C-1: What we should do?
C-2: We should move. To another house.
C-1: OK. We're moved. We moved to another house.
C-2: OK. Now we put all our stuff in. Oh, yeah.
C-1: Mother?
C-2: The ghost . . .
C-1: I think I hear a giant!
C-2: Giant? There's no giant at night.
C-1: Why?
C-2: There's no giants at morning.
C-1: Uh-huh. (Yes.)
C-2: No, there isn't.
C-1: You see one?
C-2: No, I don't.
C-1: Well, I do.
C-2: I don't see one.
C-1: I do.
C-2: I don't.
C-1: I do.
C-2: I do not.
C-1: I do.
C-2: Now, be quiet.
C-1: I'm watching the news.
C-2: No, you aren't.
C-1: Uh-huh! Uh-huh!
C-2: You aren't.
C-1: Uh-huh! Now you be quiet.
C-2: You be quiet.
C-1: You be quiet.
C-2: You be quiet.
C-1: *You be quiet!* (Screams it.)
C-2: You be quiet!

C-1: I think I'm gonna die.
C-2: No, you're not.

C-1:   Yes, I am.
C-2:   No, you won't.
C-1:   I need a nurse.
C-2:   No.
C-1:   Yeah!
C-2:   No.

C-2:   Well, better be quiet.
C-1:   Why?
C-2:   'Cuz there's a monster coming!
C-1:   OK. (whispering) I see a monster! What we should do?
C-2:   He's coming in the door—now he's in the house—wait—hide—hide.[19]

The Development of Sound System

We have said very little so far about children's acquisition of the sound system of their language. We know that children move from making sounds to making sense. But there is some debate as to whether earlier sound making is continuous or discontinuous with the "true speech" that begins at around one year of age, when children begin using identifiable words and sound strings that make sense.

There is some agreement that two distinct sound-making periods can be identified during the first year, a vocalization, or prebabbling, period and a babbling period. During the first, which lasts roughly for the first six months, children vocalize in a random way. Their vocalizations include a wide range of sounds and do not demonstrate a pattern or control.

This is what the child produces. But there is evidence that the child is making some important perceptual sound distinctions during this period also. For example, she discriminates between the sound of the human voice and other sounds, between angry and friendly verbal expression, between male and female voices, between various intonation and rhythm features, and between certain speech segments (Clark and Clark 1977, p. 377). And you remember that one-month-old infants discriminate between /pa/ and /ba/, a very subtle distinction (Eimas et al. 1971).

During the second six months, the babbling period, the vocalizations are different. The sound productions exhibit greater pattern and articulatory control as children verbalize strings of repeated consonant + vowel syllables. Their cries are more differentiated for surprise, hunger, and discomfort. They babble with more melody—the suprasegmental features of their language (intonation, stress, rhythm) are more in evidence. Some of the sounds that were present in their vocalizations in the prebabbling period are now gone.

As the child moves into "wordness," or true speech, there is a corresponding decrease in her babbling. Her first words may differ markedly from adult pronunciations, though they are likely to be simplifications of the adult pronunciations involving the omission of final consonants (/b/ + vowel for "ball"), the reduction of consonant clusters (/tik/for "stick"), the

---

[19]I am indebted to Genevieve Kerr for this example from her data.

omission of unstressed syllables, or the reduplication of syllables (Clark and Clark 1977, p. 397). At first, the child may have variable pronunciations for the same word, but gradually the form stabilizes. In fact, it is the child's use of a "phonetically constant form" (stable pronunciation) in particular situations that enables us to say that the child has "a word"—an identifiable verbal expression for an identifiable meaning. A similar general sequence in the acquisition of basic sounds is evident in many children, with each sound generally being produced at the beginning of words before it is produced in the middle or at the end of words, with /l/ and /r/ usually being among the last basic sounds acquired, and with consonant clusters (for example, /pr/, /kl/, /str/) being acquired after single consonants.

The child must learn to perceive the significant sound features of her language and she must also learn to produce them in her own speech. Examples like the following are common:

> Recently a three year old child told me her name was Litha. I answered "Litha?" "No, *Litha*." "Oh, Lisa." "Yes, Litha." (Slobin 1971, p. 65, quoting G. A. Miller)

> One of us . . . spoke to a child who called his inflated plastic fish a *fis*. In imitation of the child's pronunciation, the observer said: "That is your *fis*?" "No," said the child, "my *fis*." He continued to reject the adult's imitation until he was told, "That is your fish." "Yes," he said, "my *fis*." (Berko and Brown 1960, p. 531)

Such examples suggest that children perceive distinctions which they do not produce in their speech. Clark and Clark posit this as evidence that young children store in their minds "adult-based representations" of words, rather than representations based on their own pronunciations. They find further evidence for children's adult-based representations in the fact that (1) they identify meanings based on their perception of the sounds of the words they hear, (2) they change their pronunciation over time toward the adult pronunciation, and (3) when they begin to produce a given sound segment (such as /s/), it spreads to other words in their repertoire where it does belong, but not to words where it doesn't belong, according to the adult pronunciations.

In the development of the sound component of language, the actual practice of particular sounds and sound combinations seems to be as important as mental representations of sounds in guiding children toward adultlike pronunciations. Overt practice assumes greater importance in this area of acquisition than in the area of semantics or syntax. Articulatory skill becomes more controlled and refined with use. The development of this component is heavily physical, and as in the development of other physical abilities (standing on your head, swimming), practice helps to bring the skill under control.

It seems that early vocalizing is and is not continuous with later true speech: There is continuousness in the child's development of suprasegmentals (intonation, rhythm, stress), in her steadily increasing articulatory control, and in her mental representations of words; however, there appears to be discontinuity in the child's development of a particular set of sounds from early vocalizing to the use of these sounds in the child's first words.

THE SCHOOL YEARS

We expect that at around age five our children come to kindergarten. What sort of language users are these children? What sort of expectations might the kindergarten or first-grade teacher reasonably hold regarding her children's facility with language? One hopes she'll remember an important fact about language: Language development and use are unique and universal. She will expect, and welcome, the uniqueness of each child's language. She will recognize that each child has fashioned her language system out of a particular set of experiences in her own home and community, for particular purposes, and with particular individuals; that each child has her own range of language styles, her own ways of expressing meaning in different situations; that each child has her own personality characteristics which play themselves out in the child's ways of using language. One child's orientation is more impulsive and another's more reflective and cautious; one child inclines more toward overt expression (an abundance of talk), another toward observation, quietly building relationships in her own thinking; one child's approach toward life is more playful, another's approach is more pragmatic—and their ways of using language bear their playful or pragmatic stamp; one child is more social, using language mainly as a way of relating to others, another is more analytic, perhaps using language mainly as a way of learning about her physical environment. In short, each child's language will reflect her own individuality.

Yet the teacher will also reasonably expect some commonalities. She will expect that most of her children will have a well-developed system for relating many meanings to their verbal expression. This means, of course, that each child has a hefty vocabulary, a range of words she understands and uses, though different semantic domains will be more fully elaborated for different children, again reflecting their different backgrounds. Each child will come with a well-developed sense of syntax, a sense of the functions of different words in sentences and relations among them (such as agent or attribute or action). The teacher can expect her children to interpret and produce sentences of various types (for example, question forms, negative statements, affirmative statements, commands) and, further, to control a variety of forms within each type (for example, statements that identify what something is or that express a characteristic of something or that answer a specific question). Her children will probably be able to express their ideas in more than one way (though possibly not in response to a specific direction to do so).

In addition to having well-developed semantic and syntactic systems, her children will have phonological systems that are close to the adult's. She will probably find some developmental pronunciations among her kindergarteners (cwackers, twuck), just as she will find developmental word forms (runned, brang). But the teacher would reasonably assume that the children will be able to understand most of her pronunciation of words, and she will be able to understand most of theirs. Some of her children may speak dialects that are unfamiliar to her, but in time her "ears" will increasingly tune in to the children's expression.

Increasingly, recent research on children's early awareness of written language tells us that young children who grow up in a literate environment are aware of what written language looks like, that print is an expression of meaning, that it relates to the context in which it occurs, and that it is used for certain purposes (and also what some of those purposes are). Specifically, it would be reasonable for the kindergarten teacher to expect that many of her children will recognize "drawing" and "writing" as looking different (and in fact some of them will produce different graphic displays when asked to "draw" or to "write," though their "writing" might not include conventional letter shapes). Although she would not expect her children to be able to read a sign placed near the class plants ("Please water only once a day") she would not be surprised if her children recognized the sign as one that carried a message and probably a message relating to the plants. Some of her children will probably be aware of some of the different ways that written language is used, for example, signs that name ("Crest," "Maple Street") or that tell you what to do ("STOP"), letters, recipes, storybooks, newspapers, or birthday cards, though, again, the specific experiences children have had with uses of written language will differ.

The kindergarten teacher can expect that her children have the capacity to appreciate language play—play with sounds (rhythms, rhymes, alliteration) and meanings, though some will have had more experience of language play than others. This is to say that kindergarten children have a sense of language—its parts, its relations, how it works—so that they are able to recognize and appreciate language used in surprising and unusual ways. Finally, though much of the children's talk will be anchored in the situation of the moment, the teacher can expect that her children will, to some extent, be able to use language out of the immediate situation as well, for example, to talk about an experience they had yesterday or about plans for a coming birthday party.

You would think that equipped with such a richly developed language system, the kindergartener could get along just fine without developing any further. But of course, though language development during the elementary school years may be less dramatic than it is in the earlier years, it is no less vigorous or interesting. The very fact that the kindergartener's language is so well developed gives her so much to work with in developing language further. Language is perhaps the ultimate "gift that keeps on giving": The more one has, the greater one's potential for developing and using language in new ways. During the school years no less than before, the child develops and uses language uniquely and universally, her language marking her as part of the human community and, at the same time, marking her as a distinct individual within that community. Language development in the school years is especially evident in three areas: (1) language structure, the ongoing expansion and refinement of semantics and syntax (and to a lesser degree, phonology); (2) language use, the increasing ability to use language more effectively to serve a variety of functions in diverse communication situations; (3) metalinguistic awareness, the growing ability to consider and to talk about language as a formal code.

Language Structure

The child's semantic growth continues because her experience continues and expands, which means, of course, that school has a very special role to play. New experiences require growth in the child's semantic system in two ways. First, as she encounters new people, objects, properties, activities, information, and relationships, her language must expand to include ways of talking about them. But sometimes the new element in an experience is the act of considering a familiar experience at a conscious level. Experiences of anger, of numerousness, of weight, have been part of the child's life for a long time as she has felt frustration and she has manipulated objects in various quantities and of various weights. But considering anger as an entity—a particular type of feeling with identifiable behavioral signs, considering number as a property of collections of objects, considering weight as a characteristic of objects—these are new experiences in that they are new ways of looking at aspects of the world. "Angry," "seven," "two more," and "heavier" become part of the child's semantic system as these concepts become hers. Sometimes the new experience will involve considering specific entities as members of higher-order classes: for example, viewing oaks, maples, and birches as "deciduous"; porpoises, dogs, and cows as "mammals"; grandmother and grandfather as "senior citizens." Other times the new experience will involve further differentiation within a domain so that things that were "little" or "teeny" may be seen as—and called—"three centimeters" or "a half inch," and what was "big" might now be "wide" or "long" or "tall" or "fat," and "dogs" might now be "dalmations," "poodles," "golden retrievers," and "mutts." But the basic principle holds: As the child's experience expands, her semantic system expands also.

The child's expanding experience alters her semantic system in a second way. As she encounters categories that are in conflict with the system she has worked out, she is forced to revise her semantic system. Over-extensions continue to disappear as she modifies her system in light of new experiences. "Horse" serves well until she encounters mules and donkeys; "camel" is fine until she encounters a dromedary.

Children's syntactic growth continues during the elementary school years also. Consider the following selected excerpts from the talk of a six-year-old girl and an eleven-year-old girl as they create text for Mercer Mayer's wordless storybook *Bubble Bubble*.[20]

six-year-old	eleven-year-old

(Picture shows a boy walking by a fence.)

He's walking.	Once upon a time a boy was walking through a yard that's full of trash.

(Picture shows the boy standing beside a box by the fence and bubbles coming over the fence; next picture shows the boy standing on the box looking over the fence; next picture shows a man blowing bubbles and in front of him, a stand with the sign "Magic Bubble Maker" and "Only 25¢.")

He found a box. He stand on it and started over the gate. He saw a man with some bubbles.	Then all of a sudden he saw some bubbles coming from the fence. He wondered what the bubbles were. The boy saw the box and got onto the box and looked over the fence and he saw a whole bunch of bubbles coming over the fence and saw a man and the man was blowing all shapes of bubbles and the card said "Magic Bubble Maker," and so he wanted to blow bubbles just like the man did.

(Picture shows the boy buying a jar of bubble liquid; next picture shows the man walking off with his case under his arm and a sign that reads "Out to Lunch" protruding from the case, and the boy walking off in the opposite direction with his bubble jar.)

A man gave him the bubbles. And he went to blow some bubbles.	So he gave the man twenty-five cents and then the man left and went out to lunch. The boy took the can and walked away.

(Picture shows the boy sitting under a tree blowing bubbles.)

He bubbled under a tree.	He sat down by a tree and started making bubbles.

[20]I am grateful to Pauline Walker for the *Bubble Bubble* examples.

(Last three pictures show (1) boy dumping the bubble liquid onto the ground; (2) boy tossing empty bubble container in a can marked "Trash"; (3) ambiguous elongated bubble creature that has risen from the puddle of bubble liquid; the creature looks toward the boy, who is walking away.)

He poured all the water out and throwed it in the trash and then he saw a bubble. A snake was melting and he walked away.	So he poured out all of his bubbles and threw it all in the trash can and all was left was the snake and he went happily home. The end.

Clearly these story tellings are different in many interesting ways. Some of them have to do with syntax. The younger child tends to use sentences with only a single proposition. When she does use combination sentences, her usual way of combining is with "and (then)." The older child combines more often and more diversely. (In the examples that follow, verbs are italicized to help you pick out the propositions being combined into longer sentences.)

. . . a boy *was walking* through a yard that's full of trash.
. . . he *saw* some bubbles *coming* from the fence . . .
He *wondered* what the bubbles *were* . . .
. . . he *saw* . . . bubbles *coming* over the fence . . .
. . . and so he *wanted* to *blow* bubbles just like the man *did*.

Notice, too, the presence of developmental word forms in the younger child's text and their absence from the older child's text, despite the greater length of the second text.

Language Use

I have imposed the distinction between development of language structure and development of language use or function so that we can study language growth in manageable chunks. However, the distinction has no basis in the reality of language acquisition. Children do not learn the structure of language and then learn how to use language to serve their communication purposes. Rather, they learn language always within the context of real communication, by using particular language structures in particular ways to serve particular purposes, and by listening to and interacting with others who do the same.

Children have to build up structure and function at the same time. As they learn more about structure, they acquire more devices with which to convey different functions. And as they learn more about functions, they extend the uses to which different structures can be put. (Clark and Clark 1977, p. 373)

Like the objects they manipulate, language *is* what language *does* for young children. And for older, school-age children, language is also very much a matter of doing: persuading, informing, entertaining, seeking information. This functional aspect of language is so important that it is discussed more fully in its own section of this text (Section Four). But a few words are in order here.

The school-age child's social world is bigger and more diverse than that of the preschool child. The six- to twelve-year-old interacts with a variety of people for a variety of purposes. She interacts with an expanded group of peers, with people older and younger than herself, with familiar people, with strangers, with people of higher and lower status than hers, with individuals, with groups. She interacts with others in a wider range of settings—in classrooms, on playgrounds, in libraries, in other children's homes and neighborhoods. In this bigger social world, her language must serve some new functions and must more effectively serve some familiar ones. The child's wider world of interactants, of interaction situations, and of interaction purposes pushes her language to become more "widely adapted" (Brown 1973, p. 245), and thus a more effective and powerful communication tool.

One extension of language as a communication tool that gets particular attention in school is the development of literacy. This development is an important aspect of the child's increasing range of interaction situations and purposes. Written expression in language enables the child to interact with others across time and space; it also extends the child's ways of serving familiar communication purposes, for example, getting and giving information, requesting, persuading, entertaining, inviting, arguing. The child's increasing interaction with others through written expression is a further example of the child's language becoming more "widely adapted" in both structure and function.

The child's development of literacy supports the child's move inward as well as outward. Some uses of literacy support and extend the child's private purposes. Journal writing is a good example. Here, writing offers a way of getting one's own thought and feeling out into a form that one can reflect on and consider. Even writing which is social (intended for others to read) can serve this personal function of externalizing one's thought so that one becomes one's own reader and responder to one's own ideas. Literacy development, an important aspect of language development in the school years, contributes mightily to the ways children use language in communication with others and with themselves.

During the school years, children increasingly develop the ability to use language as an independent symbol system, to talk and write and read about situations outside of the immediate context. This aspect of development in language use is one which is typically fostered in our schools. We generally encourage children to move from more concrete uses of language (for example, to describe objects that are in view or to tell what they are doing as they do it) toward more abstract uses (for example, considering hypothetical situations: "Suppose you were a member of the First Continental Congress or the one in charge of the water control board of our city . . .").

Metalinguistic Awareness

Metalinguistic awareness has been defined as "the ability to make language forms opaque and attend to them in and for themselves" (Cazden 1974, p. 24). The adult in the following two examples is exploring the ability of children of different ages to "make language forms opaque." She is asking children to identify grammatical and ungrammatical sentences as "sounds OK to me" or "sounds not OK to me." The responses of the five- and six-years-olds in the first conversation are quite different from the responses of the eleven-year-old in the second conversation.

ADULT: "The children climbed up the jungle gym." Does that one sound OK or
        not OK to you?
CHILD: Not OK.
ADULT: Can you tell me why? What sounds not OK to you?
CHILD: There's no jungle gym.
ADULT: "All the dogs raided the garbage cans." How 'bout that one? Does it
        sound OK to you or does it sound not OK?
CHILD: No, not OK.
ADULT: Why? What sounds not OK about it?
CHILD: Well, because dogs shouldn't raid garbage cans.
ADULT: Here's another one. "What will John do with his car?"
CHILD: Beats me! It sounds OK.

As you can see, these young children are unable to focus on these forms *as forms*, rather than as communication. Now listen to the eleven-year-old.

ADULT: "John went to the store, but Mary went to the store."
CHILD: No, it should be "John and Mary went to the store." That would sound
        better.
ADULT: "We went to see him." How does that one sound? OK or not OK?
CHILD: Well, OK, but it sounds kind of cut off.
ADULT: "He hurt himself." What about that one?
CHILD: That sounds cut off too. Make it a little longer. "He hurt himself when he
        was playing football."

This child is focusing on the language as a formal code. We would expect this kind of difference in the metalinguistic abilities of children beginning and ending their elementary school years.

The child's metalinguistic awareness can be viewed as a part of children's thinking in general.[21] The developmental psychologist Margaret Donaldson suggests that young children's thinking is "embedded," that is, that children make sense of the world in terms of their ongoing, daily, real experience—familiar situations and what people do (and why) in those familiar contexts. This is the case with language as well as with other areas of the child's mental activity. The talk of the five- and six-year-olds in the preceding examples reflects this embedded kind of thinking. Their comments have nothing to do with the adult's linguistic forms but everything to do with jungle gyms, dogs, garbage cans and raids of them. But over time, Donaldson suggests, the child becomes increasingly able to think in "disembedded" modes, to engage in "thought that has been prised out of the old primitive matrix" of human sense in the real world (Donaldson 1979, pp.

---

[21]See Van Kleeck 1982 for a discussion of metalinguistic awareness within a Piagetian cognitive development framework.

75-76) to consider problems "taken as encapsulated, isolated from the rest of existence" (p. 78). It is just this "prising out" of language form that the eleven-year-old in the example is able to do. He is able to consider language as isolated from any real existence at all, in a kind of vacuum. His consideration has nothing to do with whether he knows anyone named Mary or John or whether or not they are in the habit of going to the store. This is "disembedding" the language form from ongoing human use of language in the world.

We have already seen that young children engage in some language behaviors that foreshadow more mature awareness. The same five- and six-year-olds in the preceding grammaticality task, who are unable to focus only on the forms of sentences and ignore their meanings, probably engage in playing with language elements, in correcting their own speech, and possibly in correcting the speech of others as well (for example, the speech of a younger sibling). These earlier behaviors are part of the child's ongoing business of using language in her daily life. When the child plays with language elements (for example, responds to a Dr. Seuss story or makes up rhymes) or corrects her own or another's speech, she does so in the context of using language in communication with other people. These behaviors are "embedded" in the child's action. It is not surprising that the kind of ability required by the grammaticality task develops later, for that task "disembeds" language from its context of use and requires reflection on language as an entity with no real connection with the child's life.

It is something of a problem to sort out metalinguistic development and school influence. The school places a very high value on the child's being able to deal with language as a formal code, and much time and effort are devoted to achieving this goal. Indeed, school success for many children requires this ability. In many instances, it is not enough for the child to use and interpret words effectively in speech and writing; she must also be able to define words, categorize them by part of speech, identify their vowel sounds, divide them into syllables, find synonyms or antonyms or rhymes, identify written "sentences" for punctuating or reading aloud, and so on. How would the child's metalinguistic awareness develop without this experience? For children in Western societies, this is the road not taken. If the child did not come to school, would her early sense of language elements—so evident in her embedded play with language forms, her self-corrections, and other-corrections— develop into a more conscious awareness of the forms themselves?[22] Presumably they would to some extent, for in school or out, the child's cognitive development and her experience in the world continue. But it is surely the case that the child's school experience contributes significantly to this aspect of development. Potential abilities develop largely through the use that people make of them within their society. Thus, use of metalinguistic abilities in school contexts doubtless enhances the full development of these abilities.

[22]Some fascinating research has focused on the development of cognitive and (meta) linguistic abilities by schooled and unschooled individuals, and by literate and nonliterate individuals in non-Western societies. A major purpose of these studies has been to increase our understanding of the role of schooling and literacy in cognitive and metalinguistic development. See, for example, Scribner and Cole 1981; Greenfield, Reich, and Olver 1967; and Sharp, Cole, and Lave 1979.

7

Language Acquisition: Interaction of Child and Context

INTRODUCTION

The crucial question of this chapter is, How does a child acquire his language? To deal with this question it is necessary (as the chapter title suggests) to consider the child, the context, and their interaction.

The two major parts of this chapter focus on the child and the context respectively. Yet this division is artificial. The reality of language acquisition is a complex and continuous interaction between the child and his world. Dividing up this reality is simply a matter of organizational necessity in writing a book. But try to keep the wholeness in mind as you read. The "child" and "context" sections simply bring different parts of the whole into sharper focus, each in its turn becoming foreground while the other, for a time, becomes background. The reality, however, is always child-and-context.

Let's begin with a set of examples for two reasons. First, the examples will help you to sense the wholeness of child-and-context. Think of each example as being the sudden stopping of a film. In the particular frame that is the example, you cannot see the dynamic child-and-context interaction, the ongoing process; but each example reflects that process. You can see each one as the result of the cognitively and socially active child making sense of language in use in his world.

In addition to capturing the child-and-context whole, these examples demonstrate the most basic and pervasive notion of this chapter: The child is actively and continuously engaged in a process of "creative construction" of language. Creative. Construction. Both words are important. "Creative construction" characterizes children's activity in language learning as one of active sense making. The child participates in a social world and out of diverse experience—linguistic and nonlinguistic—the child constructs, *builds*, sense. We are particularly concerned here with the sense the child makes of language, his figuring out of how cognitive and social meanings get expressed in language forms—in talk, in print, in gesture. The building

158

process is "creative" in that it is of the child's own making; it is not imposed on him, that is, "given," by another and simply "received" by the child. Rather, the child actively figures out how language *means* by observing and participating in language in many specific contexts. The process is one of invention of an abstract system relating the language expression the child encounters to the cognitive and social meanings the child infers.

Evidence of the creative construction process in children is most apparent when children's ways of expressing are different from our own. These differences are not faulty attempts to imitate adult language; they are instead the child's own fashioning of a system which is the result of the child making sense (his own sense) of experience (his own experience). The child's expression is the result of his observing, noticing, selecting, trying out, hypothesizing, testing, participating. Children *make sense* of language; that is, they construct sense in meaning-expression relations.

In the following examples, you can see (hear) the result of this active creative construction process on the part of these children. You can also see that this process did not—*could* not—work in a vacuum. Rather, the child's creative construction necessarily is the result of the child's experience in a social world, a world that he is part of, a world of language in use.

EXAMPLE 1

An English woman is in the company of an Arab woman and her two children, a boy of seven and a little girl of thirteen months who is just beginning to walk but is afraid to take more than a few steps without help . . . . The little girl walks to the English woman and back to her mother. Then she turns as if to start off in the direction of the English woman once again. But the latter now smiles, points to the boy and says: "Walk to your brother this time." . . . the boy . . . holds out his arms. The baby smiles, changes direction and walks to her brother. (Donaldson 1979, pp. 31–32)

Can you see that the child here is making sense, not of the specific verbalizations of the participants, but of the social situation itself, the human purposes conveyed through facial expressions and gestures and the overall sound of the human voice. Think about this: How could this child ever ultimately figure out the meanings of particular words and sentences in situations without already having some understanding of the situations themselves? Only with a well-developed sense of the relations of things and people and purposes in an interaction can the child begin to figure out what the particular words and sentences used in that interaction refer to and what purposes they serve (in this case, that someone is trying to get the child to do something, what the desired action is, which direction she is to move in, and so on). Without these understandings of situation, how could the child ever figure out the meanings of the specific words "walk," "to," "your," "brother," and so on. Figuring out situations is an important way into figuring out the linguistic system that represents them. Initially this child's behavior may not seem to have anything much to do with language development. Yet it does. The child has figured out meanings in this social context, and she acts on that understanding in her response to the participants here. This is creative construction in a social context.

EXAMPLES 2

a. A four-and-a-half-year-old was trying to put on his shoes but could find only one of them. He asked his father, "Where is the other shoe that rhymes with this one?"[1]

b. A grandmother was caring for her three-year-old grandson and found crayon marks on the wall.
    GRANDMOTHER: Oh, Chris. Look at this! How did this get here?
    C: I did it, Grammy.
    GRANDMOTHER: *You* did that?
    C: Yes, but it was a accident. I couldn't find a piece of paper.

The children in these two examples are dealing with meaning-expression relations at the semantic level: What chunk of experience that I know does this particular word (verbalization) convey? The children's uses here suggest what some have called a "partial analysis": The child's meanings for these words include some, but not all, of the aspects of meaning that these words include for the adult. But from the child's point of view there is no "partial" and no "analysis." The child has made sense of his experience of these words in use up to that point in his life. The child has encountered these words in real use in the real world. It may be that these words were used in conversation with the child, or it may be that they were used in conversation around the child, conversation which he observed but did not participate in. In either case, he encountered these words in real social events, in real interactions among people.

EXAMPLES 3

a. Two four-year-olds are playing.
    C-1:   That's dangerous. You know what "dangerous" means?
    C-2:   (Nods.)
    C-3:   It means you might drop it.[2]

b. Mother and her three-year-old daughter.
    M: People are always telling you to "share," aren't they, Brenda? What does "share" mean?
    C: It means I get to play with somebody else's toys.

In these examples, the children are talking about language in a conscious way. They are producing verbal definitions of what these words mean. One hears in these definitions the echoes of talk in which these children may have encountered these words. It's easy to imagine play contexts in which a mother, in the name of "sharing," took her child's toy and gave it to another child; or a situation in which the child carried a fragile object and mother hastily intervened, "Oh oh oh, honey, that's dangerous. Let Mommy help you. You might drop it." Whatever the actual specifics of these children's encounters with "share" and "dangerous," we can be sure that they were instances of real use of these words in social events that had meaning for them, and that these children have actively made their own sense of these events, including the talk that occurred in them.

[1] I am indebted to John Henderson for this example.
[2] I am indebted to Robin Rue for this example from her data.

EXAMPLES 4

A three-and-a-half-year-old, sitting at the table in a booster chair, finished her lunch and wanted to get down from the chair. Unable to push her chair back from the table, she said to her mother, "Mommy, will you unpush me?"

A four-year-old had been put to bed by someone else in her mother's evening absence. In the middle of the night she came to her mother's bed, woke her, and requested that the mother put her to bed properly, saying, "I need to get goodnighted."[3]

A six-year-old, looking at a picture in Mercer Mayer's *Bubble Bubble*, got to the page where a fat mouse that had been blown with magic bubbles had suddenly disappeared. He pointed to the visual representation of the poof where the mouse had been and said, "It's a deblown mouse."[4]

A teacher asked a four-year-old who was sweeping the nursery school floor, "Are you mopping?" The child replied, "No, I'm brooming."[5]

A four-year-old was playing with toy figures in a sandbox in a park while his mother watched from a bench nearby. The child turned to his mother and told her, "Robbers are real stealive."[6]

The children here are using some word forms that they have not encountered before. Yet you can see that these, too, are built out of real encounters with language serving social purposes. Each child has generalized to new specific instances the patterns he has noted: "I use a mop," "I'm mopping" and "I use a broom," "I'm brooming," "someone protects," "he is protective," "someone steals," "he is stealive," and so on. These are particularly striking demonstrations of creative construction, for we know that the child cannot be imitating here but must be inventing new word forms according to a pattern he has observed. Creative construction again in evidence. Clearly, the child could not have invented these forms in a vacuum; he could only have invented these forms within a world of language in use.

EXAMPLES 5

a. Allgone Mommy.
b. No like.
c. Why we gotta be careful for?

When you first encountered these sentences (in chap. 6), they may have seemed rather bizarre. Perhaps you can see now, however, that they reflect the child's using whatever linguistic devices he or she controls to express meaning. The linguistic means controlled by the children in the first two sentences are more limited than those controlled by the child in

[3]I am indebted to Sally Means for this example.
[4]I am indebted to Candy Poland for this example.
[5]I am indebted to Janet Rothschild for this example.
[6]I am indebted to Forrest Hancock for this example.

the last sentence, but all of these children are using the language materials they have to construct sentences expressing their meanings. Both the meanings and the expression are the children's own. Again we see children creatively (not imitatively) constructing meaning-expression relations out of their experience of language in their social world.

EXAMPLES 6

Here are some examples involving written expression of meaning:
    Three-year-old Nathan is shown a Crest toothpaste box. Pointing to the word "Crest" the adult asks, "What do you think this says?" Nathan answers, "Brush teeth." (Harste, Burke, and Woodward 1982, p. 110)

Scott (4 years, 10 months) is asked to write a grocery shopping list. He does.

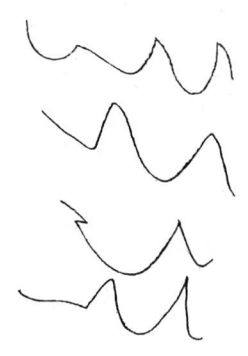

Then, reading aloud what he has written, he points to each line (top to bottom) and for each line reads one item: "milk, Halloween candy, pumpkin, juice."

Julia (5 years) is asked to write a letter and a song. She writes[7]

---

[7]I am indebted to Judith King for the Scott and Julia examples from her data.

Nathan has figured out that print means and that it means in a way which is relevant to the context of its occurrence. (This is reminiscent of the child in the first example who made a similar assumption about talk.) Scott and Julia have figured out many specifics of written language, without formal instruction, for example, that different graphic displays convey different types and purposes of writing and that units of the graphic display relate to units of messages. These are meaning-expression relations the children have constructed out of their informal experience of writing serving real social purposes around them.

I have deliberately selected a wide range of examples here as a kind of overview: prelinguistic examples and linguistic examples, talk examples and writing examples. However diverse these examples, whatever the developmental level of the child, whatever the expressive channel (talk or print), all are the result of the child's creative construction of meaning-expression relations within his experience of language in use in a social world.

Now let's look more specifically at the child's cognitive activity in learning language.

THE CHILD

The cognitive base of language acquisition is much in evidence in (1) the child's semantic development, (2) the child's early combinatory speech (early syntactic development), and (3) the child's active use of a variety of learning strategies. We consider these three areas in this section and conclude that the sequence of language acquisition is influenced by both cognitive and linguistic complexities in the learning task.

The Cognitive Base of Semantic Development

From our adult perspective, the task of creatively constructing the semantic component of a language seems immense. People sometimes suppose it is simply a matter of figuring out which labels (words) match up with which thoughts, ideas, or experiences. But thoughts and experiences don't happen in categories like those of language. Boundaries are not marked in the experience or thought itself; yet the semantic system of a language treats meanings as if they were discrete. That is, of course, what morphemes are: discrete units of meaning. Slobin gives this example from Vygotsky.

> "Thought has its own structure, and the transition from it to speech is no easy matter . . . Thought, unlike speech, does not consist of separate units. When I wish to communicate the thought that today I saw a barefoot boy in a blue shirt running down the street, I do not see every item separately . . . I conceive of all this in one thought, but I put it into separate words." (Slobin 1979, p. 147, quoting Vygotsky 1962, pp. 149–50)

The move from thought to language is a matter of translating from the wholeness and the continuous flow of thought and experience to the discrete, separate, semantic categories of language, the conventional chunks of meaning that we express as particular words. We impose divisions on the whole that is thought. These divisions are the conventional categories of our semantic system.

Remember, too, that any word or sequence of words expresses only a part of our whole notion or concept. What we conceptualize is richer, fuller, and more elaborate than what we say. Vygotsky has a fuller concept of his barefoot boy than his words tell us. His "running" doesn't tell us the look of the runner's stride or the sound of his feet on the pavement, or even whether the runner was on a paved surface at all. Both the vastness and the all-at-once-ness of our thinking mean that no small task is involved in moving from thought to the discrete and streamlined semantic categories of language.

> Working out the relations between a rich and elaborate set of conceptual categories and a system of conventional linguistic devices for talking about concepts is a complex process. (Clark 1983, p. 797)

There are many different ways that a language can categorize, that is, can divide experience into units, grouping various items as being "the same." Remember from the discussion in Chapter 3 that different languages cluster experience into differing categories and that different dimensions serve as the bases for these categories (see examples from chap. 3, p. 00). Every child must learn how his particular language divides, clusters, and labels the world.

Beyond this, the semantic component is not simply a single set of categories. Rather, it includes hierarchies of categories and subcategories—"vertical" categories (like fruit, orange, navel) as well as "horizontal" categories (orange, apple, banana) (Rosch 1978). Clearly, the child must develop both vertical and horizontal semantic relations.

Even beyond this, boundaries are often vague. You found out when you thought about various "walk" words in Chapter 3 that boundaries are not clear. Most of us would be hard pressed to articulate a clear difference between "amble" and "stroll," between "beautiful" and "gorgeous," between "child" and "youngster," or between "small" and "little." The child must figure out what the categories in his language community are, which diverse experiences will be treated as "equivalent" to one another and as distinct from other groupings or categories. He must figure out what does and also what does not get included in categories. He must learn how categories relate to one another vertically and horizontally. And, of course, he must learn the community's labels for this array of categories. As one child observer has remarked, ". . . the young child is the hardest mental toiler on our planet. Fortunately, he does not even suspect this" (Chukovsky 1968, p. 10).

We might well ask how the child deals with this seemingly impossible task. Especially if we are teachers we will ask this, since the child's school experience is diverse and thus involves him in many new experiences. New experience is precisely where semantic development occurs, which means that the child's semantic development is very active during the elementary school years.

The child does not start at zero in language. Remember that the child is born with certain genetic potential for language, including its semantic component. He is a member of the same species that originally invented human language, and it is a human language that he will learn. He is born as one who perceives and organizes and processes experience in certain ways that he shares with other humans, other language inventors and users. Thus, the nature of the semantic system itself, and the nature of the child who will learn it, both limit the semantic possibilities to a human set, the set processable by the human mind.

The child is born with a certain orientation to language and is confronted with a language which fits the child's orientation. Besides this, the child is born into a physical world that has structure. Certainly the categories that a language devises are not "given" in the environment itself. The difference between a dog and a fox or a cup and a glass is not so much in these objects themselves as it is in our decision to treat them as distinct. But just as certainly, the possible categories are constrained by existing structure in the physical world (Rosch 1978). The presence of certain properties predicts the presence of other properties; that is, certain features or properties in the world cluster more (occur together more) than others. For example, the presence of wings predicts feathers and flying, not scales or slithering. That wings and feathers and flying frequently occur together is a fact of the physical world itself, part of its inherent structure. The possible categories of a language will be constrained by such structure in the physical world. Rosch suggests that language categories include prototypes or best examples. These prototypes are category members that include more of the properties of the category and fewer of the properties of other categories. Thus, a sparrow is a "better bird" (a prototype) than a penguin or an ostrich, for a sparrow embodies more of the central bird properties and fewer of the nonbird properties, while the reverse is true of penguins and ostriches (Rosch 1978). Prototypes can serve as anchoring points for categories.

In sum, the child's task in constructing a semantic system is made manageable by the presence of structure: structure in the child (his innately specified ways of perceiving, organizing, relating); structure in the physical world (somewhat predictable clusterings or properties); structure in language in the community he is born into (an existing system for categorizing and labeling concepts and relating them in systematic ways). And the child's task is made possible by the presence of language users around him who demonstrate in their interaction with one another and with the child just what the categories and labels are in the language the child will learn.

Clark (1983) suggests that the child's work in constructing a semantic system is guided throughout by two overarching principles: (1) the principle of contrast: "the conventional meanings of every pair of words [labels] . . . contrast" and (2) the principle of conventionality: "For certain meanings, there is a conventional word [label] . . . that should be used in the language community" (p. 820). We can metaphorically think of the young child as engaged in an ongoing search for contrasting meanings and the conventional labels the community uses for them. With more experience of language in an increasing range of contexts, the child encounters further, more refined meaning contrasts and the community's labels for them. When he first encounters a sheep, the child might call it "doggie" (being already familiar with dogs). When he notices that others around him call this item "sheep," he is alerted to the fact that this object contrasts somehow with those called "dogs." The child's task is then to figure out how entities bearing the conventional label "sheep" contrast with those bearing the label "dog." He must do some reorganizing of his semantic system to make a place for this new contrast and its conventional label. You can readily think of school examples, for the school child daily encounters new meaning contrasts (and their labels, of course) across all areas of curriculum, and he must adjust his semantic system to take these new meanings and labels into account.

Over time the child's categories (meaning contrasts) and labels (conventional words) come into closer match with the adult's. This involves the child's building categories that are sufficiently inclusive. The meaning and label "dog" may originally include only his own pet but will eventually include other dogs in the neighborhood, large dogs and small ones, stuffed toy dogs, dogs in pictures, in books, on TV, and so on. And his categories and labels must also be sufficiently exclusive. "Dog" for the child will ultimately (though not necessarily at first) exclude cats and sheep and goats. Children's talk and response to the talk of others includes instances of both overextension (using a label more broadly than the adult does) and underextension (using a label more narrowly than the adult does). In examples 2a and 2b, the children's "rhyme" and "accident" were overextended to include a wider range of meanings than the adult includes for these terms.

How does the child search? What does the child notice, attend to, and use? What is *salient* to the child? To raise this question of salience is to assume that the child does not attend equally to all aspects of a situation at once; in fact, we can assume that there are some aspects of a situation that the child does not attend to at all. Evidence indicates that functional aspects of objects (what objects do or what the child can do to them) are often salient to children. These functional aspects can influence the child's creative construction of a semantic system. Katherine Nelson (1973) studied the early vocabularies (the first ten words and the first fifty words) of eighteen children over a one-year period, from the time the children were around one year old to the time they were around two. There were some surprises in her findings. Eleven of these children had "shoe" as one of their first fifty words, five of the children had "hat" and four had "sock," but only one had "crib" and not a single one had "diaper." Yet surely diapers and cribs were present in these young children's immediate environments far more than hats, shoes, and socks; the chances are that these children wore diapers constantly and spent much time in cribs but not so hats, shoes, or socks. Of these eighteen children, six—exactly one-third—had "key" in the first fifty words, but not a single one had "table," yet tables are surely more frequent in young children's experience than keys are. How are we to explain why shoes, socks, hats, and keys were much noticed and early named by these children, while many more frequently encountered items—diapers, cribs, and tables—were not?

The work of the cognitive psychologist Piaget provides an answer. He describes a predictable sequence of stages in the cognitive growth of all children. The first of these, lasting roughly from birth to two years, he calls the sensorimotor period. During this period a child builds an understanding of his world by acting upon things physically. The things of his environment *are* whatever he is able to *do* to them—some things are suckable, others biteable, others squeezeable. It is through the child's physical action upon the environment that his view of reality changes: He moves from perceiving reality as a continuousness of undifferentiated sights, smells, sounds, tastes, and tactile sensations impinging on his sense organs at birth, to perceiving reality as separate entities, actions, and people in space.

Against this Piagetian background, the presence and absence of certain items in children's early vocabularies seems less surprising. What does the one- to two-year old notice particularly? What he acts on physically. A child *acts on* hats, shoes, and socks, but a diaper is something that is *done to* him, in a sense; he "gets diapered." Keys can be grasped, jangled, shaken, and bitten, but what can a child do to a table or crib? Tables and cribs are just *there*. (I wonder what a child's notion of "table" or "crib" is anyway, since he is so small that he must be perceptually aware of only a portion of a table at any given time. If he is standing up, then "table" must be the table leg. If he is sitting in his highchair, then "table" must be a smooth surface—very different indeed from the leg. If he is standing beside his mother, who is preparing food on the table, is the "table" what he sees as he looks up, the underneath portion perhaps? How does a child put these various visual perceptions of "table" together? To some extent, this is the problem the child must solve with any vocabulary item. What any lexical item represents is different at different times and in different situations. But perhaps a child can experience, physically and sensorily, a graspable key or hat or shoe as a totality, a single entity, in a way that he cannot experience table or crib, and this may make his understanding and naming of these items easier.)

The phrase "acts on" is Piaget's: The child in the sensorimotor period "acts on" his environment. Notice that this interpretation of the child's interaction with his world sees the child as active in his own learning and experiencing. The child does not sit passively while things in the environment happen to him, but rather he reaches out, grabs, kicks, bites, squeezes, sucks, shakes. An important way of learning during the sensorimotor period is by acting on his world physically. Out of his sensorimotor experience he formulates some of the concepts and understandings he names with his first words. Perceptual aspects of situations are often salient to children also. Some researchers have observed the child's use of perceptual cues in constructing his semantic system. Young children have been observed to use a single label for a variety of objects that share a particular perceptual characteristic, apparently using that characteristic as the word's "definition." One child used a single label for a variety of round objects (moon, cakes, round postmarks, the letter O); another used one word for a variety of objects with parallel lines (crib bars, toy abacus, toast rack, picture of a building with columns); another focused on soft texture, calling a plush dog, a muffler, a cat, and a fur coat by the same name. Other children have called a variety of objects by the same name because the objects all made a hissing sound, or all were small, or all tasted sweet (Clark 1973; 1974). These examples all reflect the salience that perceptual characteristics can have for children, and also the use they may make of perceptual information as they relate new meaning contrasts to conventional labels.

Roger Brown approached the question of salience in a slightly different way. He was interested in accounting for the types of items children's early language does and does not include, and the order in which children acquire items of different types. It would be a reasonable hypothesis that a child would first learn those items he hears most frequently. These would be grammatical morphemes like articles, "be" forms, and endings on verbs and nouns. This hypothesis would be based on the assumption that the learner is a somewhat passive being whom the environment shapes and on whom it imprints language items. Since "the" and "be" are imprinted many times, they would become part of his language system early.

But, in fact, in all the language acquisition literature across the centuries, "the" and "be" forms (and comparable forms from languages other than English) have never been reported as children's first words. These are the very words that are conspicuously absent from one-word speech and from Stage 1 (two-word) speech. It turns out that there is no significant relationship between frequency—how often a child hears an item—and how early or late he acquires it. Clearly, a child must hear an item in order to figure it out and incorporate it into his developing system. But beyond some minimal level of exposure, frequency is unimportant. It is not how many times a child hears an item that is important but, rather, it is what he selects, notices, attends to, and uses—acts on—in his way that is important for his language growth.

Remember that one-word and two-word (Stage 1) speech are comprised mainly of heavy content words. When the child does begin to acquire grammatical morphemes, around Stage 2, he does so in a fairly predictable order. Brown and his colleagues have studied in depth the acquisition order in three children, from one-word speech through Stage 1 and Stage 2, and Brown (1973) suggests some language features that apparently contribute to the salience of some morphemes for the young child. One such feature is "phonetic substance": Is the morpheme a full syllable, like "on" or "here," or is it part of a syllable like the /z/ of "Mommy's" or "doggies"? Is the morpheme one which is typically unstressed, for example, articles as in "*the* big box," "*a* new one," "*some* soap"? Brown's work indicates that greater phonetic substance (full syllable, stressable) contributes to perceptual salience for the child.

The positions in which a morpheme can occur will also influence order of acquisition. Items occurring in final position gain a child's attention. We would expect morphemes which frequently occur in final position (for example, "mine" in "No, no, that's mine") to be acquired before those which generally occur initially in sentence segments ("the" or "a").

Children also seem geared to notice those items that play significant semantic or syntactic roles. A child will tend to acquire a morpheme that plays a major semantic role (pronouns which can be agents) before he acquires a morpheme that only modulates meaning (plural, or third person singular morphemes as in "goes"). And he will tend to acquire earlier those morphemes that play significant syntactic roles (subjects, verbs, objects, modifiers) than those that play lesser roles (auxiliary elements).

Morphemes vary considerably in the amount of new versus redundant information they carry. Pronouns carry more information than do third person singular verb endings, which are in fact highly redundant. In the sentence, "He goes every week," the /z/ of "goes" indicates that the subject is third person singular, but that information is already present in the word "he." The third person singular morpheme is highly redundant, and children typically acquire such redundant forms later than more informative ones.

Morphemes also vary significantly in the changeableness of their form. Many grammatical morphemes change form depending on their context. The regular past tense morpheme will be /t/, /d/, or /əd/, depending on the final sound of the verb with which it combines. However, the progressive morpheme, -ing /iŋ/ is always added to the verb in just that form. Those morphemes that are more stable in form and are not conditioned by context are earlier additions to the child's system.

Thus, it appears that children notice and earlier incorporate forms that tend to have greater phonetic substance, that can occur in final position in utterances, that are semantically significant, that are syntactically significant, that are informative rather than redundant, and that are stable in form, whatever the context of their occurrence. These features, taken together, account very well for the acquisition order from one-word speech through Stage 1 (heavy content items) and Stage 2 speech (beginning of acquisition of grammatical morphemes). Children are guided not by the frequency of forms in their environment, but by their own strategies of noticing, by what has salience for their own active processing.

Notice that the child must deal with both meaning and form—Clark's principles of contrast and conventionality, once again. The words that people around him use in various contexts signal meaning contrasts (the distinctions people make) and also the conventional forms people use to express the distinctions. And the nonlinguistic meanings that the child understands aid him in figuring out just what it is that the forms he hears possibly refer to. Clearly, the child works in two directions: from meaning (what he understands) to form (what he hears) and also from form to meaning.

At one time or another, you have probably encountered vocabulary counts for children of various ages, for example, lists of "basic words" that children of particular ages will be likely to know, or counts of how many words the "typical" x-year old knows. Such lists and counts treat children's semantic knowledge as having two states: He "has" a particular word versus he doesn't "have" a particular word. Like a light switch—off/on—he has it/ he doesn't. But this is a problem. What does it mean to "know a word"? What is the behavior test for such knowledge? Shall we say a person "knows" the word only if he can verbally define it? Define *all* of its meanings, or only some of them? Which ones? If definition is required, we will find that we fail on some of the "simplest" words. (Try defining "the," for example.) Or is it sufficient for the individual to respond appropriately to the word when he hears it? And would he have to respond to the word in all its meanings or only some of them? Which ones? (I was surprised to discover that there are meanings for "table" in the *Oxford English Dictionary* that I did not know.) Or will the test be for the child to use the word appropriately? In speech or writing, or both? In which meanings? In what situations? Must the child use a word in all of its forms, for example, friend, friendly, friendship, befriend, friendlier, friendliest, unfriendly, and so on? Or does one just have to hang onto a prescribed set of meanings for words until the test is over—the way that we "learned" vocabulary for the SAT exam or the way that teachers often require children to cram for vocabulary tests in science or social studies units? One's semantic knowledge at any given moment is far more complex than simply "having/not having" specific words. We "have" and "don't have" particular words in various contexts, meanings, and situations.

So, too, in the course of development: One does not suddenly "get" a word and then "have" it from then on. Rather, meanings build and extend gradually. The child first uses a word (with a particular meaning) in restricted ways, typically in the context in which he first encounters it. Only gradually does he extend its use to new contexts. Consider the talk of some four-year-olds in the dramatic play area of their nursery school classroom. You will sense their partial meanings for some of the words they are using.[8]

a. *C:* So we're going on a camping trip, on ummm, on . . . We're going on a million days.

b. *C-1:* He's eight.
    C-2: My big brother is ten.
    C-3: Mine is seven. Mine used to be seven and three-and-a-half quarters.

c. *C-1:* Mommy, Mommy. I want a drink of water.
    C-2: You can't 'cause a tornado's coming.
    C-3: Are you afraid?
    C-2: Come on, come on, this way! Here! I'm not afraid, I'm not scared of the monsters! We have to get our car! (inaudible)
    C-1: *Oh no!* What will we do? Or the tornado will get us, right? . . .
    C-2: Ring, ring.
    C-1: Call the operator! Ring, ring. Operator, yeah. We fixed the tornado.

[8]I am indebted to Robin Rue for these examples from her data.

It is tempting to say that these children "don't know what 'million,' 'quarters,' and 'tornado' mean." But clearly this would be a mistake. The first child knows that "million" is an amount. He probably also knows that it is an impressively large amount. C-3 in the second example knows that "quarters" is an amount word. Notice that he uses it with other fraction words ("half") and in an appropriate place: in a phrase following the whole number "seven." He clearly knows that "quarters" is a word to use in talk about people's ages. All three children in the third example know that a tornado is something scary. (Notice that C-2 connects it with monsters.) They also know that it is something that comes and that you try to get away from. This is quite a bit of knowing.

And as you know, many "words" include various inflectional and derivational affixes (for example, know, knowing, known, unknown, knew, knowable, unknowing, knowledge, knowledgeable, beknownst, knowingly, and so on). Thus, "knowing a word" involves knowing many forms of it and, just as important, knowing where the gaps are, which forms do not occur (English does not have the forms deknown, reknow, and knowness, for example). You can see from the children's unconventional word-form examples earlier in this chapter (good-nighted, brooming, stealive, unpush, deblown) that children are sensitive to patterns in expression of inflectional and derivational morphemes. They discern regularities and generalize them to new instances.

Despite all these complexities in what it means to "know a word," adults continue to do child vocabulary counts. The numbers differ greatly from one count to another, depending on the criteria each study uses to determine what words children "know." Whatever the criteria used, however, the resulting numbers are always amazing. George Miller cites one such early study as more conservative than most (Miller 1977, p. 156). According to this study, the median six-year-old knows 13,000 words, the median seven-year-old knows 21,600 words, and the median eight-year-old knows 28,300. These figures are too large to mean much to me. However, Miller helpfully breaks down these numbers: These children have learned an average of *twenty-one new words per day from birth*![9]

We must in the end, I think, stand amazed at the cognitive power displayed here. Adults (including teachers) tend to think that children learn new words because we directly instruct them in this. But children learn many words before ever coming to school, and their most powerful ways of continuing learning new words are through their activity more than through ours. The child is born cognitively active in creatively constructing a semantic system. He is born into a vast but orderly physical world. He is born into a complex but orderly social world as well, a world of people interacting with one another and with him. Many of these interactions involve language. The child is active always—attending, noticing, hypothesizing, participating, observing, testing, producing, generalizing, organizing and reorganizing—taking into account an ever-increasing

---

[9]I doubt that this is, as Miller claims, a conservative estimate. Pease and Gleason, 1985 cite Madora Smith's 1926 finding that children "during the peak preschool ages of 2½ and 4½ learn an average of two to four new words per day."

range of experience and the ways people talk about it. From his encounter with thousands upon thousands of specific instances of language in use, he fashions an underlying semantic system that the instances are examples of—an abstract system that he is never directly exposed to but must infer from his observations of how people use language in different contexts. It is a system of meaning categories and conventional words to express them, a system of vertical and horizontal relations among categories, a system of basic meanings and also refinements (inflectional and derivational morphemes). And "the staggering fact is that children acquire most of the vocabulary they will need as adults without being taught. If they were not able to learn far more than we know how to teach, they would never grow up to be like us" (Miller 1977, p. 152).

The Cognitive Base of Early Combinatory Speech

"The child's knowledge of language is deeply dependent upon a prior mastery of concepts about the world to which language will refer. . . . There appears to be some readiness . . . quickly to grasp certain rules for forming sentences, once we know what the world is about to which the sentences refer" (Bruner 1978, pp. 64–65).

Roger Brown (1973) has considered children's "prior mastery of concepts about the world" at the point at which children move into combinatory speech.[10] What must the child understand in order to express the meanings typical in Stage 1 speech (the two-word stage)? Piaget's work provides a frame of reference that makes possible a rich, coherent, and persuasive interpretation.

Think first about existence (naming; labeling), recurrence, and nonexistence. What must the child understand in order to express nomination: "this doll," "see house," "here baby"? He must at least recognize that there are separate entities in space. At first it may seem strange to think that anyone ever has to learn this; the separateness of things seems so obvious to us. But remember, we are talking about a young child who, we assume, started out as a receiver of undifferentiated sensory stimulation. Only through his interaction with things in the environment does the child come to differentiate among things. This sense of separate-thing-ness is basic to his expression of nomination. Where would this prerequisite understanding for naming come from if not from the child's experiences of physically acting on the people and objects in his environment? The notions of separateness of objects are built through the child's sensorimotor experience.

What about recurrence—"more bye-bye," "'nother raisin," "more noise"? In order to express this meaning, the child must understand that the situation which did exist but presently does not, can exist again. This is another notion that the child has built through his own repeated actions with things in his environment. The infant kicks the mobile in his crib. It moves, making interesting patterns and sounds. He kicks it again. The interesting patterns and sounds are repeated.

[10]In Brown 1973, see especially pp. 198–200, on which this discussion is based.

Brown reminds us of two apparent precursors of the language of nomination and recurrence. Piaget identifies two early "schemas" (action patterns) typically occurring around four to eight months. In the "recognition schema," the infant, in the presence of a particular object, moves his body in the way he typically acts on the object. For example, he sees the bottle, focuses on it, and begins sucking movements; or he sees his rattle and moves his arm in a shaking motion. It is as if the child provides a physical "label," through body movement, for an object he recognizes as separate and distinct. The "recurrence schema" Piaget calls "making interesting sights last." Here, the infant engages in some particular physical movement with the apparent intention of causing a pleasurable event to recur, as in the mobile example above.

When the child expresses nonexistence—"allgone egg," "allgone outside," "no juice"—he demonstrates an ability to "anticipate based on signs." Looking at an empty plate and saying "allgone egg" makes sense precisely because there was good reason to suppose there would be an egg on the plate. Children make—express—sense in terms of the way the world is. The child has come to associate specific events with specific signs—eggs with plates, outside with front doors, juice with cups—through his sensorimotor activity, his eating, drinking, opening and closing and going in and out through doors.

In expressing possession, the child acknowledges some sort of relationship or closeness between particular people and particular objects. As with his anticipation based on signs, the child is relating two different things that, in his experience, have regularly been associated in some way. While I find no basis for attributing to the child an understanding of the highly abstract notion of ownership, it does appear that the child has discerned a pattern: That particular chair has to do with Daddy ("Daddy chair"), that particular dress has to do with Mommy ("Mommy dress"), that particular nose has to do with the dog ("doggie nose").

A major cognitive understanding underlying the child's expressions of attributes of objects ("microphone hot," "animal book," "big ball") is that objects have inherent properties: The object is not the property but has the property. This seems a highly abstract notion. It is difficult to think where it comes from, if not from the child's physical encounters with objects of various sizes, textures, temperatures, and types. The variety of experience is important here. It would be impossible for a child to recognize, and verbally signal, that a ball is "big" if he hadn't had experience of balls (and other objects) of different sizes. The child is able to identify a particular book as an "animal book," rather than some other sort of book, precisely because he has experience of books which are and which are not animal books but books of some other type.

Many of the Stage 1 child's sentences involve two terms (in order) of the agent-action-object relation. It would seem that a child who says, "Kathryn stand up" (agent-action), "throw ball" (action-object), and "Kathryn ball" (agent-object meaning "Kathryn is throwing the ball") differentiates (1) between actions and entities and (2) between entities which are agents and those which are "done to" or acted on. Again, it is difficult to really believe that one ever has to learn something so obvious as the fact that objects are separate from the actions involving them. But remember that for the small child, things in the environment *are* what he *does* to them. This differentiation of actor and action is one that comes about through the child's increasingly varied physical interactions with an increasing range of objects and people. As he finds that he is able to grasp, bite, or kick a wide range of objects, grasping and biting and kicking must come to exist for him apart from the objects grasped and bitten and kicked, as well as apart from himself as the grasper and biter and kicker.

The notion of agent or causer which the child expresses in agent + action or agent + object sentences has a precursor in the child's physical expression. We often see very small children deliberately take their mother's hand and physically encourage her to do something for them, for example, to wind a toy that they themselves are unable to manage. This is clear indication of the child's recognition that people (mothers) are causers; they can make events occur. The child's later verbal symbols "Mommy push" or "Kathryn throw" express this understanding in a new way.

Finally, the child's locational expressions attest to an understanding of events and things being in distinct locations in environmental space. The child's first two years involve much in the way of picking things up and putting them down—locating, dislocating, and relocating objects in various places. Particularly interesting are the child's early "where" questions: "Where baby?" or "Where Mommy go?" At an earlier time, when a person or object was out of sight, it had simply ceased to exist for the baby. Dangle a watch in front of a small infant and then hide it behind you and the child will cry, for it is gone, nonexistent. But dangle the same watch in front of the same child a few months later and when you hide it behind you, he will crawl around behind you to find it. Now out of sight no longer means out of existence. It hasn't ceased to exist; it has simply been displaced, moved to a new location. This understanding of displacement that the baby demonstrates when he crawls around behind you looking for the watch is expressed in verbal symbols when he asks, "Where clock?" or "Where clock go?" He knows the watch has not ceased to exist; it is simply in some other location out of sight, and the question is *where*.

In summary, combinatory speech, like semantic development, is clearly cognitive in its foundation. You learned in the last section that the child's cognitive understanding underlies and is necessary to his semantic development, yet it cannot be *directly* mapped onto language. The child must also learn how those understandings get "translated" into the categories that language labels. So, too, in combinatory speech (syntax). Understanding is a necessary prerequisite but it is not sufficient. The child must also have rules for forming sentences. For example, understanding the separateness of objects is necessary to nomination, but the child must also discover that this is expressed as "this + noun," as "here + noun," and so on.

In Chapter 6 we saw continuousness in the child's movement from one syntactic stage to another. Now we see continuousness in the child's movement from early physical expressions to verbal expressions of nomination, recurrence, agent-action, and location. It is as if the child has replaced one set of expressive symbols, physical ones, with another set of symbols, verbal ones. There is continuity in what is being expressed and in the use of symbols to express. Yet the child's movement into verbal symbols represents a major advance in that his new symbol system is one that is potentially unlimited. So long as the child is dependent on the movement of his own body in relation to objects in his immediate environment, his expression must be limited to here and now. But as he grows in his understanding and in his ability to use verbal symbols to express his meanings, he moves into an expression system that will ultimately not constrain him in time or place. Perhaps it is our awareness of the greater power of linguistic symbols over prelinguistic, physical ones that is the basis for our making a sharp distinction between "linguistic" and "prelinguistic" stages in children's growth ("Is Joey talking yet?" "Suzie's first word was ———."), despite the fact that both represent continuous developmental expressions of similar kinds of meanings, and despite the fact that an important part of the child's expression will always be nonverbal, as it is for the adult.

I have dealt with the Stage 1 situation in depth, not because I expect everyone reading this book to be interested in two-year-olds, but because this rooting of language growth in cognitive growth has profound implications for any adult who works with children through elementary level. Language acquisition researchers have studied this cognitive base for language most at the very early level of development when the base is least complex, and thus we understand it best and can describe it most precisely at that level. But we know that one's real experience of the world—*whatever his age*—is the only possible basis for his developing language. We produce and interpret language in terms of our understanding of the meanings it conveys. That understanding is the sum of our experiencing in the world. As our understanding grows, so does the possibility of our producing and interpreting language more powerfully. One's continuing understanding of the world through his experiencing of it, plus one's continuing experience of language in use, are both necessary to one's construction of a meaning-and-expression system throughout life.

Language Acquisition Strategies

By systematically observing children's language behavior, researchers have been able to identify and describe some cognitive strategies that children seem to be using as they figure out how language works. Typically, researchers audiotape and/or videotape children at regular intervals (for example, once every two weeks) over a substantial period of time (perhaps a year) in interactions with others in as natural a setting as possible. The tapes are then painstakingly transcribed and the transcriptions are analyzed for recurring patterns in the children's language behavior. The identification of a recurring pattern of behavior in particular situations suggests nonrandomness in the child's functioning. Patterned behavior in children over time, along with attendant changes in the children's language systems, suggests particular ways of sense making by the children studied—particular approaches to language, if you will. These approaches or "ways of sense making" I am calling "strategies." The child does not simply drink in—imbibe—the language around him; rather, he attends to it selectively and uses it as "data" in some ways that researchers can describe. Researchers' descriptions of these strategies or approaches to language enable us to characterize more precisely what we mean by "active sense making." Just what are those cognitive actions? What does the child *do*?

There are several important things to remember as you read this section about language acquisition strategies children use. First, identified strategies cut across components; that is, a particular strategy or approach can often be observed in children's working out of semantic and/or syntactic and/or phonological aspects of language. Further, to say that a particular strategy has been observed in children is not to say that *all* children use it, or that it is the *only* strategy particular children use, or that it is a strategy that particular children use throughout the entire course of their learning of language. No. It is more accurate to see children as approaching the language-learning task in different ways at different times. One strategy is preferred by one child, another by a different child. Each child typically uses a variety of strategies, some more at earlier periods of development and others more at later periods. Also, the strategies identified comprise a fascinating but by no means comprehensive set. This is to say, of course, that children's abilities to learn language far outrun researchers' abilities to understand how they do it. Nonetheless, it is instructive, especially for teachers concerned with children's ongoing language development, to recognize the powerful and continuing active processes children employ. How children learn must ever be the starting point for how we teach. Here are some of those ways of learning—of creatively constructing language.

Use your nonlinguistic understanding as a basis for figuring out language.   You have already seen how this strategy operates at a general level in Brown's work on the cognitive base of Stage 1 speech. Understanding that objects and actions and properties and locations are separable and distinct from one another, that events can recur, that objects and persons continue to exist even when out of sight—such nonlinguistic understandings are basic to the child's "translation" of the fluidity of thought into the more fixed categories of language. Beyond this general level of nonlinguistic understanding is the child's understanding of particular situations. The child in example 1 grasped the adults' intentions in a particular situation and responded on the basis of this understanding. She was not responding on the basis of particular meanings of the words and sentences themselves. Children seem to make, and act on, the basic assumption that the talk or print they encounter in a given situation relates to that particular situation. This is a helpful working assumption; often (though not always) this assumption holds in a very direct way. Here is an example in which a mother talks to her seven-month-old daughter as she is fixing the child's lunch and the child sits in her high chair nearby.

M: Would you like something? Huh? Cottage cheese? Cottage cheese, Momma. Want some cottage cheese? Have some for you. I have some for you. Here it is. Where's your plate?

C: (variety of babbling sounds which sound insistent)

M: Are you so hungry? Hm? Are you so hungry? This is good cottage cheese. Mmmmm, this looks *good* to me. Mm-*hm.* Eeeee-*yum!*

C: U . . . . (sustained) u - u

M: Hurry? Hurry, Momma. Hurry, Momma. There you go. Here's your spoon. Here's your spoon and cottage cheese. Z'at look good? Hm?

M: Is it good? Is it good cottage cheese? Yes, mam!

C: (babble string)

M: What else would you like? Hm? Apple sauce. Applesauce and carrots. Yes.

Sometimes, especially in some nonmainstream contexts, the adults around the child talk to one another about the child: "Dis young 'un wet his britches more'n any young 'un I know"; "Dis young 'un ain't actin' right, sump'n wrong wid' im" (Heath 1983, p. 75).

Slobin has extracted an intriguing set of utterances that one mother addressed to her two-year-old daughter as she was trying to curl the child's hair.

C'mon and let me set your hair.

Don't you want to have curls for this afternoon?

Why don't you lemme put your hair up?

You won't have any curls when you go down to see Betty and Alice.

Alice has lots of little curls in her hair.

Why don't you lemme fix your hair?

You won't have any curls.

Why don't you fix his hair [a doll's] and I'll fix your hair?

You fix his hair and I'll fix your hair.

Sit up here on the chair so I can fix your hair.

You'll look like Mag Snatch with a pretty dress on and no curls.

You'll look awful.

You don't want to go out and look awful.

How would you like to have your face combed?

Lemme get the snarls out of your hair.

Can I comb your hair?

Let me comb your bangs.

Lemme fix your hair.

Why don't you lemme fix your hair?

You gotta go lemme fix your hair first. (From unpublished data of Roger Brown, in Slobin 1979, pp. 105–6)

This is quite an array of forms used to tell a child to "sit still so I can fix your hair."

In all these examples, the child lacks complete linguistic knowledge about the adult's talk; yet the child has nonlinguistic knowledge of the situation, and this nonlinguistic knowledge of what is going on enables him, ultimately, to make connections between situational meanings and language forms.

> Put very simply, the child's task in learning to comprehend the speech of others is to make the match between the messages that he can expect in well-understood contexts, and the linguistic forms of utterances . . . in such contexts. (Wells 1979, p. 78)

When language meanings are expressed in writing rather than in talk, the young child seems to make and act on the same assumption: Written language expression relates to the context in which it occurs. You can see the three- to six-year-old children in the following examples acting on this assumption. Each child is shown a Kroger's milk carton, a Crest toothpaste box, and a Dynamints box (with a picture of the mints on it) and asked, "What does this say?" Here are the three- to six-year-olds' responses: Kroger milk carton—"Some milk goes in there," "Milk," "A milk box," "Kroger," "A milk can," "Kroger's." Crest toothpaste box—"Brush," "Toothbrush," "Toothpaste," "Crest." Dynamints box—"Hot," "Vitamins/medicine," "Mints," "Tic Tacs," "Dynamints" (Harste, Woodward, and Burke 1984, pp. 24, 29). These responses may seem unremarkable at first. However, as soon as you think of the thousands of responses the children do *not* give, you recognize how powerful the child's meaningful-in-context assumption is in guiding him in making sense of print. If no such assumption were operating, then "Sesame Street," "pizza," "Corn Flakes," "Stop," and "Dear Grandma" would be just as likely to occur as the children's milk, toothbrushing, and mint responses. After all, these other possible responses involve writing that these children encounter in their lives. But these writings belong—*mean*—in other contexts. It is messages having to do with milk, toothbrushing, and mints that the child assumes are relevant and expressed in writing in the present situation. In their encounters with both oral and written expression, children use their nonlinguistic understanding of situations to make sense of the language occurring in those situations.

Fortunately for the child, the oral and written language in use around him often does relate to the child's nonlinguistic understanding of the situation. If the child were not able to make sense of the ongoing situation, one wonders how he could possibly begin to crack the language code within the situation. Understanding the situation itself, the child is able to begin relating the linguistic expression in the situation (the talk or print or gesture) to the situational meaning that he understands. He uses what he does know to figure out what he does not know. The child's readiness to assume a relation between the language expression and the situation, and his readiness to act on this assumption to construct these connections, are striking.

Using nonlinguistic understanding to figure out the meaning-expression relations of language is a very pervasive strategy for children: It operates at the general level of world knowledge and also at the level of specific situation; it operates across components of language; it operates across expressive channels (talk, print, sign).[11]

Use whatever is salient and interesting to you. Children are virtually bombarded with language embedded in particular situations, but they do not attend to it all equally. They attend selectively; they focus on particular aspects. Nelson's work on early vocabulary development suggests that two characteristics are often salient to young children and account for many of their first words: (1) objects children can act on (for example, key, sock, hat) and (2) objects that move and change (for example, car, clock). Some of Clark's work suggests that perceptual characteristics may serve as focal points for children (for example, shape, size, sound, taste). Children notice the objects that embody these salient properties, and they notice how these objects are named in the language community. Brown's work points out children's attention to language elements that play important syntactic and semantic roles in sentences. The particular focus of attention for a child may be different at different periods in his development, and the focus of attention will be somewhat different from one child to another, but what is constant is the fact of attending selectively and using the focus of attention in building a language system.

An early study by Cazden (discussed in Cazden 1972) relates to this strategy of focusing attention on what is interesting. Her subjects were twelve black children, ranging in age from twenty-eight to thirty-eight months. The children all attended a day care center eight to ten hours a day where the child-adult ratio was thirty to one. Cazden reasoned that if one evaluated these children's language and then gave them a heavy dose of a particular type of intervention, one could assume that the differences in the children's language before and after the intervention were attributable, at least in part, to the intervention strategy used. She divided the children into three groups, four children in a group; two groups were experimental (an "expansion group" and an "extension group") and one group was a control. The children in the groups were comparable in age, talkativeness, and MLU. In a playroom for forty minutes a day for twelve weeks (a heavy dose), an adult interacted with each individual child in the two experimental groups in a specified way. In interacting with each of the four children who comprised the expansion group, the adult would provide the adult form for everything the child said in his developmental form. For example, if the child said, "Dog bark," the adult would say, "Yes, the dog is barking." In interacting with the four children in the extension group, the adult would deliberately *not* "repeat" (in the adult form) what the child had said, but rather would meet the child's idea with a relevant, but different, idea. For example, if the child said, "Dog bark," the adult might answer, "Yes, but he won't bite" or "I guess he's mad at the kitty" (Cazden 1972, p. 125). The four children in the control group received no special treatment but were familiar with the adult experimenters and the

[11]We'll see in Section Five that this strategy operates in second-language acquisition as well as in first-language acquisition.

playroom and played there from time to time. The language of all twelve children was evaluated before and after the twelve-week session, so it was assumed that if greater gains were made during that time by the children in one of the experimental groups over the children in the control group, then the particular intervention strategy could be said to have contributed to accelerating the children's language growth.

The researcher's expectation at the outset of the study was that the children in the expansion group would show the greatest gains. The assumption was that the adult's provision of the adult form at the very moment when the child's attention was focused on the meaning encoded by the form would maximize the likelihood of the child's connecting that meaning with that form. It was further assumed that pairing adult form and child's meaning in this way 100 percent of the time would be maximally efficient.

The children in the expansion group did make greater gains than the children in the control group. But interestingly, the children in the extension group made slightly greater gains than the expansion group children. The children here were attending selectively, and they were attending to meaning more than form. It is noteworthy, I think, that this is attention to what is most interesting in a situation. Having a partner meet your idea with a new idea, one that goes beyond the original, is more interesting than having a partner simply repeat (in your perception) what you just said. (Remember "Nobody don't like me" and "'nother one spoon," p. 102.)

We find a similar pattern in children's early experiences in literacy. A number of language researchers have documented children's early writing at home. Typically, the young children described in this research focused on writing that was of particular personal interest to them. One four-year-old writes

(Taylor 1983, p. 73)

A six-year-old who has gotten into her mother's forbidden sewing basket in her mother's absence writes

Dar Mom
Im sre for gedin inde uor sduf. Doby mad (Dear Mom, I'm sorry for getting into your stuff; don't be mad.) (Newkirk 1984, p. 343)

And a five-year-old protects his workbench against outside intrusion by putting a sign above it that reads:

DO NAT DSTRB GNYS AT WRK (Bissex 1980, p. 23)

And, of course, it is no coincidence that many children write their own name before anything else. What could possibly have greater personal significance? In writing, as in speech, the child's selective focus is evident. The child attends to and uses what is salient, interesting, and personally meaningful.

This selective attention strategy argues strongly against a clay lump view of children. It is not what is "there" in the child's world that is important for language, not even what is "there" with considerable frequency and/or with adult insistence (as in the form correction examples). It is what is interesting, important, and engaging to the child himself. It is what he selectively attends to that he uses as the building material of a language system. (This should give every teacher pause as he reflects on the typical language arts curriculum which imposes on children a preordained sequence of activities—usually basals, workbooks, and worksheets, a curriculum that certainly does not derive from children's interests and does not get children's spontaneous and engaged attention.)

Assume that language is (mainly) used either "referentially" or "expressively" and use language data accordingly. Nelson (1973) identified two distinct groups within her eighteen children, observed from the time they were approximately one until they were approximately two years of age. She called the two groups "referential" and "expressive." The referential children were those whose first fifty words included a high proportion of common nouns (object labels) and who seemed to see the primary function of language as naming objects. The expressive children were those whose first fifty words included proportionately more words used in social expressions (formulas and social routines such as "Stop it" and "Thank you") and fewer object names and who, Nelson felt, saw language as serving a primarily social-affective function. The assumption here is that the two groups of children were "tuning in" to the language around them differently, one group attending especially to language used to refer, the other group to language used to socialize.

Since Nelson's study, a number of researchers have found contrasting groups of children that parallel Nelson's referential and expressive categories. You may be able to sense the distinction from the different labels the two groups have been given in various studies: "word versus phrase," "cognitive versus pragmatic [social]," "nominal [noun] versus pronominal [pronoun]," and "analytic versus gestalt" (Nelson 1981, p. 172). Like Nelson's expressive children, identifiable groups have emerged in other studies as having a particularly social orientation to language: children who use a number of unanalyzed wholes such as social formulas and routines like "I don't want it," "What d'you want," or "Don't do it" (Nelson 1981, p. 174); who use a higher proportion of pronouns than do groups similar to Nelson's referential, and who use language for interactional purposes more than for labeling. Groups of children similar to Nelson's referential have also been identified: children who have a higher proportion of nouns (more precise references than the expressive children's "it" or "he"), whose language is more word-oriented than whole-sentence oriented, and who use language largely for labeling and commenting.[12]

In this strategy as in the preceding ones, we can see that the child's ways of attending to and using the language around him are influenced by assumptions he has made about language. In this case, the assumption is one about how language functions in the world. Referential children make a different assumption than do expressive children, but each child apparently makes some assumption and acts on it, building his own language system that does the kind of work that he has identified as important.

It would be a serious mistake to see these differences as total. In fact, both referential and expressive children use language in a variety of ways, including both labeling and socializing. Some children have been observed to change preference from one developmental period to another. Still others have been observed to use both referential and expressive styles, but to use each style in particular contexts (Peters 1977). The referential-expressive distinction simply identifies a preference. The child's preference—overall, or during a particular period in development or in particular contexts—guides his ways of attending to and using language.

Produce language and see how others respond.   Nelson (1973) observed what she called a "productive strategy." Some of the eighteen children in her study were talking a lot and getting feedback from others' responses to their talk. The excerpt that follows, from the conversation of a nineteen-month-old girl and her mother, demonstrates a productive strategy at work.

C: I sit down.
M: Oh, you're sitting down?
C: I sit down with cup. I sitting. I sit down.
M: Uh-huh. You're sitting down there.
C: Sit down there.
C: Sit down?
M: Yeah, you can sit down.
C: (She sits down.) I sit down.
M: OK. You can sit down. OK.
C: Sit down on boat.
M: Sit down on the boat.[13]

Notice that mother informally, conversationally, provides feedback to the child.

Though this strategy is only one possibility among many, in American mainstream society it may be especially valued. Typically, the informal

---

[12]Examples of these studies include Bretherton 1983 and Corte, Benedict, and Klein 1983.

[13]I am indebted to Carole Urzúa for this example from her data.

"measure" of a child's language development is what a child *says*, rather than what a child understands. The question usually is "Is Kimmy *talking* yet?" not "Does Kimmy understand the language people use around her and with her?" It may be that this productive strategy works very well for some children because their talking elicits response, that is, talk from others. Obviously, one needs language samples in order to figure out language. A productive strategy may elicit more language "data" for some children to work on.[14] In her study of Spanish-dominant children learning English as their second language, Fillmore (1976) found that the children who talked a lot in English did get a lot of English talk back from their English-speaking friends. You can see here the difficulty of separating cognitive from social aspects of language learning: A productive strategy is "social" in the sense that it may increase interaction with others and, at the same time, is "cognitive" in that it provides the learner with feedback about his own expression of meanings and also gives him a larger sample of language to "work on."

Observe how others express meanings. "Comprehension strategy" is the label Nelson (1973) gave to those children in her study who talked less and seemed to be observing more—attending selectively, tuning in, watching to see how meanings and verbal expressions related. Both comprehension and production strategies correlated with high linguistic maturity at age two. Whatever the American mainstream preference for a productive strategy, Nelson's study does not find this strategy to have an advantage in language learning over a comprehension strategy.[15]

Adults—teachers among them—sometimes fail to recognize a comprehension strategy at work in children. Further, there is a tendency, I believe, to regard a production strategy as active but a comprehension strategy (insofar as it is recognized at all) as passive, inert. But certainly there is no cognitive doing that is more active than observing, attending. The comprehender-observer child is no less active than his producer friend. The challenge is for us to be as aware of the comprehender's activity as we are of the producer's.

[14]This is an area where one finds considerable cultural variation. High value placed on talk is characteristic of American mainstream culture, both in the early years and in the school years. Note, for example, even at college level, the value placed on "class participation"—which, of course, means how much you volunteer to talk. However, more talk is not necessarily "better" in all American cultures. See, for example, Philips's (1983) description of the Warm Springs Indians.

[15]These two strategies may remind you of different learning styles or preferences you have seen in children of other ages in other learning situations. Some children seem to "learn by doing," but many children we teach appear to prefer an observation strategy; they watch and put the pieces together in their heads. Teachers usually assume that the more overtly expressive child is brighter and the observer less so. Comments like "She's very quiet. *But* she's bright enough" are typical. "But" is the crucial word here— quiet *but* bright. We rarely hear teachers say, "Oh, she's so quiet and bright." I know of no research that supports our tendency to assume that overtly expressive children are more intelligent than children geared toward observation. Without meaning to push Nelson's research too far, I would suggest that it supports the effectiveness of an active observation strategy in one important area of learning, that of learning a language. There is no reason to suppose that an active observation strategy is not an efficient strategy for other kinds of learning as well.

The presence and effectiveness of a comprehension strategy are borne out by Fillmore's current research on Spanish-dominant and Chinese-dominant children learning English as their second language from the beginning of kindergarten to the end of second grade (Fillmore 1983). Periodic English language tests (designed and administered by the research team) showed a number of "comprehender" children (this is not Fillmore's term) to be among the more proficient English language learners and some producer children to be among the less proficient (personal communication). That is, degree of English language proficiency did not relate in a simple, direct way to use of a producer or comprehender strategy. If research evidence does not indicate that a producer strategy in language learning is superior to a comprehender-observer strategy, it is reasonable to wonder why we often see a teacher preference for a producer strategy in classrooms.

Ask questions to elicit the data you want.   Many children around age two are busy building their vocabularies. These two-year-olds don't say to us, "I'm working on labels now so would you tell me what various objects are called?" But some of the children in Nelson's study (1973) did something equally effective; they asked, "What dis?" "What dat?" That is, they used a "questioning strategy." If a child is trying to figure out the names used to label objects and actions in his world, this strategy would seem to be a particularly effective one, for every time he asks, "What dis?" or "What dat?" his conversational partner is likely to provide the appropriate label. (In Nelson's study this strategy, like the producer and comprehender strategies, correlated positively with linguistic maturity at age two. That is, questioning was a strategy used by the more linguistically developed children, which is to be expected, since it is a strategy that requires that the child have more control of language than earlier strategies require.) Not surprisingly, Nelson found questioning at age two to relate positively to vocabulary acquisition (p. 54).

An interesting pattern occurs in many children's use of "why" questions at around age three. Many children have been observed to increase their use of "why" questions dramatically, to a high degree of frequency, and then, after several months, to drop down to a moderate use of these questions. When we see a particular aspect of language suddenly come into sharp prominence for a child, we assume that the child is "working on" that aspect of the system. What is it about "why" questions that a child might be working on during this high-frequency period? It has been suggested that he might be "working" to understand causal relationships: Every time he asks "why?" his conversational partner provides an example of a "because X," a causal relationship. But some researchers have recently observed that by the time the child is asking "Why?" he has already been expressing causal relationships in nonquestion form for some time (in sentences with "and," "because," or "so") (Bloom et al. 1982). These researchers suggest that the "why" child may already have a beginning concept of cause but may still need to figure out the particular syntax of its expression in question form. And indeed, there is quite a bit to figure out about this. Comparing the earlier "What dat?" with later "Why?" reveals some of the complexities of "why."

> "What dat?" asks about one particular part of a sentence—the object (What's that? A _____); whereas "Why?" asks about an entire sentence—all the relationships within it (Why is the baby crying? Because he wants his bottle).
>
> "What dat?" can be learned as a fixed, unanalyzed routine; whereas "Why?" must be used differently (especially with a range of different verbs) for each situation (Why did she come? Go? Break it? Put it there?).
>
> "What dat?" is conversationally easy in that it can simply "drop down" anywhere as a topic initiation; whereas "Why" is "responsive to topics initiated by someone else" (Bloom et al. 1982, p. 1091)—that is, it often connects with what has preceded it in conversation (The baby's crying. Why is she crying?).

It may be that in asking so many "why" questions, the child is eliciting the very conversational contexts within which he can figure out how "why" questions are expressed in different situations (especially using different verbs) and how they connect with others' talk in the conversation. Thus, though "What dat?" and "Why?" questions are very different, both may be helpful in providing the child with important language examples.

Obviously, older children can use questions to find out specific things they want to know about language, as the two four-year-old girls do in the following examples in which their mothers read them bedtime stories. (See further examples from these children on pp. 78-79.)[16]

M: "Horton stayed on that nest. He held his head high and he threw out his chest."
C-1: What is "threw out his chest"? (Seuss 1968)

M: "But George felt sick and dizzy. His throat was hurting too."
C-2: What does "dizzy" mean? (Rey and Rey 1966, p. 26)

M: "I'll call a nurse and have her take you to the admitting office."
C-2: What's "admitting office"? (Rey and Rey 1966, p. 14)

These examples involve oral expression, but children's questions often deal with written expression as well.

Mother opens book (*Whistle for Willie*) to title page.
M: "Whistle for Willie."
C-1: Who was it written by? (She realizes that the next line of print will name the author.) (Keats 1971)

Mother is reading *Sarah's Unicorn.*
M: "He will take her on his back, and they will ride to dawn, dancing on the moon beams. Unicorns can do that you know."
SARAH: Is that the word or are you saying it? (Coville and Coville 1979)

---

[16]I am indebted to Carol Peterson and Miriam Martinez for these examples from their data.

Questioning is one powerful way of learning about the world. Clearly, many children use questioning effectively to make sense of language, both oral and written.

Imitate what other people say.   The strategy of imitation poses a major problem. What *is* imitation?[17] "That's easy," you say. "It's saying the same thing someone else said." Fine, but

> Must the imitation be exactly what someone else said?
> Must it have exactly the same words (*all* of them) in exactly the same order?
> Must the intonation and stress be the same as the model?
> What differences can occur in the "imitation" of the model for it still to be considered an "imitation"? What about substitutions? For example,

> *ADULT*:   I vacuum.
> *CHILD*:   Me vacuum. (Moerk 1977, p. 189)

> What about additions to the original?
> What about deletions—so-called "reduced imitation"?
> What about imperfections in the imitation, for example, stuttering, internal pauses?
> What about differences in pronunciation?

> *M*:   How 'bout some crackers?
> *C*:   Cwackers.

> And must the imitation follow the model utterance immediately? Or within three conversational turns? Or five? Or three days later?
> If the candidate utterance occurs after a silence, is it still an imitation? How long a silence—ten seconds? Three minutes?
> Is the child's utterance an imitation if it occurs with prompting (for example, in a sentence-repetition test in which the experimenter gives sentences for the child to repeat) or only if the utterance occurs in a natural situation?

These questions are not trivial. If you are a researcher intent on exploring children's use of imitation in learning their mother tongue, then you must decide what imitation is so that you can extract and study all instances of it from children's speech samples. In fact, all of the possibilities suggested in the preceding questions have been used to define imitation in one study or another. The research literature on imitation is replete with phrases that hint at the variety in what has been studied as "imitation": "spontaneous imitation," "elicited imitation," "immediate imitation," "delayed imitation," "imitation with expansion," "reduced imitation," and so on. It is little wonder that the results from these studies have often conflicted, for different definitions of "imitation" have led to different bodies of data to be examined. Also, the examinations themselves have differed in the ways the imitations were analyzed. One major question resulting from the conflict-

[17]For a discussion of some of the various ways that "imitation" has been defined, in research studies, see Snow 1981.

ing results of these studies was, Is imitation progressive? It was recognized that children do sometimes repeat what others say, but the question was whether this repeating advanced the child's linguistic system in any way. Some research suggests that children only imitate constructions of the types they already control. If the model is more complex than the child's system, the child does not imitate but reformulates the model sentence to fit his existing system. Consider these examples, from a two-year-old, (Slobin and Welsh 1973):

MODEL: The pencil is green.
REPETITION: pencil green (Slobin and Welsh 1973, p. 487)
MODEL: The little boy is eating some pink ice cream.
REPETITION: little boy eating some pink ice cream. (p. 487)
MODEL: This one is the giant, but this one is little.
REPETITION: dis one little, annat one big (p. 490)
MODEL: The man who I saw yesterday got wet.
REPETITION: I saw the man and he got wet.
MODEL: The man who I saw yesterday runs fast.
REPETITION: I saw the man and he run fast (p. 494)

These examples involve elicited imitation, but some researchers have made a similar observation in naturalistic settings in which the child's imitations are spontaneous (Ervin-Tripp 1964). Clearly, if a child imitates only structures he already controls and does not imitate those beyond the complexity of his current system, it makes no sense to argue that imitation helps to advance the child's linguistic system. Yet some researchers argue that sometimes children's imitations are more complex than their nonimitated utterances and thus imitation is "progressive." So, is imitation progressive or isn't it?

Our increasing understanding of the active nature of children's language learning has, I think, helped to bring some focus to this blurred picture. Our characterization of the kind of process imitation is has changed from a passive notion to an active one: from imitation as "echoism: the fact that children echo what is said to them" (Jespersen 1922, quoted in Bloom, Hood, and Lightbown 1974, p. 381) to imitation as an active, selective, child-determined process. If imitation were a mindless, automatic, echo behavior, we would expect a randomness in what children repeat. However, recent imitation studies have identified a clear, nonrandom pattern in what it is that children do, and do *not*, imitate; that is, there is selection on the part of the child, (Bloom, Hood, and Lightbown 1974; Moerk 1977). The children studied "imitated only words and structures in the speech that they heard which they appeared to be in the process of learning. They tended not to imitate words and structures that they themselves either used spontaneously and so presumably knew, or did not use spontaneously at all and so presumably did not know" (Bloom, Hood, and Lightbown 1974, p. 416). "Imitative behavior was not merely acoustic or an automatic echoing of random linguistic events" (p. 417). Again, we see a child who seems to be working on particular parts of the linguistic system, reminiscent of the child's use of questions, as discussed earlier. The structures imitated by the observed children changed over time: As the child mastered particular structures, he stopped imitating those and instead imitated others that he was in the process of learning. The course of acquisition of particular structures in children who use imitation as a learning process is that the child first uses the new structure in its adult form in imitated utterances but in a developmental form in his own spontaneous utterances; then he continues to imitate the adult form but uses both the adult and developmental forms in his own spontaneous utterances; and finally he stops imitating that structure and uses it only in his spontaneous speech (Bloom et al. 1974; Moerk 1977). This observed sequence (from imitations only, to imitations and spontaneous use, to spontaneous use only) reveals an active child using in self-determined ways the language available to him. This is vastly different from echoing behavior.

The child-determined nature of imitation is further evident in the differential use that children make of this strategy. Some children have been observed to use it very little, while other children at a comparable developmental stage use it a great deal. In one naturalistic study in which six children were observed for approximately seven months (age eighteen months to twenty-five months (MLU 1.0 to MLU 2.0), one child's imitated utterances never comprised more than 6 percent of her total during a taping session, while another child's imitated utterances never comprised less than 27 percent (Bloom et al. 1974). Also, those children who do use an imitation strategy seem to use it more at an earlier developmental stage than at a later stage (Nelson 1973).

Another line of research on imitation also sees imitation as an active strategy but characterizes the nature of the child's cognitive activity somewhat differently. Ruth Clark (1978) maintains that a child builds a supply of what she calls "stored imitations" that "constitute a child's linguistic repertoire" (p. 397). The stored imitation may be faulty in that the child may have stored only part of the content or form of the adult version. ". . . speech production, at least in the early stages, depends largely on reproducing stored sequences, or combining or fusing them in simple ways" (p. 405). Clark maintains that at first these stored sequences are unanalyzed by the child: The child simply accumulates them as fixed chunks or formulas, but eventually the child "builds up grammatical competence through examining stored fragments" (p. 409). This is an interesting idea, though it may lead one into some rather sticky problems, for example, (1) assuming that a child's speech at an early period is predominantly imitative, even though it may not closely resemble any identifiable adult speech the child has been exposed to, or (2) assuming that a child's "novel utterances" are "very simple modifications of imitations" (p. 407) rather than the result of some other process that seems equally justified by the utterances themselves. Nevertheless, it may be that this building of a repertoire of stored, unanalyzed speech chunks that the child will subsequently analyze does play a significant role as a strategy for some children.

The suggestion gains support from a similar observation made with respect to second-language learning. Fillmore (1976) found that five- to seven-year-old Spanish-dominant children learning English as their second language began by accumulating a repertoire of fixed formulas. Gradually the children "freed" parts of the formulas so that various combinations began to occur in their speech. Fillmore suggests that the basis of this approach is social: Using memorized fixed formulas appropriately in particular situations enabled these children, beginners in English, to participate in conversations with English speakers who were more proficient. This social consideration may be of importance in first-language learning as well. There are many situations in adult-adult conversation in which repetition is clearly not an attempt to copy what the preceding speaker said. Greetings ("Hi," "Hi") and leavetakings ("S'long," "S'long") are obvious examples, but Keenan (1977) identifies some less obvious examples of communication situations in which the second speaker repeats the first: self-informing ("That's Halley's Comet." "Ah, Halley's Comet."), agreeing ("That's dreadful." "Dreadful."), matching a claim ("I'm fat." "I'm fat."), querying ("Yes." "Yes?"), and answering ("Yes?" "Yes.")Keenan's (1977) examination of her twin sons' conversations (age two to age three) with each other and with adults suggests that children also may repeat others in order to contribute to the conversation in important ways. Consider some examples from these twins and their sitter.

A: And we're going to have hot dogs.
C-1:   Hot dogs!
A: And soup.
C-2:   Mmmm soup! (Keenan 1977, p. 130)

A: Aren't I a good cook? Say "Yes, the greatest!"
C-1:   Yes the greatest. (softly)
A: That's right.
C-2:   The greatest! (loudly) (p. 131)

C-1:   My hands are cold.
C-2:   Cold. (p. 131)

C-1:   My big tractors coming/
C-2:   No/
C-1:   Its coming/ *look* its coming/ its coming
C-2:   Now its coming/Its coming/Its coming/*look* its coming
C-1:   I see. (p. 135)

In the last two examples (the child-child examples), the children are following the convention they established whereby the second speaker gave some sign of attentiveness to the partner's preceding utterance. Repeating that utterance in whole or in part served as such a sign.

Notice that this work uses the term "repetition," not the term "imitation," the basic idea being that the child's repetition of others' utterances can serve many functions other than imitating or copying a model.[18]

Keenan (1977) suggests that one especially important conversational function that repetition serves in child language is to establish conversational topics.

(The twins are in their bedroom and hear their mother's alarm clock ring.)
C-1:   Was Mommy's alarm clock/
C-2:   'larm clock/yeah/goes ding dong ding dong
C-1:   No/no/goes fip fip/fip fip/ (p. 136)

A: Juji's going camping this afternoon.
C-1:   Oh yeah/ (simultaneously)
C-2:   Camping/oh exciting (p. 137)

In the first example, by repeating C-1's "alarm clock," C-2 establishes alarm clock as the conversational topic and goes on to comment about it; and in the second example, C-2 does the same with "camping." Later these children will develop other ways—syntactic ways—to establish a conversation topic. But for the young child, repetition of others' talk can help him do this important conversational work.

Again we find a strategy that is as important socially as cognitively for children. The strategy of repeating what others say may help some children to further their construction of a linguistic system while at the same time offering a way of participating in conversation. Do you get the feeling that the distinction between "cognitive" and "social" is simply an artifact of the adults' analytic tendencies, a distinction that has little basis in the reality of the child's world? You're right, of course.

We can conclude that recent research on children's imitation of others' speech indicates that imitation is, like other language-learning strategies children use, an active and selective strategy. The child's repetition of others' talk is not mindless parroting; rather, it is a matter of attending to and using those particular parts of others' speech that are helpful and relevant at the moment. And those selected parts turn out to be the items the child is currently "working on," rather than either what he has mastered already or what is still well beyond him. Repetition of others' talk supports the child's language development in another important way also: It offers the child a way to participate actively in conversation at a time when his syntactic development is minimal.

Use some general "operating principles" to figure out language.   Slobin's work on operating principles supports the notion of children as active noticers and users of patterns in language acquisition. Slobin and his stu-

---

[18]The social significance of an imitative strategy is also suggested by the finding that expressive children are more imitative than referential children. See, for example, Bretherton et al. 1983.

dents have vigorously collected their own data and have intensively studied data collected by others on first language acquisition in more than forty different languages, including Greek, Hindi, Hungarian, Turkish, Japanese, Finnish, Czech, Russian, Navaho, Samoan, Italian, Serbo-Croatian, and Swedish (Slobin 1973, pp. 177–79). Slobin looks for commonalities in the way children learn language across widely diverse languages. His assumption is that the commonalities will be a function of children's language acquisition strategies—their mental processing—rather than a function of the particular language being acquired. If children acquiring languages which are so very different are proceeding in very similar ways in the language-learning task, Slobin assumes that in these learning similarities we may be tapping those "process mechanism(s) . . . set(s) of procedures and inference rules . . . that children use . . . to process linguistic data" (Slobin 1966, pp. 87–88). He cites a number of commonalities observed and, based on these, posits some operating principles, "a sort of general heuristic . . . which the child brings to bear on the task of organizing and storing language" (Slobin 1973, p. 191).

For example, prefixes tend to be acquired later than suffixes. Children learning a language which expresses a particular meaning (such as location) as a suffix control this linguistic feature earlier than do children learning a language in which this same meaning is expressed as a prefix. This is one bit of evidence supporting Slobin's suggested operating principle (or child's self-instruction): "Pay attention to the ends of words" (1973, p. 191).[19] Another operating principle, "Pay attention to the order of words and morphemes" (p. 197), is suggested by the fact that children, whatever language they are learning, typically preserve the order of the input language. They may leave out items the adult would include, but those items children do include in their speech at any given point tend to be in the order the adult language would require.

Several of Slobin's suggested operating principles are stated in avoidance terms: "Avoid rearrangements" and "Avoid exceptions." We have already seen examples of avoiding rearrangements in those early information questions English-speaking children ask: "Where *you are* going?" "Why *he is* doing that?" And the avoidance of exceptions principle would account for the overgeneralizations applied to irregular verbs and plurals, noted earlier—the "comed," "goed," "foots," and "mans" cases that are so typical. Another interesting operating principle Slobin suggests is "Underlying semantic relations should be marked overtly and clearly" (p. 202). That is, the child seems to proceed on the assumption that if there is a particular meaning, it will find a particular expression in the surface structure. The English-speaking child's early forms like "putted" and "sheeps" suggest the use of such a principle. In the adult language, we have a surface form "put" which does not indicate past, and a surface form "sheep" which does not indicate plural. But the young child seems to assume that if the meaning of past is intended, then it should be clearly indicated in the

---

[19]This discussion is simplified from Slobin's (1973) article "Cognitive Prerequisites to the Development of Grammar." For more extensive development of the procedure, supporting data, and complete set of proposed operating principles, see the article itself.

surface structure, thus "putted"; and if the meaning of plural is intended, then it should be clearly indicated in the surface structure, thus "sheeps."

Slobin suggests more operating principles and offers more support than I have indicated here, but this should suffice to indicate that children (universally, it appears) go about the task of language acquisition using some similar mental processing schemes. They seem especially geared to noticing certain aspects of the input language data (order of parts, general patterns), and to utilizing it in building their language system.

"Make the most of what you've got"   (Fillmore 1976, p. 649). It seems remarkable that young children manage to do so much with so little: They manage to communicate a variety of meanings through very limited linguistic means. Think what the child conveys even before he uses words. He points to an object beyond his reach, looks toward the adult and vocalizes; he reaches both arms up to the adult and whimpers; he hands the adult a wind-up toy he is unable to manipulate and looks up expectantly; he takes predictable turns in games: The adult says "Wheeeeere's Trey?" and the child points to himself; The adult says, "Can you wave bye-bye?" He does. The adult claps her hands together and says, "Can you do patty cake?" He claps his hands together and grins. The adult says, "I'm gonna get 'cha" and the child scurry-crawls away. Situation plus gesture plus vocalizations convey a great deal. Words convey even more. Remember how effectively the child uses single words, especially in the later part of the one-word stage when the single word the child provides in a situation is the most informative word—literally, the most "telling." And consider this example from early combinatory speech.

A two-year-old girl is coloring on paper and talking with her mother about the crayons.

C: That green?
M: Um-hm. It's a very light green.
C: Oh. Brand new?
M: Um-hm. I think that one is brand new.
C: Those too old?
M: Well, some of them are old and some of them are new. The little ones are old and the longer ones are new.
C: Baby one old?
M: Um-hm.
C: Throw away?
M: Oh no. We're not going to throw them away yet. They are still good. We can still draw with them.[20]

This child's MLU (from a larger sample) is 2.5, yet using these short, simple constructions, she is able to make herself understood, to elicit the information she seeks, and even to take the initiative for the direction of the conversation. This is making the most of what you've got.

[20]I am indebted to Carole Urzúa for this example.

Children use words in several ways that suggest that they are "filling gaps" (Clark 1983), that is, they are extending the words they do have to convey some meanings for which they do not yet have words. Semantic overextension is a clear case. It may be that a child calls a sheep "doggie," not because he fails to recognize a sheep and a dog as different (that is, as being contrasting meanings in the language) but because he does not have a word for sheep and the label "dog" is the best of the set of labels that he does have in his repertoire. This fill-the-gap suggestion gains support from the observation that children "will not overextend a word from one category to pick out another when they already have a word for the latter in their repertoire" (Clark 1983, p. 822). Thus, if the child has both the word "dog" and the word "sheep" within his repertoire, he will not call the sheep "dog." His calling a sheep "dog" is not a matter of confusing dogs and sheep, either what they are or what they are called. It's just that he stretches the one label if he has only one, again making the most of what he has.

Another kind of semantic stretching to fill gaps is the child's use of general terms, his early reliance on all-purpose words. Thus, the child's "big" may be used for many specific kinds of bigness: wide, tall, fat, long, and so on. Lacking the words that indicate these specific dimensions of bigness, the child's general term "big" covers the range of specific cases for which he lacks more specialized terms.

A making-the-most-of-what-you've-got strategy is evident in syntax also. Think of the child's early noun + noun combinations, which he uses to convey a variety of syntactic relations. In a short time span, one child used these:

> cup glass (conjunction, meaning "I see a cup and a glass.")
> party hat (attribution, meaning "This is a party hat.")
> Kathryn sock (possessive, meaning "This is Kathryn's sock.")
> sweater chair (location, meaning "The sweater is on the chair.")
> Kathryn ball (agent-object, meaning "Kathryn will throw the ball.") (Based on Slobin 1971, pp. 46–47)

In fact, in one study a child was observed to use the very same two words in combination to convey two different meanings: "Mommy sock" spoken when the child picked up her mother's sock, and then again when her mother was putting the child's sock on the child. The contexts suggest that in the first case the child was expressing possession, while in the second case she was expressing an agent-object relation something like "Mommy's putting the sock on me" (Bloom 1970, p. 5).

Besides this semantic and syntactic stretching, children also stretch their language to do discourse work for them, that is, to enhance their participation in conversations. The best example here is perhaps the case we considered earlier of children repeating what others say to them by way of establishing a conversational topic. Lacking the syntactic means to establish the topic, the child uses what he does have, namely, the ability to repeat what the previous speaker said.

"Expressive" children, whose talk is often high in imitation of fixed formulas, may also be using this strategy for social purposes. The language formulas they use are as yet unanalyzed by them into elements and relations among them. But their "presyntactic" use of these chunks enables them to participate socially. Indeed, in her study of five- to seven-year-olds' learning of English as a second language, Fillmore found this formula use to serve important social purposes for her Spanish-dominant subjects (Fillmore 1976). It seems that the gaps that language-learning children fill are social gaps as well as linguistic ones. Notice that making the most of what you've got is a strategy that is motivated and sustained by a desire to communicate your meanings to others.

The Interaction of Linguistic and Cognitive Complexity

We have seen that creatively constructing a language is a very involving cognitive endeavor. Slobin suggests that the developmental sequence of acquisition will reflect the influence of both cognitive and linguistic complexity. Children express the "semantic intentions" or meanings of which they are capable, those which they understand. As some understandings are cognitively simpler, we would expect them to be expressed earlier in children's speech. In English, for example, the surface structure of the two questions, "Where did you go?" and "When did you go?" is similar. But, as we know, children typically ask (some form of) "where" questions before they ask "when" questions. This order is cognitively influenced. The sensorimotor child lives in a concrete, spatially oriented world, an environment of things in places. His earliest understandings include location. But "when" questions require some grasp of abstract and elusive time concepts. Understanding of time concepts develops later than understanding of location, and so, of course, their expression as "when" questions comes later also.

In some instances it is the influence of linguistic complexity that is especially clear in acquisition order. Studying young bilingual children's acquisition of their two languages, Slobin finds cases in which children express a given meaning, such as location, in one language but not in the other. Clearly, they understand the concept involved, or they would not be able to express it in either language. Looking at the languages in question, Slobin finds the syntactic devices for expressing that notion to be simpler in the one language than in the other. Thus, children master expression of location earlier in the language in which such expression is syntactically simpler, and later in the language in which expression of location is syntactically more complex.

Slobin provides an important generalization about the continuousness in language development. It is a generalization supported by his cross-cultural study of language acquisition: *New forms first express old functions, and new functions are first expressed by old forms* (Slobin 1973, p. 184). It is a sentence that takes some thinking about, but it is an important idea well worth the effort. By "functions" Slobin means something like "understandings," and by "old forms," he means forms which are already within the child's repertoire. This sentence might be paraphrased as "The child will first use a new structure to express an already familiar meaning; and he will express new meanings first by using already familiar structures." Either a new form or a new meaning, but not both. The child moves steadily, incorporating something new within a framework that is familiar. A child might first express the notion of juice being in the cup by saying, "juice cup." Later, the same child might express this as "juice *in* cup." This expression is a "new form" expressing an "old function" (understood meaning). A humorous example of the reverse—a new meaning first being expressed by the forms already within the child's control, comes from Slobin's three-year-old daughter: " 'Anything is not to break—just glasses and plates' " (1973, p. 186). She had come to a new and rather complex idea, something like "Nothing is breakable except glasses and plates." Lacking this complex expression for her new idea, she did the best she could with what she had. She used the language forms already within her control to express this new notion. And once again we see a child filling gaps by making the most of what she has in language.

Finally

One cannot but be impressed with children's development, indeed, their invention, of language. Recognizing and appreciating the active, creative construction processes children employ, we can put to rest forever the passive images of children—children as empty vessels to be filled, as clay lumps to be shaped, as blank slates to be written on. Necessarily, then, we must also put to rest the notions of teaching which these passive images imply: If children are not empty vessels, then the teacher's work cannot be to fill them up; if children are not clay lumps, then the teacher's work cannot be to shape them; if children are not blank slates, then the teacher's work cannot be to write on them.

THE SOCIAL CONTEXT

It goes without saying that a child, however well-endowed he might be for creatively constructing a language system, must be in a world of language in use in order to figure out how language is structured and used. It also goes without saying that the language he will learn is the particular language to which he has access.

In the past several decades much research has been conducted on early mother-child interaction in mainstream families, as this is thought to be a major context for language development.[21] As this research accumulated and similar patterns were observed in one mother-child pair after another, the assumption grew that the patterns observed were very widespread. It was suggested, sometimes explicitly and sometimes implicitly, that these observed interaction patterns were universal and, some even suggested, *necessary* for effective language development.

---

[21]The term "mother" is used in the sense of primary caregiver for the child. It may be someone other than the biological mother.

> It is . . . clear . . . how dependent language acquisition is upon the nature of
> the interaction that takes place between child and mother. Being a witness at
> the feast of language is not enough of an exposure to assure acquisition.
> There must be contingent interaction. (Bruner 1978, p. 64)

However, recent research on language development in American non-mainstream communities and in non-Western cultures indicates that the mother-child interaction patterns that had been described are, in fact, not universal; they are, instead, American mainstream (perhaps Western mainstream) patterns. This in no way invalidates the very rich body of mainstream mother-child interaction research; it does, however, place that work within a larger perspective: that the mainstream pattern described is one pattern among many. We currently know far more about the one than we do about the many, but already the new research on nonmainstream contexts of language acquisition has been enormously important. In addition to putting the mainstream research into a broader perspective, the non-mainstream work has suggested aspects of interaction that may differ significantly from one culture to another (for example, how much adults talk directly to young children; how adults talk to young children, whether with or without special speech modifications; who talks directly to young children and who talks "around" young children, to others within the child's hearing; how others use body language in interaction with and around young children; and so on).

This section of the chapter will describe the mainstream picture first. It may be a picture which squares with your own informal observations of children and families you know. If it is a pattern which is familiar to you, you may have difficulty remembering that the picture is only one way among many that the environment provides language around and with the language-learning child. This mainstream picture is the one we have most information about and thus the one I'll describe most fully. But for all that, try to remember as you read that the mainstream behaviors described we now know not to be universal; in fact, they do not characterize the backgrounds from which many American children come to school.

"Baby Talk" (or "Motherese")

Many adults talk differently to young children than they talk to other adults. The form of language these adults use when talking to young children is called "baby talk" (sometimes "Motherese"). Notice this is not what the lay person means by this term. Traditionally baby talk has referred to language forms we attributed to young children. This is not what we mean by the term here. Baby talk is defined as a language version that "consists only of language material identifiable as primarily appropriate for speech to young children" (Ferguson 1975, p. 7). Researchers have found baby talk to include phonological, syntactic, and semantic modifications of the adult language that adults deem appropriate for interacting with babies and young children.

Noam Chomsky's insistence in the 1960s on the gross imperfection of the language sample that the language-acquiring child was exposed to, gave impetus to this line of baby talk research. Chomsky (1965) maintained that one of the strongest supports for the view that language was to a considerable degree "innately specified" was that the language the child is exposed to—the corpus of data that he must work from to figure out expression-meaning relations and underlying linguistic structure—is such a mish-mash of false starts, backtracking, and hemming and hawing that a child could not possibly discern underlying rules from such a corpus. Chomsky claimed that the actual performance of speakers is so far removed from the idealized competence (intuitive knowledge of underlying rules) the child achieves that it is inconceivable that the child could acquire linguistic knowledge from performance data. The child must, he concluded, be born with the universals of linguistic structure already present as part of his genetic inheritance (N. Chomsky 1965).

It is undeniable that when adults engage in informal conversation, all the performance imperfections that Chomsky has noted are evident. However, it has become increasingly clear that many adults talk to young children differently than they talk to other adults. Study the two interactions that follow.[22] The first involves a mother telling an adult interviewer about her three-year-old daughter. The second involves *the same mother* talking with her three-year-old daughter with no one else present. List all the baby talk features that you can find in the second conversation. One guiding question might be, "What aspects of the mother's speech to her child would seem funny or inappropriate in conversation with me?" Those features which are appropriate in her interaction with the child but which would seem inappropriate in her interaction with you or another adult are baby-talk features. What differences do you notice between her speech to the adult interviewer and her speech to her child?

CONVERSATION 1

MOTHER: She was potty trained at one-and-a-half.
INTERVIEWER: Gee! That's good!
M: Potty trained early, walk slow. But you know, I've always heard it's better if they're a slow walker because it takes so much coordination to crawl, and I don't know if this is true or not, but I've always been told that the longer a child . . . (pause) . . . crawls, the more coordinated they'll be. I don't know if that's true or not, but I know when . . . (pause) . . . there are children who are uncoordinated, sometimes for practice, they'll make them crawl. She was a *good* crawler and she wasn't, you know, when she first started crawling she wasn't one of those that crawled on her stomach, you know. She just started crawling. She wasn't a scooter, whatever, you know. Some kids scoot and some roll, you know. (Getting out baby book.) Jill started crawling . . . (looking through book, pause) . . . I have this in here somewhere. Oh! Ah . . . (pause) . . . I think she was almost thirteen months old when she started. Okay . . . (pause) . . . sat up at six months. I remember, she, it took her a long time to sit up, too, or sit up, but she stood up at eighteen, er . . . (pause) . . . eight months, but she didn't start walking until um . . . (pause) . . . you know,

[22] I am grateful to Shirley Hollibaugh for allowing me to use these conversations from her data. (The child's name has been changed here.)

walking across the room . . . um . . . let's see . . . (pause) . . . I always meant to write all this (laughing) and just never did!

CONVERSATION 2

M: (Preparing child for bath; child has a rash.) C'mon. Take your c. . ., take your clothes off and (inaudible) your (inaudible) on. Mommy's puttin' some baking soda in it. Okay?

C: Okay. Don't take these away to me. (Refers to bathtub toys.)

M: Don't take them away to you?

C: No.

M: Why? (Drawn out with falling and then rising pitch.)

C: 'Cause I wants too many more. Right?

M: Hurry up. Take your 'jammies off.

C: I's . . . (pause) . . . take 'em off.

M: (Softly) Want me to help you?

C: Yeah.

M: (Almost a whisper) Come 'ere. You still itch?

C: Yep.

M: Wonder what's *makin'* (unusually high pitch) those bumps? They're all oooooover you!

C: Yeah.

M: What's makin' 'em, I wonder.

C: Donno.

M: Oh! My goodness! (Rising pitch, drawn out syllables.) Look! All over you! (Laughing.) Isn't it funny?

C: (Weakly) Yeah.

M: Huh?

C: Yeah.

M: Ya' wanna get in the water now and see if that helps?

C: Yeah.

M: Wadda ya wanna do today?

C: Donno.

M: Wanna go see Na-ma? (Child's grandmother.) Wadda ya wanna do?

C: Donno.

M: Go (inaudible) to Na-ma's and play?

C: (Inaudible) and put my, my, b . . . put my, that on. (M dressing child.)

M: What on?

C: My . . . new shoes.

M: Jill, those shoes don't *go* with your *pants*. Corduroy pants? You don't wear Sunday shoes with corduroy pants.

C: Do!

M: Why?

C: We do!

M: Who says?

C: M . . . m . . . Becky.

M: (Drawn out, sing-song, low to high pitch) Becky says? (Laughing.) When did Becky tell you that?

C: 'Cause she did.

M: Uh uh. (Meaning no.)
C: Uh huh! (Meaning yes.)

Some phonological features of baby talk that have often been observed and which you might have found in the mother-child conversation are exaggerated intonation contours (ups and downs of the voice), lengthening (stretching a word or syllable out in time), use of higher than normal pitch, whispering, exaggerated stress or emphasis, and substitution of sounds that are easier for children to pronounce for those that are more difficult (for example, reduction of consonant clusters). Some syntactic features that have been noted include the omission of inflections, auxiliaries, and "be"— "dolly walk" rather than the adult "The dolly is walking," or "Baby do it?" rather than "Can the baby do it?" or "You a good girl?" rather than "Are you a good girl?"

In this baby talk register, the length of sentences adults address to young children tends to be significantly shorter than the length of sentences they use with other adults. Also, the sentences they address to young children tend to be syntactically simpler than those typically used in adult-adult dialogue, including less embedding. It is interesting, too, that the adult's sentences to young children are notably more well formed than the sentences they use in conversations with adults; the child-addressed sentences contain substantially fewer performance imperfections and disfluencies of all kinds. (The differences in length, simplicity, and well-formedness of sentences are particularly evident in the foregoing sample conversations.)

One interesting feature of baby talk is the avoidance of first and second person pronouns ("I" and "you"). Expressions like "Joanie all done now?" (rather than "Are you all done now?") and "Mommy doesn't like that" (rather than "I don't like that") are common. It is plausible that the adult feels intuitively that the constant third person references ("Mommy," child's name) are simpler than the first and second person pronoun references ("I," "you") which change depending on who is speaking and who is being addressed. We often find special word forms in baby talk—"bye-byes," "tummy," and in the sample conversation above, "jammies" and "Nama"—that would be inappropriate in normal adult conversation.

A high amount of repetition, paraphrase, and question forms have been noted in baby talk. Mothers frequently repeat either exactly or with some slight alteration both what they say and what the child says. There is a high frequency of questions. This may be an unconscious attempt by the adult to maximize the likelihood of a child responding verbally and thus really conversing, for question forms more than any other sentence types pressure the listener to give a verbal response.

The content of adults' talk to young children often focuses heavily on the here and now, on objects, people, and activities present in the environment as they interact. Snow has observed another interesting aspect of the content of mainstream mothers' speech to their children. She analyzed the speech of nine Dutch mothers to their two- to three-year-old children in terms of Brown's Stage 1 meanings and relations (Snow 1974). She wondered whether mothers were sensitive to the meanings young children understand and express, and whether they would incorporate these meanings in their speech to their children. Would a high proportion of their talk with their children be about locations of entities and actions, nonexistence of things and people, agents and the actions they engaged in? If so, this would support the notion that mothers adapt their language in ways that will make it more likely the child will understand the mother's meaning. Obviously, the child is more likely to understand what his mother means when she talks with him if she expresses the same kinds of meanings that he expresses when he talks.

Snow analyzed only the mothers' sentences that were more than one word long. Of those, she found that 76 percent were adult expressions of the major meanings and relations of Stage 1 speech including the mothers' frequent nomination questions "What's this?" and "What's that?" This very high percentage suggests that mother is cueing on the child's understanding. Of course, the mothers in the sample could not tell us, "I talk with Susan a lot about what things are called and where they are located and whose they are and who does what because I know she understands these things. After all, these are the things I hear her talk about all the time." But though these mothers could not tell us this, it appears they have unconsciously picked up on the kinds of things their children understand, and they are using these as the content of their talk.

The character of baby talk is influenced by the language level of the child with whom the adult is interacting. As a child grows older and becomes more advanced linguistically, his mother's language to him includes fewer baby talk features than it did when he was younger. The mother in the foregoing conversations doubtless included more baby talk features and used them more frequently in conversing with her child when her child was younger than three than she did in this sample. Here is a short excerpt from the talk of a mother and her seven-month-old daughter. You can readily see that the presence of baby talk features is greater in this sample than in the earlier one between the mother and her three-year-old.

M: Are ya hungry? Are you hungry, little girl? You want an egg? Momma fix you egg? OK, Momma's gonna fix you egg. (pause) What is this? What is this? An egg? For you? (pause) You can't wait? You can't wait to eat? Say, "Hurry, Momma, I'm hungry. Hurry, Momma."
C: (verbal noise)
M: "Hurry, Momma. Hurry. Hurry, Momma." I'm hurrying, little girl. I'm hurrying, little girl.
C: (insistent squeal)
M: Oh, oh, oh, oh, you're mad at Momma? Are you mad at me? Are you hungry as a bear? What's Momma doing? (pause) Want an egg?
C: (mouth noises)
M: Yes, mam. *Yes,* mam! What? What? Yes? Yes, or no? An egg? You watchin' Momma make it? This is how you make it. This is how you make it. Yeah.
C: (verbal sound)
M: You're hungry. Momma's gonna let it get cold.

C: (verbal noise)

M: What else? Peaches? What else? Some peaches? Yes? OK. (pause) Or yogurt? Would you like some yogurt? Hm?

Mainstream adults talk to three-year-olds differently than they talk to seven-month-olds. This is powerful evidence of the adult shaping to the child.

A study by Cross suggests a connection between mainstream mothers' ways of responding to the child, and the child's acquisition of language structure (Cross 1975). Instead of trying to get a representative sort of cross-section for her study of mother-child interaction, Cross chose to study sixteen mother-child pairs including only very linguistically accelerated eighteen- to thirty-month-olds. What she wanted to know was what the mothers of very rapid language learners do when they talk with their children that might account for their children's rapid development. Interestingly, Cross relates that when she asked the mothers in her study this question before she began her observation, all the mothers insisted that they did not alter their speech for their child in any way. A typical comment was, "Oh, I just talk to her as if she were an adult." Of course, this turned out not to be the case. Cross identified many features of the mothers' speech that marked it as speech to young children. But the particularly interesting feature of her study was the high proportion of mothers' utterances that were directly contingent upon what the child had said. She was impressed by

> the relatively few occasions when these mothers attempted to control the focus or direction of the conversations, and by the correspondingly high proportion of interaction sequences in which they allowed the child to initiate (and terminate) the topic.
> . . . Fifty-five percent of the mothers' utterances incorporated exactly, or referred to, the child's previously expressed topic. (Cross 1975, p. 133)

Here is a picture of mothers tuning into and building on and from what their children are telling them. It is a picture of mothers following their children's initiations in conversation.

In a study of two mainstream mother-child dyads from the time the children were three months until they were twenty months, Snow focused on evidence that mothers' verbal interaction with their babies was particularly influenced by their desire to engage their children in conversation, that is, in reciprocal interaction (Snow 1977). Mother was responding to baby, but her adapting of her verbal behavior was more a response to her baby's abilities as a "conversational partner" than to her baby's ability to comprehend speech. "I would suggest that the interactions between these mothers and babies can best be described as conversational in nature, and that the changes in the maternal speech result from the development of the baby's ability to take her turns in the conversation" (Snow 1977, p. 11). Snow found that the mothers responded to many of their babies' behaviors—burps. smiles, yawns, sneezes—as if they were communication units:

C: (Smiles)
M: Oh, what a nice little smile! Yes, isn't that nice? There. There's a nice little smile.
C: (Burps)
M: What a nice wind as well! Yes, that's better, isn't it? (Snow 1977, p. 12)

Mother would often take both roles in the conversation if the baby did not participate:

M: Oh, you are a funny little one, aren't you, hmm? Aren't you a funny little one? Yes. (Snow 1977, p. 13)

They tended to phrase their questions so that any response on the baby's part could be interpreted as a reply. When the babies were over a year old and were using one-word speech, Snow noted numerous instances in which the mother would respond to her daughter's one word as initiating a new topic of conversation:

C: (Makes blowing noise)
M: That's a bit rude.
C: Mouth.
M: Mouth, that's right.
C: Face.
M: Face, yes, mouth is in your face. What else have you got in your face?
C: Face (closing eyes).
M: You're making a face aren't you? (Snow 1977, p. 18)

Snow suggested, finally, that perhaps it was these mothers' desire to converse with their children that accounted significantly for the character of their speech to their young children.

> Mothers' desire to communicate reciprocally with their children . . . may well be a crucial factor in limiting the topics discussed and thus the semantic and syntactic complexity in mothers' speech. (Snow 1977, p. 20)

Togetherness: The Mother-Child Partnership

Baby talk has been one major theme of mainstream mother-child interaction research; "jointness" has been another. In fact, the word "joint" (in the sense of together) occurs frequently: Studies include descriptions of mother and child's joint focusing of attention, their joint construction of conversation, their joint building of a repertoire of patterned interaction formats and routines, their joint construction of a shared world of experience, and their mutual influence on one another's interaction styles. Let's take these "joint" features one by one.

Joint focus of attention.   A strong tendency has been observed for mainstream mothers to talk about here-and-now objects and events that both mother and child are focusing on at the moment. The focus can be controlled by mother or by the child and can be accomplished in different ways. Mother might follow the child's gaze and then talk about what the child is looking at and, presumably, attending to. Or an action of either mother or child might become the focus of the partner. Often it is the talk of mother or of child, perhaps with accompanying action or gaze, that initiates the focus of attention for both partners. Whatever the behavior that initiates the joint focusing, mother's talk often relates to this established focus. Consider three examples from two mother-child pairs.[23] All the examples involve the child noticing his or her reflection.

Example 1: Joint focus is established when M notices and responds to C (seven months old) gazing at her own reflection in her high chair tray.

M: Do you see yourself? Hi. Did you kiss yourself? Hi. Let's see. Look. Look down there. Hi, Sarah. Hi. Hi, Sarah. Mommy says hi. Hi, little girl. Hi down there. Hi down there. That's you. In your high chair. Yeah.

Example 2: M and C (fifteen months old) are looking at a familiar book. When M turns to page with "mirror," C carries out her familiar action of leaning her face forward toward the "mirror" in the book.

C: bemamma
M: Peek-a-boo, Momma. Let's see. *Who*'s in there? *Who*'s in there? It's Sarah. Hi, Sarah. Hi.
C: uh-mama
M: Momma too. Hi

Example 3: C (eleven months old) laughs and squeals as he looks at his reflection in the oven-door window. This attracts his mother's attention and she joins his focus.

M: Who do you see in the mir—who do you see in that window? Who is that, Alan? Who is that? Hm? Is that Alan? Is that Alan?

I have deliberately selected similar events (reflection situations) in all these examples in order to demonstrate how the control of focus, even in one particular type of situation, can reside with either partner. Of course, I am assuming that the partners are responsive to each other. Indeed, this line of research has indicated a strong tendency in many mainstream mothers (though not all) to be very "tuned in" to their young children's focus of attention and to provide talk relating to that focus. The suggestion has been made that in such situations a regular pattern of mother elaborating on the focus of attention is a pattern that supports the child's developing language.[24]

---

[23]The two mothers in the examples here audiotaped interactions with their children in their homes, doing "whatever they normally did" over the course of one year. The ages of the two children during the study were seven months to nineteen months, and ten months to twenty-two months.

[24]See especially Wells 1981.

It is not clear just how pervasive this joint focusing of attention and talk may be in mainstream mother-child interaction. It is possible that it seems to be more prevalent than it actually is because of the nature of the research situations in which it has been observed. Often these are situations in which mother and child are videotaped (or audiotaped) at regularly scheduled times. Researchers try to be as unobtrusive as possible; however, when the researcher arrives in the home to "do the recording" (or when mother and child come to a laboratory situation to be recorded), it is reasonable to assume that mother does something with the child, rather than just going on about her usual business—straightening up or doing the washing or telephoning a friend or reading the newspaper while drinking a cup of coffee, or any of a number of activities that we might expect to occupy the mother.

Joint construction of conversation.   The mainstream mother-child interaction research reveals a conversational pattern that one researcher has called "vertical construction" of propositions (Scollon 1979). As we have seen already, at an early stage, the child is unable to express complete propositions but supplies one or two key words relating to the situation. Some mothers have been observed to respond to the child's contribution in such a way that the whole proposition is expressed, though it takes several conversational turns and the participation of both adult and child to accomplish this, as in these examples.

C: hiding.
A: Hiding? What's hiding?
C: balloon. (Scollon 1979, p. 221)

C: (says something close to the sound of "fan")
M: Fan! Yeah.
C: /ku/
M: Cool, yeah. Fan makes you cool. (Scollon 1979, p. 217)

You can see (literally *see*) why these joint constructions have been called vertical. The term was born from the graphic appearance of the talk in transcripts. The full idea gets expressed going down the page of the transcript, from one speaker's turn to another (vertical) rather than stretching across the page as a single sentence within one speaker's turn (horizontal).

One important factor contributing to this pattern and evident in these examples is the propensity of many mainstream adults to interpret the child's behaviors (vocalizations, gestures, gaze) as meaningful contributions to the conversation, a response pattern that you saw in the earlier examples of mother treating the infant's burps, smiles, yawns, sneezes, and so on, as meaningful conversational turns. This response pattern must stand as the clearest indication that these mothers are focused on meaning, not form. These child behaviors are certainly not models of adult linguistic forms; yet these mothers do not provide repeat-after-me drills to shape up these forms. Rather, they use the child's forms, however unconventional they may be, as opportunities to engage the child in meaning-*full* conversation. Surely this is a maternal "strategy," however unconscious, that supports the young child's strategy of "make the most of what you've got." How different mother's strategy is here from the classroom teacher's strategy the child will encounter in a few short years, in which the adult hears only the child's form and hears it as woefully inadequate and needing to be corrected rather than responded to.

Joint building of a repertoire of interaction formats and routines. Another aspect of mainstream mother-child interaction which helps the child make the most of his limited language is the development of routines or "*formats* for interaction between mother and child . . . 'expectable way[s]' of doing things together" (Bruner 1981, p. 44). Here are some routines you may be familiar with.

Child is ten months old
M: Where's Sarah?
C: (Points to herself)
M: *There's Sarah!*

M and C, fourteen months old, are looking at a picture book.
M: What's this?
C: layuh
M: Flower.
C: igi
M: What's this?
C: wiba
M: Boat.
C: ba
M: Book.
C: yaya
M: Flowers. Good girl.

M and C, fourteen months old, are playing with C's barnyard animal toys.
M: What does dog say?
C: ru (high voice)
M: Good girl. Ruff, ruff, ruff.
C: (excited huffing)
M: (laugh) What does the horsey say?
C: eeeeeeee (glides from high pitch to mid pitch)
M: Good girl. What does a *rooster* say?
C: uuuuuuuuu ("warbles" back and forth between high and mid pitch)
M: Good *girl*. (gives rooster imitation) What does a pig say?
C: (makes a throaty noise)
M: Oink, oink, oink. (spoken in a throaty snorting voice) Good girl.

The "Where's Sarah?" game in the first example involves a rigid formula on the mother's part, complete with specific intonation, stress and rhythm patterns, and a specific action response at a particular juncture on the child's part. The second example is a routine that has been called "the naming game." Notice that mother provides the labels that are most basic, though the pictures in question could be labeled in other ways. Mother uses the labels "flower" and "boat" for pictures that could be labeled at a more specific level ("petunia," "lily," or "rose"; "sailfish," or "kyak") or at a more general level ("plant"; "vehicle"). Notice that these more specific or more general labels would be appropriate in many contexts, but not this one. Mother and child participate in the same structured world. Mother labels in terms of that shared world and child attends as an inhabitant of that world. In the third example in which the child provides animal sounds in response to the mother's initiations, it is most clear that mother and child share an interaction world in which particular animal sounds have been well established as appropriate in this particular routine. In fact, the sounds that dogs, horses, roosters, or pigs make might be a matter of debate, but not for this pair in this established routine.

The particular repertoire of routines differs from one mother-child pair to another, but each is characterized by a predictable pattern of turns in sequence. Such routines provide a "format" that may help the child participate appropriately in conversation (talk and/or action turn-taking events) in that it is a reduced and simplified and predictable event. The partners' turns are predictable in where they occur in the routine and also in what each turn consists of. It has been suggested that these routines help the child make the most of his limited abilities as a conversational partner.

Joint construction of a shared world of experience. My favorite example here comes from Sarah and her mother (the pair in the preceding example). One day, when Sarah was almost nineteen months old, she was sitting in her high chair, having just finished her lunch. Mother asked Sarah if she was all finished, and then she removed the dishes from Sarah's high-chair tray. A wonderful conversation followed in which Sarah's turns made perfectly good sense to her mother, but which might have made no sense at all to an outsider to the world that Sarah and her mother shared. In the example that follows I give just Sarah's conversational turns to see if you can make sense of what Sarah was talking about. Remember, there were no physical clues in the situation—no objects present and no activities going on that would help. There was just Sarah in her high chair, mother beside her, *and*, of course, the world of experience that Sarah and her mother shared.

C: ha-hoooooooo-he (spoken in a high, sing-song voice)
M: _____
C: (blowing attempt at whistling)
M: _____
C: miomiomiowaaaaaa
M: _____
C: owaa   wiaa wa   mio*waa*miowa

M: _____
C: eh-eh-eh-eh (falling intonation, stairstep fashion)
M: _____
C: ahba
M: _____
C: uh-oh (mid-low tone)
M: _____
C: oh dis
M: _____

Can you make any sense of this at all? Probably not. But suppose I let you into Sarah and her mother's shared world a bit by telling you that story-reading events were central to this pair's interaction and that *Snow White* was a favorite at the time of this taping. Now does it make any sense to you? Well, it all made perfectly good sense to Sarah's mother. Here is the conversation in full.

C: ha-hoooooo-he (spoken in a high, sing-song voice)
M: (singing) "Hi ho, hi ho, it's off to work we go."
C: (blowing attempt at whistling)
M: (whistles next line of song) (sings) "Hi ho"
C: miomiomiowaaaaaaa
M: (very dramatically) "Mirror, mirror on the wall, who's the fairest of them all?
C: owaa   wiaawa   mio*waa*miowa
M: (very dramatically) "Mirror, mirror on the wall," the wicked old queen says that in *Snow White*. "Mirror, mirror on the wall."
C: eh-eh-eh-eh (falling intonation, stairstep fashion)
M: (Witch voice) "Eh-eh-eh. Would you like an apple, deary?"
C: ahba ("apple")
M: She takes an apple. Snow White takes an apple.
C: uh-oh ("Uh-oh")
M: What happens when Snow White takes an apple? Then what happens? What happens with Snow White? She takes an apple and falls asleep forever.
C: oh dis ("kiss")
M: Uh-hm. And then the prince comes and gives her a kiss. Yeah. And he comes on his white horse.

Sarah and her mother, like many mainstream mother-child pairs, share much beyond the specifics of the *Snow White* story. They share well-established patterns of conversational turn taking. They have built up expectations of the kinds of turns each takes in conversation. Sarah knows when she is expected to perform (verbally and/or nonverbally), when to answer, when to initiate, and so on. Sarah and her mother share a world of rhymes and songs and stories. And a world of cats, of family friends, of toys, of trips to the park, the swimming pool, the grocery store. It's a world of shared actions—bathing and dressing and eating and waking up and going to bed and watching the cat—and the talk that weaves in and through all these.

We sometimes think that we can't understand the speech of a young child but the child's mother can because the mother frequently hears the child's pronunciation and thus is familiar with it in a way that we are not. But in fact it's much more than this. The mother has expectations, as we do not, of the kinds of things the child is likely to express in different situations. These expectations grow out of the mother and child's daily encounters with each other, encounters on which they build a world of their own.

Mainstream mother-child interaction has been described extensively and thus we know more about the joint building of a shared world of experience in this social context than in some others. However, sharing a world of experience and drawing on that in interaction with others is basic to all interaction, not just to mainstream interaction. In nonmainstream families and communities, the world the members share is different, but the fact of their interactions growing out of and reflecting that world is the same.

Mutual influence on interaction style.   It is a common idea that adults in the young child's world influence the child's ways of using language. However, we are coming increasingly to understand that the child influences the adult's ways of using language also. The baby talk research discussed at some length earlier has identified a host of modifications adults make in their talk that are caused by the presence of the child.

Quite different interaction styles evolve over time with different mother-child pairs, and both partners contribute to these patterns. Mothers' talk with their young children can differ in many different ways. Mothers differ in the amount of talk they address to their children, in how much of their children's talk they respond to, in how directive (high in commands) or responsive (high in interrogatives) (Nelson 1973) their talk is, in how much they repeat their own utterances and/or their children's utterances, in how complex their talk is syntactically and/or semantically, in how much their talk focuses on objects and actions that are outside the immediate context, in the amount and type of initiating they and their children do in conversation, in how much and in what ways they extend their children's conversational contributions, in how much they correct their children for form and for content, in how routine or formulaic their talk is, in the purposes for which they use language with the child (for example, play, control, information), and so on.

Following are contrasting examples from two mother-child pairs studied over a period of about ten months (from about eighteen months to twenty-five to thirty months). In each conversation the child contributes mainly one-word utterances, but each mother responds differently. The first mother provides a lot of information around the child's single words.

MOTHER: Look, what's this?
C: Mmmm.
M: It's a little horse.
C: Mmmm.
M: Fiona gave it to you, didn't she?

C: Fo-na.
M: Your friend Fiona.
C: Fo-na.
M: She's your aunt, isn't she?
C: Fo-na-ah
M: Fiona gave you the horse.
C: Fo-na.
M: Mm.
C: Fo-na (increased urgency).
M: Fiona's not here. Fiona's at Bar Hill with Grandma.
C: Grandma. Grandma.
M: Yes, Grandma's at Bar Hill too. (Lieven 1978b, pp. 220–21)

The second mother seems more intent on getting particular answers from the child than on holding a coherent conversation.

C: Bu-la.
M: Tell us a story, what's it all about, Beth?
C: A choo-choo. Ur-naow.
M: A train what's his name?
C: Choo-choo.
M: Thomas, Thomas.
C: Choo-choo.
M: Thomas the Tank Engine.
C: Tank.
M: What's his name?
C: Choo-choo.
M: Thomas the Tank Engine, Beth, and Henry and Claribel.
C: (Sees dog, Judy) Judy. Judy. Judy. Choo Judy. Judy.
M: Judy, that's right, Judy. (Lieven 1978b, p. 221)

The researcher who studied these two mother-child pairs points out the strong influence that the children in this study exerted on how others interacted with them. Focusing on two of the children, Kate and Beth, who used language very differently, the researcher says:

> I . . . found it much easier to carry on a conversation with Kate than I did with Beth. It is difficult to respond informatively, for instance to expand or extend utterances which are extremely repetitive and seem not to relate clearly to anything in the immediate context; . . . however it was that Beth and Kate came to speak the way that they did, it is possible that they would evoke in others who were conversing with them, a speech style similar to that of their mothers . . . a child, by virtue of the way that she/he talks, may be influencing the way in which other people speak to her/him. (Lieven 1978a, p. 185)

The strong impression in the studies of mainstream mother-child interaction is that the child and mother together develop characteristic ways of interacting with each other. It is a matter of jointness again—the

togetherness in the building of expected and understood ways of expressing and of responding to each other in interaction. Again we must set aside
any notions of the child simply being acted on, or shaped, by the world
around him. Clearly the child contributes mightily—shapingly—to the
interaction. The patterns and styles of mother's and child's interaction with
each other reflect the contribution and influence of both.

Finally. Major themes thread their way through this mainstream
mother-child interaction research. They are themes of adult sensitivity and
responsiveness to the child. This research implies that the jointness patterns described here support children's language development. The picture is one of mother accepting the child's contribution as meaningful,
however unconventional its form. It is a picture of both mother and child
focusing on meaningful communication.

Recent research in children's experiences in reading and writing
before coming to elementary school enables us to ask a new question: Are
the same accepting, responding, and supporting adult behaviors evident in
mainstream interaction events involving written language as well as talk?
How typical are examples like these?

Mother and her eight-month-old daughter are sharing a book. Mother reads aloud
to the child and then invites her to read aloud.

M: Can you read this book to Momma? Read this book to Momma.

A three-year-old sits on the living room floor with a favorite book and produces the
story orally while turning the pages. His mother tells her adult friend, as they sit on
the sofa nearby, watching the child, "He just loves that book. He sits and reads it
over and over."

Mother and her four-year-old daughter are sharing a bedtime story, *Horton Hatches
the Egg*. Mother reads aloud and her daughter interrupts to provide familiar text.[25]

M: "The first thing to do is to prop up this tree and make it much stronger. That
has to be done before—"
C: I can do it! "What's the first thing to do? The first thing to do is to prop up this
tree and make it more stronger. That have to be done before I get on it. I
must weigh a ton."[26]

In all these examples, the child is being treated as a reader, as "a member of
the club" (Smith 1983). The adults here "do not expect children to be
experts in advance, nor do they anticipate failure. There are no admission

[25]I am indebted to Miriam Martinez for this example from her dissertation data.

[26]The actual text is
"The first thing to do is to prop up this tree
And make it much strong. That has to be done
Before I get on it. I must weigh a ton."

requirements" (p. 562). This is strikingly similar to mother's responding to the child's early verbalizations as meaningful conversation and treating the child as a fullfledged participant in conversation. But how typical are such examples in mainstream families? We don't know, but however widespread this pattern may be, researchers suggest that it is a fostering pattern that aids children's literacy development. Once again, it is a respond/accept adult pattern that is viewed as helpful, rather than a direct/correct pattern.

It is interesting to reflect on similarities and differences between the mainstream adult-child interaction patterns described here and those of the classroom, which is typically mainstream in its orientation (whether or not it is mainstream in its student population). Some interaction patterns are similar, for example, the "naming game" routine sounds very like many class "discussions"; in both, the adult asks questions to which she knows the answers, the child knows that the adult knows the answers, and the child responds by producing the expected answers. Yet some patterns are strikingly dissimilar. Many elementary school teachers are also parents. One wonders how it happens that the very same adult (mother) who at home accepts and responds to the child's verbalization as meaningful and disregards its unconventional form, in school (as teacher) responds primarily to the child's unconventional expression, often ignoring the meaning while correcting the form. And how does it happen that the same adult who at home supports the child's development by responding to the child's initiative often takes a very directive role at school?

We will consider some of these differences more fully in Chapter 8, but it is not too soon for you to begin to wonder about these matters.

Nonmainstream Contexts

The mainstream mother-child interaction research radiated a strong confidence that the patterns observed were very widespread, if not universal. One rarely finds qualifying statements to the effect that the observed patterns might be restricted to particular social or cultural groups. However, recent research has revealed striking differences in language-learning contexts from one culture to another. This research has typically involved researchers as "participant observers." The participant observer typically spends a great deal of time within a particular social community, trying to understand the complex workings of that social group, both by observing the day-to-day life of community members (taking extensive written field notes and audio and videorecording where and when appropriate) and by participating in the life of the community insofar as this is possible and appropriate (for example, attending social gatherings, helping individuals with their daily chores, visiting with individuals in their homes as a friend). This line of research has brought to light some fascinating contrasts in language-learning environments, especially in the ways that adults interact with the language-learning child.

The most striking example I know is the work of Shirley Brice Heath, who conducted participant observer research for ten years in three communities in a small geographical area of the Carolina Piedmont region.

The children of these three communities attended school together (following desegregation). The teachers and parents of these children wanted to understand "why students and teachers often could not understand each other, why [teachers'] questions were sometimes not answered, and why habitual ways of talking and listening did not always seem to work" for these school children (Heath 1983, p. 2). Parents would make comments like "My kid, he too scared to talk, 'cause nobody play by the rules he know. At home, I can't shut 'im up" (Heath 1982, p. 107); and teachers would make comments like "The simplest questions are the ones they [the students] can't answer in the classroom; yet on the playground, they can explain a rule for a ballgame or describe a particular kind of bait with no problem" (p. 108). Somehow, the children's and teachers' ways of using language weren't meshing.

Heath knew that in order to deal with the classroom communication problems here, it was necessary for teachers to have a better understanding of the children's different ways of learning and using language in their homes and communities, for those ways of learning and using language in the early years continue into the school years and play a crucial role in the child's learning within the school setting. Indeed, it turned out to be so: The knowledge Heath and the teachers who worked with her gained and shared with one another and with other teachers enabled them to significantly improve the children's school experience.[27]

What emerged from this ten-year research in these three communities that has special relevance for us at this point is the differences in the language-learning setting—the contexts—of these three groups of children. The examples I am drawing on here come from the community Heath calls "Trackton," (not the real name) "a black working-class community whose older generations grew up farming the land, but whose current members work in the mills" (p. 1).

The situation in which children in Trackton learn language differs from the mainstream pattern already described in some striking ways. The mainstream research focuses especially on mother-child interaction, assuming that to be a (the?) major language-learning context of the child's first few years. But the Trackton research suggests that other interaction contexts may have special significance for some other children. Much of the life of the Trackton community happens "on Trackton's stage—the plaza in the midst of their community" (p. 79).

> Most of the life of the community goes on outdoors, on the porches and in the plaza, and once boy babies are mobile and fairly steady on their feet, [twelve to fourteen months] they are put on stage in this public area . . . Young boys learn from an early age to handle their roles by getting their cues and lines straight and knowing the right occasions for joining the chorus. They learn to judge audience reaction and response to their performances and to adjust their behaviors in accordance with their need for audience participation and

[27]You will doubtless want to consult the major source in which the three communities and the changes in the school situation are described: S. B. Heath, *Ways with Words: Language, Life, and Work in Communities and Classrooms* (New York: Cambridge University Press, 1983).

approval. "The measure of a man is his mouth," so males are prepared early by public language input and modeling for stage performances. (Heath 1983, p. 79)

This is a very different picture from the mainstream one of intimate, intense one-to-one interaction between mother and child. The Trackton picture is a public picture, a picture of stage performance. And the toddler encounters many different interactants on this stage: "Boy babies toddle about from porch to porch or are 'toted' astride the hips of older brothers or sisters" and they are typically teased and challenged by adults and children alike as they move about this outdoor area. "Any sign of aggressive play or counterchallenge from the babies is acknowledged verbally by the audience" (p. 79). How different this teasing and challenging interaction pattern seems from the mainstream one, at least as it has been described in the mainstream research literature.

You remember that an important feature of mainstream mother-child interaction is mother's readiness to interpret her child's verbalizations (and even nonverbal behaviors) as meaningful contributions to their ongoing conversation. But this pattern is not usual in Trackton.

> When infants begin to utter sounds which can be interpreted as referring to items or events in the environment, these sounds receive no special attention. . . . Even in contexts where the baby's utterances can be linked to objects or events, adults do not acknowledge these utterances as labels. . . . To them, the response carries no meaning which can be directly linked to an object or event; it is just "noise." (Heath 1983, pp. 75, 76)

Not only do Trackton adults not interpret the young child's or infant's verbalizations in situations where the mainstream adult would; Trackton adults also do not address much of their talk directly to the infant.

> Encapsulated in an almost totally human world, Trackton babies are in the midst of nearly constant human communication, verbal and nonverbal. They literally feel the body signals of shifts in emotion of those who hold them; they are never excluded from verbal interactions. They are listeners and observers in a stream of communication which flows about them, but is not especially channeled or modified for them. Everyone talks *about* the baby, but rarely *to* the baby. (Heath 1983, pp. 74–75)

> Trackton adults do not see babies or young children as suitable partners for regular conversation. . . . Adults socialize with one another while the baby is in their laps or nearby, or they talk about the baby or young child. (Heath 1983, p. 86)

The Warm Springs Indian community in Oregon is another community in which this pattern of adults not interpreting babies' verbalizations as meaningful conversational contributions has been observed.

> Older kinsmen talk to infants a good deal, although probably not as much as Anglo middle-class caretakers. They less often make efforts to elicit sounds,

or words, from the babies, and make fewer attempts to incorporate the sounds the babies do make into the interaction. In other words, Indian adults less often interpret babies' vocalizations, or respond to them as if something meaningful has been said. (Philips 1983, pp. 63–64)

Also interesting in this Indian community is the greater "emphasis given to the child's receptive linguistic competence than to productive competence as he reaches first the one-word and then the two-word stages of utterance construction. Thus children are given many directions and then watched closely to see if they do what they are told. If they do what they are told, it is taken as evidence of comprehension" (p. 64).

The specific examples given here from Trackton and Warm Springs communities are only a few of many,[28] but they hint at the diversity in the social contexts in which children develop language. There are cultural differences in who talks directly with the child and who talks "around" the child to others; differences in how the child is talked to (whether with or without modification, and with what kind of modification, if any); differences in how much talk there is both to the child and around the child; differences in how the child's verbalizations are responded to; differences in the weight given to the child's comprehension versus production of talk; differences in the purposes, styles, and topics of conversation with and/or around the child; and so on. It is no longer possible to assert that particular interaction styles, contexts, and situations are universally the best for supporting children's language learning. Children develop language in many different social settings. Different communities support their children's language learning in quite different ways. Most important, children from every community learn the language of their community and do so in a comparable period of time. Each community's ways of interacting with and around its young fit into the community's larger social framework.

It is important to remember that the nonmainstream examples here do not involve so-called exotic folks who live on tropical islands somewhere. These examples involve American children whom we teach in our classrooms. Although in Section Five we will deal more with children's culturally diverse ways of using language, here it is important to underscore that the earliest and continuing ways of learning language, both how it is structured and how it is used, are directly relevant to the child in school. The language each child brings to school is precisely language as he has learned and used it in his community from birth on. It is because of this continuity and its important consequences in school that we focus here in such detail on the child's language-learning processes and the social contexts of his language learning in the early years.

We have much to learn about nonmainstream contexts in which children develop language, but already cross-cultural research has raised fascinating new questions. This research surely alerts us to dimensions of

---

[28]I have selected nonmainstream examples from within the United States. However, for an interesting example of this line of research outside of the United States you might want to see Ochs and Schieffelin's Western Samoa and Papua New Guinea research (Ochs 1982; Ochs and Schieffelin 1982).

difference in the social contexts in which the children we teach learn their language(s). Being alerted to these dimensions of difference, we may become more observant of our children's varied ways with language and thus better able to use those ways.

Children learning language and researchers learning about how children do it have much in common. As children go along, ever gaining new information about how language is structured and used in their world, they continuously reorganize, restructure, reshape the language system they are constructing, to take the new information into account. So too with child language researchers. As they encounter new insights about children learning language—the contexts in which the learning occurs and the ways the children use those contexts—researchers reorganize and restructure their system of knowledge to take the new insights into account. The growing body of studies of children learning language in nonmainstream settings is providing important new knowledge that theories of language acquisition must take into account.

Outside the Home

Child language researchers have studied the home context more than other contexts of early language learning. But clearly there are many other language contexts for children, especially after the first few years of life. Increasingly the child participates in and/or observes interaction involving people beyond the family.[29] Even very young children's social experience may include day care or nursery school, neighborhood contacts, Sunday school, trips to the grocery store, and so on. Child language research is increasingly focusing on children's language within this broader range of social contexts. This research has especially focused on social aspects of the child's language development, for example, the child's increasing use of language for various communication purposes and the child's developing ability to adapt his speaking style for various partners and situations. These aspects of language development will be our focus in Section Four. However, within this ever-expanding range of social contexts, the child's language structure continues to develop as the child continues to extend and refine his semantic, syntactic, and phonological knowledge.

Not surprisingly, in this larger world the child does not abandon the creative construction strategies so dramatically in evidence in the home contexts we have studied. No. In this ever-increasing world of social interaction, he continues to select, observe, produce, question, hypothesize, refine, revise, restructure. Obviously, school becomes an especially important context. If the child is fortunate, he will find there teachers who support his active sense-making efforts in language.

Language Acquisition: The Universal, The Unique

The learning of one's mother tongue is, at one and the same time, a universal and a unique phenomenon. Virtually every child is born with

---

[29]"Family" here is to be understood as including both nuclear and extended structures.

cognitive and social orientation toward creatively constructing language out of his experience in the world. This innate cognitive and social orientation is no small part of what it is to be a human being rather than a being of some other sort. Further, it is a universal that the physical world into which the child is born has structure. The social world the child comes into has structure too, and this fact of social structure is a universal, though the specifics of that structure differ from one social group to another. Also a universal is the fact that the child is born into a world of language—language that reflects the physical and social structure of the child's world.

Universally, children's ways of learning the language of their community could be called "learning by doing." We have explored some of the doings children engage in as they construct their language, "doings" of attending, of observing, of producing, of selecting, and so on. Individual children use specific strategies to different degrees and at different times, but the fact of the child actively fashioning a language system out of his experience in the world—this fact is universal.

If it is accurate to characterize the child in language as "learning by doing," it is accurate to characterize the social context as "teaching by doing." Universally, it appears, children are born into a world of language *in use*, language doing the work its speakers require. The child's community demonstrates language at work. This is a demonstration—*many* demonstrations, actually—in the sense of showing the learner "This is how something is done" (Smith 1981, p. 108). It is a showing, not a telling. The child figures out the structure of his language in situations of talk, as those around him use language to persuade, to comfort, to emote, to entertain, to inform, to inquire, to argue, to scold, to greet, to congratulate, to invite, and so on. And he figures it out in situations of written language in use as well—recipes, record jackets, greeting cards, grocery shopping lists, storybooks, menus, store signs, Sears catalogues, movie marqués, and so on. In writing as in talk, the child encounters language doing its real and diverse work. The specific situations differ from child to child, but the fact of the child in a world of language *in use* is universal.

Though some direct teaching has been observed (for example, adults teaching children to give specific responses to specific questions or to say please and thank you), there seems to be nothing like a structured language curriculum in which bits are extracted from the whole social fabric, sequenced, and presented and practiced in isolation, quite apart from a whole, active communication context. Language in use is the basis of children's creative construction.

> What is common to every use of language is that it is meaningful, contextualized, and in the broadest sense social; this is brought home very clearly to the child in the course of his day-to-day experience. The child is surrounded by language, but not in the form of grammars and dictionaries, or of randomly chosen words and sentences, or of undirected monologue. What he encounters is "text," or language in use; sequences of language articulated each within itself and with the situation in which it occurs. Such sequences are purposive—though very varied in purpose—and have an evident social significance. The child's awareness of language cannot be isolated from his awareness of language function. (Halliday 1973, p. 20)

The child's innate and active orientation to language, and the use he makes of his experience in the world in building a language system, all mark the child as a member of the human species. But at a specific level, the child's creative construction of language also marks him as being a unique member of that species. Each child's language is absolutely unique. It is unique in the specifics of the life experience out of which it is fashioned: each child's world includes people, things, actions, events, and characteristics that comprise an absolutely unique set, different from every other child's. And every child's doing in the world is his own: his ways of acting on, of influencing, of noticing, of using experience. In short, his ways of making (constructing) sense of language in his experience are uniquely his.

In many ways, at a general level, we share characteristics with all other humans, while, at a specific level, we are unique. We all have thumbs which are similar in structure and function, yet each of us leaves an absolutely unique thumb print. We all walk in upright position by means of alternating the movement of our two legs, yet our friends recognize us from a distance by the specific character of our walk. And so it is in our learning of language: At a general level, we are beings born to actively and creatively construct language out of our experience in a physical and social world; but the specifics of that experience and of that creative construction process will ever be unique for every human child.

8

Language Acquisition: Teachers and Children

A kindergarten teacher says, "I vacillate between the evidence continually provided by the children's behavior, and my need to conform to conventional standards." (Paley 1984, p. 11)

INTRODUCTION

The evidence that this kindergarten teacher's children provide is evidence of the active, creative construction process described in the last chapter.[1] The basic assumption of this chapter is that "evidence . . . provided by . . . children's behavior" is the only valid starting point for our teaching. Further, when that evidence conflicts with current "conventional standards," as is often the case, then we must be guided by the children and not by the standards if we would help children learn.

In many corners of the current educational scene, there is pressure on teachers to ignore what children tell us about their learning. Too often it is assumed that adults, not children, know about learning: about what children should learn, about how they should do it, about the contexts that are helpful. In the name of "raising educational standards," many adults advocate back-to-basics instruction, a renewal or strengthening of skills, drills, and practice approaches to instruction. The cry goes up for "accountability," and children's performance on standardized tests becomes the measure of the children's learning and of the teacher's teaching. But evidence from children developing language tells us that children follow their own course and employ their own processes in this complex learning; in this area of children's lives, it is children, not adults, who know

---

[1]Again remember that "what one sees depends on how one looks." It is because this sensitive teacher with twenty-some years of experience teaching young children believes that children construct their understanding through their active encounters with others, that she sees evidence of this in their behavior. This is an orientation that my knowledge of children's acquisition of language leads me to share and which forms the basis of this chapter.

218

best. It is difficult to believe deeply enough in the power of children's language learning to act on that belief in the classroom. The basic assumption of this chapter, however, is that it is children's learning processes that guide our teaching, rather than the adult wisdom encoded in conventional standards and traditions.

I frequently encounter people who feel that the preschool years are the most exciting for language development. They tell me that the early years are the most important and the most wonderful for children's language and for their learning generally. I am told that some remarkably high percentage of a child's learning—in language and in other things—happens before the age of five. (I never can remember the percentage here, only that it is big.) I have never understood how one could possibly give particular weights to particular learnings. How does one weigh the child's early acquisition of "shoe," "hat," "key," and "mommy" against the child's later development of complex relational notions and the forms that express them: "if-then," "although," "because," "unless"? How does one weigh the child's earlier interaction through talk, with her later development of ways of interacting through writing? How does one weigh the child's earlier simple, direct requests ("want juice") with her later development of more subtle and various ways of requesting—ways that take different partners and situations into account ("I just love orange juice" or "I'll trade ya my juice for your crackers")? I just don't know how anyone decides what each chunk of learning is worth (or even what a chunk is), and without knowing this, how does one total up the chunks and decide what proportion happened before age five and what proportion happened after that age? For me, this way of thinking about children's development doesn't make sense.

I personally find the elementary school years (ages five to twelve) a most exciting time in children's lives—in their learning and in their development of language to express the ever-widening and deepening world of understanding they are building. It's a time of remarkable development in children's understanding about the physical world, about others, about self, and necessarily, about ways of expressing these as children stretch their language to do new cognitive and social work. I watch with fascination as children in the school years discover new selves and new voices to express those selves. I listen to them struggle to give birth simultaneously to the new idea and to the language that expresses it, in the process creating both the idea and the language. For me, the elementary years are a very special and wonderful time for children's language.

And for me, the school is a very special place for this exciting development. In school the child finds many others to interact with—many adults, many children the same age, many older, many younger. Here the child finds—builds—many new ways of interacting with those beyond the school walls, especially through her ever-increasing competence as a reader and writer. Here the child finds many resources for her learning. Teachers often bemoan the overwhelming "manyness" of the classroom: so many children at so many different levels in so many different subject areas and from so many different backgrounds. And yet this very manyness—all the rich diversity here—can be an asset, not a liability, in children's learning.

We find it a liability only if we feel that we, as teachers, are the only or the main source of children's learning. When we recognize and act on the recognition, that other children and adults and resources within the school and outside are equally important sources, then we begin to find ways to capitalize on this diversity. Surely the diversity should support children's growth in language: so many different individuals and groups to talk with, write with, read with; so many others to listen to, to learn from and with. The child's language stretches to accommodate this wider world of others to interact with and of new ideas and wonderings to share. It is the diversity within school—in the children, in the adults, in the resources—that makes school a very special place for children to learn and language in at this exciting time in their lives.

Let's consider, then, the evidence children provide for the kinds of learning environments that support their language at this exciting period of their lives and in the potentially exciting "place called school" (Goodlad 1984).

THE SOCIAL CONTEXT

What do we know about the social contexts within which children acquire language? We know that, for all the variation from one child to another and from one culture to another, every child's social experience of language includes (1) a very wide range of social contexts: of particular settings, individuals, and communication purposes; and (2) real language, that is, language in use by the child and others in the child's community to accomplish their many kinds of social and cognitive work. The first of these aspects (the range) we will consider further in Section Four. It is the reality of language in the child's social world that we consider in this chapter.

We often find a serious discrepancy between the kinds of language events children experience in the classroom, on the one hand, and in "the real world," on the other. We find that events called by the same name in the classroom and outside are often quite different. Consider these three classroom events: a "journal," a "letter," and a "story."

> I entered a sixth-grade classroom and saw the following assignment written on the board: "Journal Writing. Topic: My Three Best Friends and Why."
>
> A class of fourth graders wrote letters, then turned them in to the teacher, who corrected them and handed them back.
>
> On the chalkboard in a third-grade classroom I found this instruction: "Write a story using as many of your spelling words as you can."

What's wrong with these? In the "real world" we *do* write in personal journals or diaries, write letters, and create stories. But the classroom versions of these social language events are poor pretenders, misleading simulations of the real events as we carry them out in our daily lives.[2] Think about these. Perhaps you keep a journal or diary. If so, you know the help

[2]See Edelsky and Draper in press for a further discussion of this idea.

it can be as you think through, on paper, the ongoing events in your life; you ponder, reflect, select, shape, and express and in the process gain some understanding or perspective or comfort, some further sense of the happenings in your life. Journal writing is an important and sustaining and clarifying language event for those who engage in it. And no one assigns topics for the writer's journal entries; entries come from within the writer herself.

We all write letters—to recognize a relative's birthday, perhaps, or to keep in touch with friends, to complain about a faulty product, to order a book. But when did you ever send a letter to someone who, instead of answering it, corrected it, and sent it back to you? Letters are for communicating, not for correcting.

There aren't many of us who write stories. Yet all of us create and tell stories often. In the course of a phone conversation we tell a friend about a movie we saw; in a letter we tell about a recent family event; we tell a child an incident from her past that happened when she was too young to remember; we create possible scenarios ("Sure, I can see it all now. You'll go walking into his office and he'll say . . .") We create mininarratives often in our interactions with others. We select details, order them, and express them, shaping our language into a little narrative. And we never select what we will tell or how we will tell it based on a set of words specified in advance.

In the "real world," it would be utterly bizarre for someone to assign us topics for journal writing, for our "topics" come from within ourselves; it would be unthinkable for a friend to return our letter with corrections; and it would never occur to us to decide what information to convey or how to convey it in order to use a particular predetermined set of words. ("I'll tell my friend something that has 'friend,' 'believe,' 'receive,' 'neighbor,' 'weigh,' and 'niece' in it.") Yet these pretender events and many others like them have become so deeply entrenched in children's school lives that we no longer recognize them as inauthentic ways of using language, as simple "figments of the curriculum" (Edelsky and Smith 1984).

The assertion of this chapter is that the most sustaining and extending social contexts of language for children in school, as outside, are those in which language is used for real social purposes, settings in which children keep real journals, not phony ones; write real letters, not simulations; read and write real stories, not pretenders.

We sometimes encounter those who tell us that research supports the effectiveness of unreal language experiences for children in classrooms, for example, vocabulary-controlled "stories" in basal readers, writing to be corrected by the teacher rather than to communicate messages, and so on. This research is the foundation of conventional standards. But when we examine that research, we find that it is research about instruction, about teaching practices; it is not research about children's learning. A typical design of such research is to compare the performance of two groups of children (usually on some sort of standardized test measure, most often a test of low-level skills) before and after each group is taught according to a different instructional method. These are studies of teaching methods, not studies of how children creatively construct their understanding of the world, including its language. These studies are born of the assumption that children's learning is the direct result of the kind of instruction teachers provide. Thus, these studies do not allow researchers the possibility of observing how children shape their own understanding and what kinds of social contexts support their learning work, for the situation observed is shaped entirely by the adult.[3] It is not this research about instructional methods, but research about children's learning that is relevant to our decisions about the social contexts and experiences that support children's language development in school. The relevant research tells us that it is in the context of authentic experience of language in the classroom that children's language development is fostered in all aspects—cognitive and social, structure and use, oral and written channels of expression.

Conflicts about the Context: Conventional Wisdom versus Child Evidence

A close look at school settings reveals some major conflicts between conventional wisdom and child evidence relating to the kinds of contexts the classroom should provide for children's language experience. We find disagreements about (1) whether the language events should involve language in its wholeness or decomposed into parts (skills); (2) whether sequences in children's language experience should come from adults' designs (sequenced curriculum objectives) or from children's engagement; (3) whether children's language growth should be assessed by standardized tests of skills or by observations of children using language for social purposes; (4) whether classrooms should be structured so children can practice or so they can communicate. We consider these four conflicts one by one.

Whole-Part Conflict

Conventional wisdom, and the conventional classroom standards based on it, tells us that whole-language events are too complex for children to use in their learning. The focus is usually on the child's development of literacy, as this is the aspect of language development that is of greatest concern in the early school years. Clearly (or so the argument runs), you can't take a child who does not know how to read and engage that child in real reading, in engagement with real literature or with the complex print of the real environment. You can't take a child who does not know how to write and engage that child in real writing, in writing notes, journals, stories, lists, and so forth. So don't overwhelm the child with the whole reading or writing events. Break literacy down into manageable parts. The child masters the parts one by one, and slowly she builds up to the complex whole. Teach the child to recognize a few words in print,

[3]For a striking recent example, you might want to see Chall 1983, a book that purports to describe children's literacy learning but in fact describes instructional practices. In contrast, see Harste, Woodward, and Burke 1984; Dyson 1982, 1983; Calkins 1983; and Ferreiro and Teberosky 1982 for research that is, in fact, about children's learning. See Lindfors 1984 for some examples of the teaching-learning distinction.

gradually add more, and, over time, the child moves up to doing "real reading" rather than reading specially contrived texts. Teach the child to write a few words at first, then add more, and eventually the child will be able to write real messages using those words. But the child can't start with whole-language events: They are too complex.

This argument makes very good sense—*until* you think about the child's development of language before coming to school. In fact, the child from the beginning has learned real language in whole contexts. She has expressed her meanings in whatever way she could from the beginning, and she has observed the expression of others, expression that was whole, not partial, expression that was real, not specially contrived for the child's benefit. It is true that many mainstream adults use simpler syntax and vocabulary when talking with young children than when talking with older children or adults, but this speaking style is motivated and sustained by a concern for communicating, not by a concern for teaching the child a language. It is but one of many examples of competent speakers adapting their speaking style to their conversational partners so as to assure the mutual understanding that sustains the conversation. The fact that the language the child encounters is invariably real and whole and communicative has led some to call language acquisition "learning without teaching."

Some educators will grant that children learn oral language by engaging in this natural communication wholeness before coming to school, but they insist that though the child "picks up" oral language, written language cannot be learned that way. Rather, written language is not "natural" and the child must consciously focus on it and the teacher must systematically and explicitly teach it, one bit at a time. It is said that

> oral language is learned in whole contexts, but written language must be learned in parts as skills;
>
> oral language is meaning-focused, but written language is learned by focusing on forms;
>
> oral language involves an active creative construction process for the learner, but written language requires the learner to take in and rehearse parts as the teacher gives them;
>
> oral language involves the forms of language becoming more conventional over time as the learner participates in communication, but written language involves the use of conventional forms from the outset and throughout the development process.[4]

To claim that written language is the exact opposite of oral language in these ways is tantamount to asserting that it is not language but something

---

[4]If you examine these claims closely, you will see that the second of each pair is a statement about instruction, a simple reiteration of traditional ways of teaching literacy; they are not, in fact, statements about children's learning. They would be accurately rephrased as "Traditionally literacy has been taught as skills, has focused on form, has required children to receive and rehearse parts as the teacher gives them, has insisted on conventional forms throughout (for example, correct spellings, word-perfect oral reading, conventional letter formation)."

else, an opposite of language. And, indeed, traditional reading and writing instruction has treated written language as if it were something quite other than language. But it is not.

Written language is language: I have yet to encounter a teacher who is not quick to agree with this statement. Yet conventional standards do not recognize the profound implications of this view. Language is, as you well know by now, meaning-expression relations. It is purposeful messages— social and cognitive meanings—and the possibilities for their expression. It is a togetherness, a whole. It occurs within the thousands of contexts and situations of people communicating with one another. You cannot have an expressive form only—a disembodied sound, a written symbol, a word or bunch of sounds or symbols or words—in a meaning vacuum. It is an erroneous notion that language can somehow be disassembled into form parts (sounds, written characters, words, sentences) and then reassembled into language again. Language is not additive. Language is not an accumulation of free-floating bits. It is complex and intricate relationships among social and cognitive meanings and expression. It is an all-at-onceness. Any breaking down is to de-language language. The child doing long and short vowel workbook pages or spelling worksheets is not working on language at all. As she engages in these communicatively empty exercises, she gets better at doing workbook pages and worksheets; she does *not* get better at producing or interpreting oral or written language. One gets better at doing language by doing language, not by doing something else. This necessarily means dealing with purposeful communication—always whole.

Chess offers an analogy. When playing chess, one grasps pieces, lifts them from the board, moves them to new locations, lowers them to the board again, and releases them. But no one would recommend piece-raising-and-lowering exercises or grasping-and-releasing exercises for people working on their chess game. Lifting and lowering, grasping and releasing only make sense as part of chess when they occur within the whole context of playing chess—engaging in a complex system of moves and rules and strategies and plans and their execution. Removed from the context of chess, lifting and lowering, grasping and releasing are only hand movements, they are not chess. It is in the context of playing chess as well as you can that you become a better chess player, including moving pieces with sufficient coordination that they don't fall over, knock down other pieces, and so on. Producing assigned sets of spelling words in lists, circling short vowels, and producing pages of a's are no more language when wrenched from the contexts that give them reason for being than lifting and lowering, grasping and releasing are chess when wrenched from the context of the game that is their reason for being. The child becomes a more effective reader and writer, not by making a's, but by making meaning in whole social contexts.

You know from reading the last chapter that even children in a one-word stage have conversations with others about topics that are of mutual interest. At this early stage, the child's talk does not include auxiliaries, prepositions, plural forms, past tenses, possessives, articles, and so on. Yet the adult does not provide skills practice on these items: "We'll work on auxiliaries, prepositions, plurals, past tenses, and articles. Then someday we'll be able to converse about our cat that you like to hold and pet, or about what we're having for breakfast, or about your reflection in the mirror, or about your bathtub toys." No. It is precisely in the whole meaningful conversations about cats and breakfast and reflections and bathtub toys that the child is enabled to figure out how the specific language elements (auxiliaries, articles, past tenses, and so on) work. Conversations provide contextualized examples of these items. Smith points out that in developing literacy (as in developing oral language), it is the authentic whole event that enables one to deal with the parts, rather than the parts enabling one to deal with the whole. His example comes from phonics, that is, systematic focus on spelling-to-sound correspondences. Instead of phonics facilitating reading for the child, it is reading—the authentic whole event—that provides information about sound-symbol relationships: "The practice of reading itself provides implicit understanding of these [sound-symbol] correspondences that readers require" (Smith 1985, p. 49). It is by participating in whole meaningful events—whether chess, oral language, or written language—that we come to understand the functioning of the parts and the relations among them; but the separate parts in isolation do not help us toward the whole.

Why is it that many adults feel it is appropriate that the child from birth acquiring oral language be an active member of a language community, observing and participating "naturally" in whole social contexts of language in use, yet feel that the same child, from age five or six on, needs to be explicitly instructed in written expression of language as disembodied bits? One important reason may be that written language is often seen as inherently more difficult than oral language, and thus the learning involved is seen as more difficult. Nothing could be further from the truth. The young child's earliest encounters with language are primarily with oral channels of expression, and so her development of an oral expression system of meaning generally precedes her development of a written expression system. In that oral language situation, the child must build a whole complex system of meanings that her language community encodes, as well as constructing the community's ways of expressing those meanings. This is an incredibly complex business and one that human children, as we have seen already, are cognitively and socially well prepared to carry out in interaction with their physical and social world. We have seen that the child in acquiring oral language has to develop notions of self and other, of separate things in space, of object permanence, of characteristics of objects, actions, people, and so on. But typically the development of literacy does not require the construction of this intricate meaning system (concepts and relations). Rather, it requires the working out of another expression system for the meanings the child has already constructed.[5] Surely it is easier to relate the meaning system you have already built to a second expression

---

[5]Obviously, as the child continues to use written language, her meanings will further develop through this important channel.

system, than it is to build a meaning system and an expression system and the relations between them in the first place.

If it is the case that developing the ability to interpret and produce written language is not inherently more difficult than developing the ability to interpret and produce oral expression, then why are children often unsuccessful in their literacy development, but rarely so in their oral language development? There are doubtless many reasons, but an important one may be that in our well-intentioned breaking down of language in order to "simplify" it for the child, we have in fact made it more difficult. Evidence from children suggests that "more complex" is not necessarily "more difficult"; that is, the complex whole written event—the totality of the social situation complete with its own communication purpose, semantic meanings, syntactic relations, and graphic displays—all these taken together to comprise an authentic language whole—maximizes the opportunities for the child to make sense of this event.[6]

Comes the outcry: "But the child cannot possibly focus on everything at once." Of course not. She doesn't—any more than she focused on "everything at once" when she acquired oral language. You have seen already that the child's language business is one of making (constructing) sense out of the language around her. She may particularly focus on what she knows about people's intentions in particular situations, or on some aspect of their nonverbal expression, or perhaps on a word she recognizes or a familiar phrase, or an intonation contour that suggests a question or a request rather than a statement, or on an overall conversational pattern or routine (for example, the naming game format), or on any combination of these. But her specific focus at a particular moment is within the context of the whole event, the interconnectedness of all its parts working in concert to express meaning. And so it is in dealing with written language. The young child may focus attention selectively, cueing especially on an aspect of the situation in which the print occurs, on the look of some part of the print, on the function the print serves, or on a semantic or syntactic relationship. One aspect of the whole event now is figure; then it shifts to ground as a different aspect commands focal attention. Children's questions and comments about print indicate some of the aspects that children attend to as they make sense of it.

The four children in the following examples are focusing on different aspects of print.

Three-year-old Matthew and his adult friend are in a department store. Matthew sees a sign hanging above the greeting card counter and explains, "That sign says 'card.'" Seeing the word "luggage" in the luggage department, Matthew tells the adult that the word must be "cases." (From Smith 1985, p. 118)

Four-year-old Sarah and her mother are reading a story together.
M: (reading the title) "Just the Thing for Geraldine."

[6]I am relying heavily here on the work of Ken and Yetta Goodman, Frank Smith, and Harste, Woodward, and Burke.

SARAH: "Just the Thing for Geraldine." (pointing to the title word by word) Just . . . the . . . Thing . . . for . . . Geraldine!

Five-year-old Julia starts to write a note to tell someone that it is raining and says, "Seeing as I don't know how to write what I need to write, then I'll draw a picture of what I need to write."

A five-year-old asks, "Mom, do you spell love l-u-v?" (Schickedanz and Sullivan 1984, p. 11)

Matthew focuses on the relation of print to its context, Sarah on the relation of printed to spoken words, Julia on the relation of writing and drawing as different representations of meaning, and the last child on spelling conventions. It is the very complexity of the whole that increases opportunities for sense making, for it offers many different ways for the child to take hold of the print event, get into it, relate to it, use it, and act on it.

Children in literate environments[7] begin figuring out how written language works long before we start "teaching" them (in the sense of providing deliberate systematic instruction). And the contexts of this early literacy learning are whole.

It's the child selecting a story she likes and climbing into the available lap of a willing partner and listening to the partner reading, and chiming in when she can and picturing the characters and events in her mind, and wondering what will happen next, and chatting about the story and commenting on the illustrations and asking why the character is so mean and chatting about lots of other things the story happens to make her think of.[8]

It's family members jotting down messages on the pad by the telephone and leaving them in designated spots for other family members to get when they come home, and it's the talk in which the skeletal jottings get clarified and elaborated later, the recipient's reaction, and so on.

It's an older sister working her way through the directions on a Simplicity pattern as she makes herself some new clothes.

It's bringing in the mail and sorting through it—the junk ads, the Sears catalogue, the notification that it's time for your dental check up, the telephone bill—and it's the talk around the mail—too much junk mail, what's the

---

[7]A "literate" environment is one in which there are many examples of people using print (reading and writing) purposefully in their lives. This may not be a "literary" environment— one in which literature plays a particularly important role. The assumption here is that the set of literacy events will differ somewhat for children from different social backgrounds, but that whatever the particulars of that set, the events will be whole and purposeful for those who use them. Thus, children may come from different kinds of literate environments, but most will have substantial meaningful contact with print and the use that people close to them make of print in their lives.

[8]It is unfortunate, I think, that some have used the term "decontextualized" to characterize the difference between written language events and oral language events (which are said to be "contextualized"). *All* language is contextualized. Watson gives this example: "Proficient readers expect to find certain kinds of messages couched in certain forms depending on the circumstances. Math books, Judy Blume stories, cereal boxes, and public bathroom walls signal specific concepts, language, and conventions . . . readers know this and use such knowledge to construct meaning, even before their eyes are on the print" (Watson 1985, p. 116).

price of sheets nowadays (such lovely floral patterns), time for the dentist already? Well, at least the phone bill's lower than last month . . .

It's eating breakfast, choosing between "Corn Flakes" and "Cap'n Crunch," cutting out the coupon and pouring your milk from the "Kroger's" carton and talking about what the day may bring; it's an adult opening the paper to the sports section and "All right! The Mets are in first place!" and then reading the comics and telling you your horoscope and checking the weather report to see if you need to wear a raincoat or sweater.

It is in these whole events and thousands of others like them, rather than in stripped down, contrived, partial contexts, that children early encounter written language in their lives. And it is in these whole contexts that they begin making sense of print.

Here are some excerpts from conversations between an adult and four-year-old Melanie, and the same adult and five-year-old Julia. Melanie and Julia have not yet been subjected to reading and writing instruction. Their talk with the adult suggests some important whole contexts in which they have encountered written language and also the kind of sense they have made of the purposes and the sounds and the look of these whole print events.[9]

The adult shows Melanie a menu and asks, "Where do you ever see something like this?"

M: At a restaurant.

A: Oh, do you? What do you do with it?

M: Um, you see what you look, the man, somebody gives it to you and you look, and you look what's in it, and you, and you get and you tell them on a list and the people write the list on it, so they won't forget and then, and then, they tell you (?), and then they and give you your food.

The adult asks Julia what kinds of things people write.

J: Some people write letters.

A: Uh-huh.

J: And some people write (pause)

A: What do they do with the letters when they write them?

J: They send them to far away people.

A: Do you write things?

J: Sometimes I write um letters to my Grandpa and, and my mom helps me by spelling them out.

A: Oh, that's neat. What do you tell your Grandpa?

J: Um, I'm working on a postcard and that postcard is going to say Dear Grandpa Bill. I, then, it's going to say, no, it's going to say I studied about bananas, from Julia.

Julia wrote a weather report which she read immediately after writing it as "That it's going to rain; that means that it's going to be cold and you'll have

---

[9]I am indebted to Judith King for these examples from her data.

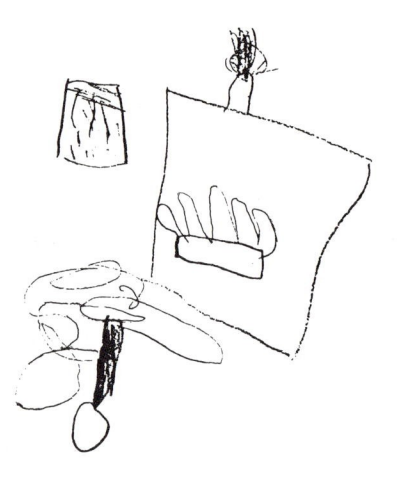

to start fires; that shows that it's going to be a wispy wind." The next day she read her weather report as, "It's going to rain, it's going to be cold, it's going to be misty wind." And a week later she read it as, "There's going to be a lot of rain, and the next one it's going to be cold, start fires, and the next one there's going to be a windy wind."

Melanie and Julia have come to know print not as isolated words or letters or sentences, but as whole events: people going to restaurants and ordering food, people writing and sending letters, people reading newspapers. If Melanie and Julia enter a kindergarten or first-grade classroom in which traditional standards override evidence from children's learning, then they will be required to confront written "language" in the form of stranger (words on flashcards, basal texts, phonics exercises), not friend. Instead of the social wholes that they know language to be —people writing notes, shopping lists, phone messages, people reading stories, hymns, announcements, birthday cards, recipes—they will find quite strange events which, amazingly, are called by familiar names ("reading," "writing," "story") yet which bear no resemblance to their authentic experience of these events. One of the most puzzling events they are likely to encounter will be basal reading material. Here we "simplify" children's beginning reading task by stripping down the text, thereby making it less "difficult" (or so we think): We give them a limited set of words, each one introduced in advance, each occurring with some controlled degree of frequency, and so on. It is interesting that the earlier the point in the child's reading development, the more disembodied and strange is the material we provide, even though research is absolutely clear on the point that the fuller and more meaningful the context of the print, the more helpful it is to the reader.[10,11]

[10]A good place to find a discussion of this research is Smith 1982a or, for a less technical version, Smith 1985.

[11]It is puzzling that we do so much in the way of contrived exercises in which children are to "use context clues," yet we deprive children of the very whole contexts of language that would be enabling and would, in fact, provide real context clues for the child to use.

Consider one basal example. The child is Sarah. You have met her before in a variety of interactions with her mother: looking at books, eating, looking at her reflection, engaging in the *Snow White* story. Audiotapes of Sarah and her mother sharing bedtime stories when Sarah is four document Sarah's active involvement as a meaning-maker in these events: She responds to the text affectively ("Yuk!" "Ooooooooo," "oh, darn") gives opinions about characters and their actions ("She's mean"), seeks clarification, acts out the actions of the story (sneezing, whistling, humming), recalls characters' sequential actions, comments on characters' feelings and motivations, corrects her mother's misreadings of text in passages she knows by heart, and asks questions about the print (p. 185). In short, she is a very actively engaged story partner.

It is two years later, when Sarah is a six-year-old kindergartner, that I observe her in her kindergarten–first-grade combination classroom. It's a classroom in which the children, during a lengthy morning period, select which of the available academic activities they will do, either individually or with friends. On this particular morning, Sarah and her best friend, Kelly, choose to read together. No adult is near—except for me, and I don't count because I sit with my back to them as I pretend to focus on some other children. My fishnet bag with the tape recorder in it sits on the table just beside Sarah and Kelly, but they don't notice it, for in this room bags and purses of visiting adults are always sitting around. Sarah and Kelly take turns "reading" by page (left column in the following example) and their "reading" sounds like this (right column in the example):

Dogs [title]	*S:* Dog - /zə/. Dogs.
I like little dogs.	*K:* I - (pause)
Little dogs sit.	*S:* like
	K: I - lick -
	S: like
	K: li - I - like - (pause) - li - *litt*le - little - *litt*le
	S: dogs
	K: dogs. Li - *litt*le - /do/ -
	S/K: dogs. (pause)
	S: it
	K: it. Its.
	S: Yeah.
	K: it. Uh. It
	S: Wait. *S*it.
	K: Sit. It
	S: Little - dogs - sit.
I like big dogs.	*S:* I - like - big - dogs. Big - dogs - jump.
Big dogs jump.	
	K: Li*tt*le - dogs - jump - too. Jump - little - dogs -
Little dogs jump, too.	jump. (pause) /də/ - /dan/(rise)

Jump, little dogs, jump!	*S:* Wait /du-*win*/
Down, little dogs, down!	*K:* /du/ (laugh)
	S: /du/ /juwin/[12]
	K: Li-
	S/K: /juwin/
	K: lit*t*le - dogs
	S: No, wait. /jen/ /jen/(decisive)
	K: (?) just read your part.
Sit, little dogs, sit!	*S:* Si*t* - lit*t*le - dogs - si*t*.
Down, big dogs, down!	*K:* /dəwin/ (pause)
	S: big
	K: big - dogs - /duwin/
	Read, read, read
I like little dogs	*S:* Okay. I like lit*t*le - dogs.
The Little Man and	*K:* Thee - lit*t*le - man - and
The Big Man [title of new story spread across two facing pages]	*S:* Thee - big - man. (They are unaware that they have moved into a new story.)

Why do they behave in this bizarre way? Because the very text that was "simplified" to help Sarah and Kelly read has made their task virtually impossible. The loss of the enabling complexity of authentic story, and the substitution of this stripped down pretender, has deprived Sarah and Kelly of the real language cues that reside in the whole event.

> When proficient readers are presented with interesting, well-written text they look like what they are—good readers reading good discourse. If these same readers are presented text that is unpredictable, lacks cohesion, is conceptually inappropriate, and holds no interest, the students will appear to be poor readers—their potential diminished by poor text. (Watson 1985, p. 116)

Dogs is a classic example of the "poor text" that makes Sarah and Kelly appear to be poor readers.

It is interesting that the author of the basal "story" was trying to help Sarah and Kelly predict. Now there is no doubt that predicting is important in children's sense making, whether they are making sense of speech, print,

---

[12] It might seem strange to you that, in attempting to read "down," Sarah tries two such different initial sounds as /d/ and /j/. But, in fact, they are not so different and her behavior here shows a very subtle awareness of the phonological system of English. Try this: Start to say "dug" and stop when your mouth is in position. Now say "jug" instead. You can feel how close /d/ and /j/ are in this case. (It is no coincidence that the first sound of "jug" is represented as /dʒ/ in some phonetic scripts.) Sarah's teacher has obviously done a lot of phonics instruction, but we can be sure that she did not suggest that " 'd' says /j/." Sarah is using her own notions of the sound system of English here.

or some other event. Surely prediction is crucial in reading. As we read, we predict on the basis of our language knowledge: our knowledge of different uses of language (in this case, our knowledge of story—of what stories are like in their purpose, organization, and style), of semantics, of syntax, of phonology. But the text *Dogs* deprives Sarah and Kelly of the possibility of using any of this language knowledge. Rather, the author of *Dogs* has substituted an inauthentic, nonlanguage basis of prediction, something like this: Expect words you have seen before in this basal context and/or words that the teacher has presented in isolation (for example, on flash cards, on chalkboard, on newsprint) in advance. There is indication from Sarah and Kelly's verbal behavior here that attention has especially been given to grapho-phonic information (sound-symbol correspondences). However, it proves self-defeating in this case because it cannot be used in meaning making, for the text offers no potential meaning to be made.

Now consider another possible text that, in striking contrast to *Dogs*, offers authentic and multiple opportunities for predicting—for reading, that is, for using language information to construct meaning from printed text. The example is *The Three Billy Goats Gruff* (Asbjørnsen and Moe 1957). I am assuming that the teacher has read this favorite to the class several times and the book is now available to Sarah and Kelly. What kind of language information would this text make available to Sarah and Kelly?

> Pragmatic information. Because this is an authentic whole story, Sarah and Kelly could predict according to their expectations about its overall structure, style, and sound. Of course, they are already familiar with the narrative line from the teacher's reading, but they know that the action and dialogue from page to page will be played out in story style. What they know about stories— how they are organized and what they sound like—will be relevant here. They will read this story to sound like story. And because it *is* story, this expectation will enable.
>
> Semantic information. The words of this story support these children's construction of powerful images: "eyes as big as saucers," "a nose as long as a poker," "gobble you up." The words also support the story sound and style: "Pray don't take me," "trip-trap," "tripping/tramping (over my bridge)," "scarce able (to walk)." The meanings conveyed and the words used to convey them fit Sarah and Kelly's expectation of the meanings and sounds of story.
>
> Syntactic information. The story uses sentence constructions that "belong" in story events: "Once on a time . . . ," "I'm too little, that I am," and the order verb-followed-by-subject so typical of story style: "A little while after came the second . . . ," ". . . under the bridge lived a great ugly troll," and "first of all came the . . ."
>
> Grapho-phonic information. In this story Sarah and Kelly would have been aided by rhyme, by alliteration, and by repetition—rhymes such as "I've got two spears, /And I'll poke your eyeballs out at your ears" and "Snip, snap, snout./ This tale's told out"; alliteration such as "I'll crush you to *b*its, *b*ody and *b*ones"; repetition as in "trip-trap" (and even "T-r-i-p, t-r-a-p").

In short, the potential for predicting by using all four kinds of language information, is inherent in this authentic, whole story.[13,14] You can readily see which of these two texts (*Dogs, The Three Billy Goats Gruff*) is the more complex. You can also see which is the more difficult.

Basal material like *Dogs* is the classic case of "nonsense" (Smith 1985), that is, material that does not provide the possibility for the child to make sense of it. No child can be expected to generate sense from nonsense. But above all, the author of *Dogs* has taken away the entire purpose of story, its reason for being in the first place: enjoyment, engagement. I know many stories that children want to read or listen to. *Dogs* is not one of them.

In classrooms guided by traditional standards, children endure endless encounters with partial and thus de-languaged events: basals, skills worksheets, drills, workbook exercises. But in classrooms guided by child evidence, I find reading and writing events that are whole:

> I find meaningful classroom print: signs by the class plants reminding the children that the plant is to be watered only once a day and providing a place for children to write the date and their name when they water it; print in the housekeeping area—the packages of food, the phone book containing the children's names and phone numbers by the toy telephone, the notepad for telephone messages, and so on; the various sign-up sheets—sheets on which the children sign up for turns at centers or to check out particular books.

> I find teachers reading stories aloud daily—an absolute minimum of thirty minutes *every* day without fail. As the teacher reads, she tapes the story, indicating auditorily the points where she turns the pages. When her reading and the children's discussion ends, while the children watch her, she writes the name of the book on the cassette tape and places the tape and several copies of the book at the listening center to join the book and tape sets accumulated over the past weeks. At least every other day she also provides simple puppets that she and/or the children have made for the story—small paper sack puppets, construction paper finger puppets, popsicle stick puppets, large paper sack puppets for children to wear, and so on.

> I find listening centers with the printed texts of song records on record jackets or in song books or song sheets the teacher has typed for the children to use as they play favorite song tapes and sing along. (Also, as mentioned earlier, I find the accumulation of story tapes and the accompanying story texts in multiple copies that friends can use together.)

---

[13]Many teachers feel that sound-symbol correspondences get a child to meaning in text. In fact the reverse is true: Meaning enables the child to figure out sound-symbol relationships. Sarah and Kelly's problem with "down" demonstrates this. They run through a variety of nonsense possibilities, never getting to "down," for "down" makes no particular sense in the senseless "story." But if there were a meaning-motivated reason for "down" to occur in the first place, then—knowing the word was "down"—Sarah and Kelly would have the possibility of noticing how the vowel sound is represented in print in this case.

[14]Story is only one kind of continuous text, but one that offers rich possibilities. Four-year-old children without much story experience in their homes can get that experience from a teacher reading orally to them daily for a period of four to six weeks (Margaret Meek, personal communication). For discussions of using children's literature rather than basals in children's early reading, see Meek 1982, Rhodes 1981, Seawell 1985.

I find well supplied and centrally located writing centers— centers with ample provision for groups of children to work simultaneously, with various sizes and shapes and types of paper for short notes, lists, reminders, cards, letters, posters, public announcements, and with various writing implements and materials for making books of various kinds such as diaries, picture books, autograph books, and telephone books with classmates' names and phone numbers.

I find thriving postal systems and children sending messages to classmates, teacher, friends in other classrooms.

I find teachers and children exchanging written messages daily in dialogue journals.

To sum up, evidence provided by children developing language tells us that in written language, as in oral, whole-language contexts enable children:

They provide maximum opportunities for children to creatively construct meaning-expression relations.

They provide continuity, allowing the child to continue using her well-developed language knowledge and powerful language acquisition processes to the full.

Above all, whole contexts provide children with *language* experience rather than with nonlanguage experience.

Sequence Conflict

The same conventional wisdom that says that decontextualized bits are helpful for children's language development says that the bits should be arranged by adults in an easy-to-difficult sequence. Like most conventional wisdom in education, this notion has a certain persuasive logic. But evidence from children indicates that such sequencing is guided by the logic of adults and that it conflicts with the psycho-logic and the socio-logic of children developing language.

Recall John Holt's mythical adult-suggested sequence in oral language development (pp. 92-93), moving children from mastering the pronunciation of specific sounds to specific syllables to specific words. No one would seriously consider such a sequence in the child's oral language development. Yet real sequences comparable to Holt's mythical one are regularly advocated, designed, and implemented in our schools; we find them in every basal series, in every reading workbook series, in every spelling series, in every language arts text series, in every district curriculum (scope and sequence) in reading, writing, and oral language. We find children's literacy experience in elementary school characterized as "a movement toward meaning" from earlier reliance on small units (for example, letter-sound correspondences) to increasing reliance on larger units (for example, sentences) (Shuy 1981, p. 922). This sequencing of bits is the logic of adults.

Now consider the psycho-logic and socio-logic of children developing their language. Their psycho-logic is that they sequence their own learning consonant with their ongoing cognitive development, and their socio-logic is that they do so in whole and purposeful social contexts. We have already seen this self-sequencing in social contexts at work in children's oral language development: We have seen that children move from shorter to longer expressed utterances according to their own internal cognitive clocks; that they work out syntactic forms and arrangements (for example, in development of negatives, interrogatives, combination sentences) according to their own observing, hypothesizing, and testing of these forms; that they predictably move from use of adult irregular verb and plural forms to overgeneralized forms and ultimately to the adult forms as they notice how these forms work; that they move from greater dependence (on concrete situation and on the help of a conversational partner) to greater independence as they figure language out; and so on. Over time they construct a language system that is increasingly elaborated and conventional. And we have seen already that this development occurs within the thousands of purposeful social situations in which children observe and/or participate—people chatting, joking, playing, teasing, comforting, swearing, arguing, and so on. Children construct language in their own specific sequence and in their own time, guided by their own developing cognition and their own social experience. This is the psycho-logic and the socio-logic of children.

However, when it comes to children's development of literacy in school settings, not only is the adult's sequencing different from children's in specifying a "logical" easy-to-difficult sequence of skills in advance; it is also different in that it is typically dominated by a concern for conventional form. Traditionally the guiding question is, What forms can the child use perfectly from the beginning? This concern influences the choice and sequencing of skills, so that the child practices producing conventional forms. Meaning is a secondary concern. Thus, children "write" pages of a's and pages of spelling words rather than journals, and they "read" vocabulary-controlled basals rather than literature. You can no doubt see the behaviorist orientation behind this. Learning, in this view, is primarily accomplished by the practice of correct responses followed by reinforcement.

In striking contrast, the child's guiding concern is not to make convention, but to make meaning. In the child's literacy development, as in her oral language development, her primary concern is to communicate and interpret messages. You remember that a striking paradox in language acquisition is that both child and adult focus on the child's meaning, yet the child, over time, develops conventional form.

The adult's form-motivated sequence (be correct, be conventional) is dramatically out of synch with the child's meaning focus. But curiously enough, it is also out of synch with the adult's meaning focus during the child's earlier development of oral language. We have seen already that adults tend to respond to the meanings young children express, whatever the forms of their expression. We have seen, too, that the child's language thrives in this meaning-oriented situation. If written language, like oral language, *is language*, and if language in school, like language outside of school, *is language*, then it is puzzling that the adult adopts such a different stance in the classroom than in the home and community. The educator's form-motivated sequence in school conflicts both with the child's meaning-motivated sequence and with the adult's meaning focus outside of school.

The notion that a child should begin by being conventional (and subsequently be meaningful) is puzzling. We would readily grant that professional writers are competent in literacy. Yet professional writers are not expected to be entirely conventional in their written forms. When a completed manuscript leaves the professional writer's hands, it goes immediately to a professional editor who deals with imperfections in the author's expression, everything from convoluted syntax to needless repetition to inappropriate vocabulary to misspelled words to misplaced punctuation. If we do not expect professional adult writers to be entirely conventional in their written forms, then on what grounds do we expect children to be? To design sequences that encourage the child to use entirely conventional forms from the beginning to the end of the education experience is to encourage children to produce form-full but meaning-empty written "language"; it is to encourage non-sense. But children's sequences are guided by making sense, not nonsense.

If adult-designed and imposed form-motivated sequences were only strange, perhaps it wouldn't matter much that many children have to go through them in school. But they are not simply strange; they are also detrimental. They deny the child's valid language behavior (expressing meaning, communicating purposefully) while requiring that the child develop invalid, nonlanguage behaviors for school (rehearsal of vacuous forms, separate skills) which will subsequently have to be dismantled or ignored if the child is to become an effective reader and writer. If Sarah and Kelly are to become fully literate, they will have to ignore the non-language behaviors required by their basal "reading" and further develop their reading behaviors from home.

Now consider a form-focused–meaning-focused pair of writing examples.

(Milz 1980, p. 181)

Es una mamó

Es una papá

Es una Tesa

Es una Ana

Es una (Med Mr.

Es una está

Es una Toy

Es una Aidi

(Translation:
It's a mom.
It's a papa.
It's a Tesa.
It's an Ana.
It's a ?
It's a it is.
It's a I am.
It's an Aida.)

(Edelsky, personal communication)

Brad's message, written on the first day of first grade, is language in that he is relating meaning and expressive form. He has been doing this in his oral expression for years, and his oral expression has become quite conventional in its form. In time, his written expression will also. Brad is "working on" language, and *language* is what he will further develop. But María in the second example is not working on language, for she produces forms with minimal regard for meaning.

Adults' form-motivated sequences are also detrimental in that they may encourage children to believe that they cannot read and write. Consider the case of Alison. Young Alison was a writer (Harste, Woodward, and Burke 1984).

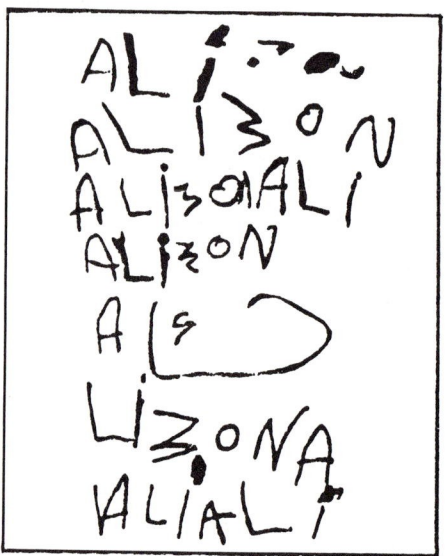

Age four, a story for a wordless book. "One day daddy came home and he said, 'Hi, Family, I'm home,' and he's gonna take us to McDonald's. I'm gonna have a Fun Meal." (p. 10)

Age five, a finger puppet on which she has written something that makes her happy: "When I see flowers." (p. 12)

Age six, a letter to her grandmother "Dear Grandma, I loved your present. Alison." (p. 13)

And as a six-year-old Alison went off to first grade and came home with a picture she had drawn of her family, under which she had copied, "Here is my home and family." At home, asked to write the very same message on another sheet of paper, Alison burst into tears and said, "I can't write . . . I don't know how to spell and write good" (p. 14). But clearly Alison had been "spelling and writing good" for some time. Alison's meaning orientation had bumped into her teacher's "assumption that control of form is prerequisite to the language process" (p. 9). The teacher's message for Alison was, "Writing is producing conventional forms. You cannot produce fully conventional forms; therefore you cannot write." It is a commonplace that we tend to do what we feel we are able to do and tend to avoid doing what we feel we are unable to do. To encourage children to believe they cannot read and write is to discourage them from reading and writing, from engaging in the very activities that will help them develop further. We do not discourage young children from talking because they do not talk conventionally. We encourage them to express themselves however they are able to and, over time, their expression becomes more elaborated and more conventional. So, too, in literacy development. "It is because Alison is and has been a reader and writer that she has a growing control of its form, and not vice versa" (p. 9).[15]

Research on the development of literacy in young children is accumulating, and it provides important information about the sequence and processes of that development. This can be helpful to teachers who try to recognize growth in their children's reading and writing and try to support the children's learning processes. Ferreiro and Teberosky (1982) have studied children's developing notions of the match between utterance and graphic display, one aspect of literacy development that is of interest to teachers. The subjects (in several studies) were 108 four- to six-year-old, Spanish-speaking Argentinian children from middle and low socio-economic-level families. All the children attended preschool, kindergarten, or first grade. The research approach was to have children individually perform specific print-related tasks and to talk with the children about what they did. In their questions and comments in conversation with the children, the researchers tried to elicit the children's own conceptions of reading and writing. (All conversations were audiotaped.) Analysis of the children's performance on the tasks and of their talk about the tasks revealed that these children constructed a sequence of hypotheses about reading and writing. According to these researchers, a child's hypothesis about some aspect of written language would hold until the child encountered a conflict: The child found either that she held two contradictory hypotheses or that her hypothesis conflicted with print she observed. In either case, such conflicts "forced" the children to revise—modify—their hypotheses to solve the problem, a behavior pattern which led the

[15]See Dyson 1982 for some further examples of "missed connections" between children's home and school writing experience.

researchers to conclude that in literacy development, "progress always occurs relative to the need to overcome a conflict" (Ferreiro and Teberosky l982, pp. 98-99).

The children's notions about written language came from two sources: the child and the social context. For some notions, the child seemed the major source. For example, these children (like others who have been studied) for a time assumed that more written symbols were required to represent a large object than a small one. Thus, more symbols would be required to write an adult's name than a child's name, because the adult is bigger. Clearly, this hypothesis is not the result of cultural transmission, since adults do not hold this view and the writing system that operates around the child does not use this principle. This notion comes from the child's own logic and is a result of the child's own creative construction. But some notions children have about print clearly depend on the social environment. For example, many children understand before coming to school that text material is read and written from front to back, and pages from top to bottom and from left to right. Obviously, this is a culturally transmitted notion. One learns these directional conventions by watching others read and write. It would be easy to characterize these two sources as cognitive-and-within-the-child, in the one case, and social and outside-of-the-child, in the other. But this dichotomy would be an oversimplification. Surely both involve (as language always does) a thinking child in a social world. The child-generated notion of larger objects requiring more symbols to represent them would not occur in a social vacuum, in the absence of experience with written language in the world. Nor would the socially generated notions of directionality in reading and writing text occur in the absence of an actively noticing and sense-making child. Child-and-context—an interaction which by now should be familiar to you as the only possible base for language development.

What developmental progression did these researchers find as the children they studied made hypotheses and modified them in response to conflicts over time? Some early notions involved what is or is not something to read. Of course, the young child encounters a wide variety of visual arrays in her environment. Only some of these are "something to read." The researchers report that the young children they studied determined which visual displays were "something to read" based on the number of characters present (usually the minimum number the child would accept was three characters) and the variation in the characters; that is, a card with the same letter repeated over and over in a string was not considered "something to read."[16] The researchers explored the children's notions of

---

[16]See Harste, Woodward, and Burke's (1984) important objection (p. 67) that the Ferreiro and Teberosky (1982) research is seriously flawed because of the research method used. For the "something (not) to read" task, children were asked to sort into two piles cards with print on them, one pile of readable cards and the other pile of unreadable cards. Thus it may be that the children thought all the cards were readable but had to make an unreadable pile to satisfy the researcher's instruction. In Harste, Woodward, and Burke's own research (in which they tried to maximize the authenticity of the print experiences they engaged their subjects in), when they asked their young subjects to read or pretend read a book, the children never indicated that they found any of the print unreadable. This is an important reminder that subjects' behavior is always influenced by the specifics of the research situation.

print in situations both with and without pictures. In the picture situation, the researchers presented the children with cards with pictures and accompanying text, some cards being pictures of single objects or persons accompanied by a single written word, other cards being pictured situations (full scenes) accompanied by a written sentence. (Notice that this task situation is not a usual print event for the child; the child typically encounters print in a communication context—a billboard, grocery list, storybook, and so forth.) A general developmental sequence was evident from the children's performance in this task. At first, the text and print constituted an inseparable unit for the children: They did not differentiate picture and text. Subsequently picture and text were differentiated, the picture being "something you look at" and the text being "something you read." But the text was seen as a single unit; the child viewed it globally. Children at this stage had different orientations to the text unit, some seeing the text as a label for the picture, others seeing the text as a sentence about the picture (regardless of whether the card bore a single word or sentence). In either case, the text was seen as a single, inseparable unit. Subsequently the children began to take into account some graphic properties of the print. Presented with a card bearing two lines of print, for example, the child would give a separate response for each line (either a different word or a different sentence for each line); or a child would read each graphic unit (word) as the name of an element in the picture. Both demonstrate the children beginning to consider the text in a nonglobal way, to break it down. The children moved toward a further breaking down of the spoken utterance and relating of the parts to graphic units, eventually matching all the graphic units with utterance parts. Ferreiro and Teberosky (1982) characterize the children's problem throughout the evolution here as "how to establish a one-to-one correspondence between the observable parts of the written text and the various segmentations of the utterance" (p. 151).[17]

In the situation without pictures, the researchers presented the children with cards bearing text only. The researcher read each card and then asked the child where various words appeared and how the child knew. Again the approach was conversational, as the researcher tried to understand what the child's hypotheses were about the print. As with the picture-and-text tasks, the children moved progressively toward further breaking down of the utterance and relating of the utterance units to graphic units.

Ferreiro and Teberosky (1982) describe the children's writing development as including five levels. The children in Level 1 wrote by making either cursivelike or manuscriptlike forms, that is, either wavy horizontal lines or combinations of circles and lines.[18] The children at this level produced larger graphic displays to represent a larger person or object, and smaller displays to represent small persons or objects. Thus,

[17]They are careful to note that the correspondences the child devises here are *not* the phoneme-grapheme correspondences that are the basis of phonics instruction.

[18]Children's early awareness of the look of print in the environment is well documented. See Harste, Woodward, and Burke 1984, p. 82, for an example (original with Yetta Goodman) in which quite different graphic displays were produced by young children from Arabic and Hebrew and English print environments, all children who did not yet write conventional symbols but captured the appearance of the writing around them.

Gustavo made a longer cursivelike string for "bear" (oso) than for "duck" (pato), and David Bernardo Mendez thought that the written representation of papa (his father) should be longer than the one for his own name (pp. 180, 184). Interestingly, at this level the children believed that only the writer could know what was written. When asked to read something the adult had written, four-year-old Gustavo said, "I don't know, because people know what they write and I knew what I was writing" (p. 180). The children in Level 2 recognized that different meanings must be written differently. They accomplished this by writing the same limited set of letterlike forms in different arrangements. This marked an important achievement, for "they had discovered . . . the antecedents of a combinatorial system" (p. 189), that is, a system which uses a limited set of basic elements that get combined in various ways. At this level the children usually knew some fixed written forms, typically their own names and possibly a few other names. Level 3 was identified by the child's syllable hypothesis, that is, her assumption that each letter represented a syllable. This level was a "qualitative leap" (p. 197) for the child in two ways: (1) She moved from considering the written representation and the utterance as global, indivisible units to an awareness of parts, and (2) she started relating writing to speech. Some fascinating conflicts occurred for the children at this level. The children viewed their own names as absolutely fixed forms; yet this fixed form conflicted with their hypothesis that each letter represented a separate syllable. Also, remember that the children thought there must be three characters in order for something to be readable. Yet the syllable hypothesis produced two-syllable words as only two letters and thus "unreadable." It was in resolving conflicts such as these that a child would move to Level 4, characterized by the alphabetic hypothesis, the child at this point assuming that letters related to segments smaller than syllables. And in Level 5, alphabetic writing, the children understood "that each written character corresponds to a sound value smaller than a syllable, and they systematically analyze the phonemes of the words they are writing" (p. 209).

It is important to remember that the developmental sequence sketched in this research is one suggested general sequence for the child's development of the "match" between utterance and graphic display—which is itself only one part of the child's understanding of written language. I have dealt with this aspect in some detail because it is one that teachers are often particularly concerned with. It is especially important to remember that every individual child follows her own specific course. This is inevitable, for every child has a unique set of experiences relating to written language, and these are an important basis for her figuring out how written language works. But besides this, every child brings a unique composite of personality characteristics to the task. Children differ in how ready they are to take risks, in how much they choose to read and write, in what purposes reading and writing serve for them, and so forth.

The developmental sequence research described here is particularly important as a dramatic affirmation that the child's way of learning is the same for written language as for oral: It involves a child actively constructing sense out of her ongoing experience of language used for real social purposes in her world. Ferreiro sums up this powerful process in a way that could apply as well to oral as to written language development:

> Children pose deep questions to themselves. Their problems are not solved when they succeed in meaningfully identifying a letter or string of letters, because they try to understand not only the elements or the results but also, and above all, the very nature of the system. (Ferreiro 1984, p. 172)

At a time when the popular notion of back-to-basics continues to mean skills-and-drills practice, one wonders what could, in fact, be more profoundly *basic* than this deep posing of questions toward an understanding of the very nature of the language system.

The research discussed at some length here is not naturalistic, for it involved special tasks designed to reveal children's notions about written language. However, observations of children learning to read and write at home in the preschool years confirm (1) the general direction of the child's move from more global to more differentiated consideration of written language and (2) the process of hypothesize→recognize conflict→resolve conflict→form new hypothesis that motivates the developmental sequence. Naturalistic research goes beyond this to indicate the importance of meaningful, authentic, conventional print in providing conflict and also confirmation of children's hypotheses.[19] Naturalistic observation confirms that

> children appear to approach reading and writing as they do most human skills—globally. They experiment and approximate, gradually becoming aware of the specific features of written language and the relationships between symbols, sounds, and meaning. They form their models of how written language works as they encounter it in specific settings. (Genishi and Dyson 1984, p. 30)

After children have started school, it becomes difficult to observe their personal learning sequences, for children are typically subjected to instructional sequences that are in direct conflict with their own ways of learning. What we observe, then, is not children's learning processes but their responses to instructional demands. Nonetheless, some important research is emerging from classrooms in which children are encouraged to explore and make sense of written language in their own ways. Kindergartners' free writing activity at writing centers shows them to be making—and revising—a variety of assumptions about print (Dyson 1981); some first graders' writing in dialogue journals reveals their move over several months from syllabic to alphabetic writing (Barbara Flores, personal communication); primary grade bilingual children's free writing demonstrates, over time, their changing hypotheses about spelling (Hudelson 1981-82,

---

[19]For examples of naturalistic studies, see Taylor 1983, Newkirk 1984, and Bissex 1980.

1984)[20] and about segmentation and punctuation (Edelsky 1983); third and fourth graders' writing— each piece moving from initial draft through subsequent revisions—shows children working through a variety of notions about writing, from overall structure of compositions to finer conventions of spelling and punctuation (Calkins 1983). This research, too, confirms that the child moves from more global to more refined, elaborated, and conventional notions of print by means of a continuing hypothesis-building and revising process. But this research also demonstrates that classroom learning environments can support this development by accepting and encouraging the children's exploration and creative construction, while at the same time providing constant interaction with real written language that provides both the conflicts and the models that the child requires. (Observe again that skills-and-drills materials—partial texts—provide neither conflicts nor models for the child.) Teachers and classroom researchers tell us of kindergartens in which

> children make books of environmental signs drawn or cut from magazines— their own books of meaningful print that they can read;
>
> children dictate their stories to their teacher, watch while she writes them, and then select classmates to act their stories out (Paley 1981);
>
> children interact with each other and with print in sociodramatic play areas— "stores" replete with shelves of canned and packaged products and materials for the necessary written transactions (shopping lists, sales slips, bargain announcements), which subsequently become other familiar environments such as home, doctor's office, or restaurant, complete with the print materials and events appropriate to those contexts;
>
> children draw/write at well-located and well-supplied writing centers;
>
> children listen to the teacher's reading aloud and then to her taped reading (at a listening center) as they follow the text (with friends) in the multiple copies of the book provided;
>
> children act out familiar texts in their own puppet play (Seawell 1985);

of first-grade classrooms in which

> children write in dialogue journals and the teacher writes daily responses from the beginning of the school year (Milz 1985; Flores, personal communication 1986);
>
> children's reading material is literature written by professional children's authors and by child authors, instead of basals (Milz 1985);
>
> children write and send letters—to friends in the classroom, to friends in other classes, to professional authors, to the teacher (Milz 1980, 1985);

of third-grade classrooms in which

> children engage in purposeful writing for forty-five minutes each day, controlling all parts of the writing process (topic selection, organization, style, editing, selection for publication) and conference with one another and with their teacher as is helpful in the process (Calkins 1983);

[20]For a classic study of children's invented spellings, see Read 1971.

of sixth-grade classrooms in which

> children read whole books "in as many sittings as necessary for purposes like 'sheer enjoyment' or preparation for 'literature study discussion' ";
>
> children carry out large projects such as planning, creating, and implementing a haunted house for the entire school;
>
> each child finds out the interests of her "assigned" first grader and then selects appropriate books to read aloud to the child (Edelsky, Draper, and Smith 1983).

Classrooms guided by conventional wisdom work very differently from those described here. Traditional classrooms give children information rather than encouraging them to actively construct their own knowledge even though "it is not . . . information itself that creates knowledge" (Ferreiro 1984, p. 171). Further, the information given the child often clashes dramatically with the knowledge structure the child has built. Beginning reading and writing instruction tends to start with bits, but, as we have seen, children begin globally. Many entering first graders are working within a syllabic hypothesis orientation, but first-grade phonics instruction assumes, and promotes, an alphabetic principle, that is, a view of print and speech relationships that is not possible for the child at this time. Most disturbing of all is Ferreiro and Teberosky's finding that school experience often divorces meaning from form.

> An imposing conclusion emerges: the phenomena of divorcing deciphering [sound-symbol decoding] from meaning and of rejecting meaning at the expense of deciphering are school products. They are the consequence of reading instruction which forces children to forget meaning until they have mastered the mechanics of deciphering. On their own, children are not inclined toward such dissociation. (Ferreiro and Teberosky 1982, p. 98)

Instances of literacy instruction divorcing meaning from form and requiring the child to focus on the latter in a meaning vacuum are often easy to identify. You observed a clear case with Sarah and Kelly's attempt to "read." The following conversation between a researcher and seven-year-old Laura provides yet another example.

ADULT: When you're reading and you come to something you don't know, what do you do?

C: We sound out the first two letters. After I gots that I try to see another word—if it has three syllables.

A: Do you ever do anything else?

C: If I do all that and I still don't get it, I try my vowel rules.

A: If you knew that someone was having difficulty reading, how would you help them?

C: I would try to whisper to them to try the first two letters.

A: What if that didn't help?

C: I would pray that God will help them find the word.

A: What would your teacher do to help that person?

C: She would say to tell them to use the vowel rules, or look for a small word, or try the first two letters.

A: What would you like to do to be a better reader?

C: I would study my vowel rules and my phonics a lot because that's mostly reading. (DeFord and Harste 1982, pp. 591–92)

One wonders whether Laura will ever resume her real work of dealing with meaning and form together.

Knowing what you already do about the sequence and processes of children's oral language development, perhaps the child's activity in constructing the written language system doesn't surprise you. And yet, children's behavior here, as in all aspects of language development, is ever surprising. That such small persons take on such enormously complex work, and that they pursue it so tirelessly and so ingeniously, finally inventing the system of language—this must ever surprise. And they carry on this work with the adults around them only minimally aware (if at all) of what the children are doing. Only with careful probing does the researcher begin to discover the child's sequences and processes of literacy development. Our beginning understanding of children constructing written language reminds us of how seriously conventional standards in education have underestimated children and the language work they do. But our beginning understanding also reassures, for it enables teachers to recognize signs of children's learning sequences and processes as they are played out in children's behavior, and to trust and encourage the child's learning work.

At times in this discussion I have focused on children's writing development, at other times on their reading development. Of course, such a distinction is artificial. We know that in the actual literacy development of children, reading and writing cannot be separated. One researcher, intent on observing third and fourth graders' writing and *not* their reading, found it impossible to observe one without the other:

> There was no way I could watch writing without watching reading. While composing, children read continually. They read to savor the sounds of their language, they read to see what they had written, they read to regain momentum, they read to reorient themselves, they read to avoid writing. They read to find gaps in their work, they read to evaluate whether the piece was working, they read to edit. And they read to share the work of their hands. . . . When children are makers of reading, they gain a sense of ownership over their reading. (Calkins 1983, pp. 153, 156)

And a first-grade teacher whose students write meaningfully from the first day of school using whatever means they have comments that though the children cannot read (in the traditional sense), they are able to read what *they write*. (Giacobbe 1981). There is a wholeness here in which the reading and writing aspects are mutually supportive. The deep, unifying fact of reading and writing is that both are activities in which one constructs text. The traditional language arts labels of writing and speaking as "productive" and listening and reading as "receptive" are wrong: Reading (listening too) is not receptive; rather, it is active creative construction of meaning as one interacts with the pragmatic, semantic, syntactic, and grapho-phonic information the author provides. Perhaps we are most dramatically reminded of the creative construction process that reading is every time we see a movie of a book that we have read. The Hollywood version never matches the "movie version" that we created in our heads as we read. It is the Hollywood version, of course, that is "wrong." This character portrayal is too gentle, that one too harsh; one character's voice is too raspy, another's face too craggy-looking; this character is too frail, that one too husky; the house is wrong and so is the yard—they didn't look like that in our heads; and where's the hovering sense of impending doom? We and the film director read the same book and because we were "really reading," we constructed different texts in our heads out of our different experiences that we brought to our reading. And what of children? Do any two of them construct the same troll or billy goats in the mind's eye? I very much doubt it. Nor should they if they are engaged in an authentic reading act.[21] "At the heart of understanding reading and writing connections one must begin to view reading and writing as essentially similar processes of meaning construction. Both are acts of composing" (Tierney and Pearson 1983, p. 568).

Indeed, observations of children reading and writing reveal that the whole is greater than just reading-and-writing; it also includes talk—children's talk that weaves in and around their reading-and-writing activity. In short, the evidence from children in classrooms where their own language development sequences are supported confirms what we intuitively "knew" all along, that reading and writing and talking and listening are all *language* and develop in inseparable and mutually supportive ways.

The classroom has tremendous potential for supporting children's own developmental sequences:

> The classroom provides new and diverse communication purposes and situations. The child finds further reasons to make and express meaning which, remember, is the very thing she is oriented toward doing. At home, most children have limited reasons to write letters and few people to write letters to; in school they may be writing to authors whose works they enjoy, to airline companies for information brochures and time schedules for social studies projects, to local government officials to inform them of how pending decisions will affect school children, to a local potter inviting her to visit, to friends from other classes, and so on. At home the child interacts with family members in various ways and for various reasons; but the classroom offers additional ways and reasons not usually found at home: Here the child participates in small-group planning sessions, serves as an expert informing a group, helps a friend clarify her thinking about a problem she has encountered in her writing. These are only a few examples; you can readily think of many more. The point is that there are rich invitations in the classroom for new ways of making and expressing meaning. This is authentic sequencing.

[21]Notice that conventional reading instruction often conveys the notion that if everyone is "really reading" the same story, then they will all have the same understanding in their heads. But I suspect the opposite is so: A "real" reading involves creation of unique text within the guidelines the author provides.

The classroom provides supportive interaction. Vygotsky writes, "What a child can do with assistance today, she will be able to do by herself tomorrow" (Vygotsky 1978, p. 87). We immediately think of the teacher as the one who plays this assisting, partnering role. We think of the teacher's well-timed comment, question, expression of appreciation, attentive listening, touch on the shoulder, suggestion. But children also play this supportive role for one another in classrooms where such interactions are encouraged, expected, and valued. We see and hear this peer support as children collaborate on projects, as they respond to one another's writing in conferences, as they help one another edit written work, as they recommend books for friends to read, and so on. Thus, as the child works on her own developmental tasks in the classroom, she has many sources of support toward ultimate independence. This is authentic sequencing.

The classroom provides abundant demonstrations of conventional purposeful print in use. The child is continually in contact with print that demonstrates both the elaboration and the convention which are the directions of her development. There is the print of books (published books of both child and adult authors), newspaper stories, ads, pamphlets and brochures, schedules, the teacher's daily response in the child's dialogue journal. In literacy development as in oral language development, the child observes and interacts with the ever-present conventional forms as she follows her developmental course toward them. This is authentic sequencing.

The classroom can provide a no-risk environment. It is in a safe, buffered setting that the child can invent, explore, question, make constructive errors, seek assistance. Being able to do her own real language work, the child shows the teacher where she is and thus the teacher is able to respond appropriately, to meet the child where she is at that moment. It is in such environments that children can get and use corrective feedback without feelings of incompetence or failure. This is authentic sequencing.

The classroom is a very special place for supporting children's developmental sequences.

Assessment Conflict[22]

If you have decided that the child should master language in discrete and sequenced bits, it is only a small next step to deciding that the child's mastery of each bit in the sequence should be tested in order to chart the child's progress. And if you believe that real language is simply a composite of the separate bits, then you believe that when you have tested the bits, you have a measure of the child's development of real language. This is the conventional wisdom, and it underlies our society's increasing reliance on standardized test scores as indicators of the level of the child's learning, the effectiveness of the teacher's instruction, the success of the school, and so on. But if you know that language development is not an accumulation of separate bits in some logical easy-to-difficult sequence, then these tests are irrelevant as measures of children's language development. At best they measure skills mastery and the ability to perform under test conditions.

Let's consider one standardized language test by way of demonstrating the problems with using this type of test to assess children's real-

---

[22]Portions of this section appeared previously (Lindfors 1983).

language development. I am going to use the 1968 Illinois Test of Psycholinguistic Abilities (ITPA) though other formal language tests would do as well. The ITPA serves as an effective example, since it is a highly reputed language assessment instrument in many educational circles, it includes subtests of various types, and it is given individually and so we would expect it to avoid some of the problems inherent in group tests.

The examiner's manual tells us that the test is "a parsimonious device by which the essential features of communication were delineated" (pp. 6–7). Let's look at two of these "essential features of communication": subtests that initially appear to be quite different from each other. The first is the grammatic closure test in which the child provides a word to complete the examiner's sentence about a picture:

Here is a dog. Here are two_____.
Each child has a ball. This is hers; and this is _____.
This boy is writing something. This is what he_____.
This man is painting. He is a _____.
This man is planting a tree. Here the tree has been _____.[23]

The verbal expression test measures another part of the language whole: "the ability of the child to express his own concepts vocally" (p. 11). At first glance this test seems more open and communicative than the language tests we may be used to. The examiner holds up each of four small objects one at a time (a ball, a block, a button, an envelope) and says to the child, "Tell me all about this." But the restricted nature of this "verbal expression" task (how far removed it is from the "real" language abilities of children which it purports to assess) becomes apparent when we look at what constitute "creditable" and "noncreditable" responses. Creditable responses include label, color, shape, composition, function, major parts, numerosity, other physical characteristics (for example, texture, weight, size), comparison, person or place or thing commonly associated with the object, or some action of that object.[24] Noncreditable responses include a reference to accidental details such as smudges, nicks, scratches, pencil marks, and the like; statements relating to the child's emotional reactions, likes or dislikes, or other people's attitudes; reference to objects other than the one the examiner is holding; and statements that are universal and apply to a large number of objects (p. 55).

I'm not sure why stating the obvious ("It's a block") is "creditable," while providing a more detailed and specific observation ("Oooooh, it's got a little smudgy place over here") is "noncreditable." Nor is it clear to me why stating the obvious ("This button has two holes") is "creditable," while relating the present object to another situation ("Mine at home has four

[23]The sociolinguist Walt Wolfram has pointed out that a fourth-grade Appalachian child who selected all Appalachian dialect alternatives in this particular subtest would be designated as functioning at a four-year-old level (personal communication). Clearly, this test measures the "standardness" of the child's dialect, but the testmaker believes one discrete part of the total set of parts comprising "language" is being assessed.

[24]You might want to see Heath 1982 for a description of a community of children for whom this approach to what counts as "creditable" would be particularly inappropriate.

holes" or "My brother hates these") is "noncreditable." What is clear is that (1) the test is not, in fact, evaluating the child's ability "to express her own concepts vocally," since the more the child expresses *her own* concepts, the more "discredited" her responses are likely to be, and (2) the examiner doesn't really mean it when she says to the child, "Tell me all about this"; what she really means is, "Tell me things about this from the set of ten preordained, arbitrary categories."

The extraordinariness of this "language" situation is apparent after only a moment's reflection. The examiner tries to provide a comfortable interactive setting for the child so that she will feel relaxed and thus be able to communicate effectively in this situation. The examiner then "invites" the child to talk about the objects in question. However, the "talk" that the child must produce in order to score well (be "creditable") is "talk" which is totally inappropriate—in fact, utterly bizarre—in a normal face-to-face conversation between two individuals. Never in "real life" do we "converse" by naming characteristics of objects which are entirely obvious to the conversational partner: "Hi, Janet. Haven't see you for ages. This is a button. It has two holes. It is yellow. It is used for fastening clothes. It is light in weight . . ." The child needs to understand that she must not be taken in by the examiner's attempt to establish an informal conversational atmosphere; rather she must set aside her well-understood rules of conversation (for example, that a conversation between two partners is a turn-taking exchange in which both partners contribute relevantly to the ongoing discourse, relating each conversational turn to the partner's preceding one and then adding something new to carry the conversation forward). How ironic that only by deliberately abandoning her knowledge of how to communicate in real life is the child deemed, by the test score, proficient in "verbal expression." If this individual "verbal expression" test is so seriously inadequate as a measure of children's real language abilities, then how much worse are the group tests of spelling, reading comprehension, and so on, which are even further removed from real-life languaging.

It is easy enough to demonstrate that the formal standardized skills tests on which child, teacher, and school evaluations increasingly depend do not, in fact, give information about children's real-language development. What, then, can we use instead as authentic demonstrations of children's progress, for we, the children, their parents, and school administrators must know that—and how—the children are progressing. Again, we look to evidence provided by children. The authentic evidence of their real language development is how they use language in real communication situations. The challenge is to develop procedures for validly sampling and preserving the children's communication behavior.

More and more, classroom teachers are developing and sharing methods that work for them. Many teachers keep ongoing anecdotal records in their children's file folders. Each is a brief, dated description of a particular incident, written or typed on a file card. (It is helpful to keep a constant supply of cards in an accessible place, as it is sometimes possible to jot down a sketchy phrase or two right after the incident occurs and then develop the notes into a fuller description later.) Many teachers develop and use their own checklists or observation forms to document children's language behaviors which are of particular interest to them. Some teachers tape record selected activities and then transcribe and/or write descriptions of the segments which are of interest. Many teachers keep samples of children's writing.[25] It is important to keep samples of both informal and formal writing. The informal samples (for example, dialogue journals, where the child's writing is not edited) will provide a record of the child's developing hypotheses about written language and will typically show an overall move toward elaboration and conventionality in the child's spontaneous writing. The more formal writing samples (for example, copies of books that the child has published, along with copies of the earlier drafts) will show how the child consciously works on particular pieces to bring them to publishable form. It is important to capture and to share with the child and her parents both the more spontaneous and the more consciously crafted writing, for both show important aspects of the child's development.

On those occasions when a testing time is set aside and the teacher "administers" something with "test" printed on the front, it is easy enough to recognize that one is testing. In fact, we tend to test children far more than we are aware. In testing, the goal is to assess the child's knowledge or skill; the goal is for the child to perform. In contrast, the goal in teaching is to help the child build knowledge or skill; the goal is for the child to learn. Performing versus learning, testing versus teaching—these are very different. Many accepted classroom events that are considered teaching-learning activities, are, in fact, testing-performing activities; their goal is for children to demonstrate whether or not they know or can do particular things. The sets of reading comprehension questions we ask in reading circle are tests. Every worksheet and every workbook exercise is a test. Reading aloud individually in reading circle is a test. Oral "discussion questions" are often tests. Every book report that we assign, collect, and grade is a test. In contrast, some teachers encourage their students to respond to books they read in ways that are not tests, ways that do not ask the child to engage in a performance that the teacher will evaluate. Rather, these teachers invite their students to dialogue purposefully about what they have read. Some teachers, for example, keep a file of manila folders by the classroom library, available to the children. Each file folder is labeled with the name of a book in the class library. After reading a particular book, a child can, if she chooses to, write her reaction to the book and put it in the appropriate file folder. Other children, considering reading that book, can consult the folder of written reactions and consult the children who wrote them for further information if they want to. Some teachers have established written dialogues with their students about what they are reading. Here are samples from the "written conversations" between one eighth-grade teacher and her student Daniel, who, as of the first day of eighth

---

[25]For descriptions of nontest ways of assessing children's language, see Almy and Genishi 1979; Jaggar and Smith-Burke 1985: *Language Arts*, 61, no. 4 (1984); Boehm and Weinberg 1977; Irwin and Bushnell 1980; and Genishi and Dyson 1984.

grade, had never bought a book or borrowed one from the town library, and estimated that he had read "maybe one or two" novels.

Sept 20/82

Dear Miss Atwell,

About David.

I liked it because it made me feil it happend to me. it was one of the first books I read that I enjoyed. Because I don't read much. I liked it when they talked about David and the feilings his friend and family (or lyns Parent's) felt.

10/1

Dear Daniel,

Do you think you'd read more if you could find more really good books? Your note about *About David* made me sad. It seems like you haven't found many books you've enjoyed. There are so many novelists who describe people's feelings as well as Pfeffer does.

For example, I think you'd like *Tex*, by S. E. Hinton. Have you read it?

Write back.

Ms. Atwell

Dear Miss Atwell,

I don't think I would read more because I an too bissee. did you ever read About David? no I have never read this book.

10/25/85

Dear Daniel,

I read *About David* on Wednesday. You're right: it's definitely a book about feelings. I couldn't imagine where Pfeffer could possibly go after opening her novel with a suicide/double murder. But the way she slowly develops the aftermath—focusing on the effects of David's actions on the people who are left— just knocked me out. Thanks for recommending it.

Ms. Atwell (Atwell 1984, p. 243)

Notice that these nontest responses of children to books help the teacher gain a sense, an authentic sense, of the child's reading. Thus they help the teacher respond appropriately to the child's reading; they help her to support and extend that reading; in short, they help her to teach effectively.

We must have a clear sense of our children's ongoing activity and progress as we teach. We must assess. But we must clearly differentiate between subjecting the child to contrived situations in which she performs in order to be evaluated, and observing and documenting the child's behavior in communication situations which are purposeful to her.

Conventional standards tell us to teach skills in sequence, testing each one, checking it off, and going on to the next. In a recent conversation with a student teacher in a fourth-grade classroom, I asked about the reading lesson I had just observed in which the student teacher had taken the children through a set of low-level, detailed questions about a story they had read in their basal: "What's the name of the boy in your story today?" "What's his friend's name?" "What did they find?" "Where did they find the _____?" I asked her why she was having the children do this. Her answer was quick and certain. "They have to answer these questions so they'll be ready for Friday's skills test." The skills test, or standardized test, becomes the end, while the teaching is the means to it. Increasingly, it seems, "language" tests are determining what and how we teach. However, evidence from children tells us that we help them most in their language development, not when we teach so that they will do well in the test, but when we "test," that is, assess, so that we will do well in the teaching. We help children when we observe their language in authentic communication situations, let our observations guide our teaching, and document our observations periodically so that we and our children can see how richly they are developing.

Rehearsal versus Communication Conflict

This conflict is an overarching one and has to do with different views of what the child's language work is in school: Is she to prepare to do language, that is, to rehearse separate skills that supposedly will prepare her to read and write and converse effectively at some later time? Or is she to *do* language, to communicate with others in written and oral channels as best she can, getting better at it as she goes along?

James Britton (1973) makes a crucial distinction between two meanings of the term "practice." His distinction puts this conflict in sharp focus. One kind of practice is "rehearsal practice," for example, the juggler "practicing" a juggling act he will later perform. This "practice" isn't the real thing; it is rehearsal for the real thing. The other kind of "practice" is the practice of "engaging in," as the doctor "practices" medicine or the lawyer "practices" law. This isn't rehearsal for the real thing; it *is* the real thing. Rephrasing our conflict in Britton's terms: Is the child's appropriate language practice in school the practice of *rehearsal* for communication, or is it the practice of *engaging in* communication? The answer to this question determines whether the teacher's job is to provide opportunities for rehearsal practice or opportunities for engaging in communication.

Conventional standards have perpetuated rehearsal activities on the assumption that one must first learn how to do something and then one will be able to do it. This seems a reasonable enough assumption—until one thinks of children acquiring language. A moment's reflection reveals the absurdity of the notion that a child first learns how to use language and then she uses it. Does a young child learn how to converse and then start interacting with others? From your reading of Chapters 6 and 7, you know that it does not happen this way. Rather, the child uses language in whatever ways she is able to in order to communicate her meanings and to interpret the expression of others; and in the process of engaging in language, her expression and understanding develop, becoming more elaborated, more conventional, more refined. This engaging-in practice is *language* practice, both during the school years and before, and in both oral and written modes of expression. Engaging-in practice provides a powerful continuity in children's language development in the school years. The school child, rightly, knows that language is doing communication.

The kind of rehearsal practice we see so much of in schools tells the child that "language" (reading, writing, speaking) in school is not real language, that it is discontinuous with what she has known and done as language all along, and that the well-developed abilities she has for constructing relations between meaning and expression are irrelevant.

Instead of engaging in reading as "a process of interpreting the world" (Cole and Griffin 1983), she will practice decoding.

Instead of making meaning from text, she will call words in sequence.

Instead of making sense of authentic written texts—signs, songs, predictable children's literature, stories she has written with her teacher's help, books her classmates have written, notes the teacher has written in her dialogue journal, letters she finds in her mailbox—instead of this she will circle pictures of words beginning with *b*.

Instead of engaging in writing as a way of communicating with others and with self, she will rehearse letter forms and sequences so that someday she will be able to write.

Instead of writing articles for the class newspaper, she will practice assigned lists of spelling words for Friday's test.

Instead of writing a grievance letter to her teacher, she will write adjectives in the blanks provided in the sentences of a workbook page.[26]

Consider this final pair of examples contrasting third graders' rehearsal practice and engaging-in practice.

EXAMPLE 1

I entered a third-grade classroom just as the teacher was starting the whole-group language arts lesson on how to make more interesting sentences.

[26]Interestingly, research studies of children engaging in language in classrooms (for example, doing sustained silent reading instead of phonics, doing self-selected reading instead of reading basals) shows that when they are tested on skills (for example, grammar, reading comprehension, word recognition, spelling), they outperform children who have been doing rehearsal practice (phonics, exercises, basal reading) (see, for example, Elley and Mangubhai 1983). I am indebted to Steve Krashen for this observation. Calkins observes that the third graders she interviewed from a classroom in which punctuation was taught by drill could explain on average fewer than four kinds of punctuation; whereas the third graders she interviewed from a classroom in which all punctuation was learned in the context of the children's own writing could explain on average eight kinds of punctuation (Calkins 1983, p. 35).

T: Today we are going to think about how we can write more interesting sentences. (On the overhead she projects "The boy ran.")
T: Now this isn't a very interesting sentence, is it?
Cs: (a general muttering of agreement)
T: But now how 'bout this one? Here's a more interesting one. (She uncovers a new sentence directly beneath the first one on the overhead. It says, "The boy raced to school." She points out the improvements in the second sentence and then goes on to give the children new uninteresting sentences on the overhead, inviting them to revise the given sentences to make them more interesting. She writes the children's suggested "more interesting" sentences under her suggested "uninteresting" sentences. Soon the overhead looks like this.)

We played the game. (Teacher's sentence)
We played the game at school.
We played Clue.
I played a fun game of Clue and I won.

I liked the story. (Teacher's sentence)
I liked the story of "Jack in the Beanstalk."
I liked the story because it was funny.

The circus was fun. (Teacher's sentence)
The circus was fun and I stayed there all day.
The circus was fun when the horses did tricks and I watched them until 7 o'clock.
The circus was fun because the clowns went on the trapeze.

EXAMPLE 2

A researcher (Calkins 1983) observes third graders in their daily writing workshop as they select topics for their writing, write, conference with peers and with the teacher, edit, revise, and publish selected works as classroom books. One morning she watches Susie.

Susie began her next piece, "The Big Fish" . . . by writing five leads . . . "Hey, Diane, listen to these," Susie said, nudging her friend. As Susie read her leads to Diane, she also read them to herself. The fifth lead went like this and it was the one Diane paid attention to:
   Our boat was drifting on the water. It was a beautiful warm day. The sun was just going behind some hills and all was peaceful. Just then I felt something on my line. I thought it was a snag but it wasn't.
   "How'd it feel like on the line?" Diane asked . . . Susie did not answer Diane's question. Instead she ducked her head back toward her paper, reread the lead, and wrote another draft adding the missing information. When Susie finished, she showed it to me . . . When she read the lead to me, she found a specific problem. "How will you know I'm fishing?" she said, not expecting me to answer. She solved the problem by writing another draft of the lead, then correcting it and recopying it . . .
   Me and my father were fishing at a lake. I looked in the water and saw a

> quick flash. It was a school of fish that looked like silver dollars. (Calkins 1983, pp. 58-59)

Which third graders are, in fact, "working on writing interesting sentences"? It is naive to suppose that the idle exercise of the first group, in which the children thrust teacher-pleasing sentences into a communication void, will in any way support their writing development. These children are not doing language; they are doing teacher pleasing. But Susie in the second example *is* doing language. It is because she is writing something for herself and others to read that she works so hard to forge new ways of expressing her meaning, much as she did as a very young child verbally expressing her meanings in new ways.

Our knowledge about what language is and how children acquire and use it motivates us as teachers to question conventional standards in language education when those standards conflict with evidence provided by children themselves. The children tell us that the classroom contexts that best support their language development are those in which

> language experience is whole, not piecemeal;
>
> language sequences derive from children's active, cognitive, and social engagement with the world, not from adults' well-intended, logical designs;
>
> language assessment is the teacher's ongoing observation and documentation of children using language in communication, not children's scores in tests of "language" skills;
>
> language "practice" is engaging in language, not rehearsing it.

Excellent classroom teachers are showing us how to provide such learning environments for our children.

SUGGESTED PROJECTS

1. *Analysis of child language sample.* In as natural a setting as possible, record, or have a mother record, a total of thirty to forty minutes' worth of language from one child (age two to four). Transcribe and analyze your recorded data. Find the MLU for your sample (see Brown 1973, p. 54, for procedure for determining MLU). Discuss the semantic, syntactic, and phonological features of the child's language system (as evidenced in the child's performance) and the purposes for which you feel the child is using his language. It will help if you number the child's utterances sequentially in your transcript, so that you can readily cite supporting examples from your data for the points you make in your discussion.

2. *Study of child-child-language.* Record twenty to thirty minutes' worth of good (audible) conversation among several children between two and five years of age playing together in as informal a situation as possible and *without an adult* in the immediate vicinity. Transcribe you tape. Then (1) analyze it for any differences you notice between the children's use of language and your own, and (2) cite as much specific evidence as you can from your recorded data of the children's knowledge of language rules— of principles underlying their verbal behavior.

3. *Replication of Berko Gleason study.* Replicate Jean Berko Gleason's (1971) morphology study (the "wug study") with four or five children, ages four to seven. You'll conduct the test with each child individually, describe your results, and compare with Berko Gleason's.

4. *Sentence repetition test.* Construct and administer a sentence repetition test of approximately twenty-five items to each of five children ages two to five. Be sure your test includes sentences of a variety of types (affirmative statements, negative statements, commands, questions), of varying lengths, and of varying complexity. Record each child's responses and transcribe them exactly. Analyze your results. Are there differences from younger to older children? What are they? What kinds of changes do the children make in their repetition of the model? Do they substitute items? Delete items? Rearrange items? Which ones? How can you account for these changes? Do you see any patterns here?

5. *Study of mother's speech to young child.* Tape record an informal conversation between yourself and the mother of a child between six months and two years of age (about fifteen minutes' worth). (You might tell the mother that you are taping because you do not like writing things down and would rather just talk with her informally, but you do want to have the information from the conversation, in case you want to refer to it later.) The focus of your conversation will be for the mother to tell you about her child. Get her to talk *as much as possible.* Then have her, at some time when you are not present, tape about fifteen to thirty minutes' worth of her informal interaction with her child—for example, child's play time after nap, child's bath, lunch time. Transcribe both tapes. Analyze the mother's language to compare the language she used when she talked with you, an adult, and the language she used when she talked with her child. Note any semantic, syntactic, phonological features of difference in her language in the two situations (length of sentences, complexity of sentences, variety of vocabulary, variations of pronunciation, stress, or emphasis, use of playful nonsense words, number of well-formed sentences).

6. *Adults' language to children of different ages.* In as natural a setting as possible, have a parent tape about thirty minutes of family interaction involving at least one parent and two children of different ages. For example, a mother and father and their one- to two-year-old and four- to seven-year-old at dinner would be ideal. Transcribe your tape. (There are bound to be points at which the sound is inaudible. Just transcribe as completely as you can, leaving blanks for the segments it is impossible to hear, and indicating by a question mark those segments of which you are uncertain.) Analyze your transcript, noting especially any differences in the adults' language with each other, with the older child, and with the younger child. Also, how does the language of the older child change when she is interacting with the adults and when interacting with the younger sibling?

7. *Survey.* We hear adults express many commonly held misconceptions about how a child acquires a language. Design a questionnaire relating to how children acquire their language and have fifteen to twenty adults respond to it. Discuss your results. What notions about language acquisition are most prevalent in your sample? Do the ideas of parents differ from those of nonparents? If so, how? Be sure to frame your questions so that they are open enough that respondents' answers will be informative (not simply yes or no) yet limited enough that people will not simply throw the questionnaire in the waste basket because it is too much trouble to respond. An appropriate item might be this: "Some researchers have observed that adults talk

differently to very young children (from birth to about two years of age) than to other adults. How do you think adults modify their talk when they interact with infants and toddlers?" You might want to consider using items that are not in question (interrogative) form, for example, "List 10 words that you think might be among a child's first words" or "Rank the following five adult behaviors from the one you think is most helpful (1) to the one you think is least helpful (5) for a child learning his or her native language." Then you might list five adult behaviors that are of interest to you (for example, reinforcing a child for the forms she uses, or listening and responding with interest to what the child says). You might want to follow a ranking item of this kind by asking the respondent to give reasons for his or her first and last choices. Or, you could provide a statement about language acquisition and have the respondent agree or disagree with the statement and support his or her position. After you have made up your questionnaire, to be sure that your items are easily understood and elicit the kind and amount of information you want, try it out with several friends before you distribute it to the respondents in your study.

8. *Study of young child's awareness of environmental print.* This suggestion builds on Smith's mention of a young child's responses to print in stores in a shopping center (Smith 1985, p. 117). You need (1) a preschool child who has not been subjected to formal reading instruction and (2) a situation rich in contextualized print (for example, a department store or grocery store, or perhaps the child's own home). Your purpose is to explore the child's awareness of print in the setting you have chosen. You might do what Smith apparently did: Simply ask the child what various signs and labels say (being sure to keep a record, either taped or handwritten, of the child's responses as you go). You might also want to take a camera with you so that you or the child can take pictures of some of the print you encounter. (The child might want to make a picture book of these to share with parents or siblings.) Then analyze your child's responses: What knowledge does each response indicate? If possible, repeat this with several other children (three to five children would be a good number in all). (You might prefer to do this with several of your classmates or fellow teachers. Each of you would take a child, or two, and then the group of you would come together to combine observations.)

9. *"Your own thing."* Design your own learning experience relating to the ideas in the section, discuss it with your instructor and/or an acquaintance knowledgeable in this area, and execute it.

SUGGESTED FURTHER RESOURCES

Books

CALKINS, L., *Lessons from a Child: On the Teaching and Learning of Writing.* Portsmouth, N.H.: Heinemann Educational Books, 1983. A description of children's authentic writing experiences during their third- and fourth-grade years.

CHUKOVSKY, K., *From Two to Five*, trans. and ed. Miriam Morton. Berkeley, Calif.: University of California Press, 1963. Anecdotal observations of early language development.

GENISHI, C., AND A. DYSON, *Language Assessment in the Early Years.* Norwood, N.J.: Ablex Publishing Corporation, 1984. A description of oral and written language development from preschool through the primary grades, in home and institutional settings, and written expressly for practitioners.

GRAVES, D., *Writing: Teachers and Children at Work.* Portsmouth, N.H.: Heinemann Educational Books, 1983. A book whose purpose is "to assist classroom teachers with children's writing"; demonstrates how teachers work with children in all aspects of the writing process (topic selection, conferencing, editing, and publishing).

GLEASON, J. B., ed., *The Development of Language.* Columbus, Ohio: Charles E. Merrill Publishing Company, 1985. An introductory, readable, and well-informed collection of chapters on various aspects of language development.

HARSTE, J., V. WOODWARD, AND C. BURKE, *Language Stories and Literacy Lessons.* Portsmouth, N.H.: Heinemann Educational Books, 1984. "An attempt to get teacher-researchers to think through the implications of recent insights into literacy and literacy learning"; focuses on young children's (mainly ages three to six) active building of an understanding of written language.

MEEK, M., *Learning to Read.* London: The Bodley Head, 1982. Supposedly a book for parents (though I think it is a book for teachers, too), it describes reading development through adolescence, with special focus on using literature. (Many of the literary works cited are British publications.)

PALEY, V., *Wally's Stories.* Cambridge, Mass.: Harvard University Press, 1981. Kindergarten children's real discussions and created stories and their sensitive teacher's observations about these and about the teacher's role.

SLOBIN, D., *Psycholinguistics* (2nd ed.). Glenview, Ill.: Scott, Foresman and Company, 1979. A fascinating presentation of research and theoretical issues relating to language, its development, and its use. This book is not oriented toward practitioners. (I'd advise skipping Chapter 1, as it is rather technical and may discourage all but the most hearty and determined.)

SMITH, F., *Reading without Nonsense* (2nd ed.). New York: Teachers College Press, 1985. Written for teachers, this book describes, in a nontechnical way, the nature of learning to read and how teachers can support the process.

SMITH, F., *Understanding Reading* (3rd ed.). New York: Holt, Rinehart and Winston, Inc., 1982. A more technical version of *Reading without Nonsense*, describing the research base of current knowledge about the nature of literacy and its development.

SMITH, F., *Writing and the Writer.* Portsmouth, N.H.: Heinemann Educational Books, 1982. An in-depth discussion of the many aspects of the writing process.

Collections of Articles Appropriate for Practicing Teachers

GOELMAN, H., A. OBERG, AND F. SMITH, eds., *Awakening to Literacy.* Portsmouth, N.H.: Heinemann Educational Books, 1984.

HANSEN, J., T. NEWKIRK, AND D. GRAVES, eds., *Breaking Ground: Teachers Relate Reading and Writing in the Elementary School.* Portsmouth, N.H.: Heinemann Educational Books, 1985.

JAGGAR A., AND M. T. SMITH-BURKE, eds., *Observing the Language Learner.* Urbana, Ill.: National Council of Teachers of English, 1985.

SMITH, F., *Essays into Literacy.* Portsmouth, N.H.: Heinemann Educational Books, 1983.

Films

Child Language: Learning without Teaching. Sterling Educational Films, Inc.

Oral Language Development: Views of Five Teachers. Agency for Instructional Television, 1111 West 17th Street, Bloomington, Indiana 47401.

Journals

Language Arts published monthly (September through April). Includes regular columns on current research, children's books, and resources for teachers. Each issue is a collection of articles focusing on a particular theme (for example, writing, children's literature, social aspects of language, assessment, language across the curriculum). Includes many articles written by classroom teachers. Subscription goes with National Council of Teachers of English membership. Write *Language Arts*, 1111 Kenyon Road, Urbana, Illinois 61801.

Teachers

Classroom teachers are surely the most important resource for one another. For a description of how a group of teachers organized themselves into a learning cooperative, and of the kinds of meetings they have found helpful, see "On Becoming Teacher experts: Buying Time," *Language Arts*, 61, no. 7 (November 1984).

Organization

National Council of Teachers of English (NCTE) is an important language education resource. The organization produces a variety of reasonably priced publications on various aspects of language education. (Contact Director of Publications, 1111 Kenyon Road, Urbana, Illinois 61801, for information about available publications.) The organization also holds annual national and regional conferences. (For conference information, contact Convention Director, same address. For additional information on services available to members, contact Director for Affiliate and Member Services, same address.)

9

Language in Learning

There is a whole set of very fundamental notions about the ways in which we relate to the world. Of these, the most important is the idea that this relation is active on our part from the beginning. We do not just sit and wait for the world to impinge on us. We try actively to interpret it, to make sense of it. We grapple with it, we construe it intellectually, we represent it to ourselves. (Donaldson 1979, p. 67)

INTRODUCTION

We saw in the last section that language acquisition is clearly dependent on cognition. Children figure out the oral and written language in their environment by using powerful processing abilities, hypothesizing, testing, confirming, disconfirming, and revising underlying rules for meaning-expression relations.

In this section, the major question for us is the other side of the language-cognition coin: *How does language contribute to cognitive growth?* Fortunately for us, psycholinguist Frank Smith provides "a conceptual framework for teachers" that deals with this question without getting bogged down in the illusive and mysterious realms of mentalism—vague wonderings about "mind," "thought," "idea" (Smith 1975). Smith's approach is the one we will use here. He assumes that every human builds, out of personal experience, a cognitive structure or *"a theory of the world in the head"* (p. 11). This theory, or personal notion of what the world is like, shapes both the way we look at past experience (recall, summarize, interpret it) and the way we look at new experience. Every human attempts (1) to *comprehend*, that is, to make sense out of the world by *"relating new experience to the already known,"* fitting new experience into our existing cognitive structure or "theory" (p. 10), and (2) to *learn*, that is, to alter our existing cognitive structure when experience does not make sense, when it does not square with our "theory." Our theory of what the world is like provides us with a set of expectations. When our ongoing experience fits our expectations, everything is fine; the new experience makes sense, we comprehend. But when the new experience is out of line with our expectations, we are forced to modify those expectations to make room for the new experience—it must fit, we must be able to make sense of it. Using Smith's conceptual framework, we can rephrase our original question: Can language help one to make sense out of the world? How does language help one *comprehend* and *learn?* In this chapter we will consider the use of language to help children comprehend and learn, especially as language is used in (1) questioning, (2) focusing attention, (3) making understandings more precise, (4) making understandings more retrievable, (5) reinterpreting past experience, and (6) going beyond present personal experience. We will also consider the important roles that interaction (in talk and writing) plays in the child's comprehending and learning, and, finally, the child's move from more action-based to more reflective modes of thinking.

How are the two little girls in the following two episodes using language to help them make sense out of their world?

A two-year-old girl is in the bathtub, playing with toys.

C: Gammy make those? (Refers to bathtub toys.)
M: No. Gammy didn't make those.
C: Gammy got those?
M: No. Mommy and Daddy got those.
C: Oh. Brand new?
M: No, they're old.
C: Throw away?
M: Well, we may think about it. They're not really good blocks. Maybe Santa Claus'll bring you some better blocks. OK?
C: OK. (Child indicates another toy.) Gammy Gammy gave those me?
M: Yes, your Gammy gave those to you.
C: Oh. Brand new?
M: Uh-huh. They're brand new. Remember, they came in that package? Before Thanksgiving?
C: (Child indicates a different toy.) Mommy Daddy get those?
M: Yea.
C: Oh. Old?
M: Not too. Got them to go on the airplane to see Gammy. 'Member?
C: OK.
M: They're pretty new. Pretty new.
C: Pretty new?
M: Uh-huh.
C: (Child indicates a different toy.) Those new?
M: No, those are old.
C: OK. (Child indicates a different toy.) Those, that old?
M: Pretty old.
C: Pretty old?
M: Uh-huh.
C: Those old? Gammy give it me?
M: No, Gammy didn't give those to you. Mommy and Daddy got those.

C: Oh. Those brand new?
M: No, they're old.
C: Still brand . . . still . . . still brand new?
M: No, they're not still brand new. They're old[1]

A four-year-old girl and her mother are reading a story that involves a rabbit and a squirrel sleeping in a tree.

M: (reading) "But the red squirrel pushed and shoved him until they were both settled snug and peaceful, high up in the tree under the stars."
C: Where do rabbits really sleep?
M: In their holes.
C: Under the ground?
M: Uh-huh. "The next day—"
C: Where do squirrels sleep?
M: In their trees.
C: Do they have nest-es?
M: They build nests in trees.
C: Squirrels do too?
M: Uh-huh.
C: But, who lays eggs?
M: Birds.
C: Ducks do too.
M: Well, ducks are birds. Fish lay eggs.
C: Nuh-uh! (meaning no)
M: Yes, they do. Right in the water.
C: What else?
M: Uh, what else lay eggs? Turtles lay eggs.
C: Nuh-uh!
M: They do. Go ask Daddy. They do![2]

Clearly, each of these little girls is trying to make sense out of her world, trying to relate new experience to the theory of the world she has built from her past experience and to further elaborate her theory—of new and old (and pretty new and brand new), of the habits of animals. Language is helping them make sense of their experience and figure out what kind of world they live in.

The claim of this chapter is that language is a powerful tool in comprehending and learning. Language helps us to comprehend and learn in various ways, and one very important way is questioning.

Questioning

Britton suggests that a child begins "with the drive to explore the world he is born into," and that speech early becomes its "principal instru-

---

[1] I am grateful to Carole Urzúa for letting me include this episode from her dissertation data.

[2] I am indebted to Carol Peterson for this example from her data.

ment" (Britton 1973, p. 93). Questioning is a particularly important instrument for exploring the world. Most children are active questioners. One four-year-old told his mother, "I'm a why-er, you are a because-er!" (Chukovsky 1968, p. 31).

A child's questioning for information gives him considerable control over his own comprehending and learning (provided, of course, that he is in an environment in which he is able to exercise it freely). By questioning, a child is able to initiate and actively search for what he wants to know in order to continue building and revising a theory of the world. We see the child once again as the active party in his own learning. It is what *he* notices and wonders about that gives rise to his questions.

We hear people talk informally of children's "innate curiosity." We do not know whether curiosity is, in fact, innate, but we do know that the child's earliest verbal language includes questioning. Even when the child is limited to one-word utterances, questioning is present (Dore 1975) and can be identified by the rising intonation contour of the voice, as well as by aspects of the situation itself (for example, waiting expectantly for a reply and looking away after the reply is given). When children move into combinatory speech, two morphemes and beyond, both yes/no and information questions are much in evidence. It is likely, initially, that one- and two-word questions serve primarily as requests for a verbal response from a conversational partner. But early on children appear to employ questions to gain information as well as simply to engage in conversation. It is difficult to escape the conclusion that the two-year-old in the earlier episode is using questions primarily for cognitive purposes—to figure out some aspect of her world.

You remember that the syntax and the semantics of questioning develop over time, with yes/no and "where" questions preceding "why" questions, with "when" questions coming still later. But children (and the rest of us) use other language forms as well as interrogatives in their inquiry, for example, "Tell me about X" or "Show me how to Y" (imperative forms) or even "I want you to tell me/show me . . ." (statement form). These forms, also, elicit information from another in conversation. There are many ways of using speech as a "principal instrument" of exploration. Yet questioning goes even beyond speech. Consider this example: I sat unobtrusively in a corner of a classroom of four-year-olds during their free activity time, watching as they interacted with one another and with a variety of materials at different centers. I was intent on gathering questions—tape recorder ready, note pad and pencil in hand. My attention went to a little girl looking intently at a variety of small rocks and seeds and leaves spread out on a table top. She didn't touch them, she just looked. Suddenly she picked up a leaf and walked briskly—purposefully—to the diagonally opposite corner of the room where there was a table with a three-legged magnifying glass on it. Carefully, she placed the leaf under the glass, looked at it through the glass for a minute, then picked it up and bustled her way back to the original table. Once there, she replaced the leaf and picked up a few seeds. Back across the room to the magnifying glass again, a second trip. Then a third. And a fourth. She never said a word.

There were no spoken questions for me to record or write, but surely this child was actively questioning.

Ferreiro carries the notion of nonverbal questioning a step further. You encountered in the last chapter her characterization of literacy development as a process of children continually posing "deep questions to themselves" as they try to understand "the very nature of the system." This is to focus on questioning as an internal cognitive process. In a similar vein, Smith describes reading as a matter of asking oneself questions, and reading comprehension as the answering of these internal and usually unconscious questions.

> Reading is asking questions of printed text. And reading with comprehension becomes a matter of getting your questions answered . . . To read we must ask questions, *implicit* questions, not ones that we are aware of. (Smith 1985, pp. 96–97)

The four-year-old examining leaves and seeds under a magnifying glass, the child figuring out how written language works to express meaning, the reader comprehending a text—all are instances of active questioning just as surely as if the individuals had verbalized their questions and had done so in interrogative form. Our questions, and children's, sometimes go outward toward others, but sometimes inward to ourselves.

> We are, by nature, questioners. We approach the world wondering about it, entertaining hypotheses which we are eager to check. And we direct our questions not just to other people but to ourselves, giving ourselves the job of finding the answer by . . . exploration of the world. (Donaldson 1979, p. 67)

Speech may, indeed, early become a "principal instrument" of the young child's "drive to explore the world," but his questioning may involve "inner speech" (Vygotsky 1962) as well as expressed speech.

FOCUSING ATTENTION

Young children's talk often serves to help them attend to and execute tasks. Consider the following examples.

> A four-year-old is drawing a picture. Her grandmother is present. The sentences in italics are addressed to her grandmother, the others to herself.
>
> *I'm going to draw a picture now.*
> Big park and another bit of it coming below. Two bits of it. Colour it in and make it all into one park. Draw St. James's Park.
> *Look! Now I'm going to draw a person walking around.*
> A little round head. A little eye and another little eye. A little nose. A little mouth. And how big the body is and there's the feet. Hands.
> *I'm drawing a little girl in the park.*
> That's a little girl walking round. What nice coloured clothes she's got on.

What lovely coloured clothes. Clothes. Coloured clothes. (Britton 1973, p. 54)[3]

Here is a child talking quietly to herself as she puts her doll to bed.

Putting her to bed. In the bed. Like that. Puts legs down. (Child looks around.) Now . . . well . . . a cover. Where's a cover? I'll have to find a cover . . . in the box (Child turns over the contents of a box) . . . here . . . *that'll* do for a cover . . . there . . . put it round . . . make you warm . . . . There . . . that's nice and warm baby. (Based on Tough 1977, pp. 48–49)

The child's talk here is clearly not directed to anyone else. It is not interactional in any way. The talk is a running commentary that seems to aid in keeping the child "aware of the actions he is performing" (Tough 1977, p. 47). Also, when the child encounters an impediment to his action, this talk seems to direct his activity toward the recognition of the problem and the solving of it. The child's talk seems to keep him on course and help him resist distraction.

It would be easy to dismiss this monitoring use of language as the child simply talking to himself idly while playing. But if we remember how important the child's activity is to his building of a theory of the world, then we are likely to see this action-related use of language as an important aid to his comprehending and learning.

Obviously, the talk of others can serve to focus one's attention also. Much of adults' talk with the child seems to be for the purpose of directing the child's attention to certain aspects of what he is doing or observing, as in the following episode.

A five-year-old and his teacher are watching a spinning top.

T: Where are all the colours now do you think?
C: Gone—they've gone away.
T: Have they really gone away?
C: No, but you can't see them.
T: The colours are really still there, do you think?
C: Mm. 'Cos you can't see them.
T: The colours are still on the top, but we can't see them. I wonder why can't we see them?
C: It's going too fast. You can't see them because it's going round fast.

(The top loses speed.)

T: Look—what can you see now?
C: The colours again—red and blue and all colours.
T: Why can you see them now?
C: Because it's nearly stopped—it's going slow—you can see them.
T: What did it look like when it was going round fast?
C: It just looked like lines—sort of white and black wasn't it? (Tough 1974, p. 82)

---

[3]Quoted with permission from Mrs. E. W. Moore, formerly of the University of London Institute of Education.

When we turn from situations of direct action (drawing, playing with dolls) or observation (of a spinning top) to situations of "thought," again we find that language can aid in directing attention as children conjecture about a situation. What instances can you find in the following two episodes of language serving to focus attention on aspects of situations that children are conjecturing about? Here are a teacher and some six- and seven-year-olds.

T: I am going to ask you a question. Here's something for you to think about. Do you think the bird was clever to choose that place [under the school roof] to build a nest?

Cs: Yes. Yes. It was a good place, etc., etc. (several taking part).

T: Why is it?

C: Because the cats can't get at it . . . Because it is too edgery to go along . . . . It's too narrow to go across, and because they've got small feet . . . Well, they wouldn't be able to get on . . . and they would just fall off.

T: You don't think the cat could balance along there? And somebody said it's out of the rain, yes? What's another good reason why the bird would build a nest there?

C: Not a very good reason . . . . Because Mark . . . he was trying to get . . . he had a big . . . he had a big cage and he was climbing up to get the bird down. (Based on Rosen and Rosen 1973, p. 49)

And here is a teacher talking with her eight-year-old students about unkindness.

T: What makes you unkind?

C-1:   Well . . . um . . . sometimes if children are older than others . . . and then they're nasty to them.

C-2:   They tease them.

T: Yes they do, don't they? I wonder why that is?

C-2:   They want to.

T: Do you think that when there are a lot of boys together that sometimes that makes a difference?

C-1:   Yes . . . . If you get one . . . one bad person . . . an . . . um . . . then all the others um . . .

C-2:   Turn bad.

C-3:   Yes . . . . Like one bad apple in the barrel turns the rest bad.

T: Yes, that's true.

C-3:   Not that to good . . . not that one good makes the rest good . . .

T: You don't think that happens if you've got one good one?

C-1:   No, that never happens.

C-3:   But if you leave one good one in with bad ones, I think the good one'll turn bad.

C-1:   Yes.

C-4:   And the . . . and the . . . an' the nasty children . . . an' . . . they'll make the . . . um . . . good children be nasty . . . or . . . or . . . they hurt and everything. They're always unkind with everybody.

C-2:   I'm never unkind. (Laughs)
C-5:   I don't believe it.
C-2:   Don't you?
C-5:   No. I don't.
C-3:   Everybody's unkind sometime in their life. I wouldn't like someone who wasn't unkind *at all*. (Based on Rosen and Rosen 1973, p. 83)

Even as adults we often find that the very act of verbalizing helps us block out distractions and focus our attention on a demanding task. Have you ever found yourself reading a poem or difficult passage of an article out loud in order to grasp its meaning more fully? In the act of verbalizing we seem to marshall our forces of attention.

In summary, then, children's own talking, as well as the talk of those they interact with, can help them focus attention on what they are doing (drawing a picture, or putting a doll to bed), observing (a spinning top), or thinking about (the location of a bird's nest, or reasons for unkindness).

MAKING UNDERSTANDINGS MORE PRECISE

One high school English teacher had a recurrent struggle with her accelerated group of students. As they wrestled with elusive poetic images, she would ask, "What do these lines *mean*?" One floundering student after another would respond, "I *know* what it means; I just can't *say* it." The teacher's answer was always the same: "If you can't say it, you don't know." I think her meaning might be more accurately paraphrased, "If you can't say it, then you don't know it in the precise and clearly delineated way that I want you to." It's possible that our theory of the world, our "knowing," involves much that we cannot articulate. But it is certain that those understandings that we can articulate, we do most surely know, comprehend. Further, it is likely that in the struggling act of representing (re-presenting) our understandings in spoken or written form, we render those understandings more precise, give our nebulous ideas a definite shape they did not have before.

You probably noticed that in the last two examples (the bird's nest and unkindness discussions) the children's talk was quite dysfluent—halting, grappling, struggling. That dysfluency reflects the children's struggle with their own ideas, their attempts to refine their understanding, to make it more precise. (Just as this refining of ideas is most evident in children's talk when that talk is most dysfluent, so in children's writing it is most evident in smudgy, often-erased, crossed-out, written-over pages, not in crisp, clean ones.) Often as teachers, in class discussions like the preceding one, our tendency is to supply the expression for the difficult idea the child is struggling to put into words. We finish the sentence for him when he pauses, or we fluently paraphrase his emerging and half-expressed idea. But I believe that the struggle itself is important both for the child's thinking and for his languaging. If we can hold our tongues, we do the child a service. There is no surer way for him to become the master of an idea than to render it expressible.

Making Understandings More Retrievable

Language aids recall. Early studies indicate that giving expression to an idea helps us to recall it later. Even beyond this, the way that we talk or write about the idea influences the way we recall it. Some early studies suggest that we remember the perceptual information from an experience, but we also remember labels given to that experience, and the associations we have for the labels become part of the recollection.

In one study, subjects were presented with line drawings and each drawing was given one of two labels for each subject (Carmichael, Hogan, and Walter 1932). One line drawing was ⊢ . Those subjects for whom this drawing had been labeled "seven," when asked to draw it later, tended to distort the figure as 7 . Those for whom it had been labeled "four" tended to reproduce it later as 4 . The subjects recalled their associations with the label "seven" or "four," as well as the perceptual image of the line drawing itself. The line drawing ⋈ was reproduced as ⋈ by those subjects for whom it had been labeled "curtains in a window," but was reproduced as ◇ by those subjects for whom it had been labeled "diamond in a rectangle." Thus the event recalled is a different event from the one actually experienced, partly because of the associations the "recaller" has for the language label that is part of the recollection. When we "recollect" an experience, part of what we "collect" are the associations that are part of the label we use to name the experience. What this research says to teachers is that in encoding his experience in language, in talking about it, the child will make an experience more readily retrievable. Also, the way the child talks about the experience—the language he uses—will influence the way he remembers it later. The associations he has with the labels themselves will become part of the remembered experience. The kind of sense the child makes out of personal remembered experience will be affected by the language that was part of its storage.

REINTERPRETING PAST EXPERIENCE

Britton tells us that "language is one way of representing experience . . . we habitually use talk to go back over events and interpret them, make sense of them in a way that we were unable to while they were taking place" (Britton 1973, p. 19). Here is language serving to aid us in making better sense of our past experience. The word "represent" is important here. Language can provide a means by which we "re-present" past experience—present it again, isolate it, consider it, reinterpret it in light of our ever changing and growing "theory of the world in the head." And of course, though our theory shapes our interpretation of past experience (contributes to comprehension), that theory is itself shaped and modified by subsequent experience (contributes to learning) in that our theory must be able to account for all our experiences, not just some of them. The symbols language provides for re-presenting our experience are a powerful means of making that experience an "object" we can "act on," shaping it to fit our theory, and also an "object" which further shapes our theory. Britton speaks of our symbolizing reality by means of language "in order to handle it" (Britton 1973, p. 20) as some sort of object. Thus, language provides one important means for our comprehending and learning, for our making sense out of our past experience.

GOING BEYOND PRESENT PERSONAL EXPERIENCE

The notion of language aiding us in going beyond the present situation is a favorite of Bruner's. He believes that, in time, children develop language as a cognitive instrument such that they can use language symbols to represent, manipulate, and transform "the regularities of experience" apart from the direct experience itself. We can see children grow in their ability to use language to "go beyond" in at least three areas: (1) going beyond the actually present here-and-now experience, (2) going beyond the personal experience, and (3) going beyond the real or possible experience.

Going beyond the Present Experience

Though much of young children's talk is closely tied to their action of the moment, there is evidence that two- to three-year-olds are beginning to go beyond the here-and-now experience in their thinking and talking. They may talk about events that have recently happened or soon will. The following two-year-old is talking with her mother, who has picked her up from the sitter, about events that happened recently.

M: What did you do today with Kimberly? Can you tell me?
C: I played toys with Kimberly.
M: You played toys with Kimberly?
C: I put the toys away.
M: You put the toys away?
C: I put the tinker toys away.
M: Oh, the tinker toys.
C: Was messy.
M: It was messy?
C: Yep.
M: Oh.
C: In Kimberly's room. (Sachs 1977, pp. 59–60)

And this three-year-old is talking with her mother about going to her grandmother's ("Na-ma's") later in the day.

C: . . . go to, to Na-ma's and play.
M: Wadda ya gonna play at Na-ma's?
C: So we (inaudible) to, to babies.
M: You gonna play with the babies?
C: Yep. To Na-ma's.

M: What else?
C: So play, play with the toys.
M: With the toys? What else?
C: Puppy.
M: Would you like to play with Skippy? (Skippy is the puppy's name.)
C: Yep.[4]

Going beyond the Personal Experience

Joan Tough's study of three-year-olds suggests that some children this young are beginning to be able to go beyond their own experience, projecting themselves into the experience of others. Here are some examples of three-year-olds using language in an empathetic way.

> Jane refers to a child who was crying before she came into the observation room:
> *Jane*: She doesn't like Terry teasing . . . that's horrible . . . and she's crying 'cos she didn't like it.

> Tim talks about the figures in the snowstorm novelty:
> *Tim*: The cowboy wouldn't like going up and down on the see-saw . . . it would make him feel sick.

> Michelle is telling the observer about an accident at home when her mother fell over their dog:
> *Michelle*: Lassie didn't mean to . . . not to hurt my mum . . . she didn't.
> (Tough 1977, p. 58)

And here are two three-year-old boys discussing the kind of garage they will make out of an available shoe box. The discussion involves one child's going beyond his own experience to incorporate the other child's experience.

C-1: Well, you know, garages have to have doors.
C-2: Sometimes they don't.
C-1: Garages have to have doors that will open and shut.
C-2: My grandad has one and he puts his car in and that hasn't doors.
C-1: But a garage has doors—and you lock the door so nobody can take it—the car you see.
C-2: My grandad has a car thing and it hasn't doors on. It just keeps the rain off you.
C-1: Oh—well—shall we make a garage or a car thing like your grandad's?
C-2: Well, I don't know how to put doors on.
C-1: I would think of glue or pins or something like that.
C-2: No—put it this way up see—and cut it.
C-1: Yes, that might be all right.
C-2: Right—Mark—right—I'll get the scissors. (Tough 1974, p. 21)

---

[4]I am indebted to Shirley Hollibaugh for this excerpt from her data.

Going beyond the Real Situation

We sometimes see young children go beyond a real situation to an imagined one. Some of the imagined ones are situations that could occur (for example, dramatic play of domestic activities), while some are situations that, for adults at least, could not occur (such as dramatic play involving monsters and ghosts).

Sapir sees the possibility of going beyond the present personal experience at being heavily dependent on language.

> If a man who has never seen more than a single elephant in the course of his life nevertheless speaks without the slightest hesitation of ten elephants or a million elephants or a herd of elephants or of elephants walking two by two or three by three or of generations of elephants, it is obvious that language has the power to analyse experience into theoretically dissociable elements and to create that world of the potential intergrading with the actual which enables human beings to transcend the immediately given in their individual experiences. (Sapir 1956, p. 7)

Because language supports our going beyond, it makes a significant contribution toward our comprehending and learning, toward our building a theory of the world which includes what *is* and what *is not*, and also what *could be* and what *could not be*.

It is a predictable aspect of children's language growth that they will gradually move from their language relying heavily on personal, present, direct experience, toward a greater independence of language from immediate situation. Perhaps this is what Bruner means by language becoming a "cognitive instrument" for children. Over time, children become better able to represent hypothetical situations and manipulate language symbols apart from an actual situation. If Bruner is right, the child becomes able to transform reality to create and consider different hypothetical possibilities through his languaging.

THE IMPORTANCE OF INTERACTION
IN COMPREHENDING AND LEARNING

One implication throughout this discussion has been that interaction, the use of language in communication, contributes to comprehension and learning. Our theory of our world grows and changes as we encounter others' experiences, interpretations, and ideas. This encounter most often happens through language interaction, whatever the expressive channel: talking and listening, reading and writing. New questions and wonderings often arise in interaction. The comments, observations, and wonderings of someone else can get me wondering about something I had not considered before. The very presence of a knowledgeable conversational partner may encourage me to express my wonderings and get feedback from my partner that starts me on some new wonderings. The provision of new information may give rise to new questions.

But it is not only in the area of stimulating us to ask new questions (expressed or implicit) that interaction can play an important role in comprehending and learning. We have seen already that our attention is often directed in an interactive situation, whether the focus of attention be a spinning top or a consideration of safe locations for birds' nests or of children's unkindness. Further, we are often motivated in an interaction situation to put words to our impressions, thus making them more precise. We will struggle to give an idea an expressible shape so that it can be communicated to someone else. Interaction (communication) is a powerful motivator. Interaction can also play an important role in one's recalling and reinterpreting past experiences. Children are eager to tell us about what they are doing or making, or to tell friends about recent experiences they have had. These interactions may serve a cognitive purpose, as well as a social one, in that they influence the way the occurring experience will later be recollected, and they provide a setting and motivation for reliving and reinterpreting the past experience.

And, of course, it is in interactive situations that we often encounter others' experiences and understandings that encourage us to extend and modify our own theory of the world. In interaction, we have access to "the beyond"—beyond the present, beyond the personal, beyond the possible. The example of the two three-year-olds making a garage from a shoe box is not a trivial one. C-1 insists that garages must have doors. His experience tells him that garages have doors that open and shut and can be locked. C-2 confronts him (insistently) with a counter example, his grandad's "one" that he puts his car in and that keeps the rain off the car, but that most definitely does not have doors. And C-1, as a result of this encounter, modifies his theory to include both garages (with doors that open, shut, and lock), and also "car things" that don't have doors. The "car thing" is beyond his personal and direct experience, but he makes a place for it in his theory. Through interaction, he has gone beyond the limits of his own personal experience. Through interaction, he has learned.

Verbal interaction, then, serves an important cognitive function for adults and for children by getting us to new ideas or observations, taking us beyond the limits of our own experience. But this is not all. Piaget has stressed the importance of cognitive conflict in a child's cognitive development. When an individual's idea or theory bumps up against a conflicting one, then the individual is pushed to resolve the conflict by modifying his original idea or theory. Ferriero and Teberosky (1982), you remember, described children's developing ideas about written language in terms of this Piagetian notion—as a continuous process of making hypotheses, encountering conflicts, and resolving them by forging new hypotheses. Interaction with others is a major source of cognitive conflict. (Again the garage doors example is relevant.)

Vygotsky (1962, 1978) suggests that yet another aspect of interaction is important for cognitive growth, one that initially seems almost the exact opposite of Piaget's cognitive conflict. Vygotsky's notion is captured in terms like "collaboration," "collective activity," and "cooperation." He identifies a "zone of proximal development" as the area of difficulty just beyond that point at which the child can solve problems independently; it is the area in which a child can solve problems in collaboration with others, especially with an adult or a more competent peer. This is the area (zone) that Vygotsky feels is especially important in a child's learning—that area where a child, with help, can go beyond himself. Interaction, then, becomes crucial in that it provides this assistance as the child stretches beyond his own limits.

> Learning awakens a variety of internal development processes that are able to operate *only* [emphasis added] when the child is interacting with people in his environment and in cooperation with his peers. (Vygotsky 1978, p. 90)

In summary, then, interaction, it appears, can help one go beyond his own limits by providing a new idea, question, or observation; by providing cognitive conflict; and by providing collaborative assistance.

Where could the potential for cognitive growth through interaction be greater than it is in the classroom community? And what period of one's life is better for it than the elementary school years? But I'll let elementary school children speak for themselves to demonstrate this. The children in the following example are fourth graders. They are with their science teacher, exploring the creek that borders the school property.[5] As you study the following excerpts from these children's creek exploration, see if you can find examples of the three ways, mentioned so far, that interaction supports children's sense making: (1) providing an encounter with a new idea or observation, (2) providing cognitive conflict, and (3) providing assistance or support.

A. *REBECCA:* Ohhhh yuck! Mrs. Westgate, there are some squirmy things under the bottom of this rock.
    T: Oh, those little jelly-like things?
    REBECCA: Yeah, What are they?
    T: We think they're snails. We're waiting to see when they hatch.
    REBECCA: These are not snails because—
    KEN: Yes, they are. Put them under water—they're going to die.
    REBECCA: No, they're *not* snails because snails have their babies in a little sack—
    KEN: No—
    REBECCA: —with all the eggs. Yes! I have millions of snails!
    KEN: That's your fault. These are, these are water, they're underwater, that's why they're there—
    REBECCA: My snails are underwater snails too!
    KEN: So what? Just leave them there.
    REBECCA: I am!! Gosh! . . . But they're not . . . snails. (spoken quietly to herself)

---

[5]I am indebted to Karen Westgate, the teacher in this transcript, for this example from her data.

B. *KEN:* Look at that rock down there.
   T: With the green stuff?
   KEN: Yeah.
   T: What is it? Touch it.
   KEN: I am not going to touch it. Move, Peter.
   PETER: Don't worry.
   KEN: Look right there that stuff . . . that is gross.
   T: All the leaves and trash have gotten caught.

C. *NILES:* Look look look over here. Look over in here.
   T: What is it?
   NILES: It's a waterfall.
   KEN: Yeah. Wait. I got some water running back here. Hey, I got some water running . . . I got some water running Ms. Westgate.

D. The children are building a dam.
   PETER: Hey wait, Ken. I want water (?) gonna get a rock out.
   KEN: Then put one big rock in front, then a small rock, then—
   PETER: All I'm doin' is blockin' off the water like I suppose to.
   MARK: Yes, I know . . . Careful 'bout that, it's not all that—
   NILES: Sturdy.
   PETER: This thing is definitely (?).
   KEN: Hey, Niles, you know that shovel you have, Niles? You know that shovel you have? Look, wait, wait, no, I want to ask him something. You know that shovel? We could have made a big hole here so (?) mud on top of it.
   MARK: Well, we're starting to build, rebuild the dam up.
   KEN: Yeah, and we're not, it's not, it's not very pleasant.
   NILES: Bombs away! (He throws a stone.)
   PETER: Niles, we could have used that.
   MARK: Use some, get some of those, get some of those chiplets, they'll work.
   T: Ken, what are you doing?
   KEN: I'm trying to dig it. So water comes out here so you can get across.

   (They all struggle with rearranging the rocks. Grunts and heavy breathing on tape.

E. *LESLIE:* Keep up the good work, Peter.
   KEN: He does better work down here than upstairs. (meaning in the school building up the hill)

F. A large tree limb stretches over the creek from bank to bank, and Matt, a somewhat timid child, is trying to find the courage to cross the creek on this limb.

   MATT: Peter, I'm going to come up there.
   BRAD: Get down. Climb down there, then start walking. Hang on to that branch. Come as close to the land as you can. Then jump.

MATT: Is it scary, Brad?

BRAD: Naaaaaaaah!

PETER: Naaaaaaaah!

MARK: It's not scary.

BRAD: The only scary part is when you look down and you see water below you.

MARK: There isn't any scary part, but there is a hard part—

MATT: How do you get down, Brad?

CHRISTA: How do you get down—(giggling)

MARK: Climb up to that branch—

BRAD: You start walking on that branch. You get close to the edge and jump.

PETER: You don't. You live there. (response to Matt's last question)

CHRISTA: Matt! Matt, did you say, "How do you get down"? You don't get down.

BRAD: Yeah, you can get down . . . No, you jump on the land.

(The children continue to talk Matt across the limb to the far side of the creek.)

The children's talk here is very close to their ongoing action. You probably noticed several instances of one individual calling another's attention to something—"squirmy things," rocks with "green stuff," a "waterfall"—or suggesting an approach that others hadn't thought of—using Niles's shovel or using the "chiplets" in constructing the dam. (You probably also noticed that the teacher here is an active participant along with the children.) In each of these cases, one individual extends another's world of the moment to include a new observation, idea, or suggestion.

Perhaps the most obvious conflict in this example is the snail disagreement in segment A. If Rebecca and Ken had agreed that the "little jelly-like things" were snails, the matter would have ended there. But because they did not agree, both were pushed to support their positions.

In this creek episode, you can see that children can, and do, support or assist one another in a variety of ways (some of which Vygotsky doesn't mention, so far as I know). The very fact of the children's cooperative effort in building the dam (segment D) is enabling to all the children involved. Notice the compliment and encouragement that Leslie and Ken provide for Peter in segment E. Especially noteworthy is the encouragement the children provide for Matt as they talk him across the tree limb above the creek (segment F). (Would you say that Peter's and Christa's humorous remarks in this segment help or hinder Matt's efforts? Why?)

It would be easy, and I think unfortunate, to dismiss this example as "just a bunch of kids messing around in a creek." These children are building: They're building a dam; they're building social relationships; they're building their understanding of the world.

Interaction, as you well know, does not involve only talk. Written language extends interaction possibilities far beyond the here-and-now, face-to-face communication. In our encounters with written language, we come to know people and their ideas that we will know *only* through their writing. And we ourselves may write to bridge space and time, giving a message permanence beyond the fast fading sounds of the human voice. Written language is an important "gift that keeps on giving." In written language as in oral, we encounter (in our reading) and provide for others (in our writing) new ideas or observations, cognitive conflicts, and assistance or support (for example, confirmation of one's ideas or an explanation that clarifies a previously fuzzy notion).[6]

In recent years, there has been keen interest in the special contribution that the writing process itself can make to the writer's own thinking. Understand that this renewed interest in writing does not exalt writing above other forms of expression; it does not see writing as inherently "better" than expression through speech or various art forms. Rather, it considers the special contribution of each expressive mode and finds that writing is particularly well suited for furthering reflective thought. Because of the permanent character of written language (in contrast to the fast-fleeting character of speech) writing supports the development of understanding in some very powerful ways. Considering the special contributions of speech and writing, Smith says:

> Sometimes speech might be considered more effective or appropriate—for example, in establishing interpersonal relations. Sometimes writing may be the preferred form, as it is for most contractual and recording purposes, or because, as I would argue, it separates our ideas from ourselves in a way that is easiest for us to examine, explore, and develop. Writing permits ideas and events to be created and manipulated in ways that would not exist if all language had to be as transient as thought or spoken words. (Smith 1982b, p. 15)

In writing, "we can fasten our thoughts onto paper" (Calkins 1985, p. 191). Writing can and does "placehold meaning" for us (Harste, Woodward, and Burke 1984). The meaning, the idea, the thought, is *there* in concrete form and keeps on being there "for us to examine, explore, develop" as we choose. Writing "overcomes limitations of memory and attention" (Smith 1982b, p. 34).

Notice that the notion of interaction has now shifted slightly. We have gone from thinking about writing as a product that provides new ideas, conflicts, and support to thinking about writing as a process of interacting with one's own ideas. There is a subtle shift here from focus on the written product (the written ideas fastened on the paper) to focus on the writing process—the process of continuing interaction between the writer (the self) and what is being written.

---

[6]You might want to think a minute about how you mark up a text you read for a course. Do you sometimes find yourself marking the new idea or observation—you highlight or underline it or put an asterisk in the margin beside it? And do you sometimes mark points of conflict, points where you and the author disagree? Don't you sometimes write "No!" or "I wonder about this" in the margin? And what about the support— confirmation or clarification, perhaps—that the text offers. Do you ever write "Yes" or "!" or "Ahhhhh" in the margin?

> Things happen when we write. Ideas can be generated and developed in the interaction between writer and what is being written that would not be possible if the ideas were left to flower and perhaps fade in the transience of the mind. Writing can be used in the same way that a rough sketch is used by a painter or an architect, because no one can plan and work on an entire painting or building in all its interrelated detail in one's head. Even when we think we are writing solely for others . . . the writing is helping us to organize and develop the possibilities of our own minds. (Smith 1982b, p. 16)

Of course. Remember that what the writer is fastening on the paper is his ideas, his thoughts. In modifying, manipulating, elaborating, and shaping the written words, the writer is acting on his own "fastened" thoughts. And so, an ongoing interaction is occurring between self and thought. The product may be intended as a communication for someone else, yet the process itself engages the writer in interaction with his own thought.

These are hefty and, I think, difficult ideas about the writing process. This powerful interaction between the writer and his own thought is particularly difficult to grasp and believe in if your own personal experience of writing has, like most people's, been limited to writing reminders, shopping lists, and lecture notes, and carrying out assignments under duress (writing term papers, taking essay exams, and so on). It seems that as a society, we do not love to write. Very few of us really get "into" writing—we rarely wrestle-write, write ourselves into new knowing.[7] Because we have not ourselves had much meaningful writing experience, it may be difficult for us to comprehend (or believe in) the powerful cognitive process that writing can be for the children we teach. However, studies are accumulating that describe children's authentic writing in elementary classrooms over time. These studies document children "learning to think through writing" (Calkins 1985, p. 190).[8]

It is difficult enough to grasp fully the potential of the writing process in the examination, exploration, manipulation, and shaping of one's ideas. But the claim goes beyond this to what may be the most difficult notion of all: "Writing creates new worlds" for the writer as he writes (Smith 1982b, p. 220). As one engages in interaction with one's own thought, one gives birth to new ideas. It may be that writing is the language mode which more than any other "not only *reflects* our knowing . . . but . . . also *causes* our knowing" (Dillon 1985, p. 9).

"We do not write [only] in order to be understood; we write in order to understand" (attributed to C. Day Lewis). This quotation suggests an important distinction in our writing purposes: writing to communicate with others (to reach out) and writing to communicate with ourselves (to reach in). Most often we write to communicate with others: We write a letter to a

---

[7]It is for this reason that classroom teachers are participating in summer writing workshops, for example, the Bay Area Writing Project or the Hill Country Writing Project. For a personal description of one teacher's experience in such a writing workshop, see Mikkelsen 1984.

[8]See especially Graves 1983 and Calkins 1983. These works will suggest additional studies you might want to read.

friend, we write a memo to send home with our students, we write a reminder for a family member. Sometimes, though, our writing is for ourselves. Journal writing is the classic example. It is private writing. We are our only reader. This writing especially may reveal us to ourselves. And we are, after all, important people for ourselves to know.

Because writing externalizes and holds our ideas so that we can act on them, writing can increase our awareness of our own thinking. There is importance not only in *what* we think but also in *how* we think. This awareness of how we think is important because "awareness of one's own thinking marks a crucial step toward directing it" (Calkins 1983, p. 136). Conscious awareness of our thinking increases our control over it. When we are conscious of it, we can make our thinking work for us in ways not possible when we are unaware of it and thus must leave its functioning more or less to chance.

"But," you ask, "haven't we moved a long way from children here? Isn't conscious awareness of one's own thinking processes the province of adults, not children?" The answer seems to be no. Adults are surely more oriented toward conscious awareness of and direction of their thought than children are. However, the development of awareness and control of one's own thinking is possible for children of elementary school age, and the elementary classroom can itself be a particularly helpful environment for fostering this development. And again, actively engaging in the writing process seems to have special advantages. Fourth-grade Birger is aware of the way he thinks and plans and acts on material as he writes, and being aware of it, he deliberately makes it work for him. He tells the researcher, "I've just made a discovery. I usually put people into my stories now because, when there are other people than me in the story, then I don't have to say 'I did this and I did that.' Instead . . . I can have the other people do the talking, keeping things explained" (Calkins 1983, p. 135). "In every story I write, I'm always thinking, 'Is this one story?' 'Is this two stories?' " (p. 153). Birger's awareness has increased his control.

We must ask ourselves whether the learning environments we provide for children actively engage them in writing for self as well as in writing for others; in writing as a way of exploring, manipulating, and even creating ideas and meanings; in writing as a way of increasing awareness and control of one's own thinking. If our learning environments do not provide for all of these writing engagements, then we deprive our children of important opportunities for both language and cognitive development.

EMBEDDED AND DISEMBEDDED THINKING[9]

Our consideration of children interacting with their own thoughts and becoming ever more aware of their thought processes as they write brings us again to a most important idea about children's thinking. It is the notion of embedded and disembedded thought, mentioned briefly at the end of

[9]The terms "embedded" and "disembedded" are from Margaret Donaldson 1979.

Chapter 6 (p. 156). Donaldson (1979) characterizes this important distinction in children's thinking this way:

> By the time they come to school, all normal children can show skill as thinkers and language users to a degree which must compel our respect, so long as they are dealing with "real-life" meaningful situations in which they have purposes and intentions and in which they can recognize and respond to similar purposes and intentions in others. . . . These human intentions are the matrix in which the child's thinking is embedded. They sustain and direct his thoughts and his speech. . . . While the child's thinking and his language remain wholly within the bounds of human sense in this kind of way, he remains largely unaware of them . . . he does not reflect upon them in abstraction from the contexts in which he employs them. (Donaldson 1979) . . . He [does not] turn language and thought in upon themselves. (Donaldson 1979, p. 90).

Clearly, there are degrees of disembeddedness, that is, language and thought not within "real-life" purposeful human activity. Formal logic would have to stand at the extreme end of disembeddedness. In the statement, "All A's are B's, all B's are C's, therefore all C's are A's," it makes absolutely no difference what A's and B's and C's are in the real world; in fact, real-world knowledge can get in the way as one deals with such a statement. Formal logic comes vacuum packed; all the relevant information is within the premises: They constitute the entire relevant world. This kind of thinking is far removed from that of young children—and, for that matter, quite removed from adult thinking in our day-to-day lives. But Donaldson's point is that disembedded, hypothetical, reflective thinking is more the province of adults than it is of children, and the younger the child, the more embedded in real-life activity his thinking is likely to be. It's interesting that if the cold and disembodied A's, B's, and C's of formal logic are replaced by warm-blooded beings and actions (such as in children's literature), the child is able to reason quite logically. Here are a few examples of young children's logic as they listen and respond to stories.

> "What a lot of things he's taking! He wouldn't have . . . he's only got two hands and he wouldn't have space for his two hands to carry all these things."

> *(PREMISES:* 1. Peter has more to carry than two hands can carry; 2. Peter has only two hands.
> *CONCLUSION:* It is not possible for Peter to carry all that he is represented as carrying. Implied criticism of the story.)

> "She must have eaten all her food on the other day."

> *(PREMISES:* 1. Houses normally have food in them; 2. This house has no food.
> *CONCLUSION:* The food must have been all eaten up.)

> "But how can it be [that they are getting married]? You have to have a man too."
> (The book contains an illustration of a wedding in which the man looks rather like a woman. The child thinks it is a picture of two women.)

(PREMISES: 1. You need a man for a wedding; 2. There is no man in the picture. *CONCLUSION*: It can't be a wedding. (Donaldson 1979, pp. 51–52)

To say that the young child's thinking is embedded is not to say that he is utterly incapable of disembedded thinking. Sometimes young children's comments do suggest that they are turning "language and thought in upon themselves." Here are a few examples of children not simply using language to accomplish their social purposes but actually reflecting on the language code itself:

TWO FOUR-YEAR-OLDS TALKING TOGETHER.

C-1: Uh oh!
C-2: What'd you say?
C-1: Uh oh!!
C-2: Uh oh?
C-1: Uh oh!!
C-2: That's a funny word!
C-1: Yeah.

FOUR-YEAR-OLD EMILY IS TALKING WITH HER MOTHER.

C: Get the old sugee bowl, the old sugee bowl.
M: Get the old what?
C: The old sugee.
M: Oh.
C: That's sugar.
M: Oh, sugar.
C: (laughs) I said it funny.

This is talk about language, language turned in upon itself. Language here has become opaque. The next two children are commenting on their own thinking.

One four-year-old tells his friend,

You know what? The first time I heard of the moonwalk, I thought that it meant a spaceship would go up to the moon and walked on it.

Two five-year-olds are working with clay and conversing as they work.

C-1: I know how to make a turtle.
C-2: How?
C-1: It's . . . I don't have . . . I, I, I can still remember it in my head. That's why I like . . . I did that . . . cause, so I can do it at other places and not just at home.[10]

[10]I am indebted to Barbara Gilstad for this example from her data.

It's no wonder that this child has some difficulty expressing the idea that she carries her knowledge of how to make a clay turtle in her head and thus she is able to employ that knowledge at other places than home. Her struggling talk reflects her struggling idea.

The claim, then, is not that the beginning-school child is without the possibility of disembedded thinking. We do see traces of such thinking, and they hint at the promise for further development here. But on a day-to-day basis, the young child lives mainly in a world of thinking which is embedded within a matrix of human real-life purposes and intentions, his own and others'.

Now think about the school situation for a minute. All educators would agree that the ability to think in reflective, detached ways is terribly important. The question becomes, How do we help children further their reflective thought? The answer provided by traditional standards is to bombard the child from the beginning of his school experience, with disembedded items. The traditional "language" curriculum is, as we have seen, a sequence of these items (skills), quite unconnected to the real-life world of human purposes and intentions as the child knows it. In the last chapter I advanced arguments against this skills orientation on the basis of its inauthenticity as language. Now I would extend those arguments to the broader domain of children's thinking. To wrench the child's school experience from the "matrix of human social purposes and intentions" that makes it meaningful to him is to provide the child with something that is nonsense—something that he has no way of making sense of. I would argue that we support the child's move into disembedded thought, not when we sever his connections with real-life human intentions and actions, but when we support those connections. It is not a new idea to you by this time that in their language development children progress by relating the new to the already familiar. They are able to interpret and act on the new precisely because and insofar as they are able to relate it to what they already know. They go beyond their present knowing by relating it to the new. It is only with one foot placed squarely, securely within the known, the familiar, that the child can place the other foot in the beyond. We have seen that

the child is able to begin to make sense of the talk around him at all because he understands the situation itself in which the talk occurs and to which it refers. He deals with what is presently beyond him (the talk) by relating it to what is already his (the understanding of the context);

the child's first words often label the very objects the child already knows by acting on them. His action-knowing enables him to bridge beyond it into a new way of encoding that knowing: in words;

the child is aided by the adult's scaffolding, that is, by the adult's provision of limited, familiar interaction routines that support the child's going beyond these very routines. The adult supports the child by holding the familiar conversational structure constant, so that the child can gradually incorporate new elements within that familiar structure. The child's reaching out into the new is supported by the steadiness of the familiar;

the child (as Slobin points out, p. 194) progresses in language by expressing a familiar meaning in a new way, or by extending a familiar expressive form to convey a new meaning. The child uses what is familiar, whether a meaning or an expressive form, to go beyond it to the new meaning or form. Something old, something new. The child again is moving into the new by relating it to his known world;

in storyreading situations in which the text is familiar, the child's attention is increasingly drawn to the code itself—which words are used, what they mean, how they are written. Knowing the story already, the child can focus on new aspects, especially the telling itself.

In all these language examples (and the many more you can doubtless think of) it is what the child has and knows and does already—his familiar word—that enables him to go beyond it. He bridges into the new in language development, not by breaking with the familiar, but by relating the new to it. And how could it be otherwise?

So, too, in the cognitive domain. Smith points out that children's comprehending and learning, their building of a "theory of the world in the head" is precisely a matter of relating "new experience to the already known." Disembedded thinking, thinking which is unsupported by immediate, real-life human activity, will ultimately be part of the child's "theory." He will make sense of detached, vacuum-packed reflections quite removed from ongoing human purposes, as well as making sense of socially embedded events. He will, in short, move from more embedded into more disembedded modes of thought. And I believe it is his "embeddedness," that is, his present intense connectedness with real-life human intentions (his present world), that will enable him gradually to go beyond into thinking that is farther removed from those human purposes that now sustain his thought. Further, school offers very special opportunities for supporting the child's enabling connectedness in two important domains: (1) the child's connection with his own ongoing experience and (2) the child's connection with others. You have already seen both of these at work in examples of children's talk. The child's own purposeful doing offers, I believe, the best "material" for the child's subsequent reflection. Our first knowing is through our own doing. It is to be expected that what the child first actively engages in is what he will then consciously consider. The child's own meaningful experience embedded within his own real-life purposes offers the very most important and enabling "material" for his conscious consideration. It is this experience, rather than the disembodied bits of the traditional curriculum, that enables the child to "turn . . . around on [his] own traces and record . . . in new forms what he [has] been doing or seeing." He will be able to say, " 'I see what I was doing now.' or 'So that's what the thing is' " (Calkins 1983, p. 136, quoting Bruner 1966).

The other main source of connectedness is others—the "social matrix" within which the child himself is embedded. The classroom offers a very special social matrix for the child. As we have already seen, it is often in the interaction with others that the child encounters the new idea, cognitive conflict, and support. The possibilities for "turning language and thought in upon themselves" are far greater in such interaction contexts than in the isolation of seatwork.

I am arguing here that we do not support the child's move into disembedded modes of thought when we sever his connections with his own familiar world of thinking and doing, simply leaving him adrift. I am arguing that we foster this move into more detached thought when we support and extend the child's connectedness, for it is the child's connectedness with his own experience and with others that provides the necessary anchoring in the known that enables his reach into the beyond.

Finally, I come back to writing and the special contribution that it may make to children's development of more detached and reflective thinking. As mentioned already, an approach to children's classroom writing that is gaining ground is what is sometimes called the "writing process approach."[11] Basic to this approach is that children write purposefully from the beginning of first grade on, and that they retain control of the writing process throughout. Children have a substantial daily writing period, during which they select their own topics, write, revise, edit, and conference with teachers and/or peers at various stages of their work. You can see that though the focus is on writing, the languaging involved goes far beyond "writing" per se and in fact includes all expressive and interpretive modes as children write, conference, and read what they and their friends (and adult authors) have written. This continuing daily "writing" experience is one which, I believe, provides the connectedness (with the child's own experience and with others) that supports the child's move into disembedded thinking.[12] The child connects with his own experience in two ways. First, much of the writing is about the child's own personal experience. In writing about the familiar experience, the child must reflect on it, that is, consider it in a new and distanced way, as he selects, orders, and shapes what he will tell his reader. He is "recording in a new form" his own actual experience. He has already lived it; now he acts on it at a slight remove. He has one foot in the already known, the other beyond it.

Second, this writing process often involves the child (on his own and in interaction with others) reworking his own piece—revising it, writing subsequent drafts, editing it for possible publication, and so on. Now the child is reflecting on (considering and reconsidering)—another personal experience: his experience of writing the piece in the first place. He is also considering the piece (the product) that resulted from that writing experience. It is within this deep and continuing connectedness with his own past and ongoing experience that the child here is able to "turn on his own traces," to reflect on what he has done.

You can see that in this writing approach the child's connections with others are strong. In conferences children and teachers raise questions

[11]This approach is most fully described in Graves 1983.

[12]I am not suggesting that this is the only way children should write in the classroom. Barrs (1983) raises two important points to keep in mind for teachers inclined toward this writing approach: that (1) the personal experience writing which is very important in this approach not be the only kind of writing done (to the exclusion of writing fiction, poetry, plays, and so on) and (2) individual differences in children's writing styles be taken into account. (For example, not all writers, whether adults or children, write several drafts of their work, edit extensively, and so on.)

about the content and the processes involved in one another's work. Vygotsky claims that "internal speech and reflective thought arise from the interactions between the child and persons in her environment." (1978, p. 90) Indeed, there is some evidence that in the context of these writing conferences children begin to ask themselves the questions that first occur in the writing conference interactions. One researcher (Calkins 1983) writes that after experience of peer conferences, first graders "anticipated questions their friends would ask." Greg said, "They'll still have questions, but at least I got rid of some of their questions" (p. 139). And first-grade Laura wrote:

> We plad a gam,
> and then, as if anticipating the question "What game?" she exclaimed, "Oh, no! They're going to kill me." . . . sounded out and spelled the name "Aggravation" . . .
> We plad agoushon (Calkins 1983, p. 139)

Across the table, Brad, writing his book "All Abt Rbts" asked himself, "And what do they eat?" and went on to write, "Rabs at cars [Rabbits eat carrots] (p. 139). As she wrote, second-grade Heather said:

> "I'm having an individual writing conference with myself . . . On each page I ask myself the questions the other kids would ask me . . . Here I wrote, 'I have a horse.' The kids would ask me if I ride it, so I'm going to add, 'I ride my horse every day unless it's raining.' " (Calkins 1983, p. 140)

And fourth-grade Diane explained, "You can conference with yourself . . . You just read the piece over to yourself and it's like there is another person there and you think thoughts to yourself of what is wrong with it" (p. 138).

It is precisely because these children have been deeply embedded within this important social matrix—intensely connected with others—that they are able to extract themselves from it, stand back and consider from a bit of a distance the pieces they write and the writing and thinking processes they engage in. They are coming to turn language and thought in upon themselves. It seems a wonderful paradox that it is through his very connectedness (to his own experience and to other people) that the child ultimately achieves the distance and disconnectedness that disembedded thinking requires.

Finally

In this chapter we have explored some ways that language, in all its expressive forms, supports the thinking child in his work of making sense of his world as he probes, attends, recalls, and interprets, and as he reflects on experience through his interaction with others and with self. We find that language aids thought; language reflects thought; language refines thought; language extends thought; language creates thought. And language even enables us to become aware of our own thinking and thus, to some extent at least, to direct it. Is this what people mean when they call language an "instrument of thought"? Some mighty instrument!

10

Language in Learning: Teachers and Children

Young children have a curiosity and an urge to find out about the world. They pry into corners, turn over stones, stare at cranes, explore empty houses and comb rubbish dumps. All too often this curiosity is not sanctioned in school and their attention is directed instead to barren collections of information which give no hint of the excitement of discovery and doubt. Small wonder then if their language becomes barren too. It is only those affairs which create real preoccupation which can make them reach out for the language to express new understanding, new questions and new perceptions. This is the language of curiosity. It may express itself as a set of observations or be explicitly speculative but it is always the result of the child's own probing into the working of the world.

Children should find school the kind of place which accepts their curiosity and makes room for it to be taken further, supplies the means for reaching deeper understanding and a climate in which an individual's enthusiasm can draw in others to participate or listen and question. The more the school is in tune with the curiosity of the children within it the greater the chance it will become the initiator of new inquiries, wider in scope and offering new possibilities. It should not be the business of school to produce a tamed and house-trained curiosity and, inevitably, a tamed and house-trained language to match. (Rosen and Rosen 1973, p. 28)

INTRODUCTION

Having considered some important ways that language fosters children's sense making in the world, we turn in this chapter to the classroom. We will focus first on the mismatch between the probing child and the traditional classroom; second, on the helpful roles the teacher can play in supporting children's sense making; and finally, on two examples that show children and teachers doing authentic languaging and learning work in the classroom.

286

CHILDREN'S CURIOSITY QUESTIONING IN SCHOOL
(DO THEY DO IT?)

If everybody in the world keeps drinking water, are we going to run out of water some day? I don't mean now, I mean years and years from now?

Why is this macaroni on my plate making steam?

What does gravity look like?

Are there more stars in the sky or in a million cans of chicken-and-stars soup?

People say that no two snowflakes look exactly alike. How do they know that? How can they tell? How could anybody possibly have looked at every snowflake?

The same nine-year-old who asked these questions at home was observed to ask very different questions in his classroom:

Do we underline the spelling words?

Do you want us to skip every other line?

Do we write the date on this paper?

Why is his curiosity and the language that expresses it so alive and vital at home yet noticeably absent at school, where his questions demonstrate an overriding concern for following the teacher's preferred procedures? How typical is this child? Unfortunately, my observations of children in elementary classroom settings suggest that he is the rule rather than the exception. The main concern of the majority of the elementary-level children I observe in school settings is to do what you are "supposed to do": finish assigned written work accurately, neatly, in the proper format, and on time.

Some undergraduate education majors who were engaged in field experiences in classrooms ranging from preschool through sixth grade (and including one Sunday school class) were asked to write down ten successive questions they heard children ask in their classrooms. (For a related project suggestion, see number 1 on page 314.) These undergraduates did not know why they were being asked to do this, so presumably they did not select the questions in any way. Their university instructor had simply told them, "At some time when you are not doing the teaching in your classroom, say to yourself, 'Now,' and then write down, verbatim, the next ten questions you hear children ask, the situation in which each question is asked, and the person to whom it is addressed." The instructor had assigned this question-gathering exercise in order to get these undergraduates to begin to *listen* to the ways their children were questioning. This was not intended as a carefully controlled study of children's classroom questioning; no careful sampling procedures were used, no interrater reliability was established.[1] Nevertheless, when the resulting questions were pooled

[1] For some controlled studies of children's classroom questioning (relating to dimensions other than the curiosity/procedural/social distinction used here), see Allender 1969, 1970; Davis 1971; Dodl 1966; Haupt 1966; Ross and Balzar 1975; Torrance 1970, 1972 and James and Seebach 1982.

and analyzed, the results were disturbing. The questions were first divided into three levels: questions asked by preschool and kindergarten children, questions asked by primary-level children (grades one through three), and questions asked by intermediate-level children (grades four through six). The questions within each level were then categorized into three groups.[2]

1. *Curiosity*: a question form functioning mainly to get information about something one wonders about, wants to know about simply to satisfy one's own self. Does not focus on satisfying any outside source.
2. *Procedural*: a question form functioning mainly to get information that will aid one in carrying out a procedure in a way that will be considered acceptable by someone else. Focuses on satisfying an external source; helps one do what one is "supposed" to do.
3. *Social-interactional*: a question form functioning mainly to initiate or maintain or clarify a relationship (for example, an invitation to joint action, a conversation starter, a challenge).

Of the 159 preschool-kindergarten questions analyzed, approximately 45 percent (almost half) were social in nature, approximately 33 percent (one-third) were curiosity questions, and approximately 23 percent (less than one-fourth) were procedural. The situation changed dramatically at primary level. Here, of a total of 253 questions analyzed, the curiosity questions comprised only 19 percent and the social only 14 percent, while procedural questions soared to 66 percent (almost two-thirds) of the total. The situation was similar at intermediate level, with 16 percent of the total (116) being curiosity questions, another 16 percent being social, and a staggering 68 percent being procedural. Here are some examples from each level and each question type:[3]

PRESCHOOL-KINDERGARTEN LEVEL

Curiosity:
(*Teacher is holding a snake.*) What do he like to eat?
(*Teacher is outside on a blanket.*) How come you took your shoe off?
(*To children in a group during play*) Where's milk come from?
(*To another child*) How come you raised your hand and you don't want to do it?
(*To an adult observer in the classroom*) Is God in cookies?

Procedural:
(*During art lesson, to teacher*) Can I do it like this?
(*During art lesson, to teacher*) Do I have to write my name up here?

---

[2]Those questions not falling into these three categories were not analyzed further, for example, questions in dramatic role-play situations, questions in which there was insufficient context to ascertain the speaker's intention, requests for aid, questions seeking repetition for hearing, rhetorical questions.
[3]"Question" here is a syntactic interrogative, that is, a form seeking a yes/no reply ("Do you have it?") or beginning with a question word (for example, what, where, when, why, how) or requiring a choice ("Do you want the red one or the blue one?").

(*During art lesson, to teacher*) Is this right?

(*During group work, to teacher*) What do I do now?

Social-interactional:

(*Outside, to another child*) Hey, Gabriel. You wanna play this till clean-up time?

(*At play-dough table, to teacher*) See mines?

(*After juice, to another child*) You like the juice?

(*Accusing, during block play, to another child*) Are you taking mine?

(*At play-dough table, to teacher*) Know what my mommy buy?

(*To student teacher*) You know how many I am?

(*To student teacher*) You didn't know I got my ears pierced, did you?

(*Free play, to another child*) Andrew, will you talk to me?

(*After an argument at art table, to another child*) I forgive you, Jenny. Do you forgive me?

PRIMARY-GRADE LEVEL

Curiosity:

(*All the following, and many more, were asked of a visiting scuba diver who had talked with the children and let them examine his diving equipment.*)

Have you seen any sunken British ships?

Do you have a collection of sea shells?

Have you seen any dead people?

Have you ever seen a shark?

What happens if your fin trips on the side of the ship?

Procedural:

(*To teacher*) Do I gotta put a heading?

(*To student teacher*) How many pages do I have to read?

(*To teacher during art project*) Do we have to color it in, teacher?

(*To teacher*) Miss, I am finished; now what?

(*To another child during seatwork time*) Is seven times seven fifty?

(*To student teacher*) Do we have to write one of them stories again?

Social-interactional:

(*To another child*) Did you watch *MASH* last night?

(*To another child, while filling out worksheet*) Why don't you sit down beside me, right here?

(*To another child*) What did you call me!?

(*To student teacher*) Everybody's angry today, right Miss?

(*To another child at recess*) What are you doing, you dummy!?

INTERMEDIATE-GRADE LEVEL

Curiosity:

(*To another child during free play, referring to finger brace*) What is this thing anyway? Is it somethin' to put on your finger so it won't break?

(*To student teacher*) Why aren't you married?

(*To adult observer, after seeing a picture of Medusa*) How come she's got a head full of snakes?
(*To student teacher*) Do you get paid for this or something?

Procedural:
(*To teacher*) Do I put a *j* right here?
(*To teacher*) Can I go on to the next color of rate builders?
(*To student teacher*) How many commas is it supposed to have?
(*To teacher*) Miss, is this right?

Social-interactional:
(*To teacher, while looking at book*) Want me to show ya' the kind of dog I like?
(*To student teacher*) You wanna play a little short game?
(*To student teacher*) Did you know he loves you?

Why would the proportion of procedural questions triple from kindergarten to intermediate (23 percent to 68 percent), and the proportion of curiosity questions drop by half (33 percent to 16 percent)? It would appear that we are saying to our kindergarten children, "Being curious and exploring your environment is appropriate here . . ." but, to our postkindergarten children we say, ". . . but not here."

Needless to say, the "results" of such an informal exercise are at best only suggestive, but they do square with my own observations of children's questioning in elementary school classrooms. Why do I hear so little of the vigorous curiosity questioning that I know the child engages in outside of school, and so much of questioning aimed at making her performance acceptable or correct to someone else? Is the child building a rich theory of the world by asking such questions? Do these questions support her comprehending and learning? Or is she simply building a theory of how to comply with conventional standards? Why is the environment such that the child's overriding concern is "How do I satisfy others' requirements?" rather than "How does this world I live in work?"

The informal exercise described here had a second part. This involved undergraduate education majors asking school-age children (preschool through grade six) the simple question, "How do you learn in hool?" (For a related project suggestion, see number 3 on page 315.)[4] Again, the students did not know why they were being asked to do this. In fact, their university instructor wanted to focus their attention on children's perceptions of what "learning" is in school and, especially, to see whether any of the children questioned would mention their own probing as a way of learning. We know that children's questioning is an important source of

[4]We can learn a great deal about children's learning experiences by simply asking them. If our goal is to understand what the child's school experience is from where *she* stands as *she* lives it, then the child herself would seem to be the most relevant and informative person to ask. Incredibly, however, the child is the one we rarely, if ever, ask. We ask teacher, principal, parent, test score, and cumulative folder and, not surprisingly, we receive the perceptions of the teacher, principal, parent . . . and so on. But it is the *child's* perceptions of her learning experience that are the most important and, if we ask her for them, we will get them more often than not.

learning outside of school; would children see it as an important source of learning in school?

The results suggested that although children may be—and in some cases may see themselves as—"why-ers" outside of school, they apparently don't view themselves as "why-ers" in school. Out of a total of eighty-four different responses given to the question ("How do you learn in school?"), only one child, a kindergartner, mentioned questioning, and apparently was thinking of procedural questions: "Ask about it . . . ask the teacher" (meaning, ask the teacher how I should do the work?).

Several responses suggested an active view of learning in school:

K: By looking at things.
3RD: Sometimes I learn from my mind.
4TH: I think.
5TH: Using my brain.

Some children, especially the younger ones, simply indicated the content of their learning—what they learned, not how:

K: We learn *a, b, c, d, e,* . . . (to *z*).
K: I go 1, 2, 3, 4, 5, 6, 7, 8, . . . (to 49).
K: We learn first-grade stuff. That's all we do. We learn first-grade stuff so we can be good in first grade.
3RD: I do math, cursive, clean the room at the end of school.
3RD: We learn our times, our division. We learn how to talk in school. We learn how to write.
3RD: Learn math, like division . . . learn manners at lunch.

Most of the children asked said they listened to the teacher, and they mentioned him or her as the major (or only) source:

K: By my teacher telling myself.
1ST: Listening to the teacher. Be real quiet and listen.
2ND: You listen to teachers and then they just teach you something.
2ND: I listen to the teacher and I don't talk much.
3RD: Pay attention. Doing what the teacher says.
3RD: The teacher tells me what to do and I do it (most of the time).
3RD: I listen to the teacher and then she screams at you and if you don't get it she sends you to the principal's office.
4TH: The teachers tell us stuff. Then most the time we write it down. Or we do a page that has the same stuff on it.
5TH: By having the teacher explain.

Many activities were named, especially reading, writing, studying, seeing films, answering questions, and doing homework. (One refreshing pre-schooler mentioned playing!) Several children mentioned "good" behavior:

1ST: I work, I do math and reading. Be careful not to get in trouble.
2ND: By not goofing off or playing around.
5TH: The teacher being strict. 'Cause if she's not strict, you'll just play around.
         'Cause instead of screaming at you she'd giggle at you.

(And how does one categorize this fourth grader's reply: "Find all the shortcuts and read the instructions two times"?)

The overall impression from the total set of responses was that the majority of the children saw the business of school more as a matter of doing what was assigned than as a matter of exercising their curiosity and initiative and engaging in active searching. The results of these informal exercises and classroom observations are certainly not definitive, but they are suggestive: They suggest that many children perceive their role as a passive one—take in information that I am given and do as I am told.

THE TEACHER'S ROLES

If the child's role is not one of taking in information and doing as she is told, then clearly the teacher's role is not one of dispensing information and telling children what to do. If the teacher is not doing this, then just what *is* she doing? Here's what: She is providing, demonstrating, learning, observing, and responding.

Teacher as provider.   The suggestion that children's language and cognitive development move along in a certain general direction is sometimes (mistakenly) thought to support the plant image of children. That image says that if adults simply provide the right greenhouse conditions—appropriate temperature and amounts of sunlight and water—children flourish, growing into full and beautiful bloom. Not so. Children develop, not by receiving warmth, sunlight, and water, but by actively engaging in their work. The environment we provide them is better seen as a workplace—a studio, a workshop, a lab—than as a greenhouse. As with doctors, artists, carpenters, and inventors, so with children: The nature of the workplace is determined by the nature of the work that is done there. So, the teacher provides a workplace that is suitable for children's work of creatively constructing a "theory of the world" (including its language) out of their ongoing active engagement with people and things in the world.

What is the structure of this workplace? It's a quite predictable place in many ways (which may surprise those adults who think that places where children do real work are "unstructured"). The child knows that she will have the time, space, and materials she needs for her work and that reasonable procedures operate for using these resources. Time, ample, unbroken blocks of time, is needed for real work, and the child needs the continuity of day-after-day time for working on continuing projects. This is only to say that children are like ourselves, not a separate species. What is more frustrating and destructive of our own serious work than really "getting into" something and then being interrupted (by the ill-timed phone call or visitor, perhaps) and having to abandon our project? And so it is with children. Yet it is the rule rather than the exception in the classrooms I observe that the day is incredibly fragmented (largely the result of the fragmented curriculum, of course). Fragmented time and fragmented curriculum foster fragmented work. Sustained work needs sustained time. Also continuity. The child needs to know that there is a tomorrow. Real reading, writing, exploring, and planning and implementing projects take time. Regularly in classrooms, I hear, "Okay, everybody put away whatever you're working on and get out your _____." And if the children groan or ask why, the teacher responds with, "But it's spelling time" or "Because it's 10:30"—which, from the point of view of children's mental development, certainly sound like nonreasons to me. Of course inauthentic work—the rehearsal practice of skills sheets, workbook pages and such—lends itself better to this fragmentation and lack of continuity than real work (engaging-in practice) does. Real work requires ample blocks of uninterrupted time and continuity over time (from day to day). We provide this kind of time for children's work if we believe in the legitimacy and integrity of their work.

The teacher provides appropriate places for the children to engage in their work—quiet, private places for solitary kinds of work and conversational areas for interactive kinds of work; areas to write in, areas to reflect in, to socialize in, and to build in; and the freedom for the child to move about, to change her location when the nature of her engagement changes. Again, this is only to provide for children the kind of environment we would need ourselves.

The teacher provides materials. She doesn't necessarily provide them herself, but she helps the children get to the materials they need. (Children working through the problem of what resources they need for their projects and how to go about getting them are engaged in a most important part of their work.) Some resources are constant (for example, writing supplies, art supplies, and listening center equipment). Some resources are specific to particular projects (for example, experts the children may consult). Some resources are in between; there are books that will rotate, drama center props that change from time to time, and story tapes in the listening center that may be added to or changed daily.

The teacher assures that children have (and know and follow) reasonable procedures for using these resources (time, space, materials). There are well-established ways of caring for equipment and of sharing materials; there are established places for materials to be kept when they are not in use; and so on. The teacher provides this predictability in the children's workplace, not to limit or constrain the children's work, but to free the children to do their real work. People doing real work in the world need appropriate and predictable time, place, materials, and procedures; school children are people doing just such work.

The teacher also provides for variety, that is, for a range of possible activities and projects within the workplace. I think immediately of Kohl's (1976) unit planning. After choosing a circus theme to explore with his class, Kohl went to the circus "to remind [him]self what it was all about" and then "speculated upon things that could be studied in conjunction with the circus . . . developed a number of starting points, and came up with a whole range of topics that could be explored depending upon the students' interests" (p. 37). The first ideas to go on paper looked like this:

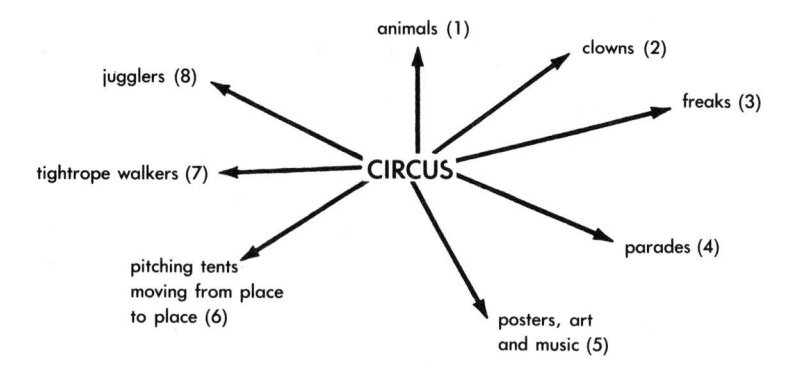

The subthemes were elaborated further. "Tightrope walkers" became "balancing" and looked like this:

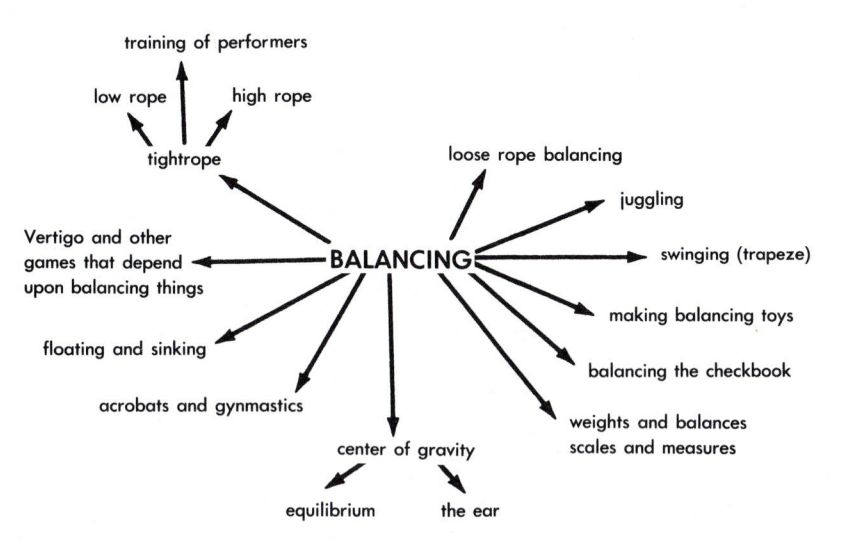

Possible experiences relating to these themes began to emerge. This is one particular teacher's way; other fine teachers work somewhat differently, but all, I think, engage in some sort of initial brainstorming with themselves, messing about, playing with ideas. When we let our children know what some of the possibilities are that we have thought of, their own thinking is often sparked so that they come up with further possibilities. The teacher is ever alert for activities and projects that extend beyond the school walls and engage children in interacting with a wider world. One teacher I know is currently making plans for her third graders to "adopt" an old folks home within walking distance of the school for the coming school year. She's also making plans for these Texas children to respond to the call that has gone out for individuals to help in a statewide program to gather and identify every kind of wildflower that grows in Texas. Her third graders will participate as scouts in this program, gathering wildflowers in their area and sending them to the state headquarters for this program. You can call these experiences "social studies" and "science" or you can call them "language," but whatever you call them, you can see that the range of activities and experiences that will evolve within this wider-world engagement will necessarily be quite diverse and real-world entrenched.

The teacher who provides for a range of possible experiences also provides support for the child's choice and initiative. The child may choose to follow up on a possibility the teacher has suggested, probably modifying and shaping it as she goes along in ways the teacher had not anticipated. Or she may initiate an activity the teacher hadn't thought of. In either case, the teacher provides support for the child's own shaping here: "Oh, so you're going to _____. Hmmm. How are you planning to _____? Had you thought about _____? I wonder if so-and-so might be helpful."

A word of caution. It is possible to think we are encouraging authentic student initiative when, in fact, we are only engaging children in a subtle form of teacher pleasing. Again my third-grade teacher, Mrs. McKenzie, provides an example. (This is the very same Mrs. McKenzie who gave me grief about sentences, p. 82). She would introduce a new social studies unit by saying something like "We're going to begin studying Eskimos. Let's think of all the questions you have about Eskimos—all the things you'd like to find out. I'll write your questions on the board." (Does this sound as if she's encouraging student initiative?) The fact is, there was nothing my class of suburban Philadelphia eight-year-olds wanted to know about Eskimos. Eskimos were quite outside the outermost edge of our wonderings. It is easy enough to think of ways that Eskimos could have been brought within the reaches of our wondering world. But they weren't. "Eskimos" just dropped down on us from out of the blue (as Plains Indians, Our South American Neighbors, and various others had done before them). What we did in this situation was to give Mrs. McKenzie her "approved questions" list, the same list every time (substitute "Eskimos" for "Plains Indians," "South American Neighbors," and so on). Some of the suggested questions seem, from my adult perspective, quite bizarre: "What do they eat for breakfast?" we'd ask, or "What do they do for recreation?" [Is it possible that third-grade suburban children who had never encountered an Eskimo for real or on TV (there wasn't any) or in a movie or book ever wondered what Eskimos ate for breakfast or did for recreation?] As the board filled with "our" questions, the task was to look carefully at the list to see if we could think of one of the approved questions that was still missing. If so, we'd provide it and Mrs. McKenzie would add it to the lenghtening list. This was teacher pleasing all dressed up in "student initiative" trappings. But the trappings don't make the experience, any more than the cover makes the book or the clothes make the individual who wears them. In striking contrast to my third-grade experience, the third graders who are going to adopt the nearby old folks home and scout for wildflowers will have abundant opportunities for exercising real initiative as they plan their activities.

The teacher also provides a no-risk environment that invites the children to explore and to play with ideas. The close connection between intellectual play and creativity is well established: " . . . creative thinking seems to entail at least a degree of regressive playfulness, impulse acceptance, and arationality" (Getzels 1964, p. 265); ". . . teachers and students need to be encouraged to play, to go crazy, and to be irrelevant. Play is a creative process. . . . Play is a form of heuristic learning. . . . Where heuristic learning is concerned, the less conventional person is more likely to generate the more original and creative meanings" (Suchman 1977, p. 269). In an environment in which children engage in intellectual play, creative thinking, and heuristic learning, they will surely generate much that is unconventional—including errors of all kinds. But because these children participate in real-world work, the conventional is also ever present and influences their work. Does this sound like a contradiction— provide for children to be unconventional *and* conventional? No, not a contradiction; rather, a balance. (It will not be news to you that teaching often involves quite delicate balances.)

A writing teacher provides an analogy for the writing process that helps to clarify this unconventional-conventional balance. This writing teacher tells her students that effective writing involves both the student's own "madman" and "judge," but the student must use each at different points and for different purposes in the writing process. The madman comes first: "He's full of ideas, writes crazily . . . gets carried away by enthusiasm . . . [He's full of] playful, creative energies, the ideas which form the basis of one's writing." But in the final stage of the writing process (after one's "architect" has organized the madman's ideas and one's "carpenter" has "nailed the ideas together, sentence by sentence"), the "judge comes around to inspect." It is the judge who is concerned with conventions. Both madman and judge are crucial for effective communication: The "outpourings of [one's] madman must be balanced by the objective, impersonal vision of the educated critic within . . . for writing is not just self-expression; it is communication as well" (Flowers 1981, p. 835).

As there is a place—a necessity, even—for both madman and judge in writing, so there is a place for both in children's exploring, planning, and implementing in other areas. Madman, judge, and the delicate balance: This is what the teacher provides. Traditionally education has fostered judge but not madman; yet the judge, "for all his sharpness of eye . . . can't create anything" (Flowers 1981, p. 834). Clearly, children are, and need to be encouraged to be, both madmen *and* judges.

The teacher, then, provides a structure for the workplace that assures resources the children need and the freedom to use them. Built into the structure is the possibility of student input and initiative and exploration.

And because the structure engages the children in authentic work, the conventional, which provides the necessary conflict and confirmation of the children's developing notions of language, is ever present. Thus the teacher provides a workplace well-suited to the kind of work school children do: creatively construct their theories of the world.

Teacher as demonstrator. "Demonstrator," not "model." When people use the term "model" in relation to teachers, they often mean a kind of performance—a role play, pretense, pretend. The teacher "models" an activity in the sense of performing it as an actress would, pretending to do it. But to "demonstrate" (a term used by Frank Smith 1983a) is to "show how something is [actually] done" (p. 102).

Graves (1978) uses the term "artisan" to convey the idea of teacher as one who actively engages in activities that are important to her, one who demonstrates by doing. A significant finding from his study of classrooms in England, Scotland, and the United States, where children were or were not writing, supports the importance of teacher as doer and active participant, the teacher as "artisan." Despite wide differences in many characteristics of the teachers in whose classrooms vigorous student writing was going on, the characteristic of "teacher-as-artisan" was common to them all.

> They had an artisan's view of the universe. There were no final states. Information and material were constantly evolving toward some expression of excellence. Compositions, drawings, experiments, mathematical problems were *not wrong, only unfinished.* This was their stance toward teaching because they either wrote themselves, painted, developed photos, or cared for plants. The children were aware of teacher crafts since they wrote, drew, painted, or acted with children. Teachers enjoyed their craft and wanted to share it. . . . These teachers provided time for writing. . . . [They] not only provided time for children, but time for themselves to participate in the [writing] process. (Graves 1978, p. 639)

One of the aspects of children's development we value most in school is children's development of literacy, but when do our students see us read or write for our own real purposes? Well, they may see us read memos from the office, daily cafeteria menus, notes from parents; and they may see us write notes to be taken to the office or sent home to parents. But the kinds of involved really-into-it reading and writing we want our students to do, they rarely see us do. It's easy enough to see that this view of the teacher as doer, demonstrator, artisan working along with her students often receives little support. School administrators often view the teacher as a people mover: Her job is to move children *through* things (workbooks, basals, curriculum objectives) and *to* things (the cafeteria, the library, the gym). This pervasive view of the teacher's role is an enormous obstacle to teacher demonstration.

However, an equally large obstacle in the area of literacy is that reading and writing may in fact have little place in our own lives. Several years ago I had an eerie conversation with an undergraduate student who was enrolled in a practicum in which she provided daily reading and writing instruction for a small group of fourth graders. She told me, "I never read or write. In my university courses I don't read the texts; I just listen to what people say in class. I've always just *hated* reading and writing." I expressed surprise that she was enrolled in the reading concentration program within our department, since she hated to read and write so. She answered, "Oh, that's exactly *why* I'm in reading concentration. I want to teach children to read and write so they won't hate it like I do." As I see it, there is no hope for this approach, however well-intentioned she may be. What she perceives, and will necessarily demonstrate, as reading and writing are skills activities (probably what she was taught as reading and writing when she was in elementary school). She mistakes traditional reading and writing curriculum for real reading and writing. This is what she will demonstrate (show, by engaging in); this is what her children will learn. They, too, will perceive the skills activities as reading and writing. She will try to make the children like these activities—the basal stories and comprehension questions, the assigned book reports, the fill-in-the-blanks workbook pages, the "stories" written using the week's spelling words, and so on. She will do this by exuding a feigned enthusiasm: "You get to do a really fun page in your workbook today." Maybe she will try to convince the children of the importance of reading and writing in their lives (reading and writing as she perceives them, though not the real thing, because that she does not know): "Suppose you apply for a job and your letter is full of spelling mistakes and somebody else with your same qualifications applies for the same job but her letter doesn't have spelling mistakes—who do you think is going to get the job?" She'll offer rewards—stars on the chart for every book read in different categories, praise, and so on.[5] The children may try to please her; they may do more worksheets or use more spelling words in their stories (which, of course, will render the stories more meaningless). But until and unless real reading and writing become *her own*, serving meaningful and welcomed purposes in her own life, there is no way that she can demonstrate these and thus foster authentic literacy development in the children she teaches.

Smith maintains that the basis for children's learning is what we in fact demonstrate—which may be quite different from what we *think* we demonstrate. The practicum student just mentioned thinks she is demonstrating reading and writing. She isn't. She can't because she herself is engaging in something else. There is another problem, too, and that is that our demonstration invariably includes how we feel about what we do.

> A teacher who stands before a class demonstrates . . . how a teacher feels about what is being taught and about the people being taught. A tired teacher demonstrates how a tired teacher behaves, a disinterested teacher demonstrates disinterest. . . . Not only do we all continually demonstrate how the

[5]One way to identify authentic experiences is to look for those that children engage in *without* the teacher's feigned enthusiasm, her talk about importance in later life, or her rewards. These teacher behaviors usually indicate inauthentic experiences that children engage in mainly when these subtle forms of pressure are applied.

things we do are done, but we also demonstrate how we feel about them. (Smith 1983a, p. 102)

Teacher as learner.   The very behavior that may be the most important of all for us to demonstrate is probably the one we demonstrate least: how *we* go about learning. Our educational system does more to promote the notion of teacher-as-knower than teacher-as-learner. Yet we all know that the children we teach know more than we do in many areas. Surely they know more about aspects of their personal lives—their home, family, friends, and community. They know more about current favorite TV programs, films, recordings, and singing groups. It would be easy to dismiss these areas of knowledge as trivial, but this would be to let our adult egocentrism take over: These areas are important to the children. Beyond this, we invariably find that our children have individual areas of expertise: a particular child is "into" rocks or stamps or car engines or computers, or knows another language, or is good at making paper airplanes. (And is there a kindergarten anywhere without a resident dinosaur expert?) It's not that we already know things that distinguishes us from our students so much as it is that we are effective and more experienced learners. We know about how people learn; even more important, we have had substantial experience doing it ourselves. We are good leaders in learning because we demonstrate our learning in the workplace we share with our students.

We have much to learn from our children. We show them that we learn from them in many ways: in the genuine questions we ask, in the attentive way we listen to what they tell us, in our responses to their talk ("Oh. I didn't know that!"), in our responses to their writing (for example, in dialogue journals we may write, "Thanks for telling me about X").

We also have much to learn from the world we inhabit with the children. Rosen and Rosen (1973, p. 28) bemoan the tendency of teachers to direct children's attention "to barren collections of information which give no hint of the excitement of discovery and doubt." It is so easy to teach as if knowledge is "conveniently packaged, stored, and guaranteed by authorities," fixed and absolute, "a closed system . . . in which a problem is solved by looking it up' " (Suchman 1977, p. 263). Yet this view of knowledge is completely untrue. We tend to stay entirely within the safety of "clear" examples, avoiding all grey areas (examples we tend to call "tricky ones"), the very problem cases that we would have to work through ourselves, thus demonstrating how we make sense of things we do not understand already (how we comprehend and learn), and also giving the children a "hint" of the "discovery and doubt"—the not-known—that is the excitement of learning. Consider these examples.

A student teacher was working with fourth graders on the prefixes "re," "un," and "dis." The topic was quite unrelated to any real-language event in the children's lives; it simply happened to "come next" in the workbook. Somehow in giving examples of words including these prefixes, the student teacher happened to use "repair." She became very embarrassed, apologized for the "bad" example and told the children to forget it because "repair" didn't mean "to pair again." The children moved on to checking over a workbook page on compound words that they had done previously. One of the words was "passageway." She asked, "What words make up the word 'passageway'?" A child answered, "Pass," "age," and "way." The teacher, again embarrassed, replied, "This is sort of a tricky one. It's actually 'passage' and 'way' " and she hurried to the next item. Two missed opportunities—the only possible bright spots in an otherwise bleak and deadening event!

Fortunately, I went next to observe a student teacher in a sixth grade. She and a small group of children were discussing a selection they had read about the partridge, "a ground bird." One of the children said, "But we sing about 'a partridge in a pear tree.' If a partridge is a ground bird, how did it get up in the tree?"[6] And for a good (*very* good) five minutes the group—including (and especially) the teacher—considered and conjectured and reflected on the different ways that birds move from place to place (flying, hopping along, walking, swimming, and so on). The teacher here was a partner in learning with these children.

My son once asked me, "Are there more things in the world we do know or more things we don't know?" The more we talked about an individual's "known" and "not-known," the more we both came to realize what a tiny speck a human's knowledge is in the universe. Why, then, do we so often give school children the impression that knowledge is already all in, accumulated and sitting there waiting for us to come get it? The teacher-as-learner gives a different impression; she gives—lives—the "excitement of discovery and doubt."

It is interesting that even the seemingly most mundane kinds of learning offer possibilities for the teacher as learner and explorer. Take handwriting. What could be more mundane than learning letter shapes and how to form them. The tendency is to convince children that there is a single way to form each letter in any script. Alphabet cards line the front of virtually every classroom, showing the one-and-only-way that each letter is supposed to look. Children are often given their own alphabet cards to keep in their desks, each letter appearing with small numerals and arrows indicating the order and direction of strokes. Doggedly children produce page after page of letters formed in the prescribed way. For me, it stands as one of the great triumphs of the individual human spirit that the result of this one-and-only-one-way training program is an individual whose handwriting is so absolutely distinctive that it identifies her, as uniquely as the fingerprint does, from among all others in the human race and thus the signature can be used on legal documents. John Holt, a teacher-learner par excellence, suggests that a teacher might approach letter forms in a different way, a way that hints at the wonderfulness of this area.

Typography is one of the great crafts or even arts, with a long history of its own. Why not give children a glimpse of this part of the continuum of experience? Why not get, from any maker of type, or printer, or commercial artist,

---

[6]I can't resist adding that the children in this group had been designated "the *low* group"!

or art supply store, some sheets of samples of type faces, so that children can see some of the many ways in which we make our letters? Better yet, why not invite the children using old newspapers, magazines, labels, and so on, to find as many different kinds of *A*'s (or other letters) as they can . . . We might start everyone thinking about the number of ways we can make a capital *A*. We could make it tall and thin, or short and fat. We could make it slant to the right or to the left. We could make the strokes thick (heavy) or thin (light), or a mixture of the two. We could put feet (serifs) on the legs, or leave them off. We could put the bar high in the letter, or low in the letter. We could weight the lefthand stroke . . . or we could weight the righthand stroke. We could make our strokes hollow, or fill them with cross-hatching, or dots. We could make our strokes out of wiggly lines, or right-angled steps, or dots, or short dashes. Or we could make our strokes out of the letter *A* itself, or some other letter—why not an *A* made out of *B*'s, and a *B* made out of *A*'s? Children like such novelties. They suggest that the world is a fascinating place, full of possibilities. Why not tempt children with the idea of making *A*'s (or other letters) in as many different ways as possible? Making letters would then be an exploration, an adventure, not a chore. (Holt 1970, pp. 194–96)

With personal computers all around (as they were not when Holt wrote this) and word processing programs with all sorts of types and fonts, this kind of activity should be more engaging than ever. The world—the *child's* world—is full of letters, not in the form of alphabet cards, but on billboards, soda cans, birthday cards, bumper stickers, and T-shirts. Children's daily encounters with print in the world must surely make them wonder why we are telling this one-and-only-one-way lie about letter formation. The teacher as learner discovers that no area is "mundane"; she approaches every area knowing that it holds fascinating promise for exploration.

It may be that those areas we know least about offer special opportunities for the teacher as learner. It is easy to feel insecure when our students move into areas of exploration that are new and unfamiliar to us. We feel "shaky." But why? We know how to learn—how to explore, how to make mistakes and try again, how to question, how to search, how to wonder. Making our own learning process obvious to our students may be the most important teaching we ever do. In the end, we don't teach information, we teach learning, and there is no more powerful way to do this than to show that process in action in our own lives.

Teacher as observer. In his article about reading called "Twelve Easy Ways to Make Learning to Read Difficult (and One Difficult Way to Make It Easy)," Frank Smith (1973) gives the following as the "one difficult way to make it easy: Respond to what the child is trying to do" (p. 195). This is as relevant and important a guideline in other curricular areas as it is in reading.[7] It involves, first, believing that the child is trying to do something, something legitimate and significant. Indeed, this has been the major thrust of the last few chapters. Beyond this, responding to what children

---

[7]See *Language Arts*, 62, no. 3 (March 1985), an issue devoted to the theme, Responding to What Kids Are Trying to Do.

are trying to do requires recognizing what it is that they are trying to do. This means observing; it means reading children's behavior; it means teacher as observer.

The classroom that is designed as a workplace and provides for variety, choice, and exploration offers rich opportunities for the teacher-observer. Children's talk, writing, and actions are all important sources of information about what they are trying to do and how they are trying to do it. What is the child "into"? How is she making sense of her experience? We learn a lot if we really tune in to the child's conversation (her initiations, her listening, her responding to others, her questions) in her one-to-one interactions with us, in her interactions with her peers (in larger and smaller groups), in her interactions with those outside the classroom. Her writing (and responses to others' writing) tells us a lot too: What does she select to write about? To read about? What does she write about in her dialogue journal and how does she respond to our written responses? In their reading and writing, children reveal much about themselves that is helpful to the teacher-observer. Their actions give us helpful insights too: What kinds of activities does the child choose or initiate? What kinds of situations does she act out in sociodramatic or puppet-related play? Whom does she choose to work with on various types of projects? How does she change roles with different partners? How does she go about planning and implementing tasks? Does she prefer to structure her own tasks, or does she seek more peer or adult structuring and guidance and approval? In which situations does she observe, in which follow, in which initiate? Our children differ in all these ways and many, many more. Some of the differences are matters of individual personality. Some relate to a child's cultural background. Some children, for example, come from social backgrounds that value children's initiative and that see children as having important status in adult-child relationships (including teacher-child interaction); while others come from homes in which children are expected, not to take initiative in adult-child interactions, but to be deferential and respectful and to look to teachers (rather than to themselves or other children) to structure and direct their learning activity. Our children teach us about themselves through their conversation, reading and writing, and actions *if* we observe carefully.

Moffett (1973) provides a good example of some second- and third-grade teachers who observed a "burning issue" for their students and built on that real concern. It was their students' concerns about the petty stealing of supplies—pencils, rulers, erasers. It would seem, on the face of it, an unpromising starting point for rich language, but in fact it was a very powerful starting point precisely because the children were extremely interested in and concerned about this issue. As the children tried to solve the problem of petty stealing, their activities included initial discussion in small groups and the recording of the main ideas from each group's discussion; discussion among the recorders from the initial groups; planning and making posters about stealing; planning a publication about stealing—brainstorming in small groups, recording ideas, presenting ideas to a panel, selecting the best ideas for what to include in the publication; going around to other classes to explain the campaign; preparing a questionnaire and conducting a survey on attitudes toward stealing; writing articles for the class publication, reading them to others, discussing the articles, offering feedback to authors of the articles, rewriting and proofreading the articles, and selecting the final group of articles to be circulated to other classes; going in pairs to other classes to get reactions to their suggestions for dealing with stealing; small-group discussion of these reactions (main ideas recorded); final discussion about specific ways to implement the campaign throughout the school (Moffett 1973, pp. 49–50, 139–42).

My favorite example of observing and building on children's interest comes from a wonderful sixth-grade teacher who wrote a new script for a familiar story.[8] It's the old paper-airplanes story. You know the one: Paper airplanes begin flying around the room, surreptitiously at first, but then more openly as more children become involved. In the usual scenario, the teacher begins with comments like "All right. Put those away now. This isn't the time for paper airplanes. We have work to do." But the paper airplanes continue and the teacher becomes more stern: "OK, I'm not going to tell you anymore. If I see any more of these airplanes I'm going to tear them up." There are more. She tears them up, throws them away, eventually names go on the board, checks beside the names, and so on. The familiar script.

But this particular sixth-grade teacher saw the paper airplanes beginning to fly around the room and figured that the children must be interested in paper airplanes. Then she asked herself, "Where can I go with that interest?" She set up a glider center. There were to be prizes: for the glider that went the farthest, the one that stayed up the longest, the one that went the fastest, the one that went the highest, and so on. The activities of the paper-airplane group over the next several weeks could be called "playing with paper airplanes"; or they could be called "exploring physical principles." In any case, the interested children designed, constructed, tested, redesigned, compared, and observed gliders of an incredible variety, each with its own subtle modification intended to carry it farther or longer or higher than its predecessor. And there were prizes. And friendships. And new discoveries, invention, and exploration and the talk that conveyed these. (I happen to know about this glider experience because, somewhere in my twenty-one-year-old son's treasures-from-childhood boxes in the attic, there's a faded blue ribbon that reads, "First Prize for the glider that went the farthest.")

What we see does depend on how we look; and *whether* we see depends on *whether* we look. It requires perceptive and continuing observation of children to recognize what they are trying to do so that we will be able to respond appropriately.

Teacher as responder. Respond how? Sometimes by giving direct assistance. Children often ask for specific help—anything from the spelling of a particular word, to where to find further information about a particular subject, to how to organize a project that has several stages. Sometimes the child lets us know that she needs help but she isn't sure just what

[8]I am indebted to Sharon Ely for this example from her class.

kind—the "I'm stuck" syndrome. She may not say "I'm stuck" but may simply demonstrate frustration. Our response may be to think-talk the problem through with the child: "Stuck, are you?" or "It looks to me like you're kind of frustrated with this. How can I help? Let's think about your goal first—What do you want to accomplish here? What do you think you want to end up with? Tell me about what you've done so far. Where are you planning to go next—what do you see as your next step here?"

Sometimes we offer assistance we feel the children can benefit from without their asking for it. Remember again Vygotsky's comment, "What a child can do with assistance today, she will be able to do by herself tomorrow" (Vygotsky 1978, p. 87). We may appropriately provide assistance at any point in the children's work: in their finding topic or focus or direction, in their planning, in their implementing, in their modifying plans and changing course, in their evaluating and reflecting on what they have done. Sometimes this help involves our convening with an individual, sometimes with a small group, sometimes with the entire class; but in any case, we're trying to support or "scaffold" the children to move beyond their current limits. I sometimes find it difficult to distinguish between "intervention" and "intrusion." When are we, in fact, helping (intervening) and when are we taking over (intruding)? I don't know any foolproof test for determining this. What one person sees as intervention, another sees as intrusion. Perhaps the best we can do is to be aware that the dividing line between intervening (helping) and intruding (taking over) is very thin and to ask ourselves regularly, "Am I intervening or intruding here?"

In the classroom that is a workshop, the children show the teacher—in their talk, in their writing, in their activity—points at which and ways in which she can offer help. One of the beauties of the workshop classroom is the opportunity it offers for good timing; because the teacher is on the spot, involved in the children's continuing activity, she can offer appropriate help at the very moment that the children can benefit from it, just when they are ready to attend to it because they can use it in their work. Writing conventions are a good example. Teaching written conventions apart from the context of real writing is, as I have argued, meaningless. But giving help with an appropriate written convention when a child wants to incorporate it in something she is writing for publication—this is maximally effective assistance. The child receives the help she wants at the time she wants it for her own purposes. Could there be a more efficient procedure than this? I often encounter the view that if children are doing real writing, then less attention is being devoted to conventional matters (grammar, sentence structure, spelling, punctuation, handwriting) than would be the case if the children had daily skills exercises. I disagree with this. It seems to me that these matters get *more* attention, not less, when they are dealt with in the context of children's real writing, for the attention they get is the *child's* attention. We have seen already that the child's development of language from birth is determined by the child's focus of attention: It is what the child focuses on, attends to, makes sense of, that is the basis of her learning. In classrooms in which children spend a lot of time on skills sheets and workbook pages devoted to these conventions, it is the teacher's attention, not the child's, that is engaged. Children do not learn from activities that switch their minds onto cruise control; they learn from activities in which their own attention is actively and purposefully engaged. It is just this kind of involved attention that the teacher triggers with her well-timed assistance to children as they work.

The teacher often responds by extending. You may remember how effective the adult's strategy of meeting-the-child's-idea-with-an-idea was in three-year-olds' language development (Cazden study described on p. 179). And so it is for older children too. Opportunities for extending abound in the workshop classroom; they are in our responses in children's dialogue journals, in conferences, and in informal conversation:

> I mentioned your interest in _____ to the librarian yesterday and she told me to tell you that . . .
>
> If you liked that book, you might enjoy _____. It's also an adventure story about a boy and his dog, but the author tells it in a very different way.
>
> Had you thought about setting up your project as an exhibit in the hallway at the front entrance, or maybe as a traveling exhibit on our pushcart so it could be in a different classroom each day? You might want to put some sort of question box with it so kids can write you any questions they might have.

Again, we need to be careful not to take over the child's project, especially with those children who feel that the teacher has such special status that they interpret her every suggestion (however casual in her view) as a directive and immediately pick up on it in an attempt to please her.

Sometimes our response is encouragement. For children's work, as for our own, there may be no greater encouragement than indication of another's genuine interest. We show our own serious interest in the child's work each time we sit with her and listen as she tells us what she has done and is trying to do, express our understanding of her purposes, raise a real question, or make an interested comment. This response reminds the child that she is doing important work and that it is—and will remain—*her* work.

I think we also encourage children by helping them to recognize ways in which they are competent. When I ask my graduate students to describe a particularly meaningful elementary school experience they had, and when they ask other adults to do the same, again and again these adults cite an experience in which they found out that they were competent. (For a related project suggestion see 7 on p. 316.)

> "I was in second grade and we were supposed to write a story. I got my paper back and on it the teacher had written, 'You have a good imagination.' " (This is a forty-two-year-old recalling—some thirty-five years later—the teacher's exact words.)
>
> "I had never thought that I could write poetry, but in third grade we started doing it and I found out that I could, and that I was actually good at it."

"There is a fundamental human urge to be effective, competent, and independent, to understand the world and to act with skill" (Donaldson 1979, p. 118). There is no more important reason to keep anecdotal records and samples of children's work than to be able to demonstrate to children how they are developing competence, independence, skill. We recognize the value of conferencing with parents about the child's development, and most schools see this as important enough that they build in time and procedure for it. But surely it is every bit as important that the child recognize her increasing competence, for it is the child, not the parent, who is the learner here. How often do we sit down with an individual child for the same kind of conference we make certain to hold regularly with her parents: to reflect on her development, her growing interests, her friendships, her plans, her perceptions of her school experience, ways she thinks we could be of help to her. As we help children recognize that they are (and are becoming) competent, we sustain them in getting on with what they are trying to do.

Sometimes our response to children is that of partner—those moments when we see what the child is trying to do and join her. We sometimes partner children in a physical task (for example, setting up some sort of exhibit or a sports event), sometimes in a creative endeavor (for example, taking a role in the children's puppet play), sometimes in an intellectual event (as in the partridge-is-a-ground-bird discussion). But one very special partnership is partner in wondering. We may think of individuals going along through life, building a theory by solving problems that arise. Donaldson points out that this is not all: "It is not only when incongruities are forced on us by events that we try to resolve them. Sometimes we positively seek them out, as if we liked having to deal with things that we do not understand, things that challenge us intellectually" (1979, p. 118). My son, as a fifteen-year-old, came in from his after-school activities one day as I was fixing dinner and asked, "Mom, what is time? I mean, what is it *really*? I know about planets and all that, but what is time itself?" As the peas burned on the stove, we talked about time—about repeated events that give us a sense of time, about the kinds of divisions of time that some other languages use (past, present, and future are not the only possibilities), about a philosophy professor at the local university who was writing a book about time and might be available to talk with him about time. The next day, again late in the afternoon as I was fixing dinner, he entered the kitchen and asked, "What *is* time?" And the day after that, the same scene, the same question: "What is time? I mean, what *is* it?" Did he want an answer? No, he asked the second and third times knowing I had none, but only wanting me to wonder along with him. Traditionally, education has done more to support children's problem solving than children's wondering. But surely the school should be the one place above all others that fosters the child's wondering. And ours. The partnership.

"Respond to what the child is trying to do." This must ever remain the continuing challenge of teaching. Now the response is to help, now to meet the child's idea with a new idea, now to suggest, now to encourage, now to partner—always sensitive to the particular child at the particular moment. However much schools may advocate one curriculum or another, one method or another, one text series or another, teaching is, finally, a person-to-person business. Adult recollections of personally meaningful elementary school experiences invariably include the adult's remembrance of feeling special to the teacher as an individual:

"The teacher had me stay after school to help her."
"The teacher drove me home in her own car."
"The teacher asked me to do a special project."
"The teacher picked me to read my story out loud to the class."

This constant theme leaves no doubt in my mind of the profound and lasting significance of the individual teacher-child relationship.

I recently was talking with Anna, a fourth-grade friend of mine, about her current school experience. A pattern quickly emerged in her talk, of comparing her current experience to her third-grade experience, and third grade was definitely winning. I finally said, "You know, Anna, as I listen to you I get the feeling that you liked third grade better than you like fourth grade." Anna answered, "Well, our teacher this year doesn't really like us very much, but last year, every one of us was teacher's pet." I do not know how that third-grade teacher made every child feel like "teacher's pet," but I feel sure that much of this occurred in the individual encounter, in her sensitive response to each child and what each child was trying to do.

Smith is certainly on target in calling responsive teaching a *"difficult way"* to make learning easy for children. There is much in the current educational scene that works against teachers being the providers, demonstrators, learners, observers, and responders described here. Preservice teacher education programs, inservice teacher education, social pressures, school administrators, and fellow teachers more often than not expect and encourage teachers to dispense prepackaged information and assign ready-made tasks. Even school children themselves often come into a new classroom expecting "teaching" of this kind. And information dispensing and task assigning are far easier than teaching that believes in, observes, and responds to what children are trying to do.

So what, then, does this responsive kind of teaching have going for it? Only this: It makes sense in terms of what we presently know about how children learn; it is more engaging to us than information dispensing and task assigning will ever be; and the feedback from our children tells us it is worth the effort. The difficulty of such teaching in no way lessens its importance. Never has such teaching been more important than it is now.

CLASSROOMS IN TUNE WITH CHILDREN'S CURIOSITY: TWO EXAMPLES

Children actively pursue their "urge to find out about the world" all the time. School is a good place to do it. I have suggested that the classroom be a workshop in which children and teachers can do their work—children "probing into the working of the world" and teachers providing, demonstrating, learning, observing, and responding. In the two classroom examples that end this chapter, the children and teachers are doing authentic work in their classroom workshop. The teacher in the first example would tell you she was "doing math"; the teacher in the second example would tell you he was "doing science." I will tell you both were "doing language." Where children and teachers are doing real work, there is no way to separate out "language" and what is sometimes called "content". The following examples will make this clear.

The first example involves a teacher who engaged a class of fourth graders in working on this question: What makes a fourth grader?[9] Her goal was to help the children develop some basic notions in statistics by having them explore an area of importance to them. Well, of course, they had to begin by planning how they would go about this task, how they would gather information, what information would be relevant, how they would compile it, analyze it, make sense of it, share it with the rest of the school. Groups got busy. Maybe what makes a fourth grader distinct from third and fifth and all other graders is what time they go to bed. Maybe it's how much allowance they get. Maybe it's height and weight. Maybe TV or movie preferences. Maybe it's which rock groups they like best. Surely *something* sets fourth graders apart from others. There was discussion, planning, note taking, and sharing with the larger group. And off they went—troops of fourth graders interviewing others up and down the school about bedtimes and heights and weights and allowances and TV and rock star preferences. More group discussion— compiling information and trying to make sense of it. Then getting the information into presentable form and sharing the results with the rest of the school. This is only a sketch, the barest hint of the children's activity. Your imagination can fill in the details. But do you get some sense of the providing, the demonstrating, the learning, the observing, the responding, this teacher was doing for the three-week duration of this project?

The second example is a partial transcript from one particular session. Thus it is in the teacher's actual words that you will be able to recognize the various roles he plays as he interacts with these children. The situation itself is one that few of us would choose to teach in—a televised science lesson using a group of children that the teacher scarcely knew. Yet despite the intrusiveness of TV cameras and lights and personnel, the teacher's divided attention between the children and the TV audience (he makes intermittent comments to the TV audience on the children's activity as it proceeds), and the unfamiliarity of the teacher and the situation for these sixth-grade Mexican-American children, their talk is full of the "language of curiosity" (especially questioning) during this half-hour activity. What is it that the teacher does in his interaction with these children that fosters their probing, their curiosity questioning?

Six sixth-grade Mexican-American children are on the floor around a large plastic tub of water in which there are five live crayfish. Several pairs of tongs are on the floor. Throughout this activity there was much conversation among the children

[9]I am grateful to Alison Claus, the superb teacher in this example, for allowing me to use it.

that I was unable to pick up. Nevertheless, the children's remarks in the excerpts that follow give the flavor of the kind of conversation that was going on. The children's questions are in *italics*. The teacher makes some introductory comments to the TV audience, and then turns to the children and asks them his first question.

T: So how would you pick up a crayfish?
C: Get them by the back.
T: Sure.
(The children are trying to pick up crayfish and are talking about it as they do so.)

T: Are there any other ways? . . . Can you pick them up with your hands?
CS: Yes.
T: How would you do that?
C: *Do they bite very hard?*
T: How would you find out?
C: Let 'em bite you.
T: That's good.
C: *Do they bite?*
C: Uh-uh (negative). They don't bite.
T: What does that feel like when you're picking him up. S—?
C: Like a rock.
T: Does it feel like a rock?
C: Yeah. With a bunch of little sticks in it.
T: Are they sharp?
C: No.
T: How do you know?
C: 'Cuz I already picked 'em up.
C: He wants to bite.
T: How do you know he wants to bite?
C: He's ready to.
C: *But how do you know he wants to bite?*
T: Well, can you get him to bite?

C: *Could you eat crayfish?*
T: Sure. What part of the crayfish do you think you'd eat, E—?
C: *Tail?*
T: Yeah, the tail. Right. What other animals . . .
C: Lobster.
T: Sure, lobster. Right.
C: Crab.
C: Shrimp.

C: His feet are . . . when I touch 'em, they're real hard.
C: Yuck.
C: They force your finger forward.
C: *Is that behind his tail some legs for if these get chopped off or something?*
T: Do you think that's what they're for? What other purpose could those legs be for?
C: Well . . .
T: Does he swim with those legs?

C: No.
T: Does he *swim?*
C: No.
C: He'd have to if he lives in water.
T: All things live in water swim?
C: No. Some things don't live in water, but they still swim.
C: Clams.
T: Clams. Do clams swim?
C: No.
T: You sure?
C: Yes. They do.
T: Do baby clams swim?
C: Yeah.
T: That's something you might want to investigate.
C: *How could you tell which one's a girl or a boy?*
T: OK. I'm going to tell you that there are four boys in there and one girl, and you
     tell me how you can tell them apart.
C: I think this one's a boy.
T: How do you know?
C: He has a little thing sticking out and this one doesn't.
T: Where?
C: It's right there.
C: That one's a girl.

T: (Giving task to two children) Could I ask you if one of you would draw what it
     looks like from the back and the other one draw what it looks like from the
     stomach? OK. Good. (T gives Cs Magic Markers and indicates two large blank
     sheets of newsprint on bulletin board. The two Cs each take a crayfish and
     begin to draw.)
T: (To another child) Well, E—. What have you decided about your crayfish here?
C: Yuck.
T: Yuck? What do you mean by that?
C: They don't stay still.
T: That's a good observation, G —.

T: M—, what would you say you're doing with him now . . . well, before he fell?
     What were you doing? What were you doing there when he was crawling on
     your arm?
C: *Observing him?*
T: What did you observe him doing?
C: *His movement?*
T: Sure. Movements. What kind of movements did he have?
T: There you go, S—. (C is getting crayfish to walk on his arm.) Good. What kind
     of movements would you call that? Good, S—. Watch what M— does. He was
     having him move in a certain way.
C: *Sideways?*
T: Does it move sideways?
C: No, back.
C: They walk backwards. A crab will run sideways, but he runs backwards.

C: *How much do they weigh?*
T: How could you find out how much one weighs?
C: They don't look like they weigh even a pound.
T: It doesn't look like it.

C: *What are these other legs for?*
T: What do you think those are for?
C: *Feelers, or what?*
C: *It's very interesting.*

(Talking about crayfish eating. One child suggests a crayfish eats cheese.)

T: Would you like to try a piece of cheese and see if they eat cheese?
C: Yeah. I will.
T: All right. Here, E —. This is cheese. You can try that. See if he'll eat that. This is a piece of chicken. Don't you people eat this food; it's not clean. How could you find out if they eat . . . here's some hamburger, if you'd like to try that.
C: *Eat the whole piece of cheese?*
T: No, just take a little piece.
C: *But where does it eat?*
T: I don't know. How would you find out where it eats?
C: (To crayfish) Open your mouth.

C: He can move his eyes in back of him, in front of him, sideways.
T: Good observation, S —. Excellent, excellent.
C: *How come it never eats?*
C: He ate something.
T: Well, maybe it is eating.
C: When I gave him a little piece of shrimp, he started eating it.
C: He's eating the chicken. He's cutting, like, the fibers.
C: Yeah, he's cutting them.
T: Did he eat anything else besides the chicken?
C: A little bit.
C: It looks like he's going to go for the chicken right now.
C: *Liver?*
C: *Can they eat liver?*
T: Can they eat liver, M—? What did you catch yours on? (Reference to child's earlier statement that he had used liver as bait when he went fishing.)[10]

What characteristics of this activity foster the children's exploration and curiosity questioning and might serve as guidelines for us?

1. *The experience is novel, yet the children can relate it to other experiences they have had.* It is sometimes difficult to hit an appropriate balance between the novel and the familiar. Curiosity is apparently stimulated by novelty (Berlyne 1965) rather than by what is quite routine; yet if the experience is too novel—too "far out" from children's experience—they can't relate to it at all and thus don't wonder about it. This science lesson hits that "delicate

[10]I am indebted to Dr. John Huntsberger, a superb teacher from the University of Texas, for allowing me to use this episode.

balance"; the experience is novel in that the children have not actually handled and investigated a live crayfish before, yet it clearly relates to experiences these California children have had fishing, seeing shellfish for sale, buying and eating seafood of different kinds, and watching shellfish on the beach. The experience is intriguing, yet it connects with the theories the children are constructing. It can be integrated there; it has the potential for children making sense of it.

2. *The activity invites real involvement through direct experiencing.* A lesson in which the teacher and children had talked about crayfish without crayfish actually being present would have stimulated fewer curiosity questions from the children. Even a lesson in which crayfish were present but the children couldn't touch them would have been less conducive to children's questioning. The direct experiencing in this lesson led to very close observation that triggered some important questions: "Do they bite?" (a question you're especially likely to ask if you're about to pick one up). "Is that behind his tail some legs . . .?" "How could you tell which one's a girl or a boy?" "How much do they weigh?" "What are these other legs for?" "Where does it eat?" "How come it never eats?" "Can they eat liver?"

3. *The objective of the lesson is to stimulate children's interest and involvement, rather than to pass on a particular body of information.* David Hawkins (1965) talks of the importance of children's "messing about" as they build understanding. This crayfish lesson was designed to provide a messing-about experience. As we all know, the goal we have in mind (or the objective we have written down) for a lesson strongly influences the teaching procedures we use. The goal here was for the children to explore. Therefore, children's moves in an exploratory direction were encouraged.

4. *The group of children involved in the experience was small.* Groups of four to six children tend to work best in such an activity. Groups smaller than four allow for less of an "idea pool" and thus offer less opportunity for children to learn from each other and to trigger each other's questions. When groups get larger than six, they tend to become less interactive and require more in the way of external controls; there is less initiating and responding conversationally, and more raising of hands, being officially recognized, and spouting an opinion; it becomes more of a performer-audience situation and members participate less spontaneously. Different size groups are appropriate for different purposes, of course, but for experiences in which we want to maximize children's interacting in an exploratory, questioning experience, groups of four to six work well.

5. *The experience invites flexibility in student input, rather than following a narrow predetermined course.* In the course of the lesson, children hit on a variety of interesting areas—what crayfish eat, how they move, whether they bite, how males and females differ anatomically, whether people can eat them, what functions the legs serve, how much they weigh. The various interests they indicate through their comments and questions, the teacher follows up on until some children are focusing on and drawing the structure of the crayfish, some are feeding it a variety of foods and observing its response, some are watching and describing the crayfish's movement on their arms. This flexibility provides a richness that will stimulate further questioning and interaction among the children.

What important things does the teacher do to foster the children's curiosity questioning here?

6. *The teacher prepares beforehand for flexibility—multidirectionality.* Clearly this relates to item 5 above: The flexibility in student input didn't just magically happen; the teacher prepared for it. The teacher had thought through and provided for some interesting areas he thought might arise, and he was ready with various food items, Magic Markers, sheets of newsprint, and an appropriate task in response to the sex differences question. He went into this lesson with a lot "at the ready," but knowing that it was only a beginning, that the children would move in some unexpected directions, and that it would be important to support their moves.

7. *The teacher interacts with the children as an interested participant more than as a director or controller.* This lesson is a balanced interaction in the sense that all participants, including the teacher, both initiate and respond. The teacher doesn't feel he has to be the one to respond to everything every child says. Often one child responds to another. The children know that their actions, comments, and questions are interesting and of value to the teacher by the ways in which he responds to and uses their contributions and exploratory activities: Sometimes the response is direct praise ("that's good," "good observation," "excellent, excellent"); sometimes it is using the child's comment or action as the basis of his next question or suggestion ("What does that feel like when you're picking him up, S—?" "How do you know he wants to bite?" "Yuck? What do you mean by that?" "Can they eat liver, M—? What did you catch yours on?"). Throughout, one has a sense of all group members participating together in an experience that is interesting and enjoyable to them all. Of course, many clues to the teacher's interested participation are evident on the videotape but cannot be captured in print—the interest conveyed by his tone of voice; the enjoyment conveyed by his laughter; the involvement signaled by his body language, moving or inclining toward a child, touching a child, establishing and maintaining eye contact. One senses a structure in the experience that evolves from the interested participation of all, including the teacher, rather than a structure set by the teacher's direction.

8. *The teacher conveys an attitude of an ongoing learner, rather than one who is all-knowing.* His talk and his actions suggest that he places a higher priority on learning and discovering in process than on simply demonstrating the knowledge one already possesses. It would be easy to simply give information in this situation. But the teacher's attitude is one of ongoing learning. He often leads the children to do the learning, rather than simply telling them things: "How would you do that?" "How would you find out?" "How do you know?" "How do you know he wants to bite?" "That's something you might want to investigate." "I'm going to tell you that there are four boys in there and one girl, and you tell me how you can tell them apart." "What have you decided about your crayfish?" "What did you observe him doing?" "Would you like to try a piece of cheese and see if they eat cheese?" "How would you find out where it eats?" When he does provide information directly, it often serves as the basis for further explanation. It is the ongoingness, the learning process, that is top priority.

9. *The teacher's questions emphasize higher-level cognitive involvement.* The teacher's questions invite the children to participate cognitively at higher levels than the level of rote recall or basic comprehension. The children are encouraged to observe, compare, apply, hypothesize, predict, test, and synthesize. Higher-level cognitive questions generally encourage greater involvement from the children, and it is when children are most actively involved mentally that they use their language most powerfully for learning.

I find as I interact with groups of children who are involved in activities that the two words which are magic words for me are "I wonder": "I wonder how come . . .," "I wonder why it doesn't . . . ," "I wonder what would happen if you . . ." For me personally, these two words work; they feel right. Sometimes they stimulate a wondering in a child, something she might not have thought of if I hadn't wondered out loud. Sometimes they don't and I know it's time for me to be quiet and leave the child alone. But at the very least, "I wonder" helps to establish that I am a wondering woman with a head full of intriguing questions, rather than Wonder Woman who has all the solutions. My guess is (and it is only a guess, though the question is a testable one) that those classrooms in which teachers ask a higher proportion of genuine curiosity questions and do a lot of wondering are those classrooms in which the children ask a higher proportion of curiosity questions too. By overtly demonstrating a wondering attitude, the teacher tells the children, "This classroom is a place for the open expression of curiosity—for questioning to better comprehend and learn, a place for our 'probing into the working of the world.' "

Finally

A teacher was having a conversation with her kindergarten students about *The Three Bears.*

T: What sort of girl is Goldilocks?
ANDREW: She's curious.
T: What does "curious" mean?
ANDREW: That you get into trouble. (Paley 1984, p. 51)

When we teach with our own sense of wonder still alive, we tell Andrew and his classmates, in the most powerful way possible, that "curious" does *not* mean "you get into trouble." Quite the opposite. "Curious" means what we are and do and express in "the place called school."

SUGGESTED PROJECTS

1. *A study of children's classroom questions.* In a classroom setting, collect the questions you hear children ask. One way to do this is to write each question on a separate index card, along with any relevant information (situation in which it was asked, to whom it was addressed). This allows for easy sorting and categorizing later. What

types of questions are the children asking? Procedural, curiosity, and social-interactional categories may be helpful ones to use (see p. 288), but don't hesitate to set up your own categories on the basis of the questions you gather. What differences, if any, do you notice between the kinds of questions children are asking each other and the kinds they ask the teacher; between the questions children ask in large-group settings and in small-group settings; between the questions children ask in formal and in informal settings in the classroom; between the questions asked by children at different grade levels (kindergartners versus third graders)? Do you notice differences in the questions children of the same grade level ask in different classrooms with different teachers? You can probably think of many interesting ways to refine this project to be carried out by two or three people, for example, each one focusing on the children's questioning in different types of activities in the same classroom, or each focusing on the questioning of children with different teachers at the same grade level, or each focusing on children's questioning at a different grade level. Where you find differences, how can you describe these, and, more important, how would you (tentatively) account for them? What in the situation is encouraging or hindering children's questioning of different kinds?

2. *Designing and implementing exploratory experiences.* Working alone or with one or two others, plan and carry out an experience or a series of experiences with children in a classroom setting, in which you deliberately incorporate the nine characteristics cited in this chapter as contributing to children's exploration and curiosity questioning. Tape the children as they engage in the experience(s) you have planned. Transcribe your tape and analyze it. To what extent and in what ways did the children get involved in exploring and expressing this through language? How can you account for this? What new directions did the children think of in their encounter with the experience(s), and how could you help them follow their new-found interests in subsequent experiences? What would you do differently if you were to involve children in this experience or sequence of experiences again? You might want to compare your results here with an analysis of transcribed tapes of children of comparable age engaging in an experience in the same content area (say, a science activity) in some other classroom with a different teacher. Did you hear more of the language of exploration and discovery and curiosity from your children as a result of your having deliberately planned for it? If not, why not? What other factors might be important?

3. *Children's perceptions of school learning.* Ask school children "How do you learn (things) in school?" Write down their responses verbatim and study them. It is important that the children you ask not think of you as a teacher. If they do, they are likely to give you teacher-pleasing replies, so don't use children who know you are (becoming) a teacher. (In fact, you might want to try using a child as the "fieldworker" who asks other children and records their replies.) What you want is honesty—as true as possible a picture of in-school learning as the *children* perceive it. It might be fun to extend this project in various ways: Ask the same children how they learn things *outside* of school, or ask the teachers of the children and maybe the principal also, "How do children learn in your classroom/school?" Or ask adults how they learned things at school when they were kids and, perhaps, how they learn things now that they are adults. You can see what comparison possibilities there might be here: children's perceptions of learning in and out of school; children's perceptions of school learning and teachers'/principal's perceptions; adults' perceptions of their remembered experiences and children's perceptions. You can doubtless think of further ways to extend this and make it more interesting to you.

Generally speaking, the greater the variety of children you ask (various ages, various types of school setting), the more interesting your responses are likely to be.

4. *A case study of language in learning.* Study the way one child uses language for learning. A child of any age will do, but choose one who is talkative. (Children who are more quiet are just as likely to be using language in their learning, but for this project you need a child you can *hear*.) Follow this child, either taping or writing bits of his or her interaction with others in typical daily situations (a bit from morning preparation-for-school routine, a bit from breakfast, a bit from the morning car ride to school, a bit from structured class discussion, a bit from informal class activity, a bit from recess or lunch, a bit from after-school play, a bit from evening family time). Your goal here is to sample the child's interaction in various typical daily situations and to observe and describe the ways the child uses language for learning throughout the day. Don't let yourself get overwhelmed with masses and masses of taped segments to deal with. Just select representative samples to deal with in depth. It is likely that you will want to enlist the child's parents to help you in taping some of the segments in the home.

5. *A study of language for learning in the classroom.* Working individually or as a small group, tape three or four different types of classroom episodes (for example, teacher with whole group, guest speaker with whole group, aide or parent volunteer with individual child, children working together on a project that involves conversation, teacher or aide or visiting adult with small group of children). Look for instances of children using their language for learning through (1) questioning, (2) focusing attention, (3) making understandings more precise, (4) making understandings more retrievable, (5) reinterpreting past experience, and (6) going beyond present personal experience. (It might be helpful for you to review pages 263-271 here.) Transcribe only those portions of the tapes that demonstrate such langauge use in action. Which of these learning-oriented functions of language occurred most? Least? Not at all? Why (not)? How might these be encouraged further? Your discussion can take a number of directions, but the major purpose of the activity is to increase your ability to *hear* language for learning when its going on.

6. *Children's interests and language experience.* If you are currently working with a class or group of children, get some index cards and write one child's name on each card. Then, below the child's name, list three special interests of that particular child. It is likely, at this point, that you will need to observe your children more closely for awhile in order to come up with three interests for each one. (This in itself is helpful, as it will clue you in to which of your children are "blending into the woodwork.") After you have at least three special interests listed for each child, think of some language experience that you can provide and help each child move into that relates to one of the three interests you have listed. Write down your ideas, one on the back of each child's card. Implement as many of these ideas as you can. Which of the ideas turn out to be on target? Which ones simply miss? Why? How does your original idea change when the child gets involved? How does it expand— for this child? For other children who join in? What might you do next?

7. *Adults' remembered elementary school experiences.* Interview a variety of adults about the most meaningful positive experience(s) they remember from their own elementary school days. You might want to focus on some particular area of interest to you (for example, reading and writing experiences) or just leave it open ended: "I'd like you to just think for a few minutes about your own elementary school days, and

then—when you're ready—describe some experience (or maybe several) that you had in elementary school that was really positive and important to you." Are there some recurrent themes or common elements in the experiences that the adults give? (When my students and I have done this, for example, some recurrent themes in the experiences given have been the feeling of being competent, the feeling of being individually special to the teacher or other children, and the opportunity to freely select or shape an experience or activity.) What kinds of activities or experiences are not mentioned at all? Obviously, many variations on this basic project idea are possible: for example, having class members all contribute personal remembered experiences and then, as a class, look for common themes; having adults write (rather than tell) brief descriptions of their selected experience(s); combining with several friends or classmates on this project, each of you interviewing several adults and then combining your results; selecting a particular population to interview (elementary school teachers, perhaps, or equal numbers of high school students and individuals over sixty-five).

8. *"Your own thing."* Design your own learning experience relating to the ideas in this section, discuss it with your instructor and/or an acquaintance knowledgeable in this area, and execute it.

SUGGESTED FURTHER READINGS

BRITTON, J., *Language and Learning*. Hammondsworth, England: Pelican Books, 1973.
CALKINS, L.M., *The Art of Teaching Writing*. Portsmouth, N.H.: Heinemann Educational Books, 1986.
DONALDSON, M., *Children's Minds*. New York: W.W. Norton & Company, 1979.
GORDON, J.W., *My Country School Diary*. New York: Dell Publishing Co., Inc., 1970.
HOLT, J., *What Do I Do Monday?* New York: E. P. Dutton, 1970.
KOHL, H., *On Teaching*. New York: Schocken Books, Inc., 1976.
ROSEN, C., AND H. ROSEN, *The Language of Primary School Children*. London: Penquin Education for the Schools Council, 1973.
SMITH, F., *Comprehension and Learning: A Conceptual Framework for Teachers*. New York: Holt, Rinehart and Winston, Inc., 1975.
Issues of *Language Arts* that relate to the ideas in Section 3 include vol. 60, no. 6 (September 1983): "Language across the Curriculum"; vol. 62, no. 1 (January 1985): "Making Meaning, Learning Language"; vol. 62, no. 3 (March 1984): "Responding to What Kids Are Trying to Do."

11

Communicative Competence

We know that as speakers of a language we have linguistic competence; that is, we know a deep system of principles for organizing sentences. These principles enable us to create and to interpret novel sentences in our language. We explored this knowledge of linguistic structure (linguistic competence) in Section One, and we explored its acquisition in children in Section Two.

But our competence in language far exceeds our knowledge of the narrow bounds of linguistic structure. We have *communicative competence* as well as linguistic competence—we know how to interact, how to communicate with one another appropriately in various situations, and how to make sense of what others say and do in communication situations. The business of communicating is not as simple as it seems. Our conversations are guided by organizational principles just as "out of awareness, yet deeply binding" (Schegloff 1972, p. 347) as those that govern our creation of novel sentences. Almost every uttered grammatical sentence is for speaker and hearer, a novel one, but it falls within the set of organizational principles for that language. So almost every conversation is new for the participants, yet it falls within the set of principles for appropriate and socially interpretable communication. Every conversation rests on underlying principles of organization known to participants.

Just as virtually every child develops linguistic competence, so every child develops communicative competence and, in fact, develops them together. Linguistic competence can be considered a part of communicative competence: In order to communicate adequately, producing and

[1]The term "communicative competence" is attributed to Hymes (1974), a sociolinguist who has been important in describing and stressing the importance of the role of situational factors in communication.

318

interpreting language appropriate to various social situations, one of the things the conversational participants must be able to do is structure sentences according to the linguistic rules of their language community. But they do far more than this when they communicate. What is the nature of the adult's communicative competence, his knowledge of how communication proceeds and of the complex interaction of speech and social situation? This knowledge is a major aspect of every child's language development. In this chapter we will explore what some important aspects of the adult's communicative competence are and how the child acquires them.

What are some of the underlying rules we, as adults, know for socially appropriate interaction? Put another way, what does our communicative competence (knowledge of appropriate interaction) include, that children ultimately acquire? And if these principles, or rules, are unconscious, how do we know they exist at all?

You remember that we were able, in Section One, to recognize some sentences as grammatical—as being in accordance with the structural principles of our language—and others as ungrammatical, not in accordance with those principles. Well, the situation is analogous in the area of our communicative competence: We are able to recognize some talk in conversatons as being appropriate, and other talk as being inappropriate.[2] To say that talk is appropriate or inappropriate is to say, among other things, that it either does or does not conform to the expectations we have for how conversation sequences proceed. Let's look at a few examples.

Two adults are standing in a cafeteria line. The first wants veal cutlet and finds there is none. He turns to the second adult and says, "Every time I come here they seem to be out of the veal cutlet." Now put an asterisk beside every one of the following responses that would be inappropriate for the second adult to make.

1. Well have you tried the fish? *That's* awfully good.
2. Tuesday I leave for Chicago.
3. Johnny's mumps are almost gone.
4. Just your luck, huh?
5. I have that problem with their cheesecake.

It is 7:30 A.M. and the phone rings. Adult answers it and says, "Hello?" Now put an asterisk beside the following responses that would be inappropriate.

1. Hi, d'I get ya' outta bed?
2. Hello, Tom?
3. How 'bout Saturday?

[2]Throughout this discussion, I am assuming that the conversational participants are English speakers with an Anglo cultural background. As specifics of linguistic competence differ from one language community to another, so specifics of communicative competence (rules for appropriate communication behavior) differ from one culture to another. I am also focusing on speech as the expressive medium, though the factors discussed here hold for other expressive channels as well (for example, writing, sign).

4. Hello. I'd to speak with Ms. Johnson please.
5. It's up to 75 now.

There is no problem with the linguistic structure of the sentences you asterisked. The problem with them is that they do not *fit* at this point in these conversations. Your ability to identify conversational responses that do and do not fit in conversational sequences is evidence of your knowledge of what to expect in conversation. What principles that we know and are drawing on are being violated here? The problem with 2 and 3 in the first example is that they are not topically relevant. The first speaker has initiated a topic and we expect that the subsequent comment will be topically related to it. Topical relevance is a guiding conversational principle for us, and we recognize when it is violated. In items 3 and 5 in the second example, the speaker has left the initial greeting ("Hello?") unresponded to. Our expectation with greetings is that they occur in pairs; each partner greets the other (these patterns are particularly conventionalized in telephone conversations). Can you describe what is communicatively inappropriate in the following incidents?

Six-year-old Michael calls up and adult answers phone.

ADULT: Hello?
MICHAEL: Is George there? (George is adult's son.)
ADULT: No.
MICHAEL: Bye.

Fifteen minutes later the phone rings again.

ADULT: Hello?
MICHAEL: C'n you tell me where he is?

A and B are in a room that is very hot and stuffy. The only window in the room is closed. A says, "Boy, we need some fresh air in here" and walks toward the window with arms outstretched, ready to open it. B says to A, "Would you please open the window?"

In the first example, we know, as Michael apparently does not, that certain relevant information has to be provided before his question, "C'n you tell me where he is?" fits. And the interaction between A and B is strange because we share the underlying assumption that we make a verbal request only in a situation where the action wouldn't be likely to occur unless we asked for it. In the incident given, the action (opening the window) is already going to happen, and so requesting it makes no sense—no communication sense, that is.

Consider one more example. You see a sign, "Free Puppy," and go to the door and inquire. The puppy owner brings a reasonable enough looking puppy and says, "He's really adorable. He's so cute—we just love him. He's cuddly and has the cutest way of looking at you. He's friendly and lovable . . ." Why is it that, after a few minutes of this, you find yourself thinking, "I wonder why this fellow is so eager to dump this puppy? It must be a real loser." It is because you have an expectation that a person will respond to your inquiry in a way that is informative but will not overwhelm you in the amount of talk. If the appropriate amount is exceeded, you suspect some further meaning in the situation. In short, we know when principles of appropriate communication have been violated. We could not be aware of rule violations without "knowing" those rules at some (usually unconscious) level.

Further evidence for the existence and nature of our comunicative competence comes from our "repair" of conversational problems when they occur. For example, in our culture we expect a summons to get an answer. When it doesn't, we attempt to repair the conversational break-down, for example, by repeating the summons louder.

Bill?

(Pause)

BILL? (louder)

It is a general guiding principle of conversation that one person speaks at a time. When two people speak at the same time, they may fix it up in some way so the conversation can proceed as it should: One speaker may stop in mid sentence to let the other continue with his turn, or one speaker (or both) may say "Excuse me" and stop talking so the other can continue. One may say loudly, *"I'm not finished,"* meaning "I am the one who is talking now so you be quiet," or he may simply keep talking in a loud voice, asserting himself over the partner. In any case, participants often move to repair the violated principle of one speaker at a time. The opposite of too many speakers at a time is silence, that is, too few speakers at a time (none). You've doubtless noticed how interactants will often fill silences with inane drivel, rather than endure the silence, especially on the phone where there are no visual supports to the conversation and the voice is the only channel. This is another instance of repair. We know that in conversation slight pauses are acceptable, but periods of silence are not and they make us uncomfortable. Notice that we could not actually say how many seconds an "acceptable" silence is, but we and our conversational partner both know this at an intuitive level.

Also, speakers of a language recognize sentences that are communicatively ambiguous, just as they recognize sentences that are structurally or semantically ambiguous (remember "Visiting relatives can be a nuisance"?). Can you find the ambiguity in the accompanying cartoon?

BORN LOSER—By Art Sansom

© 1977 Newspaper Enterprise Association, Inc.

There is no question at the level of linguistic structure about how to interpret the girl's "You know what's nice about you?" But there are clearly two possible interpretations relating to the communicative intent of the utterance. Is the question to be interpreted as a preface to a compliment (the boy's interpretation) or as an information-seeking utterance (the girl's interpretation)? Here is a single utterance that can serve more than one function in the communication situation.

We can also be sure that we know and use underlying communication principles because we can deliberately alter them to change people's speaking behavior in predictable ways. We probably do this unconsciously more than we realize. If, for example, we want a shy child to talk more in conversation with us, we will probably alter our own speaking so as to encourage the child to take more and longer conversational turns. We may use more questions, more open questions, more invitations ("Tell me about—") than we normally would, and we may do less of taking long turns of information giving.

However, the most dramatic example of the deliberate manipulating of the communication situation to alter speaking behavior that I know of comes from the work of Labov and Robins (Labov 1970). These researchers, studying the dialect of Harlem preteenagers, got their subjects to produce vigorous interactive and diverse speech in large amounts by manipulating social aspects of the communication situation. "Large friendly white interviewers" interviewing similar subjects in formal settings had reported these children to be "nonverbal" or, at best, single-word mumblers (Bereiter and Engelmann 1966). By changing aspects of the social situation, Labov and Robins elicited very different speaking behavior from their subjects. The "large friendly white interviewer" was replaced by a black one from the neighborhood (Robins), who sat informally on the floor; the "interviewer" had brought along potato chips to make the atmosphere more "party-ish" than "interview-ish"; the interviewer talked with a pair of children who were good friends, instead of bringing children in to converse with him one at a time; and the "interviewer" initiated taboo topics into the conversation to show that one could say anything in the situation. In short, the researchers had provided a situation that encouraged conversaton in these children. Presto, change-o! "Nonverbal" children were suddenly competing for the floor, jesting, arguing, initiating, and responding with gusto. There was no magic here. The fact that we can deliberately manipulate aspects of the social situation to influence speaking behavior in predictable ways attests to the presence of powerful rules relating social situation and speaking behavior, and to our knowledge of such rules.

Perhaps the most important and the most easily overlooked evidence for our knowledge of principles that guide our communication with others in our language community is the fact that we constantly communicate with a high degree of success and usually with considerable ease. Communication is a cooperative effort on the part of two or more people. Together, by following the same guiding principles for communication, the participants negotiate conversations, initiating and responding, in patterned, nonrandom ways. This would not be possible if they did not know and use shared rules for appropriate communication behavior.

We have looked at only a few examples here in order to help you explore and begin to feel the reality of your communicative competence. We know that we have a deep knowledge of how to communicate with others appropriately, because (1) we know when communication principles are broken, (2) when they are broken we attempt to repair them, (3) we recognize language situations that are communicatively ambiguous, (4) we are able to deliberately alter situations so as to effect change in participants' speaking behavior, and (5) most important of all, we *communicate* creatively and with a high degree of success. It is no wonder that vigorous study is currently under way of how people communicate with each other in real situations. We have always known that language exists for the purpose of communication. Conversation has been likened to a game. It proceeds according to certain "rules." However, unlike most games, the goal is not to win but to keep the ball in play. Partners in a conversation attempt to assure comprehension and to sustain the conversation. This is the communication game.

Researchers are attempting to understand and describe both the "context-free" and the "context-sensitive" aspects of communication—that is, the general, overall organizational structure and dynamics of communication events (context-free) and also the ways in which people's style of expression changes in response to each particular social situation (context-sensitive) (Sacks, Schegloff, and Jefferson 1974, p. 700). The exciting research of the past several decades has increased our understanding and awareness of many aspects of communication, among them (1) the purposeful nature of language in communication, (2) the underlying principles governing the structure and dynamics of communication events, and (3) the variation in discourse styles that is a part of one's communicative competence. The remainder of this chapter deals with these three aspects of communicative competence and their development in children.

THE PURPOSEFUL NATURE OF LANGUAGE

Communication is purposeful. Every day, as we go about our business and our play, we are doing things through language. We don't simply emit verbal noises and written squiggles; rather, we coax, comfort, cajole, emote, jest, threaten, argue, request, justify, scold, greet, question, challenge, inform, assert, and so on. We use our verbal and written forms to express some content, and generally do so in ways that are guided by the principles of linguistic structure in our language. But basic to all our interaction and giving it purpose and shape is a host of communication intentions. These intentions are its reason(s) for being. Our verbal utterances and written symbols are *forms* (linguistically acceptable expressions of semantic content)

expressing diverse communication *functions* (what we accomplish in inter-action through the use of language forms).

The form-function distinction is an important one. Obviously in actual communication the two necessarily occur together: We use certain linguistic *forms* to express certain *functions*. But it is instructive to consider form and function separately as components of communicating.

FORM	FUNCTION
(what X is saying)	(what X is doing in the communication by saying it)
X says "I'm sorry."	X is apologizing.
X says "I wasn't listening."	X is explaining (justifying).

What can you do with these? Study each brief example and complete the function column as indicated.[3] (After completing these fifteen items, you may want to compare your responses with a friend's.)

FORM	FUNCTION
1. (Father and ten-year-old daughter are standing beside hungry-looking dog) Father says, *"Betsy, have you fed Bruno yet?"*	Father is _____-ing.
2. (Impatiently, to noisy third-grade class) Teacher says, *"Well, do you want to go out for recess or don't you?"*	Teacher is _____-ing.
3. (First adult is in room. Second adult enters from outside, roasted and sweaty) First adult says, *"Hot, huh?"*	First adult is _____-ing.
4. (Twelve-year-old girl, her mother, and her friend. Mother has	

---

[3]Express the function(s) you recognize in whatever way you can. Your particular choice of terms is not important. The format: "X" is —ing" is used here simply to focus your attention on the function being an *action*.

FORM

said daughter can't go to party that evening) Daughter says to her friend, *"Your mother is letting you go, isn't she, Janet?"*

5. (Two adult males on telephone. They have already agreed to meet the next morning to play golf) One says to the other, *"Meet 'ya at 10:00, then."*

6. (Adult to adult) Adult says, *"C'mon over for dinner around 7:00."*

7. (Five-foot-tall wife is stretching to reach a glass on high kitchen shelf. Six-foot husband is standing beside her) Wife says, *"Oh, I just can't reach it."*

8. (Sixteen-year-old girl's boyfriend arrives to take her to a movie) Girl says, *"Hi."*

9. (Mother and eighteen-month-old son) Mother says, *"Where's your nose?"*

10. (Teacher and first-grade class) Teacher says, *"I just can't fool you today, can I?"*

11. (Two children) First child says, *"Knock knock."* Second child says, *"Who's there?"*

12. (Two nine-year-olds on school playground) First says, *"Wanna fight?!"*

13. (Mother fixing dinner. Six-year-old son enters kitchen) Son says, *"YECH! That stinks!"*

14. (Kindergartner and teacher) Kindergartner says *"Know what?"*

15. (Family eating dinner at restaurant. Thirteen-year-old sister tells eleven-year-old brother, "You have watermelon all over your shirt. You got it all wet.") Brother shrugs and says, *"So what's new?"*

FUNCTION

Daughter is _____-ing.

Adult is _____-ing.

Adult is _____-ing.

Wife is _____-ing.

Girl is _____ing.

Mother is _____-ing.

Teacher is _____-ing.

Children are _____-ing.

Child is _____-ing.

Son is _____-ing.

Kindergartner is _____-ing.

Brother is _____-ing.[4]

[4]The examples here are from conversation. You might want to go back over the functions that you have written in and think of situations in which each function might be carried out in writing, for example, situations in which one might apologize, explain, request, threaten, and so on, in writing. If you do this with several others, you're likely to come up with a more interesting variety of situations than you could think of on your own.

Our responses in conversation indicate that we understand and respond to speakers' intentions (the communication function of utterances) as well as to their forms. Take the first item in the preceding list as an example. The father is requesting (function) by using an interrogative (question) form. Interrogative forms generally get answers. But if Betsy responded to the form *only*,—if she said "No" (answer) and walked away— her response would be inappropriate. Betsy knows this. Betsy will respond to the father's request function. She may reply

Ooooops, I forgot. I'll do it now.
No, but I'll do it as soon as I finish my math homework.
Nope. We're out of dog food.
No, it's Joey's turn. I fed Bruno yesterday.
Will you please stop bugging me about that!

Whether she agrees to comply with the request or provides an explanation for not complying or expresses annoyance at the request, her response will indicate her awareness that the father has made a request. And it is the *request*, the function of the utterance, that she responds to.

Sometimes the verb in a sentence explicitly names the function of the utterance:

To say "I dare you"   is to accomplish the act of daring
To say "I challenge you"   is to accomplish the act of challenging
To say "I move that X"   is to accomplish the act of moving (making a motion)
To say "I second it"   is to accomplish the act of seconding
To say "I bet five dollars" is to accomplish the act of betting
To say "I promise"   is to accomplish the act of promising
To say "I assert X"   is to accomplish the act of asserting
To say "I beg you"   is to accomplish the act of begging
To say "I advocate X"   is to accomplish the act of advocating
To say "I propose that X" is to accomplish the act of proposing
To say "I sentence you..." is to accomplish the act of sentencing

And what about these: "I now *pronounce* you man and wife" and "And thereto I *plight* thee my troth"—not forms we use often to be sure, but forms in which the verb names the function accomplished by their being uttered. By saying, "I now pronounce you man and wife," the state of two people is changed; they become man and wife because they were "pronounced" man and wife. By saying, "And thereto I plight thee my troth," a promise is made (a troth is plighted?). You may receive a "summons" in the mail: The written words "The court summons you to appear" accomplishes the act of summoning. More often, however, the forms we use do not explicitly name their function as they accomplish it, but they just as surely carry out diverse functions. For example, I am inviting you to my party regardless of whether I say, "I invite you to my party" or "Hey, I'm having a party Friday. Can you come?" or whether I send you an invitation by mail that reads, "You are invited" or "Y' all come."[5] In all our communication with others, we intend to carry out some purpose. When we talk and write, we don't just *say* things, we *do* things with our words (Austin 1962).

ORGANIZATION OF COMMUNICATION EVENTS

An interaction is a cooperative activity among two or more people. The participants together (for example, several speakers; speaker or writer and audience) construct "text" (a conversation, a written piece). Interaction proceeds smoothly for the most part because the participants know how conversation and written discourse work.[6] Interestingly, and frustratingly, though participants "know" how interaction works (that is, they are able to negotiate sequences that accomplish their purposes), sociolinguists are still struggling to understand and describe that intuitive knowledge. We have as yet no comprehensive theory of oral and written discourse. Different researchers have focused on different aspects of communication. In the literature, one encounters different and sometimes conflicting perspectives and can come away with a bits-and-pieces feeling about this work. We still do not know how the various pieces will ultimately fit together to form a comprehensive theory. However, some of the bits and pieces have contributed significant insights in their own right. Some of the pieces important for us here include (1) the study of turn taking in communication events; (2) the positing of underlying principles that participants adhere to, such as truthfulness or relevance; (3) the positing of situational conditions for the performance of speech acts; and (4) the analysis of the structure and dynamics of communication events.

Turn Taking

Turn taking is a fundamental principle in conversation: "Turn taking seems a basic form of organization for conversation" (Sacks, Schlegloff, and Jefferson 1974, p. 700). Participants know how to initiate a conversation, taking a first turn that begins a turn-taking sequence; they know how to get a turn and how to execute a turn appropriately—how to speak relevantly, informatively, and for an acceptable length of time; they know how to pass a turn to someone else. They share the same conversational ideal that one person speaks at a time and that there should be few (if any) awkward silences, those periods with no speakers. But they also know how to violate this ideal without jeopardizing the conversation. For example, they know how and how much and at what points they can overlap each other's speech while still maintaining the interacation. You're probably quite familiar with conversations in which the two partners know each

---

[5]Different researchers have categorized language functions in different ways. For a look at some different category schemes, you might want to see Halliday 1973, Jakobson 1960, Tough 1977, and Kinneavy 1971.

[6]"Discourse" refers to stretches of language consisting of more than a single sentence.

other very well and each "knows" (or thinks he does) what the other is likely to say. The one partner may "chime in" on the end of the speaker's turn, saying along with the speaker what he "knows" the speaker is going to say; or he may start his response to the speaker before the speaker is finished, again anticipating what the speaker is going to say. (You may also be aware that this is sometimes annoying, and that—as teachers—we may do this to children more than we care to admit.) Sometimes the listener offers support and encouragement with soft "um-hms" and "yeahs" (and nonverbal signals too), given while the partner is speaking. These are violations of the one-speaker-at-a-time principle, but they are acceptable.

Conversational participants know how to introduce new topics at appropriate places in the conversation, how to move into and carry out a closing (for example, in a phone conversation), and when to begin a closing sequence rather than initiate a new conversational topic. This complex knowledge that we generally take for granted is quite remarkable. You can see that without cooperation and finely coordinated moves among the participants this complex communication that we routinely engage in every day could not occur. The flow of conversation requires each interactant to move—initiate and respond—appropriately and typically each interactant does, precisely because he shares with the others an understanding of how turn sequences are executed.

The necessity for cooperation and shared knowledge of communication rules among conversationalists is especially obvious in what some researchers have called the "adjacency pair," conversational exchanges that typically (though not always) have two parts, such as greeting-greeting, offer-acceptance or refusal, and (the teacher's favorite) question-answer. It can be disconcerting when in conversation we give the first part of a pair but our conversational partner does not respond with the second part. In fact, this is sometimes deliberately done in an effort to tease or annoy, as, for example, when one child asks another child a question and the second child repeats it as part of the age-old I'm-going-to-repeat-everything-you-say game instead of responding, as expected, with an answer.

Underlying Principles

Grice has pointed out some "maxims" that are part of the set of cooperative principles of conversation that speakers adhere to (Grice 1975). One of these is the "quantity" maxim: "Make your [conversational] contribution as informative as is required (for the current purposes of the exchange)" but "Do not make your contribution more informative than is required" (p. 45). This relates to the free-puppy example given earlier; we expect speakers to provide information in their turn, but overdoing it (violating the quantity rule) may make us suspect some further, hidden meaning.

Grice also suggests a "quality" maxim: "Do not say what you believe to be false" and "Do not say that for which you lack adequate evidence" (p. 46). We assume that we and our conversational partners are speaking the truth unless some indication is given to the contrary—for example, telling a joke or deliberately exaggerating for effect or using metaphor or being ironic. In all these cases it is usually clear that we are suspending the "truth" principle, often from the situational context itself, but sometimes from indications we give verbally (like using our voices in special ways). When we, or our partner, talk about things for which we lack adequate evidence (gossip?), we may mark this verbally in some way, as in, "Well, I didn't actually see this, but Rhonda said that Glenn, . . ." Bates gives this example of how we interpret conversation in a special way when it violates the truth principle.

> If I have just come home from walking through a torrential rain and my spouse says to me *You look terrific*, we both know that the utterance is not true. Because the sentence is false, and we both know it to be false, and because we assume that there is a conversational rule against blatant falsehoods, the sentence serves in this context as an ironic statement that I am soaking wet and look horrible. When the truth maxim is deliberately violated, we ascribe some special meaning to the speaker's utterance. (Bates 1976, p. 28)

A third maxim is that speakers will be relevant in their contributions. In the earlier examples you identified some responses that were inappropriate in that they were irrelevant at that point in the conversation. Here is another example demonstrating the strong influence the principle relevance exerts as we intrepret conversationalists' meanings.

> A woman at a bus stop says to me *Do you know what time it is?* There is a conversational rule which says that speakers do not request irrelevant information from their listeners, and I know that my own knowledge of the time is in itself irrelevant to the stranger waiting for a bus. I therefore conclude from this clear violation that the woman wants more than she has actually requested. I cannot simply answer *Yes I do know*. I must also add *It is 4:30*. (Bates 1976, p. 28)

As with the quantity and quality (truth) principles, so with the relevance principle. When the principle is violated in conversation, we "read" more and other meanings into the situation; we assume that more is implied than is explicitly verbalized. Also, notice that when we intend to make a conversational contribution that is not relevant to the preceding one, we often preface it by saying something like "Well, not to change the subject but"—and then we change the subject. We are acknowledging that we know that we are expected to contribute in a way which is relevant to what has preceded, but that we are choosing to set this principle aside at the moment in order to steer the conversation in a different direction. Notice, too, that we will abruptly change topics like this only at certain points in the conversation. We would not, for example, be likely to make an abrupt topic change if the preceding turn was the first part of an adjacency pair or if the partner's topic had just gotten started.

Grice's final maxim deals with the conversationalist's manner of speaking. We expect participants to be clear and comprehensible when they talk. If they are not, we repair the problem with devices such as inserting questions or requests for clarification: "*Who* was it who said that?" "Huh?" "Don't you mean a Rabbit, not a Dasher?" or even "Wait a minute. You've lost me. Go back over it again." And we frequently insert comprehension checks: "Ya see?" "Got it?" "Okay?"

Grice's maxims, though suggested to account for some important aspects of conversation, may also relate to written discourse. Quantity: In writing as in speech, we expect the text to be appropriately informative and we recognize when the author is providing "too much" and when "too little." (Though we may individually make different judgments as to amount, we each will make *some* judgment; we each have an appropriate-amount expectation). And in writing as in speech, the amount needed to "get the job done" differs according to the job that is being done. We would expect different amounts for personal narratives, party invitations, and mystery stories. Quality or truth: We have expectations (as readers and writers) of what constitutes "truth" and how it is indicated in written events. We hold different kinds of writing to different kinds of truth standards, but we hold each kind of writing to *some* standard. We expect a telephone message to be literally true (who called at what time and for what purpose); we expect a Mother's Day card to be an exaggeration of the truth that we care about someone; we expect a novel to be true within its own world that the author has created (we criticize the work when created characters do not behave in ways which are "true" to people of their type or when we find internal contradictions or inconsistencies). As with the quantity maxim applied to writing, so with the quality or truth maxim: We have, not an absolute standard of appropriateness, but a relative expectation for different types of written events.

Relevance in writing as in speech has to do with continuance and connectedness, a tying in to what precedes and a moving beyond it. We expect that all the parts within a written piece will "go together"—they will all belong. Think of the composition teacher's concern for unity, coherence, smooth transitions, tying devices. As we expect conversational turns to belong and to belong at the points where they occur, so do we expect this in written discourse. We may criticize an event or character for not belonging in the story ("I really just didn't see that it had anything to do with the story") or as coming at the wrong place ("That happened too soon. Their relationship wasn't developed enough yet"). Some writing conventions themselves signal shifts or breaks in connection, for example, paragraphing, chapter titles, and section headings signal topic changes, in contrast to the continuing lines of text. We expect that parts of text (like conversational turns) connect with what precedes and go beyond it. This is relevance. And finally, we expect clarity, and comprehensibility. Because writers and readers expect written text to be clear and comprehensible, writers take their audience into account and readers become annoyed when text is unclear. These behaviors attest to readers' and writers' expectations that written discourse, like spoken discourse, exists to be understood, to communicate; it must be comprehensible.

Situational Conditions
for Performance of Speech Acts

In his study of speech acts, Searle has contributed significantly in bringing to our attention some additional underlying conditions that speakers know about conversation but generally take for granted (Searle 1975, p. 71). Searle has dealt explicitly with the speech acts of requesting and of promising. Conditions that speakers know (but do not consciously know that they know) relating to the making of a request include (1) that the one to whom the request is directed is able to perform the requested action (I will not request a three-year-old to reach something for me that is on a high shelf); (2) that the one making the request does in fact want the requested act to be carried out (a truth or "sincerity condition"); (3) that the requester will indicate the future act to be carried out by the requestee; and (4) that the utterance of the request, whatever its form ("Would ja get me some water?" "I need a glass of water." "Hand me that glass of water, will ya?"), counts as an attempt by the requester to get the requestee to perform the requested act. We never think about these conditions consciously when we make a request or perform a requested action, but our behavior is predicated on these conditions, accepted by both requester and requestee.

Comparable conditions underlie the act of promising: (1) that the speaker (promiser) is able to do what he is promising and that the promised act is desired by the hearer (I will not promise to buy you a Porsche because I am unable to, and I will not promise to demolish your present car because that is an act you do not desire; I may, however, promise to bake cookies for your party, an act that I am able to perform and that I have reason to believe you would find desirable); (2) that the speaker in fact intends to carry out the promised act ("sincerity condition" for promising); (3) that the speaker will indicate the promised act that is to be carried out; (4) that the utterance of the promise actually counts as the speaker's undertaking of the obligation to perform the promised act. Often when an adult is unable to do something for a child that the child expected, we hear the child wail in protest: "But you *promised!*" The child recognizes that a promise is the undertaking of an obligation. The adult knows this too and shows it in his reply: "I didn't really *promise.* I only said *maybe* we'd be able to do it."

Discourse Structure and Dynamics

Some researchers have studied conversations as entities that can be described as hierarchical structures composed of identifiable subparts or components (Garvey, Baldwin, and Dickstein 1971). Here, the basic unit to be described is the communication event—a conversation, an interview, a telephone call, a discussion, a classroom lesson. One suggestion is that at least some communication events can be described as having several *stages:* an orientation stage, a task conduct stage, and a closing stage. Telephone calls offer the perfect example here. Typically when someone calls us, we begin by engaging in talk that gets us interacting, establishes rapport, but does not contribute to the real business of the call: "Well, how've ya been?" "Haven't talked with you for a long time." "How're the kids?" "Yeah, been really busy lately." "Have ya seen——recently?" "Gee, I was just thinking about you the other day." We know this is not the business of the call, but is an important preliminary stage. Without it, the call would seem rude or brusk, but if it goes on too long we sometimes find ourselves thinking, "I wonder what he's calling about" or "I wish she'd hurry and get to the point; I don't have all day." We usually know when we enter the next stage, the task conduct stage, because it is usually marked in the conversation. There may, for example, be a slight pause and then the caller might say, "Well what I'm really calling about is . . ." or "I'm calling to ask you a favor." Notice, it is the caller, not the receiver, who initiates this stage. It would be very rude for the receiver to ask, "Well, what are you calling about?" (unless, of course, the participants were very familiar with one another and the receiver said this in a joking way—the joke being that the receiver has broken a communication convention that they both know). When the business has been taken care of, the participants move into a closing stage. Like the orientation stage, the closing usually contributes nothing directly to our conducting the business at hand, yet without it the conversation would seem rude somehow: "Gee, it's really been good talking to you." "We've got to get together sometime." "Say 'hi' to——for me next time you see her." "Good luck in your exams." "Have a good trip." Another familiar example is the whole-group lesson (rightly or wrongly called a "class discussion") so typical in traditional classrooms. First comes an "opening phase" in which it is established that the teacher and students are going to have a lesson, then an "instructional phase" in which the teacher and children exchange academic information, and finally a "closing phase" in which the teacher and students "formulate what they have done and prepare to move on to other classroom activities" (Mehan 1979, p. 36).

According to this suggested structural analysis, each stage is composed of identifiable *chunks* or episodes, that is, sequences of conversation focusing on a particular topic. Within each chunk are clear *exchanges* (or sequences of exchanges) between the conversational partners, that is, conversational turns that are closely linked as, for example, a question and answer and response sequence (A: "Think you'll be able to come?" B: "I'll sure try." A: "Good. *Do*"). And of course in each exchange or exchange group, one can identify each partner's speaking turn, the individual utterance or *event*. Just as we can have embedded sentences (a sentence within a sentence), so we can have embedded exchange sequences (a sequence within a sequence), as in the following example:

A: Do you want this one?
B: Which one?——embedded exchange——main exchange
A: The red one.
B: Yeah, that's the one.

Some sociolinguists posit an important further unit, the *move*. This is typically an utterance stretch (though possibly a nonverbal signal) accomplishing a certain purpose in the discourse (for example, an initiation or a response to the partner's initiation). The *move* is what gets accomplished. Some events (speaking turns) will include several utterance stretches, each contributing to the discourse in a different way. For example, in the preceding sequence, B's last turn (event) might have been "Yeah, that's the one. Now wanna see what I can do with this?" If so, this event would consist of two moves, the first a response to a preceding question, and the second an initiation of a new conversational focus.

This is only one way to look at the structure of communication events hierarchically, but it is a suggestive way. Different sociolinguists have defined and labeled discourse units in somewhat different ways, but there is considerable agreement that speakers of a language have a sense of conversational structure, organization, and design. If this schematic knowledge were not part of their competence, they would be unable to construct such predictably organized conversations jointly with their partners. Yet to describe a conversation simply as a hierarchical structure is to give only one kind of picture. It is a still picture, a slide, if you like, of the conversation as an entity or a thing. At least as important is the speaker's process knowledge—knowledge of the dynamic movement of conversation, how partners shape to one another in the process of "making" or "doing" a conversation. This is the film version of conversational analysis and it captures the process aspects of a speaker's communicative competence. Again think of the game analogy: Conversational partners are playing a game that has certain rules or guiding principles that the players follow as they attempt, not to win, but to keep the ball in play. The term "negotiation" is often used to characterize the mutual shaping that the partners do in order (1) to assure comprehensibility (that is, to make sure they're understanding each other) and (2) to sustain the interaction (to keep it going). You can see both of these at work (at play?) in the following example. A-2 is a twenty-one-year-old Italian woman who is learning English as her second language while living with her cousin's family in the United States. A-1 is a neighbor of the family. Because A-2 has limited competence in English, A-1 has to work rather hard to assure comprehensibility and to keep this conversation going.

A-1: Does she make pasta?
A-2: Yes. Sometimes, but—
A-1: She can buy it?
A-2: Yes.
A-1: Does she make her uh . . . sauces? (silence) Tomato sauces?
A-2: Yes.
A-1: What's your favorite food?
A-2: Uh . . . pasta.
A-1: Pasta! Do you have a garden?
A-2: No. I don't have. No garden.
A-1: Do you have trees?
A-2: No. (Wale 1985, p. 105)

You can readily see that it is A-1 who does the lion's share of the negotiating work in this conversation. This conversation may remind you of mainstream mother-child conversations from preceding chapters, in which the mother, being the more competent partner, does most of the conversational work. In a conversation among equally competent speakers of the language, we would expect the negotiating work to be shared more equally.[7] You can see that A-1 sticks to very simple questions to carry the conversation, all requiring yes or no answers except the food question, which requires only a one-word response. These questions are likely to be ones that A-2 can understand and also answer, for they require very limited responses. Notice that A-2 falters at two points and A-1 assists each time. In A-2's first turn, it looks as if she is going to have to give an explanation, so A-1 moves in quickly to help, phrasing the expected explanation as a simple yes/no question, "She can buy it?" When A-2 does not reply to the sauces question, A-1 clarifies with "Tomato sauces?" A-1's moves are clear attempts to enable A-2 to understand and to participate in the conversation.

Various types of communication events have been identified and studied, including convergent communication, the situation in which one partner knows the solution to a problem (the knower) and must convey to the partner (the doer) how to reach the solution (as, for example, when the knower gives the doer directions for getting somewhere) (Garvey and Baldwin 1970); argument (Brennels and Lein 1977; Eisenberg and Garvey 1981; Genishi and DiPaolo 1982); sharing time or show and tell (Michaels 1981; Michaels and Collins 1984); instruction giving (Cook-Gumperz 1977); therapeutic discourse (Labov and Fanshel 1977); joke telling (Sacks 1974); teacher-led lessons (Sinclair and Coulthard 1975, Mehan 1979); children's speech play rituals (Kirshenblatt-Gimblett 1976); and story reading (Heath 1982). Evident in all these types is a describable structure (though the various researchers have described it somewhat differently), and also a dynamic sequence of moves carried out in accordance with discourse rules understood by the participants.

This discussion barely scratches the surface of what we are beginning to understand about a speaker's communicative competence as it relates to the overall organizational structure and dynamics of oral communication events.[8] Typically we are very casual about talk. It would not be at all unusual for any of us to respond to the question, "What were you and X

---

[7]This is one strong argument given in support of peer interaction in classrooms. In teacher-child interactions, it is often the teacher who assumes the major responsibility for keeping the ball in play; but when children interact with one another, they share the work and thus become more able negotiators in conversation.

[8]I have restricted this discussion to oral discourse. However, you can see that our communicative competence includes structure and dynamics of written discourse as well. We have different structure expectations for different written events: a letter, a poem, a short story, a diary, a play. And as in oral discourse so in written discourse: The partners (author and reader) have a "contract" of sorts to keep the ball in play. The author takes his reader into account, producing text devices to engage the reader's interest and tying devices to assure the flow of the prose, and so on. And the reader reads with the intention of making sense of the author's text and keeping on. It is when the contract is broken, when the text is not comprehensible and/or sustaining (because of the author's *or* the reader's activity), that the reader puts the book aside. (Do you think that basal text or children's literature more fully engages writer and reader in a contract to assure comprehensibility and to sustain the interaction? Why?)

doing?" by saying, "Oh we were jes' talkin' 'bout this an' that." But "jes talkin' 'bout this an' that" is a remarkably complex, mutually and sensitively coordinated sequence of appropriate moves. "Jes' talkin' 'bout this an' that" may be the most complex and intricate game we ever play, in spite of its being so effortless and often so pleasurable.

VARIATION IN DISCOURSE STYLES

Do you ever make (or hear others make) comments like these?

> She wasn't talking *with* me; she was talking *at* me.
>
> What a disaster that conversation was! I kept throwing him the ball, but he wouldn't run with it. All I could get was one-word answers.
>
> If you tied my hands, I just couldn't talk.
>
> I gave up on that book. I expected a story, but it reads more like an insurance policy.
>
> She talks to me like I'm a kindergartener.
>
> He writes more like a Hemingway than a Henry James.
>
> I find him hard to talk to. He's so intense—just doesn't have a talent for small talk—no gift for gab.

And what does it mean to say that someone's speech or writing is "flamboyant" or "pretentious" or "casual" or "warm" or "plodding"? These are comments about language styles, that is different ways of using language in spoken and written discourse. "It ain't what cha say, it's the way how cha say it," as the old song puts it. What's the difference between identifying someone as a "janitor" or as a "sanitation engineer"? What's the difference between calling something "unpleasant" and calling it "the pits," or between calling someone "unstable" and calling him "wifty"? Is being "blotto" the same as being "inebriated"? The differences here have social significance; that is, their use is sensitive to the social context. In some situations one form would be appropriate in other situations another form would be.

We all control a range of speaking styles. Some sociolinguists are studying what some of the specific factors of situations are that influence our choice of which speaking style to use. That is, they are trying to discover more about the speaker's underlying knowledge relating to the context-sensitive nature of communication. You can begin to explore this yourself by considering the following pairs of sentences. For each member of the pair, suggest a situation (or several) in which it would be appropriate (for example, speaker, person, or group spoken to; purpose; setting). (You may want to do this with several other people. You may find that you come up with a variety of situations for each utterance depending in part on the way the words are spoken—tone of voice, accompanying gestures, and facial expressions.)

> No way I'm gonna do that.
>
> I'd rather not do that.

I beg your pardon?
Huh?

Bye-bye.
Good-bye.

Shall we go?
Let's get out of here.

What do you want?
May I help you?

May I have your attention please?
Shut up and listen. (Williams, Hopper, and Natalicio 1977 pp. 64-65)

The changes we make in our style in different situations are not just changes in word choice. Our syntactic forms and our pronunciations are sensitive to various social factors also. In general we are more likely to use passive constructions in more formal situations (especially in writing). Speaking in a large meeting, with the purpose of recalling to the group an action taken at a previous meeting, we would be likely to say, "You may remember that, at least week's meeting, it was moved that . . ." But in telling a close friend about the action in casual conversation, we would be more likely to use the active forms: "Remember last week X moved that we . . ." And, as we saw in the previous section, if our conversational partner is a young child, we may tend to shorten and simplify our sentences. The forms we pronounce as "why don't you" and "I'm going to" when we are conversing with our new school superintendent at a reception are likely to become "wyoncha" and "I'm gonna" when we're in blue jeans stretched out on the floor of our living room in front of a cozy fire, talking with spouse or close friend while munching on Fritos. We use our voices differently, too, talking louder in some situations and more quietly in others, sometimes using a wider intonation range and sometimes a more restricted one, often conveying a special meaning—sarcasm, mockery, cynicism, irritation—by using a special tone of voice.

Nonverbal aspects of our communicaton vary from situation to situation, too, though these are aspects of communication that we understand less well. The ways in which we do (or do not) establish and maintain eye contact when we converse, the physical distance we establish and how we incline toward or away from our partner in conversation, our use of touch (whom we touch and how and when in conversation), our facial expression and use of gesture—these are only a few of many nonverbal aspects of communication that alter with the social situation we are in. Many teachers use touch a great deal when they interact with their children. We can generally recognize when the touching conveys impatience, affection, or restraint. We have much to learn about nonverbal aspects of communication. Usually we are unaware of these aspects of communication altogether.

However, sometimes we are aware that verbal and nonverbal signals are in conflict. For example, a teacher may grab and restrain a student impatiently, all the while talking in a "honeyed" tone of voice, or in an oversteady voice that tries to convey (between clenched teeth) a calm and control that the teacher does not feel. Our awareness of conflicting or inappropriate nonverbal signals suggests that these aspects of our communication are, like the verbal aspects, nonrandom and rule governed. If we know when a rule has been broken (that is, recognize when one behaves in a way that is counter to our expectations), then clearly we have knowledge of some rules or guiding principles for that behavior, however unconscious that knowledge may be. A college student once described one of her professors to me by saying, "She always tells us that she really wants us to actively participate in class and really get involved in discussion. But then, as soon as we begin to say something, she looks nervously at her watch." The student had zeroed in on a clear conflict between the verbal and nonverbal messages that professor was giving. Our unconscious knowledge of appropriate nonverbal behavior is one more aspect of our language knowledge that humorists have exploited.

Unconsciously, automatically, we slip in and out of various comunication styles, adapting our oral and written expressions and even our gestures so that they are appropriate to each social situation. We are generally no more aware of the various styles we are shifting in and out of so facilely than we are aware of the linguistic structure of the utterances we endlessly create. An example of this lack of awareness of the styles we use is the following from an adult English speaker learning Spanish. The authors of his text had translated an informal Spanish sentence with an English sentence that included "gonna." When the student encountered one of the textbook authors who was involved in doing some of the teaching for the class, the student pointed out the "gonna" translation and suggested that they must be teaching the students "substandard" Spanish if the equivalent English translations were so "substandard" as to include "gonna". The author-teacher protested that "gonna" was not substandard English but, indeed, was a form he himself used all the time. The student replied adamantly, "Well I don't. And I'm not gonna start now!" The author-teacher reports, "The effect was electric. His embarrassment at being caught was aggravated by the amused laughter of his classmates" (Bowen

1966, p. 45). For the first time, perhaps, the student heard what he actually said, not what he thought he said.

As with this student, so with ourselves. Only occasionally does our stylistic use come to the level of our conscious awareness. One such time is when we use an inappropriate style in a given situation. This is usually embarrassing and often we become flustered and/or apologetic, as in the following example. A second-grade teacher had been working very hard at trying to break the habit some of her children were in, of not listening to instructions of any kind. She had firmly resolved that every time she gave an instruction she would follow a pattern of first alerting the children to the fact that she was going to give an instruction, then give the instruction clearly and respond to any questions regarding it, and then under no circumstances would she repeat the instruction for the ever-present few who requested it over and over again. She was trying very hard to follow this firm resolve, and often heard herself say to a child, "——, I told you that already and I'm not going to tell you again. You'll have to figure it out the best you can." After dinner one evening, her husband asked her a question about something they had previously discussed. She turned to him and said in a "schoolmarmish" voice, "I've told you that already and I'm not going to tell you again." Of course he replied, with justifiable annoyance, "I am *not* a second grader!" a response which showed his clear recognition that she had used an identifiable and inappropriate style in talking with him. Her own embarrassment and mumbled apology attested to the same recognition on her part. She had clearly violated some principles of appropriate language use for that situation, principles that both she and her husband knew.

We also become consciously aware of varying our language style in different situations when we, or someone we are listening to, suddenly and dramatically shift from one style to another. Consider the teenage girl engaged in a fight with her younger brother: (sarcastically) "Oh *sure!* You weren't in my room while I was out! Then how come my records are all messed up and my jeans are on the floor? You're always . . ." (Phone rings. Sudden shift as she answers it and says in a neutral voice) "Hello?" then sweetly, "Oh hi, Paul," and an animated conversation continues.

Sometimes we deliberately assume a role in telling a story in conversation, and the role style contrasts sharply with our conversational narrative style. Here is an example in which a woman relates to several of her friends (as they are conversing informally on her porch) an incident in which a recent comer to the neighborhood suggested that the narrator's "ol' man" had been wandering:

> She holler off her porch, "Yo man, he over in Darby Sat'day nite." I say "Shit, what you know 'bout my man? My man." It was a rainy night, you know ain't no use gettin' fussied up to go out on a night like dat. Tessie 'n I go play bingo. But dat ol' woman, she ak like she some Channel Two reporter or sump'n:
>
> "P.B. Evans was seen today on the corner of Center and Main Street. He hadda bottle in each hip pocket, and one under his London Fog hat. Sadie Lou (a well-known stripper in a local topless bar) was helpin' him

across the street, holin' her white mink in front of him to keep his shiny shoes from gettin' wet. The weather tomorrow promises to be cloudy for some."

What she think she doin', tellin' *me* 'bout my ol' man? Sayin' "He lookin' mighty fine, yes sireeeeee." She betta keep her big mouf 'n stay shut up in dat house. (Based on Heath 1983, pp. 168-69)

Here, the speaker's "Channel Two reporter" style contrasts sharply with her narrative style and also with her dramatization of her conversation with the intruder. Or consider children's use of language in role-play situations. Their use of language to negotiate the play ("You be the mommy and I'll be the little girl, OK? And pretend you just came back from the store and you find me all covered with mud") is clearly distinguishable from their use of language in the assigned roles.

Our stylistic range includes written as well as spoken channels. We expect, use, and interpret a variety of written styles. We expect a biology text to "sound" different from a poem, and we respond to each on its own terms. The business letters we write and receive use a style quite different from that we use when we write to a friend. And what about the old high school yearbook? It would be unthinkable to write the truth: "I don't know you very well, but as much as I know you, you seem OK. I have no particular reason to think you're a loser or really terrific. You seem to be kind of regular" or "I've known you a long time and you're average." *Every* high schooler knows better than to do this; *every* high schooler has a language style appropriate for writing in yearbooks. And think about scripture. On one occasion one chooses the St. James version, on another, a modern version. Different written styles serve our different purposes.

Let's sum up for a moment. Our communicative competence includes knowing how to adapt our language appropriately for various situations; our communication is context-sensitive. We all control a range of communication styles. Without even thinking about it, we choose among the words, syntactic structures, phonological devices, and even gestures that we control, those which are appropriate to each situation we are in. And although our choices are not conscious ones, we know that they are non-random and rule governed, because we and our conversational partners know when those guiding principles of appropriate speaking or writing are broken.

Just what are those aspects of communication contexts that so strongly influence the ways we speak or write on different occasions?[9] You identified some when you responded to the exercise pairs on pp. 335-336, and the Labov and Robins example suggests some more. First, who are the participants in a communication event and what is their relationship to one another? Age will make a difference here. The language style that teenagers use in conversation with their peers will differ from the style they use in talking with a younger child (as in a babysitting situation) or with someone older (a friend's mother or father). How familiar are the participants with one another? Are they friends, family members, or neighbors, or are

[9]See Hymes 1974 for a classic set of situational factors that interact with language style.

they relative strangers who just happened to arrive at the same meeting early or sit beside each other on a bus or stand next to each other in a cafeteria line? What is the relative status of the participants? Are they fellow students, playmates, or colleagues, with comparable status? Or is there a status imbalance—an older child tutoring a younger one, a boss talking with a subordinate, a teacher conversing with a student, or a school superintendent with a teacher? Clearly, these aspects are not always distinct. Variables of age and status often overlap (older tends to have more status), as do age and familiarity (often greater familiarity among age mates) or status and familiarity (often greater familiarity with someone of similar status).

One intriguing feature that exerts a very strong influence and overlaps with several of the above is the shared background of the participants in a communication event. If the participants know each other very well, they can assume so much background knowledge and thus leave so much unspoken, that the outside observer might either not understand the interaction at all or else might misinterpret it, perhaps taking at face value what the participants understand to be sarcasm or jest or mockery. Consider this example.

A mother who was driving a carpool of elementary school children pulled up in front of the last rider's house and honked. The rider, an eleven-year-old girl, walked to the car. As she opened the car door, the following conversation took place between her and a nine-year-old girl already in the car:

NINE-YEAR-OLD: How long?
ELEVEN-YEAR-OLD: Ummmmm, I think till Wednesday. Maybe, if I'm good today she might cut it shorter. I might get just, you know, today. (Both laugh.) But . . .
NINE-YEAR-OLD: Did she mean nobody over there too?
ELEVEN-YEAR-OLD: Well, I thought she didn't say, "You couldn't play with anybody." She said, you know, "You cannot leave the house," and I thought, so OK, I didn't leave the house. And I invited you over and she goes, "Um . . . that wasn't part of the deal."[10]

It is not until this point that the outsider begins to be aware that these two girls (who have not seen or talked to each other for twenty-four hours) are talking about the older child's punishment by her mother. It was an exchange that made no sense to the others in the car, but the shared background of the two participants made it perfectly clear to them.

The setting in which a communication occurs also influences language usage. The time and place will make a difference; people will speak differently at an afternoon picnic in the park, at a Sunday morning church service, and at a fashionably late dinner party. The type of language event makes a difference, too. The fact that we use different terms to label various types of speaking events suggests that we think of speaking events differently. We call some speaking events "meetings,"

---

[10]I am grateful to Kay Walther for this example from her data.

some "services," some "debates," some "interviews," some "bull sessions." The same is true of writing: "documents," "letters," "reports," "textbooks," and "prose poems" are quite different written events and involve quite different styles. Each occasion has its own set of discourse conventions and the participants know (unconsciously) what they are.

Setting also includes the number of people present and/or involved. The talk in a group of three or four is likely to be a "conversation" or a "discussion," while the talk in a group of thirty or forty is likely to be a "presentation." The public or private nature of the interaction may influence the language; we would expect language that is not meant to be overheard to differ from that which is intended to be heard by many people, and a letter we write to a friend will "sound" different from a "to-the-editor" letter we write for publication in our local newspaper. The formality level of a situation (which obviously overlaps with other aspects of setting) also influences the language of the participants. The tone or spirit of the communication is important, too. How do the participants interpret the event? Is it serious, perfunctory, playful? You can see, perhaps, that aspects of setting overlap with each other, and overlap with who the participants are as well.

Further, our purposes in communicating are different and each purpose guides the language choices we make. We talk or write differently when we comfort, persuade, argue, inform, instruct, entertain, and so on. The topic we are discussing exerts its influence also. Recently I might have experienced a vacation trip to Hawaii, the death of a friend, and intense study for an upcoming economics exam. The nature of these topics, the very events themselves, would influence the way I told you about each one.

Surely the language styles we use are influenced by many aspects of the communication event. But just as surely, the language style itself influences the situation. There is a real interaction of language style and the situation, not simply one-way influence. The speaking or writing style used can render the event more formal or pretentious or friendly or routine. Have you ever found yourself in a situation that seemed formal and intimidating until suddenly someone (the host or hostess perhaps) began to talk with you in such a relaxed and comfortable way that the situation itself became more relaxed? You might even have referred to that person later as someone who was good at "breaking the ice" or "putting people at ease."

Whatever the style of speaking or writing that we use on a particular occasion, remember that we are always our individual selves using that style from our repertoire. Every discourse event we participate in, we shape in individual as well as in socially appropriate ways. The individual expressive and responsive self is an important aspect of the communication event we create together with others.

SUMMARY

This discussion has given only the barest sketch of a speaker's communicative competence, his intuitive knowledge of what is sometimes called "the universe of discourse" (Moffett 1968). It is a universe that includes a wide array of human communication purposes and expressive forms; many types of communication events, each with its own structure and each moving according to intricate dynamic principles, and a host of expressive styles that interact with every social situation, both shaping and being shaped in the interaction. Strange that this universe of discourse that we come to know so deeply and so effortlessly should be so difficult for us to become aware of at a conscious level. Yet it is so: Our communicative competence far exceeds researchers' efforts to fully observe, recognize, identify, analyze, describe, and explain it in anything like a comprehensive way. Again we face a staggering fact: Virtually every child develops this complex communicative competence and does so without explicit instruction, sequenced curriculum, skills practice, mastery tests, or any of the usual trappings of traditional instruction. And so it *must* be, for the complex workings of the communication game are "out of awareness" for the competent communicators from whom and through whom the child learns them. Once again we come face to face with the well-endowed, creatively constructing child, making sense of the social world to which he belongs.

THE DEVELOPMENT OF COMMUNICATIVE COMPETENCE

The language the child encounters is the living language of oral and written communication.

> Language comes to life only when functioning in some environment. [The child does] not experience language in isolation . . . but always in relation to a scenario, some background of persons and actions and events from which the things are said to derive their meaning. (Halliday 1978, p. 28)

Sometimes the child is participant, sometimes observer, but in either case he is regarded and treated as a "member of the club" of that communicating community. The language going on around him and with him is the all-at-onceness we have seen before: whole and purposeful communication events. Each event in its wholeness simultaneously demonstrates particular expressive forms carrying out particular communication purposes; organizational schemes and the playing out of dynamic sequences; and language styles appropriate to the specifics of the social context. Each event is a demonstration in Smith's sense of showing how something is done (communication, in this case). The thousands of communication events provide thousands of demonstrations for the child member of the club. The purposeful, functioning wholeness of communication events provides the raw material out of which the child constructs his own communicative competence.

Developing Communication Functions

It has been suggested that "a major difficulty for children" in their acquisition of language is the lack of fit between form and function (Coulthard 1977). As pointed out earlier, a single function, for example, request-

ing an action, can be accomplished by a variety of forms. On the other hand, one form can be used to express a variety of functions. Consider, for example, the various functions conveyed by the interrogatives (a particular form) in the accompanying cartoon.

I doubt that this lack of a one-to-one correspondence between form and function constitutes "a major problem" for language-acquiring children, but surely form and function relations are a vital feature of the language they must learn. The language environment provides them with plenty of data, since every oral and written language instance is both form and function.

In the following conversation between a mother and her one-year-old son as they play ball, you can see that the mother's language is serving many different purposes. She "is doing things with words." What different functions can you identify? (The child's responses are transcribed here in a very informal way. You'll notice that some of his responses seem very close to English words that would be appropriate to the situation, while others bear almost no resemblance to English words at all, though the mother generally treats his responses as if they are the appropriate words; for example, she responds to his "eh bah" as if the child really had said, "Mickey Mouse," the response she is seeking.)

M: Where'd that ball go?
C: uguh
M: Where'd it go?
C: oguh
M: D'ya have it? There it is. (Pause) D'ya wanna play catch?
C: kesh
M: Catch the ball.
C: gah
M: Oh, what a throw!
C: ebaw
M: Here's the ball. Catch.

C: wuu guh
M: Are your pants wet? (Touches child's pants to find out.)
C: kesh kesh
M: Catch.
C: guh
M: Ooooohhhhh.
C: eduh baw
M: Here's the ball.
C: bawh
M: Oh, good catch!
C: uh
M: Want me to take your hat off?
C: bawh
M: A——, let me take your hat off. (Pause while M takes child's hat off.) Let's look at what's on your hat. D'ya see all those animals that M—— and D—— were talkin' about? See?
C: yuh
M: Who's that?
C: duk
M: That's a dog (as if repeating what child said). Who's this?
C: eh bah (high-low intonation)
M: That's Minnie Mouse? (as if what child had said). And who's this?
C: ba bah (low-high intonation)
M: Donald Duck? (as if what child had said). And who's this?
C: eh bah (high-low intonation)
M: Mickey Mouse (as if repeating child.) Mickey . . . (waits for child to repeat) . . . Mouse. And who's that?
C: duk
M: A dog (as if repeating child). Who's this?
C: gee goh
M: Minnie Mouse?
C: thusuh giddy go, giddy gish?
M: A who? (as if asking child to repeat meaningful utterance)
C: bawh, kesh
M: Wellllllllll?
C: ge dula ell
M: Are you gonna tell me "well"?
C: bawh
M: Bow-wow, chuh. Hit me right in the eye ball.[11]

This is "language come to life," functioning in an environment. Through a variety of linguistic forms and actions and gestures, the mother initiates and maintains interaction; she informs, she expresses and explains, she praises, she alerts, she invites the child to action, she "tests" him, she seeks information ("Are your pants wet?" plus her action), she entertains or plays with language (see last utterance), she provides social formulas ("Thank

[11]I am indebted to Ben Blount for this episode.

you"), and she requests action ("A——, let me take your hat off," that is, come here and be still) and verbal repetition ("Are you gonna tell me 'well'?"). Given this rich kind of interactive environment—people communicating with and around the child using a variety of forms to express a variety of functions—the child figures out how conversation works in both its context-free and context-sensitive aspects. He uses this developing knowledge to guide his own communication behavior, continually hypothesizing, testing, and revising his hypotheses as he continues to get more data. Remember, the language structure (form)-language use (function) distinction is one we impose as a convenience to ourselves in trying to study a vast and unwieldy topic—language. But the distinction has no basis in the child's (or our own) experiencing of language. Forms and functions are all of a piece, quite an inseparable wholeness for the child as he interacts with others.

We cannot see into the child's head and observe his mental processes directly as he figures out how various communication purposes are expressed. But from the beginning the child leaves behavioral traces. The earliest traces are nonlinguistic; through gestures and/or vocal sounds (not yet resembling words), the child protests, requests actions and objects, and "answers" another's initiation. The child is oriented toward purposeful communication; even during his first year he behaves as if he "knows" that purposeful interaction is what language is about, that language is *doing things*. He is geared toward figuring out what those doings are and how they get done.

When the child begins to use words, linguistic traces are added to the earlier nonlinguistic ones. It is fascinating that even when children's linguistic means of expression are limited to single-word utterances, those single-word utterances serve at least the following recognizable functions: labeling, repeating, answering, requesting an action, requesting an answer, calling, greeting, protesting, and practicing (Dore 1975, p. 31). The child's word(s), intonation contour, and nonlinguistic behavior and the immediate context, taken together, make possible the (tentative) identification of these diverse early functions in children's speech. And from his observations of a child from nine to eighteen months of age, Halliday has identified the following set of language functions (in order of their emergence) as those "functions in which a child first learns to mean" (Halliday 1977, p. 37): (1) instrumental or "I want," through which the child's material needs are met; (2) regulatory or "Do as I tell you," through which the child gets others to do what he wants them to; (3) interactional or "me and you," through which the child moves into or maintains an interaction with someone else; (4) personal or "here I come," through which the child expresses his uniqueness and self-awareness; (5) heuristic or "tell me why?" through which the child explores the environment; (6) imaginative or "let's pretend," through which the child creates his own environment; and, emerging somewhat later (around two years) (7) informative or "I've got something to tell you," through which the child conveys information to someone. And Joan Tough has observed the following functions in the language of three-year-olds: directive function, including directing self and directing others; interpretative function, including reporting on present and past experiences, and also reasoning; projective function, including predicting, empathetic, and imaginating; and relational function, including self-maintaining and interactional (based on Tough 1977, pp. 68–69). Though different researchers categorize children's language functions in somewhat different ways, it is absolutely clear that from the time that children "have words," they are "doing things with words." It is also clear that an important part of children's language growth that continues through the elementary school years is (1) the adding of new functions to their range and (2) the adding of new means for expressing each function. Initially, children use a limited set of linguistic forms to express a limited set of functions; ultimately, they use a diverse set of linguistic forms to express a wide range of functions.

> Children have to build up structure and function at the same time. As they learn more about structure, they acquire more devices with which to convey different functions. And as they learn more about function, they extend the uses to which different structures can be put. But even at age seven or eight, children still have a long way to go. Acquiring a language is a long and complicated process. (Clark and Clark 1977, p. 373)

Many of the demonstrations around and with the child involve print expression of various communication purposes. The child is a member of the club that *does things* through the written language of storybooks, recipe cards, junk mail, Simplicity patterns, traffic signs, menus, birthday cards, bumper stickers, and food can labels. Children's behavior traces early responses to print that indicate awareness of the purposes print serves. When the two-year-old comes to his parent, lugging a favorite storybook behind him, it is because he is seeking the entertainment function he knows the storybook will provide; when the three-year-old gets excited as the family car turns in at McDonald's, it is because the golden arches sign has served its purpose of announcing a particular kind of place. The child figures out early that storybooks and McDonald's signs *do things*, and he responds in ways that tell us that he knows what things they do, what functions they serve. From his first year, the child's nonlinguistic and linguistic behaviors indicate that he is constantly making sense of the purpose-*full* demonstrations of spoken and written language ever in use around and with him.

Developing Communication Organization

The child member of the club observes and participates in a wide variety of types of communication events that are part of his community. There are oral events—perhaps sermons (within the larger event of church service), personal narratives and jokes (both within the larger event of informal conversation), telephone calls, and so on. And there are written events—perhaps scripture, Sears catalogs, grocery lists, and so on. Whatever the set of communication events that are demonstrated with and around the child, each type has, and reveals, its own characteristics: Each has its own overall organizational design, each has characteristic moves. The following, for example, all belong in different discourse events: "Once upon a time . . ." "So I said to him . . ." "Did you hear the one about . . ." "Here endth the reading . . ." "This week only, 50% off." In each event, individuals participate differently: Whether and how and how much they speak or listen, how they get speaking turns, how they carry them out, what constitutes relevance in a turn—all this and more differs from one communication event to the next. The set of oral and written discourse events is somewhat different for each child, but every child is involved in some set and builds his own repertoire from it.

Fascinating differences in discourse events abound in the different cultural and social communities from which our school children come. The Warm Springs Indian child's experience will include General Council meetings and naming ceremonies (Philips 1983); the Trackton child's experience will include "raised hymns" in church services and challenges (for boys) and "fussing" and playsong games (for girls) to be performed on Trackton's "stage" (the central plaza encircled by the neighborhood homes). Every community the world over has "story" events. Yet what "story" is and the nature of its performance differs from one community to another: In one group story is a fixed, fossilized entity; in another, an imaginative and embellished tale. In one group story is performed by one individual, in another, as a collaboration. In one group story is mainly a written event; in another, usually an oral rendition. And so on. So it is with other discourse events also; every group has structures for passing information, structures for joking, and so on, but the structures differ from one group to another. Virtually every child is a member of some club, some community carrying on its social work; thus every child builds a repertoire of discourse events out of the set he observes and participates in.

Because the research on children's early interaction has concentrated largely on mainstream settings, the major focus has been on mother-child interaction events (for example, the naming game, book-reading events, conversation while playing with toys). But it's interesting to note the kinds of interaction events children engage in when an adult is not a participant (and therefore does not take the major responsibility for assuring conversation-ness). One researcher has studied the tape-recorded predawn conversations of her twin sons from age two years and nine months to three years and eight months (Keenan 1974; Keenan and Klein 1975) and found them to be truly conversational in nature; they consisted of turn-taking sequences in which each turn related to the partner's previous one and influenced the next. Before age three, many of the exchange sequences (about one-third) were sound play; that is, one twin's turn would involve a nonsense sound sequence and the second twin would then incorporate that sound sequence in his next turn, sometimes repeating it, sometimes modifying it. It is significant that, without an adult present to take major responsibility for making the dialogue follow conversational norms, these very young children's interactions followed basic conversational conventions of turn taking, coherence (sequences of related exchanges), and relevance (each successive utterance relating to the preceding one).[12]

Consider the following three excerpts from the interactions of pre-school children, slightly older than Keenan's twins (three- and four-year-olds). Identify every instance you can find of the participants demonstrating their awareness of discourse structure and dynamics that is, of their engaging in a sequence of moves, each one responsive to preceding moves and influencing succeeding ones, and all occurring within a rule-governed framework.

MARK: That's my red car John.
JOHN: But it isn't really.
MARK: Well—I was playing with it—I had it first.
JOHN: Oh—well—which shall I have then? I'm going to have the blue one and I'm going to race it.
MARK: Mine's racing too —round it goes.
JOHN: Push your car faster Mark, like this. Wow—wow——mine's going fast as anything—as anything and fast as a train.
MARK: Mine's going fast as a rocket—whoosh.
JOHN: Watch out Mark—my car's coming fast—I think there'll be a crash—make yours come to mine.
MARK: Yes there will be a big crash—mine's coming—watch out—brr—there—there—crash.
JOHN: Oh, an accident, an accident—my car's on fire.
MARK: Fetch the fire engine—the cars are burning all up.
JOHN: And the people are getting all burnt up too. (Tough 1974 p. 17-18)

C-1: Guess when my birthday is.
C-2: The 4th of June.
C-1: No.
C-2: The 16th of September.
C-1: No.
C-2: The 3rd of November.
C-1: No way.
C-2: I give up.
C-1: In March. (She begins to draw on the desk top.)
C-2: Look what you did, T——. Miss S——, T—— drew on the table.
C-1: Stop, you're dumb.
C-2: You called me dumb, dummy.
C-1: Ha ha ha ha ha. Look what I made.
C-2: Ha ha ha ha ha. That isn't pretty.
C-1: Ha ha ha ha ha. That isn't pretty.
C-2: Ha ha ha ha ha. (C-1 leaves)[13]

C-1 and C-2 are playing, and their interaction occurs in an entirely playful manner.

[12]See Garvey 1984 for a book focusing on child-child interaction.
[13]I am grateful to Cynthia Postel for this example from her data.

C-1:   I will turn the light off.
C-2:   I will turn the light on.
C-1:   And I will put you into the garbage can.
C-2:   I will put you into the garbage can.
C-1:   And I will go somewhere else.
C-2:   I'll go somewhere else, where you can't find me.
C-1:   Uh-uh (meaning no). I know how ta run . . . and fight.
C-2:   Me too . . . and I'll run and jump over you.[14]

These child partners share knowledge of the structure of these events:
They know how to carry out a disagreement, how to coordinate an imagined event, and how to "play" a guessing game or a one-up-manship game.
Within each event the children move through an appropriate sequence of
turns, each turn relevant to and clearly connecting with the preceding one
and also carrying the conversation beyond it. It is because both children in
each event have similar knowledge of how these events are organized and
move along that they are able to keep the ball in play in these particular
communication games. These conversations are important traces, indicating what these children have figured out about the structure and dynamics
of these discourse events.

By the time children enter elementary school, they have observed and
participated in many different kinds of discourse events, each demonstrating its own structural patterns and moves. Some children's repertoires of
discourse events mesh closely with the events of the classroom. For others,
there will be little fit between discourse events at home and at school. But
every child comes to us with well-developed knowledge of how various
communication events work in his community. The challenge for us is to
recognize what each child's repertoire includes, what his notion is of classroom events (especially those we tend to take for granted, like information-
passing events, and story events) and, knowing this to find ways of extending each child's range. The greater the diversity in the children within a
classroom, the greater the potential for doing this extending, since children
construct their communicative competence out of their social experience.
The classroom can be an important part of that social experience.

Developing Communication Styles

Linguistic theory treats . . . the child's acquisition of the ability to produce,
understand, and discriminate any and all of the grammatical sentences of a
language. A child from whom any and all of the grammatical sentences of a
language might come with equal likelihood would be of course a social monster. With the social matrix in which it acquires a system of grammar a child
acquires also a system of its use, regarding persons, places, purposes, other
modes of communication, etc.—all the components of communicative events.
(Hymes 1974, p. 75)

"All the components of communication events" is a tall order indeed.
However, because every instance of oral and written communication dem-

---

[14]I am grateful to Genevieve Kerr for this example from her data.

onstrates all interrelated components simultaneously, the child builds a system that accounts for all these aspects and their complex interconnectedness. Every instance demonstrates language in use by particular individuals in particular relationships to one another (status, familiarity, age) in particular numbers (pairs, small groups, large groups) at particular times, in particular places, in particular modes (oral, written, nonverbal, and all possible combinatons of these), for particular purposes (arguing, informing, entertaining) about particular topics . . . on and on; every instance is an incredible all-at-onceness. Constructing such a complex system out of such complex experience seems very hefty work for very small persons. We need to remind ourselves that the small person is a *human*, which means that he is innately oriented, cognitively and socially, to construct the very kind of communication system that he encounters, and to do so out of direct social experience, the very experience that the environment provides. He is *the right kind* of being born into *the right kind* of environment: the thinking human child in a social human world. He is *the right kind* of club member in *the right kind* of club: a club of people using language to do their cognitive and social work, a club of people who accept the child as one of themselves.

Again we look for traces in the child's behavior to indicate the child's development of a system of language use that includes stylistic variation in different social situations. We often find such traces in children's sociodramatic play. The following three-year-olds are playing roles of father (F), babies (B), and mother (M).

F: I won't give you any food if you're not good.
B: I'm good.
F: No, you're not. You're crying. Only good babies get food.
B: I'm good. Put my pie on. My pie! My pie!
F: This is not what I'm cooking. The father says what's cooking.
B: Give me what you're cooking.
F: Only if you beez a good baby.
B: We won't cry, Daddy.
F: Wait till these are ready because they're too hot. But if the babies aren't good, no food.
B: We're laughing.
F: Okay. Here's some food, baby.
B: I'm good, right?
F: Yeah, you're good now. Both of you get porridge that's just right. (M enters)
M: No more food, father. No more food, babies. No more, no more.
B: I'm finished now.
M: You have to get in your bed. Daddy will cover you up.

(F. cradles a doll in his arms and begins to sway dreamily in the rocking chair. "M-m-m, go to sleep, little baby doll, m-m-m.") (Based on Paley 1986)

It is not unusual to hear children as young as three pretend-read story or picture books, using a story-reading style (for example, distinct intonation patterns, sentence structures, dialogue sequences). We also find traces in the child's conversations with different partners. Four-year-olds talk differently to two-year-olds than they talk to peers or adults (Shatz and Gelman 1973). Consider how the language style of the following five-year-old boy, E, alters as he talks to his five-year-old friend, his mother, and his infant sister.

Two five-year-olds eating lunch.

E: Do you like pickles?
B: What?
E: Do you like pickles on your hamburger?
B: Pickles?
E: Yes.
B: Yes.
E: Not me. My mommy took 'em off.
   (Now they are playing.)
B: I need a big block like that.
E: Here—because you can use those medium ones.
B: Okay, now.
E: Hey, look at this! My trailer's gonna park in here with my truck.
B: So is mine.
E: I need some medium ones (blocks). These are mine, right? Here, you need these? You have to put it just like mine. You see how I put it there?
B: How? Where are the mediums?
E: You see, there are a lot of mediums.
B: I don't have enough blocks.
E: You don't? Oh my gosh! Here's a little one. Now look! Look how many cars I have!

E is talking with his mother about the tape recorder.

E: What is that star? (Refers to the microphone on the tape recorder.)
M: What is what?
E: The star.
M: Where? Right there?
E: Yes.
M: That's the microphone.
E: It is?
M: Uh-huh. Isn't that neat?
E: But if people are far away from it, how will they talk through it, and will it still be loud?
M: Yes, because this little dial over here can make it louder or not over here. So that's what we have to do.
E: Where's our other tape recorder what we used to have— ours?
M: A long time ago?
E: Yes.
M: I don't know.
E: Can we ask Daddy? He might have took it somewhere.

M: Maybe. We'll have to find out.

E: Now?

M: Not now.

E: If he doesn't know where it is, then you know what we are just going to do?

M: What?

E: Buy another one, and it's gonna be mine!

E is talking with his infant sister.

E: You are my beautiful M——. You're a beautiful bye, you're a beautiful bye. I will get you somewhere else. Beautiful pie, beautiful pie. Beautiful girl. M——, how are you doing? Yes, you're beautiful. They are records in there. Do you know what records are? Do you know? Do you know what this is for? They are things what we listen to. Did you know that? M——, records are the things what we listen to with our ears. (Baby babbles.)

E: M——, hi there! M—— da-da-da! Da-da-da-da-ya-ya-da-da-da-da! Say "da-da," M——. (Sings) Hello, sweetie pie. We'll put some fancy socks on and you will look so pretty, my little M——. (Baby coos.)

E: M——, how are you doing this morning? That's my beautiful pie, that's a beautiful bye, right, M——? This is a sweel li'l girl. (Baby whines.)

E: Don't cry, my sweetie baby girl. Don't cry, sweet as apple pie. (Sings) I like you, my sweetie pie, pretty girl. Do you want to go to school, sister? It's a beautiful day outside.[15]

Some recent research suggests that pre–first-grade children not only *use* different speaking styles in different social situations but they may also have a beginning conscious awareness of different language styles. The following examples involve Mandy (first example) and Lem (second example), four-year-olds who live in Trackton.

> Mandy . . . was . . . playing with a mirror and talking into the mirror. She seemed to run through a sequence of actors, exemplifying ways in which each used questions:
>> How ya doin, Miss Sally?
>> Ain't so good, how you?
>> Got no plaints. Ben home?
>> What's *your* name little girl?
>> You a pretty little girl.
>> You talk to me.
>> Where's yo' momma?
>> You give her this for me, okay?
> When Mandy realized she had been overheard, she said, "I like to play talk. Sometimes I be me, sometimes somebody else." [When] asked who she was this time, she . . . said, "You know Miss Sally, but dat other one Mr. Griffin talk." Mr. Griffin was the insurance salesman who came to the community each week to collect on insurance premiums. (Heath 1982, p. 119)

> Lem was particularly fascinated by fire trucks, and in the car he would keep up a chain of questions whenever [he and the researcher] passed the fire station.

[15]I am grateful fo Debbie Strasmick for these examples from her data.

Dere go a fire truck.
Where dat fire truck go?
What dat fire truck do?
What dat dog do at da fire?
Whose dog dat is?
How da firemen know where dey going?
How come dat dog know to stay on dat truck?

At the end of the first 19 days of nursery school, in the car on the way home, he saw a fire truck. His sequence of questions ran as follows:

What color dat truck?
What dat truck?
What color dat truck?
What color dat coat?
What color dat car?

[The researcher's] response was: "What do you mean, 'What color is that truck'? You know what color that truck is. What's the matter with you?" Lem broke into laughter in the back seat, realizing his game had been discovered . . . he was playing "teacher" . . . (Heath 1982, pp. 120–121)

Mandy is consciously aware that she is talking like Miss Sally and Mr. Griffin and is able to tell the researcher so. And Lem is deliberately playing a teacher-talk game.

An indication of early and subtle awareness of written language styles comes from a study of thirteen kindergarten children (Green 1981). Their teacher read the entire class ten books (two by each of five authors) over a fourteen-day period. Then the thirteen subject children individually listened to tapes of five unfamiliar stories, written by the same authors. (To control for guessing, some children heard one story by each of the five authors and some heard two by one author and one by each of three others.) The child's task was to indicate which author he thought had written each story he heard on tape. Three of the children performed at chance level. However, four of them performed better than chance, and six performed well above chance (.06 probability level or better). After the child indicated the authorship of a particular book, the researcher asked questions like "How did you know it was that one?" or "Tell me something about the story that made you know who wrote it." (p. 146) Some responses (though certainly not all) suggested a beginning conscious awareness of style.

Because . . . uh . . . because they were talking the same.
Um, because of how they were talking.
Well, it sounds like like she's the one (pause) that was talking.
It really sounds like the Lorax girl. (Green 1981, p. 147)

It appears that the child's social environment in which language is authentically used in various ways in various communication situations supports the child's development of various styles but also supports his developing awareness of them.

IN CONCLUSION

What we don't know about children's development of communicative competence far exceeds what we do know. Yet for all that, what we do know is important and provides a solid base for learning more. We have significant beginning knowledge of

> what the child brings to the task of developing communicative competence: an orientation, both social and cognitive, that is his birthright as a human being; an orientation toward relating to others and toward actively making sense of experience, including language—perhaps the most basic human social and cognitive phenomenon.
>
> what the child encounters: language in use by members of the child's community, each language instance demonstrating the communication purposes and structures and styles of communicating within a complex social matrix.
>
> what the child does: observes and participates in communication events, actively figuring out as he does so the many ways that language is used in different social situations. Gradually he constructs the complex system we call "communicative competence."

In the area of communication development we again see the child as doer, actively engaging in, as well as he can, the very thing he is learning. For children, "communicating and learning to communicate always go hand in hand" (Labov and Fanshel 1977, p. 20).

12

Communicative Competence: Teachers and Children

INTRODUCTION

We come now to consider the dimensions of children's language growth which the school can contribute to most powerfully of all: children's growth as effective and versatile communicators. Now those very aspects of the classroom that we tend to bemoan—the large numbers of people involved and the great diversity of abilities, needs, backgrounds, and interests among them—become our staunchest allies. The child's home and immediate community provide a rich environment for her development of language. Yet, if this were the child's *entire* social and language world, then her language development might be limited in some important ways that school experience can foster. In school the child is a member of a social world beyond the family, and in this larger world her language becomes larger too. It is a basic fact of language development that one's language extends to take the whole of one's social experience into account: One's language must somehow find—must *make*—a place for this whole.

Nowhere is the potential contribution of school greater than in the area of the child's developing communicative competence. Certainly the wider world of the classroom goes well beyond the home in the particular aspects we focused on in Chapter 11:[1]

> *Communication purposes:* The child comes to school knowing that language is purpose-full and having used language purpose-full-ly from birth. But new experiences in school involve new communication purposes as well as the refinement and extension of familiar ones.
>
> *Communication events*: The child comes to school having participated actively in a variety of types of communication events (including different sets for different children, of course). In school the child will participate in some

[1] I am using the term "classroom" here not in the sense of a particular actual room bounded by four walls. I am thinking, rather, of experiences the child has in connection with school, whatever the particular location of those experiences happens to be.

events that are new to her—perhaps interviews, sharing time, peer-group writing conferences, dialogue journals, meetings of groups working on projects.

Communication situations and styles: The child comes to school having observed and interacted with a variety of individuals in a variety of situations, but her school experience will involve her in written and oral interactions with a far wider range of individuals and situations. Even her immediate classmates will include children from backgrounds quite different from her own. And her interactions will go well beyond her immediate classmates to include adults in the larger community, authors, children from other grades, and so on.

It is not the goal of this chapter to "cover" all the possibilities for children's communicative development in their school experience. This would obviously be impossible, since our understanding of communicative competence is itself limited. But perhaps even more important, such complete treatment would be impossible because in their daily interactions with children, teachers create and exploit new possibilities that we could not even imagine out of a real context. No discussion could capture the moment-to-moment responsive business that teaching is.

However, it *is* possible to suggest the potential in this rich social environment of the classroom. It is in hopes of doing this that I am focusing on three selected language functions (narrating, informing/explaining, and expressing personal feelings and opinions) and three aspects of social situations (age, status, and familiarity of the participants) in the classroom context. I am simply playing with some of the possibilities in these selected areas in hopes of sparking your own thinking and helping you to further your awareness of the many communication purposes and events and situations and styles that school experience offers.

Finally in this chapter we will consider some kinds of classroom talk, the restrictions we often place on it, and what some recent research does—and does not—tell us about classroom talk.

FUNCTION

Narrating[2]

We want children to be able to tell (or follow the telling of) a "story," a series of related events, either real or imagined, in an orderly time sequence. As adults, we use language in this way a great deal: "I had the worst dream last night. I dreamed I was. . . ." "I was reading in the paper just yesterday that the police finally caught up with X. At first they had thought . . . so they had . . . but then they found out that . . . so they had to. . . ." "You probably don't remember the time you fell on broken glass and we had to take you to the hospital. You were only little then. You see,

---

[2]I am ignoring here a distinction that some scholars have maintained between the communication goal and the means of achieving it, for example, Kinneavy's (1971) distinction between "aims" and "modes" and Tough's (1977) distinction between "functions" and "uses."

you had been out playing in your sandbox. . . ." "Saw a great movie yesterday. It was about a. . . ." "Once upon a time. . . ." "Dear Sir: Three weeks ago I requested from you. . . . One week later I was informed that. . . ."

Our narrating serves different purposes. Sometimes we narrate in order to inform someone of something; sometimes to persuade someone to change a course of action; sometimes for pure enjoyment. Whatever the ultimate purpose this use of language is serving, we certainly use this function far more than we think we do.

Harold Rosen (1983) considers narrative a "fundamental process of the human mind," a fundamental way of knowing, of making sense of the world. Indeed, given the universality of storying, he may very well be right. We know of no cultural group, either at this moment or through recorded history, that does not have well-developed ways of creating and expressing narratives (real or imagined). Groups differ in their ways of storying (see chap. 11, p. 347), but every group *has* ways of storying; that is, every group has conventions underlying individuals' production and interpretation of narratives. Whenever we encounter an aspect of language that appears to be universal in our species, we have strong reason to suspect that we have encountered an element that defines us as humans (rather than as members of some other species). Narrating may be one such element—perhaps a "fundamental process of the human mind" after all. In any case, narrating is real and ever present in our oral and written communication.[3]

Think about the effective and ineffective story tellers (and writers) you know. How do the more effective ones differ from the less effective? In many ways, no doubt, but it's likely that some of the differences have to do with selection of what to tell, with keeping "on track," with clarity in presenting the sequence of events, and with the variety of techniques used in the telling. Other things being equal, the more effective telling is likely to be one that

includes content that is clear and interesting to the listener or reader;

keeps the story line going, not getting sidetracked into unimportant or unrelated details;

conveys the events in ways that make the chronological sequence clear (though they need not be presented in chronological sequence; flashback, stream-of-consciousness, and other nonchronological techniques can be most effective);

includes variety in the ways the story is presented, for example, use of a variety of sentence types, dramatization, impersonation, and dialogue. (How many times have your children told you those monotonous "and then . . . and then . . . and then . . . and then . . ." stories?)

[3]Rosen adds another intriguing idea: that in every non-narrative kind of discourse (that is, every language event whose overarching purpose is not narrative) "there stalks the ghost of narrative," and in every narrative "there stalks the ghost of non-narrative." For example, my purpose may be to persuade you to allow me to do something, and in the course of my argument I may tell a story of someone else who did that thing with good result; or, in telling a story, the teller will surely step out of the narrative sequence to describe characters, scenery, feelings. Rosen's point is that the narrative function weaves in and out of much of our oral and written communication.

Children in school are most likely to develop these ways of using the narrative function effectively if they are accepted as full-fledged members of the club of story makers and interpreters and actively engage in narrating (reading, writing, listening, telling) in real interaction with others—with classmates, community members, published authors, child authors, and so on. Consider these examples of authentic narrative events in classroom settings.

Three-year-old Fredrick dictates a story to his teacher that he and his classmates will later act out: "First Fredrick fell off the bench, then Stuart fell off" (Paley 1986).

A kindergarten teacher has asked the children "How do you know if somebody likes you?" In the course of the discussion, the children recall some of their shared experiences as mini-narratives.

DEANA: Jill, remember when you and me were in your father's car sucking our thumbs?

JILL: Oh yeah. That was so much fun. My daddy kept singing, "Rockabye baby in the tree top." Remember?

FRED: Hey, Wally. Remember at Eddie's birthday party we put those metal kettles on our heads?

TANYA: Lisa, remember when I first came to your house and I didn't know where the bathroom was? And then we put the boats in the bathtub?

ELLEN: Remember when we were looking for the black kitty at your house, Kim? And we said, "Here, kitty, here's kitty" and we were laughing so much?

KIM: And it was in the closet? I remember that.

WARREN: Kenny, remember in nursery school we brought snow inside in our hats and the teacher was laughing?

KENNY: Hey, let's do that again. Okay? (Paley 1981, pp. 151–52)

In the same kindergarten, the children are retelling the story of Martin Luther King.

WALLY: My mom said Martin Luther King was smart and he . . . decided to throw off that sign [that said Blacks had to sit at the back of the bus] and so you could sit anywhere.

EDDIE: You forgot to say about Rosa Parks. See, she came on the bus and gave the bus driver some money and she sat in the chair and the bus driver said, "No, you're not white." And she said, "I don't care. I want to sit because I'm tired and also I gave you a dime."

WALLY: Now you can sit wherever you want. Also Martin wasn't allowed to go to any water fountain or any bathroom and he also had to have only a black grocery-store man to pay. He was separated. My mom knows all about that. She even used to *be* separated.

EDDIE: We're talking about the bus now, Wally. He told people they shouldn't go on the bus and don't pay them money. Then if they get a broken bus they can't fix it.

WARREN: And he told them to stop shopping if you can only be white. (Paley 1981, pp. 111–12)

Second-grade Juanita reads the story she is working on to her teacher and several classmates as Pam holds the picture Juanita has drawn to go with her story.[4]

JUANITA: "This is Tinkerbell. She is my friend. She is a angel and she is a puppet. She is going to read you a story. I will tell you how I got made. One day I had to be colored then I had to be cut out and then! I had to be stapled. And then she wrote a story and that is all for now."

OLIVIA: Who is "she"? (Refers to "she" in the last sentence of the story.)

JUANITA: Tinkerbell.

OLIVIA: I think it's . . . "she" is—

PAM: —that "she" means herself. (Refers to Juanita.)

OLIVIA: But then I don't know "she" means herself.

PAM: I thought "she" meant herself.

TEACHER: Who did you mean, Juanita? (She points to herself.) OK, So instead of "she," what could you do?

JUANITA: My name.

(She reads the story again with the change and the children understand.)

These examples differ in the ages of the story tellers, in whether the story is real or imagined, in whether it is collaboratively or individually created, in whether it is a new story told or a familiar story *re*told. But common to them all is the children's active engagement in narrative for purposes which are real to them. Notice that it is in such authentic storying events that the children receive important feedback about the very characteristics that enhance the effectiveness of their narrative. In her Tinkerbell story, Juanita is using a story-within-a-story framework, an interesting departure from the standard pattern. Her classmates' discussion provides the feedback Juanita needs to clarify her meaning for her listeners and readers and thus carry out her interesting technique successfully. Eddie's comment, "You forgot to say about Rosa Parks," is a reminder both about the specific content that belongs in the story and also about where it belongs in the chronological sequence of events. And Eddie's "We're talking about the bus now, Wally" is his way of saying that Wally has veered away from the story line and needs to get back on track. Story content, focus, sequence, means of presentation—these are central elements of effective narrative and they are the very elements these children are attending to. How sharply these examples contrast with the typical classroom situation in which the teacher assigns a topic ("Today you're going to write a story about X") and then returns the children's papers with corrected spelling and punctuation for the children to copy again in their "very best handwriting."

There are many ways of involving children actively in narrative events. One way I like to play with the incredible range of possibilities is to consider the elements of storying with children and then think of ways to vary each element. Story events generally include these elements: a tale, a

---

[4]I am indebted to Judith King for this example from her data.

teller, an audience (listeners and/or readers), and a way of telling, that is, some method of presentation.

The tale: What comes to mind first may be the magnificent world of children's literature available to us, and surely there is no substitute for your reading a well-selected book aloud to children *every* day during *prime* time for *at least* thirty minutes. Fine, but what about other stories? What about

wordless storybooks for which the child provides a verbal story.[5]

ongoing classroom events written in an ongoing classroom journal or in a classroom newspaper that circulates through the school and to the children's homes regularly.

dramas created spontaneously in the sociodramatic area of the classroom. (Every elementary classroom from kindergarten through grade six should have a designated area for children's creation of narratives through drama. No, sixth graders are not "too old" for this; they love it!)

favorite stories played or new ones created in the puppet area of the classroom (another area that every classroom should have, complete with a variety of puppet-making materials).

real episodes from your own experience. My experience has been that many children are fascinated with the personal incidents their teachers tell. (It's sometimes a real revelation to young children to learn that the teacher currently has a life outside of the classroom, and that she was once a child and even, on occasion, got in trouble.)

comics—to be read and to be created by the children.

narrative songs and poems.

children's own written narratives on topics, real or imagined, that they have selected themselves (as described in Graves 1983 and Calkins 1983).

picture stories. I think immediately of Polaroid pictures children took while on a walk, to which they later added text to make a picture story; or the ongoing pictures and text some kindergarten children provided over several weeks as they observed eggs and then newly-hatched chicks and a caterpillar that finally became a butterfly.

biography. There are some fine published biographies available, but also autobiography can be an important type of writing and telling for children. (Older children can be helpful scribe-partners for younger children who tell their life stories for the older children to write down for them. See Tassell 1983 for a description of such a partnering autobiographical project.)

the child's own ongoing personal journal or diary (written or taped).

plays to be read or written. The most elaborate created narrative I know of produced by school children came from a group of sixth graders. They made up a story about a difficult new child in the classroom, based on a real experience they had had that year. Their final creation involved showing a series of slides they had taken, as groups of children acted out segments of the story, accompanied by a tape of children playing the parts in the dramatized version they had written, and also including musical background selections for some of the slides.

[5]For a helpful list, see Genishi and Dyson 1984, p. 187.

oral histories. I think immediately of some school children whose study of the Depression Era included interviewing older people in their neighborhoods to gather oral histories of their experiences during the Depression.

daily events in the child's life. These are stories to be told to you, an interested listener ("Know what?" the excited child says to you. "No, what?" you reply—and she's off!), or to be told publicly to classmates (as Show and Tell, perhaps) or to be shared quietly with a friend in the classroom conversation corner. This story may be the least noticed and the most important of all.

The teller or presenter.[6] You as story reader may be the one we think of first. But what about

adults whom you and the children invite to come into the classroom to read aloud, for example, school personnel, parents, community folks, children from upper grades (including the children's high school heroes). Why not encourage your students to invite people they would like to come? (It is especially fascinating to include readers with various voices and dialects and styles. In fact, you may want to have several different people read the same story to the children, by way of demonstrating this variety.)

professionals on record or tape. (Again, there's a wonderful selection available.)

your own students who write and publish narratives for others to read, who tell narratives to their classmates, who select stories that they read to children in younger classes, who tell versions of wordless storybooks to or with classmates, and so on.

parent volunteers.

Audience: Who will hear or read the story—consider it, appreciate it, enjoy it, respond to it—and even mentally construct it from the author's words? Again, the classic picture is that of the teacher presenting a story in some way as an entire class of children listens. But what about

an individual child at the listening center.

pairs of children in a quiet corner—classmates perhaps, or maybe cross-grade partners—reading or telling stories to one another.

small groups at a listening center, following a taped story together in their accompanying books.

several children collaborating in creating a narrative, each one both audience and teller-presenter in the process.

you as audience; every time a child comes to you with "Know what?" and you answer, "No, what?" you have accepted the audience role, ready to listen and respond to the child's story with interest. And when you listen to or read the story a child is writing, again you become an important audience.

[6]In some cases there is one creator and a second presenter. For example, in the case of an adult reading a story aloud to children, the author is the "teller" in the sense of having provided the words, but the adult who reads the story aloud is the presenter, as she conveys the author's words to the children. But in the case of a child reading a story herself, the author is both the teller and the presenter.

shifting clusters of children in peer conferences, helping an individual child with her current writing—sometimes planned, sometimes spontaneous, sometimes the whole class, sometimes a few, or one.

Audiences ever shifting, forming and reforming—the possible groupings are many in a classroom where children are communicating.

The ways of telling; method: Well, one individual reads to a group in a face-to-face event. That's one way. But what about

a telling instead of a reading. Whether the tale is a story by a professional author, the child's Show and Tell, a personal event from the teacher's own childhood—a *telling* can be especially involving to the listener(s).[7] Do you and the children ever turn off the lights on a gloomy day and tell ghost stories? Rylant (1985) tells of her third-grade teacher, Miss Evans, who told the children an ongoing saga called *The Journey*: "The main characters in *The Journey* were the twenty-five of us sitting in her classroom. Once a week, Miss Evans led us on an adventure into the jungles of Africa or the glaciers of the Antarctic or some equally harrowing place, and she narrated, in a tense, mysterious, breathless voice, the epic battles we won, together and individually" (p. 460).

the tape-recorded voice. I have already suggested that you tape every story you read aloud to the children and put the taped stories in the listening center. But there are other tape-recorded voices reading or telling stories. Any of the tellers already mentioned can be on tape as well as in the face-to-face encounter.

dramatization (either spontaneous or planned)—children using their own voices and bodies to express sequences of events.

dramatization through the use of puppets.

the professional's voice on tape or record.

filmed versions of favorite stories.

the children's dramatizations presented on videotape or slide-and-tape.

More often than not, several means happen in combination. One teacher, for example, writes down her kindergartners' stories as they choose to dictate them to her individually, and then, the same day during the children's acting out time, the teacher reads each child's story aloud to the whole class as the author and several other children the author selects act out the story (Paley 1981). Another adult, working with Spanish-speaking kindergarten children combines reading aloud and dramatizing[8] (Seawell 1985). She introduces a new story (either Spanish or English) to the children by reading it to them in small groups (usually three children) so that they can be maximally involved; a child might sit in the adult's lap as she reads, or hold onto the book, or request rereadings of particular parts. Then she introduces a set of simple papersack hand puppets for the story. She puts the book and the set of puppets and an audiotape of the story at the children's listening center, and she prepares several more envelopes

[7]For a recent book on story telling, see Livo and Rietz 1985.

[8]This activity is described more fully in Chapter 15.

with book and hand puppets that the children can check out to take home. Every week she introduces a new storybook that gets added to the collection. Small groups of children select a story-and-puppet envelope and "do" their selected story. Different groups may choose to "do" their selected story in different ways. In some groups, one member may read/tell the story from the book while the others hold the puppets (and assist the reader-teller when she needs it). In other groups, the children may all take puppets and dramatize the story directly. The adult here simply introduces the stories to the children and provides copies of the books and puppets; it is for the children then to decide how to use what the adult has provided.

I have deliberately saved until last what may be the most basic narrative encounter of all: the child with a book. Now the story is whatever the author has chosen to tell, the teller is the author, the "audience" is the child, the way of the telling is the book itself—words printed on pages. The child will read many kinds of books in school, but one important kind will be narrative. Though child-plus-book may, on the face of it, seem to be the most basic narrative experience of all, it's quite remarkable how little child and book come together directly in some classrooms. In the name of "reading," children often seem to do everything *but* read: They labor through word-calling page by page in basals; they complete worksheet exercises; they do endless workbook pages on isolated skills; they look up words and read or write out definitions; they call words presented on flash cards or newsprint or chalkboard. All this in the name of back-to-basics. Yet what could possibly be more *basic* than a child reading a book she has chosen? We contribute greatly to our children's ability to read and to their love of reading, when we provide a substantial period every day without fail for children's self-chosen reading. We provide the time, the place, the model, and the materials. The place—are there cozy, inviting corners available where children curl up with their books? Are there some carpeted areas where children can stretch out? Are there inviting places for reading outside of our classroom? Are the children permitted to go to the library for their reading time, or to sit outside on the grass under a tree on a nice day? The model—do we read too? Do our children see us "get into" books of our choice? Do they see that this reading time is a special and highly prized time of our day—for *reading*, not for grading papers or arranging materials for an art activity? The materials—they need to be abundant and diverse so that children really do have choices for their reading. Obvious sources are school and public libraries. Inexpensive paperback editions of fine works abound and are an excellent investment to your ongoing classroom library. The books your own children have published will make a very special contribution, of course. Combining your resources with, or trading off with, those of another class doubles the materials available to all the children. Fader's idea is still a good one: Give each child a paperback that *belongs* to him or her, that can be traded with another child, and so, many traded books keep circulating (Fader and McNeil 1968).

The crucial thing about the self-chosen reading period is that the children really be free to choose what and how they will read during this time. This means changing materials each week—not all of them, of course, but those that seem to have served their purpose—so that the children really do have choices. This also means resisting the temptation to say to a child who is endlessly reading the same type of material, "Why don't you read a different kind of book for a change? Why here's an interesting biography. You haven't read biography for a long time." Some fifth graders may read every single Nancy Drew ever written before they move on (just as some adults do with Agatha Christie novels). Some second or third graders will go through every *Tin-Tin* and then go back to the beginning and read through them all again! And many children will read through all their favorite Dr. Seuss books that you thought they had left years earlier. But for this sacred period, that is their privilege. Most important of all, if the child is to be truly *free* in this reading time, there will be no test to take, no comprehension questions to answer, no book reports to write or present, no stars or brownie points of any kind awarded, no subtle competition gimmicks, no possibility of failure (see Holt 1969). (How much would you and I read for enjoyment if we knew that we were going to be examined at the end of each book via tedious comprehension questions, being required to write about the funniest incident or "the part I liked best"? The experience of reading a book is our own, pleasant and personal. So it should be for our children.) Will the children talk about what they are reading? Undoubtedly, just as you and I do when we really "get into" a book, but they will do it because they want to (the right reason), not because we force them to (the wrong reason).

The ideas I've played with here are, of course, only a beginning, but perhaps they suggest the possibilities for the narrative function in classrooms. It involves children in telling and listening and reading and writing and acting; in real and in imagined creations; in communication events ranging from the most informal conversation to the most carefully planned performance. Narrating can be an important way of knowing and doing for children.

Explaining/Informing

We know that we want children to be able to put something that they understand into words in such a way that their listener(s) and/or reader(s) will understand it also, and to be able to seek and interpret effectively the explanations of others in speech and writing.

As with other language functions, explaining is something we engage in frequently. Just consider the information you provide, seek, and interpret each day relating to such diverse topics as why the car won't run, what's happened to your friend's faltering marriage, why the checkbook doesn't balance, the rationale underlying a particular math text series, how your new blender functions to accomplish all those culinary miracles described in the accompanying booklet, what the nature of your illness is.

We think of school as a place where this informing/explaining function is basic. The most typical classroom instructional interaction pattern is teacher asks question and child answers it. Whether in a one-to-one, small-group, or whole-group situation, when we ask a child, "How did you arrive at that answer?" or "How do you know that—?" or "Why do you suppose that —?" we are asking the child to use language to explain something that she understands. We might paraphrase these requests as "Use your language to explain how you arrived at that answer, to explain how you know that X, to explain why you suppose that Y."

Typically the situations in which children inform/explain to us are of two different types. In the first and probably the most frequent, we ask children to explain something to us so that we can get some insight into their understanding. This is a way of using language that is special to the classroom. Underlying normal (outside of classroom) conversation is a basic condition we adhere to—that one asks for information because one sincerely wants to know that information, that is, because one doesn't know it already. If I ask you, "What time is it?" you and I both assume that I don't already know; if I ask my garage mechanic, "Why is my car making that grinding noise?" we both assume that I really don't know why and that I want to have that information. But if I ask a child in a classroom, "Mark, how could I find out which set has more members?" it is not because I myself do not know how to find out which of two sets has more members. Mark needs to know that in this classroom context, the usual operating condition of asking for information I don't already know is suspended. Mark needs to know that I am seeking information about Mark's understanding of how to determine which of two sets has more members. Notice, however, that we are both engaging in language for explaining/informing. The explanation Mark is constructing and expressing is a math concept and process for verifying; the explanation I am extracting from Mark's language is what is the nature of his understanding of this math concept and procedures for verifying.

But there is another type of situation in which children explain things that more accurately reflects "real" (nonclassroom) conversation, namely, the situation in which we really don't know the information or explanation that we explicitly seek in our question. Let's take an example. Suppose five of your fourth graders decided they'd like to start a regular program for presenting a story to a kindergarten class each day for two weeks. They've been working on this project for several days. They've talked with the kindergarten teacher to see if she'd like them to do this, they've arranged with you and the kindergarten teacher for a particular daily time block for presenting and also for scheduling their own practice and preparation sessions. They've dealt with the problem of what stories to present: They've talked with the kindergarten teacher about the children's favorites and which have and haven't been read to them this year; they've talked with school and local librarians to find out which books seem to be the current favorites of five- and six-year-olds; they've looked over a catalogue and a few new children's books the public librarian has given them; they've recalled their own kindergarten favorites and talked with classmates about what their favorites were when they were in kindergarten. They've decided to present the selected stories in different ways—one person reading aloud, several people reading in parts (for a poetry session), dramatizing one story, presenting another with puppets, telling several short folk tales (instead of reading them) while another group member shows the pictures on the overhead projector. They've arranged for who will do what in each presentation, and for how they'll provide suggestions for one another in their practice sessions.

All this has involved a lot of languaging—talking, listening, reading, writing—for various purposes. Throughout all this, you've been somewhat in the background. You are aware of how their plans are gelling in a general way; you have responded to their ideas with enthusiasm when they've told you about them; you have provided realistic limits when they were moving in directions that weren't feasible ("You know, since it's only a half-day kindergarten and the teacher has a lot of things for the children to do in that time, you'll have to think in terms of twenty-minute presentations each day. Maybe it would be a good idea to time each one when you practice it to be sure you're close to the twenty-minute mark.") You have probably thrown in a suggestion or two to carry the children's ideas further ("You know, it might be fun to tape your presentations and leave the tapes with the children as a start for their own tape library"). But there comes a point at which you need to know in more than a general way what their plans are. Now you sit down with them for the purpose of having them inform you about things you don't already know: what their planned procedure and schedule will be, what stories and poems they've finally chosen and why, and what their plans are for each presentation. Here they are explaining to you what they have been doing and what they plan to do and why, because you really don't know. Situations like these, in which teacher and children confer and in which the children are the knowers and explainers/informers and the teacher is the nonknower, are extremely valuable. They tend to be frequent in classrooms where the teacher feels that an important aspect of the job is to support and extend the children's initiatives and ongoing plans for their learning experiences. In this situation in which you, the teacher, are the learner, the children have the invaluable opportunity of watching you learn, seeing how you listen, analyze, question relevantly, request information, synthesize what they are telling you. ("Let me make sure I have it straight so far. You feel it's important for little children to—so you're going to—. What about—? What are you going to do if—?")[9]

Of course, much of children's textbook material is explanatory and informative in nature, whether the explanation deals with a mathematical process, the structure of social organization of an African tribe, or the human body's use of food. We sometimes think of this kind of language as being boring, and something we have to force on children because they wouldn't engage in it otherwise; and indeed, some of this material is poorly written and very boring. (It must stand as a credit to children's good taste that they do not choose to read much of this material.) Yet clearly it is not the case that this language function itself is not engaging to children. They seek it on their own. We all know children who pour over auto manuals.

[9]As Carole Edelsky reminds me and I remind you, we carry our teacher status with us in all our interactions with children. Even when we are nonknowers and our children explain to us, we all know that the final approval for the children's plans is ours. Thus in interactions like the one described here, there is an element of "approval seeking" as well as "explaining/informing" on the children's part.

We know that children are eager to talk or write about personal hobbies and interests, which involves language heavy in explaining/informing. Consider the following titles of explanatory/informing type articles from (now defunct) *Kids* magazine: "How to Make a Moon Goon" (no. 9), "Water, Our Lifeline in Danger: Water Pollution" (no. 4), "How to Make Rubbings" (no. 7), "Countdown to Extinction" (no. 8), "How I Made My Movie" (no. 7), "Making Giant Totem Poles" (no. 10), "Life with a Boa Constrictor" (no. 14), "What's It Really like to Be a Twin" (no. 14), "The Wonderful World of Shells" (no. 15), "Sun Blackout July 10" (no. 15), "My Pet Raccoon" (no. 17). Not only did children choose voluntarily to write on these topics, but child editors selected them for publication in the magazine, presumably because they found these articles interesting and thought other children would too. And think of children's self-selected writing topics in classrooms: First grader Steve writes an informing piece called "Whales," while his classmate Gary writes "All About Alligators" (Sowers, 1985). Children working together on some project of importance to them inform each other a great deal. Each has a special contribution to make to the project; each must keep the others informed about what she is doing and how and why, and how that part fits in with the others. Each child must also respond to the information provided by other group members. The "burning issues" and "What Makes a Fourth Grader?" projects described in Chapter 10 are good examples of projects that involved a hefty amount of informing/explaining as the children carried out the many facets of their work.

Children working on individual or small-group projects will want to make their work available to others. A display format of some type might be useful: a bulletin board area or a table displaying the child's written material, perhaps some interesting books that she had found during the writing, some books with paper-clipped pages where interesting pictures could be found, any models or related art work that she might have done, a cassette tape on which she had read/told a relevant folk tale or provided explanatory comment relating to the selected pictures or to her art work. Providing areas where children can make available to other children what they are researching, and providing opportunity for children to explore those works of others which they choose to explore, will facilitate children's learning from the work of their classmates. Sometimes children will want to prepare a "traveling exhibit" on a pushcart to take around to other classes. Whatever the specifics of these informing events, what we need to aim for is more in the way of following children's interests and less in the way of coercing them to follow ours.

Much of explanation is the how-to-do-it type, steps in a process. Children are "practicing" explanation every time they read, write, listen to, or tell someone else how to play a particular game, how to construct a model, how to make chocolate chip cookies, how to make a kite. Our tendency is to give instructions for these activities to all the children at once. But we provide an important opportunity for our children to explain if we give instructions to only one or two children who then explain it to one or two other children they choose to play the game with. If a child who knows how to play a particular game wants to play that game with a friend who does not know how to play it, the "knower" will use language purposefully to explain the game to the friend, and the friend will interpret the instructions and provide immediate and clear feedback as to the success of the first child's explanation. And remember, you can be an important example of a learner if you share with your students your own experience of figuring out from the written instructions how to use a new piece of classroom equipment or how to play a new game or how to prepare for a new gerbil. How do you gather and use explanatory material? It's valuable for your students to see.

Too often school children come to think that all important information/explanation lives in books. Obviously books are important sources of information; but living, breathing people are good sources too. When children gather information directly from others, through interviews or written (or taped) correspondence, they then have much to share with one another. There are many people resources in every community. There are many more resources children can get to by letter. Many children's authors *do* answer children's letters. So do U.S. presidents (or, at least, those relegated to do this in their place). Use of firsthand resources can make research exciting for children (as for adults), and it often provides children with an especially interesting body of information to convey to others.

Traditionally the teacher has been seen as the information-giver and the child as the receiver. There has been a pervasive notion of teaching as giving and learning as receiving what is "given." As we have come to rethink this notion of the child as a passive receiver and to see the child instead as an active shaper and builder of her own understanding, we have come, I think, to value more equal balance of teachers and children engaged in information dialogue. Even very young children have much to inform us about. One kindergarten teacher is particularly aware that her five-year-olds think differently than she does and that it is *their* world of thought that is the relevant one for the children's learning (Paley 1981). So, she actively seeks information from the children about their ways of thinking:

When Wally says he's going to be a mother lion when he grows up, this teacher asks Wally and a number of his classmates whether they believe this can happen (p. 7).

When she hears the children arguing about whether it is possible to fool the tooth fairy, she asks the children individually what they think about this (p. 39).

Eddie's comment, "Sometimes I hate myself," sparks her curiosity about what constitutes naughtiness in the children's view: "When (do you hate yourself)?" "What do you do that's naughty?" (p. 54).

And in discussions about stories read aloud, her questions elicit valuable information from the children about their concepts of fairness, often quite different from her own ideas: "Was it fair for the fox to chase everyone out of the house?" (p. 27). "Why can't [Tico] decide for himself what kind of wings he wants?" (p. 26).

This teacher sincerely seeks information from the children, and they readily provide it—much to her benefit and to their own.

As with all language functions, so with informing/explaining: It is in authentic communication situations that children become more effective in its use. I have suggested only a few of many situations that can provide authentic experience in informing/explaining: children responding to our questions, interacting with information texts, writing informing material for others to read, working with friends on projects, displaying their own research, interpreting or giving how-to instructions, using firsthand sources, and explaining themselves to us. Only in such authentic contexts do children have reason to select and order ideas carefully, to clarify, elaborate, expand, rephrase, and exemplify them in their speaking and writing, and to seek order, clarity, and so on, in the information and explanations provided in the talk and writing of others.

Expressing (Personal)

We know that we want children to be able to express personal feelings and opinions in ways that make it possible for others to understand "where they are coming from," and also to be able to respond to, to feel into, the personal expressions of others. It would be impossible to underestimate the importance of language growth in this function. As the child's sense of self and her awareness of others continue to develop, and as she experiences new depths and heights of feeling (fear, joy, awe, frustration, humor, sympathy, anger), her language grows to find more adequate ways of expressing these feelings.

Some excellent children's literature is available to feed this personal understanding and expression. Children's fiction specifically focusing on children's feelings abounds and often helps children find ways to express personal experience. In fact, all excellent fiction, whether or not its specific purpose is to deal with some difficult emotional experience common to most children, presents characters who are *real* and thus experience a range of feelings. In reading or hearing such works, children are having the invaluable experience of feeling into another's life.

Much of children's own expression and interaction in this personal function will be intended to be read or heard by others (though sometimes the source will remain unidentified). Children writing for other children in (now defunct) *Kids* magazine came up with regularly appearing "Dear Dr. Loker" and "Don't You Hate . . ." sections. Here are a few samples:

Dear Dr. Loker:

I have just moved. And it is hard to find a friend because I am shy. What should I do? Signed, Shy. (no. 17)

Dear Dr. Loker:

In school I am no good in math. I try and try to do it, but I just can't do it right. Do you have a good solution? I sure do need it. Your friend Math-Whiffer. (no. 7)

Dear Dr. Loker:

I have three brothers and no sisters. That can be a real problem! They always beat up on me but I never get revenge on them. How can I? Signed, Revenge. (no. 10)

Don't You Hate . . .

Being bawled out for something your friend did (no. 11)
Kids that copy your papers (no. 9)
When your mother "screams" at you (no. 9)
When your parents treat you like a child, even though you're five (no. 9)
Forgetting your lines in a school play right in front of the whole P.T.A. (no. 10)
On Christmas getting excited over a lot of presents for you, but finding out it was nothing you wanted (no. 10)
When your mother sends you to school with a raincoat on, and no one else in the world is wearing a raincoat . . . and then it gets sunny (no. 10)

It's easy enough to provide a "Dear—" box or bulletin board area, and a box or area where children can put their responses. A "Don't You Hate . . ." caption on an empty bulletin board will elicit a lively response from some children.

Sometimes you might want to provide a very involving item intended to evoke personal responses from your students—perhaps a sensory item for younger children (such as, slime), or an emotional or ideational item for older children (an inflammatory editorial or article relating to serious ethical or moral conflict, perhaps). Your purpose here is to stimulate individual personal expression and response. Perhaps you'll write down what your young students say and make it available for others to read (or hear you read). Other times the expression and response may take the form of conversation or debate. Older children may be moved to write their personal responses for others to read. But whatever the form, the purpose is the same: a personal expression (emotion or opinion) and/or response to someone else's.

Poetry is a rich resource for language in the personal function. Exposure to a wide range of personal poetic expression conveyed in various forms is important here. Poetry written by children, especially by your own school children, speaks meaningfully to children. We often forget that poetry is all around us. Our school children often talk poetry; we can simply write down, exactly, snatches of their own talk—a line here, a line there—if our ears are tuned to hear the poetry in their talk. A group poem can provide a rich means of personal expression relating to a particular shared experience.

On a Walk Today . . .
I found a smooth white pebble—a bright spot in a patch of mud. (Jamie)

I found some moss that feels soft when I rub it on my cheek. (Tim)
I found an orange and black speckled butterfly wing. (Celia)
And I found a baby leaf, the size of my thumb nail. (Jody)

Treasures in our pockets.

It is important not to equate poetry with rhymed and metered verse. Much of the poetry we love—from Dr. Seuss to Shakespearean sonnets—is rhymed and metered. Much of it is richly beautiful; much of it is simply hilarious great good fun. But much of poetry, especially children's poetry, does not and should not have to conform to strict formal constraints. Even young children seem so naturally to provide the vivid word picture, the unique personal expression that captures an individual perception. Preserve it! It is a poem in its own right. If we provide exposure only to jingles in the name of "poetry," we will find our children substituting "fat cats wearing hats and sitting on mats" for real personal expression.

Much of our personal use of language is intensely private. Conversation between friends is often a private matter. Our children may engage in this a great deal in school, but often they are forced to do so surreptitiously; often private personal conversation is not sanctioned in the classroom. We would do well, I think, to legitimize it, to support this as a valid and welcome interaction activity. A conversation corner might help. An area so labeled and demarked by a carpet scrap would do, to be recognized as a place for private conversation among friends.

Personal journal writing is perhaps the most private and intensely personal writing activity of all. It is imperative that we respect the children's privacy here. The child's writing is not for our eyes unless the child specifically asks us to read it. Then more than at any other time, we must remember that what the child has chosen to share with us is a meaning, not a form; we respond to the meaning *only* and are careful not to see spelling "errors" or immature grammatical constructions. There are many ways to support and encourage this important means of personal expression. One is by simply providing time for it. A simple diary makes a lovely Christmas or un-Christmas or unbirthday gift for each child. Basically, it's a bunch of blank pages, after all, but made special in some way—a blank cover front and back for the child to decorate in a personal way and you to laminate? Or a cover you have personalized with a snapshot you have taken of the child? A personal note from you inside the front cover? Your own word-picture description of the child to accompany your gift?

Another gift many teachers give their students is a book to be used as a dialogue journal. I have mentioned dialogue journals before but cite them here as an important way of providing for children's personal expression of their wonderings, opinions, grievances, anger, anticipation. In one fifth-grade classroom, the first day the children turned in their dialogue journals, Larry's first page was blank. His teachers wrote back, "How can we answer you if you don't write?" Larry responded (in writing), "I don't like writing." The written interaction continued.

TEACHER: "Does anything bother you about writing?"

LARRY: "I don't like to write because I can't not spell right. that's bother me about writing."

TEACHER: "Don't worry about it right now. The more you read and write the better your spelling will get. Just worry about getting your ideas written down . . ." (Hayes and Bahruth 1985, p. 99)

Apolinar, in the same class, began his journal with

> I like writing because we do art on it sometimes an I love writing and reading books because I love stories and I love draw in pictures alot because you can learn to draw pretty pictures and writing to other people and i hait writing what the teacher said to us to do because i like to write wat i like to do at my paper. (Hayes and Bahruth 1985, p. 99)

I find this a fascinating classroom "genre." In a way, it seems strange to carry on a personal written correspondence with someone who is only a few feet away, someone you can see even as you write to her. Typically, we use writing rather than speech either because those we are communicating with are not present or because we have "something to say [that is] important enough to last longer than conversation" (Meek 1982, p. 17), or because we want to examine our own thoughts on paper. But in dialogue journal writing, the person the individual is writing to is a few feet away, the ideas are not usually important enough to preserve, and the writer is typically not examining the ideas that she writes. How, then, can this be an authentic way of using language in the classroom? As I have argued already, if it is authentic, then it will serve a genuine communication purpose for the participants.

And so it does. Dialogue journal writing serves to keep teacher and child in touch with each other in a very special way. Though teacher and child are in close proximity for much of each school day, the opportunities for their real one-to-one dialogue about matters of the child's interest may be few. (So many children, so little time.) There are factors other than physical distance that separate people who want to communicate with one another. Dialogue journals provide a way for teacher and child to keep in close continuing contact across the time and people demands of the classroom. The classroom is a very special kind of community and requires some special ways of communicating. Dialogue journals are a striking example of the creative power of language users as they devise new ways of making language work for them. This classroom "genre" was born out of teachers' concern to interact with their students more fully, more personally. Indeed, this genre enables both teacher and child to get to know each other better as individuals and to stay in close touch, even as it engages both in authentic personal expression of their own feelings and opinions and in personal response to the partner's. Authentic indeed!

To me, one of the most intriguing types of personal writing that children seem to engage in so naturally is note passing. I find it interesting that we try so hard to stamp out this activity that is written personal communication at its very best! That it is so resistant to our stamping out efforts should tell us how meaningful this activity is to our children. Note passing is alive and well—thriving—in most of the classrooms I visit. And it should be! It involves everything we would ask of a communication experience: It is purposeful and relevant communication for the child; it is language used for a valid function (personal); it receives relevant and immediate feedback in the response of the receiver. Why, then, do we pounce with such zeal on the note being passed from hand to hand under the desks and across the aisles? Usually so that the children can get back to their assigned task, which is often one that engages their interests and language abilities far less—a worksheet involving comprehension questions on a reading assignment, a spelling exercise, or a "language arts" exercise on verb forms or parts of speech or sentence types. (I have been amazed at the high level of personal writing in many of the note-passing series my own three children have kept and have let me read. I have found vivid imagery and sophisticated wit and humor that these children rarely attained in assigned writing tasks. One such series involved lengthy personal ritual insults, written in the style the teacher had taught them was used by Eskimos, clear evidence that these children had grasped far more from the Eskimo study than the teacher dreamed!) So why don't we use note passing, legitimize it?[10] A personal mail envelope on every desk might do and the understanding that getting up and going over to another child's desk to deliver a letter was OK, just like going to sharpen a pencil or get a drink. I know one teacher of young children who uses a carpenter's apron with great ingenuity, regularly putting a surprise (usually a note) in each pocket one for each child. Carpenter's aprons are easily made (by your students, perhaps?) and each pocket can be a mail pocket for a different child. You can doubtless think of more and better ideas than these, but the point is to capitalize on children's real use of an important language function, rather than to punish it.

How much do your students see you engage in personal writing? Do you do any personal journal writing in class, or sometimes write a line or two of poetry? Do you express personal feelings and responses verbally, out where the children can hear them? Do your students hear/see you respond sensitively to the personal expressions you read or hear? Your own use of this function (as all functions) is important to your students' communication growth.

One obvious way that your students might see you engage in personal language is by your writing them notes— quickies, even one-liners, that you dash off as the spirit moves you.

You're sure grinning a lot today. Do you have some special secret?

Sorry if I jumped on you pretty hard this morning, but—
 I meant what I said

---

[10]A word of caution. I don't know how much of the joy of note passing comes from the fact that it is forbidden. If making it "above board" lessens its desirability for children, then let's just ignore it and let it thrive.

And I said what I meant.
You're driving me up the wall today
One hundred percent!
Let's talk for a minute in the conversation corner after lunch about how we can get through the afternoon better.

Thanks for helping to comfort Celia. I know you made her feel better.

I think—I just think maybe you have a new friend today. Am I right?

How do you think up so many unique ideas? Your idea about_____was an interesting and valuable contribution to your group's discussion this morning.

Dear Jess,
This is a hint!
There once was a student named Jess,
Whose desk was a terrible mess
By the end of the day
He'd cleared it away
And now his teacher nags less.
Today, Jess?!

It's unique, it's personal, it's your thoughts and perceptions and feelings spilling over into writing in a way that's natural and comfortable and fun for you. If your students see that this is an easy and natural way of expressing for you, it's likely to become an easier way of expressing for them too.

Narrating, explaining/informing, expressing personal feelings and opinions—these are obviously just a few of many uses we make of our language and will encourage in our children. These are the three I have chosen to discuss at some length because they are different enough from one another to reflect the wide range of language use. But whatever the uses chosen as examples for discussion, the basic principles would remain the same. Using language effectively

1. involves expressing in speech and writing, and also interpreting and responding to the writing and speech of others;
2. involves developing an awareness of another's perspective and shaping expression appropriately for the listener/reader; or interpreting the language of others from the producer's perspective;
3. develops through the active involvement of children figuring out through using language in meaningful interaction how they can make language work effectively—how they can accomplish what they want to accomplish with words.

SITUATION

We use language always for some purpose(s) and always in some situation. It is through interaction in a wide variety of social contexts that the child's language becomes a more widely adapted communication instrument. We have identified a few of the many situational variables that influence the talking style we use on a given occasion (for example, the age of the conversational participants, their respective status, the topic of conversation, the time and place.) How can we deliberately incorporate a diverse range of these variables in the communication experiences we provide for our school children? To deal with this question, we will consider, in an exploratory way, several selected situational dimensions, much as we did in the previous portion on language uses. My hope is that you will be spurred to consider ways you can incorporate within your classrooms other aspects of social situations not discussed here, as well as additional ways to incorporate those discussed. Remember that the goal here is to involve the children as fully as possible in real communication experiences that are maximally diverse situationally. The hypotheses that children build, test, and revise will grow to account for the ways speech and writing are adapted to these diverse social situations. Let's take age, status, and familiarity as examples, remembering that they are only three among many, and that, like all situational variables, they often overlap.

Age

We tend to think of a classroom as a giant peer group. It is, and this is doubtless important. But it can be much more, especially for language. My mind runs immediately to the grandparent generation and the rich contribution the older members of our community can make to our children's growth as competent communicators. One school I know instituted Grandparents Week. It was exciting to watch grandparents participate in the children's school activities and to see new cross-age friendships grow up on the playground or at lunch. When we talk about a friendship, we are talking about a relationship in which language plays a vital role. A friendship is a languageship. More and more I find myself wondering why we in education have so little used people of retirement age in our classrooms. Why have we so quickly forgotten the rich educational resource "the older generation" was not so long ago when we were a more rooted, less mobile people, and several generations of one family lived in one home or neighborhood? This potential resource is greater now than it has ever been. The number of vigorous, interesting, and highly skilled retired people is steadily growing. Many of them are eager to contribute to the community in ways that the demands of their steady jobs had previously made impossible. Many of them care about children and their growth. We have failed to see the potential contribution of this virtually untapped resource.

Sometimes we have used older people as resources for specific projects, for instance, as primary sources in a unit on local history. One kindergarten studying lullabies from around the world relied heavily on local grandmothers (many of whom had strong European ties, and many more of whom were fuzzy on their ancestry but knew plenty of non-American lullabies). But why limit our children's classroom interaction with older people to a special week or to special units or to blood relations? Older people can contribute much in our classrooms—talking with (listening to?) individual children, sharing personal experiences and interests with the children in an informal way, reading/telling stories and listening to children read stories individually, helping with small-group projects that need some overseeing (cooking experiences, perhaps), but most important of all, just being friends who come by to visit and participate because they enjoy it. My experience has been that these friendships are as enriching to the adult as to the child.

Younger children offer another important source of relationships. Just as we rarely involve older people in our classrooms, so we rarely involve preschoolers in elementary classrooms. What about the younger brothers and sisters of our children? Couldn't we work out times that they would be welcome in our classrooms so that our children could build meaningful relationships and languageships "downward"? (And think of the important languaging that would be involved as our children planned for activities that would be interesting and involving to younger children.)

We have always known that younger children often look up to older ones. We can use this. Involving fifth graders significantly in second-grade classrooms helps children at both age levels; the fifth grader gets an ego boost, and the second grader gets a new hero or heroine. Language is at its best in a relationship that is mutually satisfying. We are using older children more and more as tutors for younger ones, and this is good. How can we use our intermediate-level children more as classroom aides, as story tellers/readers, with small groups or individuals, as friends who stop by to visit or who join the younger children for picnic lunches on nice days, as walking partners for the younger children when they go on local field trips, as helpers for younger children working on projects that place heavy demands on their reading and writing abilities? And of course, whatever a fifth grader can be to a second grader, the second grader can be to a kindergartner.

The relationships between children and their peers, children and older people, children and younger children will be different. The language that lives in and fosters these relationships will be different also. And that's what we want!

Status

When older children interact with younger ones, the older ones usually hold the position of higher status. But what provisions do we make for their interactions with people of higher status than theirs? Do we do as much as we might by way of inviting school board members, city government officials, or the principal to come and visit, to have lunch with us, to participate in our activities for a day? Having started relationships through these visits, do we then make return visits?

Do our children have many opportunities for interacting in writing with people of higher status? If they wonder why an author "made the story end sad," do they write and ask him or her? If they have questions relating to actions taken by city, state, or federal government officials, do they write or call up and ask for explanations? If they are concerned by these actions, do they write to explain the implications they feel the actions will have for them when they are adults? Or to point out the ways these decisions affect children? If the decisions are made by local officials, do they make an appointment to discuss their concerns with them, either at school or at the official's office? If their local newspaper discontinues a favorite comic strip, do they write to protest? Our children should know that those who hold high-status positions are usually only a telephone call or a postage stamp away.

Interviewing activities offer endless possibilities for interacting with people of different status precisely because you can interview *anyone* about *anything*. Taped interviews are sometimes best because they can be conducted individually or in a small group and then made available to everyone in the class.

It is fascinating to watch children of all ages in dramatic play as they assume high-status roles and role play interactions in various status relationships. They play with various language styles, deliberately changing style when they are queen or subject, teacher or pupil, boss or employee, parent or child. Such play is an important support for the children's growing ability to express and to interpret language expressions of role relationships, one of many reasons that sociodrama should be an ever-present opportunity in *every* elementary and preschool classroom.

Familiarity

A shared background of experience is the basis of familiarity. To say that a friend is more familiar to us and the grocery store cashier is less familiar to us is to say that we share a greater background of experience with the friend than we do with the grocery store cashier. We may talk to both. Our talk will reflect our greater familiarity with the friend and our lesser familiarity with the cashier.

In an interactive classroom, teacher and children steadily build a rich background of shared experience during the year. Sensitive teachers know how important it is to get a picture of each child outside of school as well as inside. That's why we encourage children to talk about outside interests, hobbies, and concerns; that's why we try to establish contact with the child's parents and, where possible, visit the child at home. In becoming more familiar with our children's lives, we are expanding our interaction range with each child beyond the confines of what we do together in school.

It is important to us that we know our children as people, not just as students. Yet we seem less concerned that our children know us as people, not just as teachers. I was struck one day by how limited children's views of their teachers can be when I walked my five-year-old daughter up the walk to her kindergarten class and she asked me, "Where does Miss J_____ (the teacher) keep her pajamas? And where is her bed?" I suddenly realized that she had no concept of Miss J_____ apart from school, and she assumed that Miss J_____ lived there. As it happened, several weeks later Miss J_____ invited her class to her home for part of the morning and for lunch. She showed them her home, her interests—the books she was reading, the dress she was making, the art work she had collected. She had them prepare the lunch in her kitchen. They played with her dog, ate lunch on the floor of the living room, cleaned up, went for a walk (Lucky for Miss J——, she lived on a California beach!). It was an important shared experience for both teacher and children, and opened new areas of communication. Miss J—— and her students had more to talk about because they were more familiar with each other as friends, rather than simply knowing each other in teacher-student roles.

We help to extend our children's language when we make provision for interaction with people with whom they are less familiar also. Communicating effectively with someone with whom we share little background of experience often requires greater explicitness, for we can't assume the listener will know what we're talking about in the way that a friend does. Bringing "outsiders" into the classroom is valuable, whether as "guest speakers" or as "consultants" to work on a specific project with a group of children, or just as interested visitors. Providing for interaction with children from other schools can be helpful also. I have known same-grade children from different schools to get together for lunch and to exchange jump-rope rhymes and hand-clap games. The actual visit was preceded by exchanges of letters and was followed by a return visit—and then several more as the children found other areas of common interest.

Negotiating with outsiders about field trips, both prior to and during the field trip, provides many real reasons for the children to communicate with people they know less well. We tend to assume that it is for us to arrange field trips for our students, and the value to them begins when they board the bus or start the walk. But this is not so, especially for language. Much of the value for our students is in their planning and follow-up—requesting information, selecting places to visit and persuading others of the value of their choice, arranging (by phone? by letter?) for the trip itself, and communicating with other classes the advantages and disadvantages of such a trip and how other groups might modify the arrangements (based on their experience).

Again, the point is the range of communication experiences we provide. As children's social experience becomes more diverse, so does their language. We want the children's language use to include styles appropriate to interaction with people familiar and with people unfamiliar to them. We can provide for this if we decide to. Language arts, the art of producing and interpreting language effectively in spoken and written forms, is everywhere and always; it is not something that happens during a particular time of day. If we are providing truly interactional environments for children, they are languaging all day long, with each other, with outsiders, with you, with themselves.

SOME TALK ABOUT TALKING
(OR, UP ON THE SOAP BOX AGAIN)

In some ways tradition works against those of us who want interactive, talky, environments for our children. It is interesting that traditionally many teachers who have all along sincerely professed an intense concern for children's oral language development, punish children more for talking in school than for any other single "offense." More children miss recess, stay after school, have their seat moved to an isolated area of the classroom, or write paragraphs about what constitutes good (quiet?) behavior, for their "offenses" relating to talking, than for any other "misbehavior," including a host of various deliberate and calculated unkindnesses. The "offender" talked when she "should have been working" ("Stop talking and do your work"; maybe some talking *is* her work). She talked too loud ("_____, I can hear your voice above everyone else's"). She talked in the wrong place ("We don't talk in the halls"). She talked about the wrong thing ("We're talking about social studies now, not about what you are going to do after school"). She talked to the wrong person ("_____, you're supposed to be working with Jenny now; Susan isn't in your group"). She talked without raising her hand and being recognized first ("Did I call on you? I don't remember seeing your hand up!" or "I called on David. Is your name David?"). She talked too much ("Margaret, can't you *ever* be quiet and just listen!").

Am I suggesting here that there should be no constraints on talking in the classroom? *Absolutely not.* I am suggesting, rather, that we be sure that our restrictions are in line with the very definite talking constraints that already exist in the society which our classrooms supposedly reflect, many of which constraints the young child is already aware of. Consider:

1. *Talking when working.* There are kinds of work that are enhanced by a quiet atmosphere. But in the "real world" much of our work involves talk. I know we provide for work requiring silence. Do we provide adequately for work that talk is a vital part of?

2. *Talking when one should be listening.* Remember that conversational turn taking is learned early. Turn taking makes sense to children. It is part of their sociolinguistic understanding. But if *all* turn taking involves teacher to child 1, teacher to child 2 . . . teacher to child 28, this means that for every fifty-six turns (twenty-eight for the teacher and twenty-eight for the children, assuming one turn for each child), the child has only *one*. One out of fifty-six is hardly a reasonable proportion and does not correspond to many kinds of social encounters outside the classroom. Are our questions always in the context of whole-group "discussions"? Are classroom interactions always teacher-directed and teacher-centered? Also, we need to ask ourselves what it is that we are requiring the child to be quiet and listen to. In the real world there is usually a reason to listen, and when there isn't a reason, we stop listening. We listen to find out something we don't already know, or to establish a caring relationship with someone else. But in school the child is often supposed to listen to other children read (usually bumblingly) a passage from a story she has already read. Why? She is supposed to listen to other children answer the teacher's questions designed to find out whether the children have learned the facts the teacher hopes they have learned. Why should we expect a child to listen to this? Put another way, why are we surprised that the child only "listens" in these situations through greater or lesser coercion: "Listen so you'll know where we are when I call on you," or "If I catch you not listening again, you'll have to miss recess." Would you or I *"listen"* if we were in the child's

place? Maybe I should rephrase that: *Did* you and I listen when we were in similar situations as students in elementary school or even in college? Listening to someone read poorly a passage you have already read and in many cases found only minimally interesting anyway, could only be described as a colossal bore. That children don't *listen* in these situations is surely a tribute to their intelligence and demonstrates that they know what reading aloud is for, namely, for conveying new and interesting information, or for enjoying fine literature together.

All too often when we tell children to "listen," what we actually mean is, "Don't talk and keep minimally aware of what's going on so you'll be ready to perform when your turn comes." (You and I were very good at this as elementary school students. In classes where our teachers went systematically around the room calling on each child in turn, we got very good at counting how many children were left before the teacher got to us, and at anticipating what question we would have to answer or what passage we would have to read. Remember? This made it unnecessary for us to listen to the intervening stuff. And woe to us when we found we had counted wrong or the teacher suddenly changed tactics!) We often make listening a negative thing, refraining from talking. But listening, real listening, is far too important to be treated this way. Real listening requires mental activity, the processing of new information, the integrating of new information into one's existing cognitive structure, the encounter with the new idea that triggers a new question one never had before. This active process is *listening*.

3. *Talking too loud.* Another early and real learning about talking is that there are some places where one talks quietly and other places where one does not. One whispers in church and in libraries; one talks in a moderate voice at the dinner table; one talks loudly in an outdoor game where the participants are widely separated. But we need to ask ourselves if our volume requests are reasonable. Children know that there are good times and reasons for quiet voices; this is *not* a new idea to children when they come to school. But loud voices are appropriate on the playground, and moderate voices, not whispers, are appropriate in group work or in the cafeteria.

When many children talk at once in moderate voices (in the cafeteria, say), the overall noise level will be, must be, significant (just as it is at a cocktail party where we never ask people to quiet down). It is important, and at first difficult, when the overall volume is up (as in a class where children are all working and talking in groups simultaneously) to learn to hear the difference between simple *noise* and the sound of meaningful verbal interaction.

4. *Talking in the wrong place.* Examine where children can and cannot talk. In many schools I visit, the cafeteria is the "wrong place," yet we value mealtime conversation in our homes. Are all areas of the classroom the wrong place? I visit many classes where there is no right place for talking. If we sit down and actually list the right and wrong places for talking, and find more wrong places than right ones, we need to look again and do some revising. If the child's only right time for talking in the classroom is "After

you have finished your work you can go to a center and play a game with a friend," then children who never finish their work (and every classroom has them) never get to talk with their friends, and they may be the very children who need it most.

5. *Talking about the wrong thing.* Children need to learn to be relevant. But some wondering aloud about fringe areas to the discussion may lead to relating one area to another. Do we sometimes restrict too narrowly what is "on the subject"? Are we sometimes worried by laughter when children are supposed to be working on a social studies project? Why? In terms of real talk in the real world, don't we inject humorous remarks or tell related anecdotes while we work jointly toward some serious goal? And if our children are, in our view, continually "off the subject," perhaps we need to reexamine the subject itself: Is it one that is of genuine interest to the children in the first place? Children are generally pretty good at staying on topics or tasks that are of interest to them.

I have known situations in which a teacher rejected a child's comment for being "off the subject" when in fact it would have been more accurate to say that the comment was simply off the *teacher's* subject—not where the teacher wanted the group's discussion to go; yet the child's comment was clearly on the *children's* subject— on the topic that the children were interested in discussing. Paley points out that it is valuable for the children to see the teacher make explicit the connection between the ongoing topic of the discussion and the child's seemingly irrelevant remark.

> Any sudden switch in topics is a challenge for the teacher, who must try to find a common element between the new idea and the ongoing discussion. This is done not to soften the children's non sequiturs but to demonstrate logical connections. . . . Even when the teacher's reasoning is incorrect, the children witness the process by which such inferences are made. To dismiss a statement as being "off the subject" forfeits a valuable teaching moment. (Paley 1981, p. 216)

So when her kindergartners are discussing how to choose cubby partners without hurting peoples' feelings, and Deana suddenly asks, "Why can't we pick our own actors to be in our own stories?" instead of telling Deana that she is off the subject of cubby partners, Paley responds with "I think I know what reminded you of that, Deana. Choosing your own actors *is* a bit like picking a cubby partner" (p. 216). In giving this response, she demonstrates for the children a logical connection between the discussion topic and Deana's contribution. When we do not immediately see the connection between the ongoing discussion and a child's remark, rather than dismiss the child's remark as "off the subject," we might do better to encourage the child to help us see the connection: "I wonder how come you thought of that just now."

6. *Talking to the wrong person.* Who is this "wrong person"? It is the "wrong person" from the teacher's point of view, but clearly not from the child's, or the child wouldn't be talking with this person. Children elicit conversation for purposes that are real to them and carry on these con-

versations with the appropriate people, just as you and I do. If we have children working in groups on some kind of project, and a child from one group is consistently going to another group to interact with someone there, we need to ask what the basis for our grouping was. Were the children working with people they wanted to talk and work with?

After observing a student teacher engaging her fourth graders in some small-group work, I asked her how she had decided which children to put together. She answered my question in a negative way: "Well, I had to put Albert and Kevin in different groups because they get too loud when they're together, and I had to separate Melanie and Kendra and Dolores, and . . ." It turned out that she did not really have *groups* at all, only conglomerations of individuals who "wouldn't get in trouble" (interact? talk?) if they were together. Now surely it is strange to deliberately group children on the basis of their *not* wanting to interact with each other. Further, in what situations do we appropriately assign children to groups rather than letting them form their own groups? Another question that arises when children are working in groups is this: Are the children talking about something other than the project they are supposedly working on? If so, what is it they are talking about? Obviously, it is something that, at that moment for those children, is more important than our purposes. We need to know what the children's important purpose is at that point so that we can respond to it. It is where the children's purpose is that the more powerful opportunity for their learning is. Is there some way we can focus on that purpose? Now? Later? How can we provide for these children who have sought each other out to work together in ways that are interesting to them? Our reaction should be "Aha, here's a real interest and a real relationship—the real bases for meaningful communication. Where can we go with this?"

7. *Talking without raising one's hand.* Again, turn-taking conventions are well understood by children. Such conventions are especially necessary in large groups. Notice that we have well-established formalized conventions for turn taking in adult meetings and other large-group settings. But do we have too much of large group in our classrooms? How much of our typical social encounter in the real world is large-group meetings where these formalized conventions are required? (One evening at dinner I asked, "Who would like some more peas?" and out of habit, my daughter's hand flew up.) Another question: Do we require the hand-raising-teacher-recognizing convention the same way of everyone? I suspect not. I remember a nine-year-old describing to me the usual situation in teacher-led whole-group discussions in her classroom. The two children whom she described the teacher as treating very differently were two children I knew and had observed in class: Tracy—tiny, bright, very talkative, "cute" in every way, with two bouncing ponytails, self-confident, outgoing—and Thomas—large, friendless, whiney and babyish, emotionally troubled, receiving significant psychiatric help outside of school. (On one visit I had watched him kick and hit the teacher during a violent emotional outburst.) My nine-year-old friend told me, "When we have class discussions, Tracy just says her ideas right out without even raising her hand, and Miss B_____

says, 'That's an interesting idea, Tracy.' But whenever Thomas says his ideas out, Miss B_____ says, in an angry voice, 'Thomas, I didn't see *your* hand up' or 'Did I call on you, Thomas? I've told you before, don't talk until I call on you.' "

8. *Talking too much.* I think immediately of Cazden teaching in a combined first, second, and third grade, wistfully wishing out loud "for a key to turn Greg on and off"—mostly off (Cazden 1975). Every teacher who draws breath on this planet has been there, and many times! We would only want to be sure that we provide plenty of opportunities for acceptable talk within our classrooms.

All teachers need to have noise levels that they are comfortable with. Probably this is different for each one of us, and certainly it is different for various types of activities. That's fine; that is reality and we live with that. But we do need to ask ourselves whether and in what ways we are being held to the typical silence-dominated situations we knew as elementary school students, and how we can assure that our classrooms reflect and encourage the kinds of interaction that are appropriate in the larger society of which our children are members.

Classroom Interaction Research

Sociolinguists interested in interaction among members of a community are contributing a growing body of research on interaction patterns in classroom communities.[11] What does this research tell us about classroom talk? It will probably come as no surprise to you that it tells us that (1) teachers' talk dominates; (2) teachers' talk is high in known-answer questions, in evaluation, and in control; and (3) the most usual interaction pattern is teacher initiates (typically by asking a known-answer question), student responds, and teacher evaluates student's response (called the IRE pattern, Mehan 1979). You can readily identify these characteristics in the following example.

Teacher has placed one large ball to represent the sun and is using a smaller one to represent the earth.

T: Now here we have the earth revolving around . . . (pregnant pause). What does the earth revolve around?

C-1: The sun.

T: The sun. Right, Marie. But as it moves around the sun, it also keeps turning, like this (turns ball) on its own . . .

C-2: Center.

T: Well, it's kind of . . .

C-3: AXIS!

T: Its own *axis*. Right. And do you know what we call that? (pause) When it goes around on its own axis? We say the earth ro . . . (hopeful pause)

C-2: Revolves?

T: No, not revolves. We say it ro . . .

[11]For a helpful overview of this work see Cazden in press.

C-3:   Rotates!

T: Rotates! That's right. It rotates on its own axis. And that makes day and night. Now if we live right here on this side of the earth where my finger is, are we having day or night when the earth is like this? (T indicates spot away from sun.)

CS: Night.

T: We're having night. Yes. And when we're turned like this so that the side we're on is facing the sun . . .?

CS: Day.

T: Day. We're having *day*. Very good.

The bulk of recent classroom interaction research studies focus on teacher-directed large- or small-group lessons.[12] (That classroom interaction is perceived mainly as teacher-directed large- or small-group instruction events is itself interesting). This research provides detailed transcripts of teacher-child interactions (from audiotapes and/or videotapes) and systematic descriptions of the patterns that occur. This would seem to be very helpful information for classroom teachers. It is . . . and it isn't. It is important for us to be very clear about what this research does and what it does *not* tell the classroom teacher. What it does tell us is what *is* in classrooms—the norm, the typical, the most frequent. What it does *not* tell us, is what the *best* is like—how excellent teachers interact authentically with their children. This work does not (and does not claim to) provide any sort of models for teachers. The sociolinguist's purpose in doing this research is to describe interaction as she finds it occurring. It is not the sociolinguist's purpose to evaluate interaction situations, or to select and describe the most effective situations, or to advocate particular ways of interacting in various settings.

Teachers' purposes are very different from sociolinguists' purposes. Teachers are in the business of trying to make classrooms better places for children to learn and grow in. The classroom interaction research can help us do this if we take and use that research for what it is: systematic and detailed descriptions that bring the typical into sharp focus. These descriptions enable us to consider the norm, to reflect on it, to evaluate it. But we would make a serious mistake if we unthinkingly took these descriptions of the norm as teaching demonstrations for us to emulate. This would be to misuse this research. Excellent teaching is what we are trying for. Excellence is not the norm, and it has not typically been studied in sociolinguists' classroom interaction research.

Our growing understanding of children's language and learning suggests that the most supportive interaction patterns in the classroom will be those that recognize and encourage the child's orientation toward active sensemaking. Helpful situations are likely to be those in which teacher talk does not heavily dominate the interactions and does not serve mainly to ask performance questions, to evaluate children's responses, and to control the

---

[12]There are some striking exceptions. For example, see Garvey 1984 for research focusing on nursery school children's interactions with one another; Michaels and Collins 1984 for student-run sharing-time research, and articles in Wilkinson 1982.

direction of the discussion. Some extremely perceptive teachers are providing examples for us of how such interactions *sound*. They sound strikingly different from the previous example in which a teacher and children "discussed" the movement of the earth. You can hear the difference in the following example in which a teacher and her kindergarten children discuss lack of freedom—Martin Luther King's and their own.

WALLY: I want to tell the part about when [Martin Luther King] was in kindergarten. Tommy's mother said, "Go away, bad boy." And he said, "I'm his friend." And she said, "No, you're the wrong color." He was only a little boy so he cried. So he went to his mother and she said, "I have to tell you something sad. There's a rule against us."
ROSE: Why did they have that?
WALLY: It was their habit. Anyway Martin changed all the rules.
LISA: All the *bad* rules.
FRED: But not the one for the bathroom. The girls have to separate from the boys.
DEANA: Tommy's mother was mean to Martin. Very mean.
EDDIE: She wanted to boss him.

DEANA: Did even Martin Luther King have to sit in the back of the bus?
TEACHER: All black people did.
DEANA: That was really no fair.
JILL: That reminds me. Why do we have to always sit at the same lunch table?
TEACHER: What would you rather do?
JILL: Sit anywhere we want. That's more fair.
TEACHER: That might become confusing. Most people would rather know exactly where they sit, Jill.
DEANA: I don't would rather know.
EDDIE: Me neither.
TEACHER: How does everyone else feel about this? (There is unanimous approval.) Well, then, it's okay with me.
JILL: Free at last! (Paley 1981, pp. 112–13)

This, I believe, is the excellent, not the typical, and it has not been much described in sociolinguists' classroom interaction research. Sociolinguistic research may help by revealing the interaction patterns we typically engage in and perpetuate, thus helping to bring these patterns to our attention. However, in the end, we may learn more from teachers' demonstrations of the excellent than from sociolinguists' descriptions of the typical.

This is easy to say, but where do demonstrations of the excellent come from? They come from classroom teachers, that's where. The term "teacher-as-researcher" has become fashionable. The reality of teachers-as-researchers is deeper than fashion, however. More and more, committed classroom teachers are recording interaction events in their classrooms and making these available to others. They are observing, recording (by audiotape, videotape, in personal journals) analyzing, reflecting, and raising new questions. And they are communicating their observations to others—at local, regional, and national conferences; at inservice workshops; in published articles; at teacher group meetings. This work provides data in the form of real talk and writing of teachers and children, and it also provides teachers' perceptive comments on that talk and writing. Both the data and the comments are invaluable.

Finally

As our knowledge of children increases, our ways of looking at children change and grow and we inevitably come to see new implications for classrooms. When conscientious teachers—those who set the highest standards for themselves—encounter new classroom implications from ongoing research, it is easy for them to think, "I always thought I was a good teacher, but I haven't been doing X so I guess I'm not a good teacher after all." Clearly, it would be a mistake to think this way. We can only teach at any given time in terms of what we know *at that time*. Good teaching is to do that: to teach in terms of the best we know at that moment. New knowledge informs our teaching in new ways. It will—it must—ever be so. It has been suggested that teachers "are like sailors who have to rebuild their ships at high sea, without being able to seek port" (Harste, Woodward, and Burke 1984, p. 50). And that building is continuous. We build, not one ship, but many—ship after ship in the midst of a perpetual storm. Good teaching, like good learning, is not something achieved, but something ever in process; good teaching is not a particular built ship, but the continuous shipbuilding process. In the end, I suspect that excellent teachers will do what they have always done: grow. And the growing will be as it has ever been: the result of their tuning in to their students, responding to them, and learning from and with them even as they "teach" them. The classroom that is an authentic social community fosters the adult's continuous development as a teacher, even as it fosters the children's continuous development as competent communicators.

SUGGESTED EXERCISES AND PROJECTS

1. *Language functions exercise.* Alone or with several friends, study the following conversations involving children from three to ten years of age. Identify the various functions the children are using in each interaction. You may find Halliday's categories, or Tough's categories helpful, or you may choose to "call it like you see it," without any preconceived category scheme. Remember that usually several language functions are involved simultaneously, though it may be possible to identify one as dominant.

Adult and three-year-old.

A: What are the babies doing? Your baby dolls.
C: Shhhh . . . they are sleeping (low voice).
A: They are sleeping, so we cannot talk loud. OK, so why don't we go to . . . Pull the other chair. (Pretending to have breakfast.) OK, let's have some breakfast.
C: Put your coffee right here (on little table).
A: Well, let's have a good breakfast. What do you want?

Ten-year-old and adult riding in car on the way to school.

C: Hey look! They're flying in a V. (Refers to birds.)
A: Yeah, birds often fly in formation like that.
C: Why?
A: Instinct. Which doesn't really tell you anything, of course.
C: (Laughs)

Four-year-old and adult.

C: Do you wanna know why I'm sucking on my thumb?
A: Why are you sucking on your thumb, Rebecca?
C: 'Cuz I got a hurt on it.
A: How did you hurt your finger?
C: I don't know.

Ten-year-old at dinner table with his family.

C: (Looking at steam coming from plate of hot macaroni from dumped over aluminum foil dish.) Why is it making steam?
A-1:   'Cuz it's hot.
C: Yeah, but why is it making steam?
A-2:   Because it has moisture in it and it's evaporating. Like when you boil water and it makes steam.
C: Oh. So that's why, when you heat things up over and over again they get so dry. If you heat an egg up again and again, it gets like rubber.

Adult and friend sitting in a booth at a restaurant. Aquarium next to booth. Three-year-old comes to look at fish and starts conversation with two adults.

C: I never seen big fishes like them. Did y'all?
A: No, we didn't.
C: Look at them big fishes. Them are angel fishes. Ahhhh. Them are pretty.

Eight-year-old and her father.

C: Look over there!
A: Where?
C: In the corner! There is a spider!
A: (turning around) Where?
C: April Fool
      Go to school
      Tell your teacher
      That you're a fool.

Several four-year-olds.

C-1:   Everybody get on the bus. Here we go. (She sits on a bookcase that serves as the bus.) Somebody get on the bus!
C-2:   OK. We're on the bus ready to go off on the bus. We're ready on the bus. (Other children get on the "bus" also.)

C-3:   OK.
C-2:   OK.
C-4:   OK. (Giggles)
C-2:   OK. (Giggles)
C-3:   OK. (Giggles)
C-2:   Kay, kay, kay, kay. We're going now.
C-3:   OK. Honk, honk, honk, honk.

Four-year-old and mother in supermarket.

C: I want some candy.
A: You may have gum but not any candy.
C: I want candy!
A: No, no candy.
C: I want that gum.
A: OK (gives child gum).
C: Let me have it. I want life savers, Momma (pointing).
A: The doctor says you can't have candy. You've got gum.
C: Open it. (A pours out gum pieces.) I want one more.

Nine-year-old doing chalk picture at table with several friends in classroom.

C: Yech!!! Phew!!! I *hate* workin' with chalk. It's irritating!

Four fourth-grade girls are sitting at table, trying to get going on a writing assignment in which they are to use metaphoric language to describe owls in a picture. (Mrs. K_____ is their teacher.)

C-1:   Mrs. K_____, how could you really say an owl's like anything else?
T: I'll give you one we had last week. "He's as thin as a rail."
C-1:   But he's *not* thin.
T: But maybe part of him reminds you of something else.
C-2:   Maybe he's square as a box.
T: Right! Good. His body's as square as a box. You compare (inaudible). (T leaves group.)
C-3:   You should call him Blockhead.
C-?:   His foot is as thin as a worm.
C-?:   He's fatter than his wife.
C-?:   Oh I wish we didn't have to do this!
C-?:   Oh I know! The ugly one looks like V_____. (V_____ is one of the four girls.) (Laughter)
C-?:   His face is triangular.
C-?:   He's thinner than a worm. (Laughter) That's a good one.
C-?:   How 'bout "He is as smart as an owl?"
C-?   Who is?
C-?:   You.
C-?:   He's as wise as a pig.
C-?:   He's as pink as a pig's rump.

Adult holding infant. Two-and-a-half-year-old approaches.

C: Let me see the baby.
A: You may see her, but please be careful with her.
C: Look at her little feet and tiny toes. Can she wear shoes?
A: Yes, she can wear shoes if her mother wants her to.
C: Look, she can blink and stick out her tongue.
A: She can do a lot of things you can do.
C: She cries a lot but I don't, because I'm not a baby.

Five-year-old and teacher are looking at fish tank.

C: They're eating it. Look.
C: They must be hungry.
C: Will they grow fat if they eat a lot?
A: I expect so.
C: Will they get bigger and bigger?
A: Do you think they will?
C: Yes, they'll get bigger and fatter until they're as big as *that.*

Ten-year-old and adult.

C: Why do you go to school?
A: To learn things. Like how to read and how to write and how to work with numbers.
C: Yeah, but you could learn that anyway.
A: It's true you can learn in other ways too, but if people didn't go to school, some of them would learn those things, but some wouldn't. We have schools so everyone can have the chance to learn.
C: Yeah, but when will we ever use those things?
A: Well, I'd sure hate not to know how to read. I use that every day.
C: But when will we ever use things like finding the factors of a fraction and things like that? (A slight pause and he changed to new topic.)

2. *"Language function environment" study.* Working individually or as a group, do a "case study" of one child that focuses on his or her "language function environment." First select typical portions of the child's day (you may need to talk with the child's mother or father to get this information), and then get a language sample from each portion—morning school preparation routine, breakfast, car pool ride to school, whole-group teacher-directed lesson, small-group discussion in class, recess, lunch, afterschool play, dinner, evening conversation with family members. It is helpful to get taped samples and then transcribe them for study. However, for some activities (such as recess), it is impossible to keep the child in taping range without highly sophisticated equipment, so a written record would have to suffice. Also, some activities might best be taped by the child's parent (morning routines, dinner) so you might want to leave a tape recorder and several cassette tapes with her. When you have gathered and transcribed your language samples, study them for the purpose of identifying and describing the range of language functions the child is using in his or her interactions with others. Your goal is to describe the

child's typical daily language function environment. (If you do this project individually, you might want to limit yourself to four or five different situations and about half an hour of taped interaction from each. If you work as a group, you can gather, transcribe, and analyze more conversation from more situations, of course. Remember that transcribing tapes is very time consuming. Keep the project scaled to a feasible size so that the major part of your creative energy goes into insightful analysis and description, rather than into transcribing time.)

3. *Child observation: classroom interaction.* Individually or as a group, observe a selected child in his or her school experience for one morning or afternoon (or one day, if possible), keeping a written record of the child's interactions, the people involved in each, the time and place of each, the nature of the activity, the topics discussed, the formality level, and so on. Then analyze your record for the purpose of describing the range of situational variables in the child's typical interaction experience in a school day. Include such information as age, status, and degree of familiarity of interaction partner(s); the time and place of the interactions; the number of participants in the interactions; the formality level, tone, type of activity, and topical focuses of the interactions; and the channel of the interactions (written or oral or both). When you have analyzed and described the child's school interaction experience in this way, suggest ways of expanding that experience to include more situational diversity. For example, you may find that the written channel is rarely used for interaction (but only for exercises), or that the child has little or no opportunity to interact with people who are relatively unfamiliar to him or her, or with people of lower status. How might interaction experiences in these areas be strengthened?

4. *Repeated language experience study.* Record a child engaging in the same language activity three times and then analyze and describe how the child's language changes over the three times. Some activities you might want to try are these: (a) The child teaches another child to play a new game (three different children in turn); (b) the child tells another individual or group of children about his or her hobby display (three different children or three different groups); (c) the child tells a story for a wordless storybook to three different small groups of younger children.

5. *Adult-present and adult-absent child interaction study.* In a home or a school setting, tape record a group of children engaging in an activity when an adult is and is not present. What differences do you notice in the children's language in the two situations? In what they talk about? In how they talk? [One university student did this in a nursery school setting with four-year-olds. She placed the tape recorder near the children's play-dough table with the microphone suspended above the center of the table. She left the equipment there—sometimes on and sometimes off—for several weeks before she started collecting the tapes she was intending to analyze. By then the children had become oblivious to the tape recorder, which seemed to be just another piece of furniture. The children went on with their play-dough activity and their conversation in a completely natural way. The student taped for several days, just pushing the record button and *leaving the area* from time to time. Parent volunteers drifted in and out of the play-dough area as usual. Thus it was possible to compare the children's language in adult-present and adult-absent situations that were very natural, and in which the children's activity was the same. Because the area was small, the microphone close, and the number of children

limited (by the activity itself), it was possible to pick up almost everything that was said—which is not usually the case when taping children in classroom settings.][13]

6. *Language experience in the "content" areas.* If you are a teacher or are a student involved in a teaching field experience, collect your social studies, science, and math lesson plans for a week (a semester if your teaching in these areas is limited). Viewing these as plans for language experiences (*which they are*), identify all the (a) language functions and (b) situational variables these lesson plans engage your students in. What special language opportunities do these lessons provide? How could they be extended?

7. *Adult as "function model."* If you are a teacher or a student teacher, record samples of your own classroom languaging with your students. Then transcribe your samples and study them to see which language functions you do and do not "model" for the children; that is, which functions they do or do not see you actually engage in (in speech, in writing). Try to think of ways that you can increase your range. (If you are not involved in teaching children yourself, you might want to observe the "function modeling" of another classroom teacher.)

8. *Classroom language functions study.* Tape children and teacher (yourself, if possible) languaging in various types of classroom activities—in a whole-group teacher-led social studies lesson, in a small-group session with no teacher present, at a center, at free play, at lunch. Transcribe and analyze your taped samples to see whether the activities provided daily involve the children in as wide a range of language functions as possible. Do they provide opportunities for children to narrate, to report observations, to explain or inform, to justify, to persuade, to evaluate, to entertain, to establish and maintain social rapport, to express feelings, to question, to imagine, and so on? What language functions seem to be dominant in each type of activity? Why? How could the activity types be modified or expanded to provide opportunities for a wider range of language functions among the children?

9. *"Knower-doer" communication study.* View the film *Shared Nomenclature* (See "Suggested Further Readings and Resources" that follows). Then conduct the same (or a similar) experience using three pairs of subjects: ages four to six, ages eight to ten, and adult. Tape record the experience and transcribe your tape. Discuss and compare the performance of the subject pairs, including their descriptions of the block designs, their descriptions of the placement of the blocks, and aspects of the interaction between each pair.

10. *Wordless storybook.* Tape record five or six children telling a story based on the same wordless storybook. You might want to select children of different ages in order to focus on developmental factors, or you might want to choose children who are all approximately the same age in order to focus on individual stylistic differences. For each child, introduce the tape recorder and the task and then leave the room while the child tapes his or her story. (Stay nearby so that the child can come get you when the taping is done.) The reason you do not want to be present during the taping is that if you are there, the child may look to you for help instead

[13]I am indebted to Victoria Perry for this description of a successful way of executing this study.

of performing the task on his own from beginning to end. Thus, you may unintentionally structure the story task yourself. For example, when the child pauses you might ask, "And *then* what happened?" thereby imposing an actions-in-sequence structure where the child himself might have done something quite different (for example, he might have thought a bit and then added more descriptive detail to the part he just told, or he might have changed his mind and gone back to redo the preceding part, or he might have simply named pictured objects and not dealt with actions at all—as many young children do in this task). If you feel that you really must be present with some of your younger children to sustain them through the task, try to say as little as possible. If the child says something about a page and then looks at you expectantly, you might say, "Anything else?" or "Oh" or "Hmmm" or just smile and turn the page. If after a time the child has not said anything about the new page, you might ask, "And here?" or "What now"— questions that do not force the child into an action framework. When the taping is done, transcribe your tape(s). Analyze the story tellings, comparing and contrasting them on such dimensions as sentence length, syntactic complexity, syntactic variation, semantic variation, fluency, elaboration (inclusion of detail), explicitness, use of dialogue, and going beyond the page (for example, giving names to the characters or providing motives and feelings). For a helpful list of wordless storybooks, see Genishi and Dyson 1984, p. 187.

11. *"Your own thing."* Design your own learning experience relating to the ideas in this section, discuss it with your instructor and/or an acquaintance knowledgeable in this area, and execute it.

SUGGESTED FURTHER READINGS AND RESOURCES

Some interesting works relating to communication include

BRITTON, J., *Language and Learning.* Harmondsworth, England: Pelican Books, 1973.
BROWN, G., AND B. YULE, *Discourse Analysis.* New York: Cambridge University Press, 1983.
COULTHARD, M., *An Introduction to Discourse Analysis.* London: Longman, Inc., 1977.
ERVIN-TRIPP, S., AND C. MITCHELL-KERNAN, EDS., *Child Discourse.* New York: Academic Press, Inc., 1977.
GARVEY, C., *Children's Talk.* Cambridge, Mass.: Harvard University Press, 1984.
HEATH, S. B., *Ways with Words: Language, Life, and Work in Communities and Classrooms.* New York: Cambridge University Press, 1983.
HYMES, D., "Models of the Interaction of Language and Social Life," in *Directions in Sociolinguistics: The Ethnography of Communication,* ed. J. Gumperz and D. Hymes. New York: Holt, Rinehart and Winston, Inc., 1972.

Some interesting works focusing on children's languaging in school settings include

CALKINS, L. M., *Lessons from a Child: On the Teaching and Learning of Writing.* Portsmouth, N.H.: Heinemann Educational Books, 1983.
GORDON, J. W., *My Country School Diary.* New York: Dell Publishing Co., Inc., 1970.
GRAVES, D., *Writing: Teachers and Children at Work.* Portsmouth, N.H.: Heinemann Educational Books, 1983.
GREEN, J. L., AND C. WALLAT, EDS., *Ethnography and Language in Educational Settings.* Norwood, N.J.: Ablex Publishing Corporation, 1981.

Language Arts, elementary journal of the National Council of Teachers of English, Urbana, Illinois.

PALEY, V. G., *Boys and Girls*. Chicago, Ill.: The University of Chicago Press, 1984.

————, *Mollie Is Three: Growing Up in School*. Chicago, Ill.: The University of Chicago Press, 1986.

————, *Wally's Stories*. Cambridge, Mass.: Harvard University Press, 1981.

ROSEN, C., AND H. ROSEN, *The Language of Primary School Children*. London: Penguin Education for the Schools Council, 1973.

SPINDLER, G., ED., *Doing the Ethnography of Schooling: Educational Anthropology in Action*. New York: Holt, Rinehart and Winston, Inc., 1982.

WILKINSON, L. C., ED., *Communicating in the Classroom*. New York: Academic Press, Inc., 1982.

Two films of interest are

Oral Language Development: Views of Five Teachers. Agency for Instructional Television, 1111 West 17th Street, Bloomington, Indiana 47401.

Shared Nomenclature. Ohio State University. Film Lab Service, Inc., 4019 Prospect Avenue, Cleveland, Ohio 44103.

A source of interesting materials relating to children's school language experience is

Teachers and Writers Collaborative Catalog, 5 Union Square West, New York, New York 10003.

13

Dialect Variation

"I knowed you wasn't Oklahomy folks. You talk queer kinda. That ain't no blame, you understan'. Ever'body says words different . . . Arkansas folks says 'em different, and Oklahomy folks says 'em different. And we seen a lady from Massachusetts, an' she said 'em differentest of all. Couldn' hardly make out what she was sayin'." (Steinbeck, Grapes of Wrath)

REGIONAL AND SOCIAL DIALECTS

Folks from Oklahoma, Massachusetts, Arkansas "say [English] words different"; and so do folks from Alabama, Oregon, and Arizona. And what about folks from England, Scotland, and Australia, or the millions of folks for whom English is a second language in India, Kenya, Saudi Arabia? And in the United States. They all "say words different," yet we would agree that they are all speaking English. If we can "make out what people are sayin'," but their way of speaking calls attention to itself and we are as aware of how they are speaking as we are of what they mean, then we say they are speaking a different dialect of the language.

Some dialect differences will be in the pronunciation of words: while we take *vit-* (rhymes with "bite") -amin pills, many Britishers take *vit-* (rhymes with "bit") -amin pills. And many people from England work in science la-*bor*-a-trees, follow time *shed*-jules, and wrap their leftovers in al-yew-*min*-i-um. And while some of us object to "greasy" (with /s/) French fries, others of us complain about "grea/z/y" ones.

Some differences will be in the words and word combinations used. Some of us eat hoagies, others eat submarine sandwiches. Some of us fry our eggs in a skillet, others in a frying pan, and others in a spider. Some of us eat green peppers while others of us eat bell peppers. Some of us order "donuts" and get something cakey; others of us order "donuts" and get something puffy. Some of us wish on chicken wishbones, and others of us wish on pulley bones. And some of us eat (or know people who eat) cottage cheese, pot cheese, farmer cheese, or even smearcase—and we're all eating the same thing. While some of us "are able to" do something, others of us "might (maht) could" do it. And from a Texas first grade comes this example: The teacher is giving the class instructions as they take a standardized multiple-choice test that involves circling pictures.

T: Draw a circle around the picture of someone getting ready to take a bath.
C: Is that the same as "fixin' to"?

Some regional dialect differences are more subtle than the differences in the particular words people use and the ways they combine and pronounce them. These more subtle differences are stylistic and involve such aspects of speaking as "when you start and stop talking; how fast you talk; how you use pitch, loudness, tone of voice, rhythm: what your 'point' is likely to be and how you get to it; what you talk about, when, and to whom" (Tannen 1981, p. 30). These stylistic features, too, can differ from region to region. One sociolinguist, herself a New Yorker, has studied interactions between New Yorkers and Californians. She has this to say about a prevalent New York style.

> New Yorkers have lots of ways of being friendly that put non–New Yorkers off, such as the way we ask questions. When we meet someone, we think it's nice to show interest by asking questions. Often we ask 'machine-gun questions': fast, with an unusually high or low pitch, in a clipped form, and often thrown in right at the end of someone else's sentence, or even in the middle of it. (Tannen 1981, p. 31)

She gives this example of conversation between Diane (from New York) and Chad (from Los Angeles) who had just met.

DIANE: You live in L. A.?
CHAD: Yeah.
DIANE: Y'visiting here?
CHAD: Yeah.
DIANE: Whaddya do there?
CHAD: I work for Disney Prese—Walt Disney.
DIANE: You an artist?
CHAD: No, no.
DIANE: Writer?
CHAD: Yeah. (Tannen 1981, p. 31)

Chad later told the researcher that this conversation made him feel like he was "under interrogation," yet Diane was only being friendly and she wondered why Chad was being so *un*friendly.

The differences discussed so far are all geographically based. People from one geographical region will speak differently from people from another region. The more widely separated they are and the less contact they have with one another, the more distinct their dialects tend to be. Geographical regions are rarely clearly demarked; neither are dialectal "regions." Nevertheless, the general notion of regional dialects is helpful.

We often identify other people as "speaking with an accent," yet we sometimes fail to realize that we also "have an accent"; that is, we too speak a distinct regional variety of the language. Sometimes this is called to our attention when we travel to a different area and people living in that area will recognize our speech as nonlocal. You'll fall into casual conversation with a post office clerk or bus driver in the area you're visiting and he'll suddenly ask, "Where're you from?" and when you've answered, he'll say, "Well, I knew you didn't sound like you came from around here." But notice, too, that the longer you stay in the new area—say, if you move there—the more your speech takes on the characteristics of that region, the more you blend in language-wise.

You have probably heard people speak of "the standard dialect" or "standard English." This is a notion that gives trouble as (1) "standard" is so variously defined and (2) the term suggests that there is some preferred "correct" variety of English and deviations from this variety are inferior. But we know that no dialect is inherently superior to or more "correct" than any other; each variety of English (or any language) is simply an alternate way of expressing meanings in speech and writing, and no way is more or less effective than any other. As for defining "standard English," some of the favorite definitions are these: "Standard English is a dialect that doesn't call attention to itself" or "Standard English is the kind of English Walter Cronkite (or some other national newscaster) uses." (One definition that is infrequently stated but may, in fact, be the most common is "Standard English is English as I speak and write it.") You can see what the problems are here. *Every* dialect of English "calls attention to itself" in some situation. Walter Cronkite's speech calls attention to itself in Boston or Alabama. Thus the notion of a "regional standard" dialect (rather than just a standard for the language in general) seems to better reflect the situation of dialect diversity in that it recognizes that there are many identifiable varieties of English (or any language), and that they are all valid linguistic systems. Think of a regional standard as that language variety used by the majority of adults in the community—the language as you hear it on the bus, on local radio stations, in local department stores, in your doctor's office, at PTA meetings; the language as you read it in the newspaper or in office memos. Of course, no two people speak or write a language in *exactly* the same way, but the expression of the majority of adults in any region will be more alike than different.

We tend to have preconceived attitudes toward different regional dialects and the people who use them, though these attitudes are usually unconscious. They are the result of many factors in our backgrounds—how much contact we have had with speakers of a particular dialect, what the nature of that contact has been. We hear (and perhaps even make) comments like "His speech is so *quaint.*" "She sounds so *provincial.*" "I love to listen to him talk; he sounds so *charming* and *genteel.*" "She has such a *high-flown* way of talking—a little *stuck up.* Oh, it sounds very *intelligent* and all, but she makes me a little bit nervous." "I guess he's bright enough but he talks so *slow* and *lazy-like* with a sort of a drawl." Initially these attitudes about particular dialect varieties tend to color our impressions of the people who speak these varieties; we see the *speaker*, as well as the speech style, as quaint, provincial, genteel, stuck up, intelligent, slow, lazy.

Worse yet, in some instances (like the New Yorker example) we are not consciously aware of differences in language use at all and simply perceive the *person* as pushy, loud, or unfriendly.

In the case of regional dialects we can usually manage to get past these initial impressions. Jimmy Carter speaks differently from Walter Cronkite and so did John F. Kennedy, but we don't think of them as quaint, lazy, unintelligent, or whatever because of their dialects. For the most part we can, in time, accept regional dialects and their speakers; for the most part, regional dialects "ain't no blame, you understan'."

However, this is generally not the case with social dialects. A social dialect is a way of speaking (and writing) that is closely associated with a particular social group. As with regional dialects, various social dialects develop and are perpetuated because of distance between the speakers of the different varieties. However, that distance is geographic distance in the one case, but social distance in the other. Both types of distance limit interaction between dialect groups and thus reinforce each group's distinct language system. Typically that dialect used by the more powerful social group in an area is more prestigious. Notice that a more socially prestigious dialect is not more expressive, or more cognitively powerful, or more abstract, or more anything else. Different dialects are simply different expression systems for conveying meaning. No dialect is inherently better or worse than any other. Each dialect serves the intellectual and social purposes of its speakers with full adequacy and effectiveness. But dialects spoken by social groups that hold less of the power and prestige within a society tend to be regarded by the mainstream group (and often by themselves) as inferior ways of speaking. In fact, these less prestigious dialects are often regarded not as intact linguistic systems (which they are), but as error-ridden, garbled, inadequate attempts of a group of people to use a regional standard dialect (which they are not). A speaker of a less socially prestigious dialect of English will often not be perceived as using a valid, rule-governed variety of English, but rather as trying unsuccessfully to use a more prestigious variety. Those semantic, syntactic, and phonological aspects of his dialect that are different from the regional standard are regarded as "mistakes," rather than as linguistic forms that result from a different set of language rules than the standard dialect employs. In short, what is in fact a *different* linguistic system from the regional standard comes to be mistakenly heard as *deficient*.

Nowhere has this been more true in American society than in the case of what has come to be known as "black English." It may be that with regional dialects there "ain't no blame." But in the case of "black English," there has been considerable "blame" and profound misunderstanding that has had serious negative consequences for many children in our schools. For that reason and because the majority of elementary teachers will at some time teach "black English"-dominant children, we will look further at this dialect.

FEATURES OF BLACK ENGLISH

Much has been written about "black English." But what is it, this so-called "black English"? The label suggests that it is the speech of black people, but in fact the label has typically been applied only to *one particular* version of communication that *some* black Americans *sometimes* use (many features of which nonblack people also use), the version that one linguist defines as "that relatively uniform grammar found in its most consistent form in the speech of black youth from 8 to 19 years old who participate fully in the street culture of the inner cities" (Labov 1972, p. xiii). This linguist argues that

> the term "black English" is not suitable for this dialect, since that phrase implies a dichotomy between Standard English on the one hand and black English on the other. "Black English" might best be used for the whole range of language forms used by black people in the United States: a very large range indeed, extending from the Creole grammar of Gullah spoken in the Sea Islands of South Carolina to the most formal and accomplished literary style. A great deal of misunderstanding has been created by the use of this term, "black English." (Labov 1972, p. xiii)

And so he chooses to call the black inner-city street speech he describes, "black English vernacular." Other linguists and scholars have used other labels in their attempts to designate more precisely the particular variety of black speech they describe: "black street speech" (Baugh 1983); "Africanized (black) English" (Smitherman 1985); "inner-city English" (Edwards 1985); "Negro nonstandard English" (Labov 1970); or the speech of "'community' inner-city blacks" (Kochman 1981, p. 13).

Labels are problematic. However, there is the further problem of the severe limitations on what it is that has been described. One black linguist points out

> tne paucity of research on black speech by contemporary black scholars. Seeing the value and distinctive African character of black English, white researchers have produced a sizable body of data attesting to the systematicity, use, and functions of black English. Not all of this research has been to our betterment. In particular, blacks have decried treatments . . . [that] focus on the sensational words and phrases in black speech. Black language is, after all, more than "jive-ass" lingo of ghetto teenagers or the "pussy-coppin" raps of prisoners. The "more than" awaits the treatment of black scholars who can continue in the black intellectual tradition. (Smitherman 1985, p. 57)

One aspect of this "more than" is surely the style shifting that black English vernacular speakers engage in. As you already know from reading Section Four, all speakers of a language use a range of speaking and writing styles depending on the social situation—for example, whether the situation is more or less formal, who the participants are, what the speaker's or writer's purpose is, and so on. A linguist describing regional standard English would be likely to recognize and describe both the more and the less formal varieties of this dialect. But such a recognition has been noticeably absent from descriptions of "black English," possibly because many of these descriptions have been done by white mainstream linguists who are subject to the usual psychological phenomenon of being sensitive to the rich, subtle variation within the (language) behavior of their own social group yet are unable to perceive comparable subtle variation in the behavior of the less familiar group; that is, they perceive the less familiar group's (language) behavior as a simple, single, uniform "other." One black linguist, whose research on "black street speech" has focused largely on stylistic variation, acknowledges a common dialectal core, on the one hand, and, on the other, both the flexibility of street speech as an ever-fluctuating dialect and the "chameleon quality" of its speakers as they shift styles in different social situations.

> There can be no question that a majority of black Americans share some aspects of what is commonly thought of as street speech, although different aspects may appear with different frequency for various speakers. This is the natural result of the social diffusion of black America. . . .
> American blacks have long been aware of dialect differences within the racial group; in fact, such folk terms as "city rap," "country talk," and "talking proper" distinguish different types of black speech. . . . Street speech is the nonstandard dialect that thrives within the black street culture, and it is constantly fluctuating. . . . Street speech survives because there is a population of speakers who use it in their daily lives . . . but it would be wrong to suggest that most street speakers exhibit identical styles. All the [speakers] whom I have interviewed adopt more standardized speech while simultaneously eliminating aspects of street speech in very formal circumstances. (Baugh 1983, pp. 5–7)

As teachers, we need to be aware of some prevalent phonological, syntactic, semantic, and stylistic characteristics "that a majority of black Americans share," "aspects of what is commonly thought of as street speech"; and we need a concommitant and equal awareness that "different aspects . . . appear with different frequency for various speakers" and do so in different social situations.

Just as what we see depends on how we look, so what we hear depends on how we listen. I have selected some black English vernacular forms to describe here that are prevalent in the speech of many school children and that are often jarring to teachers' ears. We need to work on our ears, which often hear only regional standard speech forms as "correct," so that we may come to hear the forms that follow as correct also. These forms, too, are part of our children's rule-governed communication systems; they are not "mistakes" that need to be eradicated. First, some prevalent pronunciation features.[1,2]

1. *Final consonant sounds*, especially when they are part of a consonant cluster, will frequently be deleted. This means that for some children, the

[1]Throughout this discussion you will probably be aware that many of the features described here are used by speakers of other dialects as well.

[2]I am using Labov's label BEV ("black English vernacular") and the generally accepted label SE (standard English). However, it is important for you to remember that SE is actually a *regional* standard English. Though standard dialects share some features from region to region, they also include regional differences.

words "men," "mend," and "meant" may all be homonyms (sound alikes), all pronounced /mVn/. The words "six" (/sVks/) and "sick" (/sVk/) may be sound-alikes, both pronounced like "sick" for the same reason, namely, the /s/ dropping out of the final /ks/ consonant cluster in "six." (Remember, we are talking about sounds, not about spellings.) "Bowl" and "bold" may be homonyms for some BEV-speaking children (just as "know/no" or "there/-their" are for some SE speakers), and so on. When, in reading, we ask a child whether two words are "sound-alikes," we might do well to listen to the child's pronunciation of the two words before we evaluate his response to our question. The child's sound-alikes and ours may be different.

A particularly interesting situation arises when the final consonant that is deleted is one of the following: /t/, /d/, /s/, /z/. Can you see why? In SE, these four sounds often express syntactic information: past tense ("walk*ed*" /t/ or "cried" /d/), plural ("balls" /z/ or "bats" /s/), possessive ("Johnny's" /z/ or "Janet's" /s/), third person singular subject of a verb ("walks" /s/ or "cries" /z/). We sometimes hear people say of a BEV-speaking child who says, "She walk yestiddy" that this child "doesn't have an understanding of time, doesn't differentiate between what happens in the present and what happened in the past." But clearly this is absurd. There are verb forms for SE speakers that have a single form for present and past. We would not think of questioning an SE speaker's knowledge of present and past because he says "I *put* my books on my desk every day" and "I *put* my books on the desk yesterday." The case is similar with plural. We sometimes hear people comment that BEV-speaking children "don't know the difference between one and more than one" because they say "one cent" and also "five cent." But again, comparable examples exist in SE where the speaker expresses both the singular and plural with the same form—"one sheep" and "five sheep," or "a fish" and "several fish." Both SE and BEV include instances where a single verb form expresses past and present, or a single noun form expresses singular and plural. The particular nouns and verbs that work this way are simply a slightly different set in each dialect, but the speaker's linguistic knowledge in each case is the same.

2. *The consonant sounds /l/ and /r/ are frequently not pronounced* or else pronounced very lightly in the middle or at the ends of words. We might hear a BEV-dominant child say something like "Mah schoo teachuh she hep me wif mah wok." Again, the child who deletes /l/ and /r/ sounds medially and/or finally may have different homonyms than the teacher has, for example, "hep" and "help"; "sore" and "saw"; "whole," "hole," and "hoe"; "toe" and "toll"; and "carrot" and "cat" all may be homonym sets for some BEV-speaking children. (Can you tell how each set would be pronounced?)

3. *The "th" sounds* show interesting variation, also. Remember that there are two "th" sounds, a voiced one like the first sound in "*thy*," and a voiceless one like the first sound in "*thigh*." The sound /d/ often occurs in BEV at the beginning of words that SE speakers would start with the voiced "th." Thus, words that an SE speaker would usually pronounce as "this," "that," "these," "then," "them," "the," some BEV speakers would sometimes pronounce with /d/ as the first sound (as would speakers of various

other dialects, of course). In the middle of words, voiced "th" becomes /v/ for some BEV speakers; thus SE "bro*th*er" might become BEV "bro*v*ah."

Voiceless "th" as in "*th*ing" and "*th*ank" for SE speakers, may sometimes be pronounced as /t/ at the beginning of words by some BEV speakers. In the middle of words we sometimes hear /f/ as a BEV variant of voiceless "th" as in "nu*f*in" ("nothing"). And in word final position we may hear BEV speakers pronounce /f/ where the SE speaker would use voiceless "th." Thus, "dea*th*" and "deaf," "Ru*th*" and "roof," and "wi*th*" and "whiff" might be sound-alike pairs for some BEV speakers, each ending in /f/.

4. We sometimes hear it said that BEV *speakers "drop the g" in progressive verb forms* like "walking," "coming," "going," "thinking." Here is a sound-spelling confusion. There is no /g/ sound in these verb forms, only the alphabet letter "g" in their spelling; in fact, the "ng" spelling combination represents a single sound, /ŋ/ as in the last sound of "ki*ng*." The pronunciation feature being referred to here, and one which is common in the speech of many people other than BEV speakers, is the substitution of one nasal sound (/n/), for another /ŋ/, thus yielding verb forms that are often misleadingly represented in print as "walkin'," "comin'," "goin'," "thinkin'." Our traditional spelling representation suggests, mistakenly, that something has been left out. In fact, one sound has been substituted for another.

5. *Some BEV speakers tend to use "a" before words beginning with consonant or vowel sounds*—"a box," "a apple," "a egg"—while SE speakers use "an" to precede words beginning with vowel sounds. Stress in some words occurs differently for some SE and BEV speakers also; the words usually pronounced "ho*tel*" or "po-*lice*" by an SE speaker may be pronounced "*ho*-tel" and "*po*-lice" by a BEV speaker. Sometimes multisyllable words beginning with an unstressed syllable get reduced in BEV by deletion of the first syllable. Thus "important" may become "portant," "suppose" may become "pose" or "spose." One word that often stands alone in BEV, not as part of a general pattern but just as a particular case, is the word "ask." Often this word is pronounced as "axe" by BEV speakers; that is, the final two consonant sounds are reversed ("ask" /Vsk/ becomes "axe" /Vks/).

For some obscure reason, the syntactic differences between BEV and regional standard dialects are often more jarring to teachers' ears than the pronunciation differences. One of the most disconcerting to many teachers is the expression of negative more than once in a sentence. Sentences like "I ain't got no pencil" are likely to be censured or corrected. The simple fact is that BEV is a dialect whose rule system permits inclusion of more than one negative element in a sentence.

My favorite example is the following:

a young woman . . . was angry at the prospect that another woman, a rival, would be going to an amusement park with a man whom both of the women liked. Before leaving with this man, the rival stopped at the pool to show off some new clothes that she had purchased for the occasion. Part of her attire consisted of a new pair of platform shoes, and when the couple finally departed the first woman uttered the following remark: "It ain't no way no girl can't wear no platforms to no amusement park." (Baugh 1983, pp. 82–83)

It's interesting that multiple negatives are so abhorrent to some SE speakers, though they use multiple negatives themselves, but do so in different types of sentences and are unaware that they do it. Sentences like "It is not impossible that they'll still make it" contain two negative elements (can you find them?) yet would be regarded as quite OK by most SE speakers. And what about sentences including "any": "I don't want any." Clearly, "any" is a negative element, for in the affirmative case the SE speaker would use "some": "I want some." (And, of course, the SE speaker has no difficulty accepting the fact that French speakers express negative twice per sentence, placing *ne* before the verb and *pas* after it.) Obviously, the issue is not whether one "should" express negative once or more than once per sentence. Both BEV and SE use multiple negatives in some cases; however, their rule systems differ as to which types of structures they are used in, and as to just what the negative elements will be.

It's interesting that in the case of BEV negative, some SE speakers will, out of ignorance, criticize BEV for expressing a meaning—negative—*more than once* in a sentence; yet these same SE speakers will also criticize BEV for expressing *only once* in a sentence some elements that SE expresses more than once in a sentence. In each of the following three SE sentences, one syntactic meaning is expressed twice. Can you find it in each one?

> She is going now.
> I have three blocks.
> He rides his bike to work every day.

In the first, the syntactic information that the action of going is in process at the time of speaking is indicated by the "is" before the verb and also by the "-ing" at the end of the verb. In the second, plurality is indicated by the "three" preceding the noun an also by the /s/ added to the end of the noun. And in the third sentence, the fact that the subject is a third person singular is indicated both by the pronoun "he" and also by the addition of /z/ to the verb "ride." Here we have three examples of SE expressing syntactic information more than once in a sentence, a situation comparable to the BEV speaker's expression of negative more than once per sentence. These same three sentences in BEV would be cases where each element might be expressed only once. In BEV these sentences could be

> She going now.
> I have three block.
> He ride his bike to work every day.

In short, some syntactic information will be expressed more than once per sentence in BEV and only once per sentence in SE, and vice versa. The rules of each system simply delineate a different set of particular structures for each case. But "there ain't no blame, you understan'," just different rule systems operating.

The pervasive third person singular pattern (he go, she have, Mama say) is only one of the interesting patterns relating to verbs in BEV. In some cases where the SE speaker uses a variety of verb forms, a BEV speaker may choose one verb form and stick to it. The BEV speaker may use "have" or "go" whatever the person and number of the subject (I have/go, he have/go, they have/go), where the SE speaker uses "have" and "has" or "go" and "goes" depending on the subject. With irregular past tense forms a BEV speaker will sometimes use the present tense form for both present and past. For example:

he say . . .
yesterday she come . . .
he get . . .
she run . . .

whereas most SE speakers would use the special irregular past tense forms "said," "came," "got," and "ran" in these cases. Many BEV speakers use a single form of the verb "be" across a variety of situations (as main verb and as auxiliary, as present and past tense), whereas the SE speaker would use different forms. Thus, the following would all be possible in the speech of some BEV speakers.

She *be* busy now. (Main verb)
They *be* busy now. (Main verb)
She *be* coming tomorrow. (Auxiliary)
They *be* coming tomorrow. (Auxiliary)

Sometimes a form other than "be," such as, "was," or "is," is used in various situations. In any case, an SE speaker should not be surprised by this BEV reduction of SE "am" "is" "are" "was" and "were," to one or two of these forms used throughout all "be" situations.

One very helpful rule is, "If it's contractable in SE, it's deletable in BEV." Consider the following.

SE	BEV
She will come at 6:00. (She'll)	—She come at 6:00.
She is coming at 6:00. (She's)	—She coming at 6:00.
She will be coming at 6:00. (She'll)	—She be coming at 6:00.
She has gone. (She's)	—She gone.
She had gone. (She'd)	—She gone.

But notice, what can't be contracted in SE can't be deleted in BEV. Consider the following pair. The "be" in the first is contractable (therefore deletable in BEV) and the other is not.

I know where he is going. (I know where *he's* going becomes I know where he going.)
I know where he is. (Cannot become I know where *he's* and therefore cannot become I know where he.)

In BEV we can get "I know where he going," but never "I know where he."

Pronouns are interesting in BEV also. We sometimes hear the forms "mines" (counterpart of SE "mine") and "hisself/theirself" (counterpart of SE "himself/themselves"). These forms seem to "regularize" an SE paradigm. Consider the SE possessive set: "they're your*s*, hi*s*, her*s*, our*s*, their*s*" but "they're *mine*." In BEV, the "mine" case works like the others and becomes "mines" rather than being an exception to the pattern as in SE. Consider also the SE set "*my*self, *your*self(ves), *her*self, *our*selves," but "*him-*(not *his*)-self" and "*them-*(not *their*)-selves." Again in BEV there's a tendency toward regularization and we may hear "He did it all by hisself" or "They did it all by theirself."

BEV speakers frequently use pronoun apposition. Don't be frightened by the term. The concept is simple, as you'll see from these examples:

> Miz Jones, *she* always be sayin' . . .
> Randy, *he* say dat.
> Daniella, *she* be sick today.

It is a double subject in a sentence—a noun subject followed by the appropriate pronoun. There are also cases where SE "there" is expressed as "it" in BEV.

> *SE:* There's a door by the window.
> *BEV:* It's a door by the window.
> *SE:* There's some children in here.
> *BEV:* It's some children in here.

A final syntactic feature of BEV that is prevalent enough to deserve mention here is the expression of conditional. SE conditional sentences like

> She asked him *if he wanted to go.*
> She asked him *if he went.*

are expressed by some BEV speakers as

> She axe him *do he want to go.*
> She axe him *did he go.*

This discussion of pronunciation and syntactic features frequently heard in the speech of BEV speakers has just touched on a limited set of particularly prevalent features of BEV.[3] Remember, these features do not occur in the speech of *all* black Americans, nor do they occur *only* in the speech of black Americans, nor do they occur *always* in the speech of someone fluent in BEV. What is important for us is to hear the BEV forms our students use as regular features of a different dialect than SE, rather than as a poor attempt to speak SE. BEV speakers are not speaking SE;

---

[3]For detailed discussions of pronunciation and syntactic features of BEV see Baratz 1969; Fasold and Wolfram 1970; Labov 1969, 1970; Dillard 1972; and Baugh 1983.

they are speaking something else, a valid systematic something else. In her autobiography Maya Angelou says:

> My education and that of my Black associates were quite different from the education of our white schoolmates. In the classroom we all learned past participles, but in the streets and in our homes the Blacks learned to drop *s*'s from plurals and suffixes from past-tense verbs. We were alert to the gap separating the written word from the colloquial. We learned to slide out of one language and into another without being conscious of the effort. At school, in a given situation, we might respond with "That's not unusual." But in the street, meeting the same situation, we easily said, "It be's like that sometimes." (Angelou 1970, p. 191)

With this brief discussion of some important BEV features behind you, consider the talk of the following kindergarten children. (A portion of the second example was quoted in chapter 1.) Both episodes were taped without the children's knowledge and without an adult present in the immediate area. The episodes were recorded in two different kindergarten classrooms. See which BEV features you can identify in these conversations. From the first class:

C-1: Nobody gonna mess wid mah dawg. Whoever mess wid mah dawg gonna, they gonna git bite—bit.

C-2: Whoever mess wid mah dawg gonna git bit.

C-3: Whoever mess wid mah dawg gonna git bit on da boody.

C-2: Whoever mess wid mah aintie (aunty) dawg, what . . .

C-1: My aintie, my aintie dawg, boy, boy Midnight tear you up.

C-2: My aintie got a doberman picher, boy.

C-1: My aintie do too, boy. She, she, las, las time she thought dere was a robber in da garage. Boy, Midnight tore 'im up. It was one in da garage.

C-3: What?

C-1: A robber.

C-4: A robbery.

C-1: Boy, Midnight came aftuh 'im an RRRRRRRRRR, Arf - arf - arf - oh-oh-oh-oh.

C-1: Look at D——.

C-2: Dat a wig?

C-3: Nuh-uh. Dat's mah real haih. Ain't no wig.

C-1: Dat ain't no wig.

C-2: It's you wig.

C-1: Cain't ya'll see da real hair stickin' on her?

C-4: M——, dat a wig.

C-1: Naw.

C-4: Sure ain't.

C-1: I see dat. I see dat hair stickin' on.

C-5: It's you Afro.

C-1: It's you Afro. Let me see it (refers to picture card). Let me see it.

C-2: I'll keep if'n it ain't nobody's.

C-1: Dat's a mama. Dat's a mama. She gonna be a mama. She gonna be a mama, D——— (C-2 pulls on C-3's wig).

C-3: Stop!

C-2: I be seein' if it be a wig.[4]

From the second class:

The children are playing with toy cars.

C-1: Tol' ya dat's woner bug, he rollin' by hisself, ain't he? Woner bug, he a bad lil ol cah. He be catchin' all up wit you. 'Cause I . . .

C-2: Bettah watch out, boy!

C-1: Woner bug, he'll 'tack dat cah, righ'?

C-3: Um-uh. Woner bug is *mean*!

C-1: He'll be mean ta . . .

C-2: A-o-o-o-o he fixin' to dribe (drive) hisself. Rum—m-m-m.

C-3: Git 'way from baby wit dat cah, gir'. My baby, she, she want dat cah.

C-1: Dat's my baby's bottle. I put some milk in here fo mah baby.

C-2: Here dat kine (kind). You bettah hush you mout.

C-1: Leabe her 'lone. She sleepin'.[5]

How did you interpret the child's "Woner bug is *mean*!" in the second class? The term "mean" (probably more like "meeeeeeeeeean") expresses admiration. The term "bad" in BEV is also frequently a complimentary one. It is high praise to say of someone "He baaaaaaaaaad!" One often encounters this pattern of using a term in BEV with a meaning opposite to its meaning in SE.

You know by now that any language is not just the linguistic forms—semantic, syntactic, and phonological—its speakers and writers use. Any language is also the ways in which its speakers and writers use those forms in communication. And so we move beyond BEV-speakers' words to consider now some of their "ways with words"—their "styles" (Kochman 1981), "rhetorical qualities," and "Black modes of discourse" (Smitherman 1977). A variety of ritualized speaking events have been described, each type of event having its own structure and dynamics (for example, "the dozens").[6] Smitherman, a black linguist, points out that "while the rituals of black discourse have an overall formulaic structure, individuals are challenged to do what they can within the traditional mold. Centuries-old group norms are balanced by individualized improvisational emphases . . . unique contributions to the group approved communication structure" (Smitherman 1977, pp. 103–4). She describes both the deep traditional communication structures (the overall interaction patterns) and the rhetorical devices that individuals use as they play out their roles within these communication structures.

[4]I am indebted to Brenda Cone for these excerpts from her data.

[5]I am indebted to Lenora Burkhart for these excerpts from her data.

[6]For discussion of these events, see Kochman 1972, 1981; Smitherman 1977; Baugh 1983; and Abrahams 1974, 1976.

The communication structures, or "black modes of discourse," that Smitherman (1977) describes include call-response, signification, and narrative sequencing. (Though it is in the next chapter that we will be focusing specifically on the classroom situations involving dialect diversity, you might want to keep the classroom in mind as you consider these interaction patterns that are markedly different from the communication structures of the traditional classroom.) Call-response is an "African-derived communication process" involving "spontaneous verbal and nonverbal interaction between speaker and listener in which all of the speaker's statements ("calls") are punctuated by expressions ("responses") from the listener" (p. 104). The traditional black church service is the prime example of this pattern, though surely not the only example, for this communication mode is "such a natural, habitual dynamic in black communication that blacks do it quite unconsciously when rapping with other blacks" (p. 118).

"Signification" Smitherman defines as "the verbal art of insult in which a speaker humorously puts down . . . the listener" (p. 118). Now a mainstream individual might be unlikely to regard insulting people as a form of "verbal art"! But those who engage in this discourse mode with one another understand that the insults are not to be taken to heart. "Sometimes signifyin . . . is done to make a point, sometimes it's just for fun" (pp 118–19), but in either case its basic characteristics surely justify the designation "verbal *art*" for those characteristics include the "metaphorical-imagistic (but images rooted in the everyday, real world); [the] humorous, ironic; rhythmic fluency and sound; . . . punning, play on words; introduction of the semantically or logically unexpected" (p. 121)—a set of characteristics very similar to the set I remember my undergraduate introductory literature professor using to describe poetry.

Smitherman describes the important role that narrative sequencing, yet another discourse mode, plays for many black Americans:

> Black English speakers will render their general, abstract observations about life, love, people in the form of a concrete narrative. . . . The story element is so strong in black communicative dynamics that it pervades general everyday conversation. An ordinary inquiry is likely to elicit an extended narrative response where the abstract point or general message will be couched in concrete story form. The reporting of events is never simply objectively reported, but dramatically acted out and narrated. (Smitherman 1977, pp. 147, 161)

The rhetorical devices individuals exploit as they participate in these interaction structures include a variety that, taken together, may go a long way toward accounting for the playful and artful verbal character of these events frequently noted by researchers. To the earlier list of devices often used in signifying (verbal-insult rituals), Smitherman adds these: exaggerated language, mimicry, proverbial statements, spontaneity and improvisation, bragging, and "tonal semantics" or "the use of words and phrases carefully chosen for sound effects" (for example, repetition, alliteration, rhyme) (pp. 94, 99). These expressive forms seem a far cry from the verbal flatness that pervades much of traditional classroom talk.

   This discussion barely scratches the surface of one dialect within the wide range of spoken and written forms and uses called "English." It is an important dialect, yet only one among many. This discussion hints, I hope, at something beyond BEV to suggest the range of possible forms and styles and uses that versions of English can include. I could have chosen a different dialect to describe, but whatever the selected dialect, it would necessarily be a communication system that shares many features with other English dialects (and thus is understood by speakers of other dialects) yet at the same time preserves some phonological, syntactic, semantic, and stylistic features that, taken together, comprise a distinctive set.

   Speakers who share a particular dialect share a particular "world" as well. You know already that any communication system is rooted deeply within the experience of its speakers. A particular dialect is maintained and reinforced because its speakers have substantial and continuing interaction with one another. That shared communication lives within the group's shared lifeways—their mutual understandings of what is of value, of what behavior is appropriate in different social situations, of what is sacred or humorous or routine, of what constitutes "work" and "play," and of how work and play are carried out; a shared history, shared assumptions for the present, and shared expectations for the future. Any group's dialect, their distinctive ways with words, reflects and is inseparable from their ways of experiencing in the world. And so it is that every school child brings not simply his ways of talking but also his ways of *being*—his ways of thinking and doing and interpreting and valuing and experiencing in the world. What Smitherman says of the black vernacular she describes could be said of any dialect: "language is identity."

> The children's language is them is they mommas and kinfolk and community and black culture and the black experience made manifest in verbal form. (Smitherman 1985, p. 58)

Our children bring their talk to school; they bring their worlds as well.

MYTHS

   A number of myths abound in education (and the larger society as well) about children who use nonstandard dialects of English. They are myths about children like Kendra, the fourth grader in the following example. Kendra is having trouble in reading (as it is taught in her school), and so the university student in the example below tutors Kendra each day. One day they have this conversation.

C: I pick some dewberries and some plums and I ate 'em up. But firs my daddy . . . my daddy made some dewberries. He put some dewberries and bashed 'em up and den put a couple o' milk and den a couple o' sugar and den mash it down and they turn purple and I ate it all up; my brother messed in it.
A: He messed in it? How'd he do that?

C: He go (makes noise and accompanying gestures to demonstrate).

A: Oh, he just got and played in it?

C: Uh huh.

A: Where'd you get your dewberries?

C: Uh, we picked 'em down ta our our grammaw house . . . we go (demonstrates) . . . and den he throwed dem dewberries in the truck and I had to get (inaudible) I had to pick 'em (inaudible) he missed.

A: He did?

C: Uh huh.

A: What else'd you do down at your grandmother's at Easter?

C: Uhmmmm . . .

A: Did y'all go to church?

C: We went to church. And my mama went, went to work.

A: She did? She had to work?

C: Uh huh. But everyday we haf to go ovah Co' Madabee's. I *hate* dat.

A: You have to go where?

C: Ovah Co' Madabee's. She keeps ma . . . she keeps ma brothah and ma sistah when I don' have ta go ta school. And when I have to go ta school, she don't keep me, but when I don't . . . when I when I have to . . . when I when I don' have to go ta school, den she have to keep me too. So I don' like huh.

A: How come?

C: Because she won' let us bring our bikes over dere n' ride.

A: Oh.

C: So all we has to do is jes' sit aroun' and *wait* and *wait* and *wait*; den when we get home we play wid our Play-doh, go boomp (demonstrates). I'm gonna bring my Play-doh if it's all right wid you.

A: You're gonna bring your Play-doh to school?

C: Uh huh.

A: Well, you'd have to ask Ms. —— first, probably.

C: OK.

C: Now, I I killed two hairy worms, dat makes six all together. My sistah say "Ahhhhh". And den he, and den he got crawlin', I went . . . I was walkin' over dere and he go POW, and I stepped on it.

A: Oh, wow, was he . . .?

C: He was a-ah, honey we yelled and that juice went sliiiiiidin' all out.

A: Yuk!! Oooh!

C: It was a green caterpillah but he look like a hairy worm but he didn't have no hair up on him. And den I, I put it in a in a cup and I kep' it. It was on a flower at firs' and I got it off, my cousin picked it up and we kep' on playing wid it and den I wan I wanted ta bring it ta schoo' but it die and we went ashes ta ashes an' dus' ta dus'.

There is no way I can convey the *sound* of Kendra's talk. She plays her voice like some wonderfully expressive instrument—its highs and lows, its rises and falls, now sustained, now staccato, now heavy, now light. However, from the transcript alone, you can recognize that Kendra's speech in this excerpt includes many features of BEV. There are myths about Kendra and the many children (and adults) who talk as she does. They are myths about these children's language, their cultural backgrounds, and their cognitive abilities. Consider the following:

> The language of [BEV-speaking children] is usually *informal or restricted*. Simple in nature, it lacks the breadth and depth necessary for precision about ideas or emotions. It tends to be severely inhibited because of a deficiency in concept development. The language of these children tends to be repetitious and dull, colorless and unimaginative—reflecting the environment within which they exist.
>
> On the other hand, middle-class children tend to use formal, elaborate, and imaginative language patterns, learned from their parents and peers. Their language is grammatically more precise, more complex, and allows for elaborations of meaning and subjective feelings. Therefore, the disadvantaged child's language development is delayed during infancy and early childhood because of the absence of formal language interaction. Their world is a noisy world *but* a relatively fixed verbal world. (Frost and Rowland 1968, p. 379)

It is not only the child's language that is regarded as deficient here but his cultural background and cognitive development as well. (Notice, too, what a striking example this is of the fact that what we see and hear does indeed depend on how we look and listen.)

These mistaken notions about children's nonstandard forms of English were more strongly voiced by educators and educational psychologists in the 1960s than they are today. Yet one wonders whether much has changed beyond the voicing. Have the notions themselves significantly changed? Many educators are now sufficiently sophisticated to avoid making explicit statements about nonstandard-speaking children's "deficient language." But many of these same educators advocate the use of Distar and other similar materials.

Though the Distar program is not used only with BEV-dominant children, the impetus for its development came from the "deficits" attributed to "disadvantaged" populations. Drills like the following are clearly aimed at substituting SE for BEV, though the authors apparently feel that they are teaching the child *language*. (What is italicized in the following is the teacher's speech, written in blue lower case in the original. The remainder tells the teacher what to do as she talks.)

> *Let's find out if you can really listen*
> *Note*: Pronounce *sss* as *zzzz*.
> a. *My turn. I'll tell you if I hold up fingersss or finger. Listen carefully.*
> Hold up two fingers. *Fingersss.*
> Hold up three fingers. *Fingersss.*
> Hold up four fingers. *Fingersss.*
> Hold up your index finger. *Finger.*
> Hold up your little finger. *Finger.*
> b. *Your Turn. Tell me if I hold up fingersss or a finger.* (Book B, p. 19)

> *Now we are going to name some objects. Listen carefully.*
> a. Point to the apple.

My turn. What is this? An apple. Listen again. What is this? An apple.
b. *Say it with me. What is this?* Touch.
Respond with the children. *An apple. Again.* Touch. *An Apple.*
Repeat *b* until all children are saying *an apple.*
c. *All by yourselves. What is this?* Touch. *An apple. Again. What is this?*
Touch. *An apple.* Repeat *c* until all children are saying *an apple.* (Book
A, p. 56)

To advocate such approaches is to act on a belief that the child's nonstandard language is inadequate and he must learn a better one. It is our *beliefs*,
not our words, that we act on. Have beliefs changed? Or do we have a case
of wolves in sheep's clothing? I wonder. Wolves dressed in the fashionable
clothing of currently acceptable phrases are still wolves and may be potentially more dangerous than naked wolves because they are harder to recognize. The endless skills sheets and workbook pages that children are
required to do in the name of back-to-basics surely foster the notion that
regional standard forms of English are more "basic" than other forms and
not simply a subsystem that is useful and appropriate— even necessary—in
certain contexts for some important purposes.

Language myths are not the only ones. There are cultural myths also.
During the 1960s we were told many negative things about BEV-speaking
children's cultural background. The picture painted was one of chaos
reigning where a culture ought to be. Much was made of the fact that in
many homes the father was not present and the mother worked. The
conclusion was that the children were pretty much neglected and did not
receive adequate psychological and emotional support, and that there was
no adult present to talk with the children, which was said to be why the
children "had no language" when they came to school. We were told that
the children received little or no "stimulation" in their homes, had few
interesting toys. Interestingly, when researchers actually began to go into
urban black communities they found many people interacting in children's
homes—a variety of people coming, going, often staying a while. There
was, in fact, a great deal of stimulation and activity, many people and things
for the children to interact with. At this point, we were told that the "problem" with urban black children's background wasn't that there was *too little*
stimulation; rather, the problem was that there was *too much* stimulation
and therefore the children couldn't focus their attention on any particular
thing and learn from it. We were told these environments were "noisy" and
therefore not well suited to learning. In retrospect, this sudden 180-degree
turnabout is remarkable. Surely one must be suspicious on purely theoretical grounds when some observed behavior is "explained" by "reasons"
that are diametrically opposed: not enough stimulation/too much stimulation.

As in the case of the language deficit myths, so in the case of the
culture deficit myths. Educators and educational psychologists saw behaviors that followed different norms from their own mainstream patterns,
and they assumed those behaviors to be deficient insofar as they differed
from their own accepted behavioral norms.

And is the situation any better today than it was in the 1960s? I don't know, but I do know that I become anxious when I encounter mainstream-oriented individuals (whether black, brown, or white) who go into low-socioeconomic urban homes to introduce nonmainstream mothers (or other primary caregivers) to particular ways of interacting with their children, for example, to particular toys and ways of using them with their preschool children. How can one see this as anything other than I'm-bringing-you-a-better-way-of-being-a-caregiver? And is there anything more basic in a culture than caregiver-child relationships? I am told by the well-intentioned, mainstream-oriented individuals who provide this kind of "parent education" that a major goal is to "enhance the child's cognitive development so that the child will do well in school." This brings us smack up against what may be the most damaging myth of all: cognitive deficit.

There has been and continues to be in our society a deep and pervasive confusion of "cognitive ability" with "school success." In the name of "developing children's cognitive abilities" or "helping children learn," well-meaning adults (educators at the forefront) have, instead, worked to equip nonmainstream children with mainstream trappings that will help them deal with educational nonsense—nonsense which is very mainstream oriented. But the crucial point here is the misunderstanding of what they were, and are, doing. They see their work as "cognitive catch-up operations" rather than as "training in mainstream trappings." It is mainstreamness, not cognitive development, that is being dealt with here. Of course, you only try to help someone "cognitively catch up" if you think that someone is cognitively lagging.

There are considerable pressures today that reinforce notions of cognitive deficit in nonmainstream children. The society's educational concerns for "basics," for teacher accountability, for teacher merit pay, for "raising standards," all work against nonmainstream children, for these concerns are played out as greater pressures for inauthentic assessment measures—the grade level number on a child's basal reader, a score on an achievement test, the number of skills sheets and workbook pages successfully completed. I have already argued that such assessment measures are inauthentic for all children (see chap. 8); they do not measure children's language or their learning or their cognitive development or anything else that schools are supposedly trying to foster. It will be misleading in the case of any child to take an *inauthentic* measure as an indication of his *authentic* development. But these inauthentic measures are especially punishing to nonmainstream children; for being unfamiliar with these particular kinds of nonsense, these children are likely to play these games less well than their mainstream counterparts. Their performance is rarely if ever seen as an indication that the game itself is wrong, or that the game has only indicated the child's mainstreamness. Rather, the performance is seen as indication of cognitive deficit, learning problems, laziness, below gradeness, and so on.

But back to Kendra. As long as her cognitive abilities are seen as a number on a basal, as skills sheets and workbook pages correctly completed, as scores on achievement tests, there is no way that she will be seen—or treated—as bright. But what happens if, instead of amassing meaningless numbers, we *listen* to Kendra? What do you hear of inadequate cognitive development in this child, whose observations of ill-fated caterpillars would rival most adults'? Or what do you hear of inadequate cultural background—an experiential vacuum or perhaps chaos? This is a child who picks dewberries with family members at her grandmother's house, who goes to church, who stays at a relative's after school, who rides her bike and plays with play-dough, who catches—and kills and buries—unwary caterpillars. Engaging in interesting experiences with a variety of other people certainly sounds like "culture" to me. And what of her language? "Restricted"? "Simple"? "Inhibited"? "Repetitious"? "Dull"? "Colorless"? "Unimaginative"?

Kendra is one child. There are many more whose language and backgrounds are not mainstream and thus don't mesh very well with the school's ways and expectations. If so many of these children are, like Kendra, bright, observant, and articulate, then we must ask why so many of them, like Kendra, fail in our schools.

14

Dialect Variation: Teachers and Children

Homogeneity is fine in a bottle of milk, but in the classroom it diminishes the curiosity that ignites discovery. (Paley 1979, p. 56)

INTRODUCTION

We know that a child's developing language extends to take into account the whole of her language experience; she creatively constructs language out of *all* of her experience of it, not simply out of some selected segment of that experience. We know, too, that the children we teach come to school from a variety of cultural backgrounds. This is simply one way of saying that they bring to the classroom a variety of lifeways and the range of communication purposes, events, and styles that reflect and carry out those lifeways, their various ways of being social in the world.

Now, if all this is so, then it logically follows that the greater the linguistic and cultural diversity of the classroom, the more powerful it should be as an arena in which children's language can grow. The potential here is especially noteworthy in two areas of children's developing language that are important for children of elementary school age. First is the child's developing communicative competence: her ability to use language effectively across a range of communication situations. The more diverse the child's communication experience, the more extended her language becomes as a social and cognitive instrument. However "inconvenient" language and cultural diversity within a classroom may be for teachers, there is no better social environment for elementary-age children's development of communicative competence.

Second, think about the child's development of metalinguistic awareness, her developing conscious, reflective awareness of that powerful social and personal instrument which is her language. It's easy enough to see that if everyone we encounter uses language in the same ways we do, then those ways do not draw attention to themselves; they remain transparent; we do not see them. We're the fish who don't discover the language water we are in; it is simply *there*. It is when we encounter ways of using language that are different from our own that we have a special opportunity to become consciously aware of the medium itself. We can notice language—see and hear it as a communication system at work. And so it is with children. The socially and linguistically diverse classroom offers powerful possibilities that the child's conscious and continuing discovery of language may be ignited and sustained.

The basic argument of this chapter is that if we, as teachers, do not recognize the language differences our school children bring, we can neither appreciate nor use them. Some differences are easy to recognize. These are mainly differences in the forms of English our students use, for example, their words, their combinations of words, their pronunciations (some of which were discussed in the last chapter). Far more difficult to recognize, however, are differences in the children's "ways with words" (Heath 1983), their various ways of using language forms in communication. And every teacher, like every child, brings his or her own ways of using language to the classroom too. What we think of as *the* appropriate way to carry on a large-group discussion or interact in a reading group may in fact be only *our own way*—*one* way among many.

The good news is that we can increase our awareness of our own and our students' various ways with words. This heightened awareness is our starting point. It is a first and necessary step toward our appreciating and fostering those diverse ways. And this is a goal well worth our best efforts, for in supporting our students' culturally distinct ways with words, we validate and further develop a child's own ways, while encouraging that interaction across "ways" that works to extend the child's communication abilities and awareness.

A BROAD LOOK[1]

The aspect of dialect we are concerned with in this chapter is not the particular linguistic forms our school children use, but their various ways of using those forms in communication. When the child's ways of using English in communication with others are different from our own ways and also are not obvious to us, we may be left with only a vague sense of something being amiss, yet be unable to pinpoint what's wrong. Teachers in such situations have made comments like these:

They [the students] don't seem to be able to answer even the simplest questions.

I would think some of them have a hearing problem; it is as though they don't hear me ask a question . . .

I sometimes feel that when I look at them and ask a question, I'm staring at a wall I can't break through. (Heath 1982, pp. 107–8)

[1]Portions of this chapter have appeared in Lindfors 1986.

Parents express their awareness of classroom communication problems in remarks like these:

> The teachers won't listen . . .
> Miss Davis, she complain 'bout Ned not answerin' back. He say she asks dumb questions she already know 'bout. (Heath 1982, p. 107)
> They [our children] sure do have a hard time in school . . . We send the children to school to read and write and talk English—not to just get punished. (Dumont 1972, p. 363)

And children's own words express classroom communication difficulties:

> [The teachers] pick on me . . . [they] just scold us. (Boggs 1972, p. 326)

These teachers, parents, and children understand each other's words; they fail to understand each other's "ways with words." Their language forms are recognizable English words and sentences, but their systems of using these forms in communication are different. These are different systems of English-in-use, and they are differences that may give rise to a sense of the conversational partner not listening, scolding, punishing, asking dumb questions, or being "a wall I can't break through."
Tannen points out that

> The goal of all conversation is to make clear to others the intentions of the speaker; the degree to which one's meaning is understood as intended depends upon the degree to which conversational strategies, and hence use of devices [particular ways of speaking and listening] are similar . . . the similarity of such devices [among conversational partners] makes for . . . smooth interaction . . . creat[ing] the satisfying sense of harmony that often accompanies conversation among people who share social, ethnic, geographic, or class background. By the same token, the use of strategies and consequent devices that are not understood or expected creates a sense of dissonance, which often leads to negative or mistaken judgments of intent. (Tannen 1984, p. 150)

One parent who knows this "sense of dissonance" exists in her child's classroom interactions says, "My kid, he too 'scared to talk', cause nobody play by the rules he know" (Heath 1982, p. 107). Recent research is providing some information about culturally distinct ways of communicating that can help us move from a vague "sense of dissonance" in classroom communication to a sharper awareness of the different ways of using English that we and our school children employ.

Every child comes to school with a complex system of "rules he know" for communicating. That system includes a variety of functions and ways of expressing them; for example, the child knows ways to inform, to inquire, to invite, to comfort, to argue, to assert, to joke, and so on. The system also includes a variety of types of written and oral communication events that the child has observed and/or participated in, in her community. Each type of event has its own organizational structure; for example, telephone calls, letters, bedtime stories (the reading and the talk), and sermons are different events, each with its own organizational design. Further, each event involves the participants in different ways: how one gets a speaking turn, how one listens (and demonstrates listening), how one executes a speaking turn (for example, making it appropriate in amount, in its connections to others' turns, in relation to the other people present), how one introduces a new topic—all these aspects of participating and many, many more are part of a child's knowledge of how to use language with others in different communication events. And the child's communication system also includes some knowledge of how to adapt her language behavior, her style, to be appropriate in each social situation, taking into account the status, familiarity, age of the participants, the setting and topic and tone of the event, and so on. In the child's "ways with words" she conveys respect or warmth or solemnity or involvement. She conveys messages in her ways with silence, too—how and when she attends and signals her attention. What is especially important for us to recognize is (1) that all of our children have well-developed ways of using language in communication and (2) that their ways of communicating that they bring to the classroom are different. The ways of requesting, informing, inquiring, and arguing differ from one community to another. Communication events differ too. Children from one community may have observed and participated in communication events that are special to their own group, for example, hymn raising (Heath 1983) or ritual insults (Baugh 1983; Labov 1982; Smitherman 1977; Heath 1983) or council meetings (Philips 1983). But also events that go by the same name in different communities may be quite different from one group to another (and thus from one child's repertoire to another). For example, "story" occurs in every community, but whether stories are individually or collaboratively created and performed, whether they are typically oral or written, whether they are "supposed to be" realistic renderings of actual events or imaginative and highly embellished productions—all these "story" differences and more occur from group to group. And though all children will to some degree adapt their communication behaviors to the specifics of social situations, again their adaptations will differ; how and when and with whom to express respect or warmth or involvement will differ from child to child. All these differences are variations in the children's "ways with words," and they all come to the classroom.

Let's take a closer look now at some "ways with words" that have special relevance for the classroom: ways of questioning, ways of storying, ways of participating in classroom groups, ways of cooperating and competing, and ways of engaging in teacher-child interaction.

A CLOSER LOOK

Ways of Questioning

In the classroom, children are sure to find ways of questioning. The teacher's way may be to ask performance questions, that is, test questions. Children from communities in which adults do not ask questions in this way may very well see these as "dumb questions she already know 'bout."

Not recognizing these questions as requests (demands?) for public performance of a particular type of knowledge, to be delivered in a particular style, the child may give an "inappropriate response" (from the teacher's point of view), for example, silence perhaps, or telling a personal anecdote—information not already known to the group. Many teachers use question forms as indirect requests: "Why don't you do the next one?" "Can you find a seat?" or even "Who's ready?" (that is, "Sit up straight and be quiet") or "Don't you like the way Jana is sitting?" But many English-speaking children's ways of requesting are more direct, not in question form. If the child does not recognize the teacher's question form as a request, she may not comply with it and may then be perceived as uncooperative.

You have already met four-year-old Lem, a resident of Trackton (a black milltown in the Carolina Piedmont region). A third grader from Lem's community made this comment: "Ain't nobody can talk about things being about theirselves" (Heath 1982, p. 105). If one of your students said this to you, what sort of sense would you make of it? This child's comment highlights some important differences in the ways of questioning that this child found at home and at school.

This child's and Lem's teachers came from mainstream backgrounds.[2] In their homes, these teachers asked many questions and often even directed them to infants. They typically engaged their own young children in routines (for example, book routines) in which they asked many questions requiring the child to provide known information about labels and colors and other properties of pictured objects. They also issued many directives in question form and asked many unanswerable, wondering-out-loud questions ("Why is it things can't be simpler that they are?" Heath 1982, p. 111).

But the adults in Lem's community didn't ask questions in these ways. They didn't direct questions to infants, and when they asked children questions it was not for the purpose of getting them to produce known information (performance or test questions). Rather, the adults asked questions they didn't already know the answer to; their questions were real requests for information (for example, "What do you want?"). They also asked story-starter questions: First speaker: "Did you see Maggie's dog yesterday?" Second speaker: "What happened to Maggie's dog?" The second speaker's story-starter question gave the initial speaker the floor so that she could tell her story (rather like "Know what?" "No, what?" question pairs do). Analogy questions were frequent too: "What's that like?" Lem's teachers asked "What's that like?" too, but they wanted a different kind of response than Lem and his friends were used to. When the teacher asked, "What's that like?" she typically had a very specific item of shared information in mind, whereas when adults in Lem's community asked "What's that like?" they were seeking a nonspecific comparison of one item or event with another. Compare these two cases:

[2]I am drawing heavily on Heath 1982 in this discussion. Heath's article is a most important one for teachers to read.

TRACKTON ADULT: What's that like? (referring to a flat tire on a neighbor's car)
ANSWER: Doug's car, never fixed.

TEACHER: (pointing to a new sign to be used in arithmetic) What was it we said
   earlier this sign is like?
EXPECTED RESPONSE: The mouth of an alligator. (an explanation used earlier
   in the day by the teacher) (Heath 1982, pp. 116–17)

   So children from Lem's community came to school with notions of
questioning quite different from their teachers notions. They had different
notions of the purposes that question forms served and of the kinds of
responses that were appropriate. Perhaps most important was that Lem
and his friends came to school with little (if any) experience of the kind of
question that is a great favorite of teachers: The teacher asks a question to
which she already knows the answer to see if the child knows the answer (as
she is supposed to). Most of these questions require the child to identify
attributes and provide labels. Now does the child's earlier comment make
sense to you: "Ain't nobody can talk about things being about theirselves."
It expresses the child's puzzlement about the questions that ask the child to
provide known information such as labels and characteristics (color, shape,
function)—"talk about things being about theirselves."[3] These questions
were not used in this child's community.
   What would you expect the Trackton child's behavior to be like in the
classroom in which her community's ways of questioning met her teacher's
ways? Heath tells us that Lem and other Trackton children "either did not
respond or gave minimal answers" when their nursery school and primary-
grade teachers asked get-acquainted questions of the "What's your name?
Where do you live?" type. Then the teachers moved to questions in which
"colors, numbers, letters, and elements of pictures in books became the
foci." These questions required students to "pull the attributes out of context and name them" (p. 122). But because the objects pictured and the
ways they were pictured were unfamiliar to the Trackton children, the
teachers were now asking "foreign questions about foreign objects" (p.
122). And when their teachers made requests in question form ("Why don't
you hang up your coat?" or "Can you hang your coat up over there?"),
"Trackton students generally ignored these questions and did not alter
their behavior until given explicit directives" (p. 123). In short, these children's "communicative competence in responding to questions in their own
community had very little positive transfer value to these classrooms" (p.
123). These children were unfamiliar with the teachers' most basic ways of
questioning: asking children to give back information the teachers already
knew, using questions to control behavior, and requiring specific knowledge of talk about books.
   We have become so accustomed to the preponderance of known-
answer questions teachers typically ask that we may take this kind of ques-

---

[3]Think again of the ITPA Verbal Expression Test (p. 249). Do you remember the
"creditable categories"? How well do you think Lem and his friends will do on this test? And
how will their performance be interpreted?

tioning for granted in school. Yet it is not to be taken for granted. From a reflective perspective, it seems odd for a group of people to sit around and say already-known things to one another by way of public display. You can probably see that this is one particular way of questioning, and one that, however pervasive it may have become in the classroom, might well seem peculiar to many children.

Less important than the specifics of the differences in ways of questioning between Lem's community and his teachers' community is our awareness of the dimensions along which teachers' and children's questioning can, and do, differ. Is the purpose of the question to elicit a display of knowledge, to request a behavior change, to solicit a specific shared item of knowledge, to start a story, to elicit a nonspecific or specific comparison, and so on? How is one expected to respond? Should one give a specific known answer or provide new information, tell an anecdote, be silent, change one's behavior? If we recognize these dimensions of variation, we can then perhaps tune in more closely to these aspects of our own questioning and of our school children's. When we sense a mismatch between our question and the child's response, or when we sense a child's puzzlement at our response to her question, we can at least pause and ask ourselves: What sense is this child making of this exchange? What did I intend? How does my intention differ from the child's sense of what is going on here? How can I use what this child olfers? How can I modify my ways so that she can use what I offer?

What could possibly be more basic to the teacher's trade than questioning? It is reasonable to expect that our children know important ways that questioning works in communication; but it is just as reasonable— even necessary—to expect that our children bring various ways of questioning. It is well to remember, too, that our own questioning is not simply "questioning", rather, it is "a way of questioning."

Ways of Storying

School children are sure to find story events in the classroom, but the teacher's ways of storying, like her ways of questioning, may be unfamiliar. When the teacher says, "We're going to write stories today. Pretend you're . . ." she has in mind an imaginary narrative. But some children's communities do not see this way of storying as legitimate. Third-grade Sally and Wendy come from a Southern white milltown community in which stories include straight reporting of actual events, or realistic fictional stories, both with a clear moral. Sally reprimands Wendy for having told a different kind of story, an embellished account of a personal experience. Their talk brings two conflicting ways of storying (the teacher's and the community's) into focus.

SALLY: That story, you just told, you know that ain't so.
WENDY: I'm not tellin' no story, uh-er-ah, no I'm tellin' the kind Miss Wash [her teacher] talks about.
SALLY: Mamma won't let you get away with that kinda excuse. You know better.

WENDY: What are you so, uh, excited about. We got one kinda story mamma knows about, and a whole 'nother one we do at school. (Heath 1983, pp. 294-95)

When the teacher says, "Now we're going to have Show and Tell," she has another kind of story in mind. She typically intends that individual children will provide mini oral compositions about real personal events, and that the "audience" will focus attention on each child speaker, listening quietly and speaking themselves only at specified points (for example, when the floor is explicitly opened to ask the "teller" questions) and only when recognized in particular ways (for example, raising hand and being called on). Now virtually all school children will have observed and/or participated in events in their own communities in which one individual holds forth, recounting a personal experience to a group of listeners. Thus, such events become part of a child's communication repertoire. But different classroom "tellers," having had different experience of such events, have different expectations for how to "tell," and some of their ways with words in these events do not match the teacher's expectations. Michaels and Collins (1984) characterize two contrasting styles: (1) topic-associating, "discourse consisting of a series of implicitly associated topics" and used more by the black first graders in their study and (2) topic-centered, discourse focused "on a single, clearly identifiable topic" and used more by the white first graders in their study (p. 224). Many teachers favor the topic-centered style (Michaels and Collins 1984; Cazden 1985). Some "tellers" expect that their stories should be, like stories in comparable events in their communities, elaborate exaggerations of fairly mundane events, an expectation which is likely to conflict with the teacher's.

Recently I had the task of observing, weekly, two (mainstream) student teachers who dealt quite differently with their students' ways of storying during whole-group instruction. The differences may be illuminating. Their classrooms, a first grade and a second, were in an integrated suburban school with roughly equal numbers of children from low-socioeconomic black and middle-class Anglo families (along with a sprinkling of Mexican-American children). In the first-grade classroom, the student teacher regularly grouped the children around her on the floor for some whole-group science lessons. The following was typical.

TEACHER: We're going to talk about clouds today, all different kinds of clouds. (She picks some pictures up from the floor and puts them face down on her lap.) I have pictures here for you today, of different kinds of clouds. Do you ever just look up at the sky sometimes and just look and look at the clouds? (Children all begin to chatter somewhat noisily. Apparently they do indeed look up at the sky.) Oh-oh-oh, wait a minute. Remember what we do when we have something to say. We raise our hands, don't we? (Hands fly up.) Well, now wait a minute until I show you my first picture. (She holds up the first picture.) This is a picture of cumulus clouds—you know those puffy kinds of clouds you sometimes see—all cottony-like. Did you ever go outside and see clouds that look like this? Cumulus clouds? (Children are straining and hands are waving. They *do* see those kinds of clouds and they want to tell about it.) OK now, remember what we said yesterday. If I call on you it's so you can ask a question. This is science time, isn't it, so it's not the time for telling stories. (Sam looks especially eager.) Sam, is it a *question* or a *story?*

SAM: A question.

TEACHER: OK, Go ahead.

SAM: Yesterday me and my cousin—

TEACHER: Ah-ah. Saaaaaaam (rising intonation that cautions). This sounds like a story, not a question. We're having science now and that's the time for questions, not stories.

Over the weeks, science content took a back seat to lessons on question versus story. But I kept wondering why storying couldn't be incorporated as a legitimate mode of talking about clouds. Why couldn't the children use storying as they considered new ideas, acted on new information, related it to their existing knowledge, and came to know more fully? Why couldn't they use storying to demonstrate what they knew and how they were making sense of new information? Why couldn't storying be an appropriate way of inviting children to think in new ways? In short, why couldn't the teacher use storying to do all the things a teacher tries to accomplish in whole-group science discussions? And so I wondered.

Down the hall, in the second-grade classroom, another (also mainstream) student teacher frequently grouped her children around her on the floor for whole-group discussion also. On one particular occasion the subject was "social studies" and the focus was on differences in American life fifty years ago and today. She held up a *Foxfire* book photo of a ninety-seven-year-old woman and explained that the woman had been interviewed about life in her area when she was young.

TEACHER: I'm going to read you some things this lady said in her own words. Now she comes from a different part of the country, and she didn't go to school very long, so her way of talking sounds a little different from ours. (Bobby's hand goes up. Bobby is a black child who, when I had observed on a previous occasion, the student teacher had "explained" to me was "not bad, just really sociable.") Bobby?

BOBBY: Does she have a toilet and furniture?

TEACHER: She *does* have a toilet. But ya know what? It isn't in the house. It's out away from the house in a little house of its own. And ya know what we call that?

JAMES (BOBBY'S FRIEND):   An outhouse.

TEACHER: Right. An outhouse.

LISA: How did he know that?

TEACHER: I don't know. James, how *did* you know that?

JAMES: My grandpa used to have one. He lives in the country.

TEACHER: Well ya know, when I was a little girl, I used to go visit my grandmother, and she had an outhouse. And you'd be lying in bed on a cold, cold night. (Now the group is absolutely still. They know from the dramatic sound of the teacher's voice that she has moved into a story mode—and they're with her, lying in that bed on a cold, dark night.) And you'd wake up, and you'd have to go, but it was so cold and you just wanted to stay under the warm covers. And it was scarey, too, going out there in the middle of the night . . . [4]

And so it continued. This student teacher happened to be unusually "tuned in" to her children. In contrast to the first student teacher, who expected her children to conform to her conventional view of "appropriate" ways of sharing information in whole-group discussion, this second student teacher not only accepted her children's storying mode as a legitimate way of demonstrating and of sharing information, but she also used that mode herself, the result, I believe, of her tuning in to the ways the children used. My guess is that those second graders will shudder at the thought of scarey trips to outhouses on cold, dark nights long after the first graders have forgotten that puffy clouds are called "cumulus." But the point is to raise the question of whether a storying mode need conflict with the information-passing goals of whole-group instruction situations.[5]

One has to wonder whether appreciation and encouragement of various ways of storying wouldn't lessen the "flatness" of classroom life as well as enhancing our children's development of communicative competence and metalinguistic awareness. Isn't there—shouldn't there be—a place for the sharing of information that is "objective" factual reporting, but also informing that relates personal narrative and conveys the speaker's personal involvement? A place for the relating of personal events that is straightforward and unadorned, but also relating that embellishes, dramatizes, invents? For storying that preaches and moralizes, but also for storying that engages and entertains? For storying through writing and for storying through talk? For storying that involves an individual creator and performer, and for storying which is collaborative? Do we too narrowly define "appropriate contexts" and ways of storying? Storying offers wonderful, and diverse, ways of knowing and ways of sharing for our children. And for us.

Ways of Participating in Classroom Groups

Teachers often give their children conversational guidelines when they feel the children's communication behavior has been inappropriate. The teacher tends to assume that the guidelines are self-explanatory. Are they? Consider a few.

"Don't interrupt." But what is an interruption? Clearly, it is not simply two people talking at the same time, for this is often acceptable—for example, a teacher eliciting a choral answer to her question, or one partner "um-

---

[4]I am grateful to Catherine Buck, the fine student teacher in this example, for allowing me to include it.

[5]For a description of a classroom setting in which reading lessons were modified to incorporate young Hawaiian children's "talk story"—a cultural speech event that is a "rambling personal experience narrative mixed with folk materials" see Au 1980.

hmming" along in support of the speaker, or the "listener" chiming in at the end of a "speaker's" turn. It takes two to make an interruption, the "interrupter" and the one who interprets the behavior as an "interruption," that is, as an unacceptable overlap. What counts as interruption in a given stiuation is different for individuals from different backgrounds. And, of course, the acceptability in overlaps is different from one situation to another even within a single classroom. An overlap that the teacher considers an "interruption" in a formal whole-group, teacher-directed lesson, she may not consider an interruption in an informal peer-group interaction. How is a child to know?

"Stay on the subject." Every community values "relevance" in communication events and has its ways for speakers to contribute to established topics and to introduce new ones. But, again, the ways are different, as reflected in the topic-associating and topic-centered show-and-tell styles already mentioned. I well remember a conversation I had with an English graduate student after he had gone to a first-grade classroom to show the children his slides of African animals. I asked him how his visit had gone. He answered, "Well, it was sort of strange. Little kids don't stay on the subject much. I showed a picture of a camel and one kid said, 'I saw a camel once.' Then another one said, 'I rode a camel once' and another said, 'I rode a pony once,' and then someone said, 'My cousin has a pony' and I didn't know where we were. So I showed another slide. 'Now here are some crocodiles by the water.' So one kid asks, 'Do crocodiles vomit?' It was pretty weird, actually." No doubt it was weird to this adult, but I doubt that it was weird to the children. They were "staying on the subject" (*their* subject) in their own way, and it was a different way from his way.

Again, teachers and children are likely to have a variety of different perceptions of how to contribute relevantly to an established topic and how to introduce a new topic in different classroom interaction events. In a teacher-directed lesson (especially with a large group), many teachers control the introduction of topics almost entirely, and a child's introduction of a new topic, however much the child may see it as connecting naturally with the teacher's topic, is often seen and treated as inappropriate ("We're talking about X now, Melissa. We'll talk about Y some other time"). In such situations the teacher may be reacting to the child's having taken over topic initiation—*her* preserve—rather than to the appropriateness of the topic itself. But surely the child's introduction of a topic indicates her eagerness to be involved, to contribute to the action. Because such a desire is important to the child's learning within the classroom, the teacher would do well to heed it and to make a place for it, rather than to discourage it.

Beyond the matter of introducing new topics, there is the question of how to contribute to the topic already on the floor. Often what the teacher expects (especially in the teacher-directed group interaction) is very narrow. (We saw an example of this earlier in some teachers' asking, "What's that like?") Many teachers in the classrooms I visit begin whole-group lessons with questions such as "Remember we were talking about X yesterday? What did we say about that?" This seems to be a very open invitation, but make no mistake: the teacher typically expects a very particular item and her responses to the children's suggestions give evidence of the particularity of her expectation: "Nooooooo (rising intonation), that's not it, but you're close." "Yeeees, but what *else*? Jenny, can you help?" "Well, we *did* say that, but that's not it." "I think you need a hint." "*Nobody* remembers? Well, I guess I'll have to tell you." Most often I find that the children do suggest things that were talked about the day before. But this is not really what the teacher means: In *this* situation she has something very particular in mind. The child must know this in order to have her contribution accepted and/or in order to know why it is not accepted. Teacher-directed group lessons often require very specific ways of contributing to the teacher's established topics.

"Wait until it's your turn to talk." I think immediately of Daryl, a black fourth grader in a class I observed over several months. Daryl was a child I noticed immediately, as any observer would have. He was bright and confident, highly interactive, aware of everything going on around him, and above all, articulate and expressive (constantly) of his observations. This last proved to be his downfall with his classroom teacher. During the first month of my weekly observations, I watched the teacher's frustration with Daryl steadily increase: "Daryl, I didn't call on you. I called on _____. Is your name_____? How many times do I have to tell you to raise your hand? Daryl, is that your voice I hear again? If I want your opinions I'll ask for them." By the second month, Daryl spent as much time alone for disciplinary reasons (in the hall, in the office, missing recess) as he spent with the other children. Into the second month, the corporal punishment began. But the situation between Daryl and his teacher was not the "fault" of either one so much as it was a *mismatch* of expected behaviors that became compounded over time: The teacher saw Daryl's overt expressiveness in the group setting as inappropriately unruly and as a challenge to her authority and control. Daryl saw the teacher as being against him ("You always takin' up fuh ev'body else. How come you nevuh take up fuh me?") and all her actions reinforced his interpretation.

How do you know when it's your turn to talk? What are the signals? The fact is that they are different from one situation to another in the classroom (to say nothing of how these differ from home) and sometimes even from one person to another. In some instances you raise your hand. Other times you do not; the teacher calls your name. Sometimes she looks toward you and smiles or nods. Sometimes she expects everybody to respond, sometimes all saying the same thing and sometimes not. Getting a turn is often different in small groups and large ones, and very different in groups with and without the teacher present. I suspect that many teachers, like Daryl's teacher, misperceive a child as disruptive because her ways of getting turns at talk do not match the teacher's expectations, expectations which she may be completely unaware of.

"Speak up so everybody can hear you." In teacher-directed groups (large and small) much of what is going on is "public performance," that is,

an individual demonstration of knowledge in front of an audience. Children, for a host of personal and cultural reasons, have very different orientations toward public performance. Some children are eager to perform verbally before the group. They stretch and wave and grunt to be called on, and then—proudly grinning—speak up and out in strong sure voice. But there are other children for whom individual performance in the classroom is uncomfortable, even painful. Some children come from communities in which one does not set herself apart from the group in this way: It is group cohesion, not individual distinction, that is valued in this setting (Dumont 1972). In her autobiography, *The Woman Warrior*, Maxine Hong Kingston recalls:

> It was when I found out I had to talk that school became a misery . . . I did not speak and felt bad each time that I did not speak. I read aloud in first grade, though, and heard the barest whisper with little squeaks come out of my throat. "Louder," said the teacher, who scared the voice away again. The other Chinese girls did not talk either, so I knew the silence had to do with being a Chinese girl. (Kingston 1975, p. 193)

Another example comes from the Warm Springs Indian community in Oregon. Children in this community

> are raised in an environment that discourages drawing attention to oneself by acting as though one is better than another. The efforts children are expected to make to get the teacher's attention to be given a turn at talk require them to draw attention to themselves, to lay claim to knowing more than their peers, and to demonstrate a desire to display that knowledge, all of which is unseemly by Indian adult standards for behavior. (Philips 1983, p. 118)

If the discussion so far has focused mainly on formal whole-group teacher-directed lessons, it is because these situations are the ones that have been most observed and most fully described. (They also seem to be the type of instructional event that is seen as the most central to the educational endeavor. One colleague of mine is fond of saying, "There is no substitute for *the teaching act*," by which she means what the teacher does in whole-group formal instruction.) But, we would hope such interaction structures constitute only a small part of classroom interaction. We would hope to find small groups of children working on projects together—sometimes with a teacher and sometimes without. And we would hope to find groups interacting informally (again sometimes with teacher and sometimes without) in situations that have no goal beyond that of being together. I believe that small-group activity that is not under the teacher's direct control is terribly important, for in these group situations the children create the structure of the event: what the topics are, how one introduces a new topic (and who does it), how one contributes to an established topic, how one gets a speaking turn, executes a turn, responds to another's turn, and so on. Of course, it is especially valuable when groups include children from different backgrounds (though one must not force this), for the children may then have to deal with—accommodate—group members' different ways of accomplishing communication. This may be more valuable than the social studies or science project that was the ostensible reason for the group's interaction in the first place, for in the process of building an interaction structure that accommodates the children's different ways of participating, the children may become both more competent communicators (extending their own range) and more aware of means of communicating.

I want to close with a final example, a frightening example, which may indicate why it *matters* for us to increase our awareness of differences in children's expectations for how to participate in classroom interaction events. A student I had had in class the previous semester came by to visit with me one day. She had just started her student teaching and was eager to tell me about it. She was teaching in an all-black kindergarten in a poor section of the city. She told me that she had discovered right away that "You just have to set your goals lower for 'these' children." She went on to describe the situation in which she had made this "discovery."

> I had the children sit in a circle on the floor and we went around the circle and each child had to say, "I am so-and-so, I am a boy" or "I am a girl." I really had to work with them on it for a long time. They just couldn't get it. But I've learned. I know now that it just takes much longer with these children.

The inescapable question is *why*: Why would any adult have any children engage in such a bizarre ritual? This is educational nonsense at its very worst. The student teacher is correct in her assumption that mainstream children would more quickly have carried out this ritual in the way she anticipated. They would have done so because, though the ritual is rank nonsense, it is nonsense of a familiar kind, a kind that mainstream adults often perpetrate on children, an event in which the child is called upon to tell the adult things that are altogether obvious to everyone present. What is most frightening to me about this situation is the student teacher's misinterpretation of the children's lack of participation. She is unable to see this event from the children's perspective—as an event altogether unlike any they know. She is unable to see the event as an instance of classroom nonsense. She is unable to see that it is a very particular kind of event requiring a particular kind of interpretation and participation. She sees it, rather, as obvious and straightforward: When it is your turn you say X. Failing to see this event from any perspective other than her own, she looks at the silent children and concludes that "these" children are less able than others. What we see depends on how we look. The challenge, again: to look and see through the children's eyes. The crucial question ever: What kind of sense is this child making of this event? Like ourselves, the child will—must—make sense of communication events in the classroom in terms of the ways of communicating in her community. It *matters* that we be aware of our expectations and our children's expectations of how to participate in classroom interaction events.

Ways of Cooperating and Competing

I came into the sixth-grade classroom as the student teacher was introducing a new activity. She had given the children a set of words, and they were to have twenty minutes to write down as many synonyms and antonyms for those words as they could. Her final instruction before they began was this: "Work independently so your partner [the person seated next to the child] won't have an edge." An unremarkable comment, perhaps. But then again, perhaps not. Her comment reflects the competition that is so pervasive in our educational system that, like so many aspects of classroom interaction, we do not even notice it. School children compete for the number of A's on report cards, for the number of spelling words correct on Friday's test, to be the last one left standing in the spelling bee, for reading the most "free reading" books and getting the most stars, for moving into a higher-level reading book, for scoring high on standardized achievement tests, for working ahead in the math workbook. Their school work is a highly individual and competitive venture: "Do your own work." "Don't look on anyone else's paper." "This is a test." "Work independently so your partner won't have an edge."

A system that turns on grades is, by definition, a competitive system, for grades are a way of ranking each individual against every other. And, of course, the more entrenched our grading system becomes, the more teachers, too, are drawn into competitive rather than cooperative ways of functioning. Increasingly, it seems, a teacher's "merit" depends on how high her children's test scores are compared to the test scores of children in other classrooms. This would hardly seem to encourage cooperative feelings among teachers. Mainstream culture encourages competition, and prizes individual achievement and, for better or for worse, our schools tend to reflect this cultural value. The child who comes to school eager to "shine"—to stand out from among the others—is well suited for this. (I am reminded of the first school day of a kindergarten friend of mine. The mothers had been invited to visit for the children's first morning. When the teacher called the children to sit on the rug, my little friend scurried over and sat up in an abnormally straight and rigid posture, behavior which was very puzzling to her mother, until the child explained, in a stage whisper that carried across the room, "I'm going to get an *A*!" Neighborhood children had initiated her well in their games of playing school. Sitting on the rug was not to be taken lightly!)

All of us teach children who have different culturally influenced notions of which kinds of situations call for cooperation and which call for competition, and also how cooperation and competition are carried out in those situations. Our own notions (rooted in our own cultural backgrounds) may differ from those of individual children. Think about cooperative versus competitive contexts first. In many classrooms, "work" is something we expect children to do individually—and competitively (the goal being to outshine others)—while "play" is something we expect children to do cooperatively ("Do your own work" versus "You're playing together so nicely.") (And I'm setting aside here the obvious and important question of what different individuals view as "work" or as "play"; we differ in this too, and some of the differences relate to cultural background.) But many children come from social backgrounds in which work is an endeavor in which people help one another; whereas it is in playful contexts that one competes, shines individually. Recall the art of verbal ritual insult that some BEV-speakers engage in. This highly competitive event occurs in a playful context. And it is in this playful context that the "man of words" performs and establishes his reputation. Many who would compete in this play setting would find it appropriate to collaborate in their work. Teacher-led "discussions" (for example, whole-group "lessons" or smaller reading groups) are typically situations in which teachers expect children to perform individually. But one education program for young Hawaiian children increased the children's participation in reading groups by incorporating more joint verbal performances, that is, responses given by several children together. This was a modification that included some features of "talk story," an event in the children's culture in which a narrative is produced by several speakers (Au 1980).

Besides the matter of which contexts are perceived by teacher and children as calling for collaborative effort or for individual distinction is the matter of how cooperation and competition are "appropriately" carried out. One often misunderstood expression of competition is BEV verbal insult events. However intense these events may be, the participants themselves understand that these events are not hostile. However, mainstream observers, including teachers, may mistakenly perceive these interactions as fights.

Goodlad (1984) bemoans the intensely competitive nature of American public education. Doubtless some of us would moan along with him and welcome moves toward greater cooperation among children as they work. But whatever our personal preference, we must at the very least recognize that our notions of appropriate arenas and ways of cooperating and competing within the classroom will differ from many of our children's notions. Our ways and our children's ways are deeply rooted in our differing social experience.

Ways of Engaging in Adult-Child Interaction

It may be that both the most frequent and the most important interactions we have with our children are one to one. We meet individual children may times each day—in our gaze, smile, touch, gesture, facial expression, spoken or written words that suggest, criticize, appreciate, inform, challenge, soothe, amuse—there is no end to the list. It is awesome. And all these encounters, from the most fleeting to the most prolonged, are deeply rooted in our and our children's notions of how adults and children appropriately relate to each other for these purposes. The families and communities that nurtured and socialized us taught us these ways and, being different families and communities, they taught us different ways. We all come carrying these ways to our classroom encounters. Now if we came carrying these ways *outside* of ourselves, like a sweater we chose to bring along and which we can put on or take off at will, then we could see the ways we bring. But we do not carry them outside, like extra sweaters;

we carry them inside as the fabric of our social selves. We can not put them on and take them off at will; they are us and thus difficult to see as particular ways among many possibilities for engaging in adult-child interactions.

In Chapter 7 we considered some different ways that adults interact with young children. We find differences in how much adults talk to young children and whether they do at all; in what kinds of things adults feel are appropriate to talk with children about; in whether—and how—adults shape to the child (for example, modify their manner of speaking or focus on objects of the child's attention) or expect the child to shape to the adult; in whether the child is to be an active participant with the adult or a listener/observer. And so on. In all their verbal and nonverbal ways of interacting, the adult and child participants convey attitudes such as respect, involvement, attention, and authority. They play out what their community sees as their social relationships.

In every society I know of, adults have some authority and children interact with adults in ways that "acknowledge" that authority. But ways of doing this are very different, which means, of course, that teachers' and children's notions of how they should appropriately interact with one another will be very different also. One misunderstanding I encounter frequently has to do with "eye avertance," that is, the child's failure to make direct eye contact with the adult. In adult-child interaction in some communities, it is an indication of respect for the child to lower her gaze and look down at the floor when the adult is talking to her, especially in reprimand situations. Meeting the partner's gaze would be regarded as disrespectful, even hostile in some situations. But teachers from some other backgrounds interpret this eye avertance as an indication of "sneakiness" or "slyness," not as the indication of respect that the child intends. And in frustration and anger the teacher blurts out, "You *look* at me when I'm talking to you," thereby requiring the child to behave in a way that, for her, expresses *dis*respect.

Children and teachers from some backgrounds expect children to take considerable verbal initiative in teacher-child interactions, actively asking questions or introducing topics of interest, so sharing with the teacher a balance of control in conversation. But in some communities such behavior in interactions with outside adults (especially teachers) is regarded as inappropriate. In his autobiography, *Barrio Boy*, Ernesto Galarza recalls being reprimanded by his landlady for asking her many questions. When he told his mother about the reprimand and the questioning that had prompted it, she tried to clarify the distinction between "asking about things you don't understand" and "minding other people's business." "It is not good to be nosy. It is good to ask. Just be careful who you ask and what you ask" (p. 95). And he recalls being taught respectful behavior with adults, including "to speak only when addressed and not to put my spoon into adult conversation" (p. 147).

The teachers whom these more- and less-initiating children encounter will value children's initiation and control in adult-child interaction differently; some teachers will value such behavior more and others less, depending largely on their own backgrounds, which have shaped their communication expectations for adult-child interaction.

This discussion of cultural differences in our and our children's ways with words barely scratches the surface of this fascinating area. Yet even such a limited scratching may help sensitize you to the many ways your own students bring to your classroom. It may also convince you that such increased cultural sensitivity *matters*. Which brings us again to your role as teacher.

The Teacher's Role (Revisited)

The teacher's roles suggested in Chapter 10 take on additional significance against this background in the culturally oriented, different ways of using language that come to our classrooms.

Teacher as provider.   How do we provide in ways that capitalize on the rich cultural diversity of the classroom? In Chapter 10 I suggested that teachers provide a workplace in which children can do their work of creatively constructing a theory of the world—including language—by engaging with people and things. Now you can see that this must surely include

providing, validating, and using a variety of participation structures. Having children work in pairs or in small groups has special potential here, for the groupings can shift so easily and often, allowing children to be in a variety of interaction constellations and so encounter the various interaction ways of other individual children. Whole-group teacher-directed situations tend to constrain flexibility.

providing and accepting a wider range of language behaviors as appropriate within existing structures. (Recall the earlier example of the teacher's acceptance and use of a storying mode within a teacher-directed whole-group instruction time.) The familiar IRE (initiate, respond, evaluate) pattern that characterizes whole-group "discussion" is certainly not a necessary one. The kindergartners' discussion (p. 385) demonstrates a participation structure that is much more open and responsive to children's shaping than the typical IRE-dominated, teacher-controlled event. Whole-group writing conferences in which the child author is in "the author's chair," reading her work to the group in order to get feedback, offers another whole-group structure that invites a wider range of possibilities for children's shaping of the event.

providing new structures that evolve to meet the special communication needs and potentials of the classroom community. The dialogue journal is a superb example here. It is a structure that allows a sensitive teacher to shape to and support individual children's ways with language. When one reads the dialogue journals from a sensitive teacher's class, one is struck by the variety of ways that children use this medium—to complain, suggest, share, joke, play with language and ideas, invite, justify, explain, apologize. One is also struck by the various ways that different children use to express these purposes.

providing opportunities for children to work and play with those from their own social group, thus validating and encouraging those children's shared ways of work and play, and also, providing opportunies for children to work and play with those from social backgrounds different from their own and so extend their own ways and their awareness of ways of languaging. This one can be difficult. It is easier and often more pleasant to interact with someone from your own group than with someone from a different background. "You [as a teacher] cannot manufacture friendships to suit some notion you have of what a child needs" (Paley 1979, p. 109). But if we are alert to children's interests, we will find that some interests are shared by individual children from different backgrounds. Shared interests provide authentic reasons for these children from different social backgrounds to interact.

providing encounters with children's literature about children from a variety of social backgrounds. Some of the richest children's literature available today focuses on nonmainstream children. I think immediately of the literature about urban black children—the literature provided by Clifton, Steptoe, Greenfield, and Myers.[6] We would go a long way to find literature that more authentically captures the language of these children. It is important for our children to see and hear themselves and each other in books so their own ways may be validated and their awareness of others' ways increased.

Teacher as observer.   If our intention is to provide for cultural diversity, it is likely that we will observe our children more closely. And differently. We'll look with a readiness to see behaviors that differ from our expectations, as possibly making sense from another cultural perspective. We'll be less quick to label a child "disruptive," "uncontrolled," "aggressive," "disinterested," "inattentive," "passive," "sneaky." We'll ask ourselves instead, "What is this child doing that I interpret as evidence of unruliness, lack of control, aggressiveness, disinterest, inattention, passivity, sneakiness?" (Is it "calling out," not answering when I call on her, talking in a very loud or soft voice, socializing during work time, averting my gaze when I reprimand her?) And we'll go back and look again. This is the teacher as observer, and it takes a lot of looking. Our looking will include

observing individual children participating in a variety of interaction events— formal and informal, work and play (serious and playful), fleeting and sustained; large group, small group, pairs. In which situations does the child lead and/or follow? *How* does she lead and follow? Which children does she choose to work or play with in formal or informal situations? Does she seem more comfortable in large- or small-group events and with or without a teacher present?

observing children's personal interests and concerns. This means noticing which activities the child chooses to engage in and with whom; what she chooses to read, what she writes about, what she tells us; what she tells others—all of which means, of course, that children must have the opportunities to reveal themselves to us in these ways, to choose what they will do and read and write, and to talk with us and with others in the classroom.

[6]You might want to see Sims's *Shadow and Substance* for a discussion of this literature. Also see Tway 1981 for a bibliography including sections on ethnic, religious, regional, and world cultures.

Elementary school children spend in excess of thirty-five hours a week in school. Yet I know adults who do not consider the classroom "the real world" but think of it only as *preparation* for "the real world." Of course this is absurd; the classroom must be "the real world" for the child if she is to learn there. And the classroom cannot be the real world for any child who must leave her home ways (of languaging, of interacting) outside the classroom door like some unwanted pair of muddy boots. And so we invite children to bring their ways inside; then—believing that their ways make sense—we can observe in order to better understand and incorporate those ways, thereby creating with the children a real world for them to learn in.

Teacher as demonstrator. I would guess that it is when we are *least* aware of it that we *most* demonstrate "how the things we do are done" and "how we feel about them" (Smith 1983a, p. 102). Our demonstrating is our own real doing.

> The student teacher who quite naturally fell into a story mode during the social studies lesson with her second graders was demonstrating. In her doing story to share information, she demonstrated storying-as-way-of-informing.
>
> The teacher who is interested in the personal anecdotes that all children tell and write responds to these children in ways that necessarily demonstrate her valuing of the children and their personal lives.
>
> The teacher who herself enjoys the wonderful, socially diverse children's literature now available and shares this literature with her children demonstrates her own valuing of this literature in which the children can see themselves and each other.

Our every interaction with every child and every group of children demonstrates how we feel about the children and the ways of their interacting.

Teacher as responder. Recall Smith's difficult way to make learning easy: "Respond to what the child is trying to do." This takes on special importance when the child is from a background that mainstream schools traditionally have not been designed for in their tests, their curriculum, their teaching materials, and their interaction expectations. It is reasonable to assume that one thing the child is trying to do is interpret and participate in the many classroom interaction events in ways that make sense to her. We have explored a few of these ways in hopes of increasing our own awareness of the ways in which children's communication behaviors can differ. The point is that, being more aware of children's culturally-influenced ways of communicating, we will be better able to read these behaviors accurately and thus respond more appropriately. This means responding to the child's behavior in terms of the meaning the behavior has for the child, *not* on the basis of what that same overt behavior would mean if *we* engaged in it. This is admittedly difficult to do, but we can learn.

Teacher as learner. One kindergarten teacher in a culturally diverse classroom concluded: "Teaching children with different cultural and language experiences kept pushing me toward the growing edge" (Paley 1979, p. 118). One child this teacher learned from was Wally, a black child who

> had been taught to feel a close kinship to his people that most five-year-olds did not have yet. He was conscious of his own racial and personal attributes and identified other children by theirs in an easy, natural way. . . .
>
> "Give it to the black girl in the red dress," he would say, before he knew everyone's name. Or, "Tell the white boy over there it's his turn." He told Akemi he liked her "Japanese paintings" and Warren that he liked "Chinese eyes." He found out from Earl why "Kosher Jews" could not have milk with meat sandwiches. (Paley 1981, p. 109)

Every teacher would be lucky to have a Wally in her class. His "easy, natural way" of dealing with ethnic differences is difficult for some teachers to develop in themselves. Many teachers feel uncomfortable when explicit reference is made to children's racial or ethnic characteristics. They feel that to treat all children fairly and respectfully is to treat them as all the same. But surely not: It is, rather, to treat each child as a quite unique combination of cultural and personal characteristics.

And so we open avenues through which our children can reveal themselves to us. Our children become our teachers. From them we learn new ways of being human in a complex social world. And in the process, we necessarily learn more about ourselves and our own ways of understanding and communicating—our own ways of being human.

15

Different Languages: Teachers and Children

"Why, Huck doan' de French people talk de same way we does?" "No, Jim, you couldn't understand a word they said—not a single word—" "Well, now, I be ding-busted! How do dat come?" "I don't know, but it's so. I got some of their jabber out of a book. S'pose a man was to come to you and say Polly-voo-franzy. What would you think?" "I wouldn't think nuffin, I'd take en bust him over de head—dat is, if he warn't white. . . ." "Shucks, it ain't calling you anything. It's only saying, do you know how to talk French?" "Well, den, why couldn't he say it?" "Why he is a-saying it. That's a Frenchman's way of saying it." "Well it's a blame ridicklous way, en I doan' want to hear no mo' bout it. Dey ain't no sense in it." (Twain, Huckleberry Finn)

INTRODUCTION

Sometimes linguists define different languages as "mutually unintelligible" systems; Huck expresses this idea more simply: If you "couldn't understand a word they said—not a single word—" you would know that you and "they" were speakers of different languages.

We laugh at Jim's naiveté in the above conversation, and yet we know that a great deal of naiveté abounds among more "sophisticated" folks than Jim where different languages are concerned. Have you ever heard someone say that a certain language is "more expressive" or "more poetic" or "more difficult" or "more analytical" or "more abstract" than some other? Think a minute. Languages are simply expressive systems for their speakers to use to communicate in. The language—every language—does whatever its speakers want it to. Every language serves poetic, analytical, social, and cognitive purposes because its speakers are poetic, analytical, social, cognitive beings. If some languages were, in fact, more difficult than others, how could we explain the fact that children acquire different first languages by about the same age? It is true that there is considerable individual variation in rate of acquisition from child to child, but the variation is *not* from language to language; Chinese-speaking children do not as a group take longer to learn Chinese than German-speaking children take to learn German, nor do Swahili speakers take longer to learn Swahili than Portuguese speakers take to learn Portuguese. As with different dialects, so with different languages: Each is a rule-governed system for relating expression and meaning and serves adequately all the purposes its speakers put it to. No language is inherently more difficult, or more logical, or superior, or inferior to any other. However, as in the case of dialect differences, in a society in which several languages are spoken and the speakers of the one exercise less control in that society (if they are poor, hold fewer political positions, hold fewer prestigious jobs), that language and its speakers may be stigmatized and regarded as less "good." Understand, this has nothing to do with the language; rather, it has to do with the misguided attitudes of people toward that language. French is a fully intact language system. Parisians know this, but people in Montreal, Quebec, or areas of Maine may regard French and French speakers in their area as "inferior" because as a group they are socially less powerful in that region. And so it is with many languages our school children and their families speak. Spanish may be regarded one way in Spain, Mexico, or Puerto Rico, but a different way in New York, Texas, or California. Tagalog may be regarded differently in the Philippines and in Portland, Oregon, and Japanese regarded differently in Japan and on the California coast. These differences have to do not with the language in question, but with deep-rooted and often unconscious attitudes toward the people who speak them.

As our classrooms become socially, ethnically, and racially more diverse, many more of us as teachers have opportunities to work with children speaking different dialects of English. Some of us even have the opportunity to work with children who speak different languages as well. For those fortunate teachers, the possibility exists for their children's language range to expand to include not only stylistic and dialectal variation but also more than one language.

Traditionally, American public schools have fostered the melting pot approach, the goal being for language and cultural differences to be minimized. To be American was, above all else, to speak English, and it was a major concern of the public school that all children who entered with a home language other than English should learn to read and write in English. Traditionally, English has been the major (or sole) medium of instruction for all school children, regardless of whether they were monolingual speakers of Navajo, Spanish, German, Swedish, or Chinese. But over the last two decades we have seen a move toward salad bowl thinking, the idea being that the whole that is the United States of America is enriched by the unique and distinct contributions that various ethnic groups make, and that ethnic diversity should be preserved. Nowhere has the move toward salad bowl thinking become more evident, perhaps, than in the state and federally legislated dictates that children whose dominant language is not English shall receive instruction in their own language as well as expanding their range to include English. But there is a great gap between the federal voice saying, "Children who come to school dominant in a language other than English shall receive instruction in both their home language and in English," and educators actually devising and implementing bilingual programs in our schools. Currently there are more questions than answers regarding bilingual education, and the various programs that call themselves "bilingual" reflect these questions: How shall we identify the child who is monolingual in language X or dominant in language X? How much instruction should be given in each language? Should the amount of instruction be the same in each of the languages, or should there be more of one than the other? Should the amounts change as the child moves to a higher grade? How? Or should some subjects be taught entirely in one language and other subjects entirely in another? Should children be taught to read and write in their home language or only in English? How shall the parents' desires be taken into account? What do we do with children whose parents do not want their children to be instructed in the home language? What can we do to assure that, in this society in which English is the dominant and prestigious language, children will acquire English *in addition to* their home language, rather than *in place of* it; how can we assure that the children continue to develop their home language?

The focus in this chapter is the English-as-a-second-language (ESL) part of this bilingual concern. I am not dealing with the various models of bilingual education or with the philosophical and political debates relating to bilingual education. As the label "English as a *second* language" suggests, the assumption is that the children we consider in this chapter are acquiring English in addition to their home language. Our major consideration in this chapter is how a child goes about acquiring a second language and how we can support that process.[1]

In this chapter we will consider two distinct views of (1) the second-language learning *task* (what does second-language learning involve?), (2) the second language *learner* (what does the learner bring to the task and how does he use it?), and (3) the role of the second language *environment* (what can the environment contribute to second language learning?). Then we will reconsider these two distinct views of the second-language learning task, learner, and environment in light of some important recent research. And finally, we will consider some classroom implications for second-language learning suggested by that recent research.

TWO VIEWS

Following are two episodes involving a teacher and several children. These episodes are vastly different, yet both purport to help second-grade Spanish-dominant children acquire English as their second language. It seems

---

[1]Krashen and Terrell (1983) have insisted on a distinction between "acquisition" (that is, "developing ability in a language by using it in natural, communicative situations" p. 18) and "learning" (that is, " 'knowing the rules,' having a conscious knowledge about grammar" p. 18). I am not maintaining such a distinction, but am using "learning" and "acquisition" interchangeably, as I have done throughout the preceding chapters on first-language development. As you will see in the next section focusing on two different views of second-language development, one view relates more to Krashen and Terrell's "learning," and the other more to their "acquisition."

438 *Different Languages: Teachers and Children*

incredible that two such diametrically opposed approaches can be thought to serve the same ultimate goal. The two approaches are based on different assumptions about the three basic ingredients: the task, the learner, and the environment. Study the two episodes carefully and, if possible, discuss your observations with several other students.

EPISODE 1

Two children are saying a poem.

T: Are they saying words, class?
C: (Class): Yes, they are saying words.
T: Now, ask me, "Are they saying words?"
C: Are they saying words?
T: Yes, they are saying words.
T: Aren't they saying words?
C: Yes, they are saying words.
T: Group 1 ask Group 2, "Aren't they saying words?"
G: Aren't they saying words?
G: Yes, they are saying words.
T: Is language made of words, class?
C: Yes, language is made or [sic] words.
T: Isn't.
G: Isn't language made of words?
G: Yes, language is made of words. (Southwest Educational Development Laboratory, *Oral Language*, Book 3, pp. 53-54)

T: I tasted the lemon. Passive.
C: The lemon was tasted by me.
T: She tasted the candy. Passive.
C: The candy was tasted by her.
T: I heard the bells. Passive.
C: The bells were heard by me. (Southwest Educational Development Laboratory, *Oral Language*, Book 2, pp. 39-40)

T: Class, ask [Juan/Maria], "How do you feel?"
C: How do you feel?
P: (individual pupil): I feel [fine/good/well].
T: Class, ask [him/her] "Are you happy?"
C: Are you happy?
P: Yes, I am.
T: Ask [him/her], "Do you need to lie down?"
C: Do you need to lie down?
P: No, I don't need to lie down.
T: Ask [him/her], "Do you need food?"
C: Do you need food?
P: No, I don't need food.
T: Class, ask [him/her], "What do you need?"
C: What do you need?
P: I don't need anything.

C How do you feel?
P: I feel [find/good/well].
C: Are you happy?
P: Yes, I am.
C: Do you need to get warm?
P: No, I don't need to get warm.
C: Do you need to go to sleep?
P: No, I don't need to go to sleep.
C: What do you need?
P: I don't need anything (Southwest Educational Development Laboratory, *Oral Language*, Book 1, pp. 77-78).

EPISODE 2[2]

The children and teacher are looking at a film strip of *Put Me in the Zoo* and discussing the pictures.

C-1: The dog is walking. The dog is going to the zoom.
C-2: No. It is *zoo, zoo* not zoom.
C-1: Zoo.
T: Right. The dog is going into the zoo. Why is he going into the zoo, C-2?
C-2: To see the animals.
CS: Animal.
T: Very good, C-2.

T: What are the men doing here?
C-1, C-4: Cut the hair.
T: The man is cutting the hair.

T: What is the dog doing now?
C-5: He is looking. Laughing.
C-3 He is laughing and looking at something.
T: What do you think that something is?
C-3: A lion.
T: Good thought. True. What is the other man in the back doing?
C-2: Eating the fish to the . . .
CS: Giving the fish to the . . . Feeding the fish to the . . .
T: Seal.
CS: Seal. (Relieved to know the word in order to finish the sentence.)
T: Giving the fish to the seal. Feeding the fish to the seal.
C-1: The men . . . no . . . the zoo men . . . see the dog.

T: Why are they looking at the dog?
C-4: (Answers in Spanish and asks for translation.)
T: Because he is sticking out his tongue.
C-4: Because he is sticking out his tongue.
C-2: (Says his idea in Spanish and asks for translation.)
T: Yes, because he is not supposed to be there. Very good, C-2.

[2]I am grateful to Michelle Hewlett-Gomez for this episode.

C-3:   Because the dog don't belong there.

T: Right, because the dog doesn't belong there. What is that thing there?

C-1   The girl and the boy is look at the dog.

C-6:   And the man . . . the two man . . .

C-4:   . . .is looking the dog.

C-1:   And the boy and the girl is eat popcorn.

T: Yes, the boy and girl are looking at the dog. The boy and the girl are eating popcorn.

C-1:   Falling down the popcorn.

C-3:   Come falling down the popcorn.

C-4:   Come down the popcorn.

T: Yes, the popcorn is falling out of the box. They turned the box upside down.

C-4:   The girl have circle red. The boy have circle red. The shirt . . . the hair . . . the hair . . . the dress . . . the box . . . has red circles.

T: Very good. They all have red circles.

C-5:   The tree have circle red.

CS: *Red circles.*

T: Right. The tree has red circles.

C-1:   The girl and the boy don't have red circles. The tree don't have too red circles.

T: Nothing has red circles. Good.

T: What's happened here?

C-3:   The dog is playing with little circles red.

T: Little red circles, right.

C-3:   Red circles little.

C-1:   Little circles red. Little red circles.

C-2:   Little red circles.

T: Yes. Little tiny red circles.

Views of the Task

Underlying the first sample, episode 1 (exemplifying what is often called the "audiolingual" method), is the assumption that the learner's major task is to make the structures of the second language matters of unconscious, automatic habit; the major focus is on mastery of utterance form. In contrast, underlying the second sample is the assumption that the goal is communicative competence; that the learner be able and want to communicate with speakers of the second language. Remember that linguistic competence, the acquisition of linguistic structure, can be regarded as one component of communicative competence. In order to be understood in a language, one must eventually select and organize language elements in the ways that speakers of that language do it.

Advocates of the first approach would probably say that the communication goal is important but that the child can't use the language in communication until he *has* the language, that is, until he controls its structure. Once he has mastered this, he will use it in communication situations. Advocates of the second approach feel that, as with first-language development, such separation of structure and use is impossible; all language for the first-language learner is "contextualized"; that is, it is language used in a communication context. They feel that that is the nature of the system the second-language learner must acquire also.

It's easy to identify items in the first sample that demonstrate the assumption that learning language structure is the primary task. The drills are designed to make language structures maximally obvious to the learner (Are they verb-ing X? Yes, they are verb-ing X. Aren't they verb-ing X? or Is X made of Y? Yes, X is made of Y. Isn't X made of Y?).It does not matter that the sentences themselves are communicatively empty or absurd. "The bell was heard by me" is not only a sentence that no native English speaker *has* ever said in a natural situation; it is a sentence that no native English speaker *would* say, for the passive construction simply would not be used in a situation where one heard a bell ring and later related that information. However, the sentence serves to demonstrate the structural relation between active and passive sentences, and this is what is considered most important. In a real conversation, on finding out that you were feeling fine, I would not proceed to ask questions intended to discover your nonexistent problem and help you solve it (do you need to lie down/get warm/go to sleep). But the drill provides controlled practice of specific structures and is therefore considered helpful.

Also underlying the first approach is a strong belief that learning a language is learning a set of habits that become more firmly entrenched through practice. It is assumed that the second-language learner has already mastered a set of first-language habits (semantic, syntactic, phonological) and that where these differ from the patterns of the second language, they will interfere with the learning of the second language. The learner will tend to impose the habits of his first language on the patterns of the second. Therefore, a major job for the second-language learner is to practice the patterns of the second language, especially those which are different from the first, so that second-language habits will become automatic. In contrast, the second approach, episode 2, sees the learner's task as a more cognitive one, namely, to discern the underlying regularities (both structural and social) of the second language as it is used around him and with him in interaction.

In summary, the first approach assumes the learner's task is to make the structural patterns (especially syntactic) of the second language automatic habits, and then he will be able to use them in interacting with people who speak the second language. The second approach assumes the learner's task is to learn how the new language is used by its speakers, and that he will learn the structure as well as the communicative appropriateness of expression together in interactive contexts.

Views of the Learner

Advocates of both approaches demonstrated here acknowledge that the language learner already basically controls one language. But whereas advocates of the second approach see this as an advantage in some important ways, advocates of the first approach see this as being largely a disadvantage. The purported disadvantage is that the learner has well-entrenched language habits that will interfere with establishing new habits appropriate in the second language. Encountering a new linguistic form in the second language, the learner is likely to impose the nearest equivalent from the first language. For example, in Spanish the adjective follows the noun it modifies rather than preceding it as is generally the case in English. Thus, the Spanish speaker learning English is likely to talk of the "circle purple" rather than of the "purple circle," making the second-language structure conform to the first. The Spanish speaker's "I have hunger" might occur as a direct translation from first language to second.

The advantages that the proponents of the second approach see in the fact that the learner has already acquired one language are (1) that he does not need to develop basic concepts and understandings about the world as he did in learning the first language—he already has these and mainly needs to develop new ways of expressing these (which of course includes some reorganization of semantic domains)—and (2) that he has had solid experience in using cognitive processes well suited for language learning (as evidenced by his having successfully learned one language) and these same well-developed cognitive processes are basic to the acquisition of an additional language. While the first approach focuses on children's previous practice of particular forms (semantic, syntactic, phonological) specific to that language, the second approach focuses on children's process "practice" (engaging in), their "practice" in using cognitive processes basic to the learning of any language. Thus the first view sees well-practiced *specific content*—forms and patterns—interfering with the mastery of new specific forms and patterns, while the second view sees the development of *general processes* of language learning as aiding further language learning.

Proponents of the first approach see the learner as one who must practice (rehearse) new forms required by the new language. The more practice he has in using new forms correctly, the more firmly they will be entrenched and the more likely he will be to continue to use these correct forms. Thus a great deal of practice in error-free responding will be the learner's major occupation.[3] Group response increases the number of times the learner gets to practice saying particular forms exemplifying new language patterns. Reinforcement for the second-language forms he uses will help to establish the new language habits. (You can probably see the behaviorist orientation here.)

Proponents of the second approach see it as the learner's job to engage in interaction that will provide natural language samples for the

---

[3]The example here is oral, but a similar orientation holds in children's writing development as well, in which practice of error-free written forms is the goal, whether or not these forms express real meanings for the child.

child to exercise his language-figuring-out abilities on. The "reinforcement" the child receives will be responses to the meanings he conveys, not to the forms he uses. As he did when he acquired his first language, he will make hypotheses about how the new language operates and will test and revise these in interactive contexts.

In summary, then, according to proponents of the first approach, what the learner *brings* to the second-language learning task is a set of first-language habits and forms that will in many instances interfere with the habits and forms the second language requires; what the learner *does* is intensely practice the new language forms until they become unconscious, habitual ways of responding. According to proponents of the second approach, what the learner *brings* to the second-language learning task is a well-developed conceptual base and a set of well-developed cognitive processes for figuring out how a language works; what the learner *does* is observe and interact with speakers of the new language and make, test, and revise hypotheses about how their language is structured and how it is used.

Views of the Environment

Each approach above is a different way of providing a situation intended to help the learners (as they are characterized) to accomplish the task (as it is characterized). Different views of the learners and their task result in different approaches to helping them accomplish that task. Thus, those favoring the first approach provide an environmental situation in which the children's attention is carefully directed to the oral and written patterns of the new language, which provides large amounts of practice in error-free responding in talk and writing, which corrects—immediately— all errors of oral and written form. Structured drill becomes a major activity; the "audiolingual" approach is to listen to a pattern ("audio") and say it and others like it ("lingual"). Those favoring the second approach provide an environmental situation in which the children are immersed in interactive experiences that involve diverse forms embedded in diverse communicative contexts, and in which the children are responded to and interacted with according to the meanings they are conveying in their talk and writing (rather than on the basis of the correctness of the forms they are using). Conversation with children about things they are doing and are interested in becomes a major activity.

Two Views: A Pulling Together

The two contrasting views discussed here are sometimes called the *interference* view and the *creative construction* view. The interference view and its well-developed audiolingual methodology has been with us for a long time. It has been basic to adult second-language learning programs—for foreign students in American universities or high school students in Commonwealth countries (Kenya, India, Nigeria) learning English as a second language. It has also been basic to high school foreign language programs in the United States in which students learn some French, German, or Spanish as a college entrance requirement, but with little intention of really using that language in communication with native speakers. It is also probably the most prevalent view and methodology encountered in bilingual education programs in American elementary schools today.

The interference view is rooted in observations of errors learners make as they acquire the second language. According to this view, these errors are mainly the result of learners trying to make the new language structures (semantic, syntactic, phonological) conform to those they already know from their first language. Lacking a particular structure in the second language, learners will use the nearest equivalent from the first language. The audiolingual methodology based on the interference view was a logical outgrowth that took shape and steadily gained prominence during the past several decades when behaviorist approaches to learning were prevalent. Also, a view of learning that identifies (possible) "trouble spots" (points of interference or difference between the first language and the second) and provides ways of either avoiding or remedying them (audiolingual drills) is, of course, likely to flourish in an educational milieu in which teachers see their job as diagnosing and treating children's problems. The audiolingual method provides ways of diagnosing (potential) problems and treating them: Identify points of difference between the first language and the second, and then provide drill on those second-language structures. The interference view and its resultant audiolingual methodology took shape and gained ground as the result of a composite of factors including (1) observations of second-language learners' errors (especially by adult learners), (2) the prevalence of a compatible behavioristic theory of learning—what learning is (building habits) and how one does it (practice)—and (3) the presence of a compatible educational philosophy of diagnose, prescribe, treat.

The creative construction view maintains that children acquire a second language as they do a first, namely, by discerning the underlying rules of language structure and use in the language surrounding them and by continually hypothesizing, testing, and revising in the light of subsequent interaction. They "creatively construct" novel sentences on the basis of the rule system they are building. This will, of course, involve errors in the second language (as it did in the first). Since the learner already has one language, when he lacks the means of expression in the second language, he will use the resources of his first language, which provide a reasonable guess as to what the expression might be in the new language.

This view is more recent than the interference view; in fact, it is stretching the point a bit to suggest that it really has a developed methodology.[4] This view has grown out of our observations and insights relating to young children's acquisition of a first language. Whereas the interference view originated from observations of *adult* learners in *second-* (and foreign) language situations, the creative construction view originated from observations of *child* learners in *first*-language situations. As we came to know more about the sequences and processes of first-language acquisi-

---

[4]For a six-level ESL series for children that implements the creative construction orientation described here, see Hudelson's *Hopscotch* (1985).

tion, some researchers began to ask whether the sequence and processes of second-language learning by young children might not be similar. Early research revealed some similarities. For example, some researchers (Dulay and Burt 1974a, b, c; Milon 1974) identified some general similarities in sequence of acquisition by children learning English as a first language and children learning English as a second language, and also between children from different first-language backgrounds (for example, Spanish and Chinese) learning English as a second language. The sequential acquisition of the fourteen grammatical morphemes identified by Brown, and the sequential development of stages in acquisition of negation as identified by Klima and Bellugi-Klima (see chap. 6), have been observed in children learning English as a second language, and some significant similarities have been found. However, sequential differences have also been found. In the excitement at having found significant similarities, researchers have sometimes glossed over the differences. The sequence evidence does not suggest a strong hypothesis that children's acquisition of a second language follows *the same* sequence of stages that children's learning of that language as a first language follows, but it does support a weaker version of the hypothesis, suggesting that there is similarity in the sequence, and that *one* factor operating may be a simpler-to-more-complex sequence inherent in the language itself.

More impressive than the research looking at similarities in sequence of acquisition is the research relating to similarities in the acquisition processes children learning first and second language's seem to be using. Here we find some rather compelling similarities between first- and second-language learning. For example, we find children moving in the second language as they did in the first, from shorter utterances composed of heavy content items toward longer utterances including more "ivy"—inflections, articles, and so on. We find the familiar overgeneralization—the early regularizing of exceptional forms in the language. We also see over-extension of terms so that initially a child's word denoting a category will include members that, for the native adult speaker, would belong to other categories. We see children refine both the overgeneralized syntactic cases and the overextended vocabulary items over time, as is the case with first-language learners. In short, the second-language child seems to be making sense of the second language by using many of the strategies that served him well in making sense of his first language.

SECOND-LANGUAGE ACQUISITION RECONSIDERED

The Task Reconsidered

What is it that second-language learners must learn? After intensively observing during an entire school year five Spanish monolingual children (ages five to seven) acquiring English as their second language, one researcher summed up the second-language learner's task this way. The learner must figure out how the sound system of the new language is organized, how units of meaning are organized into words, by what principles these words are put together to form sentences, how these sentences can be used appropriately in given settings, and in what ways meanings can be conveyed in the new language and culture. (Fillmore 1976, p.634)

This sounds remarkably similar to the first-language learner's task, namely, to develop communicative competence—the ability to use and interpret well-structured sentences appropriately in various social settings. It also sounds like an enormous task: In Fillmore's words, "the [second language] learner has everything to learn" (p. 634). But does he? There are some aspects of the first-language learner's task that the second-language learner's task does *not* include.

Second-language learners must learn how to express meanings and how to interpret the expressions of others, but they don't have to develop those basic meanings in the first place as first-language learners do. Their task, unlike the first-language learners', does not include prerequisite maturational development, development of perceptual control, or development of muscular control. They already possess the ability to sort out, remember, and produce signals, and they know the kinds of work language does for its speakers, for example, the work of referring, informing, and seeking information.

Some recent research reminds us that the second-language learner's task involves making sense of written language as well as oral language (Edelsky 1981, 1982, 1983; Hudelson 1984; Flores et al. 1985). This research suggests that, as with his oral language development, the second-language learner doesn't "have everything to learn" in his literacy development. The school-age child already knows that print *means*, regardless of whether it is print of his first language or his second. He also knows the kinds of purposes print serves: He has encountered the purposeful print of street signs, can labels, bumper stickers, menus, billboard ads, hymnals, newspapers, Safeway specials, greeting cards, scripture, and record jackets. Now he must go on to learn how the second-language print expresses those purposes and meanings; however, he has a very good start on the task.

The Learner Reconsidered

In addition to his experience of learning his first language, the school-age second-language learner brings to the second-language learning task (1) certain attitudes and (2) certain personality characteristics (including learning style and social style).

First, consider attitudinal factors. The learner brings certain attitudes toward the second language and its speakers as well as toward his own language and culture. These attitudes are an important factor in the child's success in learning the second language. The learner who is positively predisposed toward the second language and culture is more motivated to become like its speakers and is likely to experience greater success in second-language acquisition than is the learner who has negative feelings about the second language, its speakers, and their culture.[5] Also, the learner who feels strongly positive toward speakers of the second language is more likely to actively seek interaction with them, and this interaction is the basic "stuff" of his second-language learning. Notice that there is an important difference here between the first- and second-language situation. It doesn't make much sense to talk about the first-language learner's "attitude" toward the first language and its speakers. The young child becomes more of a participating member of his community as he acquires language. There is not the possibility of deciding whether or not he chooses to identify with this group. It is his only group. He simply develops as a more social human being, with increased social skills, one of which is language. To be able to interact and to be like *the* group (his only group) is to speak its language. But the second-language learner already belongs to a social group, is a fully participating member of it, including speaking its language. Only at this point at which the child has an awareness of different social and language groups does it make sense to talk about his having positive or negative attitudes toward them.

Second, consider personality factors, which give rise to particular ways of learning (preferred learning styles and strategies) and particular ways of socializing. Both learning style and social style influence the way a child learns the second language. Fillmore's 1976 study of the five Spanish-speaking children learning English demonstrates this.

Each of the five monolingual Spanish children in the study was paired with an English-speaking friend.[6] The five pairs of children were in a bilingual school in which half of their instruction was given in Spanish and half in English, with Spanish-dominant and English-dominant children in classrooms together. There was no explicit instruction in either language as a second language; both languages were used as mediums of instruction for all the children. Fillmore followed the Spanish monolingual children's development of English during the course of one school year. She gathered data on these children's second-language development in several ways, but the richest source of data consisted of tape recordings and accompanying observational records of weekly sessions for each Spanish-English pair of friends in a well-equipped playroom. Only the observer and the two children were present in the room for each weekly play session. The five Spanish-speaking children demonstrated wide variation in their approaches to learning the second language. At one end of the continuum was a subject who produced almost no English for the first six weeks of the study and then suddenly began to speak in English a lot and to do so with considerable skill, demonstrating that he had been actively noticing and remembering all along in his own way. At the other end of the continuum was five-year-old Nora who appears to have talked her way nonstop in English from the first moment of the study to the last.

In a more recent study (Fillmore 1983) Fillmore and a team of

[5]For further study relating to attitude and its relation to second-language learning, see Gardner and Lambert 1972.

[6]The one exception here was a child whose partner was bilingual.

researchers have closely observed the ESL development of forty-three Chinese (Cantonese)-speaking and Spanish-speaking children from the beginning of kindergarten until the end of second grade. The study involved extensive videotaping and focused especially on the relation of success in second-language learning to "learner characteristics" of two kinds: "language learning style characteristics" and "social style characteristics." Language-learning style characteristics involve

> aptitudinal characteristics such as verbal memory (defined here as the ability to remember and to reproduce linguistic materials produced by others), verbal fluency and flexibility (ease of production, facility with words, and the ability to think of alternative ways of saying things), and sensitivity to linguistic context and patterning (the ability to guess at meaning, and to find patterns in linguistic materials). These are cognitive characteristics that affect the learner's ability to handle the analytical activities that have to be carried out in determining how the new language is structured and how meanings get expressed in it (Fillmore 1983, pp. 160-61).

Social-style characteristics involve

> interactional characteristics of learners as in their social skills (outgoingness and desire for contact with others), communicative needs (talkativeness, etc.) and activity preferences (whether they prefer activities that involve a lot of interaction and talk with others, or activities that are largely solitary and nonverbal in nature). (Fillmore 1983, p. 161)

Based on the findings from the earlier one-year study of the five Spanish-speaking children learning English, the researchers expected that in the more extensive three-year study they would find that the more sociable, outgoing, and talkative children would be the more effective second-language learners. Interestingly—and ever-so-importantly for us— only about half of the children identified as "good learners" in the second study fit this description. The researchers concluded that "there is no single way to characterize either the good or the poor learners." (p. (161). It seems that, as with first-language acquisition, there are many ways to be an effective second-language learner. What are some of those ways? You may remember from Chapter 7 that though different children use different strategies to different degrees and at different times in their development of their first language, it is possible to identify a set of strategies that have been observed in many first-language learners. Well, it may not surprise you that many of these are evident in second-language acquisition as well. Though the second language is new to the learner, ways of learning language are not new, it appears. Thus, a child's experience of creatively constructing his first language may be very relevant to his creatively constructing a second language also. Let's consider now how those first-language strategies from Chapter 7 may apply to second-language acquisition.

Use your nonlinguistic understanding as a basis for figuring out language. Remember that the school child comes to the second-language learning task with considerable knowledge of the physical and social world. This means that he already understands much of the meaning that people around him will express in their talk and writing in the language which is new to him. In Fillmore's earlier study of the five Spanish-speaking children acquiring English, her observations led her to posit some cognitive strategies she believed the children were using. The first of these was this: "Assume that what people are saying is directly relevant to the situation at hand, or to what they or you are experiencing." (p. 634). You can see that this is another way of phrasing the strategy we have called "Use your nonlinguistic understanding . . .". The children in this study had ample opportunity to use this strategy in their classroom experience and they did. In the children's classrooms, the teachers followed a predictable daily routine, and the language of this routine was predictable also—signaling the end of one activity or the initiation of another, giving directions or suggestions, and so on. The children were able to relate the predictable language to the predictable situation, and "because they paid attention to contextual cues, the children were able to function as if they understood what was going on in the classroom long before they understood the language used in it" (p. 637).

In her later three-year study of the Cantonese- and Spanish-speaking children learning English, Fillmore describes one subgroup of the good learners as studious children who "while not downright unsociable, seldom went out of their way to be with other children" (1983, p. 162). Apparently their effectiveness in acquiring English was largely due to their being able to figure out the situation, even when they didn't know the language being used in it. Fillmore gives the example of an animated film on tooth decay that some of the children in her study saw one day (the children who were in a class with equal numbers of English-speaking and non–English speaking children). The action in the film

> began with a view of a screen-sized open mouth, and as the camera zoomed past the lips and in on the teeth (which did not look like real teeth at all), a writhing ghostlike apparition appeared from between the teeth, a Placque-Man spreading the pall of tooth-decay, gum disease, and bad breath throughout the gaping cavern. (Fillmore 1983, p. 163)

Not surprisingly, few of the non–English speaking children got the message of the film, for "because of the way the message was being presented . . . the viewer had to be able to understand the voice-over narrative in order to know what was going on" (p. 163). But when members of the research team interviewed the non–English-speaking children after this film, they found that a few of the children *had* figured out what the film was about.

> Those non-English speakers who . . . were able to figure out more or less what the film's message was, were among the subjects who eventually became the best language learners. They might have known some of the words they were hearing, and they must have been able to figure out why they would be seeing, in school, a movie about bad things happening in someone's mouth.

450 Different Languages: Teachers and Children

Those who turned out to be the poorest language learners had no good guesses as to what the movie was about.[7] (Fillmore 1983, p. 163)

It appears that at least some second-language learners attend closely to the contexts in which the unfamiliar language occurs and make good guesses about what is going on. Understanding the contexts, they can begin to figure out the expression within those contexts.

Use whatever is salient and interesting to you. Evidence for second-language learners' use of this strategy comes from both oral and written language events. The activities that were most interesting to Nora, a particularly effective language learner in Fillmore's first study, were activities that "involved almost constant verbalization—play-acting, arguing, complaining, gossiping, and general chit-chatting" (Fillmore 1976, p. 573). These were the activities she chose to engage in, and so they were the activities through which her second language developed.

In a recent study by Seawell (1985), low SES (socio-economic status) Spanish-speaking kindergarten children became tremendously interested and engaged in a literature and puppet activity that Seawell carried out with them over a twelve-week period. I am going to describe this study in some detail because I feel it offers rich possibilities for children's language development in the classroom. There were twenty-five children in the class: eighteen categorized as monolingual Spanish, two as Spanish dominant, two as Spanish-English bilingual, and three as English monolingual. After becoming very familiar with the children, Seawell would come to the class each Monday and Tuesday and introduce a new book to the children, three children at a time[8] in a separate small room so that the children could interact fully with the book and with her (for example, turning pages, asking about pictures, asking her to reread it, echoing her, and so on) (Since the goal was to support and observe the development of both English and Spanish within this literature activity, six of the selected books were in English and six in Spanish, presented alternately over the twelve-week period.) When Seawell and the three children had finished reading the new book, she would show the children simple paper-sack hand puppets that she had made to go with the story. Then Seawell and the children would enact the story using the hand puppets. When all the children in the class had been introduced to the week's story and puppets in this way, Seawell placed the book, the puppets, and an audio cassette tape of the story in a listening center that the children were free to use during free choice activity periods. Each week a new book, set of puppets, and audio cassette tape were added to the center.

[7]A moment's reflection will probably suggest to you that there are some classroom activities in which the context itself gives clues to the meaning of the talk or print within it and thus support children's use of this strategy; and there are other classroom activities in which the context gives few, if any, clues to meaning and thus do not support the child's use of this strategy.

[8]There were two dyad groups; the rest were trios. These groups were constant throughout the twelve weeks.

From week 5 of the study on through the remaining weeks, Seawell placed in a "circulating library" eight packets for each of the books already introduced. Each packet contained a copy of the book and a set of hand puppets. The children could check out these packets to take home.

On Thursday and Friday of each week Seawell would take the classroom sets of familiar books and puppets into the small room in which she had originally introduced the stories to the groups of children. One group would come in at a time and Seawell would tell them, "It's time for your puppet shows. Each of you may choose a book you'd like to act out together while I record you" (p. 57). The children's "puppet shows" were videotaped for research purposes.

The videotapes documented impressive language growth within this activity over the twelve-week period. It might have been expected that the children's story telling/enactment would have come closer and closer to the exact original text over time. Indeed, the children increasingly chanted together—and more exactly—the sing-song recurring phrases (for example, "Then I huff, and I puff, and I blow your house down"). However, one of the most striking changes was the children's increasing paraphrase and extension of the original text. The following excerpts come from Erica (classified as bilingual) and Oscar (classified as Spanish monolingual) retelling *The Three Little Kittens* in week 2 and week 12.

Week 2

E: "Oh, Mother, dear, we sadly fear, our mittens we have lost." "You naughty kittens, then you shall have no pie. Then you shall have no pie." The three little kittens they lost their mittens. "You naughty kittens. Then you shall have no pie." The three little kittens, they hung their mittens. The three little kittens they washed their mittens. The three little kittens, they hung their mittens. (p. 139-40)

Week 12

E: "You naughty kittens! You dirty kittens! My kids are dirty kittens."
O: "Oh, my gott!"
E: "Then you shall have no pie. Aren't y'all embarrassed for me to be ironin' and washin' y'all's own clothes? Y'all should know how. You dirty kittens!"
O: "You dirty kittens! Washie! Washie!"
E: "Scrub on those mittens! Scrub on those mittens! And hang them out to dry." (p. 140)

Another example comes from Jesse (who spoke very little in any language but was classified as bilingual) enacting *Caps for Sale* during week 10. Shaking both fists, he shouted at the "monkeys," " 'You give me back my hat now or I'll kick your ass!' "—which could certainly be called a paraphrase or extension of the original text! Clearly, these children were making these stories their own.

I am sure that this literature-puppet activity supported the children's language development for various reasons, not the least of which is that it offered the children flexibility within a predictable, understandable, and manageable context. But above all, the children's enthusiasm was unmistakeable: They were most eager to take the book-and-puppet packets home with them (averaging two packets home per child per week); they often chose the listening center with the books, puppets, and audiotapes of the stories, though many other interesting activities were available; and they were most enthusiastic about doing their "puppet shows." This activity, as introduced by the researcher and shaped by the children, held high interest and that interest sustained their total engagement in using their first and second language.

Seawell was not surprised either by the children's enthusiastic participation or by the gains evident in their use of oral language in this context. What she had not anticipated were the contributions that this activity clearly made to the children's literacy development. The three "emergent literacy patterns" that Seawell observed in these children were (1) pretending, "engaging in conventional reading behavior such as holding a book upright, turning pages, and/or pointing to the text while retelling a story" (p. 125); (2) matching, "showing an awareness of the relationship between the written word and its oral counterpart'" (p. 128); and (3) anticipating, "showing an awareness of reading as a desirable accomplishment" (p. 132). Seawell reports that all the children engaged in pretending during every puppet show session during the twelve-week period. The following is an example of this pretending as P (Spanish speaking) "reads" *The Little Engine That Could* during week 9.

> El choo-choo train think I can. Once a choo-choo train so happy. Oso, [bear] and elephant, two dolly and own-uh-own [orange], apple, milk, candy. Said, "Why you stop?" "Wait, wait." "Wha happen?" "You help us?" "No, I too tired for that. I too tired for that." "Stop! Stop! Stop! Stop! De engine broken. Fix it, please. Help me, please." "No, I too tired for that." "Stop! Stop! Stop! Stop!" "Wha happen?" "The engine broke. Can you help us?" "I, I, no, I too little. I think . . . all right, I can. Think I can, think I can, think I can, and then I can, and then I can, can, caaaan." (P was singing softly). "I think I can, can, can. Now." The end. (pp. 127–28)

Like pretending, matching occurred in all the groups and in both Spanish and English texts, but it clearly increased in the later weeks. Here is an example from week 10 in which C and F are retelling *The Little Engine that Could.*

C: And then the blue one. Choo-choooooo, choooo-ee, choo-choo-chooooo. I think I can. I think I can.

F: Ah, noooo. No, esa no dice. La otra. [Ah, nooo. No, that one doesn't say it. The other one.] (F is referring to the page with the text "I think I can.")

C: La otra? [The other one?] (C thinks F is referring to a character in the book.)

F: No, hombreeeee. [No, maaaaaan.] (F is impatient with C for not understanding him.)

C: "I think I can."

F: Donde están (?). Esta. Acá comienza. [Where there are (?) This one. It starts here.] (F is still attempting to match what C is saying with the printed words in the book. He is turning the pages of the book forward.)

C: "Woooooooooo."

F: Acá! [Here!] (F continues turning pages, attempting to find the appropriate lines in the text.)

C: "Wooooooo. I think I can. I think I can."

F: Acá dice "I think I can." Acá, mira. [Here is where it says "I think I can." Here, look.] (F is pointing to the appropriate lines of the text.)

C: "I . . . think . . . I . . . can. I . . . think . . . I . . . can." (Based on pp. 131-32)

Anticipation was evident from week 4 on. It was during week 4 that the children began to announce that they were able to read. Such announcements were made with increasing frequency during the remaining weeks. Erica (bilingual) and Oscar (Spanish monolingual) were partners during the study, and both of them came to feel confident that they could read.

Week 11

(Oscar is retelling the Spanish translation of *Are You My Mother?*") Y cuando llegó la pájara, "¿Quién soy yo?" "¡Mi mamá!" Y le contestó. Le dio comida su mamá. Y ahí estaban solitos. Y'cabé mi trabajito. Ya sí puedo leer. [And when the mother bird arrived, "Who am I?" "My mother!" And she answered him. His mother gave him food. And there they were, just the two of them. Now I finished my little job. Now I can read.] (Oscar said this with a happy smile on his face.) (p. 133)

Week 12

(Erica had just helped Oscar read *The Gingerbread Man*.)

E: I'm gettin' smart now that I got books at home and I'm practicin' reading. It has . . . like 10 pages and I can read them all. (p. 152)

Indeed, there was some evidence that Oscar and Erica and their classmates were right. Many of these children were beginning to read even in the sense of interpreting print in the conventional way. The children would write their names beside the titles of the book packets they wished to take home, correctly identifying the listed titles and also the packets with the titles written on them. Surely it would be simplistic to conclude that these children demonstrated this growth in the oral and written aspects of their languages *only* because the literature-puppet activity held high salience and interest for them; but just as surely it would be impossible to conclude that the salience-interest factor was not contributing in a major way to this language growth.

Additional classroom evidence of children using what is salient and interesting to them as they develop written aspects of their first and second languages in bilingual classrooms comes from children writing in dialogue journals (Hayes and Bahruth 1985) and on topics they select themselves

(Edelsky n.d.). Edelsky, studying first, second, and third graders' writing in their bilingual classrooms (in their first and second languages), observed that the kinds of writing the children engaged in and the level of their involvement in their writing were influenced by the amount of control they were given over the writing.

> When teachers allowed children more control over their own writing, they wrote genres such as jokes, sincere invitations, and songs (these did not appear in assignments). . . . Not only was genre different, but when teachers made it possible for children to write based on their own intentions . . . the writers seemed to be more involved with the piece. (Edelsky n.d., p. 17)

Given control, the children were able to write about topics and in genres that were purposeful and interesting to them. Such interest sustains a child's involvement in the writing process.

Hudelson (1984) cites the role of "what is salient and interesting" in ESL children's awareness of English print. Earlier studies[9] had found that "even children who were virtually non-speakers of English in such isolated areas as the Navajo Nation in Northern Arizona could read items such as *Crest, Coca Cola, McDonald's, Cheerios, Wonder Woman, Dracula,* and *Spider Man.* . . . They were able to do this because these items from the media and real-life were salient for them" (p. 223). Hudelson cites the example of a third grader, recently arrived in the United States, who knew that a sign in his neighborhood, "Beware of the Dog," meant "que no se acerque al perro" ('don't get close to the dog') (p. 223).

Given the opportunity, second-language learners can—and do—use what is salient and interesting to them as they learn to express themselves in speech and writing in the new language. Like first-language learners, while focusing on meaning and purpose in situations that are interesting to them, they acquire expressive forms as well.

Assume that language is (mainly) used either "referentially" or "expressively" and use language data accordingly. You may remember that the referential/expressive distinction is one that is apparent at an early stage in children's acquisition of their first language. Some children ("referential") appear to be working on the assumption that language is used mainly for labeling, while other children ("expressive") seem to be working on the assumption that language is used mainly for socializing. But though children show an early referential or expressive preference, remember that by the end of their second year their language does both referring and socializing kinds of work for them.

We would assume that the child learning English as a second language in school knows from his own first-language experience that language serves both referential and expressive purposes. If, early in his second-language acquisition, a child is more oriented to single-word learning or to phrase learning (characteristics of referential and expressive chil-

---

[9]See Y. Goodman 1980; Y. Goodman and B. Altwerger 1981; and Goodman, Goodman, and Flores 1979.

dren respectively), presumably it is not because he believes that the second language does mainly one kind of work or the other, but rather for reasons of learning style (for example, he finds one easier than the other) or social style.

In her early study of the five Spanish-speaking children learning English, Fillmore (1976) identified three stages in second-language acquisition (overlapping and not clearly demarked, of course) that seemed to motivate and guide the learners' strategies. The three stages are perhaps best characterized as evolving concerns of the learner. Briefly, the learner's earliest concern (first stage) was to establish social relationships with speakers of the second language; his next concern (second stage) was to communicate content, that is, messages, to second-language speakers; and the final concern (third stage) was to be correct in speaking the second language. In the first stage, when the learner was intent on establishing social relations, he would often engage in activities with second-language speakers that were more "interactional" than "informational" (p. 659), relying heavily on fixed verbal formulas (such as "You know what?" "Guess what!" "You know what dese doing?" "Shaddup your mouth," "Oh goody," "This is mine," "Stupid"). Fillmore reported that the learner in this stage also relied on nonverbal communication and on learning key words—labels—that would be useful in the interaction situations of the immediate environment. In the second stage, when the learner became more concerned about communicating messages, he began to create more novel sentences, moving away from socially useful intact formulas toward new combinations including parts of those formulas and some acquired lexical items. It appears, then, that the second-language learner's use of the new language is guided by his concern stage (either socialize or convey messages), and that he will use whatever means he has—fixed whole phrases and/or single key words—as he interacts with speakers of the language he is learning. Apparently it is the learner's concern stage (along with his learning style and social style) rather than an assumption about the main purpose of language (analytic/referential or social/expressive) that guides his ways of using the new language.

Produce language and see how others respond and/or observe how others express meaning. Fillmore (1983) gives the following characterization of the "good language learners" in her three-year study of the forty-three Cantonese and Spanish-speaking children:

> About a half of these children had the characteristics that would have led us to predict success for them; they were highly sociable and outgoing; they were talkative and eager to communicate with anyone who was reasonably receptive to them. Most of the children in this subgroup were highly verbal; several had mouths that seemed to operate non-stop around the clock.
>
> But not all of the good learners were like that. At least 4 of our "good learners" were very quiet: they were children who had seemed to have little to say about anything, and they rarely spoke unless they were prodded. . . .
>
> It seems that while these four children were shy and uncommunicative, they were, at the same time, also inclined to be attentive listeners and quite

observant. These children tended to pay close attention when their teachers talked to them, and they seemed to be observing, if not participating in, most of the activities that took place in the classroom around them. Thus, as bystanders, they observed and listened, and were apparently picking up the language they heard their classmates and teachers using, although they seldom used it themselves. (pp. 162, 164–65)

Fillmore seems to be describing "producer" and "observer" strategies at work. We've seen these two strategies in first-language learning, some children mainly using the first and others mainly using the second. And, no matter how much our society may favor talkativeness in language learning, it appears that an observer strategy can be quite effective in second-language learning as in first. (Notice that the researchers themselves predicted success for producer children and were initially less aware of the second-language competence of the observer children.)

It would seem that a producer strategy would increase the amount of verbal interaction the child has with second-language speakers. We think of more talkative children as initiating and sustaining interaction more than quiet children do. Clearly, in order to learn the second language, the child must hear it. Yet two important points emerge from the second Fillmore study. First, some of the observer children were quite popular and had no lack of social opportunities (Fillmore, personal communication). Second, though a child must "participate" in the language in order to learn it, that "participation" does not have to be talk: "Participation" does not equal "verbalization." A child also actively participates in the language situations by listening and observing attentively. Fillmore's four observer children let the research team know "that there is more than one way to learn a new language" (1983, p. 165).[10]

There is evidence that active observation is an important strategy in the second-language learner's development of the written language as well as the oral language. In one major study of first-grade, second-grade, and third-grade Spanish-dominant children's development of writing in Spanish and in English, Edelsky and her research team found that the children had observed some important differences in the orthographies of Spanish and English and they maintained these differences in their own writing (Edelsky 1982). (The children in this study were in classrooms in which they wrote from one to three hours a day, they wrote in whichever of their languages they chose, they were allowed to write on topics of their own choosing, and to use unconventional written forms, for example, invented spellings, unconventional segmentation and punctuation). Of the twenty-six children whose writing was closely observed during one academic year, all but one used the letter *k* only in their pieces written in English; they

---

[10]See Krashen and Terrell 1983, Chapter 2, for a discussion of ESL approaches stressing the importance of (1) providing "comprehensible input" (that is, talk that focuses on meaning in natural contexts, not on grammatical form) and (2) providing a "silent period" during which second-language "acquirers build up competence by active listening" (p. 36). Though Krashen and Terrell do not use the label "observer strategies," they appear to be providing a situation in which the acquirer can figure out how the language works by observing its use in meaningful contexts.

represented the sound of /k/ in their Spanish writing by using either the letter *q* or the letter *c*. Further, they used tildas and accents only in their Spanish writing. These systematic differences in the children's Spanish and English writing suggest an observation strategy at work. And, indeed, these children had had ample opportunities to observe conventional print in both languages: Materials written in both languages were abundantly displayed in the three classrooms, and the children were provided with substantial reading materials (and time to read them) in both languages.

Frank Smith has pointed out repeatedly that one learns to write by *reading*: "Reading seems to me to be the essential fundamental source of knowledge about writing, from the conventions of transcription to the subtle differences of register and discourse structures in various genres" (Smith 1982b, p. 177). This is apparently true of both first-language and second-language learners. The children in the present study did not have reading instruction in the second language (English) until literacy in their first language (Spanish) was well established (through the second grade). Thus, the fact that these children made these English writing-Spanish writing distinctions is more readily accounted for as the result of their own observations of conventional print in the two languages than as the result of direct instruction. This seems a strong argument for the importance of surrounding children with a multitude of examples of meaningful conventional print in the languages they are developing, and providing ample opportunity for the children to interact with that print.

Ask questions to elicit the data you want.   Though I am not aware of any child second language studies that have focused explicitly on children's questioning, Fillmore's early study of the five children indicates that the learners were questioning (in the sense of using syntactic interrogatives). Fillmore identified a number of formulas the children used early in their acquisition of English. These formulas helped the children participate socially with English-speaking children in the class before they actually knew much English. One category of formulas Fillmore cites is questions: All five children had formulas in this category (ranging from four question formulas for one child to twenty-six question formulas for another). Except for the label-eliciting questions "What is it/this/that?" "What are these?" "What's that one thing?" and "How do you do this in English?" (listed in the Language Management category), the children's question formulas don't appear to be oriented toward helping the child gather language structure "data" as we saw with the first language learners' questions in chapter 7 (the high instance of "What dis/dat?" and "Why?"). These children's question formulas seemed mainly to either seek information that was not specifically about language (for example, "How does dese work?" "How you do dese?" "Who got it?" "What do you want?" "Where'd he go?") or to involve the children socially (for example, "Can I have one?" "What are you doing?" "You wanna X?" "Do you want a X?" "Whatsa matter?" "What you wanna play?" "Can I get some these?"). In fact, Fillmore lists some question formulas in other categories, all of which are strongly social: Name exchanges ("What 'cha/What's your name?"), politeness routines ("How are you?"), conversation management (nine in this category including "You know what?" and "You know why (X)?"), responses to comments, questions ("Oh yeah?" "So?" "So what?" "Why not?" "I don't know, why?"), attention callers ("See this here?" "Will you stop doing that?"), and play management ("Can I play wi' dese?" "My turn?" "Can I be the X?"). Of course, by their very nature, question forms elicit a verbal response from the conversational partner: they are the first part of a question-answer adjacency pair. Thus they give the child an initiating move in conversation. It appears that question formulas helped these children learning English as their second language to be social activists.

Imitate what other people say. You may remember that imitation appears to be both a social and a cognitive strategy for some children in their acquisition of a first language. As a social strategy, repeating what another says gives some children important ways of participating in conversation at a time when their first language is in an early developmental stage: It provides a way for the child to establish a conversational topic, and it provides "expressive" children with socially effective expressions to use in interactions with other people. As a cognitive strategy, Clark (1978) suggests that "stored imitations" may provide linguistic material for the child to subsequently analyze.

There is some evidence that an imitation strategy may serve social and cognitive purposes for the child acquiring a second language also. In her earlier study, Fillmore found that her five Spanish-speaking children initially built up an extensive repertoire of formulas which were basically imitations. These formulas "functioned wholly or partly as unanalyzed, fixed or automatic units for the speaker" (Fillmore 1976, p. 295). (You saw examples of this in the children's questions.) These formulas enabled the children to be active verbal participants in interactions with their English-speaking classmates, and to do so long before they had figured English out. Remember that Fillmore saw the children's first concern as a social one—to belong to the social group. The children's use of these imitated formulas helped them to achieve this. Because the Spanish-speaking children used these formulas so effectively, the English-speaking children believed that they understood English even before they did, and so the English-speaking children kept interacting with the children learning English. Use of formulas thus helped the Spanish speakers to get a hefty amount of talk—"data"—from the English-speaking children.

The children's use of formulas led Fillmore to suggest the following as a strategy the children were using: "*Get some expressions you understand, and start talking*" (p. 639). Notice that this is a producer strategy; it was in Fillmore's later study of the forty-three children that the observer strategy became apparent. But it would seem that heavy use of formulas in the social interactions of the first and second language speakers would aid the observer child in his interpreting as well as helping the producer child in his talking. In order to participate appropriately in social situations, one must accurately interpret what's going on, and the predictable, routinized speech of formulas may have helped the observer children to interpret situations and the talk within them.

Fillmore posited another strategy based on the five children's use of formulas: *Look for recurring parts in the formulas you know* (Fillmore 1976, p. 644). (Notice that this is not phrased as a producer strategy.) The children in this study gradually freed "recurring parts" (elements, constituents) from the original intact formulas. Here is an example of one child's (Nora's) gradual "freeing" of "how" from her original formula "How do you do dese?" (based on pp. 647-48). At first Nora used this question often but always and only in this fixed form. After awhile she began to add elements to this fixed frame:

How do you do dese	little tortillas?
	in English?
	September por mañana?

Then the part of her sentences following "you" began to show variation from the original fixed "do dese," yielding sentences like

How do you	like to be a cookie cutter?
	make the flower?
	gonna make these?

or sentences with "did" instead of "do"

How did you	lost it?
	make it?

Then she began to vary her sentences after the do/did/does, with the "you" no longer necessary in the developing frame.

How did	dese work?
How do	cut it?
How does	this color is?

And finally Nora freed "how" from the original formula, using it in sentences like

Because when I call him, how I put the number?
How you make it?
How will take off paste?

Though these last sentences may sound no more nativelike than Nora's original formula, "How do you do dese," you can see that they represent a tremendous advance in her figuring out the structure of the new language and how to use it flexibly to convey her own meanings. Thus, these imitated formulas served an important cognitive as well as social function for these children: The formulas provided language material that the children subsequently "analyzed."

In the Seawell study, described in detail earlier, Seawell found the children using a variety of "simulation strategies" in their "puppet shows."

"Simulation strategies" were "any situation in which a child repeats all or part of a speech utterance originated by some other speaker" (Seawell 1985, p. 64). There were four distinct types of simulation strategies the groups of children used as they did their "puppet shows" together, sometimes in English and sometimes in Spanish. The following examples demonstrate the four types of repeating.

1. Prompting
(Oscar and Erica are enacting the Spanish translation of *Are You My Mother?*)
O: "¿Tú eres mi mamá?" ["Are you my Mother?"]
E: ¿Tú eres mi mamá?" "No, yo soy una gallina." Así es que siguió su camino. El gato no era su mamá, la gallina no era su mamá. ["Are you my mother?" "No, I am a chicken." So he continued along the road. The cat wasn't his mother, the chicken wasn't his mother.]
O: Se encontró el perro. [He met the dog.]
E: Se encontró el perro. "¿Tú eres mi mamá?" [He met the dog. "Are you my mother?"] (p. 98)

2. Echoing/repeating
(C, P, and J are retelling *The Gingerbread Man.*)
C: "Run, run, as fast as you can. You ca——
C, P, and J: ——can't catch me, I'm the Gingerbread Man." (based on p. 103)

3. Creative constructing
(JA, J, and E are retelling *The Three Little Pigs.*)
JA: Five o'clock, five o'clock . . . go get apple.
J: Go get apple, y'all! (p. 105)

(Oscar and Erica are retelling *The Little Engine That Could.*)
E: Then the dolls got happy.
O: Happy dolls. (p. 105)

(Oscar and Erica are retelling *The Three Little Kittens.*)
E: I smell a rat close by. Yes, I smell a rat close by.
O: Yes, a rat close by, little kittens (p. 145)

4. Recalling
(A and E are retelling *The Three Little Kittens.*)
A: The three little kittens, they washed their mittens, and hung them out to dry. Oh, oh, Mother, dear, can you not hear? Our mittens we have washed. (p. 107)

Can you see the differences in these four types? In prompting, "a child would pause in the reading apparently unsure of how to proceed; another child would prompt by saying the next word or phrase of the story; the first child would repeat the word or phrase and continue with the story" (p. 64). In echoing/repeating, a second child would "echo" what the first child said either as that child was speaking or else immediately after the child had finished. The "creative constructing" child would use a phrase from the first child's utterance as the basis for a new phrase. And in recalling, the child simply attempted to reproduce a phrase or expression exactly as it occurred in the original text.

These quite different ways and purposes of repeating what someone else has said suggest that imitation ("simulation") may more accurately be considered a *set* of strategies than a single one. It is interesting to see how repetition of another's speech helped these children to jointly carry out this literature/puppet task, both in their first language and in their second: Repeating another enabled one monolingual Spanish child to be *in* the second language event (echo/repeat); it enabled another to use a friend's help (prompt); it enabled another to reproduce an original text (recall); and it enabled another to act on and modify an original utterance (creative construction). Again one has the sense of these strategies serving both social and cognitive purposes for these children.

Use some general "operating principles" to figure out language.

In studying four- to nine-year-old English monolingual children acquiring French as their second language while living in France, Ervin-Tripp (1974) found that

> the functions of early sentences, and their form, their semantic redundancy, their reliance on ease of short term memory, their overgeneralization of lexical forms, their use of simple order strategies all were similar to processes we have seen in first language acquisition. In broad outline then, the conclusion is tenable that first and second language learning is similar in natural situations. (Ervin-Tripp 1974, p. 126)

This observation suggests that these second-language learners were using "operating principles"—"a sort of general heuristic . . . which the child brings to bear on the task of organizing and storing language" (Slobin 1973, p. 191)—as they did in acquiring a first language. Child second-language learners seem to be guided by some of the same operating principles that Slobin suggests for first-language learners, for example, "Pay attention to the order of words and morphemes," "Avoid rearrangements," "Avoid exceptions." Fillmore (1976) suggested five cognitive operating principles that she felt her five Spanish-speaking children were using in learning English (several of which I have mentioned already):

> "Assume that what people are saying is directly relevant to the situation at hand, or to what they or you are experiencing." (p. 634)
> "Get some expressions you understand, and start talking." (p. 639)
> "Look for recurring parts in the formulas you know." (p. 644)
> "Make the most of what you've got." (p. 649)
> "Work on big things; save the details for later." (p. 655)

But Fillmore went beyond a cognitive set to suggest some social operating principles, or strategies, as well:

"Join a group and act as if you understand what's going on, even if you don't." (p. 667)
"Give the impression—with a few well-chosen words—that you can speak the language." (p. 669)
"Count on your friends for help." (p. 688)

The first social strategy is important because in order to be included in the conversations of the speakers of the second language, those speakers have to believe that the learners understand them. The speakers will believe this if the learners do appropriately what the others in the group do. The children in Fillmore's study watched and copied the second-language speakers' actions closely, thus giving the impression that they understood the language of the situations. The children's "formulaic speech" comprised the "few well-chosen words" of the second social strategy. In order to continue interaction opportunities, second-language learners must convince the group that they speak (as well as understand) the language. And the second-language speakers in this study were convinced, frequently commenting that the learner understood English, or getting annoyed with the learner for not saying something in English, assuming that the learner was in fact able to and simply chose not to.

The English-speaking friends that the learners "counted on for help" aided the language learners in many ways. Obviously, they provided the second language in interaction contexts. They believed that the Spanish-speaking children were learning English, and so they kept the interaction coming. They provided encouragement and made every effort to understand what the learner was trying to say in English.

The specifics of the suggested operating principles (or "guiding heuristics") may be less important than the fact that second-language acquisition—like first-language acquisition—demonstrates a nonrandomness in the ways children go about the task. In short, second-language learners give evidence of an active sense-making process at work that we have called creative construction. They do seem to be using "guiding heuristics," or operating principles.

And, of course, these operating principles are not limited to the second-language learner's acquisition of oral language; they extend to his making sense of the written language as well. Recent research on young children's writing in the second language demonstrates a hypothesis-making and -using process that we have seen already in written language development in first-language acquisition (Edelsky 1982, 1983; Hudelson 1984; Flores et al. 1985). In many bilingual programs, children's initial literacy instruction is in the child's first language. When the child then begins to read and write in English, the second language, the child applies the same sorts of principles that he has already figured out for the first language.

Once a Spanish-speaking child "breaks the code," for example, uses the alphabetic hypothesis, the child does not need to progress through the different conceptual interpretations of written language again . . . the child applies his/her schema to the second language. (Flores et al., 1985, p. 4)

Here is an example from a first grader whose initial literacy in a bilingual program included a great deal of writing in Spanish but no formal literacy instruction in English. One day in late Spring the child's teacher asked the children if they could write in their journals in English instead of in Spanish. Here is what the child wrote.

Today is Wednesday.
la Tichrabrina motosrayco
damorosaycoes purti.
Mesesilba tucmaypicher
chy Tayms
en gey mi Cendi

Today is Wednesday.
La teacher bring a motorcycle
The motorcycle is pretty.
Mrs. Silva took my picture
two times
and gave me candy

(Hudelson 1984, p. 230)

And ten-year-old Rosa, also Spanish dominant, writes the following in her dialogue journal.

Rosa Oct. 1, 1984
 Oame happy tha Halloween is come min up. I maet be Frankenstein Waif. I'm not sher wat am i going to be da you na wat Nikki is goin tu be cen you ascer. Miss. Krasmerekk wat wer you wen ye wear a little gril.o i forgat to ta you if wer a teacher 2 yers ago wat grat did you tech do you lake bien a teacher vave. You go en tech anweraos.

(Flores et al. 1985, p. 20)

You can readily see that these children's writing in the second language is guided by the kinds of hypotheses (operating principles) that they built for written expression in their first language.

Edelsky (1982) suggests that the first-, second-, and third-grade Spanish-dominant children in her writing study were demonstrating their use of another general principle: "The hypotheses one makes should be based on past input" (p. 225). You remember that these children used the letter *k* only in their English writing (representing the sound /k/ as *q* or *c* in their Spanish writing), and that they used accents and tildas only in their Spanish writing. The "past input" that they were using was English print that used the letter *k* and Spanish print that did not, and Spanish print that used accents and tildas and English print that did not.

"Make the most of what you've got"   (Fillmore 1976, p. 649). This strategy originated in Fillmore's earlier study, though, as we've seen in Chapter 7, it works well in accounting for children's behavior in acquiring a first language also. Fillmore found evidence for the children's use of this strategy in their semantic overextensions (use of "sangwish" to refer to all food, "no good" extended to mean "dead" and "gotcha" extended to mean "kill") as well as in their overuse of acquired expressions, which they would sprinkle about generously in their conversations whether they were appropriate or not ("if we want" or "already" got attached to many sentences where they helped make the child sound fluent but were semantically empty). One child's "Wha' happen?" and "Wha' sa matter?" served to ask all questions he had in mind.

> The children managed to get by with as little English as they did because they made the greatest use of what they had learned—and in the early part of the acquisition period, what they had learned was largely formulaic. (Fillmore 1976, p. 654)

Oscar (Spanish monolingual), a particularly intriguing child in the Seawell study, shows us that talk in the second language is not the only resource the language learner can "make the most of" in expressing his meanings in the new language. Oscar uses his first language as a resource when his partner, Erica (bilingual), is retelling *The Three Little Pigs* in English and leaves out an important part of the story.

E: *The Three Little Pigs.* The mother said, "Bye, my little pigs got to go." The first little pig met a little man with a bundle of straw. "Please, please leave me have those straw. I can build a house." "Okay, that's a good idea." "Little pig, little pig, let me in." "Not by the hair of my chinny, chin, chin." "Then I'll . . . huff . . ."

O: Se lo comió. [He ate him.]

E: ". . . and I'll huff, and huff, and I'll blow your house in." The second little pig met a little man with sticks. "Little man, can I have those sticks?" "Sure, what will you build with it?" "I can build a house." "Okay, that's a good idea." "Little pig, little pig, let me in." "Not by the hair of my chinny, chin, chin." "Then I'll puff . . ."

O: Se lo comió. [He ate him.]
E: ". . . and I'll puff, and I'll blow your house down."
O: Se lo comiooooooooó! Erica, Erica, se lo comió. El, el marranito. [He aaaaate him! (shouting) Erica, Erica, he ate him. The, the little pig.] (Seawell 1985, pp. 84–85)

(Notice that though Oscar was speaking very little English by this time, he was able to follow Erica's story enough to know that she had left something out, what it was that she had left out, and that she continued to leave it out despite his prompting.)

Oscar also uses gestures as a resource.
(Erica and Oscar are retelling *The Three Little Kittens.*)
O: "Mother, watch! Meme!" (Holds up his hands to show his imaginary dirty mittens.) Oh, my gott! (Grabs the sides of his head with his hands and grimaces.) Laddle kit, "Meow, meow, meow, meow." (Wipes imaginary tears from his eyes.) Washie washie, washie, washie. (Scrubs imaginary mittens between his fists.)
E: Hung them out to dry. See. Les cuelgaron para que se secaron. [They hung them up so they would dry.]
O: Aaaaahhhhhh. (based on Seawell 1985, pp. 115–16)

And Oscar uses his partner as a resource as he builds on the language she provides.

E: The three little kittens, they washed their mittens.
O: They wash their mitts. Washie, washie washie. (Seawell 1985, p. 144)

And, of course, he uses the enabling context the adult has provided in this literature/puppet activity. Oscar brings new meaning to the word "re-sourceful" ("resource-*full*?").

THE ENVIRONMENT RECONSIDERED: CLASSROOM IMPLICATIONS[11]

Obviously, some kind of classroom experiences will invite and support the child's use of these language-learning strategies more than others will. Since children learning a second language seem to use some strategies that are very similar to those of first-language learning, it should not surprise us if general characteristics of the supportive classroom are similar too. Again the conflicts from Chapter 8 are relevant.

[11]For a discussion of the complex interaction of children's learning styles and personality styles, with the type of classroom structure, see Fillmore 1982. Fillmore considers factors such as a child's "adult orientation" versus "child orientation" in interaction with classroom aspects such as whether the structure is mainly centers or mainly teacher-directed activities and whether the classroom population is mainly non–English dominant, mainly English dominant, or an equal mix of both.

Whole versus Part Conflict

Which offers the second-language child the better opportunities for using his nonlinguistic understanding, for making sense of the situation itself,

Activities involving language *parts*	or	Activities that are *whole*
oral ESL drills	or	sociodrama
basals	or	literature
workbook exercises	or	dialogue journals

Does the "partial" set or the "wholeness" set support the child's use of nonlinguistic knowledge? Which set offers better contextual support? In the oral drill, there is no nonlinguistic context, only practice of forms in a social vacuum; in the basal, context has been stripped away to make the task "easier." The workbook page is devoid of meaningful context. In the part activities, the child has very little meaningful nonlinguistic information for this strategy to work on.

The whole activities stand in striking contrast to the part activities, offering opportunities for the child to use his knowledge of human behaviors, intentions, concerns, and the expression of these through gesture, voice, pictures, and so on.

Which set—whole or partial—is more salient and interesting to the child? This is a most important question, since it is what is interesting and engaging to the child that he uses for his language learning. Which set offers the more authentic referential and expressive uses of language? The skills activities are heavy in referential/single-word language use, but offer little in the way of expressive/social use. Which set of experiences offers the better opportunities for producer *and* for observer strategies? In the skills activities, neither the producer child nor the observer child gets what he needs—real language in use. Real language is what the producer child produces and it is what the observer child observes. What about questioning: In which type of situation is the child's questioning supported? Clearly, the child questions in both. But what kind of questioning? That is the real issue. The skills activities will be high in questions concerning how to do the exercise to please the teacher: "Is this right, Miss?" "Do we do the next page?" "Do I put a circle here?" As Fillmore's early study clearly indicated, in whole contexts such as sociodramatic play, both social questions and true information questions come into play: "What are you doing?" "Whatsa matter?" "What you wanna play?"

What about imitation/repetition strategies? There are really two questions here. The first is, What kind of language are we offering for the child to imitate in these two types of activities (partial or whole)? Do we really want children who imitate the language of skills and end up speaking the English of oral ESL drills and writing basal prose? The other question is, Which type of situation offers the better opportunities for imitation? The Seawell study, described at length here, surely answers that question.

Like producer and observer strategies, use of operating principles requires real-language samples, and this means authentic language in use. The restricted, nonreal "language" of skills activities gives operating principles very little to operate on. Finally, there's the strategy, "Make the most of what you've got." I think of Oscar. I know Oscar makes the most of what he's got in a literature/puppet experience. But what—oh *what*—can Oscar do with a skills sheet?

Sequence Conflict

In many examples in this chapter you have seen second-language learners following their own sequences of development within the context of language experiences that were meaningful to them.

> Recall the five Spanish-speaking children in Fillmore's first study, whose changing concern stages (be part of the group, convey messages, be correct) guided their ways of constructing the new language. Remember, too, that this sequence of concern stages was the opposite of the traditional ESL curriculum that *begins* with a concern for correctness of form and subsequently moves toward expressing meanings and engaging in social interactions.
>
> Recall these children's early use of language formulas, which enabled them to participate in social events in the classroom, and their gradual "freeing" of elements from these formulas toward a more flexible use of the new language.
>
> Recall the Seawell children, moving, during the twelve weeks of her study, toward more elaborated and flexible expression in English within the literature/puppet activity Seawell provided.
>
> Recall the examples of children writing in English, their second language: low SES Spanish-speaking children writing in dialogue journals (Hayes and Bahruth 1985; Flores et al. 1985; Hudelson 1984) and primary-grade children writing on topics of their own choosing (Edelsky n.d., 1982). Their writing moved toward fuller elaboration, flexibility, and conventionality.

All of these examples have involved an adult providing authentic, whole, and meaningful interaction situations for the child and then responding to the child's use of these experiences.

The traditional ESL sequence, reflecting adult logic, has been for the learner to engage in listening, *then* speaking, *then* reading, and *then* writing. But some recent research on ESL children's literacy development suggests that this traditional sequence needs serious rethinking. Hudelson points out that "even children who speak no or very little English are reading some of the print in their environment and are using that reading to increase their English" (Hudelson 1984, p. 222). "ESL learners are able to read English before they have complete oral control of the language" (p. 224). This means that "ESL teachers do not need to wait until children are highly fluent in English before offering reading materials" (p. 226) and also that "ESL learners can (and should) write English before they have complete control over the oral and written systems of the language" (p. 231). (Hudelson follows her own advice in her *Hopscotch* series, in which children engage in meaningful literacy experiences from the outset.) Again it appears that sequences derived from adult logic often fail to be in tune with the active sense-making experiences of children.

In her study of first-, second-, and third-grade children's writing development (in their first and second languages), Edelsky observed that this "development in writing seems to have occurred through individual construction of succeeding hypotheses" (n.d., p. 5)—a basic sequencing process that is, by now, familiar to you. However, the classroom teacher influenced—and often interfered with—the children's sequencing in a variety of ways. One especially important factor was the teacher's expectations about the children's writing abilities; these expectations determined what the children wrote.

> The first grade study teacher believed that entering first graders could not write. Therefore the September data for first grade consists entirely of labeled or signed pictures. By November, she believed they could compose their own journal entries if guided by a teacher-established structure. The second collection from first grade is made up of one assigned thank-you letter and journals [in which the children listed] surface features of what [they] did the day before. In February she began to believe she could "take the lid off." The variety and richness of the third and fourth collections reflect the "removed lid." From what happened in two other non-study first grades, we can tell that this change is not simply a function of the children's own maturation. In one class, the teacher turned major writing decisions over to children from the beginning of the year. That classroom produced pieces that reveal that the writers were taking major risks in genre, syntax, and topic. In the other class the teacher believed that children need to spell conventionally and decode accurately in reading in order to write. Writing from that classroom as late as April still resembled texts in phonics workbooks. (Edelsky 1981, pp. 90–91)

Thus, the sequence followed in these first-grade classrooms derived from the teachers' belief. Only in the classroom in which the writing process belonged to the children from the beginning were the children able to play out their own developmental sequences, building and testing and revising their own hypotheses about written language.

Assessment Conflict

Presumably we assess children's ongoing development of language in order to get information. What kind of information do we get about our ESL children from skills tests or standardized tests? Think again of Oscar. It's about time for Oscar to have a "reading readiness" test. If he is given such a test, for sure the result will be this message: Oscar is not "ready." The diagnosis. In fact, the results will probably specify a number of specific ways in which Oscar is not "ready." The "prescribed treatment" is likely to be skills and drills to get Oscar "ready" to begin reading and writing. But observations of Oscar tell a very different story. As we have seen already, Oscar already is actively engaging in making sense of print in the new language: he is actively participating in producing the stories he understands are "held" in the print; he is selecting from lists of book titles the ones he wants to check out and take home, and so on. The reading readiness test would give us "information" about Oscar that would lead us to deprive Oscar of the very experience that he is using so powerfully in his learning of the new language.

Skills tests and standardized tests do not measure the second-language learner's use of English any better than they do the first-language learner's use of English. These tests give a child a label: high/low, ready/not ready, gifted/remedial, proficient/Chapter 1, LEP, TAG, and so on. But the label is not based on the child's use of language. If we want to know how a child is using English in interacting with others, then there is no valid alternative to observing the child interacting with others; and if we want to know how the child is making sense of print in English, then we will have to observe him interacting with English print.

Providing labels based on inauthentic, nonlanguage behaviors is what standardized and skills tests do. Here is what they don't do: They don't give the teacher information about what the second-language learner is *doing*—the process—the ways in which he is making sense of the second language. This is the teacher's most important kind of information and what it is most important for her to assess. The better the teacher understands how the child is going about his business of constructing the new language, the more effectively she can support the child's work—by providing, observing, and responding appropriately.

Earlier and later taped samples of the Seawell children doing their "puppet shows" showed what these children were *doing*; regular observations of Fillmore's children playing together showed what these children were *doing*; regular dialogue journal writing and writing on self-selected topics showed what these children were *doing*. This is assessment.

Rehearsal versus Communication Conflict

The conventional wisdom that says first-you-must-learn-language (train) and then-you-can-use-it (communicate) is nowhere more evident than in second-language instruction. The oral ESL practice drills provided at the beginning of this chapter offer a typical example. Often ESL materials begin with identification drills of the "This is an X" variety. Clearly, this is not done to help the learner actively engage in communication with others, for it is difficult to think of a more sure-fire conversation stopper than "This is a desk." These drills are provided, rather, as training for later communication.

But evidence from children acquiring English as their second language suggests that it is not rehearsal practice, but the engaging-in practice of communication that is their first concern. Left to their own devices, Fillmore's Spanish-speaking children used socially useful formulas in English. Taken together, the formulas these children used form a motley set, strikingly different from the neatly tailored oral-language drill sets of traditional ESL materials. The single feature common to all the formulas was that they enabled the children to participate in situations they wanted to be part of.

Not only is engaging-in practice (communication) the second-language learner's major concern. It is also, apparently, his greatest ally. You've already seen the children in the Fillmore and Seawell studies actively engaging in communication. Their talk was not practice for the real thing; it *was* the real thing. And it was by engaging in the real thing that these children became more able communicators in the second language. There is increasing evidence that this active engagement in real communication facilitates written development, too. Edelsky's first, second, and third graders, over time, moved toward more conventional ways of segmenting and punctuating their writing. Now, in many classrooms, segmentation and punctuation are likely candidates for rehearsal practice. Many children are much drilled on these "rules of writing." But not the children in Edelsky's study: "One thing that was *not* going on was direct teaching of segmentation and punctuation." Edelsky asks, "If no one instructed these children to separate propositions with stars or to put a period after every word, how then did such usage come about?

> Although it was invented, it was not "totally new under the sun." Existing means (capitals, periods, stars, one message per line, running text, etc.) were used; they were simply used unconventionally via particular hypotheses based on input from conventional "environmental" and "book" print. The changing character of these hypotheses over time came about as a consequence of interaction with print, since there were no lessons on spacing or sentence boundaries. Here is an example, then, which shows that even "rules of writing" . . . were *acquired* [that is, developed naturally within meaningful communication contexts]. . . . Moreover, these hypotheses moved toward conventionality through real use rather than practice/training. (Edelsky 1983, p. 155)

It's a commonplace that we get better at doing what we engage in doing. Second-language learners who do rehearsal practice drills get better at doing rehearsal practice drills; but it is the second-language learners who engage in communicating in the second language who get better at doing that: communicating in the second language. A child develops language— first or second—by engaging in *language*, and that means engaging in communication.

And so we have come full circle. The second-language learner, like the first-language learner, is a child creatively constructing language in a social world. The classroom is a wonderful social world for the bilingual child to do this first and second language work in.

SUGGESTED PROJECTS

1. *Interviews with educators: BEV.* Tape a sample (approximately ten minutes) of one or several BEV-dominant children in as natural a situation as possible. Design a set of informal interview questions to ask educators representing different groups—student teachers, classroom teachers, school principals, classroom aides, college education professors. For each

person you interview, first play the taped sample (you might want to provide a transcript as well, to help the interviewee follow and then recall the sample), and then tape your interview with the person. You might want to ask some questions relating to the child's background such as "Just from hearing this small sample, would you feel able to make any tentative guesses about this child's home background? What kinds of experiences do you think she might have had prior to coming to·school? What might her family be like?" You might want to ask some questions about the interviewee's perceptions of the child's school experience: "Would you expect that this child might have found any particular areas of adjustment to school difficult when the child first arrived? How? Why? Would you be willing to make any guesses about what this child may be strong in or weak in, in school? How would you expect this child to perform socially in school—in relations with peers? in relations with adults? Why? What sort of educational program would you want to provide for this child? Why?

These are only a few suggestions to get your thinking started. What you want to see is what kinds of attitudes and knowledge the educators hold relating to BEV-dominant children. It is important that you not force the interviewees into biased responses. You want to phrase your questions in such a way as to allow for responses like "Just listening to ten minutes of a little girl talking on tape I couldn't possibly tell you what she'd be good at or poor at in school." This kind of comment would tell you a great deal about the attitudes held by the interviewee. You might want to follow such a comment with a question like "What kind of information *would* you need to make such a guess?"

Analyze your taped interviews. Do you see any similarities within groups and differences between groups? What are they? Or do you find similar attitudes and suggestions across groups? Or is there no particular pattern, but simply an interesting range of responses? Describe the patterns, similarities, differences, and so on.

2. *Interviews with educators: Bilingual.* Adapt suggestion 1 to focus on language difference (rather than dialect difference) by taping a child or children whose first language is not English. Be sure to include some native speakers of the child's dominant language in your interviewee group. You might want to see whether interviewee responses differ in any significant and interesting way between the native speakers of the child's first language and the native speakers of English. (I am assuming that English is the child's second language, though this project could be done with an English-dominant child acquiring another language.)

You can doubtless see ways of doing suggestions 1 or 2 with several friends working together—for example, each of you interviewing a different group of educators and then listening to each other's taped interviews and discussing them together.

3. *A study of preferred educational approaches to ESL.* Prepare a brief description of a mythical (or real) school child (or several) in your class—maybe six or seven years old, who speaks a language other than English: family background, language background, personality, special abilities and interests observed. Present your description to various educators (as in

above projects). Then present a variety of second language oriented experiences and get the educator to discuss the merits or demerits of each for use with the child you have described. You might also want to have the educator rank the activities from most to least effective. It might be particularly helpful to work as a group on this project so as to come up with an interesting range of suggested activities initially. (Your results can not be any more interesting than the range of possible activities you suggest.) You may want to include some typical audiolingual drill activities, some typical whole-group teacher-directed lessons, some structured independent types (seatwork, worksheet, and workbook exercises), some small-group (about five in a group) projects (perhaps one more structured and one less structured), some free activities like talking with other children on the playground or at lunch, and some play activities in which children are paired with friends from the second-language group (as in Fillmore's 1976 study). Try to vary the suggested activities along these dimensions: (1) the degree of imposed structure, (2) the number and language background of people involved, (3) the meaning-full-ness—interestingness (versus form-full-ness) of the activity. Again, taping your discussions with the educators you interview might be the most helpful way to capture and preserve their ideas. See whether for each activity selected as helpful you can infer what the respondent's assumptions are about how a young child acquires a second language. For example, if a respondent suggests thirty minutes a day of audiolingual drill "so the child will learn to not make so many mistakes and say things backwards," you might assume the respondent considers language learning largely a matter of establishing correct habits. If the respondent says, "Well, I'd want the child to have plenty of time to just talk and play with friends who speak the second language," you might assume the respondent sees second-language learning as largely a social communication process.

4. *Bidialectal Sentence Repetition Test.* Have a bidialectal (BEV and SE) speaker tape record Joan Baratz's Bidialectal Sentence Repetition Test (Baratz 1969), leaving after each model sentence ample space on the tape for a child to repeat the model sentence. Then have three to five BEV-dominant children and three to five SE-dominant children take the test, preferably without you or any other adult present. This will involve two tape recorders, one on which the model sentences are played and one that is recording the taped model sentences *and* the child's repetitions of them. Then analyze the differences between the children's repetitions and the model sentences.

5. *Analysis of black English Vernacular sample.* Tape record and transcribe thirty minutes of language from a BEV-speaking child or group of children. Analyze and discuss the dialectal features in your transcript.

6. *Social interaction for second-language learning.* Collect thirty minutes of language from a child who is learning a second language, when he or she is engaged in an informal play activity with one or several children who speak the child's second language (the language being learned). An ideal situation would be the housekeeping or dramatic-play area of a classroom. Your data collection will have to include both a tape recording and your

own supplemental handwritten observational notes as the interaction proceeds. (Of course, videotape would be ideal if you have access to it and can arrange a situation in which the equipment is minimally intrusive.) Your goal is to observe and describe (1) how the child uses language and other means to become and remain part of the social group. For example, does the child use some pat formulas in the second language ("Hi" "Can I play?" "Me too")? Does the child watch and copy the actions of the others (if one child picks up a dish and pretends to wash it, does the subject child do the same)? Does the child use whatever devices he or she has in the second language to express new ideas? How? Does the child pantomime? What? How? (2) How do the other children adapt their behavior for the child's benefit: Do they use simpler structures and vocabulary? Do they repeat and/or paraphrase? Do they accompany their words with extra gestures that help to make their meanings clear? Do they ever physically guide the child through an appropriate action sequence?

7. *Language switching.* If you have access to a bilingual child, do a short case study to see how the child uses each of his or her two languages in oral and written channels. This will involve gathering data on the child both at home and at school, so you will want to be sure you have the parents' support for your study. Your study will not involve taping and transcribing, but it will be observational and descriptive in nature. You will "follow" the child through one day (possibly the parents will need to fill you in on the child's morning activities before school and on the evening or bedtime events). What topics does the child use each language to discuss? What does the child read in each language? What does she write in each? With which different persons does the child use each language? In what settings does the child use each language? What seems to influence the switch from one language to another in the child's talk, reading, and writing? In what situations are both languages used—switched within a single conversation or written piece, or even within a single spoken or written sentence? In what situations does the child reply in a language other than the one he was addressed in?

8. *Your own questions.* Discuss in depth any questions and wonderings you now have about language—what it is, how it is learned, and how it is used.

9. *"Your own thing."* Design your own learning experience relating to the ideas in this section, discuss it with your instructor and/or an acquaintance knowledgeable in this area, and execute it.

SUGGESTED FURTHER READINGS AND RESOURCES

ANGELOU, M., *I Know Why the Caged Bird Sings.* New York: Bantam Books, Inc., 1973. A powerful autobiography of a black woman's childhood and young adult years.

ASHTON-WARNER, S., *Teacher.* Middlesex, England: Penguin Books, 1963. A classic personal account by a teacher of Maori children in New Zealand.

BAUGH, J., *Black Street Speech: Its History, Structure, and Survival.* Austin, Tex.: University of Texas Press, 1983. A quite readable description of black English, based on the author's collection of data in a variety of natural settings.

CAZDEN, C., V. JOHN, AND C. HYMES, EDS., *Functions of Language in the Classroom*. New York: Columbia University Teachers College, 1972. A collection of articles focusing on the educational situation (especially language) of American children from various ethnic backgrounds.

Council on Interracial Books for Children, Inc., 1841 Broadway, New York, N.Y. 10023. A good source of information and materials (for example, books, filmstrips, pamphlets) relating to racism, sexism, classism, and various other "isms."

GALARZA, E., *Barrio Boy*. Notre Dame, Ind.: University of Notre Dame Press, 1971. The autobiography of a Mexican child who comes to the United States and grows up here, or—as the author puts it—"a true story of the acculturation of Little Ernie."

HUDELSON, S., *Hopscotch*. New York: Regents Publishing Company, Inc., 1985. A six-level ESL series for children that engages children actively in using oral and written language in meaningful communication.

KINGSTON, M.H., *The Woman Warrior: Memoirs of a Girlhood among Ghosts*. New York: Vintage Books, 1975. The autobiography of a Chinese-American woman.

KOCHMAN, T., *Black and White Styles in Conflict*. Chicago: The University of Chicago Press, 1981. The conflicting "styles" the author describes are cultural, including, but not restricted to, ways of using language.

LABOV, W., "The Logic of Nonstandard English," in *Report of the Twentieth Annual Round Table Meeting on Linguistics and Language Study*, ed. J. Alatis. Washington, D. C.: Georgetown University Press, 1970. Also reprinted in *Language and Poverty*, ed. F. Williams. Chicago: Marxham Publishing Company, 1970. A fascinating and classic study of the language of Harlem preteenagers.

Pizza Pizza Daddy-O, University of California, Extension Media Center, Berkeley, California 94720. An intriguing film of black children's playground games.

SIMS, R., *Shadow and Substance: Afro-American Experience in Contemporary Children's Fiction*. Urbana, Ill.: National Council of Teachers of English, 1982. A discussion of themes, styles, and selected authors in the field of black literature for children.

SMITHERMAN, G., *Talkin and Testifyin*. Boston: Houghton Mifflin Company, 1977. A description of black English—its forms, styles, and uses. Abundant examples.

References

ABRAHAMS, R. D., "Black Talking on the Streets," in *Explorations in the Ethnography of Speaking*, ed. R. Bauman and J. Sherzer. London: Cambridge University Press, 1974.

————, *Talking Black*, Rowley, Mass.: Newbury House Publishers, Inc., 1976.

ALLENDER, J. S., "A Study of Inquiry Activity in Elementary School Children," *AERA*, 6 (1969), 543–58.

————, "Some Determinants of Inquiry Activity in Elementary School Children," *Journal of Educational Psychology*, 61, no. 3 (1970), 220–25.

ALMY, M., and C. GENISHI, *Ways of Studying Children*. New York: Teachers College Press, 1979.

ANGELOU, M., *I Know Why the Caged Bird Sings*. New York: Bantum Books, 1970.

ASBJØRNSEN, P. C., and J. E. MOE, *The Three Billy Goats Gruff*. New York: Harcourt Brace Jovanovich, Inc., 1957.

ATWELL, N., "Writing and Reading Literature from the Inside Out." *Language Arts*, 61, no. 1 (1984), 240–52.

AU, K. H., "Participation Structures in a Reading Lesson with Hawaiian Children: Analysis of a Culturally Appropriate Instructional Event," *Anthropology & Education Quarterly*, 11, no. 2 (1980), 91–115.

AUSTIN, J. L., *How to Do Things with Words*. Oxford: Oxford University Press, 1962.

BALLARD, L., *The New True Book of Reptiles*. Chicago: Children's Press, 1982.

BARATZ, J., "Teaching Reading in a Negro School," in *Teaching Black Children to Read*, ed. J. Baratz and R. Shuy. Arlington, Va.: Center for Applied Linguistics, 1969.

BARNES, S., M. GUTFREUND, D. SATTERLY, and G. WELLS, "Characteristics of Adult Speech Which Predict Children's Language Development," *Journal of Child Language*, 10, no. 1 (1983), 65–84.

BARRS, M., "The New Orthodoxy about Writing: Confusing Process and Pedagogy," *Language Arts*, 10, no. 7 (1983), 829–40.

BATES, E., *Language and Context: The Acquisition of Pragmatics*. New York: Academic Press, Inc., 1976.

BAUGH, J., *Black Street Speech: Its History, Structure, and Survival*. Austin, Tex.: University of Texas Press, 1983.

BELLUGI, U., "Simplification in Children's Language," in *Language Acquisition: Models and Methods*, ed. R. Huxley and E. Ingram. New York: Academic Press, Inc., 1971.

BEREITER, C., and S. ENGELMANN, *Teaching Disadvantaged Children in the Preschool*. Englewood Cliffs, N.J.: Prentice-Hall, Inc., 1966.

BERKO, J., and R. BROWN, "Psycholinguistic Research Methods," in *Handbook of Research Methods in Child Development*, ed. P. H. Mussen. New York: John Wiley & Sons, Inc., 1960.

BERKO, GLEASON, J., "The Child's Learning of English Morphology," in *Child Language: A Book of Readings*, ed. A. Bar-Adon and W. Leopold, Englewood Cliffs, N.J.: Prentice-Hall, Inc., 1971.

BERKO, GLEASON, J., and S. WEINTRAUB, "The Acquisition of Routines in Child Language," *Language and Society*, 5 (1976), 129–36.

BERLYNE, D. E., "Curiosity and Education," in *Learning and the Educational Process*, ed. J. D. Krumboltz. Chicago: Rand-McNally & Company, 1965.

BETTS, E. A., "Ride In," in *Time to Play*. Second Preprimer, Betts Basic Readers (3rd ed.), Language Arts Series. New York: American Book, 1963.

BETTS, E. A., and C. M. WELCH, "Stop and Go," in *All in a Day*. Third Preprimer, Betts Basic Readers. New York: American Book, 1963.

BISSEX, G. L., *GNYS AT WRK: A Child Learns to Write and Read*. Cambridge, Mass.: Harvard University Press, 1980.

BLOOM, L., *Language Development: Form and Function in Emerging Grammars*. Cambridge, Mass.: The MIT Press, 1970.

——, "Language Development Review," in *Review of Child Development Research (vol. 4)*, ed. F. D. Horowitz. Chicago: The University of Chicago Press, 1975.

BLOOM, L., L. HOOD, and P. LIGHTBOWN, "Imitation in Language Development: If, When, and Why," *Cognitive Psychology*, 6 (1974), 380–420.

BLOOM L., P. LIGHTBOWN, and L. HOOD, *Structure and Variation in Child Language*. Monographs of the Society for Research in Child Development. Chicago: The University of Chicago Press, no. 160, v. 40, no. 2, 1975.

BLOOM, L., S. MERKIN, and J. WOOTEN, "Wh-questions: Linguistic Factors that Contribute to the Sequence of Acquisition," *Child Development*, 53, no. 4 (1982), 1084–92.

BOEHM, A. E., and R. A. WEINBERG, *The Classroom Observer: A Guide for Developing Observation Skills*. New York: Teachers College Press, 1977.

BOGGS, S. T., "The Meaning of Questions and Narratives to Hawaiian Children," in *Functions of Language in the Classroom*, ed. C. B. Cazden, V. P. John, and D. Hymes. New York: Teachers College Press, 1972.

BOWEN, J. D., "English Usage and Language Learning among the Navajo," in *Workpapers in Teaching English as a Second Language*, 2. Los Angeles: University of California Press, 1966.

BRAINE, M. D. S., "On Two Types of Models of the Internalization of Grammars," in *The Ontogenesis of Grammar*, ed. D. Slobin. New York: Academic Press, Inc., 1971.

BRENNEIS, D., and L. LEIN, "'You Fruithead': A Sociolinguistic Approach to Children's Dispute Settlement," in *Child Discourse*, ed. S. Ervin-Tripp and C. Mitchell-Kernan. New York: Academic Press, Inc., 1977.

BRETHERTON, I., S. McNEW, L. SNYDER, and E. BATES, "Individual Differences at 20 Months: Analytic and Holistic Strategies in Language Acquisition," *Journal of Child Language*, 10, no. 2 (1983), 293–320.

BRITTON, J., *Language and Learning*. Hammondsworth, England: Pelican Books, 1973.

BROWN, G., and B. YULE, *Discourse Analysis*. New York: Cambridge University Press, 1983.

BROWN, R., "Introduction," in J. Moffett, *Teaching the Universe of Discourse*. Boston: Houghton Mifflin Company, 1968.

——, *A First Language*. Cambridge, Mass.: Harvard University Press, copyright © 1973.

BROWN, R., C. CAZDEN, and U. BELLUGI-KLIMA, "The Child's Grammar from I to III," in *Child Language: A Book of Readings*, ed. A. Bar-Adon and W. Leopold. Englewood Cliffs, N.J.: Prentice-Hall, Inc., 1971.

BROWN, R., and C. FRASER, "The Acquisition of Syntax," in *The Acquisition of Language*, ed. U. Bellugi and R. Brown. Chicago: The University of Chicago Press, 1964.

BRUNER, J. S., "Learning How to Do Things with Words," in *Human Growth and Development*, ed. J. Bruner and A. Garton. Oxford: Oxford University Press, 1978.

——, "The Pragmatics of Acquisition," in *The Child's Construction of Language*, ed. W. Deutsch. New York: Academic Press, Inc., 1981.

BRUNER, J. S., C. ROY, and N. RATNER, "The Beginnings of Request," in *Children's Language (vol. 3)*, ed. K. Nelson. Hillsdale, N. J.: Lawrence Erlbaum Associates, Publishers, 1982.

BUSWELL, G. T., *An Experimental Study of the Eye-Voice Span in Reading*. Supplementary Educational Monographs, No. 17. Chicago: The University of Chicago Press, 1920.

CAIRNS, H. S., and J. R. HSU, "*Who, Why, When* and *How*: A Development Study," *Journal of Child Language*, 5, no. 3 (1978), 477–88.

CALKINS, L. M., *Lessons from a Child: On the Teaching and Learning of Writing.* Portsmouth, N.H.: Heinemann Educational Books, 1983.

————, "Learning to Think through Writing," in *Observing the Language Learner*, ed. A. Jaggar and M. T. Smith-Burke. Urbana, Ill.: National Council of Teachers of English, 1985.

————, *The Art of Teaching Writing.* Portsmouth, N.H.: Heinemann Educational Books, 1986.

CAMPBELL, R., AND J. LINDFORS, *Insights into English Structure: A Programmed Course.* Englewood Cliffs, N.J.: Prentice-Hall, Inc., 1969.

CARMICHAEL, L., H. P. HOGAN, and A. A. WALTER, "An Experimental Study of the Effects of Language on the Reproduction of Visually Received Form," *Journal of Experimental Psychology*, 15 (1932), 73–86.

CARROLL, L., *The Complete Works of Lewis Carroll.* New York: The Modern Library, Random House Inc., n.d.

CAZDEN, C. B., *Child Language and Education.* New York: Holt, Rinehart and Winston, Inc., 1972.

————, "Play and Metalinguistic Awareness: One Dimension of Language Experience," *The Urban Review*, 7 (1974), 23–39.

————, "Classroom Teaching Relived," *Harvard Graduate School of Education Association Bulletin*, 19, no. 3 (Spring/Summer 1975).

————, "What Is Sharing Time For?" *Language Arts* 62, no. 2 (1985), 182–188.

————, "Classroom Discourse," in *Handbook of Research on Teaching* (3rd ed.), ed. M. C. Wittrock. New York: Macmillan, Inc., in press.

CERF, B., *Book of Laughs.* New York: Beginner Books, Inc., 1959.

CHALL, J., *Stages of Reading Development.* New York: McGraw-Hill Book Company, 1983.

CHOMSKY, C., *The Acquisition of Syntax in Children from 5 to 10.* Research Monograph No. 57. Cambridge, Mass.: The MIT Press, 1969.

CHOMSKY, N., *Aspects of the Theory of Syntax.* Cambridge, Mass.: The MIT Press, 1965.

————, "Current Issues in Linguistic Theory," in *The Structure of Language*, ed. J. Fodor and J. Katz. Englewood Cliffs, N.J.: Prentice-Hall, Inc., 1964.

————, "A Review of B. F. Skinner's *Verbal Behavior*," *Language*, 35, no. 1 (1959), 26–58.

CHUKOVSKY, KORNEI, *From Two to Five*, trans. and ed. Miriam Morton. Berkeley: University of California Press, 1968.

CLARK, E. V., Review of *The Acquisition of Syntax in Children from 5 to 10* by C. Chomsky. Research Monograph No. 57. Cambridge, Mass.: The MIT Press, 1969. In *Language*, 47 (1971), 742–49.

————, "Some Aspects of the Conceptual Basis for First Language Acquisition," in *Language Perspectives—Acquisition, Retardation, and Intervention*, ed. R. L. Schiefelbusch and L. L. Lloyd. Baltimore: University Park Press, © 1974 University Park Press, Baltimore.

————, "What's in a Word: On the Child's Acquisition of Semantics in His First Language," in *Cognitive Development and the Acquisition of Language*, ed. T. Moore. New York: Academic Press, Inc., 1973.

————, "Meanings and Concepts," in *Cognitive Development* (vol. 3) ed. J. Flavell and E. Markman. New York: John Wiley & Sons, Inc., 1983.

CLARK, H., and E. V. CLARK, *Psychology and Language.* New York: Harcourt Brace Jovanovich, Inc., 1977.

CLARK, R., "What's the Use of Imitation?" *Journal of Child Language*, 4, no. 3 (1977), 341–58.

————, "Some Even Simpler Ways to Learn to Talk," in *Development of Communication: Social and Pragmatic Factors in Language Acquisition*, ed. N. Waterson and C. Snow. London: John Wiley and Sons, Inc., 1978.

COLE, M., and P. GRIFFIN, "A Socio-Historical Approach to Re-mediation," *The Quarterly Newsletter of the Laboratory of Comparative Human Cognition*, 5, no. 4 (1983), 69–74.

CONFORD, E., *Just the Thing for Geraldine.* Boston: Little, Brown & Company, 1974.

COOK-GUMPERZ, J., "Situated Instructions: Language Socialization of School Age Children," in *Child Discourse*, ed. S. Ervin-Tripp and C. Mitchell-Kernan. New York: Academic Press, Inc., 1977.

CORTE, M. D., H. BENEDICT, and D. KLEIN, "The Relationship of Pragmatic Dimension of Mothers' Speech to the Referential-Expressive Distinction," *Journal of Child Language*, 10, no. 1 (1983), 35–43.

COULTHARD, M., *An Introduction to Discourse Analysis*. London: Longman, Inc., 1977.

COVILLE, B., and K. COVILLE, *Sarah's Unicorn*. New York: J. B. Lippincott Company, 1979.

CROSS, T., "Some Relationships between Motherese and Linguistic Level in Accelerated Children," *Papers and Reports on Child Language Development*. Stanford University, Stanford, Calif., no. 10 (1975).

CUMMINGS, e. e., "hist whist," in *More Poems, Interaction*. ed. J. Moffett, B. Thorpe, and P. F. Neumeyer. Boston: Houghton Mifflin Company, 1973.

DALE, P. S., *Language Development: Structure and Function* (2nd ed.). New York: Holt, Rinehart and Winston, Inc., 1976.

DAVID, R. M. S., "A Study of the Relationship between Pupil Questions and Selected Variables," *Dissertation Abstracts*, 31A (1971), 5027–28.

DEFORD, D., and J. HARSTE, "Child Language Research and Curriculum," *Language Arts*, 59, no. 6 (1982), 590–600.

DILLARD, J. L., *Black English*. New York: Random House, Inc., 1972.

DILLON, D., "Editorial," *Language Arts*, 62, no. 1 (1985).

DODL, N. R., "Questioning Behavior of Elementary Classroom Groups," *California Journal for Instructional Improvement* (October, 1966), 167–79.

DONALDSON, M., *Children's Minds*. New York: W. W. Norton & Company, 1979.

DORE, JOHN, "Holophrases, Speech Acts and Language Universals," *Journal of Child Language*, 2, no. 1 (April 1975), 21–40.

———, " 'Oh Them Sheriff': A Pragmatic Analysis of Children's Responses to Questions," in *Child Discourse*, ed. S. Ervin-Tripp and C. Mitchell-Kernan. New York: Academic Press, Inc., 1977.

DULAY, H. C., and M. K. BURT, "Errors and Strategies in Child Second Language Acquisition," *TESOL Quarterly*, 8, no. 2 (June 1974), 129–36.a

———, "Natural Sequences in Child Second Language Acquisition," *Language Learning*, 24, no. 1 (June 1974), 37–53. b

———, "A New Perspective on the Creative Construction Process in Child Second Language Acquisition," *Language Learning*, 24, no. 2 (December 1974), 253–78.c

DUMONT, R. V., "Learning English and How to Be Silent: Studies in Sioux and Cherokee Classrooms," in *Functions of Language in the Classroom*, ed. C. B. Cazden, V. P. John, and D. Hymes. New York: Teachers College Press, 1972.

DYSON, A. H., *A Case Study Examination of the Role of Oral Language in Writing Processes of Kindergarteners*. Unpublished doctoral dissertation. The University of Texas at Austin, 1981.

———, "Teachers and Young Children: Missed Connections in Teaching/Learning to Write," *Language Arts*, 59, no. 7 (October 1982), 674-80.

———, "Reading, Writing, and Language: Young Children Solving the Written Language Puzzle," *Language Arts*, 59, no. 8 (November/December 1982), 829–39.

———, "Research Currents: Young Children as Composers," *Language Arts*, 60, no. 7 (October 1983), 884–91.

EDELSKY, C., "From 'Jimosalsco' to '7narangas se calleron y el arbol-est-triste en lagrymas' " Writing Development in a Bilingual Program," in *The Writing Needs of Linguistically Different Students*, ed. B. Cronnell. Los Alamitos, Calif.: SWRL Educational Research and Development, 1981.

———, "Writing in a Bilingual Program: The Relation of L1 and L2 Texts," *TESOL Quarterly*, 16 (June 1982), 211–28.

———, "Segmentation and Punctuation: Developmental Data from Young Writers in a Bilingual Program," *Research in the Teaching of English*, 17 (May 1983),135–56.

———, *The Teacher's Role in Young Children's Writing*. Unpublished paper. Arizona State University, Tempe, Arizona, n.d.

EDELSKY, C., and K. DRAPER, "Reading/'Reading', Writing/'Writing', Text/'Text'," in *Reading and Writing: Theory and Research*, ed. A. Petrosky. Norwood, N.J.: Ablex Publishing Corporation, in press.

EDELSKY, C., K. DRAPER, and K. SMITH, "Hookin' 'em in at the Start of School in a 'Whole Language' Classroom," *Anthropology and Education Quarterly*, 14, no. 4 (1983), 257–81.

EDELSKY, C., and K. SMITH, "Is That Writing—Or Are Those Marks Just a Figment of Your Curriculum?" *Language Arts*, 61, no. 1 (January 1984), 24–32.

EDWARDS, W. F., "Inner-City English," in *Tapping Potential: English and Language Arts for the*

Black Learner, ed. C. Brooks. Urbana, Ill.: National Council of Teachers of English, 1985.

EIMAS, P. D., E. R. SIGUELAND, P. JUSCZYK, and J. VIGORITO, "Speech Perception in Infants," *Science*, 171 (1971), 303–6.

EISENBERG, A., and C. GARVEY, "Children's Use of Verbal Strategies in Resolving Conflicts," *Discourse Processes*, 4 (1981), 149–70.

ELLEY, W., and F. MANGUBHAI, "The Impact of Reading on Second Language Learning," *Reading Research Quarterly*, 19 (1983), 53–67.

ELLIS, R., and C. G. WELLS, "Enabling Factors in Adult-Child Discourse," *First Language*, 1 (1980), 46–62.

ENGELMANN, S., and J. OSBORN, *Distar Language I* (2nd ed.). Chicago: Science Research Associates, Inc., 1976.

ERVIN, S. M., "Imitation and Structural Change in Children's Language," in *New Directions in the Study of Language*, ed. E. Lenneberg. Cambridge, Mass.: The MIT Press, 1964.

——, "Discourse Agreement: How Children Answer Questions," in *Cognition and the Development of Language*, ed. J. R. Hayes. New York: John Wiley & Sons, Inc., 1970.

——, "Is Second Language Learning like the First," *TESOL Quarterly*, 8, no. 2 (June 1974), 111–27.

ERVIN-TRIPP, S., and C. MITCHELL-KERNAN, eds. *Child Discourse*. New York: Academic Press, Inc., 1977.

FADER, D. N., and E. B. MCNEIL, *Hooked on Books: Program and Proof*. New York: Berkeley Publishing Corporation, 1968.

FASOLD, R. W., and W. WOLFRAM, "Some Linguistic Features of Negro Dialect," in *Teaching Standard English in the Inner City*, ed. R. W. Fasold and R. W. Shuy. Arlington, Va.: Center for Applied Linguistics, 1970.

FERGUSON, C., "Baby Talk as a Simplified Register," *Papers and Reports on Child Language Development*. Stanford University, Stanford, Calif., no. 9 (1975).

FERREIRO, E., "The Underlying Logic of Literacy Development," in *Awakening to Literacy*, ed. H. Goelman, A. Oberg, and F. Smith. Portsmouth, N.H.: Heinemann Educational Books, 1984.

FERREIRO, E., and A. TEBEROSKY, *Literacy before Schooling*. Portsmouth, N.H.: Heinemann Educational Books, 1982.

FILLMORE, L. W., "Instructional Language as Linguistic Input: Second-Language Learning in Classrooms," in *Communicating in the Classroom*, ed. L. C. Wilkinson. New York: Academic Press, Inc., 1982.

——, "The Language Learner as an Individual: Implications of Research on Individual Differences for the ESL Teacher," in *On TESOL 82: Pacific Perspectives on Language Learning and Teaching*, ed. J. Handscombe and M. Clarke. Washington, D.C.: Teachers of English to Speakers of Other Languages, 1983. Reprinted by permission of the publisher and Lily Wong Fillmore.

——, The Second Time Around: Cognitive and Social Strategies in Second Language Acquisition. Doctoral dissertation. Stanford University, Stanford, Calif., 1976.

FLEMING, J. D., "Field Report: The State of The Apes," *Psychology Today*, 7, no. 8 (January 1974), 31ff.

FLORES, B., E. GARCIA, S. GONZALEZ, G. HIDALGO, K. KACZMAREK, and T. ROMERO, *Bilingual Holistic Instructional Strategies*. Phoenix, Ariz.: Exito, 1985.

FLOWERS, B. S., "Madman, Architect, Carpenter, Judge: Roles and the Writing Process," *Language Arts*, 58, no. 7 (October 1981).

FROMKIN, V., and R. RODMAN, *An Introduction to Language*. New York: 1974 Holt, Rinehart and Winston, Inc., (3rd. ed.).

FROST, J., and T. ROWLAND, "Cognitive Development and Literacy in Disadvantaged Children: A Structure-Process Approach," in *Early Childhood Education Rediscovered*, ed. J. Frost. New York: Holt, Rinehart and Winston, Inc., 1968.

GALARZA, E., *Barrio Boy*. Notre Dame, Ind.: University of Notre Dame Press, 1971.

GARDNER, R. C., and W. E. LAMBERT, *Attitudes and Motivations in Second Language Learning*. Rowley, Mass.: Newbury House Publishers, Inc., 1972.

GARVEY, C., *Play*. Cambridge, Mass.: Harvard University Press, 1977.

——, *Children's Talk*. Cambridge, Mass.: Harvard University Press, 1984.

GARVEY, C., and T. BALDWIN, *Studies in Convergent Communication: Analysis of Verbal Interaction*. Baltimore: John Hopkins Center for the Study of Social Organization of Schools. Report No. 88, 1970. ERIC ED 045 647.

GARVEY, C., T. BALDWIN, and E. DICKSTEIN, "A Structural Approach to the Study of Convergent Communication," paper presented at AERA, 1971. ERIC ED 056 555.

GENISHI, C., and M. DIPAOLO, "Learning through Argument in a Preschool," in *Communicating in the Classroom*, ed. L. C. Wilkinson. New York: Academic Press, Inc., 1982.

GENISHI, C., and A. H. DYSON, *Language Assessment in the Early Years*. Norwood, N.J.: Ablex Publishing Corporation, 1984.

GETZELS, J. W., "Creative Thinking, Problem-solving, and Instruction," in *Theories of Learning and Instruction*, 63rd Yearbook, Part I, ed. E. R. Hilgard. National Society for the Study of Education, 1964.

GIACOBBE, M. E., "Kids Can Write the First Week of School," *Learning*, 10 (1981), 130–32.

GLEASON, J. B., ed., *The Development of Language*. Columbus, Ohio: Charles E. Merrill Publishing Company, 1985.

GOELMAN, H., A. OBERG, and F. SMITH, eds., *Awakening to Literacy*. Portsmouth, N.H.: Heinemann Educational Books, 1984.

GOLDIN-MEADOW, S., and H. FELDMAN, "The Development of Language-like Communication without a Language Model," *Science*, 197 (1977), 401–3.

GOODLAD, J. I., *A Place Called School: Promise for the Future*. New York: McGraw-Hill Book Company, 1984.

GOODMAN, K., Y. GOODMAN, and B. FLORES, *Reading in the Bilingual Classroom: Literacy and Biliteracy*. Rosslyn, Va.: National Clearinghouse for Bilingual Education, 1979.

GOODMAN, Y., "Making Connections," *Language Arts*, 59, no. 5 (May 1982).

———, "The Roots of Literacy." Keynote address to the Claremont Reading Conference, March 1980.

GOODMAN, Y., and B. ALTWERGER, "Print Awareness in Preschool Children: A Study of the Development of Literacy in Preschool Children." Tucson, Ariz.: Occasional Papers, Program in Language and Literacy, Arizona Center for Research and Development, 1981.

GORDON, J. W., *My Country School Diary*. New York: Dell Publishing Co., Inc., 1970.

GRAVES, D., *Writing: Teachers and Children at Work*. Portsmouth, N.H.: Heinemann Educational Books, 1983.

———, "We Won't Let Them Write," *Language Arts*, 55, no. 5 (May 1978), 635–40.

GREEN, G. M., "Competence for Implicit Text Analysis: Literary Style Discrimination in Five-Year-Olds," in *Analyzing Discourse: Text and Talk*, ed. D. Tannen. Washington, D.C.: Georgetown University Round Table, 1982.

GREEN, J. L., and C. WALLAT, eds., *Ethnography and Language in Educational Settings*. Norwood, N.J.: Ablex Publishing Corporation, 1981.

GREENFIELD, P. M., "Informativeness, Presupposition, and Semantic Choice in Single-word Utterances," in *Development of Communication*, ed. N. Waterson and C. Snow. London: John Wiley & Sons, Inc., 1978. Also in *Developmental Pragmatics*, ed. E. Ochs and B. Schieffelin. New York: Academic Press, Inc., 1979.

GREENFIELD, P. M., and J. H. SMITH, *"The Structure of Communication in Early Language Development*. New York: Academic Press, Inc., 1976.

GREENFIELD, P. M., L. C. REICH, and R. R. OLVER, "On Culture and Equivalence: II," in *Studies in Cognitive Growth*, ed. J. S. Bruner and others. New York: John Wiley & Sons, Inc., 1967.

GRICE, N. P., "Logic and Conversation," in *Syntax and Semantics: Volume 3: Speech Acts*, ed. P. Cole and J. Morgan. New York: Academic Press, Inc., 1975.

HALLIDAY, M. A. K., *Learning How to Mean*. New York: Elsevier North-Holland, Inc., 1977.

———, *Language as a Social Semiotic: The Social Interpretation of Language and Meaning*. Baltimore: University Park Press, 1978.

———, *Explorations in the Functions of Language*. London: Edward Arnold, 1973.

HANSEN, J., T. NEWKIRK, and D. GRAVES, eds., *Breaking Ground: Teachers Relate Reading and Writing in the Elementary School*. Portsmouth, N.H.: Heinemann Educational Books, 1985.

HARSTE, J., C. BURKE, and V. WOODWARD, "Children's Language and World: Initial Encounters with Print," in *Reader Meets Author: Bridging the Gap*, ed. J. A. Lange and M. R. Smith-Burke. Neward, Del.: International Reading Association, 1982.

HARSTE, J., V. WOODWARD, and C. BURKE, *Language Stories and Literacy Lessons*. Portsmouth, N.H.: Heinemann Educational Books, 1984.

HAUPT, DOROTHY, *Relationships between Children's Questions and Nursery School Teachers' Responses*. Detroit, Mich.: Wayne State University, 1966. ERIC ED 046 507.

HAWKINS, DAVID, "Messing About in Science," *Science and Children*, 2, no. 5 (February 1965).

HAYES, C. W., and R. BAHRUTH, "Querer Es Poder," in *Breaking Ground: Teachers Relate Reading and Writing in the Elementary School*, ed. J. T. Hansen, T. Newkirk, and D. Graves. Portsmouth, N.H.: Heinemann Educational Books, 1985.

HEATH, S. B., "Questioning at Home and at School: A Comparative Study," in *Doing the Ethnography of Schooling*, ed. G. Spindler. New York: Holt, Rinehart and Winston, Inc., 1982a.

——, "What No Bedtime Story Means: Narrative Skills at Home and School," *Language in Society*, 11, no. 2 (1982).b

——, *Ways with Words: Language, Life, and Work in Communities and Classrooms*. New York: Cambridge University Press, 1983. Copyright 1983 by Cambridge University Press. Reprinted by permission of the publisher.

HOLT, J., *How Children Learn*. New York: Pitman Publishing Corporation, 1967.

——, "Making Children Hate Reading," in *The Underachieving School*. New York: Dell Publishing Co., Inc., 1969.

——, *What Do I Do Monday?* New York: E. P. Dutton, 1970.

HOWE, C., Review of P. M. Greenfield and J. N. Smith, *The Structure of Communication in Early Language Development*. New York: Academic Press, 1976, xi and 238.

HUDELSON, S., "An Examination of Children's Invented Spellings in Spanish," in *National Association for Bilingual Education Journal*, Winter 1981-82.

——, "Kan yu ret an rayt en ingles: Children Become Literate in English as a Second Language," *TESOL Quarterly*, 18 (June 1984), 221–38. Copyright 1984 by Teachers of English to Speakers of Other Languages. Reprinted by permission of the publisher and Sarah Hudelson.

——, *Hopscotch*. New York: Regents Publishing Company, Inc., 1985.

HYMES, DELL, "Models of the Interaction of Language and Social Life," in *Directions in Sociolinguistics: The Ethnography of Communication*, ed. J. Gumperz and D. Hymes. New York: Holt, Rinehart and Winston, Inc., 1972.

——, *Foundations of Sociolinguistics: An Ethnographic Approach*. Philadelphia: University of Pennsylvania Press, 1974.

INGRAM, D., "The Acquisition of Questions and Its Relation to Cognitive Development in Normal and Linguistically Deviant Children: A Pilot Study," Stanford University, Stanford, Calif., *Papers and Reports on Child Language Development*, 4 (April 1970).

IRWIN, D. M., and M. M. BUSHNELL, *Observational Strategies for Child Study*. New York: Holt, Rinehart and Winston, Inc. 1980.

JAGGAR, A., and M. T. SMITH-BURKE, eds., *Observing the Language Learner*. Urbana, Ill.: National Council of Teachers of English, 1985.

JAKOBSON, R., "Linguistics and Poetics," in *Style in Language*, ed. T. A. Sebeok. New York: Published jointly by the Technology Press of MIT and John Wiley & Sons, Inc., 1960.

JAMES, S. L., and M. A., SEABACK, "The Pragmatic Function of Children's Questions," *Journal of Speech and Hearing Research*, 25 (March 1982), 2–11.

KEATS, E. J., *Whistle for Willie*. New York: Viking Press, 1971.

——, *Whistle for Willie*. New York: Puffin Books, 1977.

KEENAN, E. O., "Making It Last: Repetition in Children's Discourse," in *Child Discourse*, ed. S. Ervin-Tripp and C. Mitchell-Kernan. New York: Academic Press, Inc., 1977.

——, "Conversational Competence in Children," *Journal of Child Language*, 1, no. 2 (1974).

KEENAN, E. O., and E. KLEIN, "Coherence in Children's Discourse," *Journal of Psycholinguistic Research*, 4, no. 4 (1975), 365–80.

Kids Magazine. Childpub Management Corp., 747 Third Ave., New York, N.Y. 10017.

KINGSTON, M. H., *The Woman Warrior: Memoirs of a Girlhood among Ghosts*. New York: Vintage Books, 1975.

KINNEAVY, J. L., *A Theory of Discourse*. Englewood Cliffs, N.J.: Prentice-Hall, Inc., 1971.

KIRK, S. A. and others, *Illinois Test of Psycholinguistic Abilities* (Rev. ed.). Urbana, Ill.: University of Illinois Press, 1968.

KIRSHENBLATT-GIMBLETT, B., *Speech Play*. Philadelphia: University of Pennsylvania Press, 1976.

KLIMA, E. S., and U. BELLUGI-KLIMA, "Syntactic Regularities in the Speech of Children," in *Child Language: A Book of Readings*, ed. A. Bar-Adon and W. Leopold. Englewood Cliffs, N.J.: Prentice-Hall, Inc., 1971.

KOCHMAN, T. ed., *Rappin' and Stylin' Out: Communication in Urban Black America*. Urbana, Ill.: University of Illinois Press, 1972.

——, *Black and White Styles in Conflict*. Chicago: The University of Chicago Press, 1981.

KOHL, H., *On Teaching*. New York: Schocken Books, Inc., 1976. Reprinted by permission of Schocken Books, Inc.

KRASHEN, S. D., "Lateralization, Language Learning, and the Critical Period: Some New Evidence," *Language Learning*, 23, no. 1 (1973), 63–74.

KRASHEN, S. D., and T. D. TERRELL, *The Natural Approach*. Hayward, Calif.: The Alemany Press of New York (Pergamon Press), 1983.

LABOV, W., "Some Sources of Reading Problems for Negro Speakers of Nonstandard English," in *Teaching Black Children to Read*, ed. J. C. Baratz and R. W. Shuy. Arlington, Va.: Center for Applied Linguistics, 1969.

——, "The Logic of Nonstandard English," in *Report of the Twentieth Annual Round Table Meeting on Linguistics and Language Study*, ed. J. Alatis. Washington, D.C.: Georgetown University Press, 1970. Also reprinted in F. Williams, ed., *Language and Poverty*. Chicago: Marxham Publishing Company, 1970.

——, *Language in the Inner City: Studies in the Black English Vernacular*. Philadelphia: University of Pennsylvania Press, 1972.

LABOV, W., and DAVID FANSHEL, *Therapeutic Discourse*. New York: Academic Press, Inc., 1977.

LENNEBERG, E. H., "The Capacity for Language Acquisition," in *The Structure of Language*, ed. J. A. Fodor and J. J. Katz. Englewood Cliffs, N.J.: Prentice-Hall, Inc., 1964.

——, *Biological Foundations of Language*. New York: John Wiley & Sons, Inc., 1967.

LIEVEN, E. V. M., "Conversations between Mothers and Young Children: Individual Differences and Their Possible Implications for the Study of Language Learning," in *The Development of Communication: Social and Pragmatic Factors in Language Acquisition*, ed. N. Waterson and C. Snow. London: John Wiley & Sons, Inc., 1978a.

——, "Turn-Taking and Pragmatics: Two Issues in Early Child Language," in *Recent Advances in the Psychology of Language: Language Development and Mother-Child Interaction*. New York: Plenum Publishing Corporation, 1978b.

LIMBER, J., "The Genesis of Complex Sentences," in *Cognitive Development and the Acquisition of Language*, ed. Timothy Moore. New York: Academic Press, Inc., 1973.

LINDFORS, J. W., "Assessing Children's Language Abilities: A Consideration of Two Faulty Basic Assumptions," *Kansas English*, 68, no. 2 (Winter 1983).

——, "How Children Learn or How Teachers Teach? A Profound Confusion," *Language Arts*, 61, no. 6 (October 1984).

——, "English for Everyone," *Language Arts*, 63, no. 1 (January 1986).

LIVO, N. J., and S. A. RIETZ, *Storytelling: Process and Practice*. Littleton, Colo.: Libraries Unlimited, Inc., 1985.

MACNAMARA, J., "Review of C. Chomsky, *The Acquisition of Syntax in Children from 5 to 10*," *General Linguistics*, 10 (1970), 164–72. (Research Monograph No. 57, Cambridge, Mass.: The MIT press, 1970.)

McNEILL, D., "Developmental Psycholinguistics," in *The Genesis of Language*, eds. F. Smith and G. Miller. Cambridge, Mass.: The MIT Press, 1966.

MARATSOS, M. P., "How Preschool Children Understand Missing Complement Subjects," *Child Development*, 45 (1974), 700–706.

MAYER, M., *Bubble Bubble*. New York: Parents' Magazine Press, 1973.

——, *Hiccup*. New York: Dial Press, 1976.

MEEK, M., *Learning to Read*. London: The Bodley Head, 1982.

MEHAN, H., *Learning Lessons: Social Organization in the Classroom*. Cambridge, Mass.: Harvard University Press, 1979.

MICHAELS, S., " 'Sharing Time': Children's Narrative Styles and Differential Access to Literacy," *Language in Society*, 10 (1981).

MICHAELS, S., and J. COLLINS, "Oral Discourse Styles: Classroom Interaction and the Acquisition of Literacy," in *Coherence in Spoken and Written Discourse*, ed. D. Tannen. Norwood, N.J.: Ablex Publishing Corporation, 1984.

MIKKELSEN, N., "Teacher as Partner in the Writing Process." *Language Arts*, 61, no. 7 (November 1984).

MILLER, G., "Some Preliminaries to Psycholinguistics," *American Psychologist*, 20, no. 1 (January 1965).

———, *Spontaneous Apprentices: Children and Language*. New York: A Continuum Book, The Seabury Press, 1977.

MILLER, P. J., *Amy, Wendy, and Beth: Learning Language in South Baltimore*. Austin, Tex.: The University of Texas, 1982.

MILNE, A. A., *Winnie-the-Pooh*. Copyright 1956 by A. A. Milne. New York: E. P. Dutton, 1956.

MILON, J. P., "The Development of Negation in English by a Second Language Learner," *TESOL Quarterly*, 8, no. 2 (June 1974), 137–43.

MILZ, V. E., "First Graders Can Write: Focus on Communication," *Theory into Practice*, 19, no. 3 (1980), 179–85.

———, "First Graders' Uses for Writing," in *Observing the Language Learner*, ed. A. Jaggar and M. T. Smith-Burke. Urbana, Ill.: National Council of Teachers of English, 1985.

MOERK, E., "Processes and Products of Imitation: Additional Evidence That Imitation Is Progressive," *Journal of Psycholinguistic Research*, 6 (1977), 187–202.

MOFFET, J., *Teaching the Universe of Discourse*. Boston: Houghton Mifflin Company, 1968.

———, *A Student-Centered Language Arts Curriculum, Grades K-6: A Handbook for Teachers*. Boston: Houghton Mifflin Company, 1973.

MOFFET, J., and B. J. WAGNER, *Student-Centered Language Arts and Reading, K-13: A Handbook* (2nd ed.). Boston: Houghton Mifflin Company, 1976.

———, "Individual Differences in Language Development: Implications for Development and Language," *Developmental Psychology*, 17 (1981), 170–87.

NELSON, K., *Structure and Strategy in Learning to Talk*. Monograph of the Society for Research in Child Development No. 149. Chicago: The University of Chicago Press, 1973b.

The New Roget's Thesaurus, ed. N. Lewis. New York: G. P. Putnam's Sons, 1964.

NEWKIRK, T., "Young Writers as Critical Readers," *Language Arts*, 59, no. 5 (May 1982).

———, "Archimedes' Dream," *Language Arts*, 61, no. 4 (April 1984), 341–50.

OCHS, E., "Talking to Children in Western Samoa," *Language in Society*, 11 (1982).

———, "Cultural Dimensions of Language Acquisition," in *Acquiring Conversational Competence*, ed. E. Ochs and B. Schieffelin. London: Routledge and Kegan Paul, 1983.

OCHS, E., and B. SCHIEFFELIN, "Language Acquisition and Socialization: Three Developmental Stories and Their Implications." Sociolinguistic Working Paper No. 105. Southwest Educational Development Laboratory, 211 East Seventh Street, Austin, Texas, 1982.

Oral Language Development: Views of Five Teachers. Agency for Instructional Television, 1111 West 17th Street, Bloomington, Indiana 47401.

PALEY, V. G., *White Teacher*. Cambridge, Mass.: Harvard University Press, 1979.

———, *Wally's Stories*. Cambridge, Mass.: Harvard University Press. Reprinted by permission of the publishers. Copyright 1981 by the President and Fellows of Harvard College.

———, *Boys and Girls*. Chicago: The University of Chicago Press, 1984.

———, *Mollie Is Three: Growing Up in School*. Chicago: University of Chicago Press, 1986.

PARISH, P., *Amelia Bedelia*. New York: Harper & Row Publishers, Inc., 1963.

———, *Thank You, Amelia Bedelia*. New York: Harper and Row, Publishers, Inc., 1964.

PATTERSON, F. G., "Conversations with a Gorilla," *National Geographic*, 154, no. 4, (1978), 438–65.

PEASE, D., and J. B. GLEASON, "Gaining Meaning: Semantic Development," in *The Development of Language*, ed. J. B. Gleason. Columbus, Oh.: Charles E. Merrill Publishing Co., (1985) 103–38.

PETERS, A., "Language Learning Strategies," *Language*, 53 (1977), 560–73.

PHILIPS, S. U., *The Invisible Culture*. New York: Longman, Inc. 1983.

READ, C., "Pre-School Children's Knowledge of English Phonology," *Harvard Educational Review*, 41, no. 1 (1971).

REY, M., and H. A. REY, *Curious George Goes to the Hospital.* Boston: Houghton Mifflin Company, 1966.

———, *Curious George.* Boston: Houghton Mifflin Company, 1966.

RHODES, L. K., "I Can Read! Predictable Books as Resources for Reading and Writing Instruction," *The Reading Teacher*, 34, no. 5 (February 1981), 511–18.

ROGERS, S., "Self-initiated Corrections in the Speech of Infant-school Children," in *Early Childhood Development and Education*, ed. M. Donaldson, R. Grieve, and C. Pratt. New York: The Guilford Press, 1983.

ROSCH, E., and B. B. LLOYD, ed., *Cognition and Categorization.* New York: Academic Press, Inc., 1978.

ROSEN, H., "The Nurture of Narrative." Lecture given at the Institute of Education, University of London, 1983.

ROSEN, C., and H. ROSEN, *The Language of Primary School Children.* London: Penguin Education for the Schools Council, 1973.

ROSS, H. S., and R. H. BALZAR, "Determinants and Consequences of Children's Questions," *Child Development*, 46 (1975), 536–39.

RYLANT, C., "Thank You, Miss Evans," *Language Arts*, 62, no. 5 (September 1985), 460–62.

SACHS, J., "Talking about the There and Then: The Emergence of Displaced Reference in Parent-Child Discourse," *Papers and Reports on Child Language Development*, Stanford University, Stanford, Calif., no. 13 (August 1977).

SACHS, J., and J. DEVIN, "Young Children's Use of Age-Appropriate Speech Styles in Social Interaction and Role-Playing," *Journal of Child Language*, 3, no. 1 (1976), 81–98.

SACKS, H., "An Analysis of the Course of a Joke's Telling in Conversation," in *Explorations in the Ethnography of Speaking*, ed. R. Bauman and J. Sherzer. Cambridge: Cambridge University Press, 1974.

SACKS, H., E. SCHEGLOFF, and G. JEFFERSON, "A Simplest Systematics for the Organization of Turn-Taking for Conversation," *Language*, 50 (1974), 696–735.

SAPIR, E., "Language," in *Culture, Language and Personality*, ed. D. G. Mandelbaum. Berkeley, Calif.: University of California Press, 1956.

SAVIĆ, S., "Aspects of Adult-Child Communication: The Problem of Question Acquisition," *Journal of Child Language*, 2 (1975), 251–60.

SCHAFFER, H. R., ed., *Studies in Mother-Infant Interaction.* London: Academic Press, Inc., 1977.

———, "Early Interactive Development," in *Studies in Mother-Infant Interaction*, ed. H. R. Schaffer. London: Academic Press, Inc., 1977.

SCHAFFER, H. R., G. M. COLLIS, and G. PARSONS, "Vocal Interchange and Visual Regard in Verbal and Pre-Verbal Children," in *Studies in Mother-Infant Interaction*, ed. H. R. Schaffer. London: Academic Press, Inc., 1977.

SCHEGLOFF, E., "Sequencing in Conversational Openings," in *Directions in Sociolinguistics*, ed. J. Gumperz and D. Hymes. New York: Holt, Rinehart and Winston, Inc., 1972.

SCHICKEDANZ, J. A., and M. SULLIVAN, "Mom, What Does U-F-F Spell?" *Language Arts*, 61, no. 1 (January 1984), 7–17.

SCOLLON, R., "A Real Early Stage: An Unzippered Condensation of a Dissertation on Child Language," in *Developmental Pragmatics*, ed. E. Ochs and B. Schieffelin. New York: Academic Press, Inc., 1979.

SCRIBNER, S., and M. COLE, *The Psychology of Literacy.* Cambridge, Mass.: Harvard University Press, 1981.

SEARLE, J., "Indirect Speech Acts," in *Syntax and Semantics: Vol. 3: Speech Acts*, ed. P. Cole and J. Morgan. New York: Academic Press, Inc., 1975.

SEAWELL, R. P. M., *A Micro-Ethnographic Study of a Spanish/English Bilingual Kindergarten in Which Literature and Puppet Play Were Used as a Method of Enhancing Language Growth.* Doctoral dissertation. The University of Texas at Austin, 1985.

SEUSS, T. G., *Dr. Seuss's Sleep Book.* New York: Random House, Inc. 1962.

———, *Horton Hatches the Egg.* New York: Random House, Inc. 1968.

Shared Nomenclature, Ohio State University, Film Lab Service, Inc., 4019 Prospect Avenue, Cleveland, Ohio 44103.

SHARP, D. W., M. COLE, and C. LAVE, *Education and Cognitive Development: The Evidence from Experimental Research.* Monographs of the Society for Research in Child Development, Serial no. 178, vol. 44 (1979).

SHATZ, M., and R. GELMAN, *The Development of Communication Skills: Modifications in the Speech of Young Children as a Function of Listener.* Monograph of the Society for Research in Child Development, Serial no. 178, vol. 44 (1979).

SHUY, R., "What the Teacher Knows Is More Important Than Text or Test," *Language Arts,* 58 (1981), 919–29.

SIMS, R., *Shadow and Substance: Afro-American Experience in Contemporary Children's Fiction.* Urbana, Ill.: National Council of Teachers of English, 1982.

SINCLAIR, J. McH., and R. M. COULTHARD, *Towards an Analysis of Discourse: The English Used by Teachers and Pupils.* London: Oxford University Press, 1975.

SKINNER, B. F., *Verbal Behavior.* Englewood Cliffs, N.J.: Prentice-Hall, Inc., 1957.

SLOBIN, D. I., "Comments on 'Developmental Psycholinguistics,'" in *The Genesis of Language: A Psycholinguistic Approach,* ed. F. Smith and G. Miller. Cambridge, Mass.: The MIT Press, 1966.

———, *Psycholinguistics.* Glenview, Ill.: Scott, Foresman and Company, 1971.

———, "Cognitive Prerequisites for the Development of Grammar," in *Studies of Child Language Development,* ed. C. A. Ferguson and D. I. Slobin. New York: Holt, Rinehart and Winston, Inc., 1973.

———, *Psycholinguistics* (2nd ed.). Glenview, Ill.: Scott, Foresman and Company, 1979.

SLOBIN, D. I., and C. A. WELSH, "Elicited Imitation as a Research Tool in Developmental Psycholinguistics," in *Studies of Child Language Development,* ed. C. A. Ferguson and D. I. Slobin. New York: Holt, Rinehart and Winston, Inc., 1973.

SMITH, FRANK, "Twelve Easy Ways to Make Learning to Read Difficult* (*and One Difficult Way to Make It Easy)," in *Psycholinguistics and Reading,* ed. Frank Smith. New York: Holt, Rinehart and Winston, Inc., 1973.

———, *Comprehension and Learning: A Conceptual Framework for Teachers.* New York: Holt, Rinehart and Winston, Inc., 1975.

———, "Demonstrations, Engagement, and Sensitivity: A Revised Approach to Language Learning," *Language Arts,* 58, no. 1 (January 1981), 103–12.

———, *Understanding Reading* (3rd ed.). New York: Holt, Rinehart and Winston, Inc., 1982a.

———, *Writing and the Writer.* Portsmouth, N. H.: Heinemann Educational Books, 1982b.

———, *Essays into Literacy.* Portsmouth, N. H.: Heinemann Educational Books, 1983a.

———, "Reading like a Writer." *Language Arts,* 60, no. 5 (May 1983).b

———, *Reading without Nonsense* (2nd ed.). New York: Teachers College Press, 1985.

SMITH, M. E., *An Investigation of the Development of the Sentence and the Extent of Vocabulary in Young Children.* (Studies in Child Welfare, vol. 3, no. 5) Iowa City: University of Iowa, 1926.

SMITHERMAN, G., *Talkin and Testifyin.* Boston: Houghton Mifflin Company, 1977.

———, "'What Go Round Come Round'" *King* in Perspective," in *Tapping Potential: English and Language Arts for the Black Learner,* ed. C. K. Brooks. Urbana, Ill.: National Council of Teachers of English, 1985.

SNOW, C. E., "The Uses of Imitation," *Journal of Child Language,* 8 (1981), 205–12.

———, "The Development of Conversation between Mothers and Babies," *Journal of Child Language,* 4 (1977).

———, "Mother's Speech Research: An Overview." Paper presented at the Conference on Language Input and Acquisition. Boston, Mass., September, 1974.

Southwest Educational Development Laboratory. *Oral Language Development Bilingual Educational Program.* Austin, Texas, 1971–72.

SOWERS, S., "The Story and the 'All About' Book," in *Breaking Ground: Teachers Relate Reading and Writing in the Elementary School,* ed. J. Hansen, T. Newkirk, and D. Graves. Portsmouth, N. H.: Heinemann Educational Books, 1985.

SPINDLER, G., ed., *Doing the Ethnography of Schooling: Educational Anthropology in Action.* New York: Holt, Rinehart and Winston, Inc., 1982.

STAATS, A. W., "Linguistic-Mentalistic Theory versus an Explanatory S-R Learning Theory of Language Development," in *The Ontogenesis of Grammar,* ed. D. Slobin. New York: Academic Press, Inc., 1971.

STEINBECK, J. *The Grapes of Wrath.* New York: Viking Press, 1971.

SUCHMAN, J. R., "Heuristic Learning and Science Education," *Journal of Research in Science Teaching,* 14, no. 3 (1977), 263–72.

TANNEN, D., *Conversational Style: Analyzing Talk among Friends.* Norwood, N. J.: Ablex Publishing Corporation, 1984.

————, "Talking New York: It's Not What You Say, It's the Way That You Say It." *New York*, March 30, 1981.

TASSELL, F. V., "A Writing Assignment with a Different Flair." *Language Arts*, 60, no. 3 (March 1983), 354–56.

TAYLOR, D., *Family Literacy*. Portsmouth, N. H.: Heinemann Educational Books, 1983.

TERRACE, H. S., "How Nim Chimpsky Changed My Mind," *Psychology Today*, 13, no. 6 (November 1979), 65–76.

THOMAS, D., "Fern Hill," in *Collected Poems*. Philadelphia: J. B. Lippincott Company; London: J. M. Dent & Sons. Copyright 1946 by New Directions Publishing Corporation. Reprinted by permission of New Directions.

THURBER, J., *The 13 Clocks*. New York: Harcourt Brace Jovanovich, Inc. Copr. © 1950 James Thurber. Copr. © 1978 Helen W. Thurber and Rosemary Thurber Sauers.

TIERNEY, R. J., and P. D. PEARSON, "Toward a Composing Model of Reading," *Language Arts*, 60, no. 5 (1983), 568–80.

TORRANCE, E. PAUL, "Freedom to Manipulate Objects and Question-Asking Performance of Six-Year-Olds," *Young Children*, 26 (1970), 93–97.

————, "Influence of Alternate Approaches to Pre-Primary Educational Stimulation and Question-Asking Skills," *Journal of Educational Research*, 65, no. 5 (January 1972), 204–6.

TOUGH, JOAN, *Focus on Meaning*. London: George Allen & Unwin Ltd., 1974.

————, *The Development of Meaning*. London: George Allen & Unwin Ltd., 1977.

TREVARTHEN, C., "Descriptive Analyses of Infant Communicative Behaviour," in *Studies in Mother-Infant Interaction*, ed. H. R. Schaffer. London: Academic Press, Inc., 1977.

TWAY, E., ed., *Reading Ladders for Human Relations* (6th ed.). Washington, D. C. and Urbana, Ill.: American Council on Education and National Council of Teachers of English, 1981.

TYACK, D., and D. INGRAM, "Children's Production and Comprehension of Questions," *Journal of Child Language*, 4, no. 2 (1977), 211–24.

UMIKER-SEBEOK, J., and T. A. SEBEOK, "Introduction: Questioning Apes," in *Speaking of Apes: A Critical Anthology of Two-Way Communication with Man*. New York: Plenum Publishing Corporation, 1980, 1–59.

VAN KLEECK, A., "The Emergence of Linguistic Awareness: A Cognitive Framework," *Merrill-Palmer Quarterly*, 28, no. 2 (April 1982), 237–65.

VYGOTSKY, L. S., *Thought and Language*. Cambridge, Mass.: The M.I.T. Press; New York: John Wiley and Sons, Inc., 1962.

————, *Mind in Society: The Development of Higher Psychological Processes*, ed. M. Cole, V. John-Steiner, S. Scribner, and E. Souberman. Cambridge, Mass.: Harvard University Press, 1978.

WALE, W. M., *The Interaction of an Adult Non-native Speaker with Adult and Child Native Speakers: A Naturalistic Study*. Doctoral dissertation. The University of Texas at Austin, 1985.

WARD, M. C., *Them Children: A Study in Language Learning*. New York: Holt, Rinehart and Winston, Inc., 1971.

WATSON, D., "Watching and Listening to Children Read," in *Observing the Language Learner*, ed. A. Jaggar and M. T. Smith-Burke. Urbana, Ill.: National Council of Teachers of English, 1985.

WELLS, G. C., "Describing Children's Linguistic Development at Home and at School," *British Educational Research Journal*, 5 (1979), 75–98.

————, *Learning through Interaction: The Study of Language Development*. Cambridge: Cambridge University Press, 1981.

WILKINSON, L. C., ed., *Communicating in the Classroom*. New York: Academic Press, Inc., 1982.

WILLIAMS, F., R. HOPPER, AND D. NATALICIO, *The Sounds of Children*. Englewood Cliffs, N. J.: Prentice-Hall, Inc., 1977.

Index